CONTEMPORARY'S
World History

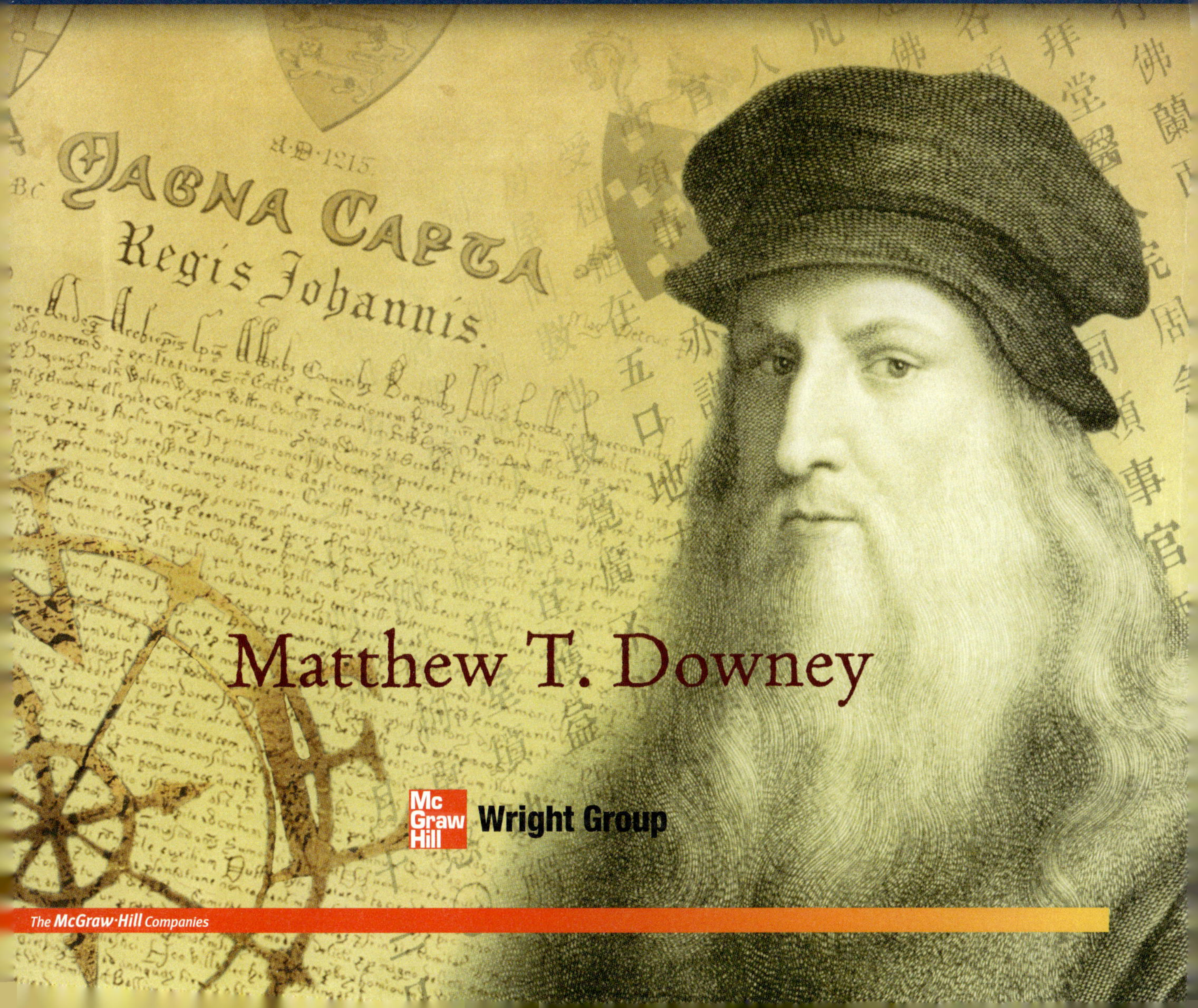

Matthew T. Downey

McGraw Hill / Wright Group

The McGraw·Hill Companies

Author

Matthew T. Downey received his Ph.D. in American History from Princeton University. He served as Director of the Clio Project in History–Social Science Education in the Graduate School of Education at the University of California, Berkeley. He also directed the U.C. Berkeley site of the California History–Social Science Project. He has taught at the University of Colorado, the University of California at Los Angeles, and at Louisiana State University. Currently, he directs the Social Science Program and the William E. Hewitt Institute for History and Social Science Education at the University of Northern Colorado.

Senior Editor: Mitch Rosin
Executive Editor: Linda Kwil
Composition: Matt McCarthy
Cover Design: Tracy Sainz
Interior Design: Linda Chandler

Photo credits are on pages 474–475.

Reviewers

Jill DeLuccia
　Social Studies Instructor
　Atlanta, Georgia

Jeffrey J. Johll
　K–12 District Social Studies Supervisor
　Dubuque Community School District
　Dubuque, Iowa

Jill Mott-Smith
　Social Studies Instructor
　Giddings, Texas

Eleanor Nangle
　Social Studies Instructor
　Chicago, Illinois

Brian Silva
　Social Studies Instructor and
　Technology Coordinator
　Long Beach, California

About the Cover

The images on the cover include (from left to right): Charlemagne, Queen Elizabeth I, Nelson Mandela, Simón Bolívar, Empress Wu, and Leonardo da Vinci.

ISBN: 0-07-704447-9 (Student Softcover Edition)
ISBN: 0-07-704449-5 (Student Softcover Edition with CD)
ISBN: 0-07-704519-X (Student Hardcover Edition)
ISBN: 0-07-704520-3 (Student Hardcover Edition with CD)
ISBN: 0-07-704450-9 (Annotated Teacher's Edition)
ISBN: 0-07-704448-7 (Teacher's Resource Binder)

Copyright © 2006 by The McGraw-Hill Companies.

All rights reserved. Except as permitted under the United States Copyright Act, no part of this publication may be reproduced or distributed in any form or by any means, or stored in a database or retrieval system, without the prior written permission from the publisher, unless otherwise indicated.

Send all inquiries to:
Wright Group/McGraw-Hill
P.O. Box 812960
Chicago, Illinois 60681

Printed in the United States of America.

3 4 5 6 7 8 9 10 QPD/QPD 11 10 09 08 07

Contents

To the Instructor v
About the Student Book vi
About the Student CD xiii
The Annotated Teacher's Edition xv
The Teacher's Resource Binder xvii
Spanish Introduction and Activities xviii

To the Student 1

Unit 1: The Beginning of Civilization 2
Chapter 1:   The Earliest Humans (Prehistory to 2500 B.C.) 4
           Biography: The Leakeys: Time Travelers 9
           Skill Builder: Identifying the Main Idea and Supporting Details ... 15
Chapter 2:   Southwest Asia: Beginnings (1200 B.C.–500 B.C.) 16
           Primary Source: The Code of Hammurabi 22
           Skill Builder: Analyzing Timelines 27

Unit 2: The First Civilizations 28
Chapter 3:   Ancient Civilizations of North Africa (2700 B.C.–500 B.C.) ... 30
           Biography: Hatshepsut 32
           Skill Builder: Comparing and Contrasting Information Using a Table ... 39
Chapter 4:   The Indian Subcontinent (2500 B.C.–A.D. 500) 40
           Primary Source: From the *Arthashastra* 53
           Skill Builder: Outlining Information 55
Chapter 5:   Early Chinese Civilizations (1750 B.C.–A.D. 200) 56
           Biography: Qin Shihuangdi 66
           Skill Builder: Using Special-Purpose Maps 69
Chapter 6:   Ancient Greek City-States (1750–133 B.C.) 70
           Primary Source: Sparta 73
           Skill Builder: How to Write a Persuasive Essay 85
Chapter 7:   Ancient Rome (500 B.C.–A.D. 500) 86
           Biography: Tiberius and Gaius Gracchus 93
           Skill Builder: Analyzing Cause and Effect 103

Unit 3: Later World Civilizations 104
Chapter 8:   The Byzantine Empire (330–1618) 106
           Biography: Empress Theodora 110
           Skill Builder: Analyzing Special-Purpose Maps 117
Chapter 9:   Islam and Muslim Civilizations (622–1699) 118
           Primary Source: The Poetry of Rumi 127
           Skill Builder: Reading a Circle Graph 131
Chapter 10: Civilizations of Africa (750 B.C.–A.D. 1570) 132
           Primary Source: A Visit to Timbuktu 145
           Skill Builder: Summarizing and Paraphrasing 147
Chapter 11: The Americas (1400 B.C.–A.D. 1570) 148
           Biography: Pachacuti (?–1471) 153
           Skill Builder: Drawing Conclusions 161
Chapter 12: The Spread of Cultures in Asia (500–1650) 162
           Primary Source: The Travels of Marco Polo 166
           Skill Builder: Analyzing Sequence Using a Flowchart 179

Unit 4: The Global Age 180
Chapter 13: Medieval Europe (500–1300) 182
           Primary Source: The Magna Carta, 1215 195
           Skill Builder: Synthesizing Information 199

Chapter 14:	Renaissance and Reformation (1300–1650)	200
	Biography: Elizabeth I (1558–1603)	210
	Skill Builder: Fact and Opinion	215
Chapter 15:	Age of European Explorations (1415–1800)	216
	Primary Source: A Spanish Attack	223
	Skill Builder: Analyzing a Line Graph	237

Unit 5: Monarchies and Revolutions 238

Chapter 16:	Political Revolutions (1600–1815)	240
	Biography: François-Dominique Toussaint L'Ouverture (c. 1743–1803)	258
	Skill Builder: Analyzing Paintings and Photographs	263
Chapter 17:	Social Revolutions (1750–1910)	264
	Primary Source: Factory Conditions	272
	Skill Builder: Analyzing a Bar Graph	277

Unit 6: A New Age 278

Chapter 18:	Nationalism in Europe (1815–1914)	280
	Biography: Otto von Bismarck (1815–1898)	288
	Skill Builder: Analyzing a Political Cartoon	291
Chapter 19:	Imperialism and Modernization (1800–1914)	292
	Biography: Menelik II (1844–1913)	300
	Skill Builder: Creating and Analyzing Tables	315

Unit 7: The World at War 316

Chapter 20:	World War I and the Russian Revolution (1914–1919)	318
	Primary Source: The Fourteen Points	327
	Skill Builder: Analyzing Propaganda	335
Chapter 21:	Between the Wars (1919–1939)	336
	Primary Source: Inflation in Germany	345
	Skill Builder: Identifying Point of View	349
Chapter 22:	World War II and the Cold War (1931–1955)	350
	Biography: Sir Winston Churchill (1874–1965)	358
	Skill Builder: Comparing Points of View	367

Unit 8: The World Today 368

Chapter 23:	The World Enters the 21st Century (1945–)	370
	Skill Builder: Problem Solving and Decision Making	395
Chapter 24:	The World: Opportunities and Challenges	397
	Case 1: Developing Nations	398
	Case 2: The Environment	402
	Case 3: Human Rights	406
	Case 4: Genocide and Other Crimes Against Humanity	410
	Case 5: Terrorism	414

Documents and Maps 418

The Declaration of Independence	419
The United States Constitution	422
Universal Declaration of Human Rights	437
Map: The United States	441
Map: The World	442
Map: North America	443
Map: South America	444
Map: Africa	445
Map: Europe	446
Map: Asia	447
Map: Antarctica	448

Glossary/Index	449
Acknowledgements	474

To the Instructor

This book is a survey of world history from prehistoric through modern times. I have tried to make it as comprehensive in coverage as space permits. It includes important economic, social, and intellectual developments, as well as wars and political events. I also have tried to make the book broadly inclusive. It tells the story of ordinary people as well as of the rich and famous. It demonstrates that people of different ethnic groups, races, and cultures helped make the world what it is today.

The book also strives to be inclusive in another sense. I have tried to write a book that struggling readers will be able to read. Each chapter begins with a pre-reading activity to help students find a purpose for reading or activate their prior knowledge by letting them anticipate what is to come. Many pages include comprehension strategies designed to help students better understand what they are reading. Each chapter ends with activities that sharpen their understanding of what they have learned.

World History is the story of individuals as well as groups. To emphasize this, each chapter includes either a brief biography of a person who left her or his mark on society or a primary source account by an individual who lived during the time period covered by the chapter. These sections help to give students a feel for the times.

This text tries to reach students who learn in different ways. Each chapter and virtually every page delivers historical information in multiple forms—text, visual images, maps, and charts. Many of the pictures are rich primary sources. The final chapter of the book introduces five case studies. The topics included in the case studies represent important issues that continue to challenge our world.

The people included in this book shaped our world. My goal is to help your students understand that they, too, can shape the future.

Matthew T. Downey

About the Student Book

The Student Edition of *World History* was created for those students who need extra help in reading and comprehension. The text is written at a fifth- to eighth-grade reading level, but it contains the key concepts and basic facts necessary for the study of world history at the high school level. Key support is given with pre-reading activities that guide students through a preview of the text and illustrations. These activities activate prior knowledge.

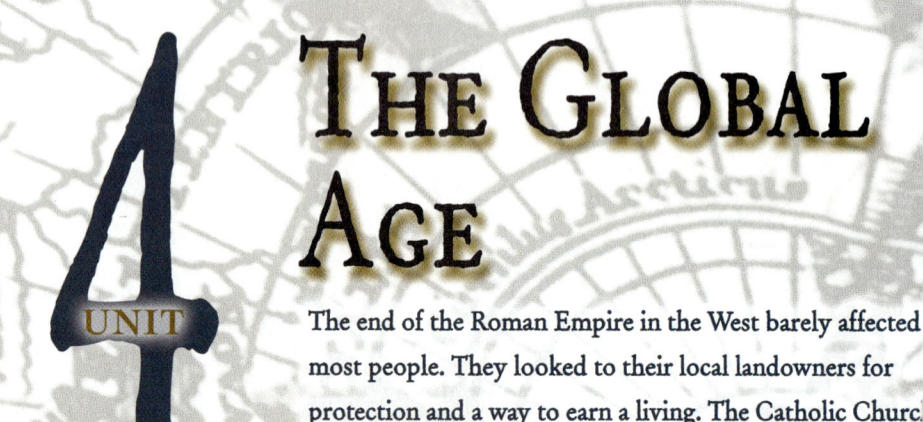

UNIT 4

THE GLOBAL AGE

The end of the Roman Empire in the West barely affected most people. They looked to their local landowners for protection and a way to earn a living. The Catholic Church remained a governing force in people's lives. But change was creeping across Western Europe.

By the 1500s, change came more rapidly—and not just to Western Europe. Europeans began to search out routes to rich trading nations in Asia. By accident, they bumped into the Americas. The race was on among European nations to establish colonies and gain riches.

Unit Opener
Units begin with a summary of the chapters included in the unit. Key concepts are identified and an overview of topics is introduced.

Timeline
Each unit presents a timeline. The timeline includes important events that are discussed in the chapters. The Annotated Teacher's Edition provides extension activities that relate to the timelines.

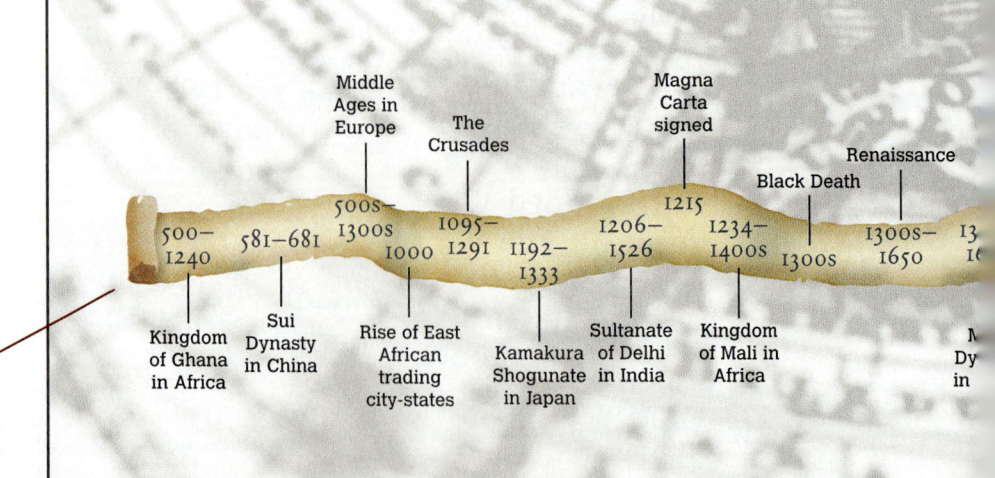

Timeline events:
- 500–1240: Kingdom of Ghana in Africa
- 500s–1300s: Middle Ages in Europe
- 581–681: Sui Dynasty in China
- 1095–1291: The Crusades
- 1192–1333: Kamakura Shogunate in Japan
- 1000: Rise of East African trading city-states
- 1206–1526: Sultanate of Delhi in India
- 1215: Magna Carta signed
- 1234–1400s: Kingdom of Mali in Africa
- 1300s: Black Death
- 1300s–1650: Renaissance

Pre-reading questions and vocabulary focus students' reading. Opportunity is given halfway through each lesson to stop and organize ideas, and again at the end of each lesson to summarize. Additional support is provided for remedial readers on the Student CD, and with Blackline Masters and Overhead Transparencies in the Teacher's Resource Binder. Extra help for English Language Learners is provided on the Student CD and on additional Blackline Masters on the Teacher's CD.

Collage

The collage of illustrations and accompanying questions should be used to generate a discussion about the chapters and develop students' prior knowledge about the topics covered. Each image represents a major event in the unit and provides information related to the question accompanying it.

Chapter 15
AGE OF EUROPEAN EXPLORATIONS
(1415–1800)

Getting Focused

The Getting Focused section of each chapter should be used as a pre-reading activity. Students are directed to read the lessons and subheadings, look at illustrations and read captions, examine maps, and review vocabulary words. Then students are asked to complete an activity in preparation for reading the chapter.

Getting Focused

Skim this chapter to predict what you will be learning.
- Read the lesson titles and subheadings.
- Look at the illustrations and read the captions.
- Examine the maps.
- Review the vocabulary words and terms.

Every continent in the world except Antarctica is discussed in this chapter. You have been making a world map. By now some part of every continent should be colored in. Make a list of each region that you have added to the map. Next to each region on your list add the name of the earliest human civilization in that region and its dates. With a partner, quiz each other on where the civilizations began and how long ago each one existed.

Chapter Opener Images

Each chapter begins with one or two images. These images are explained in the Annotated Teacher's Edition and represent events discussed in the chapter. The images should be used to generate classroom discussion about the chapter topics. The images provide connections with key chapter concepts and help to further develop students' prior knowledge.

LESSON 1

New European Trade Routes

European Explorations, 1415–1800

Thinking on Your Own

Turn each subheading in this lesson into a question. Write them in your notebook. As you study each section of the lesson, write the answers to the questions.

The Renaissance was marked by a spirit of adventure and curiosity. This spirit was the result of a number of influences. In turn, it created an outcome of huge importance: the beginning of the **global age**. During the 1400s, for the first time, Europeans had direct contact with Africans, Asians, and by the end of the century, Americans.

focus your reading

Discuss what prompted Europeans to explore the world.

What successes did the Portuguese have in their voyages of exploration?

What European nations set up trading routes in Asia?

vocabulary

global age   astrolabe
compass   cargo

The Time Is Right

A number of developments took place that made the 1400s the right time for the global age to begin. The first development, or influence, was the Crusades. Large numbers of Europeans went to the Holy Land to fight the Muslims. Their travels showed them the marvels of other places. When they returned home, they told stories of what they had seen. The ships that returned from the Holy Land carried luxury goods like spices and silks. These goods were sold in European markets. Marco Polo's journal also told Europeans about life outside Europe.

But it was more than excitement about new lands that moved Europeans. For many, it was riches. Merchants in northern and western Europe wanted to sell goods like silks and spices without having to pay Arab and Italian merchants. Goods from Asia

Age of European Explorations 217

Thinking on Your Own

This section is a pre-reading activity. Students are encouraged to familiarize themselves with the Focus Your Reading questions and the Vocabulary words and terms. Some of these activities include working with a partner, doing a short writing assignment, or helping to organize students' reading of the lesson.

Focus Your Reading

Focus Your Reading questions should be read prior to reading the lesson. Students should be encouraged to use the questions as a guide as they read through the lesson text. The questions can also be used as a review after reading.

Vocabulary

Vocabulary words and terms are listed in a box at the beginning of each lesson. The words and terms appear in boldfaced print in the lessons. All the vocabulary words and terms are defined in the Glossary at the end of the book. Many are defined in the context of the lesson.

ix

Stop and Think

Stop and Think activities are designed to help students organize and interact with the material they have just read so that they can remember it. The activity provides a stopping point midway through the lesson and encourages students to think about what they have read.

stop and think

The Spanish, French, Dutch, and English settlers in North America were not alike in how they treated the Native Americans. How and why were they different? With a partner, look for information to answer this question. Write a one-paragraph answer.

People came to the English colonies to make a better life for themselves. They looked for economic opportunities as farmers, fishers, and crafts people. Many people in the New England and Middle Colonies were the owners of small farms. However, a plantation system developed in the Southern Colonies. The climate and soil were well suited to growing crops like rice and indigo. Eventually, tobacco became a major crop. To work their plantations, owners began to import enslaved Africans. As a result, the colonies became part of the trans-Atlantic slave trade.

As more colonists immigrated, they wanted more land. The only way to get land was to push the Native Americans off. This resulted in a number of wars between colonists and Native Americans. By the 1700s, most Native Americans had been killed or forced west.

While taking away the freedom of Africans and killing Native Americans, the colonists were working to keep and enlarge their own rights. About half the colonies were **proprietary colonies**. They were owned by individuals or private companies. The other colonies were **royal colonies**. They belonged to the English monarch.

Putting It All Together

Play "Ten Questions" with a partner. Write ten questions and answers about the information in this lesson. Then take turns asking and answering the questions.

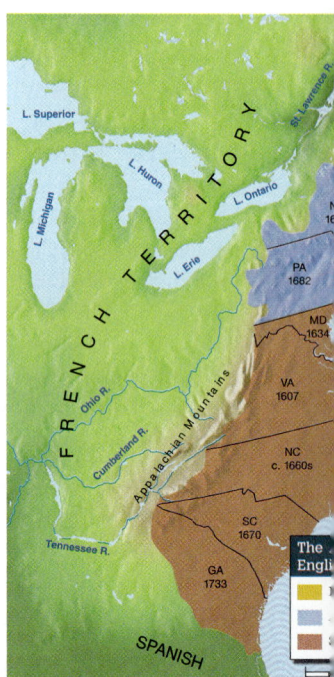

Putting It All Together

A Putting It All Together activity appears at the end of each lesson. These activities tie together the key concepts of the lessons. They often involve using a graphic organizer or creating a piece of written work. They frequently ask students to work together or to discuss ideas with a partner to expand their viewpoints or understanding. Students should be encouraged to incorporate key elements from each lesson into the Putting It All Together activities.

Biography

Biographies are included in select chapters. The biographies draw attention to individuals who lived during the time period discussed in the chapter.

Chapter 1: The Leakeys
Chapter 3: Hatshepsut
Chapter 5: Qin Shihuangdi
Chapter 7: Tiberius and Gaius Gracchus
Chapter 8: Empress Theodora
Chapter 11: Pachacuti
Chapter 14: Elizabeth I
Chapter 16: François-Dominique Toussaint L'Ouverture
Chapter 18: Otto von Bismarck
Chapter 19: Menelik II
Chapter 22: Sir Winston Churchill

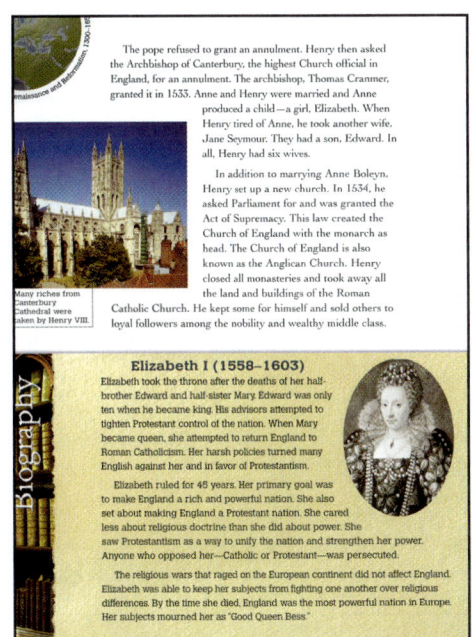

Primary Source

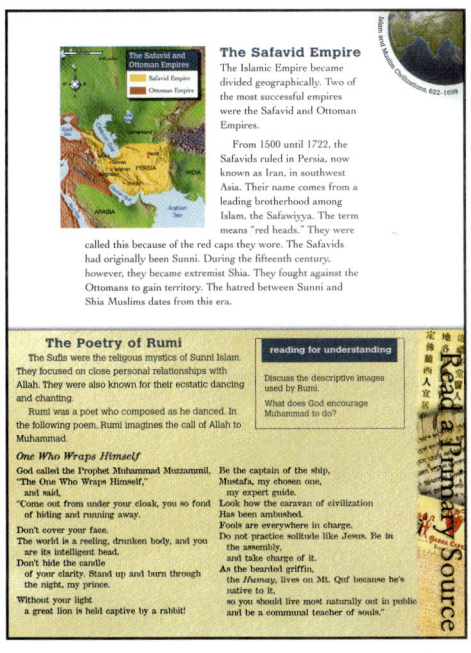

Select chapters include a Primary Source page. The documents represent the time period covered in the chapter and are often used to enhance the content of the chapter.

Chapter 2: The Code of Hammurabi
Chapter 4: From the *Arthashastra*
Chapter 6: Sparta
Chapter 9: The Poetry of Rumi
Chapter 10: A Visit to Timbuktu
Chapter 12: The Travels of Marco Polo
Chapter 13: The Magna Carta, 1215
Chapter 15: A Spanish Attack
Chapter 17: Factory Conditions
Chapter 20: The Fourteen Points
Chapter 21: Inflation in Germany

Chapter Summary

- During the Shang Dynasty, the Chinese developed a writing system based on characters, not letters. The Shang also practiced **ancestor worship**.
- The Zhou overthrew the Shang ruler.
- The **Mandate** of Heaven explains the **dynastic cycle** that developed in China.
- The family was the basic unit of Chinese society. The **extended family** included all related family members. Each family member had a duty and responsibility to every other family member. This duty was known as **filial piety**.
- During the early period of Chinese history, three important **philosophies** developed: **Confucianism**, **Daoism**, and **Legalism**. A philosophy is different from a **religion**.
- After the Zhou were overthrown, China entered the Warring States Period. Rival **warlords** fought for power.
- Qin Shihuangdi united and expanded China. He declared himself China's first **emperor**. He set up a **centralized government** and used **bureaucrats** to run it. **Censors** made sure that officials did their jobs.
- Qin Shihuangdi began the building of the Great Wall of China.
- The Qin Dynasty was overthrown by the Han. The Han adopted Confucianism. They kept the idea of appointed civil servants and set up **civil service** exams.
- Trade became important under the Han. Many trade goods flowed back and forth along the Silk Road.

Chapter Review

1. Review the questions that you wrote at the beginning of the chapter. Talk with a partner about your questions and possible answers. Then write an answer for each question.
2. Imagine you are a headline writer for a Chinese newspaper. Write a two-line headline for each of the following: (a) the overthrow of the Zhou, (b) the Mandate of Heaven, (c) the teachings of Confucius, (d) a trading trip on the Silk Road.

Chapter Summary

This is a summary of the events discussed in the chapter. It includes vocabulary words, key concepts, important events, and significant people.

Chapter Review

The questions in the Chapter Review help to summarize the key events in the chapter and provide a review of important facts. Students are often asked to conduct further research, to represent their ideas visually, or to write about their opinions.

Skill Builder

Skill Builder pages address key skills necessary for successful mastery of social studies concepts. Skills include:

Chapter 1: Identifying the Main Idea and Supporting Details
Chapter 2: Analyzing Timelines
Chapter 3: Comparing and Contrasting Information Using a Table
Chapter 4: Outlining Information
Chapter 5: Using Special-Purpose Maps
Chapter 6: How to Write a Persuasive Essay
Chapter 7: Analyzing Cause and Effect
Chapter 8: Analyzing Special-Purpose Maps
Chapter 9: Reading a Circle Graph
Chapter 10: Summarizing and Paraphrasing
Chapter 11: Drawing Conclusions
Chapter 12: Analyzing Sequence Using a Flowchart
Chapter 13: Synthesizing Information
Chapter 14: Fact and Opinion
Chapter 15: Analyzing a Line Graph
Chapter 16: Analyzing Paintings and Photographs
Chapter 17: Analyzing a Bar Graph
Chapter 18: Analyzing a Political Cartoon
Chapter 19: Creating and Analyzing Tables
Chapter 20: Analyzing Propaganda
Chapter 21: Identifying Point of View
Chapter 22: Comparing Points of View
Chapter 23: Problem Solving and Decision Making

Skill Builder

Using Special-Purpose Maps

There are many kinds of maps. There are road maps, historical maps, land-use maps, natural-resources maps, and the list goes on. Most of the maps in this book are historical maps.

To read and use the information on the map, follow these steps:
1. Read the title of the map to find out what it is about.
2. Look at the map to see what colors and symbols are used.
3. Match the colors and symbols to the map key. This explains what the colors and symbols represent.
4. Read the map scale. This tells you the distance between places shown on the map.

1. What is the title of each map?
2. What symbol is used to show the Great Wall?
3. How do you know which area was ruled by the Zhou?
4. What is the greatest distance from east to west that the Shang ruled?

About the Student CD

The Student CD contains several instructional tools:

Student Book with Audio Files
The entire student edition is available on screen in PDF format. Next to each paragraph is an icon of a speaker. When the icon is clicked, the paragraph will be read aloud. Students with reading difficulties or English Language Learners will benefit from having the text read to them.

Spanish Introduction and Spanish Activity
Research has shown that English Language Learners benefit from verbally generating prior knowledge about a given topic in their first language before learning new concepts in English. Coupled with the generation of prior knowledge is a writing component. By writing about a concept in their first language, students increase comprehension and are better prepared for content acquisition in English. The last component is writing about acquired knowledge in English.

At the beginning of each chapter are two icons. The first icon is for a Spanish Introduction. This activity is designed to generate prior knowledge for Spanish speakers. It introduces the key concept of the chapter and presents lesson overviews. The second icon is for a Spanish Activity. This activity asks students to write about the key concept in Spanish. Students are instructed to revisit their Spanish paragraph after completing the chapter by completing an English writing activity that incorporates their prior knowledge with the new concepts learned. See pages xviii–xxxii in this section for English translations of the Spanish Introductions and Activities.

Key Concepts Introduced in Spanish

Chapter 1: Prehistory
Chapter 2: Civilization
Chapter 3: Empire
Chapter 4: Social Class
Chapter 5: Dynasty
Chapter 6: Democracy
Chapter 7: Military Strength
Chapter 8: Conquest
Chapter 9: Culture
Chapter 10: Migration
Chapter 11: Adaptation to Environment
Chapter 12: Closed Society
Chapter 13: Feudalism
Chapter 14: Renaissance
Chapter 15: Colony
Chapter 16: Revolution
Chapter 17: Social Change
Chapter 18: Nationalism
Chapter 19: Imperialism
Chapter 20: Conflict
Chapter 21: Economic Depression
Chapter 22: Global War
Chapter 23: Interdependence
Chapter 24: Global Issues

Hot-linked Vocabulary Definitions

Vocabulary words at the beginning of each lesson are hot-linked to provide Glossary definitions. To access the Glossary definition of each word, students should click on the vocabulary word. A dialog box will then open that provides the Glossary definition.

Audio Captions

Captions for each photograph, painting, and cartoon are read aloud when the student clicks on the speaker icon.

Reading Comprehension and Vocabulary Reinforcement Activities

Each chapter is accompanied by four interactive activities that reinforce reading comprehension and provide vocabulary reinforcement. They vary among the following: Fill in the Blank, Crossword Puzzle, eFlashcards, Multiple Choice, Text Identification, Concept Columns, Matching, and Vocabulary Concentration.

Interactive Timeline

The Interactive Timeline can be accessed by clicking on the timeline at the bottom of the Unit Opener pages. The Interactive Timeline provides additional information about events in world history, as well as additional images. This is a powerful tool for enhancing the curriculum and provides students with the opportunity to conduct research on the topics covered in the Student Edition.

Student Presentation Builder

Student Presentation Builder utilizes PowerPoint technology and allows students to create presentations using images and maps from the chapters. An introductory lesson is included to teach students how to use this technology.

The Annotated Teacher's Edition

The Annotated Teacher's Edition provides answers to questions in the student text and extension activities to enhance the lessons. The extension activities are designed to help remedial students better understand the text material and to assist English Language Learners in developing a broader understanding of the text content.

Unit Objectives
Skills and concepts targeted in the chapters in each unit are identified at the beginning of each unit.

Getting Started
Getting Started provides teachers with a method of introducing the unit to students. This section often includes an introduction to key vocabulary terms and concepts. Students are encouraged to read the unit introduction to generate prior knowledge.

Measuring Time
Measuring Time introduces the unit timeline. Often questions are posed that will help students to better understand the period of history covered by the chapters in the unit.

Timeline Extension
Understanding a timeline is an important social studies skill. Timeline extensions provide additional information about the timelines at the beginning of each unit and questions that can be used to generate classroom discussion.

Collage Answers
The three illustrations that begin each unit, and the accompanying questions, should be used to generate students' prior knowledge about the topics covered in the unit. The Collage Extension activities can be used to enhance this instructional tool. Additional information is provided about the illustrations, and questions to the students are presented.

Related Transparencies
The Related Transparencies box lists the transparencies from the Teacher's Resource Binder that relate to the chapter.

Key Blacklines
Each chapter is accompanied by eight Blackline Masters from the Teacher's Resource Binder. These include: Biography or Primary Source, Reading Comprehension, Vocabulary Reinforcement, Map/Graphic Activity, Chapter Review, Chapter Activity, and Chapter Quiz. The topics of the Biography and Primary Source are indicated in the Key Blacklines box.

CD Extension
The CD Extension box is a reminder that students will benefit from the material presented on the CD.

Pre-Reading Discussion
The Pre-Reading Discussion is designed to provide questions and topics that generate prior knowledge among students. Often students are asked to review specific sections of text, images, or charts within the chapter.

Bio Facts
The student book contains a half-page biography in select chapters. The Bio Facts and Biography Extension include additional background information about the person highlighted in the Student Edition. The material can be used to supplement classroom discussion and to provide additional material for student research.

Reading for Understanding
Each Primary Source half-page contains reading comprehension questions to guide students through the text. Answers to the Reading for Understanding questions will vary, but suggestions of key facts are provided.

Lesson Summary
Summaries are provided at the beginning of each lesson to help the teacher understand the overall themes and key concepts.

Lesson Objective
The Lesson Objective identifies the key goal for student learning.

Lesson Vocabulary
Vocabulary words and terms are explained at the beginning of each lesson. Teachers are provided with techniques to introduce each vocabulary word and a method of linking the terms to a key concept of the lesson.

Putting It All Together
Answers and/or suggestions are provided for the Putting It All Together activities at the end of each lesson.

Stop and Think
Answers and/or suggestions are provided for the Stop and Think activities that appear in each lesson.

Picturing History

The illustrations—photographs, cartoons, graphs and charts, and paintings—in *World History* can be used to enhance student understanding of the topics covered and to generate classroom discussion. Selected illustrations are identified in the Picturing History boxes, and additional information is presented about the illustrations.

Map Extension

Geography skills are an important component of social studies instruction. Map Extension activities are included with each map throughout the Student Edition. These activities target key skills students must have to ensure academic achievement in the social studies.

Biography Extension

The Biography Extension box includes additional background information about the person highlighted in the Student Edition. The material can be used to supplement classroom discussion and to provide additional material for student research.

Novel Connections

At the end of each chapter is a list of supplemental reading materials for students. These books correlate to the concepts and topics of each chapter. The Thematic Strands of the National Council for the Social Studies are identified.

Classroom Discussion

The Classroom Discussion section provides teachers with questions to help wrap up the chapter. These questions incorporate key concepts from the chapter and guide students through making connections to related topics in world history.

The Teacher's Resource Binder

Blackline Masters

There are 168 Blackline Masters in the Teacher's Resource Binder. Each chapter contains one Blackline Master for each of the following topics: Biography or Primary Source, Reading Comprehension Activity, Vocabulary Reinforcement Activity, Map/Graphic Activity, Chapter Review, Chapter Activity, and Chapter Quiz. An Answer Key is included at the end of the Blackline Master section.

Overhead Transparencies

There are 20 Overhead Transparencies in the Teacher's Resource Binder. They include key maps that relate to the chapters, images that can be used to enhance classroom instruction, and graphic organizers: Concept Web, Venn Diagram, and a Three-Column Chart. Each Overhead Transparency is noted in the chapters where relevant, although many can be used repeatedly throughout the text.

CD

Included with the Teacher's Resource Binder is a CD. The CD contains the entire Annotated Teacher's Edition in PDF format, so it is not necessary to carry around the Annotated Teacher's Edition. Also on the CD are additional PDF Blackline Masters that can be printed. Included are Vocabulary Reinforcement pages designed for ELL instruction, Reading Comprehension pages designed for ELL instruction, Chapter Puzzles, Chapter Assessments, Unit Assessments, and a Book Assessment.

End-of-Book Assessments Correlated to State Standards

Final book assessments in PDF format, are available on the McGraw-Hill/Contemporary website: www.mhcontemporary.com. These 50-question tests assess skills outlined by the state standards of select states.

Spanish Introduction and Activities

Each chapter on the Student CD is accompanied by an audio introduction in Spanish and an audio activity in Spanish. The introductions are designed to generate prior knowledge in the English Language Learner's first language. The activities are designed to link prior knowledge with the chapter being studied. The English and Spanish versions of each chapter's Introduction and Activity are provided below. They can also be used to assist non-English Language Learners.

English	Spanish
Chapter 1 – Introduction	
The lessons in this chapter are about the people who lived on Earth prior to 2500 B.C. and how we learn about them. The key concept in this chapter is "prehistory." *Prehistory* refers to the time before writing was invented. Lesson 1 describes the earliest humans and their way of life. In Lesson 2, you will learn how farming and domesticating animals revolutionized the lives of the earliest humans and contributed to the beginning of civilization.	Las lecciones en este capítulo son acerca de la gente que vivió en la Tierra antes de 2500 a.C. y cómo aprendemos acerca de ellos. El concepto principal en este capítulo es la "prehistoria." La *prehistoria* refiere al tiempo antes de la invención de la escritura. La lección 1 describe los primeros seres humanos y sus formas de vida. En la lección 2, aprenderás cómo la agricultura y la domesticación de los animales revolucionó las vidas de los primeros seres humanos y contribuyó al principio de la civilización.
Chapter 1 – Student Activity	
With a partner, discuss in Spanish three things you would take into prehistoric times to help you survive. In Spanish, write a brief paragraph explaining how each of these items would help you survive. After reading the chapter, write a brief paragraph in English explaining how your list has changed based on what you have learned about the prehistoric world.	Con un compañero, discute en español tres cosas que te llevarías a los tiempos prehistóricos para ayudarte a sobrevivir. En español, escribe un párrafo breve explicando cómo cada una de estas cosas te ayudaría a sobrevivir. Después de leer el capítulo, escribe un párrafo en inglés explicando cómo tu lista ha cambiado en base a lo que has aprendido acerca del mundo prehistórico.

Chapter 2 – Introduction

In this chapter, you will read about the beginning of civilization in Mesopotamia—a region now known as the Middle East—from 1200 B.C. to 500 B.C. The key concept in this chapter is "civilization." *Civilization* is a term used to describe a complex culture and includes the beliefs, traditions, government, religion, and social classes of a group of people. In Lesson 1, you will read about the people who settled on the floodplain between the Tigris and Euphrates Rivers and how their civilizations developed. Lesson 2 describes the history and religious beliefs of a group of people in Mesopotamia who became the Israelites.	En este capítulo, vas a leer acerca del principio de la civilización en Mesopotamia – una región que ahora se conoce como El Medio Oriente – de 1200 a.C. hasta 500 a.C. El concepto principal en este capítulo es la civilización. La *civilización* es un término que se usa para describir una cultura compleja e incluye las creencias, tradiciones, gobierno, religión y clases sociales de un grupo de personas. En la lección 1, vas a leer acerca de la gente que se colocó en la llanura de inundación entre los ríos Tigres y Eufrates y cómo sus civilizaciones se desarrollaron. La lección 2 describe la historia y creencias religiosas de un grupo de personas en Mesopotamia que serían más tarde los Israelitas.

Chapter 2 – Student Activity

With a partner, discuss in Spanish how you might be able to find out more about prehistoric people. What clues might they have left behind that would tell us more about them? Write a bulleted list in Spanish of five things you could look at or study that would tell you much more about their lives. After reading the chapter, write a brief paragraph in English explaining three key differences between prehistoric groups and civilizations.	Con un compañero, discute en español como podrías aprender más acerca de la gente prehistórica. ¿Qué pistas pudieron haber dejado que nos digan más acerca de ellos? Escribe una lista en español de cinco cosas que podrías ver o estudiar que te digan mucho más acerca de sus vidas. Después de leer el capítulo, escribe un párrafo breve en inglés explicando tres diferencias principales entre grupos prehistóricos y civilizaciones.

Chapter 3 – Introduction

The lessons in this chapter are about the earliest civilizations in northern Africa, which developed from 2700 B.C. to 500 B.C. The key concept in this chapter is "empire." *Empire* is the term for a major political unit that controls a great amount of territory under one leader. Lesson 1 is about ancient Egyptian civilization. In Lesson 2, you will read about the Kush civilization that flourished at approximately the same time as the Egyptian civilization.	Las lecciones en este capítulo son acerca de las primeras civilizaciones en el norte de África, que se desarrollaron de 2700 a.C. hasta 500 a.C. El concepto principal en este capítulo es el "imperio." El *imperio* es un término para una unidad política importante que controla una cantidad grande de territorio bajo el mando de un líder. La lección 1 es acerca de la civilización antigua de Egipto. En la lección 2, vas a leer acerca de la civilización Kush que floreció aproximadamente al mismo tiempo que la civilización egipcia.

Chapter 3 – Student Activity

All of the Egyptian pyramids were monuments to kings. Building them took many years and the labor of thousands of workers. Think like an Egyptian. With a partner, discuss in Spanish what the pyramids say about Egyptian civilization. After reading the chapter, think about one American monument, and write a brief paragraph in English explaining what it says about us as a civilization.	Todas las pirámides egipcias eran monumentos a los reyes. La construcción de ellas tomó muchos años y el trabajo de millares de trabajadores. Piensa como un egipcio. Con un compañero, discute en español lo que las pirámides dicen acerca de la civilización egipcia. Después de leer el capítulo, piensa en un monumento americano y escribe un párrafo en inglés explicando lo que éste dice acerca de nuestra civilización.

Chapter 4 – Introduction

This chapter is about the civilizations that developed from 2500 B.C. to A.D. 500 on the Indian subcontinent, in what are now the countries of India, Pakistan, and Bangladesh. The key concept in this chapter is "social class." *Social class* refers to a rank or order of people in a society based on common traits. In Lesson 1, you will learn about the geography of the Indian subcontinent and how the early civilizations developed along the Indus and Ganges Rivers. Lesson 2 describes the beginnings and basic beliefs of Hinduism. In Lesson 3, you will learn about the early history of Buddhism.	Este capítulo es acerca de las civilizaciones que se desarrollaron de 2500 a.C. a 500 d.C. en el subcontinente indio en lo que hoy son los países de India, Pakistán, y Bangladesh. El concepto principal en este capítulo es la "clase social." La *clase social* refiere a un rango o a un orden de gente en una sociedad que se basa en rasgos comunes. En la lección 1, vas aprender acerca de la geografía del subcontinente indio y cómo las primeras civilizaciones se desarrollaron a lo largo de los ríos Indo y Ganges. Lección 2 describe los principios y las creencias básicas del hinduismo. En la lección 3, aprenderás acerca de los principios de la historia del budismo.

Chapter 4 – Student Activity

Look at the map of India on page 42. With a partner, discuss in Spanish what geographic features would have isolated India and contributed to its unique culture. In Spanish, write a brief summary of your ideas. After reading the chapter, think about three items from the Eightfold Path that appeal to you. Write a brief paragraph in English explaining how practicing those three items would help to improve your relationships with other people.	Mira el mapa de la India en la página 42. Con un compañero, discute en español que rasgos geográficos pudieron haber aislado a la India y contribuido a su cultura única. En español, escribe un resumen breve de tus ideas. Después de leer el capítulo, piensa acerca de tres artículos de la trayectoria óctupla que te atraen. Escribe un párrafo breve en inglés explicando cómo practicando estos tres artículos ayudarían a mejorar tus relaciones con otra gente.

Chapter 5 – Introduction

This chapter is about early Chinese civilizations from 1750 B.C. to A.D. 200. The key concept in this chapter is "dynasty." A *dynasty* is a succession of rulers from the same family. In Lesson 1, you will read about the rule of several dynasties in the earliest Chinese civilizations. Lesson 2 describes several Chinese philosophies that developed at this time. In Lesson 3, you will learn about the Qin and Han Dynasties and China's participation in international trade.	Este capítulo es acerca de las primeras civilizaciones de China de 1750 a.C. a 200 d.C. El concepto principal es en este capítulo es la "dinastía." La *dinastía* es una sucesión de gobernantes de la misma familia. En la lección 1, vas a leer acerca del gobierno de varias dinastías en las más primeras civilizaciones de China. La lección 2 describe varias filosofías chinas que se desarrollaron en ese tiempo. En la lección 3, aprenderás acerca de la dinastías de Qin y de Han y de la participación de china en el comercio internacional.

Chapter 5 – Student Activity

Civilizations grow and prosper by trading with other civilizations. With a partner, discuss in Spanish how trade contributes to a civilization to make it more powerful. Write a brief summary of your discussion in Spanish. After reading the chapter, revise your summary to show what you have learned about the connection between trade and great civilizations. Then rewrite your summary in English.	Las civilizaciones crecen y prosperan por medio del comercio con otras civilizaciones. Con un compañero, discute en español cómo el comercio contribuye a hacer una civilización más poderosa. Escribe un resumen breve en español de tu discusión. Después de leer el capítulo, revisa tu resumen para mostrar lo que aprendiste acerca de la conexión entre el comercio y las grandes civilizaciones. Escribe tu resumen de nuevo en inglés.

Chapter 6 – Introduction

The lessons in this chapter are about the beginnings of the Greek civilization, from 1750 B.C. to 133 B.C. The key concept in this chapter is "democracy." A *democracy* is a government in which citizens have power and exercise their power directly or indirectly through a system of representation. In Lesson 1, you will learn about the early Greek city-states, how people lived and worked, and how ideas about democracy (representative government) developed. Lesson 2 describes a period in early Greek history known as "classical" Greek civilization, which included achievements in the arts and science as well as two major wars. In Lesson 3, you will read how Alexander the Great's conquest of the Persian Empire led to the spread of the Greek language and culture far beyond Greece.	Las lecciones en ente capítulo son acerca de los principios de la civilización griega, de 1750 a.C. a 133 a.C. El concepto principal en este capítulo es la "democracia." Una *democracia* es un gobierno en el cual los ciudadanos tienen el poder y el poder de ejercerlo directamente o indirectamente a través de un sistema de representación. En la lección 1, aprenderás acerca de las primeras ciudades-estados griegos, cómo la gente vivía y trabajaba, y cómo ideas acerca de la democracia se desarrollaron. La lección 2 describe un periodo en la historia temprana griega que se conoce como la civilización griega "clásica" que incluyó logros en las artes y las ciencias también como dos guerras importantes. En la lección 3, vas a leer cómo la conquista del imperio de Persia por parte de Alejandro el Grande promovió la difusión del lenguaje y la cultura griega más allá de Grecia.

Chapter 6 – Student Activity

The roots of democracy first began in ancient Greece. Democracy puts power in the hands of individuals. With a partner, discuss in Spanish how this is a much different concept of government from any that you have read about so far in this textbook. Write a brief paragraph in Spanish summarizing your ideas. After reading the chapter, imagine that you are an Indian Buddhist missionary sent to Greece to preach and convert people to Buddhism. Write a letter in English to a friend back home explaining how Greek democracy works.	Las raíces de la democracia empezaron primero en la Grecia antigua. La democracia pone el poder en las manos del individuo. Con un compañero, discute en español cómo la democracia es un concepto de gobierno muy diferente de lo que han leído hasta ahora en este libro. Escribe un párrafo breve en español dando un resumen de tus ideas. Después de leer el capítulo, imagínate que eres un misionario budista de la India que ha sido enviado a Grecia para predicar y convertir la gente al budismo. Escribe una carta en inglés a un amigo de tu pueblo explicando cómo funciona la democracia griega.

Chapter 7 – Introduction

This chapter introduces the earliest Roman civilizations, from 500 B.C. to A.D. 500, as well as the idea of a representative form of government. The key concept in this chapter is "military strength." *Military strength* refers to the size of a nation's military force. In Lesson 1, you will learn about the beginnings of the Roman civilization, its republican form of government, and why Rome was successful in extending its control of land and people far beyond the Italian peninsula. Lesson 2 explains the changes that occurred over time in the Roman form of government and how Rome became an empire. In Lesson 3, you will read about the causes of the decline of the Roman Empire. Lesson 4 introduces the beginnings of Christianity and explains how this new religion eventually became the official religion of the Roman Empire.	Este capítulo introduce las primeras civilizaciones romanas, de 500 a.C. hasta 500 d.C., y también la idea de una forma de gobierno representativo. El concepto principal en este capítulo es la "fuerza militar." La *fuerza militar* refiere al tamaño de la fuerza militar de una nación. En la lección 1, aprenderás acerca de los principios de la civilización romana, su forma de gobierno republicano, y porqué Roma fue exitosa extendiendo su control de tierra y gente más allá de la isla italiana. La lección 2 explica los cambios que ocurrieron a través del tiempo en la forma de gobierno romano y cómo Roma se hizo un imperio. En la lección 3, vas a leer acerca de las causas de la declinación del imperio romano. La lección 4 introduce los principios del cristianismo y explica cómo esta religión nueva finalmente se volvió la religión oficial del imperio romano.

Chapter 7 – Student Activity

With a partner, discuss in Spanish why a group of people—a tribe, nation, or ethnic group—might choose to become part of an empire. In Spanish, write a bulleted list of 10 reasons. Focus your reasons on economics, geography, politics, religion, technology, society, and culture. After reading the chapter, write a paragraph in English comparing the advantages of becoming part of the Roman Empire to the advantages of remaining independent.	Con un compañero, discute en español por qué una grupo de personas – un tribu, una nación, o grupo étnico – escogería formar parte de un imperio. En español, escribe una lista de diez puntos. Enfoca tus razones con relación a la economía, la geografía, la política, la religión, la tecnología, la sociedad, y la cultura. Después de leer el capítulo, escribe un párrafo en inglés comparando las ventajas de formar parte del imperio romano con las desventajas de seguir independiente.

Chapter 8 – Introduction

The lessons in this chapter are about the eastern part of the Roman Empire that came to be known as the Byzantine Empire. This civilization lasted for more than 1,000 years, from 330 to 1618. The key concept in this chapter is "conquest." *Conquest* comes from the word "conquer" and means "to take by force." In Lesson 1, you will read how the Roman Emperor Constantine moved the Roman capital to Byzantium, in what is now the country of Turkey, and how the new Byzantine Empire grew and prospered. Lesson 2 is about the people and early history of what is today known as Russia.	Las lecciones en este capítulo son acerca de la parte este del imperio romano que vino a ser conocido como el imperio bizantino. El concepto principal en este capítulo es la "conquista." *Conquista* viene del verbo "conquistar" y quiere decir someter por la fuerza. En la lección 1, vas a leer cómo el emperador romano Constantino traslado la capital romana a Bizancio, en lo que hoy es el país de Turquía, y cómo el nuevo imperio bizantino creció y prosperó. La lección 2 es acerca de la gente y la historia de la tierra que hoy se conoce como Rusia.

Chapter 8 – Student Activity

The Germanic tribes that conquered Rome were not a seafaring people—they did not navigate ships on the seas. On a map, find the location of Constantinople, the new capital of the surviving Roman Empire. With a partner, discuss in Spanish reasons why Constantinople was not conquered by the Germanic tribes that conquered Rome. Write a summary of your reasons in Spanish. After reading the chapter, write a paragraph in English explaining why the eastern empire survived.	Los tribus germánicas que conquistaron a Roma no eran gente que viajaban por el mar—no navegaban barcos por el mar. En un mapa, coloca a Constantinopla, la capital nueva del imperio romano que sobrevivió. Con un compañero, discute en español las razones por qué Constantinopla no fue conquistada por las tribus germánicas que conquistaron a Roma. Escribe un resumen de tus razones en español. Después de leer el capítulo, escribe un párrafo en inglés explicando por qué el imperio del este sobrevivió.

Chapter 9 – Introduction

In this chapter, you will learn about Islam and the Muslim civilizations that developed and flourished from 622 to 1639, in what is now Saudi Arabia. The key concept in this chapter is "culture." *Culture* refers to the way of life of a group of people and includes their customs, language, traditions, and beliefs. In Lesson 1, you will read about the life of the Prophet Muhammad, the beliefs of Islam—the religion he founded—and how the Muslim Empire grew and was ruled. In Lesson 2, you will learn how the Muslim dynasties contributed to the expansion of the Muslim Empire and about conflicts among various groups. You will also learn about the artistic and scientific achievements of this civilization.	En este capítulo, aprenderás acerca del Islam y las civilizaciones musulmanas que se desarrollaron y florecieron del año 622 hasta 1639, en lo que hoy es Arabia Saudita. El concepto principal en este capítulo es la "cultura." *Cultura* es el modo de vida de un grupo de personas e incluye sus costumbres, su lenguaje, tradiciones y creencias. En la lección 1, vas a leer acerca de la vida del profeta Muhammad, las creencias del Islam—la religión que el fundó—y cómo el imperio musulmán creció y fue gobernado. En la lección 2, aprenderás cómo las dinastías musulmanas contribuyeron a la expansión del imperio musulmán y acerca de los conflictos entre varios grupos. También aprenderás acerca de los logros artísticos y científicos de esta civilización.

Chapter 9 – Student Activity

With a partner, discuss in Spanish five important differences you have noticed between your native culture and the mainstream American culture. Write a summary of these differences in Spanish. After reading the chapter, write a paragraph in English explaining why differences in cultures affect the way people interact with each other.	Con un compañero, discute en español cinco diferencias importantes que has notado entre tu cultura y la cultura americana. Escribe un resumen de estas diferencias en español. Después de leer el capítulo, escribe un párrafo en inglés explicando porqué las diferencias en las culturas afecta la manera en cual la gente se interrelaciona.

Chapter 10 – Introduction

The lessons in this chapter are about the civilizations that developed in Africa from 750 B.C. to A.D. 1570. The key concept in this chapter is "migration." *Migration* refers to the movement of people from one region to another. In Lesson 1, you will learn about the geography of Africa and the migration of early Africans. Lesson 2 describes different groups that were involved in trade along the eastern coast of Africa. In Lesson 3, you will read about the people and the trade of the kingdoms of West Africa.	Las lecciones en este capítulo son acerca de las civilizaciones que se desarrollaron en África de 750 a.C. hasta 1570 d.C. El concepto principal en este capítulo es la "migración." La *migración* refiere al movimiento de gente de una región a otra. En la lección 1, aprenderás acerca de la geografía de África y la migración de los primeros africanos. La lección 2 describe diferentes grupos que fueron involucrados en el comercio a lo largo de la costa del este de África. En la lección 3, vas a leer acerca de la gente y del comercio de los reinos del oeste de África.

Chapter 10 – Student Activity

Since the beginning of human history, people have moved from place to place, often looking for a better life. Most Americans have ancestors that came from another country. Think about the history of your family. What were some of the reasons your family first came to the United States? Discuss these in Spanish with a partner. Then write a summary of your discussion in Spanish. After reading the chapter, write a paragraph in English comparing your family's reasons for migrating with those of Africans long ago.	Desde el comienzo de la historia humana, la gente se ha trasladado de un lugar a otro, frecuentemente buscando una vida mejor. La mayoría de los americanos tienen ancestros que vinieron de otro país. Piensa acerca de la historia de tu familia. ¿Cuáles eran algunas razones por las cuales tu familia vino a los Estados Unidos? Discute estas en español con un compañero. Entonces, escribe un resumen de tu discusión en español. Después de leer el capítulo, escribe un párrafo en inglés comparando las razones de inmigración de tu familia con las de los africanos en épocas pasadas.

Chapter 11 – Introduction

The lessons in this chapter describe the early civilizations in the Americas from 1400 B.C. to A.D. 1750. The key concept in this chapter is "adaptation to environment." *Adaptation to environment* refers to the adjustments that people make over time to the surroundings in which they live. Lesson 1 describes the Mayans, the Aztecs, and the Incas. In Lesson 2, you will read about three of the several civilizations that developed on the North American continent.	Las lecciones en este capítulo describen las primeras civilizaciones en las Américas de 1400 a.C. hasta 1750 d.C. El concepto principal en este capítulo es la "adaptación al ambiente." La *adaptación al ambiente* se refiere a los ajustes al ambiente que la gente hace a través del tiempo en el lugar donde habita. La lección 1 describe los mayas, los aztecas, y los incas. En la lección 2, vas a leer acerca de tres de las muchas civilizaciones que se desarrollaron en el continente norteamericano.

Chapter 11 – Student Activity

Think about what you already know about early civilizations in Central and South America. With a partner, discuss in Spanish at least five things that make these civilizations great. Write a paragraph in Spanish summarizing your discussion. After reading the chapter, write a paragraph in English comparing one of these civilizations to the Roman Empire.	Piensa acerca de lo que ya sabes acerca de las primeras civilizaciones en centro y Sudamérica. Con un compañero, discute en español al menos cinco cosas que hacen estas grandes civilizaciones. Escribe un párrafo en español dando un resumen de tu discusión. Después de leer el capítulo, escribe un párrafo en inglés comparando una de estas civilizaciones con el imperio romano.

Chapter 12 – Introduction

The lessons in this chapter describe the spread of cultures that took place in Asia from 500 to 1650. The key concept in this chapter is a "closed society." A *closed society* refers to a group of people who live together, share a common culture, and exclude outsiders. Lesson 1 continues the history of Chinese civilization begun in Chapter 5. It describes life under five separate dynasties that ruled China over a period of almost 1,200 years. In Lesson 2, you will read about the early Japanese and Korean civilizations. In Lesson 3, you will learn how the Arab and Mongol invasions affected the lives of people in India.	Las lecciones en este capítulo describen la difusión de culturas que se llevó a cabo en Asia de 500 hasta 1650. El concepto principal en este capítulo es la "sociedad cerrada." Una *sociedad cerrada* es un grupo de personas que viven juntos, comparten una cultura en común y excluyen a los extraños. La lección 1 continúa la historia de la civilización China que comenzó en el capítulo 5. Describe la vida bajo el mando de cinco distintas dinastías que gobernaron a China por un tiempo de casi 1,200 años. En la lección 2, vas a leer acerca de las primeras civilizaciones en Japón y Corea. En la lección 3, aprenderás cómo las invasiones árabe y mongólica afectaron la vida de la gente en la India.

Chapter 12 – Student Activity

In earlier chapters, you learned about how civilizations developed through contact with other people. Imagine that you are part of a group of people who have a closed society. As long as you continue to trade with others, what are the advantages of shutting out outsiders? With a partner, discuss this in Spanish. Write a paragraph in Spanish summarizing your discussion. After reading the chapter, write a paragraph in English explaining the disadvantages of a closed society.	En capítulos anteriores, aprendiste acerca de cómo civilizaciones se desarrollaron por medio del contacto con otra gente. Imagínate que eres parte de un grupo que tiene una sociedad cerrada. Mientras continúan el comercio con otros, ¿cuáles son las ventajas de excluir a los extraños? Con un compañero, discute esto en español. Escribe un párrafo en español dando un resumen de tu discusión. Después de leer el capítulo, escribe un párrafo en inglés explicando las desventajas de una sociedad cerrada.

Chapter 13 – Introduction

This chapter is about the period of world history in Europe from 500 to 1300 known as the Middle Ages. This period is also called the Dark Ages because there was little advancement in the arts or knowledge in Europe at this time. The key concept in this chapter is "feudalism." *Feudalism* refers to the political system in Europe during this time, when most people depended on the landowner, who was usually a noble, for protection and the use of his land in exchange for their loyalty and service. In Lesson 1, you will learn how feudalism and manorialism kept Europe free of rebellion among the common people for almost 700 years. You will also learn how the Catholic Church became very powerful during this time. Lesson 2 describes the Crusades—Christian wars against the Muslims to regain control of the Holy Land—and how these voyages to and from the Middle East contributed to an interest in exploration, an increase in trade, and the growth of cities. Lesson 3 describes the development of nation-states in particular, England and France.	Este capítulo es acerca del período de la historia mundial en Europa del año 500 hasta 1300 conocido como la Edad Media. Este período también se llama la Edad Oscura porque hubo muy pocos adelantos en las artes o el conocimiento en Europa en este tiempo. El concepto principal en este capítulo es el "feudalismo." El *feudalismo* se refiere al sistema político en Europa durante este tiempo, cuando la mayoría de la gente dependía del dueño de la tierra, quien usualmente era un noble, para su protección y el uso de su tierra a cambio de su lealtad y servicio. En la lección 1, vas aprender cómo el feudalismo y el señorío mantuvo a Europa libre de la rebelión entre la gente común por casi 700 años. También vas aprender cómo la Iglesia Católica se volvió muy poderosa durante este tiempo. La lección 2 describe las Cruzadas—guerras Cristianas contra los Musulmanes para recuperar el control de la Tierra Santa – y cómo estos viajes para y del Medio Este contribuyeron a un interés en la exploración, un aumento en el comercio y en el crecimiento de las ciudades. La lección 3 describe el desarrollo de los estados-naciones, en particular, Inglaterra y Francia.

Chapter 13 – Student Activity

Imagine living in a small village where there is very little technology, except manual labor. Your family has lived there for generations. Few people have been beyond a day's walk from the village. With a partner, discuss in Spanish the advantages and disadvantages of living this way. Create a chart in Spanish outlining the advantages and disadvantages. After reading the chapter, consider this: If you could go back to a German village in 798, you would see people in homes made of sticks and mud, and they would be dressed in leather. If you returned in 998, nothing would have changed. Now, if you visited Philadelphia in 1798, you would see carriages pulled by horses, brick streets, and buildings no taller than three stories. If you returned in 1998, you would see skyscrapers, trains, cars, and highways. Based on your reading, why do you think the medieval world did not change for centuries? Write a paragraph in English explaining your reasons.	Imagínate que vives en un pueblo pequeño donde hay muy poca tecnología, con la excepción del trabajo manual. Tu familia ha vivido allí por generaciones. Muy pocas gentes han salido más allá de lo que se puede caminar en un día. Con un compañero, discute en español las ventajas y las desventajas de vivir de esta manera. Haz una tabla en español de las ventajas y desventajas. Después de leer el capítulo, considera esto: Si pudieras regresar a un pueblo alemán en 798, verías gente en sus casas de palo y lodo y estarían vestidos en ropa de piel. Si regresaras en 998, nada habría cambiado. Ahora, si visitaras la ciudad de Filadelfia en 1798, verías coches tirados por caballos, calles hechas de ladrillo y edificios no más altos de tres pisos. Si regresaras en 1998, verías rascacielos, trenes, automóviles y autovías. En base a tu lectura, piensa: ¿Por qué no cambió el mundo medieval por siglos? Escribe un párrafo en inglés explicando tus razones.

Chapter 14 – Introduction

The lessons in this chapter describe major changes that took place in Europe from 1300 to 1650. The key concept in this chapter is "renaissance." *Renaissance* means "rebirth" and refers to the great revival of the arts and learning that took place in Europe during this time. Lesson 1 discusses some of the ideas and events that contributed to the Renaissance. In Lesson 2, you will read about Martin Luther, whose ideas about reforming the Catholic Church led to the Protestant Reformation, and how these ideas also resulted in changes in the governments of some nations. In Lesson 3, you will learn why reforms to the Catholic Church were initially made in England. You will also learn about the Catholic Reformation.	Las lecciones en este capítulo describen cambios importantes que se llevaron acabo en Europa de 1300 hasta 1650. El concepto principal en este capítulo es el "renacimiento." *Renacimiento* quiere decir resurgimiento y se refiere al gran resurgimiento de las artes y el conocimiento que se llevo a cabo en Europa durante este tiempo. En la lección 1 se discuten algunas de las ideas y eventos que contribuyeron al Renacimiento. En la lección 2, vas a leer acerca de Martín Luther, cuyas ideas acerca de la reforma de la Iglesia Católica trajeron como consecuencia la Reforma Protestante, y cómo estas ideas también resultaron en cambios en los gobiernos de algunas naciones. En la lección 3, vas aprender porqué las reformas a la Iglesia Católica se hicieron inicialmente en Inglaterra. También aprenderás acerca de la Reforma Católica.

Chapter 14 – Student Activity

You could say that people's curiosity, or interest in something new, is what led to the Renaissance. Think about what you do when you get really interested in something, like sports, or music, or collecting baseball cards, for example. Select one thing. What do you do to expand your knowledge or satisfy your curiosity about this one thing? With a partner, discuss this in Spanish. Write a bulleted list in Spanish of five things you do. After reading the chapter, write a paragraph in English explaining how your list is similar to or different from the things people did to satisfy their curiosity during the Renaissance.	Se podría decir que la curiosidad de la gente, o el interés en algo nuevo, fue lo que llevó al Renacimiento. Piensa acerca de lo que tú haces cuando ves algo que te interesa, como por ejemplo los deportes, la música o coleccionar tarjetas de béisbol. Selecciona un aspecto. ¿Qué haces para extender tu conocimiento o satisfacer tu curiosidad acerca de este aspecto? Con un compañero, discute esto en español. Escribe una lista en español de cinco cosas que haces. Después de leer el capítulo, escribe un párrafo en inglés explicando cómo tu lista es similar o diferente a lo que la gente hizo para satisfacer su curiosidad durante el Renacimiento.

Chapter 15 – Introduction

This chapter is about a period of almost 400 years when Europeans explored the world and began what is now called "the first global age." The key concept in this chapter is "colony." A *colony* refers to a group of people who settle in another land but who still remain citizens of their own country. Lesson 1 describes the early trade routes of the Portuguese, who wanted to trade directly with India, China, and Southeast Asia. This direct trade reduced the costs of goods and increased profits. In Lesson 2, you will read about Columbus's discovery of a new world and the conquest of the native people who lived there. Lesson 3 describes the results of the Spanish colonization of Central and South America. In Lesson 4, you will learn about the colonization of North America by the Spanish, French, Dutch, and English. Lesson 5 discusses the effects that European exploration had around the world.	Este capítulo es acerca de un período de casi 400 años cuando los europeos exploraron el mundo y comenzaron lo que hoy se llama "la primer época global." El concepto principal en este capítulo es la "colonia." *Colonia* se refiere a un grupo de personas que se colocan en una tierra extranjera pero continúan siendo ciudadanos de su propio país. La lección 1 describe las primeras rutas comerciales de los portugueses, quienes querían comerciar directamente con la India, China, y el sureste de Asia. Este comercio directo reducía el gasto de los productos y aumentaba las ganancias. En la lección 2, vas a leer acerca del descubrimiento de Colón de un nuevo mundo y la conquista de la gente nativa que vivía allí. La lección 3 describe los resultados de la colonización española en centro y Sudamérica. En la lección 4, vas a aprender acerca de la colonización de Norte América por parte de los españoles, los franceses, los holandeses, y los ingleses. La lección 5 discute los efectos que tuvo la exploración europea alrededor del mundo.

Chapter 15 – Student Activity

Imagine that you and your partner are going to a far-away land to search for gold. However, you need money to buy supplies, equipment, the advice of guides, and transportation. With a partner, write a proposal in Spanish for a wealthy investor that includes reasons why he or she should invest in your search. Be sure to describe how you will make this an ongoing source of profit. After reading the chapter, write a letter to your investor in English explaining how you will make sure that the investment is protected from competitors.	Imagínate que tú y tu compañero van a viajar a una tierra muy lejana para buscar oro. No obstante, necesitan dinero para comprar suministros, equipo, el consejo de guías, y transportación. Con un compañero, escribe una propuesta en español a un inversionista rico que incluya razones por las cuales el o ella debe de invertir en tu búsqueda. Asegúrate de describir cómo van hacer que esto sea una fuente continua de beneficios. Después de leer el capítulo, escribe una carta en inglés a tu inversionista explicando cómo vas asegurar que la inversión será protegida de los competidores.

Chapter 16 – Introduction

The lessons in this chapter provide details about the political revolutions and social changes that took place in Europe and the New World from 1600 to 1815. The key concept in this chapter is "revolution." *Revolution* means the overthrow or replacement of a government or political system by the people. In Lesson 1, you will read about important developments in the way England was governed. Lesson 2 describes some of the scientific discoveries that were made during this time. It also introduces some of the philosophers and the ideas that contributed to an expansion of knowledge. Lesson 3 is about the American Revolution and the founding of an independent nation. In Lesson 4, you will read about the French Revolution. Lesson 5 describes the revolutions that took place in Mexico and South America at this time.

En las lecciones de este capítulo se dan detalles acerca de las revoluciones políticas y los cambios sociales que se llevaron a cabo en Europa y en el Nuevo Mundo de 1600 hasta 1815. El concepto principal en este capítulo es la "revolución." *Revolución* quiere decir el derrocamiento o sustitución del gobierno o sistema político por parte del pueblo. En la lección 1, vas a leer acerca de los desarrollos importantes en la manera que Inglaterra fue gobernada. La lección 2 describe algunos de los descubrimientos científicos que se hicieron durante este tiempo. También introduce algunos filósofos y las ideas que contribuyeron a la expansión del conocimiento. La lección 3 es acerca de la revolución americana y la fundación de una nación independiente. En la lección 4, vas a leer acerca de la revolución francesa. La lección 5 describe las revoluciones que se llevaron a cabo en México y en América del Sur en este tiempo.

Chapter 16 – Student Activity

In Chapter 13, you learned about the Middle Ages — a time when learning was limited. Chapter 14 was about the intellectual rebirth of Europe, and in Chapter 15, you read about how the Europeans set out to explore the whole world. This chapter deals with political revolutions. With a partner, discuss in Spanish five ways that the events described in Chapters 13–15 set the stage for political revolutions. Write a summary of your discussion in Spanish. After reading the chapter, pretend that you are a historian. Think of another name for this chapter that better describes the main idea of what took place during this time. Write a paragraph in English explaining your choice of a new title.

En el capítulo 13, aprendiste acerca de la Época Medieval — un tiempo cuando el aprendizaje fue limitado. El capítulo 14 fue acerca del renacimiento intelectual de Europa, y en el capítulo 15, leíste acerca de cómo los europeos se pusieron a explorar todo el mundo. Este capítulo se trata de revoluciones políticas. Con un compañero, discute en español cinco razones cómo los eventos descritos en los capítulos 13–15 prepararon el terreno para las revoluciones políticas. Escribe un resumen de tu discusión en español. Después de leer el capítulo, finja que eres un historiador. Piensa en otro nombre para este capítulo que describa mejor lo que se llevó acabo durante este tiempo. Escribe un párrafo en inglés explicando tu elección del titulo nuevo.

Chapter 17 – Introduction

This chapter is about the social revolutions that took place between 1750 and 1850 and how they changed the way people worked and lived in Europe and the United States. The key concept in this chapter is "social change." *Social change* refers to any major change in the way a society is structured or organized. In Lesson 1, you will read about the Industrial Revolution that changed the way goods were manufactured. Lesson 2 describes some important changes brought about by the Industrial Revolution, including the population shift from rural areas to the cities and the emergence of a working class. In Lesson 3, you will learn about some of the philosophies that developed at this time, as well as some important discoveries and inventions related to the Industrial Revolution.	Este capítulo es acerca de las revoluciones sociales que se llevaron acabo entre 1750 y 1850 y cómo estas cambiaron la manera que la gente trabajaba y vivía en Europa y en los Estados Unidos. El concepto principal en este capítulo es el "cambio social." El *cambio social* se refiere a cualquier cambio importante en la manera que la sociedad se estructura o se organiza. En la lección 1, vas a leer acerca de la Revolución Industrial que cambio la manera de cómo los productos eran fabricados. La lección 2 describe algunos cambios importantes causados por la Revolución Industrial, incluyendo el desplazamiento de la población de las áreas rurales a las ciudades y el surgimiento de una clase obrera. En la lección 3, vas aprender acerca de algunas de las filosofías que se desarrollaron en este tiempo también como algunos descubrimientos e invenciones relacionados a la Revolución Industrial.

Chapter 17 – Student Activity

Think about what happens when people can make decisions for themselves, like where to live and what kind of work to do. Can having the freedom to make choices also create some problems? With a partner, discuss this in Spanish. Write a bulleted list in Spanish of five problems you might have because you have the freedom to make choices. After reading the chapter, think about the way we live today in the United States. What programs are available today that might have helped the people who lived during the Industrial Revolution? Write a paragraph in English explaining your ideas.	Piensa acerca de lo que pasa cuando la gente puede tomar decisiones por sí mismos, cómo donde vivir y qué clase de trabajo tener. ¿Será posible que teniendo la libertad de escoger también pueda crear algunos problemas? Con un compañero, discute esto en español. Escribe una lista en español de cinco problemas que podrías tener si tuvieras la libertad de escoger. Después de leer el capítulo, piensa acerca de cómo vivimos hoy en los Estados Unidos. ¿Cuáles programas están disponibles hoy que pudieran haber ayudado a la gente que vivió durante la Revolución Industrial? Escribe un párrafo en inglés explicando tus ideas.

Chapter 18 – Introduction

The lessons in this chapter describe Europe from 1862 to 1914 and the events that led to various groups of people wanting to establish their own independent countries. The key concept in this chapter is "nationalism." *Nationalism* refers to the idea of political independence for a group of people with a separate identity and culture. In Lesson 1, you will read about attempts by various groups in Europe to establish their own independent countries. Lesson 2 describes how Germany went from over 40 distinct and disconnected small states to the largest industrial nation in Europe in a period of about 50 years.	Las lecciones en este capítulo describen a Europa de 1862 hasta 1914 y los eventos que llevaron a varios grupos de personas a querer establecer su propio país independiente. El concepto principal en este capítulo es el "nacionalismo." El *nacionalismo* se refiere a la idea de independencia política para un grupo de personas con una identidad y cultura separada. En la lección 1, vas a leer acerca de los esfuerzos por parte de varios grupos en Europa para establecer sus propios países independientes. La lección 2 describe cómo Alemania después de tener más de 40 estados pequeños, distintos y desconectados se hizo la nación mas grande industrialmente hablando en Europa en un periodo de alrededor de 50 años.

Chapter 18 – Student Activity

Think about the various groups of students in your school. Think about the students involved in sports teams or academic teams. Have you noticed that many clubs, for example, have members who share common interests? With a partner, discuss in Spanish what benefits a student might get by joining a club or student group. Write a list in Spanish of five benefits. After reading the chapter, write a paragraph in English explaining at least five benefits of a unified Germany.	Piensa acerca de los varios grupos de estudiantes en tu escuela. Piensa acerca de los estudiantes involucrados en los equipos de deportes o equipos académicos. ¿Has notado que muchos clubes, por ejemplo, tienen miembros que tienen intereses en común? Con un compañero, discute en español qué beneficios un estudiante pudiera obtener si forma parte de un club o grupo estudiantil. Escribe una lista en español de cinco beneficios. Después de leer el capítulo, escribe un párrafo en inglés explicando por lo menos cinco beneficios de una Alemania unificada.

Chapter 19 – Introduction

This chapter describes efforts during the 1800s to increase European control and influence all over the world. The key concept in this chapter is "imperialism." *Imperialism* refers to the practice of extending the power and control of a nation. This is done by acquiring more territory or getting control of the political or economic life of other nations. In Lesson 1, you will learn about the British colonization of India. Lesson 2 describes how several European countries agreed to colonize most of the African continent. In Lesson 3, you will read how Japan adapted to modern Western ideas in order to remain independent and become a major industrial nation. Lesson 4 is about European efforts to control China and how the Chinese responded to these efforts. In Lesson 5, you will read about outside influences on countries in Central and South America.	Este capítulo describe los esfuerzos durante el siglo XVIII para aumentar el control y la influencia europea en todo el mundo. El concepto principal es el "imperialismo." El *imperialismo* se refiere a la práctica de extender el poder y el control de una nación. Esto se hace adquiriendo más territorio o consiguiendo el control de la vida política o económica de otras naciones. En la lección 1, vas aprender acerca de la colonización británica de la India. La lección 2 describe cómo varias naciones europeas se pusieron de acuerdo para colonizar casi todo el continente africano. En la lección 3, vas a leer cómo el Japón se adaptó a las ideas modernas del oeste para mantenerse independiente y hacerse una nación industrial importante. La lección 4 es acerca de los esfuerzos europeos para controlar a la China y cómo los chinos respondieron a estos esfuerzos. En la lección 5, vas a leer acerca de las influencias externas en los países del Centro y del Sur de América.

Chapter 19 – Student Activity

Consider the following questions: What are the advantages and disadvantages for the country that is building an empire? What are the advantages and disadvantages for the countries that are brought into the empire? With a partner, discuss these questions in Spanish. Make a list in Spanish of at least five advantages and disadvantages for each. After reading the chapter, think about how Africa was colonized. Write a paragraph in English supporting or opposing the European colonization of Africa.	Considera las siguientes preguntas: ¿Cuáles son las ventajas y las desventajas para el país que está construyendo un imperio? ¿Cuáles son las ventajas y las desventajas para los países que vienen a formar parte del imperio? Con un compañero, discute estas preguntas en español. Haz una lista de a lo menos cinco ventajas y desventajas para cada una. Después de leer el capítulo, piensa acerca de cómo África fue colonizada. Escribe un párrafo en inglés apoyando u oponiendo la colonización europea de África.

Chapter 20 – Introduction

The lessons in this chapter describe a short period in world history that includes a major world war and a political revolution in Russia. This revolution influenced world events for the remainder of the century. The key concept in this chapter is "conflict." A *conflict* is a fight or a disagreement. Lesson 1 describes the events before and during World War I. In Lesson 2, you will read about the end of the war and the Treaty of Versailles that set the stage for the next world war. In Lesson 3, you will read about the Russian Revolution and the beginning of a Communist government.	Las lecciones en este capítulo describen un periodo corto en la historia mundial que incluye una guerra importante y una revolución política en Rusia. Esta revolución influenció eventos mundiales para el resto del siglo. El concepto principal en este capítulo es el "conflicto." Un *conflicto* es un pleito o desacuerdo. La lección 1 describe los eventos antes y durante la primera guerra mundial. En la lección 2, vas a leer acerca del fin de la guerra y del Tratado de Versalles que fue el antecedente a la próxima guerra mundial. En la lección 3, vas a leer acerca de la revolución rusa y los principios de un gobierno comunista.

Chapter 20 – Student Activity

In the previous chapter, you read about Europe's need for raw materials and new markets. You also read about increased feelings of nationalism. How do you think these contributed to conflict among European nations? With a partner, discuss this in Spanish. Write a summary of your discussion in Spanish. After reading the chapter, write a paragraph in English explaining why the League of Nations did not survive.	En el capítulo anterior, leíste acerca de la necesidad europea de materias primas y nuevos mercados. También leíste acerca del aumento de sentimientos nacionalistas. ¿Cómo piensas que estos contribuyeron al conflicto entre las naciones europeas? Con un compañero, discute en español. Escribe un resumen de tu discusión en español. Después de leer el capítulo, escribe un párrafo en inglés explicando porqué la Liga de Naciones no sobrevivió.

Chapter 21 – Introduction

This chapter is about conditions in Europe between 1919 and 1939 that led to the rise of totalitarianism. The key concept in this chapter is "economic depression." During an *economic depression*, there is a period of low general economic activity marked by rising levels of unemployment and falling wages and prices. Lesson 1 describes how Benito Mussolini rose to power in Italy and established a Fascist government. In Lesson 2, you will read about life in the Soviet Union under the totalitarian government of Joseph Stalin. In Lesson 3, you will learn how and why Adolf Hitler became the head of the German government.	Este capítulo es acerca de las condiciones en Europa entre 1919 y 1939 que llevaron al ascenso del totalitarismo. El concepto principal en este capítulo es la "depresión económica." Durante una *depresión económica*, hay un periodo de actividad general económica marcado por niveles de desempleo y la caída de sueldos y precios. La lección 1 describe cómo Benito Mussolini tuvo acceso al poder en Italia y estableció un gobierno fascista. En la lección 2, vas a leer acerca de la vida en la Unión Soviética bajo el gobierno totalitario de José Stalin. En la lección 3, vas aprender cómo y por qué Adolf Hitler se hizo jefe del gobierno alemán.

Chapter 21 – Student Activity

Sometimes, when countries are in economic or political trouble, people look for strong leaders to get them out of trouble. What are the advantages and disadvantages of choosing a strong leader? Discuss this in Spanish with a partner. Write a bulleted list of five advantages and five disadvantages. After reading the chapter, compare your list with what actually happened in Europe between the two world wars. Write a paragraph in English explaining how your list compares to actual events.	A veces, cuando países están en dificultades económicas o políticas, la gente busca líderes fuertes para que los saquen de sus problemas. ¿Cuáles son las ventajas y las desventajas de escoger un líder fuerte? Discute esto en español con un compañero. Escribe una lista de cinco ventajas y desventajas. Después de leer el capítulo, compara tus listas con lo que realmente pasó en Europa entre las dos guerras mundiales. Escribe un párrafo en inglés explicando cómo tus listas se comparan con eventos actuales.

Chapter 22 – Introduction

This chapter covers the events around the world that took place between the beginning of World War II and the end of the Cold War. The key concept in this chapter is "global war." *Global war* means that many nations from several continents are involved in a war. In Lesson 1, you will learn how Japan, Italy, and Germany began to take control of other countries and how this led to war. Lesson 2 describes many of the events of World War II as well as American involvement in the war. In Lesson 3, you will read about the hostility between Russia and the United States that became known as the Cold War.	Este capítulo cubre los eventos alrededor del mundo que tomaron lugar entre el principio de la segunda guerra mundial y el fin de la guerra fría. El concepto principal en este capítulo es la "guerra global." La *guerra global* significa que muchas naciones de varios continentes están involucradas en una guerra. En la lección 1, vas aprender cómo Japón, Italia y Alemania comenzaron a tomar control de otros países y cómo esto llevó a la guerra. La lección 2 describe muchos de los eventos de la segunda guerra mundial igual como la participación americana en la guerra. En la lección 3, vas a leer acerca de la hostilidad entre Rusia y los Estados Unidos que se vino a conocer como la Guerra Fría.

Chapter 22 – Student Activity

In previous chapters, you have read about wars between countries that were near or reasonably close to each other. What developments allowed countries to extend their fight into different hemispheres? Discuss this with a partner in Spanish. Write a paragraph in Spanish summarizing your discussion. After reading the chapter, write a paragraph in English explaining how the development of nuclear missiles made the Cold War possible.	En capítulos anteriores, has leído acerca de guerras entre países que estaban más o menos cerca uno del otro. ¿Cuáles desarrollos permitieron a los países extender sus pleitos a otros hemisferios? Discute esto con un compañero en español. Escribe un párrafo en español dando un resumen de tu discusión. Después de leer el capítulo, escribe un párrafo en inglés explicando cómo el desarrollo de misiles nucleares hizo la Guerra Fría posible.

Chapter 23 – Introduction

The lessons in this chapter are about the social, economic, and political changes that took place in the second half of the 20th century. The key concept in this chapter is "interdependence." *Interdependence* in this chapter refers to the idea of nations being dependent on each other for economic and political reasons. Lesson 1 describes some of the conflicts between European nations after World War II, some of the economic changes that took place in Europe, and the breakup of the Soviet Union. In Lesson 2, you will read about the economic and political problems in Central and South America. Lesson 3 is about the conflicts that took place in Asia during this time, including the Korean and Vietnam Wars, which involved the United States. In Lesson 4, you will learn how many African nations established independence from their European colonizers. Lesson 5 describes events in the Middle East.	Las lecciones en este capítulo son acerca de los cambios sociales, económicos y políticos que se llevaron acabo durante la segunda parte del siglo XX. El concepto principal en este capítulo es la "interdependencia." La *interdependencia* en este capítulo se refiere a la idea que las naciones dependen unas de las otras por razones económicas o políticas. La lección 1 describe algunos de los conflictos entre las naciones europeas después de la segunda guerra mundial, algunos cambios económicos que se llevaron acabo en Europa, y la caída de la Unión Soviética. En la lección 2, vas a leer acerca de los problemasacabo en Asia durante este tiempo, incluyendo las guerras de Corea y Vietnam, que involucraron a los Estados Unidos. En la lección 4, vas aprender cómo muchas naciones africanas establecieron su independencia de sus colonizadores europeos. La lección 5 describe eventos en el Medio Este.

Chapter 23 – Student Activity

In the previous chapter, you read how many nations, both large and small, were drawn into a global war. You also read about the Cold War. How do you think future conflicts between nations might be resolved? Discuss this with a partner in Spanish. Write a summary of your discussion in Spanish. After reading the chapter, write a paragraph in English explaining the steps that major powers took in the second half of the 20th century to prevent another world war.	En el capítulo anterior, leíste cómo muchas naciones, grandes y pequeñas, estuvieron involucradas en una guerra global. También leíste acerca de la guerra fría. ¿Cómo crees que conflictos futuros podrían ser resueltos? Discute esto con un compañero en español. Escribe un resumen de tu discusión en español. Después de leer el capítulo, escribe un párrafo en inglés explicando los pasos que las grandes potencias dieron durante la segunda parte del siglo XX para prevenir otra guerra mundial.

Chapter 24 – Introduction

This chapter is about some of the major problems facing the world today. These problems and how they are being addressed are presented in the form of case studies. A case study is a particular way to try to understand a problem by looking at it from different angles. The key concept in this chapter is "global issues." *Global issues* are concerns or problems that affect most of the world's population. In Case Study 1, you will read about some issues that developing nations are facing, such as infant mortality and malnutrition. Case Study 2 describes some of the environmental issues facing the world today. In Case Study 3, you will read about human rights. In Case Study 4, you will learn about crimes against humanity and genocide. Case Study 5 is about terrorism.	Este capítulo es acerca de algunos de los problemas más importantes que se confrontan en el mundo hoy en día. Estos problemas y cómo se están tratando se presentan en forma de estudios de caso. Un estudio de caso es una manera particular de intentar de entender un problema mirándolo de diversos ángulos. El concepto principal en este capítulo es "problemas globales." *Problemas globales* son cuestiones o problemas que afectan la mayoría de la población del mundo. En el caso de estudio 1, vas a leer acerca de algunos problemas que los países en desarrollo están enfrentando, como la mortalidad infantil y la desnutrición. El caso de estudio 2 describe algunos de los problemas del ambiente que se enfrentan en el mundo hoy en día. En el estudio de caso 3, vas a leer acerca de los derechos humanos. En el caso de estudio 4, vas aprender acerca de los crímenes contra la humanidad y el genocidio. El estudio de caso es acerca del terrorismo.

Chapter 24 – Student Activity

From the list of global problems described above, think of six specific problems you have heard or read about that are facing the world today. With a partner, discuss these in Spanish. Write a list of these problems in Spanish. After reading the chapter, identify a problem in your neighborhood that fits into one of the categories of problems discussed in the chapter. Write a persuasive paragraph in English about why this problem would make a good case study. How would the neighborhood benefit as a result?	De la lista de los problemas globales descritos arriba, piensa en seis problemas específicos de los cuales has oído o leído que se enfrentan en el mundo hoy en día. Con un compañero, discute estos en español. Escribe una lista de estos problemas en español. Después de leer el capítulo, identifica un problema en tu vecindario que pertenezca a una de las categorías de los problemas discutidos en el capítulo. Escribe un párrafo persuasivo en inglés explicando porqué este problema sería un buen estudio de caso. ¿Cómo beneficiaría al vecindario por consecuencia?

To the Student

This textbook is a history of the world's people and major cultures from early times to the present. It begins with Stone Age people of prehistoric times. Prehistory is that time before people made written records. We know about these people mainly from the artifacts they left behind.

The book next looks at the early civilizations that developed writing, agriculture, and towns and cities. It traces the rise of the ancient Middle East, North Africa, Asia, and the Americas. These civilizations developed separately with little or no outside contact.

However, at the beginning of what we call the Global Age, the people of Asia, Africa, Europe, and the Americas came into contact with one another. Some of these contacts were peaceful, with people trading goods. Often contact led to wars, the enslaving of people, and death by diseases brought by the invaders.

World history is a story of change. Civilization began as the change from hunting and gathering to farming and town life. As towns grew into cities, the way people lived changed again. More people lived by making and selling goods. That led to the Industrial Revolution as people worked in factories instead of at home. We continue to live in a changing world. Many of these changes have brought us a higher standard of living and a better life.

While change brings opportunities, it also causes problems. This book examines many world problems of the past and of today. These include revolutions, brutal dictatorships, world wars, economic hard times, and environmental disasters.

Fortunately, world history is more than the story of disasters and defeats. It also is an account of how people solved or learned to manage the problems they encountered. I hope that this book helps you to better understand the opportunities and problems of the world in which you live.

Matthew T. Downey

Unit Objectives

After studying this unit, students will be able to

- explain how scientists have learned about the earliest humans
- describe the first civilizations in Southwest Asia

Unit 1 focuses on the rise of civilization.

Chapter 1, The Earliest Humans (Prehistory to 2500 B.C.), examines the early stages of human development.

Chapter 2, Southwest Asia: Beginnings (1200 B.C.–500 B.C.), explores the development of civilizations in Mesopotamia and the beginnings of Judaism.

Getting Started

Have a student read aloud the title of this book. Explain that it is a history of the world. Use a world map to show students the continents of the world. Then have a student read aloud the title of the unit and the paragraph that follows on page 2. Ask students what they think a civilization might be. Ask students to record their ideas in their notebooks. They might also jot down any questions they have about the content of this unit. Encourage them to answer the questions as they read Unit 1.

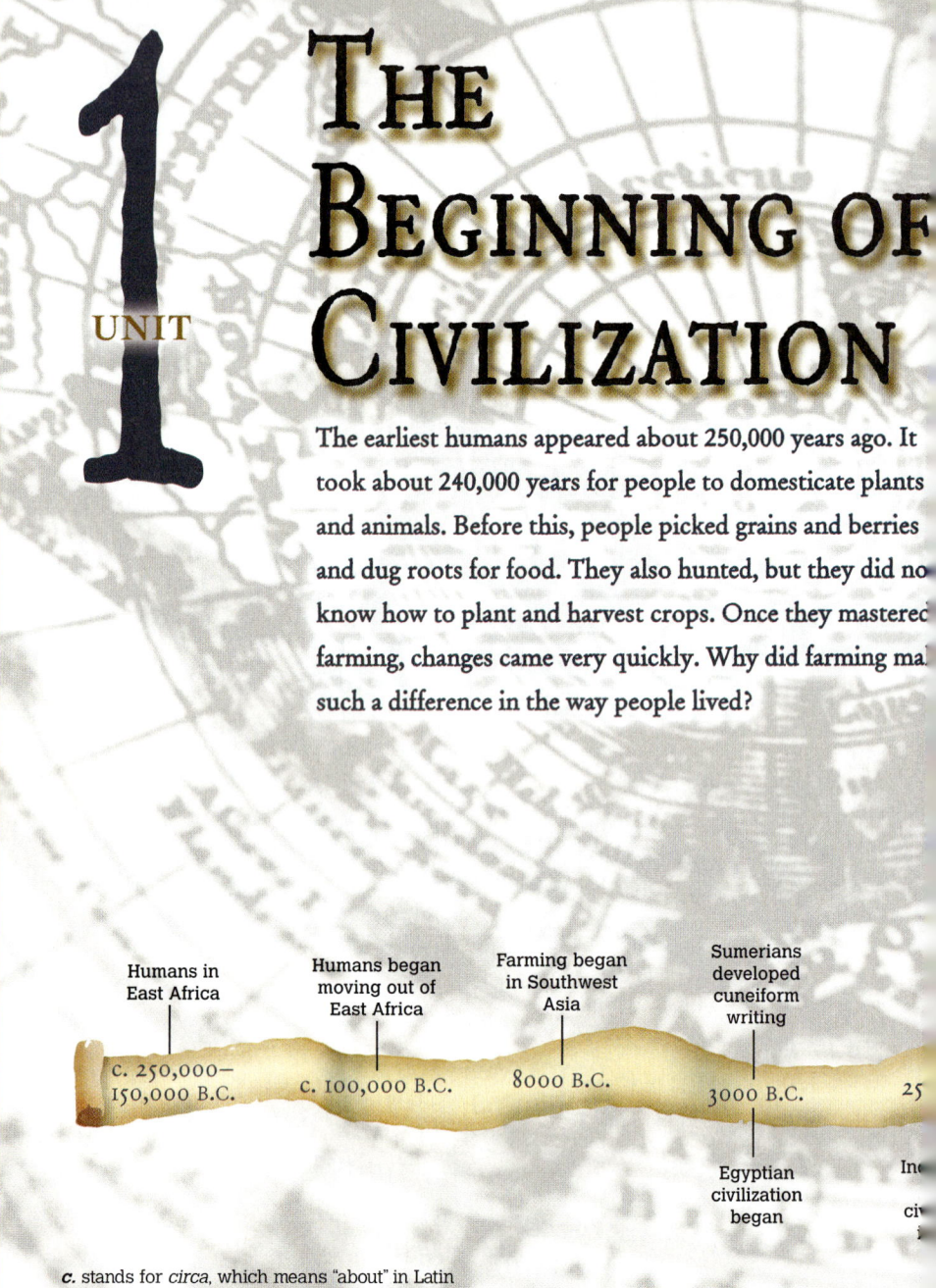

UNIT 1: The Beginning of Civilization

The earliest humans appeared about 250,000 years ago. It took about 240,000 years for people to domesticate plants and animals. Before this, people picked grains and berries and dug roots for food. They also hunted, but they did not know how to plant and harvest crops. Once they mastered farming, changes came very quickly. Why did farming make such a difference in the way people lived?

Humans in East Africa — c. 250,000–150,000 B.C.
Humans began moving out of East Africa — c. 100,000 B.C.
Farming began in Southwest Asia — 8000 B.C.
Sumerians developed cuneiform writing — 3000 B.C.
Egyptian civilization began

c. stands for *circa*, which means "about" in Latin

Measuring Time

Explain to students that Chapter 1 focuses on the beginnings of human civilizations. Chapter 2 examines the first civilizations in Southwest Asia. Explain to students that the events at the bottom of the timeline describe what was happening in other parts of the world at the same time. This is the case for each Unit Opener timeline throughout the book.

Timeline Extension

Ask students to use the timeline to preview each chapter in the unit. Then have them answer the following questions:

- What were the key events in Southwest Asia in this period?
- What were the key world events during those years?
- Where did civilizations arise?
- How many years passed between the first event and the last event on the timeline?

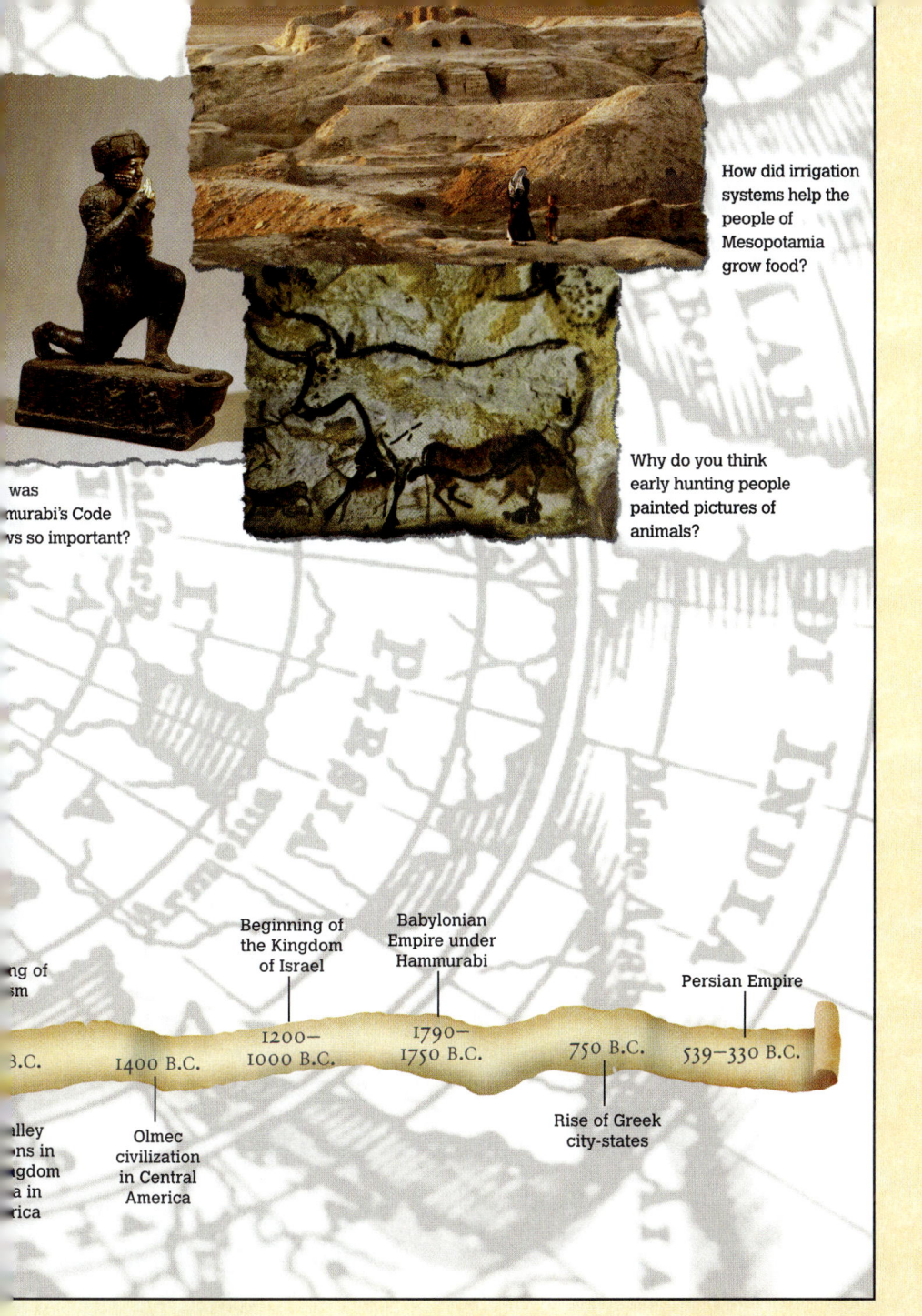

How did irrigation systems help the people of Mesopotamia grow food?

Why do you think early hunting people painted pictures of animals?

was murabi's Code vs so important?

Collage Answers

1 The land of Mesopotamia was too dry for some crops. Learning how to bring water into the fields allowed people to grow more crops despite the small amount of rain and the unpredictable floods.

2 Hammurabi's Code of laws was the first written set of laws, establishing a number of legal principles still in effect today.

3 People of early civilizations were dependent on animals for food and clothing. The paintings of animals may have been a sign of respect or a way to gain greater knowledge about the animals.

Collage Extension

Use the images and questions on page 3 to preview the unit. Discuss what the questions and pictures suggest about the earliest civilizations.

Beginning of the Kingdom of Israel — 1200–1000 B.C.

Babylonian Empire under Hammurabi — 1790–1750 B.C.

Rise of Greek city-states — 750 B.C.

Persian Empire — 539–330 B.C.

Olmec civilization in Central America — 1400 B.C.

ng of sm — 3.C.

alley ns in gdom a in rica

Picturing History

The three images on page 3 represent people and countries that will be discussed in the unit.

1 The top image is a picture of ancient buildings in modern-day Iraq. Iraq is one of the countries in what was ancient Mesopotamia. The land is still desert where very little will grow.

2 The figure in this image is King Hammurabi, who ruled in Babylon around 1790 B.C. He is known as the first ruler to codify the laws of the land. Stone and bronze images of him have survived, so historians have an idea of what he looked like.

3 This is a photograph of an ancient cave painting in prehistoric Africa. Cave paintings of animals, done by prehistoric people, are found in many places in the world. Animals were an important source of food for the people who created these paintings.

The Beginning of Civilization

Chapter Summary
Refer to page 14 for a summary of Chapter 1.

Related Transparencies

T-1 World Map

T-2 Outline World Map

Key Blacklines

Biography–Donald C. Johanson

DVD Extension

Encourage students to use the reading comprehension, vocabulary reinforcement, and interactive timeline activities on the student DVD.

Picturing History

The photograph on page 5 shows an archaeological dig in Egypt. The pans at the bottom of the photograph are used for sifting dirt. The remains of pottery, bones, and food stay in the pan, while the dirt goes through. These are artifacts that the archaeologists will study. Ask students to notice the tools the archaeologists use: the brushes, the measuring rod, and the bag (held by the man in the dark shirt). Ask students what they think the structure might be.

Chapter 1
THE EARLIEST HUMANS
(PREHISTORY TO 2500 B.C.)

Getting Focused

Skim this chapter to predict what you will be learning.
- Read the lesson titles and subheadings.
- Look at the illustrations and read the captions.
- Examine the maps.
- Review the vocabulary words and terms.

What do you think this chapter is about? Do the subheadings and pictures raise any questions for you? In your notebook, write at least two questions you want answered as you read this chapter.

Pre-Reading Discussion

1 Have students complete each bulleted direction on page 4. Remind them that Chapter 1 focuses on the prehistory of civilization—an age that ended with the development of writing.

2 Ask students to read major headings, tables, and captions for clues to the main ideas highlighted in this chapter. Have students record their ideas in their notebooks and then revise their notes as they read the chapter.

3 Have students write their questions in their notebooks.

Lesson Vocabulary

Introduce each vocabulary word for students. Encourage students to begin a list of prefixes and suffixes, along with their meanings, as they encounter them in the vocabulary terms. Review the meaning of the prefix *pre-*. (*Pre-* means "before.") Have students suggest several words beginning with this prefix, such as *precaution* and *preview*.

Ask students what they think the word *prehistory* means.

LESSON 1

Prehistory

Thinking on Your Own

Read the vocabulary words on this page. While you read this lesson, use each vocabulary word in a sentence. Write the sentences in your notebook. Share your sentences with a partner.

Africa, Prehistory–2500 B.C.

The time before writing was invented is called **prehistory**. Writing is only about 5,200 years old. The earliest humans evolved on Earth between 150,000 and 250,000 years ago. If there was no writing for most of this time, how do we learn about the earliest people? Answering this question is the work of specially trained scientists.

focus your reading

How do people learn about prehistory?

What do anthropologists think are the stages of human development?

How did early people live?

vocabulary

prehistory   artifacts
anthropologists   fossils
culture   hominids
archaeologists   nomads

How We Know About Early Life

Anthropologists study the beginnings and development of humans and their **cultures**. In this context, *culture* does not mean movies or music. As anthropologists use the word, *culture* means the way of life of a group of people. It includes their beliefs, traditions, government, religion, and social classes. A way of life is what makes a group unique.

Archaeology is a branch of anthropology. **Archaeologists** study past societies by examining the things people made and left behind. These things are

Archaeologists dig for artifacts in Egypt.

Lesson Summary

Scientists such as anthropologists and archaeologists study prehistory—the time before the invention of writing. These scientists study fossils and artifacts.

The earliest humanlike creatures were called hominids. They learned how to start fires and keep them burning. They were hunters and gatherers. Over time, they developed language and tools.

Lesson Objective

Students will learn about the methods that scientists use when studying prehistory and the development of humans as we know them.

Focus Your Reading Answers

1 People study the artifacts and fossils left behind by early peoples.

2 Anthropologists believe that the first hominids, called *Australopithecus*, lived in Africa about three to four million years ago. From that group, *Homo habilis* came. *Homo erectus* appeared about 1.9 million years ago. *Homo sapiens* were the next stage, while modern humans are *homo sapiens sapiens*.

3 Early people lived as nomads, moving from place to place gathering and hunting food. They often lived in caves. They developed language and simple tools.

Lesson Vocabulary, continued

Prehistory means "the time before writing was invented."

Explain to students that the suffix *-ologist* refers to someone who studies. An *anthropologist* is one who studies humans and how they live, while an *archaeologist* is one who studies *cultures* using materials that survive, such as tools, weapons, and buildings. Ask students to name other areas of science that include the suffix *-ologist*. (biologist, pharmacologist)

Culture refers to the ways of life of a group of people. Ask students what contributes to a group's *culture*. (music, food, clothes, etc.)

Ask students if they have ever heard of anyone burying a time capsule. Tell them that the items in a time capsule are *artifacts*. *Artifacts* are things that were made by humans. *Fossils* differ from *artifacts* in that they are not made by humans. Rather, they are preserved by natural conditions.

Hominids were the earliest humans. Point out to students the prefix *homo-*, which refers to human beings, in *homo erectus* and *homo sapiens*. *Nomads* are people who wander in search of food. They have no permanent homes, but travel to where food is available.

The Earliest Humans 5

Picturing History

The Alps Iceman, pictured on page 6, was discovered by hikers in 1991 in the mountains along the Austria-Italy border. Scientists believe he lived more than 5,000 years ago. He died after being hit with an arrow. Found with the body were three layers of well-constructed clothing, the first evidence researchers have of Neolithic clothes. He also had simple weapons and tools with him. The body is now preserved at a museum in Italy in a cold-storage vault. Scientists wishing to study the iceman can remove him for no more than 11 minutes at a time.

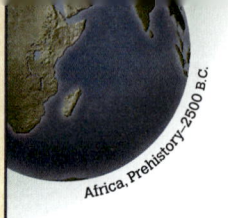

Africa, Prehistory–2500 B.C.

called **artifacts**. An artifact can be anything from a building to an earring. Anthropologists use both artifacts and **fossils** in their work. Fossils are the remains of humans, plants, and animals that have become hard like stone.

Over the years, scientists have set up scientific methods for finding and studying artifacts and fossils. The search begins with a dig, or excavation. Scientists carefully remove layers of dirt looking for evidence of human activity. They use a small hand tool called a trowel and different-sized brushes. Each find, or discovery, is labeled and packed for later study.

The remains of Otzi, the world's oldest mummy, have been preserved for study of what life was like 5,300 years ago.

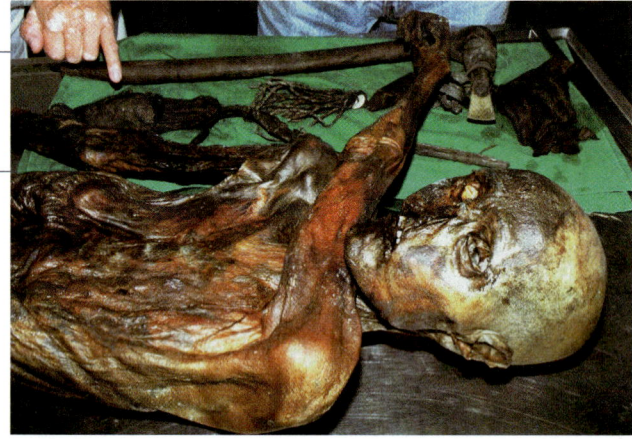

Back in the lab, scientists carefully examine the artifacts and fossils. To understand human developments, scientists need to date their finds. Anthropologists try to figure out if one culture lived earlier than, later than, or at the same time as another culture. To date items, they often conduct radiocarbon dating. Other methods of dating include tree-ring dating and stratigraphic observations.

Early Stages of Development

Anthropologists have found evidence in Africa of the ancestors of modern humans. These early humanlike creatures are called **hominids**. They walked upright and made stone tools. Anthropologists believe that hominids went through three stages of development.

Extension

The iceman was named Otzi because it was found near the Ötztal Valley. At first, the importance of the discovery was not known, and the corpse was left where it was found for a week before scientists arrived. Both police and hikers tried to free the body from the ice with whatever tools they had, including a jackhammer, ski poles, and the iceman's own possessions. In the process, some of Otzi's clothing was torn.

Scientists used Otzi's weapon to date the find. The weapon was an ax, a wedge-shaped metal blade attached to a yew wood handle with cow leather and glue made from birch tree gum. The ax blade was made of copper, used nearly 2,000 years before the Bronze Age. Scientists knew that Otzi must be 5,000–5,500 years old.

The first hominids are called *Australopithecus*. They lived in eastern and southern Africa, possibly 3 to 4 million years ago. They walked upright and made a few simple tools from stone.

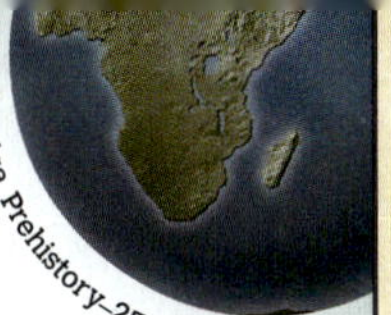

Evidence of later hominids has also been found in Africa—as well as in Europe and Asia. They are known as *Homo erectus*. They appeared about 1.5 million years ago. *Homo erectus* walked upright, too, and made more advanced stone tools. Anthropologists believe *Homo erectus* began in Africa and moved to Asia and Europe over time. It was during this period that fire was discovered. Lightning could start a fire and so could sunlight on dry branches. But these fires started naturally. *Homo erectus* figured out how to start fires and keep them burning. This was an important turning point in history.

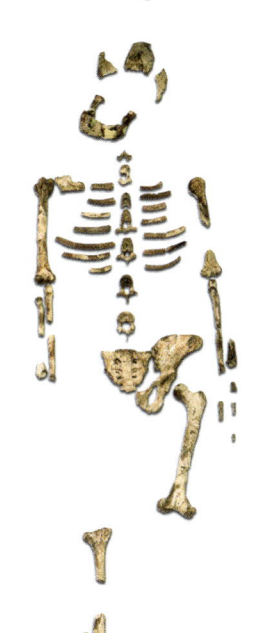

The last stage of development is called *Homo sapiens*. Anthropologists have found evidence of these humans in East Africa between 150,000 and 250,000 years ago. One branch of *Homo sapiens* became modern humans, known as *Homo sapiens sapiens*. About 100,000 years ago, *Homo sapiens sapiens* began moving out of Africa. By 50,000 years ago, humans had reached Australia. By 40,000 years ago, they were living in Europe. Humans also moved east, reaching Asia 25,000 years ago. From Asia, humans moved into North America and then South America. By 10,000 years ago, they had reached the tip of South America.

Hominids used stone hand axes as tools.

Lucy, a member of the *Australopithecus* genus, lived about 3.3 million years ago in Ethiopia, Africa.

The Earliest Humans   7

Picturing History

Early people used hand axes, like the one pictured on page 7, to shape other tools, to clean animal skins, and to plant crops. They most often used flint, which flaked when chipped but was widely available. Using a hammer, they struck the flint to trim and shape it. Hand axes were later attached to handles and used to clear forests for farming.

Picturing History

Donald Johanson and Tim Gray unearthed several hundred bone fragments, about 40 percent of a hominid skeleton, over a two-week period in late 1974. The team had been working in Hadar, Ethiopia, when they discovered Lucy, pictured on page 7. Because there was no duplication of any of the human bones, scientists believe all the fragments to be a single skeleton. The skeleton resides at the National Museum of Ethiopia in the capital, Addis Ababa. Casts have been made of her bones so that scientists in other parts of the world can study her.

Extension

Lucy received her name because, during the celebration of the find, the Beatles' song "Lucy in the Sky with Diamonds" was playing. Invite students interested in music to find a CD or recording of the song and share it with the class.

Ask other students to use library resources or the Internet to learn more about how "Lucy" was found.

The Earliest Humans   7

Stop and Think

Sentences should reflect the idea that tools made it easier to hunt and kill animals and to use plants to feed families and tribes.

Picturing History

In the days before large mills, women used hand grinding tools, such as the ones in the photograph at the top of page 8, to make flour from wheat or other grains. Unleavened bread, which contains no yeast, was a staple food during this time.

Picturing History

The photograph at the bottom of page 8 shows a burial site dating back 10,000–15,000 years. People were often buried with the goods they were thought to need in the afterlife. Food, vessels such as the one shown here, and even servants and pets, were often buried with the deceased.

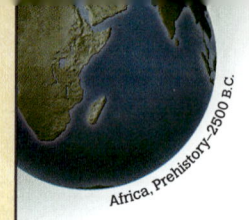

Stone tools help archaeologists to learn about ancient cultures.

Africa, Prehistory–2500 B.C.

Hunters and Gatherers

The earliest people were **nomads**. They lived in groups of 20 to 30 people. Nomads do not live in one location. They move from place to place. The earliest people had to move around because they lived by hunting and gathering their food. The men hunted big-game animals like woolly mammoths and bison. They also hunted smaller game like deer and rabbits. If a group lived near water, the men might also fish. The women dug up plants and roots, and gathered berries, nuts, fruits, and grains to add to the meat. All the plant foods grew wild. The earliest people did not know how to farm. People who live this way are called hunters and gatherers.

Many ancient burial sites contain items for the deceased to use in the afterlife.

stop and think

Why do you think learning to make tools for grinding grain and killing animals was important? Talk over your ideas with a partner. Write a sentence to answer the question.

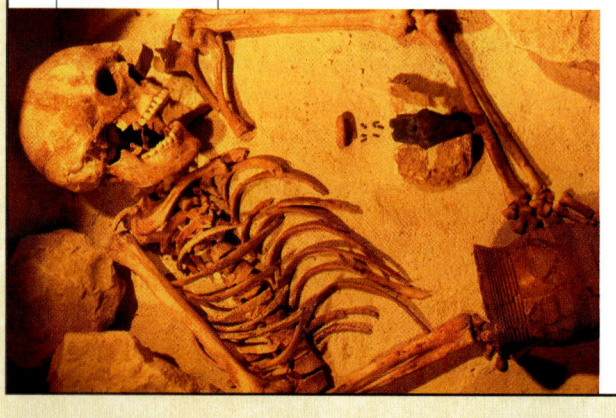

Prehistoric people spent most of their time finding and preparing food. As a result, there was little time for anything else. Over thousands of years, however, people made discoveries that made

Extension

Explain to students that an afterlife is life, or existence, that some people believe follows death. In order to prepare for the afterlife, early humans were buried with the items they would need in their afterlife. Ask students what items they think would be most important for living in the afterlife.

Extension

Divide students into small groups. Provide each group with a world map. Have them use markers to trace the possible journeys of *Homo sapiens sapiens*. Give each group time to explain its map.

8 | Chapter 1

their lives easier. They invented speech so they could communicate plans for the hunt. They learned to make tools from stone and fishhooks from bone. The invention of the spear made it easier to bring down large animals on the run. So did the invention of the bow and arrow. As people moved into colder areas, they learned to make clothing from the skins of animals. They invented needles and used thin strips of animal sinew as thread to sew skins together.

Women had a central role in prehistoric groups. Like men they were responsible for finding food. Archaeologists also speculate that women prepared the food and took care of the children. Some archaeologists think that women had a role in running the groups and making decisions.

Putting It All Together

Choose one photograph from the lesson. Write a paragraph to explain what it shows. Use information from the text and the caption. Share your paragraph with a partner.

The Leakeys: Time Travelers

The Leakeys are a family of anthropologists who work in East Africa. The first anthropologist in the family was Louis (1903–1972). His wife, Mary Douglas Nicols, (1913–1996) soon joined him in looking for fossils. Their son, Richard, (1944–) found his first fossil when he was six. Richard married a fellow scientist, Meave Epps. Their daughter Louise has also joined in the family's work.

The Leakeys' work has changed the way science describes the ancestors of modern human beings. Louis and Mary made their first important discovery in 1959. Each discovery pushed the age of human ancestors farther and farther back in time.

After her husband's death, Mary Leakey continued their work. Her discoveries have been dated to 3.6 million years ago. Richard Leakey also worked in East Africa and made important finds. He dug up what may be a separate group of human or humanlike creatures.

Biography Extension

Louise Leakey, daughter of Meave and Richard Leakey, is the third generation of Leakeys to work in Africa. Louise first visited the Turkana Basin in Kenya, where her parents were working, when she was only two weeks old. Eventually, she and her mother joined together to lead expeditions to the Turkana Basin. In 1999, mother and daughter located a 3.5 million-year-old skull and part of a jaw. Louise's work in Kenya has sparked concern for the indigenous people. Funds for a local school and medical center have been raised.

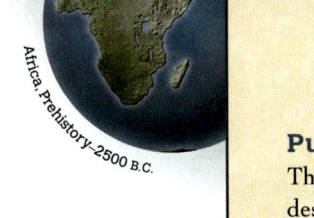

Putting It All Together

The paragraphs should describe or explain one of the photographs used in the lesson.

Bio Facts

- Louis S. B. Leakey was born in Kenya in 1903.
- His parents were English missionaries to the Kikuyu tribe.
- He was initiated into the Kikuyu tribe at the age of thirteen.
- He graduated from Cambridge University with degrees in anthropology and archaeology in 1926.
- He encouraged Jane Goodall, English ethologist and zoological biologist, in her early studies of chimpanzees in the wild.
- Mary D. Nicols was born in England in 1913.
- Her father was a landscape artist. From him, Mary got her drawing ability.
- At seventeen, she worked on an archaeological dig as an illustrator. She met Louis Leakey when he asked her to illustrate a book he had written.
- In 1959, the couple found a hominid skull that brought interest and funding from the National Geographic Society.
- Mary's greatest finds came after her husband's death in 1972.
- In 1979, footprints discovered at Olduvai Gorge indicated that walking upright was an older human trait than had been thought.
- Mary Leakey died in 1996 in Nairobi, Kenya.

The Earliest Humans

Lesson Summary
The ability to farm changed the way people lived. No longer required to follow herds or search for edible plants, people settled into villages and towns. They domesticated animals for food and work. The population increased, as there was a steady food supply. In addition, they developed arts and crafts. Civilization developed as these groups grew and needed organization.

Lesson Objective
Students will learn about the Neolithic revolution and the changes it brought about.

Focus Your Reading Answers
1 No one is certain how farming began. Some think that early people observed plants coming back in the same place each year. Others think that they planted seeds, either by digging holes or by scattering the seeds. In Southwest Asia, people began growing rice; in Mexico and Central America, people grew corn, beans, and squash.

2 People learned to farm and domesticate animals. They no longer had to wander to find food. They formed communities and began working with metals. Metalworkers created weapons and jewelry, which traders sold to others. As people stayed in one place, the population grew.

3 A civilization involves six aspects: cities, a central government, religion, economic and social classes, arts and architecture, and writing.

Africa, Prehistory–2500 B.C.

LESSON 2
Farming and the Beginning of Civilization

Thinking on Your Own
Once people learned to grow their own food, they knew that food would be available to eat. How do you think their lives changed? Write your prediction in a sentence. As you read this lesson, check your prediction against what you learn.

Early people were hunters and gatherers. Farming did not develop until about 10,000 years ago. When people were able to give up roaming in search of food, dramatic changes occurred in their lives. The development of farming created so much change that it is considered a revolution. Anthropologists call it the **Neolithic revolution**.

The practice of farming evolved over many thousands of years.

focus your reading
How did people learn to farm?
How did new technologies affect early people?
What is a civilization?

vocabulary
Neolithic revolution
domesticate
surplus
deities
social hierarchy
artisans
civilization

First Farmers
Farming began about 8000 B.C. in Southwest Asia. Some scientists think farming spread from there to other regions. Other experts think that people in different regions figured out on their own how to farm. Experts do agree that people began farming in different regions at different times. There is also agreement that people were farming in Africa, Europe, Asia, and Central America by 5000 B.C.

Experts can only speculate at how people initially learned to

10 | Chapter 1

Lesson Vocabulary
Introduce each vocabulary word to students. Ask students to add the prefix *neo-* (new) and the suffix *-tion* (act or process) to their lists of prefixes and suffixes. Read through the list of words, and discuss their meanings with students.

The *Neolithic revolution* refers to the development of farming, which brought about change in many areas of life and the beginnings of *civilizations*. *Civilization* is a complex culture of beliefs, traditions, government, religion, and social classes. Similar words include *civic, civil,* and *civilian*.

To *domesticate* an animal is to tame it. Share with students other words such as *domestic* and *domicile* to enlarge their vocabulary.

A *surplus* is anything extra or left over. A *surplus* in food resulted in population growth.

The gods that early people worshiped are known as *deities*.

A *social hierarchy* defines the status of various groups of people in a particular area.

Artisans are craftspeople who work in the arts and help create architecture.

10 | Chapter 1

domesticate, or tame and control, seeds. It is possible that someone noticed that the same plants came up in the same place each year. People might have tried throwing some seeds on the ground and putting dirt over them. Or maybe they dug holes and placed seeds in the holes. No one knows for sure. But over time people in Southwest Asia began growing wheat and barley. By around 5000 B.C., people in China were growing rice, while people in Mexico and Central America were growing beans, squash, and maize—a form of corn.

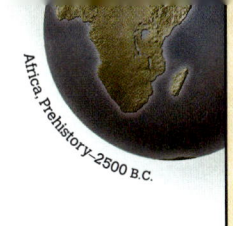

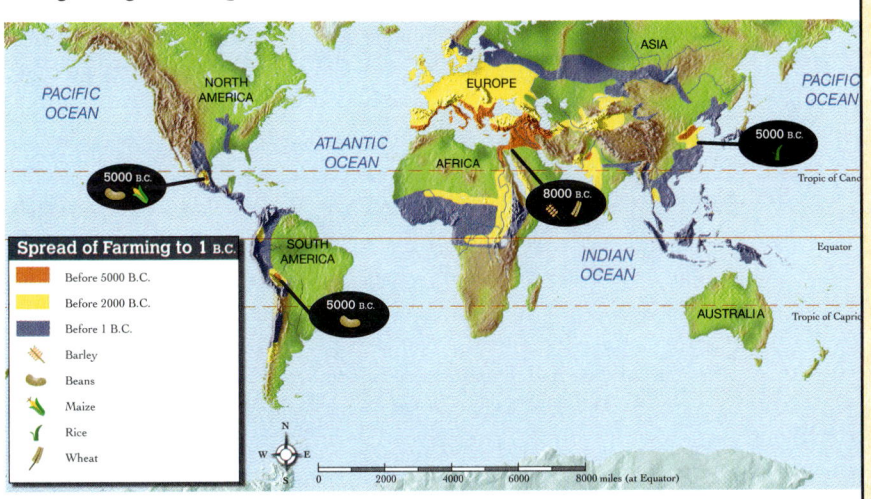

Along with learning how to grow crops, people learned to domesticate animals. Instead of moving from place to place to hunt animals, hunters captured them alive. The hunters penned up the animals and fed them. The animals were killed as their meat was needed. The first evidence of domesticated animals is in Southwest Asia. By 8000 B.C., people there were keeping cows, goats, pigs, dogs, and sheep.

In time, people found that animals provided other sources of food besides meat. Cows and goats provided milk. People also found other uses for animals besides food. Horses, reindeer, camels, and even dogs could be trained to carry loads. The wool from sheep could be woven into clothes. The skins of cows, goats, pigs, and sheep could be used as blankets and made into clothing and bags.

The Earliest Humans 11

Map Extension

Ask students to use the map on page 11 to answer the following questions:

- Where did farming first develop? (along the Mediterranean coast of Europe and Africa, in China, and in Arabia at the Fertile Crescent)

- What crops were being raised around 5000 B.C. in what is now Mexico? (beans, maize)

- Where was rice first grown? (China)

Extension

Early people probably practiced slash-and-burn agriculture, which is still used in some developing nations today. People cut rings around the trunks of trees so that the trees would die. Then they set fire to the dead trees. The ground was fertilized by the ashes and was free of weeds, but only for a time. Within a few years, when the soil was exhausted and the weeds returned, communities would move to another part of the forest to begin the process again.

Picturing History

The miniature oxcart, pictured on the bottom of page 10, is an artifact from Mohenjo-Daro in the Indus Valley. Have students identify the activity that the carving shows. Ask students why they think someone chose to make this carving of a common scene. Do they see any parallels in contemporary art, especially folk art, around them?

The Earliest Humans 11

Stop and Think

Students' lists may include creating a surplus of food, allowing people to live in permanent communities, and offering freedom to work in other areas such as craftworking and trade. They may also mention that the population increased along with the food supplies.

Picturing History

The Aztec civilization in central Mexico developed two calendars. One is shown at the top of page 12. It is an agricultural calendar with 365 days, used for calculating solar time. A second, ritual calendar had 20 months, each with 13 days, for daily affairs. The two calendars both returned to their original places in 52-year cycles, which were regarded as significant. The end of a cycle was thought to be a time of great change.

Picturing History

Have students look at the photograph of bronze artifacts at the bottom of page 12. Explain that metalworkers in Mesopotamia were looking for a metal to replace copper, which was too soft to be effectively used in weapons or tools. They discovered that by combining tin with copper, they produced a stronger material, bronze. Since both tin and copper were rare, bronze did not immediately have a wide use. It did change warfare, however, and over time had an impact on agriculture.

Africa, Prehistory–2500 B.C.

New Ways of Life

By farming and raising animals, people were able to control the sources of their food. Once they could control their food, people did not have to be nomadic. Instead, they settled where they grew their crops. If they were going to stay in one place, people could build permanent homes. They would no longer have to abandon their shelters when they moved. Nor would people have to take down their shelters and move them to another camp. People began building sturdy homes of long-lasting materials like mud bricks.

With a steady food supply, people began to have more children. The population of villages grew. Little villages became bigger villages and then towns and cities.

With a larger population, not everyone had to farm. People with special skills became craftworkers. For example, some people learned to make baskets from reeds and pots from clay. Some learned to spin thread from certain plants and to weave cloth.

Around 4000 B.C., craftworkers in Asia learned to make bronze. Copper was already in use in some places in the world. Bronze is a combination of copper and tin and is a very soft metal. With the development of bronze, metalworkers could make a living by creating bronze weapons and jewelry. Other people became traders. They made their living by exchanging **surplus** food and other goods like jewelry.

These skills developed in different regions at different times. Like the knowledge of farming, some of these skills may have spread from one region to another. Or some may have developed independently in different parts of the world. Archaeologists are still working to solve these mysteries.

> **Calendars**
>
> A calendar is a way of measuring the passage of time. Many cultures and religions have developed calendars over the centuries. Today, the Gregorian calendar is the one used by nations around the world. It measures time backwards and forwards from the year 1.
> - Time before year 1 is indicated as B.C.
> - Time since year 1 is indicated as A.D.
>
> The phrase "about 10,000 years ago" means about 8000 B.C. Today is about 2,000 years since the year 1. To find the date, subtract 2,000 from 10,000. The date is about 8000 B.C.

Bronze was used to make goods like weapons, jewelry, and mining tools.

Ancient civilizat— includin— the Azte— develop— calenda— to keep track of seasons—

stop and think

What changes resulted when peop— began to farm? List the changes in your notebook. Check them with a partner to be sure you listed at least five.

12 Chapter 1

Extension

Encourage students interested in science to find out more about metals and their alloys. Ask them to report to the class about other alloyed metals that were used in farming and war by using the Student Presentation Builder on the student DVD.

12 Chapter 1

The Six Characteristics of Civilization

Cities	As populations grew, cities became the centers of early civilizations.
Central government	Large numbers of people need a single government. Government keeps order and helps people work together.
Religion	Early people developed religions to explain nature. Early people also believed that **deities**—or gods—would help them. Rulers said their right to rule came from the deities.
Social and economic classes	As people began to do different kinds of jobs, some became wealthier than others. A **social hierarchy** was set up based on wealth. At the top was the ruler and his family. They were the wealthiest and the most important people. Next came priests and warrior nobles. Merchants and craftworkers were the third level. Farmers were the least wealthy. Below them were slaves.
Arts and architecture	Large buildings such as palaces for the ruler and temples for the deities were built. Craftworkers and **artisans** decorated them with statues, paintings, and beautiful furniture.
Writing	Not all civilizations developed writing, but many did. Writing was used to keep tax records for the government.

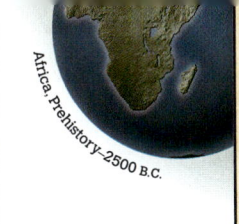

Africa, Prehistory–2500 B.C.

What Is a Civilization?

Civilization is a term that anthropologists and archaeologists use to describe a complex culture. Lesson 1 explained that culture is the way of life of a group of people. It includes their beliefs, traditions, government, religion, and social classes. The early farming people had simple cultures. They lived in small groups and worked their fields together. Women took less part in decision making for the group than they had during the hunting and gathering stage. Male heads of families began to meet as councils and make decisions for the village.

As villages grew, they needed more leadership and more organization. The result was the development of civilizations. Historians have studied early civilizations and found that most share the same six developments: cities, central government, religion, social and economic classes, art and architecture, and writing.

The remains of the granaries at Harappa, Pakistan.

Putting It All Together

In three or four paragraphs, describe how early people went from hunting and gathering to farming to living in cities. First, list information about each step in your notebook. Then check your list with a partner.

Chart Extension

Ask students to make charts in their notebooks with these six characteristics. Have them fill in the information for the civilizations they will study in subsequent chapters. As they study later civilizations, they should write the name at the top of a column and fill in the chart. This will make reviewing for an exam or writing a paper much simpler.

Putting It All Together

Students' paragraphs will vary but should include information from the chapter about the changes that resulted in the move to cities and towns.

Picturing History

Cities such as Harappa, in the Indus Valley, were laid out on a grid as shown in the photograph on the bottom of page 13. Granaries were used to store excess grain. During the city's high point, from 2500 B.C. to 2000 B.C., about 40,000 people lived there.

Extension

Buildings in Harappa and Mohenjo-Daro were made of mud bricks. Homes ranged from one-room, tenement-style buildings to large, multi-room structures of two or three stories. These larger dwellings had at least one interior courtyard, along with wells and built-in brick ovens. Nearly all houses included private bathrooms with toilets that drained into the city sewage system, which was among the more advanced in the ancient world. The cities also had temples, marketplaces, and public buildings.

The Earliest Humans | 13

Chapter Review

1 Paragraphs will vary but should include facts from the chapter about hunters and gatherers.

2 Answers will vary, but possible words could include *weapon, animal, quiet, aim, food, skins*.

3 Paragraphs will vary but should be based on one of the characteristics of civilization listed on page 13.

Chapter Summary

- The time before writing is known as **prehistory**.
- **Anthropologists** study the beginnings and development of humans and their **culture**. They use **fossils** and **artifacts**.
- **Archaeologists** study the past by examining artifacts.
- Anthropologists believe that the first **hominids** lived in Africa about 3 to 4 million years ago.
- An important turning point in prehistory was the discovery of how to start a fire and keep it burning.
- Prehistoric people were **nomads** who lived by hunting and gathering their food.
- The development of farming is called the **Neolithic revolution** because it changed the way people lived.
- Early people learned to **domesticate** animals and crops.
- Because of farming, people (1) were able to control their food supply, (2) stopped moving from place to place, and (3) built permanent homes. (4) Populations grew and (5) cities developed. (6) Not everyone had to farm. A **surplus** of food allowed artisans to create other goods.
- **Civilizations** are complex and have the following six characteristics: (1) cities, (2) central government, (3) religion based on **deities**, (4) social and economic classes, (5) arts and architecture created by **artisans**, (6) writing.
- The development of social and economic classes is a **social hierarchy**.

Chapter Review

1 Write a paragraph to describe what life was like for a group of hunters and gatherers.

2 Language had to be invented. The first people did not have words to speak to one another. Imagine you are a hunter. Make a list of words you would need to talk to another hunter.

3 Select one characteristic of civilization. Write a paragraph about the characteristic.

Novel Connections

Below is a list of books that relate to the time period covered in this chapter. The numbers in parentheses indicate the related Thematic Strands of the National Council for the Social Studies (NCSS).

Fiorenzo Facchini. *A Day with Homo Habilis: Life 2,000,000 Years Ago*. Lerner, 2003. (I, III, VIII)

David Lambert. *The Encyclopedia of Prehistory*. Facts On File, Inc., 2002. (I, II)

Betsy Maestro. *The Story of Clocks and Calendars*. HarperTrophy, 2004. (I, II)

Milton Meltzer, Sergio Martinez. *Weapons & Warfare: From the Stone Age to the Space Age*. HarperCollins, 1996. (VI, VIII)

Norah Moloney. *The Young Oxford Book of Archaeology (Young Oxford Books)*. Oxford University Press, 2000. (I, II, III, VIII)

Margaret Poynter. *The Leakeys: Uncovering the Origins of Humankind*. Enslow Publishers, Incorporated, 1997. (I, II, III, VIII)

Skill Builder

Identifying the Main Idea and Supporting Details

The main idea is the theme or idea that a piece of writing is mostly about. Look at the organization of this textbook. It has chapters and each chapter has lessons. Each chapter has a main idea; so does each lesson. Each section within a lesson also has a main idea.

The chapter title tells you the main idea of the chapter. The lesson title tells you the main idea of the lesson. Each paragraph also has a main idea. Often it will be stated in the first sentence of the paragraph. This is similar to the way a chapter title states the main idea of a chapter. Sometimes the main idea of a paragraph is unstated. Then you have to figure out the main idea from the details in the paragraph. The details explain or describe the main idea. For this reason, they are called supporting details.

> To find a main idea of a paragraph or a piece of writing, ask yourself the following:
> 1. Is there a single sentence that states what the piece is about? If there is, then you have found the main idea. To be sure, restate the sentence in your own words. Does it tell what the paragraph is mainly about?
> 2. If there is no single sentence main idea, what does the piece seem to be about? What are the details describing or explaining? When you think you know, restate the main idea in your own words. This will help you be sure you have the main idea.

1 What is the main idea of (a) Chapter 2? (b) Chapter 6? (c) Lesson 1 of Chapter 4? (d) Lesson 3 of Chapter 19?

2 Read the section "How We Know About Early Life," pages 5–6. Identify the main idea in each paragraph. Decide whether the main idea is stated or unstated. Then write a bulleted list of supporting details.

The Earliest Humans

Classroom Discussion

Discuss with students some of the broader topics covered in this chapter.

- Based on what you read in this chapter, how do history and science work together?
- Why is it important to study earlier civilizations?
- Why do all six characteristics of a civilization need to be present?

Skill Builder

1 (a) Chapter 2: the beginning civilizations of Mesopotamia and the development of Judaism
(b) Chapter 6: the development of ancient Greek city-states
(c) Chapter 4, Lesson 1: Ganges and Indus River civilizations
(d) Chapter 19, Lesson 3: Japan's modernization and the Meiji Restoration

2 **Paragraph 1** Anthropologists study human cultures—stated.
Supporting Details:
- Culture refers to a way of life.
- Culture involves beliefs, traditions, government, religion, and social classes.
- Culture makes a group unique.

Paragraph 2 Archaeologists study past societies—stated.
Supporting Details:
- Archaeologists examine artifacts.
- Fossil remains also provide clues.

Paragraph 3 Scientists use scientific methods to study artifacts and fossils—stated.
Supporting Details:
- Dirt layers are carefully removed at a dig.
- Scientists use trowels and brushes to search.
- Finds are labeled and packed to study later.

Paragraph 4 Scientists need to date their finds—unstated.
Supporting Details:
- Scientists use radiocarbon dating, tree-ring dating, and stratigraphic observations.
- Anthropologists compare finds to place them in the right cultures.

The Earliest Humans

Chapter 2

SOUTHWEST ASIA: BEGINNINGS

(1200 B.C.–500 B.C.)

Chapter Summary
Refer to page 26 for a summary of Chapter 2.

Related Transparencies
- T-1 World Map
- T-3 Persian Empire
- T-18 Three-Column Chart
- T-20 Concept Web

Key Blacklines
Primary Source–The First Farming Villages

CD Extension
Encourage students to use the reading comprehension, vocabulary reinforcement, and interactive timeline activities on the student CD.

Picturing History
The picture on page 16 is a modern photograph of the ruins of the ziggurat at Nippur. The Mesopotamian city-states built buildings that were used for worship, storing surplus food, and as administrative centers. New ones were built over old ones until they reached monumental proportions.

Getting Focused
Skim this chapter to predict what you will be learning.
- Read the lesson titles and subheadings.
- Look at the illustrations and read the captions.
- Examine the maps.
- Review the vocabulary words and terms.

Sumerians lived in city-states. Israelites spent many years moving from one place to another. Create a T-chart. Label one side "Sumerians" and the other side "Israelites." Think about what ancient city dwellers might need in order to live. Think about what ancient nomads might need. Review Chapter 1 for ideas if necessary. Then complete your T-chart.

Pre-Reading Discussion
1 Have students complete each bulleted direction on page 16. Remind them that Chapter 2 focuses on the earliest civilizations in Southwest Asia.

2 Ask students to look over major headings, tables, and charts in this chapter for clues to the main ideas. Have students record their ideas in their notebooks and then revise their answers as they read the chapter.

3 Tell students to review their T-charts as they read.

Picturing History
Ask students to identify the activities represented by the figures in the mural on page 17. What kinds of murals have they seen in their daily lives? Why might farming be considered a good subject for a mural?

LESSON 1

Mesopotamia: The Land Between the Rivers

Thinking on Your Own

Turn each of the subheadings into questions. Write them in your notebook. As you read the lesson, answer each question in your notebook. Compare your answers with those of a partner.

Mesopotamia means "land between the rivers." The rivers are the Tigris and Euphrates. They are located in what is now Iraq in Southwest Asia. Each year the rivers flooded their banks. This flooding left **fertile**, or rich, soil on the **floodplain** in the river valleys. The floodplain is the area the rivers flooded. People began to settle on the floodplain and farm around 8000 B.C.

People soon realized that they needed to control the rivers. The floods were good for the soil, but they were also destructive. The floods did not come at exactly the same time each year. In order to be sure to have enough food, the people

focus your reading
How did people use the Tigris and Euphrates Rivers?
Why was the development of writing important?
Why is Hammurabi remembered?
What did Darius do?

vocabulary
fertile — deities
floodplain — ziggurat
city-states — cuneiform
scribes — codify

Farming was an important part of the culture in Mesopotamia.

Southwest Asia: Beginnings

Lesson Summary
This lesson focuses on the achievements of the Mesopotamians. Sumer, in southern Mesopotamia, was a loose federation of city-states ruled by kings. It was one of the earliest civilizations. The Sumerians developed cuneiform writing.

Hammurabi united Mesopotamia into the Babylonian Empire. Hammurabi codified the laws and had them recorded in stone.

Under the rule of Cyrus the Great, the Persians invaded and conquered Babylon. Darius enlarged the Empire and set up the first centralized system of government.

Lesson Objective
Students will learn about the Mesopotamian civilization that developed along the Tigris and Euphrates Rivers in what is present-day Iraq.

Focus Your Reading Answers

1 Mesopotamians used the Tigris and Euphrates Rivers to irrigate their crops.

2 The development of writing meant that accurate records could be kept. In addition, people began writing down the stories and poems that had been handed down orally through many generations.

3 Hammurabi is remembered as the person who first codified laws by having them recorded. This allowed Mesopotamians to know the laws.

4 Darius expanded the Persian Empire and then divided it into satrapies. The satraps who governed the areas reported to a centralized government.

Vocabulary
...d explain each of the vocabulary terms to students.

...lain is the flat area whose soil is enriched by regular floods. *Floodplains* are extremely *fertile*. ...oil means crops will grow easily.

...all regions ruled by kings were known as *city-states*. People often lived within the walls or ... by land.

... worshiped numerous *deities*, or gods, in Mesopotamia. A *ziggurat* was a pyramid-shaped ... built in Sumerian *city-states*. A *ziggurat* was made of mud bricks. The top was called the ... but over time, the whole building took on this name.

...m writing used wedge-shaped characters on clay tablets. The *scribes* used *cuneiform* to keep ... and write stories. *Scribe* was an actual job. You may wish to discuss other words that relate ...g with the same root word, such as *inscribe, scripture, scriptorium*.

...ct and organize material, such as laws, is to *codify* it. Discuss with students other ...at are *codified*, such as library books.

Southwest Asia: Beginnings

Map Extension

Ask students to use the map on page 18 to answer the following questions:

- How might the location of the ancient shoreline have affected life in Ur and in Eridu? (The towns would have been on the sea, possibly serving as ports or fishing towns.)

- What landforms bordered the Fertile Crescent to the north and south? (mountains to the north, desert to the south)

- Into what body of water do the Tigris and Euphrates Rivers empty? (Persian Gulf)

Extension

Ask students to find out more about contemporary irrigation systems, both locally and in foreign countries. Have them investigate dam projects such as the Aswan Dam in Egypt or the Three Gorges Dam in China. Research the dams' impact on the agricultural economy of the regions.

Have students create a poster to report their findings to the class.

---

had to plant by a certain time of the year. The crops also needed water while they grew. Mesopotamia had little rainfall and the summers were very hot.

The Mesopotamians figured out how to build dikes to hold back the flood waters. They also learned to use irrigation to bring river water to their crops. By building dams with gates, the people could direct water to their fields.

To build the dikes and the dams, the people had to cooperate. As they learned to work together, they began to gather in villages, towns, and cities. The formation of cities is one characteristic of civilization.

Sumer

Sumer was the southern region of Mesopotamia. The people of Sumer were the first to build a civilization. Sumer was a series of **city-states**. A king ruled over each city-state. The armies of rival kings often battled each other for power over a city-state.

Time Box

3200 B.C.
　Beginning of Sumer

3000 B.C.
　Development of writing

1792–1750 B.C.
　Babylonian Empire

539–330s B.C.
　Persian Empire

18 Chapter 2

Time Box Extension

Use the Time Box material to review with students the time divisions of B.C. and A.D. Explain that some scholars and books today use the terms BCE (before the common era) and CE (of the common era) instead. Have students figure out the time span represented by the events in the Time Box. (2,870 years)

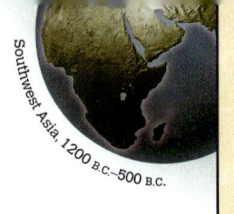

Bricks made from mud were used to build houses and buildings in the Sumerian city-states.

The cities were walled. Houses and the walls were made of mud bricks. The bricks were made by shaping mud into long, thick rectangles. The bricks were then left in the sun to bake, or harden. Most Sumerians were peasants, or farmers. They lived in small houses just outside the city walls. In the city were a number of larger houses and large buildings. Most of the larger buildings were temples to the gods and goddesses. The Sumerians worshiped several gods and goddesses.

Although most people were farmers, there were other social classes. Below the ruler were priests and soldiers. Next were **scribes**, merchants, and craftworkers. Priests were both men and women. Their task was to hold ceremonies to honor the Sumerian gods and goddesses. Their **deities** were very important to the Sumerians. The deities oversaw the well-being of a city. They made sure that the harvests were good and the people were prosperous. The Sumerians believed that the king received his power to rule from the deities. The Sumerians developed the **ziggurat** as a special temple to honor their deities. Ziggurats were built of mud bricks and shaped like a pyramid.

One of the most important inventions of the Sumerians was a form of writing. As towns and cities grew, a system for

The ziggurat of Ur, Iraq, was built to honor Sumerian gods and goddesses.

Southwest Asia: Beginnings

Picturing History

The Sumerians learned to build with mud bricks, such as those shown in the photograph at the top of page 19. They used mud, straw, and water to form the bricks. These were then dried in the sun. Ask students how the climate of the region helped the people in making bricks.

Picturing History

The ziggurat of Ur has been rebuilt in modern times. It is shown in the photograph at the bottom of page 19.

Have students suggest reasons behind rebuilding the ziggurats.

Extension

Ask students to find out more about the deities that the Sumerians worshiped. Have them present their findings to the class by using the Student Presentation Builder on the student CD.

Extension

The land of Sumer was under British control during the nineteenth and early twentieth centuries. Archaeological work in Mesopotamia was under the supervision of Gertrude Bell, an employee of the British Crown. Bell granted permission for site research and helped establish the kingdom of Iraq after World War I ended. Have students find out more about Gertrude Bell and other early archaeologists in Mesopotamia.

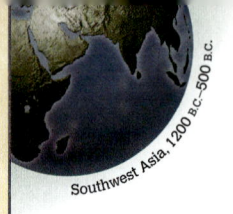

record keeping was needed. The ancient Sumerians developed **cuneiform** writing around 3000 B.C. *Cuneiform* means "wedge-shaped." The Sumerians did not use an alphabet like ours. Their writing was based on pictures. Scribes used a reed, or stick, to draw the shapes on clay tablets. The tablets were then allowed to bake, or harden, in the sun. Only men could be scribes. They were the people who kept the records for the king. They also wrote down the stories, songs, and poetry of the people. The *Epic of Gilgamesh* is one of these early stories. Gilgamesh was a Sumerian king.

Cuneiform is one of the earliest systems of writing.

The Babylonian Empire

In 1792 B.C., Hammurabi decided to create an empire. He was the ruler of Babylon, a city-state in Sumer. He and his army set out to unite Mesopotamia under his rule. He succeeded in taking over much of central and southern Mesopotamia. Many other kings attempted to control parts of Mesopotamia before and after Hammurabi. He is remembered, however, because of his code of laws.

Hammurabi was the first ruler to **codify**, or bring together, a set of laws. He did not write the laws. He gathered them from the many parts of his empire. The 282 laws were then carved on stone pillars and placed throughout the Empire. By reading the laws, Hammurabi's subjects would know what was and was not lawful.

The laws set up a strict system of justice. Those who broke the law were punished. Often the punishment was severe. Punishments were worse for public officials and wealthy men than for peasants. The laws also

Hammurabi is remembered for arranging the first written set of laws, now known as Hammurabi's Code.

Picturing History

The tablet shown at the top of page 20 has cuneiform writing on it. Cuneiform was not an alphabet but a system of symbols. It was used for at least three different languages, including Old Persian.

Extension

Deciphering the cuneiform tablets of Mesopotamia was the work of many scholars. They were greatly aided by the discovery of a royal library in Assyria, in what today is northern Iraq. Archaeologists in the nineteenth century discovered around 24,000 tablets in King Ashurbanipal's seventh-century B.C. library. In 1976, researchers at the University of Pennsylvania began to compile a dictionary of the Sumerian language. The dictionary is expected to be 18 volumes long and will take some time to complete. The first two volumes came out in 1984 and 1992, respectively. Dictionary workers assembled one million cards of information that were then fed into a computer.

Ask students to research the early work of decoding cuneiform by using library resources or the Internet.

Picturing History

Hammurabi, shown in the image at the bottom of page 20, was the sixth of 11 kings who made up the first dynasty of Babylon. Although he eventually controlled much of Mesopotamia, the rulers who succeeded him could not keep the Empire together.

stop and think

Make up symbols to stand for the letters A, B, C, D, and E. Then use your symbols to write four simple English words. Show your symbols and words to a partner. Ask your partner to figure out the words using the symbols. Have your partner read the words aloud or write them in English.

Stop and Think

Students' symbols and words will vary but should include symbols for the letters *A, B, C, D,* and *E*.

regulated marriage and the family. Every marriage was governed by a marriage contract. Fathers had absolute rule over the family. Women had fewer rights than men.

Achievements of Mesopotamia

Many different people lived in Mesopotamia over the centuries. They made important discoveries. They also developed many important concepts, or ideas.

DISCOVERIES	CONCEPTS
• the arch • the dome • the wheel • bronze and copper for tools, weapons, and jewelry • iron for tools and weapons	• cuneiform writing (Sumerians) • alphabet (Phoenicians) • division of the circle into 360 degrees • geometry concepts for measurement • calendar • code of laws

The Persian Conquerors

The power of city-states rose and fell in Mesopotamia. First, one ruler would take control of other city-states and perhaps even large parts of Mesopotamia. He would die and the next king might be powerful enough to keep the Empire together. Then later kings would be weak and the Empire would fall apart. That is what happened to the Babylonian Empire after Hammurabi's death.

It took an outsider to create another large empire in Mesopotamia. Between 559 and 539 B.C., Cyrus the Great of Persia created a large empire in what is today southwestern Iran. In 539 B.C., he and his army invaded Mesopotamia. Within nine years, Cyrus added Mesopotamia to his Persian Empire. Cyrus was known as Cyrus the Great because of his just treatment of the people he conquered.

Several years after Cyrus, Darius took command of the Persian Empire. He ruled from 521 B.C. until 486 B.C. Darius enlarged the Empire so that it reached from Europe to

Southwest Asia: Beginnings   21

Table Extension

Discuss with students the Mesopotamian discoveries and concepts from this table. Then pair students, assigning each pair one of the items in the table, to further research its influence on contemporary society. Ask students to give a report to the class when they are finished.

Map Extension

Ask students to use the map on page 21 to answer the following questions:

- Where did the Royal Road begin and end? (It began at Susa and ended near the Mediterranean coast.)
- What country was the farthest western point of the Persian Empire? (Egypt) On what continent is that country located? (Africa)
- How far north did the Empire extend? (Greece)
- How many miles did the Empire reach from west to east? (about 2,750 miles)

Southwest Asia: Beginnings   21

Picturing History

Discuss with students the changes a uniform system of coinage would bring to a nation. Be sure they understand how trade was conducted before coins were used (bartering goods). Then have students use library resources or the Internet to find out about the effects of some European countries adopting the euro rather than each nation having its own monetary system.

Putting It All Together

Concept maps should include information from the lesson about Mesopotamia, Sumer, the Babylonian Empire, and the Persian Empire. Check the Lesson Summary on page 17 for ideas.

Reading for Understanding

1. To "bear false witness" means to lie.

2. Answers will vary but should mention that the builder will have to pay the cost of repairs.

3. Answers will vary but students should use the laws to support their opinions.

India. Mesopotamia became a small part of the Persian Empire.

Darius made an important contribution to the development of ideas about government. He set up a centralized government to rule over his empire. He organized his empire into 20 provinces called satrapies. A governor, or satrap, ruled each one. A royal road linked the parts of the empire to Susa, the capital of the Persian Empire. The satraps reported to the emperor. Each one collected taxes and paid the royal army in his satrapy. The royal army protected the Empire from invaders. It also maintained the power of the emperor.

The Persian Empire was the first to use a uniform system of coin

Putting It All Together

Create a concept map to help you remember the information in this lesson. Draw a large circle and label it "Mesopotamia." Label three smaller circles "Sumer," "Babylonian Empire," "Persian Empire." As you review the lesson, add information to your concept map.

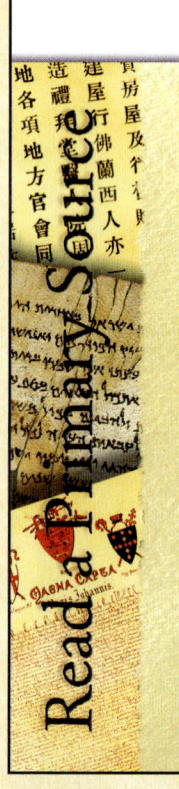

The Code of Hammurabi

The following are some laws from the Code of Hammurabi. Subjects of the Babylonian Empire could find a law to govern just about everything they di

1. If a man brings accusation against another man, charging him with murder, but cannot prove it, the accuser shall be put to death.

4. If he bear [false] witness concerning grain or money, he shall himself bear the penalty imposed in that case.

22. If a man practices robbery and is captured, that man shall be put to death.

195. If a son strikes his father, they shall cut off his hand.

233. If a builder builds house for a man and does not make it construction sound, and a wall cracks, that builder shall strengthen that wall at his own expense.

reading for understanding

What is another way to say "bear false witness"?

What is the punishment for Code 233?

Do you think the punishments are fair? Use the laws to support your opinion.

Picturing History

The Torah, sometimes called the Book of the Law of Moses, is made up of the first five books of both the Hebrew and the Christian Bibles. The word *Torah* means "teaching." Traditionally believed to have been written by Moses, it was a guide to a moral life. More realistically, the Torah was likely written down when the Israelites went into captivity in Babylon in 586 B.C.

The Torah, pictured at the bottom of page 23, is written on parchment. When the scribes first wrote the law, they used pieces of parchment. The parchment was then stitched into large scrolls. A reader unrolls the scroll to reveal the proper reading selection for the day, a practice that is still followed. In Judaism, the feast of Simchas Torah marks the close of the year's reading of the Torah. The men of the congregation dance with the scrolls as part of the joyous celebration.

Chapter 2

LESSON 2

The Israelites and the Beginning of Judaism

Southwest Asia, 1200 B.C.–500 B.C.

Thinking on Your Own

Look at the pictures and read the captions. Do you know anything about any of the objects or events shown? If you do know something, write a sentence to tell what you know about each object and event. If they are all unfamiliar to you, list what you want to know more about.

The Jewish religion, or Judaism, began in Mesopotamia. It is one of the oldest of the world's religions. What we know about its beginnings comes from the Hebrew Bible, known as the **Torah**. Christians call it the Old Testament. Archaeologists have also helped us to learn more about the historical beginnings of Judaism.

focus your reading

What was the historical beginning of Judaism?

What are some basic beliefs of Judaism?

How were Jewish beliefs different from other early people's beliefs?

vocabulary

Torah   monotheistic
Yahweh   covenant
famine   prophets

The Israelites

Judaism began around 2000 B.C. with a leader named Abraham. He and his family moved from Mesopotamia into a region called Canaan. Later, this area was called Palestine. Hebrew writings state that **Yahweh**, the Hebrew word for God, promised this land to them. Since the third century B.C., the Jewish people have avoided saying *Yahweh*. Out of respect, they use the term *Lord* or *God*.

The Hebrews were nomadic herders. They raised sheep and goats. When a **famine** came, the Hebrews migrated to Egypt in search of land and water for their herds. In the 1300s B.C., the Egyptians enslaved the Hebrews. In the 1200s B.C., a Hebrew leader named Moses led them out of Egypt and back into Canaan. This journey is called the

The Torah is the Hebrew Bible.

Southwest Asia: Beginnings 23

Lesson Summary

The Hebrew Bible records the beginnings of the Jewish people. It begins with the call of Abraham to leave Ur and go to Canaan. The lesson details Moses leading the people out of slavery in Egypt and the rule of David and Solomon, as well as the conquest of the nation of Israel by the Assyrians and Babylonians. The lesson also summarizes the beliefs of the Jewish people.

Lesson Objective

Students will learn about the founding of the Hebrew nation and the beginnings of monotheism.

Focus Your Reading Answers

1 Judaism began with the call of Abraham to leave Mesopotamia and go to Canaan. Jewish people believe that God promised them this land.

2 Judaism believes in one God and in a covenant between that God and the Jewish people.

3 In contrast to the people around them, the Jewish people worshiped one God, not many gods. Elements of nature were thought to be created by God and not for worshiping. Jewish people also remained faithful to their religion, rather than adding the gods of the nations that conquered them.

on Vocabulary

ss each of the vocabulary terms with students.

is the name that the Hebrews use for God. The *Torah* is the Hebrew Bible.

ne is a lack of food, usually caused by climate conditions that destroy the t. Use as an example pictures of the *famine* in Ethiopia and the Sudan to help ts understand the concept.

otheistic religion worships only one God rather than many gods.

ant is an agreement, such as the one that the Jews and God entered into. nts can be religious, political, or social.

ebrews had several *prophets*, or holy leaders, who taught them God's ments. Many of the world's religions have *prophets*, or religious speakers.

Southwest Asia: Beginnings 23

Map Extension

Ask students to use the map on page 24 to answer the following questions:

- What body of water formed a shared western border for both kingdoms? (Mediterranean Sea)

- Of which kingdom was Jerusalem the capital? (Judah, or southern)

- What landform was located east of both kingdoms? (the Syrian Desert)

Stop and Think

Students' letters will vary but should include a plea for the end of high taxes, forced labor, and building projects.

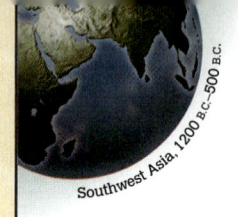

Exodus. It is honored in the Jewish holy time of Passover.

Sometime between 1200 and 1000 B.C., David united the twelve Hebrew tribes into the Kingdom of Israel. His son Solomon built a temple to God in the city of Jerusalem. The temple became the center of the Israelite religion. Soon after Solomon's death, the kingdom split apart. By about 922 B.C., the two southern tribes had become the Kingdom of Judah. Jerusalem remained their capital. The ten tribes of the north kept the name of Israel. They set up their capital at Samaria.

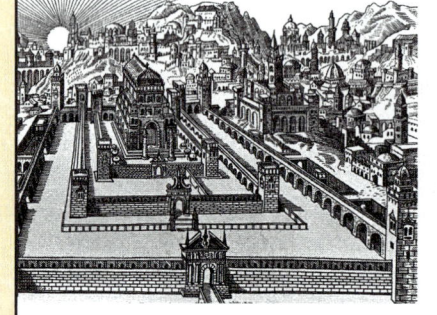

In 722 B.C., invaders from Assyria, an empire in northern Mesopotamia, moved into the Kingdom of Israel. They forced out the Israelites. Over time, the Israelites married into other groups and were lost as a distinct people.

In 586 B.C., new invaders overran the Kingdom of Judah. They destroyed Jerusalem and the temple. These invaders took many Jews as captives to Babylonia in Mesopotamia. Some 50 years later, the Persians conquered Babylonia. It was Cyrus the Great who allowed the Jews to return to their homeland. They were able to rebuild Jerusalem and the temple.

Jewish Beliefs

There are certain beliefs that are central to Judaism.

1. Judaism is **monotheistic**. This means that Jews believe in one true God.

Solomon's temple in Jerusalem, Israel, was built in 953 B.C.

stop and think

The northern and southern tribes split because of differences over how Solomon ruled the kingdom. The northern tribes objected to high taxes and forced labor on building projects. With a partner write a letter to King Solomon. Ask him to stop his huge building projects and to lower taxes.

Picturing History

The sketch at the bottom of page 24 is of Solomon's temple, a lavish structure built in the tenth century B.C. It was destroyed by invaders in 586 B.C. In 536 B.C., Cyrus the Great, the Persian conqueror, allowed the temple to be rebuilt. In A.D. 70, the Romans destroyed the temple.

2. God and the Jews entered into a **covenant**, or agreement. Under the agreement, they would be protected if the Jews obeyed the Ten Commandments. This covenant gave the Jews their sense of being God's chosen people.

Over time, holy leaders known as **prophets** arose among the Israelites and later the Jews. The people believed that the prophets transmitted and interpreted God's teachings to them. These teachings included a strong sense of right and wrong, both for individuals and for the community. The idea of social justice—looking out for others—became a core value of Judaism. The rich and powerful had a duty to help the poor and needy.

The Ten Commandments

1. Thou shalt have no other gods before me.
2. Thou shalt not make unto thee any graven images.
3. Thou shalt not take the name of the Lord thy God in vain.
4. Remember the Sabbath day, to keep it holy.
5. Honor thy father and mother.
6. Thou shalt not kill.
7. Thou shalt not commit adultery.
8. Thou shalt not steal.
9. Thou shalt not bear false witness against thy neighbor.
10. Thou shalt not covet any thing that is thy neighbor's.

Differences with Other Early Religions

Judaism	Other Early Religions
Judaism was monotheistic.	Other early religions were polytheistic. They worshiped many male and female gods.
Judaism believed that the things of the natural world—sun, moon, stars, rain, thunder, trees, and so on—were examples of God's work. God was far greater than any of these things. The things of the natural world were not deities and were not to be worshiped.	Other early religions believed that the things of nature—sun, moon, stars, and so on—were deities. These religions worshiped the things of the natural world.
Jews remained faithful to their religion. Their belief in the one true God and their sense of being the chosen people separated them from their neighbors.	Other people put aside their own deities and worshiped those of their conquerors.

Putting It All Together

Create a T-chart. Label the left side "Event" and the right side "Importance." Choose four events in the history of the Israelites and Jews. List them on the left side of the chart. On the right side explain why each one was important.

Chart Extension

Discuss with students how each of the differences between Judaism and other ancient religions might have influenced daily life.

Putting It All Together

T-charts will vary but should include four events from early Israelite history and their importance. Possible answers include: Abraham being called to Canaan—it was the beginning of the Hebrew people; Moses leading the people out of slavery in Egypt—the people returned to the land promised them; Solomon building the temple—the temple became the center of worship and national unity; the Assyrian captivity of the ten northern tribes—these tribes were assimilated and lost.

Chapter Review

1 Paragraphs about laws will vary but should include laws that focus on teenagers and give reasons why the laws are important.

2 Lists will vary depending on which group is chosen but might include: one god, many gods; farming, temples.

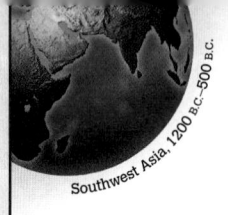

Chapter Summary

- The earliest civilization began in Mesopotamia in Southwest Asia. It arose along the **fertile floodplain** in the river valleys of the Tigris and Euphrates Rivers.
- Sumer was in the southern part of Mesopotamia. It was made up of **city-states** ruled by kings.
- The top social class was the king-ruler. Then there were priests, soldiers, **scribes**, merchants, and craftworkers. Most people were peasants.
- The people worshiped many **deities**. They built temples shaped like pyramids to honor their deities. These temples were called **ziggurats**.
- A form of writing called **cuneiform** developed around 3000 B.C. in Mesopotamia.
- In 1790 B.C., Hammurabi created a single set of laws for the Empire. It was the first time laws were **codified**.
- Judaism began in Mesopotamia around 2000 B.C. When a **famine** struck, the Hebrews migrated into Egypt. In the 1300s B.C., they were enslaved by the Egyptians, but Moses led them out of Egypt and back to Canaan.
- The Hebrew Bible is known as the **Torah**.
- The Jews believed they had a **covenant** with **Yahweh**. It was part of their obedience to the Ten Commandments.
- Judaism was a **monotheistic** religion whereas other early religions were polytheistic.
- The Jews believed that **prophets** were sent by God to transmit and interpret his teachings.

Chapter Review

1 Imagine you are writing laws for Hammurabi's empire. Write laws that teenagers would have to obey. Write a paragraph to explain why you think the laws are important. Share and discuss your laws and your paragraph with a partner.

2 Write a bulleted list that compares and contrasts the people of Sumer or Babylonia with the Israelites. Then write a short paragraph including key concepts.

Novel Connections

Below is a list of books that relate to the time period covered in this chapter. The numbers in parentheses indicate the related Thematic Strands of the National Council for the Social Studies (NCSS).

Erica C. D. Hunter. *First Civilizations*. Facts on File, Incorporated, 1994. (I, II, VIII)

John Malam. *Ancient Mesopotamia (Historic Civilizations)*. Gareth Stevens Publishing, 2004. (I, II, III)

Geraldine McCaughrean. *Gilgamesh the Hero*. Eerdmans, William B. Publishing Company, 2003. (I, III, IX)

Martha Morrison, Stephen F. Brown. *Judaism*. Facts on File, Incorporated, 1997. (I, III, IV)

Don Nardo. *The Persian Empire*. Gale Group, 1997. (I, II, VI)

Virginia Schomp. *Ancient Mesopotamia: The Sumerians, Babylonians, and Assyrians (People of the Ancient World)*. Franklin Watts, 2004. (I, II, III)

Skill Builder

Analyzing Timelines

Sequence is the order in which things happen. Knowing the sequence of events can help you understand the causes of events. Sequence can also tell you the effects of events. If you know when something happened in one place, you will be able to tell if it was before or after a similar event in another place. For example, writing developed in Mesopotamia around 3000 B.C. The Chinese developed their writing system about 2000 B.C. By knowing the dates, you can see that writing developed in Mesopotamia first.

A timeline is a quick way to see the sequence of events. A timeline arranges dates and events in chronological order. Chronological order is time order. The earliest dates are first.

The following timeline was created from the dates in the section titled "The Israelites."

Skill Builder

1. 1300s B.C.

2. 136 years

3. Moses leading the Hebrews out of Egypt happened first.

4. The Jews were sent to Babylonia.

5. 1,470 years

Use the timeline to answer the following questions:

1. When did the Egyptians enslave the Hebrews?

2. How many years did the Kingdom of Judah exist after the Kingdom of Israel was destroyed?

3. Which happened first: Moses leading the Hebrews out of Egypt or the founding of the Kingdom of Israel?

4. Which of these events happened after the destruction of the Kingdom of Israel: the Hebrews were enslaved or the Jews were sent to Babylonia?

5. What is the time span of the events shown on the timeline?

Timeline events:
- 2000 B.C. Beginning of Judaism
- 1300s B.C. Egyptians enslaved Hebrews
- 1200–1000 B.C. Hebrews united into Kingdom of Israel
- 1200s B.C. Moses led Hebrews out of Egypt
- 922 B.C. Southern tribes separated and formed Kingdom of Judah
- 722 B.C. Assyrians destroyed Kingdom of Israel
- 586 B.C. Kingdom of Judah captured; Jews sent to Babylonia
- 539–530 B.C. Cyrus the Great conquered much of Mesopotamia; Jews returned to homeland

Classroom Discussion

Discuss with students some of the broader topics covered in this chapter.

- How have rivers and other bodies of water influenced the development of civilization?
- What concepts of civilization were exemplified by the Sumerians?
- What is the role of law in the life of a society and an individual?
- How did the development of writing affect the Mesopotamian city-states?
- What are the key events in the development of Judaism?
- How has religion affected the growth of nations?

Unit Objectives

After studying this unit, students will be able to

- explain the ancient Egyptian and Kushite civilizations
- describe the early settlements of India and the importance of Buddhism and Hinduism
- compare the civilizations of ancient Greece and Rome

Unit 2 focuses on early civilizations in North Africa, India, China, Greece, and Rome.

Chapter 3, Ancient Civilizations of North Africa, examines the cultures of Egypt and Kush.

Chapter 4, The Indian Subcontinent, explores the development of settlements along the Ganges and Indus Rivers, as well as the role of religion in daily life.

Chapter 5, Early Chinese Civilizations, traces the development of Chinese dynasties and the importance of Confucius.

Chapter 6, Ancient Greek City-States, presents an overview of the growth of Greece from city-states to the empire of Alexander the Great.

Chapter 7, Ancient Rome, describes the rise and fall of the Roman Empire and the founding of the Christian religion.

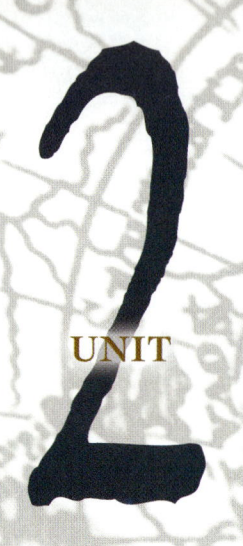

UNIT 2
THE FIRST CIVILIZATIONS

The earliest civilizations developed in river valleys. The first civilization was Mesopotamia. It grew up around the Tigris and Euphrates Rivers. Other important river valley civilizations arose along the Nile River in North Africa, the Indus River in India, and the Huang He and Chang Jiang Rivers in China.

Geography was also important in the development of Roman and Greek civilizations. The city of Rome developed on seven hills near the banks of the Tiber River. However, the area of ancient Greece did not have any great rivers. The Greeks lived in mountainous areas and on islands. The sea helped to shape Greek civilization.

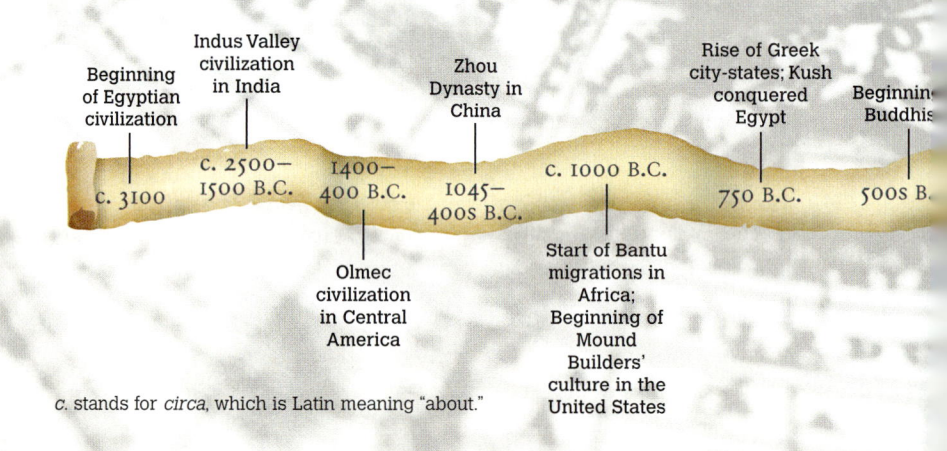

Timeline:
- c. 3100 — Beginning of Egyptian civilization
- c. 2500–1500 B.C. — Indus Valley civilization in India
- 1400–400 B.C. — Olmec civilization in Central America
- 1045–400s B.C. — Zhou Dynasty in China
- c. 1000 B.C. — Start of Bantu migrations in Africa; Beginning of Mound Builders' culture in the United States
- 750 B.C. — Rise of Greek city-states; Kush conquered Egypt
- 500s B.C. — Beginning of Buddhism

c. stands for *circa*, which is Latin meaning "about."

Getting Started

Have a student read aloud the title of the unit and the two paragraphs on page 28. Review with students the six characteristics of a civilization from Chapter 1. Also review why civilizations developed along rivers and river valleys. Ask students to write any questions they have about the content of this unit in their notebooks. Encourage them to answer those questions as they read each chapter in the unit.

Measuring Time

Explain to students that Chapter 3 focuses on the development of civilization in Egypt, and Chapter 4 examines the early cultures of India. Chapter 5 introduces early Chinese civilizations. Chapter 6 presents the formation of the ancient Greek city-states, and Chapter 7 introduces ancient Rome. The top portion of the timeline represents the major events of these early civilizations. The bottom of the timeline indicates parallel events around the world.

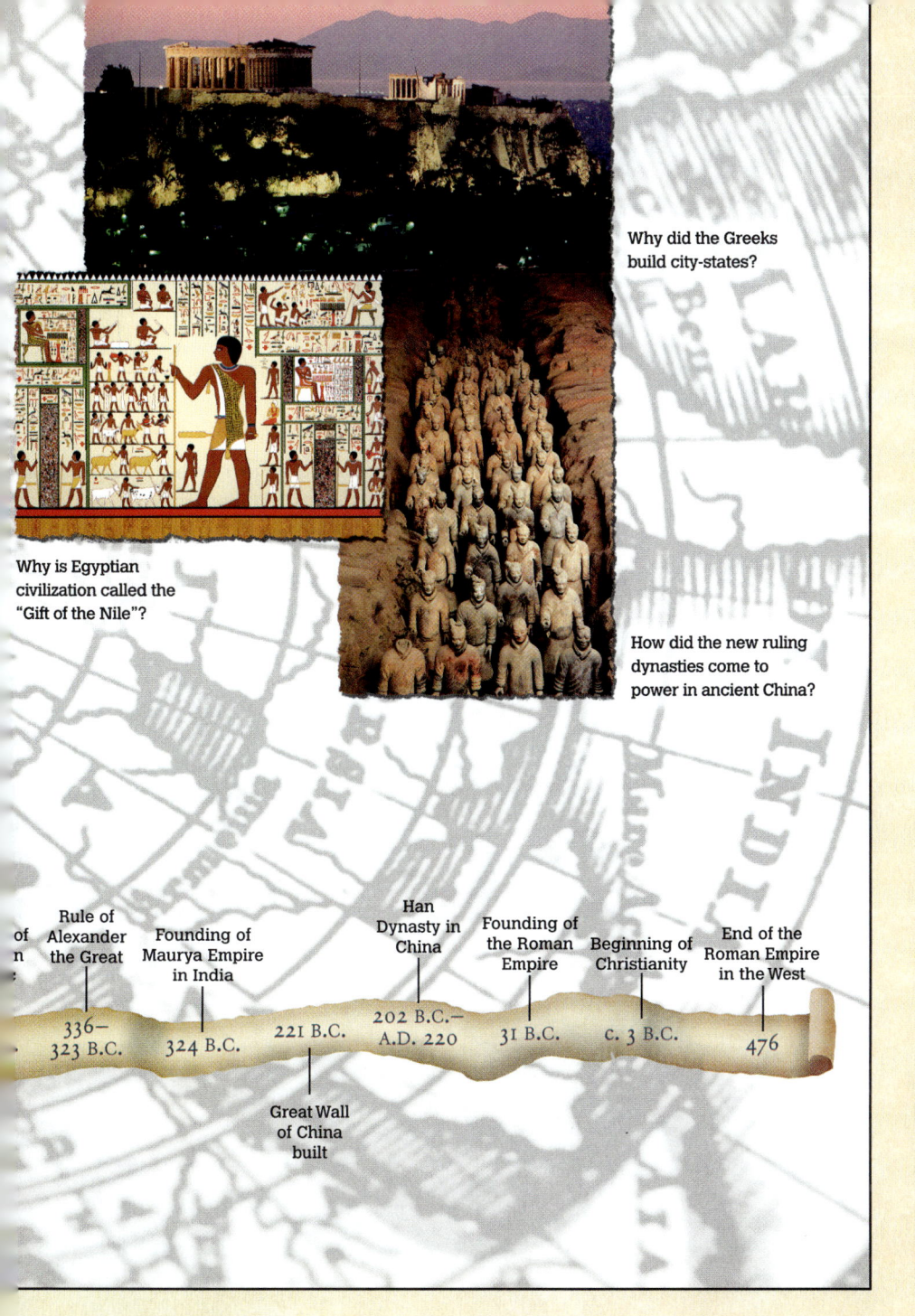

Why did the Greeks build city-states?

Why is Egyptian civilization called the "Gift of the Nile"?

How did the new ruling dynasties come to power in ancient China?

Rule of Alexander the Great	Founding of Maurya Empire in India		Han Dynasty in China	Founding of the Roman Empire	Beginning of Christianity	End of the Roman Empire in the West
336–323 B.C.	324 B.C.	221 B.C.	202 B.C.–A.D. 220	31 B.C.	c. 3 B.C.	476

Great Wall of China built

Picturing History

The first image is of the remains of the Parthenon in Athens, Greece. The second image is an example of Egyptian hieroglyphics. The third image shows some of the thousands of terra cotta warriors at the mausoleum of Emperor Qin Shihuangdi in Xi'an, China. Students will learn about each of these in more detail as they read the unit.

Collage Answers

1 The Greeks built city-states because the rough, mountainous land separated each city.

2 Egyptian civilization is called the "Gift of the Nile" because the regular flooding of the Nile allowed people to plant crops and build cities along its banks.

3 New ruling dynasties came to power in ancient China through power struggles.

Collage Extension

Use the images and questions on page 29 to preview the unit. Ask students what the pictures suggest about the first civilizations on different continents.

Timeline Extension

Ask students to use the timeline to preview each chapter. Then have them answer the following questions:

- What were the key events that shaped Egypt's growth?
- When did the Indian civilizations develop along the Ganges River?
- Were the first Chinese civilizations developing at the same time as the early Egyptian and Indian civilizations?
- What civilization in Europe developed at the same time as the Chinese?
- Which civilization developed last?
- What were the key world events during the years indicated on the timeline?

The First Civilizations

Chapter Summary

Refer to page 38 for a summary of Chapter 3.

Related Transparencies

T-1 World Map

T-18 Three-Column Chart

Key Blacklines

Primary Source–The Egyptian Book of the Dead

CD Extension

Encourage students to use the reading comprehension, vocabulary reinforcement, and interactive timeline activities on the student CD.

Picturing History

The photo on page 30 shows the Sphinx at Giza, flanked by two pyramids. Built by King Khephren, the Sphinx is 66 feet (20 m) high and 240 feet (73 m) long. It combines the body of a lion with the face of a man. Some people think that it was meant to suggest that the king had the grace and power of a lion. The Sphinx was considered a god. It is slowly being destroyed by weather and air pollution. Attempts to restore it in recent years have caused more damage.

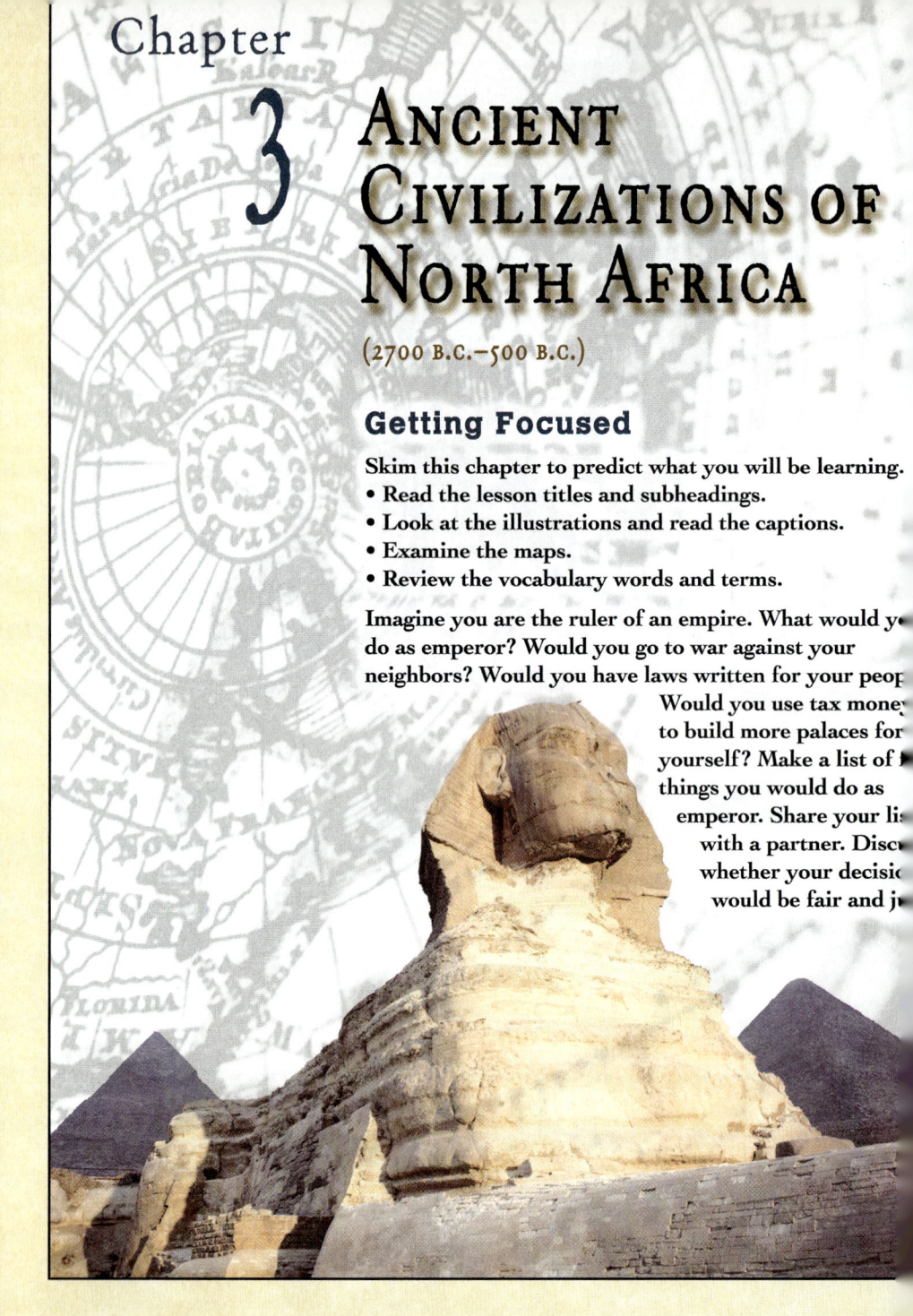

Chapter 3

ANCIENT CIVILIZATIONS OF NORTH AFRICA

(2700 B.C.–500 B.C.)

Getting Focused

Skim this chapter to predict what you will be learning.
- Read the lesson titles and subheadings.
- Look at the illustrations and read the captions.
- Examine the maps.
- Review the vocabulary words and terms.

Imagine you are the ruler of an empire. What would yo do as emperor? Would you go to war against your neighbors? Would you have laws written for your peop Would you use tax money to build more palaces for yourself? Make a list of t things you would do as emperor. Share your lis with a partner. Discu whether your decisio would be fair and ju

Lesson Vocabulary

Read aloud each of the vocabulary terms and discuss their meanings.

A *dynasty* is a family of rulers. Menes began the first *dynasty* of Egypt. The *pharaoh* was the supreme ruler. A *pharaoh's* power was believed to come from the sun god Ra.

After death, wealthy people were *mummified* because it was believed that they would need a body for the afterlife. *Mummifying* involved the removal of organs and the drying of the corpse. These actions preserved the body.

The *pyramids* were large tombs that the *pharaohs*, priests, and other nobles built for the afterlife. They were large structures built of stone, without the use of modern equipment.

Scribes were the recordkeepers of Egypt. The *scribes* were members of the middle class. They used *hieroglyphics*, a writing system of symbols. This picture writing survived on tombs and papyrus.

LESSON 1
Pharaohs and Egypt

Thinking on Your Own

Make a three-column chart in your notebook. Label the first column, "What I Know About Ancient Egypt," the second column, "What I Want to Learn About Ancient Egypt," and the third column, "What I Learned About Ancient Egypt." Fill in columns one and two now, and column three as you read. Discuss what you learned with a partner.

The Egyptian civilization grew up along the banks of the Nile River. Ancient Egypt is sometimes called the "gift of the Nile." The Nile River Valley is located in the Sahara, a huge desert in North Africa. The climate is hot and dry. Without the waters of the Nile, the Egyptians could not have planted and harvested crops.

focus your reading

What features did the Old, Middle, and New Kingdoms have in common?

Why were pyramids built?

What was daily life like in ancient Egypt?

vocabulary

dynasty   pyramids
pharaoh   scribes
mummified   hieroglyphics

Like the Tigris and Euphrates Rivers, the Nile flooded each year. When the river flowed back within its banks, it left rich soil behind. The Egyptians planted their crops in this soil.

Like the ancient Mesopotamians, the Egyptians learned to build dikes to control the flooding of the Nile. They also learned to build dams and irrigation ditches to bring the river water to their fields.

Pharaohs

Around 3100 B.C., Menes united the peoples along the Nile into the Kingdom of Egypt. He began the first **dynasty**, or family of rulers. Over time the Egyptian ruler became known as

Ancient Civilizations of North Africa | 31

Lesson Summary

The lesson presents information about the early civilization of Egypt. The Nile River provided water for crops through flooding and irrigation.

The pharaohs of ancient Egypt were part of several dynasties. The history of Egypt is divided into Old, Middle, and New periods.

Ancient Egyptians were polytheistic. Wealthy Egyptians prepared elaborate tombs and were mummified at death. They had a strong belief in the afterlife.

At the top of Egyptian social structure was the pharaoh and ruling family; next were priests and nobles; then came merchants, artisans, scribes, and tax collectors; then came the largest group, the peasant farmers. Finally, slaves were at the bottom of the social structure.

Egyptians developed paper and writing and built the pyramids.

Lesson Objective

Students will learn about the ancient Egyptian civilization that grew up along the Nile River.

Pre-Reading Discussion

1 Ask students to suggest activities a government might undertake in times of peace. Help them understand that resources could be used for building projects or for improving citizens' quality of life.

2 Have students identify the advantages of location for a local business. Using this concept as a springboard, tell students that in this chapter they will learn about the advantages of some ancient cities located on trade routes.

Map Extension

Ask students to use the map on page 31 to answer the following questions:

- How far was it from Egypt to Kush? (about 700 miles)
- What direction is the Mediterranean Sea from Nubia? (north)
- What body of water is east of Nubia and Kush? (Red Sea)

Focus Your Reading Answers

1 All three periods featured strong pharaohs, peace, large building projects, and intellectual and cultural achievements.

2 The pyramids were constructed as tombs to honor dead pharaohs and other wealthy citizens.

3 Life in Egypt was governed by a strict class system.

Ancient Civilizations of North Africa | 31

Picturing History

Ramses II ruled for 66 years after taking the throne at age twenty-five. He was the greatest builder of all the pharaohs. The photograph at the top of page 32 shows one of his most famous works, a temple called Abu Simbel in Nubia, carved of rock, with four 67-foot (20 m) seated statues of himself gazing out over the Nile. The United Nations Educational, Scientific, and Cultural Organization (UNESCO) rescued the rock temple from destruction in the 1960s when Egypt was going to flood the area as part of the Aswan High Dam project.

Bio Facts

- Hatshepsut was a female ruler born in 1503 B.C.
- She married her half-brother, common practice at that time.
- Hatshepsut's reign was a prosperous one. She sent traders to other lands.
- One famous expedition to Punt, probably in modern-day Ethiopia and Somalia, is recorded in her tomb. The carvings show Egyptian ships taking weapons, tools, and jewelry to Punt. They returned with dogs, monkeys, apes, a panther, and live myrrh trees.
- Hatshepsut is also known for her monuments, temples, and obelisks.
- She ruled for 30 years.
- After her death, images and records were destroyed by her stepson Thutmose III.

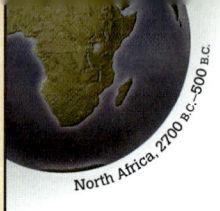

North Africa, 2700 B.C.–500 B.C.

the **pharaoh**. Pharaohs had absolute and unquestioned authority over their subjects. Egyptians believed that the pharaoh's power came from the sun god Ra. The pharaoh represented the god on Earth and was considered divine.

Historians divide ancient Egyptian history into three periods. See the time box on this page for the names and dates of these periods. These periods have the following features in common: (1) strong pharaohs, (2) peace with Egypt's neighbors, (3) large building projects, and (4) great cultural and scientific achievements.

Between these periods, Egypt suffered from weak pharaohs and invasions by stronger neighbors like the Hyksos. The region was in a state of chaos, and as a result, there were few intellectual achievements. There was also little money and time to build temples for the deities and palaces for the pharaohs.

Time Box
2700–2200 B.C. Old Kingdom
2050–1652 B.C. Middle Kingdom
1567–1085 B.C. New Kingdom

Ramses was pharaoh when Moses led the Hebrews out of Egypt.

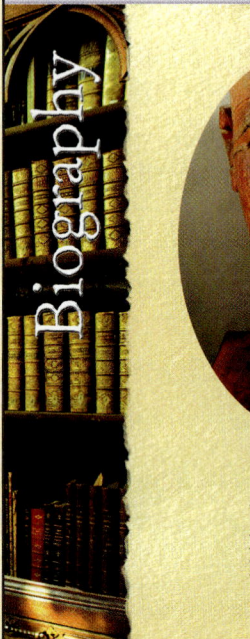

Biography

Hatshepsut

Hatshepsut was the daughter of Pharaoh Thutmose Egyptian royal families could marry only among themselves. As a result, she married her half-brother who in time succeeded their father. Wh Thutmose II died, Hatshepsut's stepson became Thutmose III. However, Hatshepsut seized powe and had herself crowned pharaoh. She ruled fo the next 30 years, from 1503–1482 B.C..

Statues show Hatshepsut both as a woman ar as a figure with a beard. Like male pharaohs, she sometimes taped a long narrow beard to her chin. S was called "His Majesty."

During Hatshepsut's reign, Egypt expanded its power and wealth. She sent a trading expedition south along the Nile, possibly as far a present-day Somalia. She may even have commanded the trip. Hatshepsut had a huge temple built near the capital to house her tomb.

Biography Extension

Ask students to research other women who ruled as pharaohs. They can use library resources or the Internet to do so. Challenge students to present their findings in a creative manner, perhaps as a television interview or radio play.

Time Box

Ask students to calculate how long each kingdom lasted. Which was the longest? (Old Kingdom) the shortest? (Middle Kingdom)

32 Chapter 3

Egyptian soldiers used chariots to defend against invaders.

North Africa, 2700 B.C.–500 B.C.

Picturing History

The illustration at the top of page 33 shows Egyptians fighting the Hyksos.

Hyksos is a Greek term meaning "rulers of foreign nations." Some people believe the Hyksos were Palestinians or Semitic people. In addition to horses and chariots, the Hyksos introduced a new type of fortification, new forms of swords and daggers, bronze weapons, and the compound Asian bow. They also improved the Egyptians' skill in pottery, weaving, and metalworking. Bronze, which is made by combining tin and copper, can be molded into various shapes. Prior to the invention of iron, bronze was the metal of choice. The development of the sword resulted from the longer, narrower knife blades that bronze could produce.

Egyptian Religion

Religion was a very important part of Egyptian life. Like most ancient people, the Egyptians were polytheistic. They worshiped deities in the natural world around them and in the sky above them. The sun gods and land gods became the chief deities of the Egyptians. Ra was the sun god. Osiris was the god of the Nile. He brought the annual flood. His wife Isis was also a deity. Together, they represented resurrection, or a new beginning.

The Egyptians believed in life after death. They thought it was similar to life on Earth. As a result, the pharaohs had themselves buried with all the things they would need in the afterlife. Their tombs were filled with food, clothing, and jewels. Their servants and even their pets were killed and buried with them.

Osiris (left); Horus, the god of the sky, and Isis (below)

Because they would need their bodies in the afterlife, pharaohs were **mummified**. Mummification is a process that preserves, or saves, the body. The internal organs were removed and spices were placed in the body. Then the body was dried and wrapped in linen cloth. In the beginning, only pharaohs and nobles were allowed to be mummified. Later the custom spread to other Egyptians.

Ancient Civilizations of North Africa 33

Extension

Ask students to use library resources or the Internet to find out more about the gods of Egypt and their responsibilities. Have them present the findings of their research to the class.

Picturing History

The images at the bottom of page 33 are of Egyptian gods.

Osiris was god of both the underworld and vegetation. He is sometimes shown with green skin because of his connection to plants. His enemy, the rival god Seth, killed him and scattered 14 pieces of his body, perhaps an allusion to scattering seeds. Osiris was brother and husband of Isis. In his role as god of the underworld, he was also a judge of the dead.

Isis was the mother goddess of Egypt. She reassembled the dismembered Osiris long enough to become impregnated with Horus, who in time defeated Seth and ruled over the first united Egypt. Thus she is protector of pharaohs, as well as the goddess of the dead and of funeral rites.

Ancient Civilizations of North Africa 33

Picturing History

The Great Pyramid at Giza built by King Khufu, shown on page 34, and a second pyramid are the oldest of the Seven Wonders of the Ancient World. They are also the only ones that have survived to the present day.

Extension

Have students use library resources or the Internet to find out more about the Seven Wonders of the Ancient World. Have students share their findings with the class by using the Student Presentation Builder on the student CD.

Stop and Think

Students' paragraphs on the effects of war on Egypt will vary but should discuss the likely results of war, such as a shortage of labor and materials for domestic building projects.

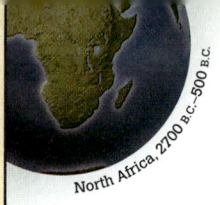

The Great Pyramid at Giza

North Africa, 2700 B.C.–500 B.C.

Paint and goldwork adorned the coffinettes of many pharaohs, such as King Tutankhamen.

The pharaohs were buried in tombs within large structures called **pyramids**. The Great Pyramid at Giza contains the tomb of King Khufu and was finished about 2540 B.C. It is made of over two million blocks of limestone. Each block weighs about two tons. The pyramid stands 481 feet high. Each side is 756 feet long. The whole structure covers 13 acres. That is about the size of 12 football fields. The pyramids are one of the greatest achievements of the Egyptians. They built these huge structures without any of the labor-saving equipment of today like cranes and other construction equipment.

Egyptian Society and Daily Life

At the top of Egyptian society was the pharaoh and other members of the royal family. Next came the upper class of priests and nobles. The priests took care of the temples and celebrated religious ceremonies. The nobles oversaw the government. The ruling, or upper class, was small in number.

The middle class was slightly larger and made up of merchants, craftworkers, scribes, and tax collectors. The **scribes** kept records using **hieroglyphics**. This was the writing system that the ancient Egyptians developed.

stop and think

The lesson says that there was little money and time to build during certain periods in ancient Egyptian history. How would invasions and war affect what went on in Egypt? With a partner think about the effects of invasions and war. Write a paragraph to answer this question.

34 Chapter 3

Picturing History

The sarcophagus pictured on page 34 is that of Tutankhamen, the boy pharaoh who died at about age eighteen. He is commonly known as King Tut. The Egyptians placed the internal organs they removed from dead bodies in four ceremonial alabaster jars. The jars were sealed so that the organs could be used in the next life. They discarded the brain, however, because they believed a person thought with the heart. The heart was not removed from the body.

Extension

Suggest to students that they find online museum exhibits about the treasures found in the tomb of King Tut. Other students may wish to investigate the 1922 archaeological dig that recovered Tutankhamen or the results of the 2005 CT scan of King Tut's mummy.

Hieroglyphics was an early form of Egyptian writing.

Egyptian life was culturally rich.

The largest class of people were peasant farmers. Land belonged to the pharaoh who gave some of it to the nobles and priests. The farmers worked the fields for the upper class. They also maintained the irrigation systems. Both men and women worked in the fields. The women were also responsible for taking care of the home and children. During nonfarming seasons, farmers worked on the pharaoh's building projects. Slaves were the lowest social class, below the peasants.

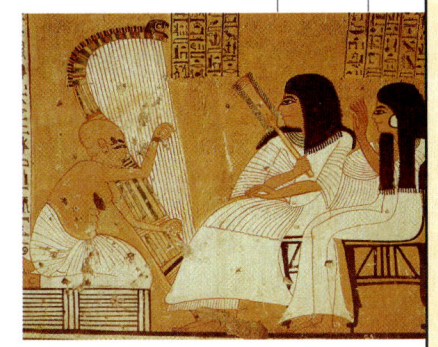

Achievements of the Ancient Egyptians

Some concepts, such as writing, did not develop in one region and spread to other world regions. Often, a concept developed independently in different parts of the ancient world.

INVENTIONS	CONCEPTS
• papyrus, a paper-like material • pyramid • mummification • medical advances such as surgery and the use of splints for broken bones • metal working in copper, bronze, and gold	• hieroglyphic writing • geometry concepts for measurement • calendar of 12 months, each containing 30 days with 5 days at the end

Putting It All Together

Women in ancient Egypt had many rights. However, they could not become scribes or work for the government. With a partner, discuss reasons why you think women were kept from these jobs. Write a paragraph to explain your ideas. Conclude by stating whether you think this was fair or unfair.

Ancient Civilizations of North Africa

Picturing History

The mural from an Egyptian tomb shown at the top of page 35 demonstrates the importance of hieroglyphics and pictures to tell the story of a person's life. Encourage students to learn more about hieroglyphics using library resources or the Internet.

Picturing History

The mural on page 35 shows two women who are being entertained by a musician playing a harp. This would be a common scene in a wealthy Egyptian home, where women were sometimes kept in seclusion.

Table Extension

1 Have students work in small groups to create posters showing some of the discoveries and concepts of the Egyptians. Display completed projects in the classroom and refer to them often during the course of the lesson.

2 Ask students to find out how papyrus is made and why its discovery was so important to Egypt. Instruct students to use library resources or the Internet to find information.

Putting It All Together

Paragraphs will vary but should include reasons to support students' positions as to the fairness of the rule against women working in government and as scribes.

Ancient Civilizations of North Africa

Lesson Summary
Kush, which was called Nubia in early times, was largely a farming society. Some Nubians, however, were merchants.

Once part of Egypt, Nubia gained its independence around 1000 B.C. It became known as Kush. A few hundred years later, Kush, in turn, conquered Egypt. Kushite pharaohs ruled for about a century. Assyrians from Mesopotamia, who had iron weapons, conquered the Kush, who retreated from Egypt to the south.

The Kushites built a capital at Meroë, where trade routes intersected. Located near large iron ore deposits, Meroë became the center of ironworking and exporting.

Lesson Objective
Students will learn about the history and contributions of the Kingdom of Kush.

Focus Your Reading Answers
1 Nubia was important to Egypt because of its rich trading network and the luxury goods it provided.

2 Meroë's location was ideal because it was near large deposits of iron ore and was also the place where two trade routes met.

North Africa, 2700 B.C.–500 B.C.

LESSON 2

The Kingdom of Kush

Thinking on Your Own
Find the general location of ancient Kush and Nubia on a world map. Find the following areas: North Africa, West Africa, Southwest Asia (Arabian Peninsula), and South Asia (India). Create a T-chart to organize bulleted notes about each region.

The land of Kush lay to the south of Egypt. The area is today part of the nation of Sudan. The kingdoms of Egypt and Kush were connected for many centuries through trade and politics.

focus your reading
Why was Nubia important to Egypt?
Why was the location of Meroë ideal?

vocabulary
trade
iron
trade routes
export

Nubia
The area that became Kush was first called Nubia. Like the Egyptians, the people of Nubia and later Kush were mainly farmers. However, over time, some Nubians became wealthy through **trade**. As early as 2000 B.C., Nubian merchants were providing Egypt with such luxury items as ivory, ebony (a black wood), leopard skins, and slaves.

Farming was an important part of life along the Nile River.

During the New Kingdom, 1567–1085 B.C., Egypt conquered Nubia. Egypt wanted to control Nubia's rich trading network. By about 1000 B.C., Nubia fought for and won its independence from Egypt. It became known as the Kingdom of Kush.

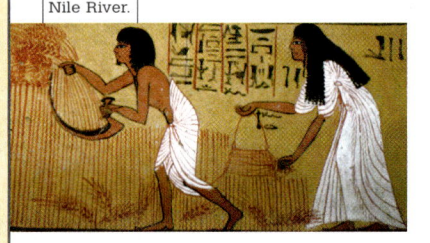

The Expansion of Kush
In 750 B.C., King Piankhi of Kush succeeded in conquering Egypt. The Kingdom of Kush spread its power all the way to the Mediterranean Sea. A dynasty of Kushite pharaohs took over the Egyptian throne. The rule of the five Kushite pharaohs lasted for about 100 years.

Lesson Vocabulary
Discuss each of the following vocabulary terms with students.

The business of buying and selling is known as *trade*. Nubian and Egyptian *trade* involved luxury goods such as ebony, ivory, and animal skins. When traveling with goods to sell, merchants used roads called *trade routes*. Cities often grew up along these *trade routes*.

Iron is a metal ideal for use in weaponry. It is made from *iron* ore and is stronger than bronze.

To *export* goods is to *trade* or sell goods to other nations. The Kushites *exported iron* goods.

The pyramids [at] Meroë [held] non-[m]ummified [re]mains of [th]e Kush.

North Africa 2700 B.C.–500 B.C.

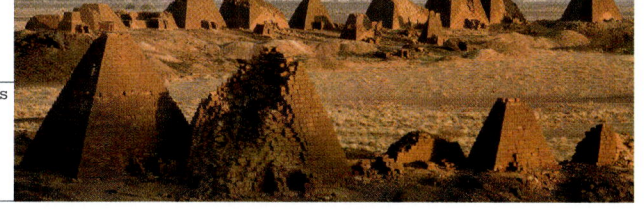

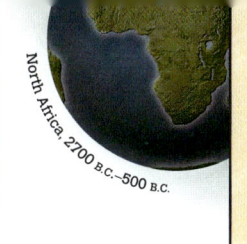

In 663 B.C., the Assyrians from Mesopotamia invaded Kush. They easily defeated the Kushites. The Assyrians had mastered **iron** working and were using iron weapons. Iron is a metal that is much stronger than bronze. The bronze and stone weapons of the Kushites were no match for the Assyrians' iron swords and spears. The Kushites had not yet learned how to make things from iron. The Kushites were pushed back into their own lands south along the Nile.

Around 500 B.C., the Kushites built a new capital at Meroë. The location was ideal for two reasons. First, it was where two **trade routes** crisscrossed. One route went north and south along the Nile. The other route went east and west from the Red Sea across North Africa and into West Africa.

Over time these routes connected Kush with the Roman rulers of Egypt. The routes also connected Kush with the Arabian Peninsula in Southwest Asia and with India in South Asia. Merchants carrying gold, ivory, ebony, jewelry, slaves, and iron goods traveled along these routes.

Iron was the second reason that Meroë's location was ideal. Meroë was built near large deposits of iron ore. The Kushites had learned iron working from their enemies, the Assyrians. The Kushites then turned to making iron tools, weapons, and other iron goods for their own use and for **export**. *Export* means "to trade or sell goods to other nations."

The Kingdom of Kush ended around A.D. 350. It was invaded and conquered by the neighboring kingdom of Axum.

Putting It All Together

Make a timeline of important dates in this lesson. With a partner, figure out how many years passed between sets of dates.

stop and think

The use of iron changed the ways of life for the Kush. With a partner, write a bulleted list of five reasons why iron was important.

Iron tools and weapons were introduced by the Assyrians.

Stop and Think

Students' lists will vary but may include the importance of iron's strength in making weapons or tools. An iron hoe, for example, would allow farmers to break up soil more easily. Additionally, students may note the importance of trade exports of iron items and the use of iron items in defense.

Picturing History

The Kushite pyramids at the top of page 37 are located near Meroë. Although influenced by Egyptian pyramids, those that the Kushites built were smaller, often with flattened tops.

Putting It All Together

Timelines will vary but may include the following:

- 2000 B.C. Nubian traders provided Egyptians with luxury goods
- 1567–1085 B.C. Egypt conquered Nubia
- 1000 B.C. Nubia gained independence and became Kush
- 750 B.C. Kush conquered Egypt
- 663 B.C. Assyrians invaded Kush
- 500 B.C. Kushites created new capital at Meroë

Calculations of time between events will vary based on the events chosen.

Picturing History

The farmer in the illustration on page 36 is using a scythe to harvest grain. Explain to students that this labor-intensive process is still used in many parts of the developing world. Have students discuss the process of harvesting without the large machines that are used during harvest season in the United States today.

Chapter Review

1. Kush was south of Egypt, west of the Arabian peninsula, and west of India.

2. Egypt was north of Kush. It was west of the Red Sea. It was north of Central Africa.

3. 2000 B.C. Nubian traders provided Egyptians with luxury goods; Middle Kingdom in Egypt

   1567–1085 B.C. Egypt conquered Nubia; New Kingdom in Egypt

   1000 B.C. Nubia gained independence and became Kush

   750 B.C. Kush conquered Egypt

   663 B.C. Assyrians invaded Kush

   500 B.C. Kushites created new capital at Meroë

Chapter Summary

- Early civilizations were built in river valleys.
- The Egyptians used irrigation ditches to water their crops.
- Egyptian rulers were called **pharaohs** and were part of **dynasties**.
- Egyptian history is divided into three kingdoms: the Old, Middle, and New.
- The three periods had the following features in common: (1) strong pharaohs, (2) peace, (3) large building projects, and (4) cultural and intellectual achievements.
- The Egyptians were polytheistic.
- Egyptian pharaohs were **mummified** and buried in **pyramids.**
- Egyptians developed **hieroglyphics**.
- The pharaoh and royal family were at the top of the social structure. Next came nobles and priests. Then were merchants, craftworkers, **scribes**, and tax collectors. Peasant farmers were the largest class. At the bottom were slaves.
- Conquering Nubia gave Egypt control of Nubia's **trade**.
- The Assyrians' **iron** weapons defeated the Kushites and drove them out of Egypt.
- Kush built its new capital, Meroë, on two **trade routes** and near iron deposits. Iron tools, weapons, and other iron goods became important **exports**.

Chapter Review

1. Go back to the world map you used for "Thinking on Your Own" in Lesson 2. Write sentences using directions to tell where Kush was in relation to (1) Egypt, (2) the Arabian Peninsula, and (3) India.

2. Using the same map, write sentences using directions to tell where Egypt was in relation to (1) Kush, (2) the Red Sea, and (3) Central Africa.

3. Create a timeline to combine important dates for ancient Egypt, Nubia, and Kush.

Novel Connections

Below is a list of books that relate to the time period covered in this chapter. The numbers in parentheses indicate the related Thematic Strands of the National Council for the Social Studies (NCSS).

Rosalie F. Baker, Charles F. Baker. *Ancient Egyptians: People of the Pyramids.* Oxford University Press, 2001. (I, II, VIII)

Miriam Greenblatt. *Hatshepsut and Ancient Egypt.* Marshall Cavendish Inc., 2000. (I, II, IV)

Zahi Hawass. *Curse of the Pharaohs: My Adventures with Mummies.* National Geographic Society, 2004. (I, II, III)

Julius Lester. *Pharaoh's Daughter: A Novel of Ancient Egypt.* Harcourt, 2000. (III, IV, V, VI)

Time-Life Books (Editor). *What Life Was Like: On the Banks of the Nile, Ancient Egypt (4000–30 B.C.).* Time-Life Books, 1997. (I, III)

Richard E. Trout. *Falcon of Abydos: Oracle of the Nile (Harbor Lights series).* Langmarc Publishing, 2001. (II, III, VIII)

Skill Builder

Comparing and Contrasting Information Using a Table

To compare information is to look for similarities. To contrast information is to look for differences. Tables are very useful tools for comparing and contrasting information. By reading down the columns and across the rows, you can determine how things are the same or different.

To use a table for comparison and contrast, follow these steps:

- Read the title of the table to learn what it is about.
- Read across the first row to learn exactly what people, places, or events are being described in the table.
- Read down the first column to see what category, or type, of information is given for the people, places, or events.

Ancient Mesopotamian and Egyptian Civilizations

Category	Mesopotamians	Egyptians
Geographical location	• Southwest Asia	• North Africa
River valleys	• Tigris River Valley • Euphrates River Valley	• Nile River Valley
Political organization	• city-states ruled by kings	• empire ruled by pharaoh
Economy	• mainly farming • some trade	• mainly farming • some trade
Religion	• polytheistic • kings considered divine	• polytheistic • pharaohs considered deities
Social structures	• king and royal family • priests and nobles • merchants, craftworkers, scribes • peasant farmers • slaves	• pharaoh and royal family • priests and nobles • merchants, craftworkers, scribes, tax collectors • peasant farmers • slaves
Writing system	• cuneiform	• hieroglyphics

1. What is this table about?
2. List five things that the Egyptians and Mesopotamians had in common.
3. List five things that were different about the two civilizations.

Skill Builder

1. The table compares and contrasts Mesopotamian and Egyptian civilizations.

2. Five things in common: located in river valleys; mainly farming, though some trade; polytheistic; ruler and royal family at top of social structure; slaves at bottom of society.

3. Five things that were different: Mesopotamia located in Southwest Asia, Egypt located in Africa; Mesopotamia consisted of city-states, Egypt was an empire; Egypt had pharaohs, Mesopotamia had kings; Egyptians allowed tax collectors in a middle class, Mesopotamians did not; Mesopotamians used cuneiform, while Egyptians used hieroglyphics.

Classroom Discussion

Discuss with students some of the broader topics covered in this chapter.

- What makes a good ruler?
- How are people divided into social classes today?
- What does a community need in order to be a successful trade center?
- Why do times of peace lead to growth for a country?

Chapter Summary
Refer to page 54 for a summary of Chapter 4.

Related Transparencies
T-1 World Map
T-2 Outline World Map
T-19 Venn Diagram
T-20 Concept Web

Key Blacklines
Biography–Aryabhata

CD Extension
Encourage students to use the reading comprehension, vocabulary reinforcement, and interactive timeline activities on the student CD.

Picturing History
Buddhism is a worldwide religion. The carved statues shown on page 40 represent Buddha. Statues of Buddha take many different forms. These statues are from a Buddhist sculpture park outside the city of Vientiane, Laos. Buddha Park, or Xiang Khouan as it is known, hosts hundreds of images of Buddha. The park is located along the Mekong River about 15 miles (24 km) outside the capital of Laos.

Chapter 4
THE INDIAN SUBCONTINENT
(2500 B.C–A.D. 500)

Getting Focused
Skim this chapter to predict what you will be learning.
- Read the lesson titles and subheadings.
- Look at the illustrations and read the captions.
- Examine the maps.
- Review the vocabulary words and terms.

Studying world history takes the reader all over the world. To help you remember where you have been and where you are going, use an outline map of the world. Start a map key. To indicate different regions, use shading or a design. Choose two ways to show regions and mark the two world regions you have studied so far: Mesopotamia, Egypt, and Kush. Label the two boxes in your map legend.

Pre-Reading Discussion
1 Have students complete each bulleted direction on page 40. Tell students that Chapter 4 discusses the development of early civilizations in India.

2 Ask students to write in their notebooks any questions that occur to them as they preview the chapter. As they read, ask them to record the answers to their questions.

LESSON 1

Civilizations Along the Indus and Ganges Rivers

Indian Subcontinent, 2500 B.C.–A.D. 500

Thinking on Your Own

Create a concept web. In the center write "Indian Subcontinent." As you read this lesson, add information to your web. Include all the factors that influenced life on the Indian subcontinent.

The large Indian **subcontinent** is part of the larger continent of Asia. It is called a subcontinent because it extends out from the continent. Today, India, Pakistan, and Bangladesh are the major nations of the Indian subcontinent. To better understand the history of the region, it is important to know something of its geography.

focus your reading

How did monsoons affect people on the Indian subcontinent?

What were Harappa and Mohenjo-Daro like?

How did Aryans affect Indian society?

vocabulary

subcontinent   monsoons
plains   Brahman
plateau   castes

Geography of the Indian Subcontinent

The Indian subcontinent is shaped like a huge triangle. The base of the triangle lies in the north along the Himalaya Mountains. These are the tallest mountains in the world. Below the mountains lie **plains**, or flat land. The plains are watered by the Indus River to the west and the Ganges River to the east.

South of the plains is the Deccan **Plateau**, an area of high, mostly flat land. The sides of the triangle face the Arabian Sea on the west and the Bay of Bengal on the east. To the south is the Indian Ocean. The climate is hot and dry in winter and

The Indian Subcontinent 41

Lesson Vocabulary

Read and discuss each of the vocabulary terms with students.

A *subcontinent* is part of a larger continent. Tell students to add the prefix *sub-* to their list of prefixes and suffixes, along with other sample terms such as *submarine, submerge,* and *subterranean.*

Plains are flat lands. The Ganges *Plain* is watered by both the Ganges and Indus Rivers. A *plateau* is a region of high and mostly flat land. The Deccan *Plateau* is located south of the *plains*.

The *monsoons* are seasonal winds. The *monsoons* of India bring heavy rains in winter and summer.

A *Brahman* is the highest *caste* in India. The *Brahmans* were the priestly class.

Castes are divisions of people based on social class and occupation. There were four major castes. (This might be a chance to discuss homonyms—words that sound the same but have different meanings and spellings. Point out that a *cast* and a *caste* are two different things. Extend even further with multiple-meaning words, such as a *cast* of a play, a *cast* of a statue, and a *cast* on a broken limb.)

Lesson Summary

The lesson discusses the geography and climate of the Indian subcontinent. Summer and winter monsoons bring both rain for crops and the danger of flooding.

The earliest civilizations in India were at Mohenjo-Daro and Harappa in the Indus River Valley. The cities were very sophisticated with plumbing, apartment buildings, and large public baths. The economy of both cities was based on farming.

Aryan invaders from Central Asia arrived about 1500 B.C. They developed a caste system that continues to affect India today.

Lesson Objective

Students will learn about the climate and geography of India, as well as the early history of civilizations along the Indus and Ganges Rivers.

Focus Your Reading Answers

1 The monsoons provided rain for crops. However, too much rain often led to flooding, endangering the lives of people and crops.

2 Harappa and Mohenjo-Daro were cities built of mud bricks, laid out on a grid. Their houses had indoor plumbing and running water. The cities included a building that served as fort, palace, and temple. Farmers lived in villages and worked in the fields around them. The economy was based on farming and trade.

3 The Aryans brought a caste system to India. It was based on social class and occupation. There were five levels in the caste system.

The Indian Subcontinent 41

Map Extension

Ask students to use the map on page 42 to answer the following questions:

- Over what mountain range do the winter monsoons travel? (the Himalaya Mountains)
- From what body of water do the summer monsoons begin? (Indian Ocean)
- What parts of India seem to be less affected by the pattern of monsoons? (northwest corner, east central coastal plain)

Picturing History

The photograph on page 42 shows the flooded streets of modern Guwahati, India, during the summer monsoons. Ask students to imagine how life would be affected after a monsoon.

Extension

Have students find out more about weather patterns in India or Sri Lanka. They can use library resources or the Internet to locate facts about monsoons and the subsequent flooding that can occur.

Indian Subcontinent, 2500 B.C.–A.D. 500

warm and wet in summer. The change in climate is caused by **monsoons**. These are seasonal winds that blow across the Indian Ocean. The winter monsoons begin in October. The summer monsoons begin in late May or early June.

Monsoons have played an important role in the history of the subcontinent, and they still affect people living there today. The farmers of the subcontinent have always depended on the monsoons to bring rain to grow their crops. The monsoons are both life-giving and life-threatening. Without the rain, crops wither and die. With too much rain, the rivers flood. Thousands of people die and crops are destroyed in the swirling flood waters.

The summer monsoon floods still impact life in India.

The Geography of the Indian Subcontinent
- Indian subcontinent
- Winter monsoons (dry winds)
- Summer monsoons (wet winds)

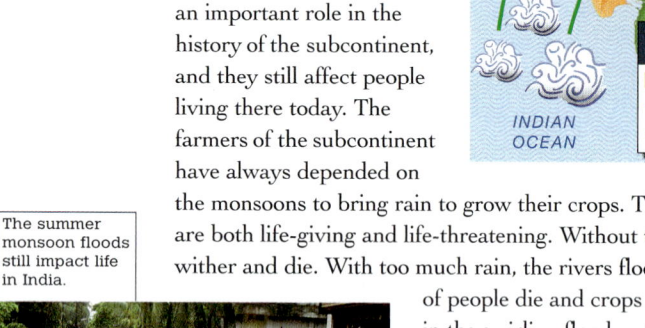

The First Civilization

The earliest civilization on the subcontinent began in the Indus River Valley. Archaeologists have found more than one thousand sites there. They date the civilization around 2500 B.C. to 1500 B.C. Much of what is known is based on two cities, Harappa and Mohenjo-Daro. More is still to be discovered as archaeologists continue to study other settlements.

Harappa and Mohenjo-Daro are 400 miles apart and may have been twin capitals. The two cities were carefully planned and very similar. Both were laid out on a grid pattern. Wide streets ran north and south and smaller streets ran east and west.

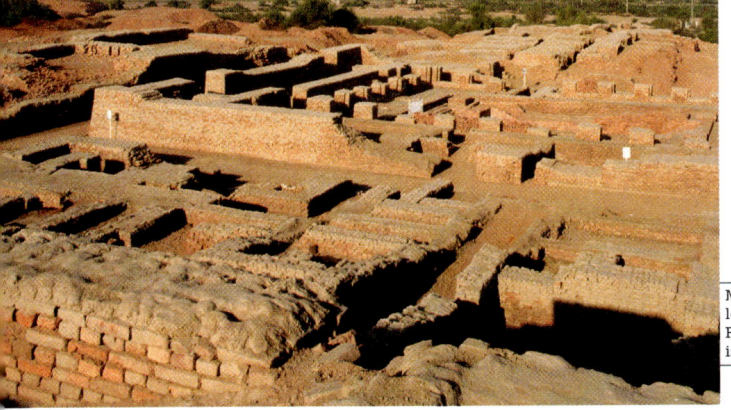

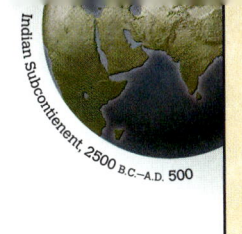

Mohenjo-Daro was located in the Indus River Valley in what is today Pakistan.

Private homes and public buildings were made of mud bricks. Some houses were three stories tall. All houses had a center courtyard. Rooms were built around the courtyard and opened onto it. Houses had running water and indoor plumbing that drained into a citywide sewage system.

A combined temple, palace, and fort stood over each city on a nearby hill. Both cities had villages and fields scattered around them. Farmers lived in the villages and worked the fields. Each city had large warehouses where the crops were stored.

The economies of Harappa and Mohenjo-Daro were based on farming. Like the Tigris, Euphrates, and Nile Rivers, the Indus flooded each year. Farmers used the rich soil left behind to grow crops such as wheat and barley. The farmers of the Indus Valley were the first to grow cotton. Spinners turned the cotton boll, or seed pod, into thread. Weavers wove the thread into fine cloth.

Cotton cloth became one of the trade goods of Indus merchants. Other trade goods included grain, copper, and pearls. A trading network developed between the Indus Valley and the city-states of Sumer. Merchants sent trading ships along the coast of the Arabian Sea to the Persian gulf. The ships then sailed north through the Gulf as far as Sumer.

Evidence tells archaeologists that Harappa and Mohenjo-Daro had some form of central government. A strong,

A carving found at Mohenjo-Daro

The Indian Subcontinent | 43

Picturing History

Like the Sumerians, the people of Mohenjo-Daro built with bricks. The photograph at the top of page 43 shows the grid layout of the city. Discuss with students the advantages of a grid layout for a city. Use contemporary western cities as examples of a grid system: Philadelphia, Chicago, or Washington, D.C.

Extension

About 700 different Harappan settlements have been the focus of archaeological work. Harappan lands covered some 502,000 square miles (1.3 million sq. km) and included land in what is now Pakistan and north India. It was larger than both the Mesopotamian and Egyptian societies that grew up along the Euphrates and Nile Rivers.

Picturing History

The photograph at the bottom of page 43 depicts a carving of a priest-king of Mohenjo-Daro. The statue was carved of sandstone. Ask students to identify any marks of status they see on this bust, such as the jewelry on the head. The sculpture is now in the Karachi Museum in Pakistan.

Extension

Although archaeologists have found hundreds of writing samples, no one has yet decoded the Harappan language. A few symbols have been identified, but not enough to decipher the inscriptions. Scholars have had to rely on illustrations on carvings and figurines to better understand Harappan society.

The Indian Subcontinent | 43

Map Extensions

1 Have students use the maps in their textbooks to locate the places mentioned in the chapter as trade partners with Harappa and Mohenjo-Daro.

2 Ask students to use the map on page 44 to answer the following questions:

- Which Aryan invasion swept through the Ganges Plain? (the second invasion, from 1500–1000 B.C.)

- From which geographic direction did the first invasion come? (north)

- What was the movement and destination of the final invasion? (west from the Ganges River region near the Bay of Bengal to the Deccan Plateau)

Stop and Think

Students' tables should include:

- Geographical Location: Indian subcontinent
- River Valleys: Indus and Ganges
- Political Organization: kingdom
- Economy: farming and trade
- Religion: polytheistic
- Social Structures: king, priests, craftspeople, peasants, slaves, caste system
- Writing System: not yet decoded

---

organized government was needed to plan and lay out the cities. The government was probably headed by a king or priest-king. No one has been able to decipher the written language of the Indus Valley people. All we know about life in these cities comes from archaeological records.

The people of the Indus Valley were polytheistic—meaning they worshiped many gods. A major deity was a god of creation. They also worshiped animals.

The Impact of Aryan Invaders

Around 1500 B.C., Aryans from Central Asia invaded and conquered the Indus Valley. They were nomadic warriors. Over time they moved eastward into the plain around the Ganges River and then south into the Deccan Plateau.

Most of what is known about the Aryans comes from the *Vedas*. The *Vedas* are a collection of books containing prayers, songs, and other writings of the Aryans. The Aryans brought with them their own language, religious beliefs, and social system. They spoke an Indo-European language known as Sanskrit. English, German, Persian, Spanish, and French are some of the languages that are based on the Indo-European language.

Like other ancient people, the Aryans were polytheistic. Their chief deity was Indra, the god of war. Other deities represented the natural world such as the sky, air, and water. Priests called brahmans offered sacrifices to the deities. Over time, the people began to worship a single force or power in the world known as **Brahman**.

The Aryans developed a social system that has had a lasting impact on Indian culture.

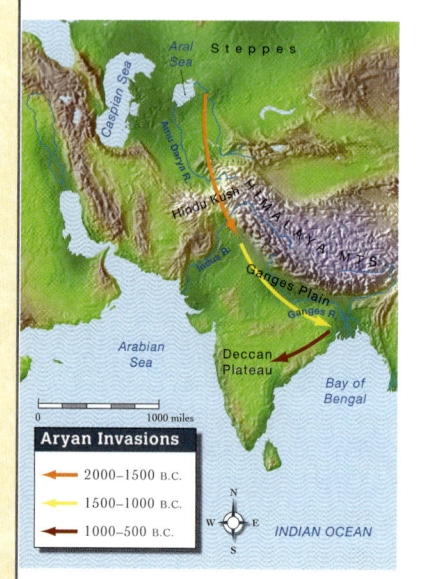

> **stop and think**
>
> Look back at the table on page 39 of Chapter 3. Draw a fourth column in your notebook. Label the new column "Indus Valley People" and add information from this lesson. Work with a partner to complete this column.

They divided the population into four major categories, or **castes**. These four castes were further divided into thousands of subcastes. The castes determined a person's occupation and social class. Those not included in the caste system were called Untouchables.

Over time, Aryan culture and its caste system expanded across much of the Indian subcontinent. Aryan kingdoms grew up in several areas, especially on the vast plain around the Ganges River. These became important centers of farming and trade.

Mahabharata, Indian epic, details classic Indian culture.

Indian Subcontinent, 2500 B.C.–A.D. 500

Five Major Categories of Aryan Society

Caste	Characteristics	Work
Brahman	• priests • highest caste and smallest in number	• oversaw religious ceremonies
Kshatriya	• warriors	• defended kingdom
Vaisya	• commoners, or ordinary people	• mostly farmers or merchants
Sudra	• largest group of people • non-Aryans	• earned a living by doing farm work and other manual labor
Untouchable	• outside the caste system • about 5 percent of the people	• did jobs no one else would do, such as garbage collecting • lived separate from others

Putting It All Together

Imagine you are a member of the Sudra caste or an Untouchable. The only reason you are not a member of a higher caste is that you are not an Aryan. The Aryans conquered your people. How would you feel (a) about your life and (b) about the Aryans? Discuss the questions with a partner. Write a bulleted list of notes as you talk. Use your notes to write a paragraph that answers the questions.

The Indian Subcontinent 45

Picturing History

The illustration at the top of page 45 is from the *Mahabharata*, the most famous piece of classical Indian literature. It is also the longest poem in any written language, with more than 90,000 stanzas. The main subject of the poem is the war between cousins wishing to control the kingdom around 1200 B.C. The poem was probably written down about 100 B.C.

Extension

Show students a reproduction of Picasso's painting of the Spanish Civil War of the 1930s, *Guernica*. Ask them to note any similarities in style or mood to the illustration on page 45, done thousands of years apart.

Table Extension

Ask students to compare and contrast the categories of Aryan society with those of Egypt and Mesopotamia.

Putting It All Together

Students' lists and paragraphs will vary but should include feelings about the Aryans and about life as a member of a lower class or as an Untouchable. Encourage students to include the topic of discrimination in their analyses.

Extension

Suggest to students that they use library resources or the Internet to investigate the current status of the Untouchables in India, known now as Dalit.

The Indian Subcontinent 45

Lesson Summary
The four basic tenets of Hinduism are explained in this lesson. Hindus believe that Brahman is the eternal and supreme force of the universe. They also feel that union with Brahman is the goal of all souls. The soul's next life is determined by karma, the actions of this life. Following dharma, divine law, affects one's karma. Hinduism reinforced the caste system and encouraged the poor to hope for a better life in the future, not fight for one in the present.

Lesson Objective
Students will learn about the major beliefs of Hinduism and about Hinduism's effect on Indian society.

Focus Your Reading Answers

1 Hinduism developed over centuries, blending the religion of the Aryans with that of the people already living on the Indian subcontinent.

2 Hinduism teaches that Brahman is the eternal and supreme force of the universe. Union with Brahman is the goal of all souls. The soul's next life is determined by karma, the actions of this life. Following dharma, divine law, affects one's karma.

LESSON 2

The Beginning of Hinduism

Thinking on Your Own

Skim the lesson by reading the subheadings, captions, and vocabulary words. Write five questions that you have about this lesson. Share your questions with a partner. As you read, answer all of the questions.

Hinduism is one of the two major world religions that began on the Indian subcontinent. The other religion is Buddhism.

Hinduism developed from a blending of Aryan religious beliefs with those of other people who lived on the subcontinent. Unlike Judaism or Buddhism, no one person founded Hinduism. The teachings, prayers, hymns, and ceremonies of Hinduism developed over centuries. In time, they were collected in four long *Vedas* and three other works.

focus your reading

How did Hinduism develop?

What are the basic beliefs of Hinduism?

vocabulary

Hinduism   karma
atman   dharma
reincarnation mobility

The Ganges River is sacred to people of the Hindu faith

46 Chapter 4

Lesson Vocabulary
Read aloud and explain each of the vocabulary terms to students.

Hinduism is one of the major religions of India. The teachings of *Hinduism* have been collected long *Vedas*, or sacred writings. The Hindu word for "soul" is *atman* (atma). The *atman's* goal unite with Brahman after dying. Thus, *Hinduism* teaches *reincarnation*, the belief in the soul's birth and death. The number of *reincarnations* a soul must pass through is determined by beha

The sum of actions of a person's life is known as *karma*. *Karma* determines whether a soul mu reborn, and if so, into what state.

Dharma refers both to the divine law and to a person's keeping that law. Each person's *dharm* different, depending on his or her social class, job, and so on. The ability to move from one s class to another is known as social *mobility*. This social *mobility* is hindered by the beliefs of H

Basic Beliefs of Hinduism

Hinduism is a very complex religion with many deities and different rituals and practices. However, Hindus share certain beliefs.

1. Brahman is the supreme and eternal spirit, or force, of the universe.

Because this is a difficult idea to understand, Hinduism has a large number of lesser deities. People find it easier to worship deities that are shown as humans or animals. Hindus believe that these deities are all forms of Brahman.

2. The goal of every soul is to become part of Brahman.

The Hindu word for soul is **atman**. The goal of every atman is to unite with Brahman after death. Before it can achieve this, the soul must free itself from earthly desire, such as wanting to be wealthy or popular. It may take many lives to complete this journey. This cycle of birth and death is called **reincarnation**.

3. **Karma** determines a soul's next life.

Karma is the sum of a person's actions in life. These actions determine whether a soul is reborn into a higher or lower life or whether it has to be reborn at all. The answer depends on how close the soul comes to freeing itself from earthly desire. For example, a commoner who has worked hard at being good could be born into the warrior caste.

Brahma

Shiva

Vishnu

Indian Subcontinent, 2500 B.C.–A.D. 500

The Indian Subcontinent 47

Picturing History

Statues of Brahma show him with four heads; three are shown in the photograph at the top left of page 47. The god of creation, Brahma originally had one head. However, when he created woman, he fell in love with her. Wanting to be able to see her at all times, even when she hid, he grew additional heads facing in every direction.

Picturing History

The photograph on the top right of page 47 shows Shiva as "Lord of the Dance," Natarajah. The dance is the cycle of life and destruction; Shiva is both destroyer and re-creator. A legend says that he danced on the demon of ignorance, thus subduing 10,000 heretics.

Picturing History

The image on the bottom of page 47 is Vishnu, the goddess with many hands, all posed in the gesture of blessing.

Picturing History

The modern Hindus shown on page 46 are enacting a ritual cleansing at the Ganges River. It is believed that by bathing in the sacred Ganges River, one's sins will be washed away. One of the most popular places to bathe is Varanasi (Benares), a pilgrimage site. The Ganges is named for the goddess Ganga. It is a sacred river, meant to symbolize unending life.

Extension

Have students use library resources or the Internet to find out more about the gods of Hinduism. Ask students to consider the following questions:

- What are their roles and responsibilities?
- How are they best worshiped?

Have students present their findings to the class by using the Student Presentation Builder on the student CD.

The Indian Subcontinent 47

Extension

Hindus believe everyone should have four ashramas, or stages, in life. The first is being a student who studies the sacred literature. The second involves developing responsibility within society as a householder (a man who marries, earns a living, has sons, takes care of his family, and gives alms to the poor).

The third stage is being a contemplative (a man who becomes a forest dweller and pays homage to his ancestors). The final stage is the ascetic (a man who withdraws from society and spends time in personal devotion, reflection, and meditation), who renounces worldly pleasures.

Putting It All Together

Students' responses will vary but may suggest that the third and fourth beliefs were most important in supporting the caste system. If karma determined the next life, then having no earthly desire, including advancement, was the best response. If following dharma, based on one's current social class, affected karma, then people remained in their own class and worked hard.

Picturing History

The idealized painting of Buddha on page 49 sitting under his banyan tree meditating demonstrates high regard for Buddhism's founder. Note the light rays coming from his body and head. This painting is located in the Temple of Yongju in Suwon, South Korea.

---

4 Karma is determined by following **dharma**.

Dharma refers both to divine law and to a person's obedience toward divine law. Dharma sets up certain moral and religious duties for every person. These duties depend on one's caste, job, gender, and age. A person is supposed to behave according to his or her dharma. How well a person performs these duties helps in his or her journey toward union with Brahman. If a person behaves according to one's dharma, then he or she will move toward union with Brahman. Disobey one's dharma and move backward on the cycle of reincarnation.

> ### The Hindu Trinity
>
> Brahma, Vishnu, and Shiva make up the Hindu trinity, or Trimurti. These are not separate gods, but three faces of the same god.
>
> **Brahma:** the creator, who breathes out the universe to make it come into existence.
>
> **Vishnu:** the preserver or caretaker of the universe, who must balance everything that exists, and whose constant action–karma–keeps everything running.
>
> **Shiva:** the destroyer: god of opposites–light and darkness, good and evil, creation and destruction, rest and activity, mild and terrible, male and female.

Hinduism has social as well as religious importance. Hinduism links union with Brahman to behavior on Earth. For centuries, this link encouraged people to stay within their castes, behave better, and work hard. Social **mobility** is the ability to move from social class to social class and better one's life. Hinduism made this difficult, if not impossible. It supported keeping things the way they were. The ruling caste and the wealthy did not have to worry about being pushed out by people working their way up. The promise of reincarnation gave hope to the poor. Their lives could be better the next time.

Putting It All Together

The last paragraph says that Hinduism "supported keeping things the way they were." What two basic beliefs of Hinduism were most important in supporting the caste system? Talk this question over with a partner. Write your answer in a sentence in your notebook.

Lesson Vocabulary

Discuss each of the vocabulary terms listed on page 49 with students.

Buddhism is a religion based on the teachings of the "Enlightened One," or Buddha.

Stories and customs passed from generation to generation become *tradition*. Much of what we know about Buddha is based on *tradition*. Ask students to describe one of their family's *traditions*.

A *rajah* is a ruler. Siddhartha's father was a *rajah* in what is now Nepal.

Meditation is thinking intensely about spiritual things. During the practice of *meditation*, Siddhartha became enlightened. Being released from a cycle of reincarnation is *nirvana*. Buddha did not believe that *nirvana* was achieved only by moving upward through the caste system.

A *dynasty* is a ruling family. The Maurya *Dynasty* united much of the Indian subcontinent.

A *missionary* is one who teaches religion to others in an attempt to convert them. Asoka sent *missionaries* throughout the empire to teach *Buddhism*.

LESSON 3

The Beginning of Buddhism

Thinking on Your Own

Look through the lesson for vocabulary words in bold type. In your notebook, write the words you do not know. Read the definitions in the text and in the Glossary. Write a sentence for each word. Be sure you use the word in context and spell it correctly.

Unlike Hinduism, **Buddhism** was founded by a person. It began in the 500s B.C. by Siddhartha Gautama. Much of what we know about him comes from **tradition**, or stories passed from one generation to the next. According to tradition, Siddhartha was born around 563 B.C. His father was the **rajah**, or ruler, of a small kingdom in what is today Nepal.

Siddhartha lived the life of a prince until he was about twenty-nine years old.

focus your reading

What was Siddhartha searching for?

What are the four basic principles of Buddhism?

Why is Asoka one of India's greatest rulers?

Why is the Gupta period in Indian history important?

vocabulary

Buddhism   nirvana
tradition   dynasty
rajah   missionaries
meditation

One day while out riding, he came upon a sick person, then an old person, and finally a dead body. He wanted to know why people like this suffered and died. Siddharta gave up his life as a prince to search for the answer to his question.

Lesson Summary

The lesson explains the origins of Buddhism and its major beliefs. Siddhartha Gautama, who became known as the Enlightened One, or Buddha, was an Indian prince who lived during the sixth century B.C. He set out to find an answer to suffering and death, which he found after a six-year search. He taught the Four Noble Truths and the Eightfold Path. Buddhism spread through the word of missionaries that Asoka sent throughout the Maurya Empire that he governed. After the decline of the Maurya Empire, the Gupta Empire flourished. These Hindu rulers emphasized trade, expanding as far as the Mediterranean.

Lesson Objective

Students will learn about the development of Buddhism, India's other major religion. They will also learn about the Maurya and Gupta Empires.

The Indian Subcontinent | 49

Focus Your Reading Answers

1 Siddhartha wanted to know why people suffered and died.

2 The Four Noble Truths are:
- Life is full of suffering, pain, and sorrow.
- Suffering is caused by human desires.
- Conquering desire is the only way to end suffering.
- Following the Middle Path, or the Eightfold Path, is the way to conquer desire.

3 Asoka is considered a great ruler because he was devoted to the principles of the Four Noble Truths. After attempting to conquer more land, Asoka converted to Buddhism and decided not to fight any more. He had laws carved on stone pillars so that everyone could know them. He sent Buddhist missionaries to other parts of the world. He built roads with rest houses for travelers, as well as hospitals.

4 The Gupta period was a Golden Age of India. The rulers encouraged trade, developing a trade network that included Southeast Asia and China. They were also responsible for discovering a smallpox vaccine and for mathematical and astronomical discoveries.

The Indian Subcontinent | 49

Picturing History

The photographs at the top of page 50 represent the wide range of styles of depicting Buddha favored by various nations. The statues demonstrate that Buddhism is still practiced in many parts of the world. The Buddha images on this page are from the following locations:

Po Fook Hill, Hong Kong (top left)

Thai statue on display in Genoa, Italy (top center)

Pak Ou Caves, Laos (top right)

Buddhist shrine, Sri Lanka (bottom right)

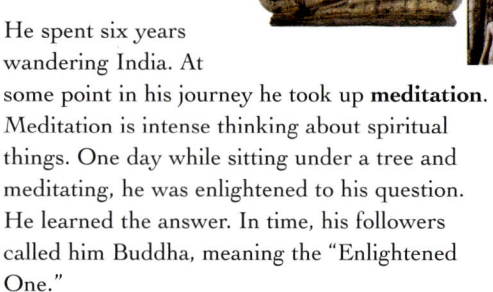

He spent six years wandering India. At some point in his journey he took up **meditation**. Meditation is intense thinking about spiritual things. One day while sitting under a tree and meditating, he was enlightened to his question. He learned the answer. In time, his followers called him Buddha, meaning the "Enlightened One."

The Four Noble Truths and the Eightfold Path

Buddha lived to be about eighty years old. He spent his life teaching the answer he had learned. His words became the basis for Buddhism. Its basic principles can be summed up in the Four Noble Truths and the Eightfold Path.

The Eightfold Path is also called the Middle Path. The eight steps include having the

The Four Noble Truths

1. Life is filled with suffering, pain, and sorrow.
2. Suffering is caused by our desires.
3. The only way to end suffering is to conquer desire.
4. The way to conquer desire is to follow the Middle Path.

(1) right belief: A person must know the Four Noble Truths.

(2) right intention: A person must commit to living by the Four Noble Truths.

(3) right speech: A person must always speak the truth and must not gossip or use bad language.

(4) right behavior: A person must not kill, steal, or do anything that is not moral and right.

(5) right occupation: A person must quit a job that is not good for him or her and find one that will help the person live according to Buddhism.

Buddha takes many forms around the world.

50 Chapter 4

Extensions

1 Some students may be interested in using library resources or the Internet to find out more about the design of Japanese gardens attached to Zen Buddhist monasteries. Ask them to share their findings with the class.

2 Have interested students find out more about the life and teachings of the Dalai Lama, the spiritual head of Tibetan Buddhism. Ask them to create a poster for the class.

(6) right effort: A person must develop good attitudes and behaviors and keep bad ones from developing.
(7) right mindfulness: A person must be constantly aware of the senses in order to control the body.
(8) right concentration: A person may receive enlightenment by meditating.

Buddha accepted the Hindu ideas of karma and dharma. However, he rejected the many deities of Hinduism. Like Hindus, Buddha believed in reincarnation. The goal of Buddhists is to reach union with the universe. However, Buddha did not accept the caste system. He taught that a person could achieve **nirvana** without having to move upward through the caste system in each new life. Nirvana was Buddha's name for release from the cycle of reincarnation. Over time, Buddhism spread throughout Asia as far as Korea and Japan. Hinduism remained an Indian religion.

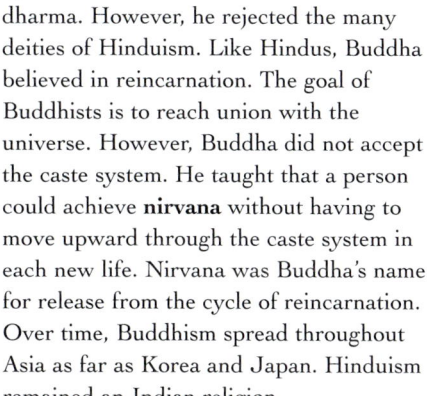

stop and think

Use a Venn diagram to compare and contrast Hinduism and Buddhism. Work with a partner to make sure that you include all the information from Lessons 2 and 3.

Buddhism and the Maurya Empire

A major reason that Buddhism spread so far was Asoka. He was the grandson of Chandragupta Maurya. In 324 B.C., Chandragupta founded the first **dynasty**—or ruling family—to unite much of the Indian subcontinent. He began his conquest in the Ganges Valley.

Asoka continued his grandfather's struggle against the other rulers of India. However, after one very bloody battle, Asoka gave up fighting. He converted to Buddhism and committed himself to living by the Four Noble Truths. He used these principles to rule his empire. Among other actions, he improved medical care by setting up hospitals. To aid travelers, he built roads and rest houses along the roads. He had his laws carved on stone pillars so everyone could see them. His laws followed Buddhist teachings. Asoka also sent **missionaries** throughout

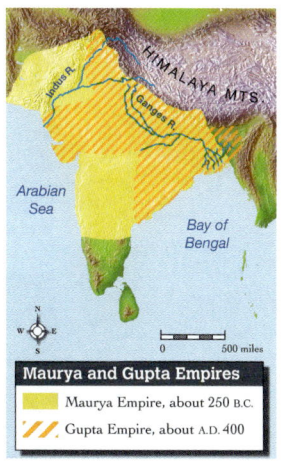

Maurya and Gupta Empires
- Maurya Empire, about 250 B.C.
- Gupta Empire, about A.D. 400

The Indian Subcontinent | 51

Stop and Think

Students' diagrams will vary but may include the following ideas:

- **Alike:** both begin with four basic ideas; both believe in reincarnation, karma, and dharma; both feel that the goal is to reach union with Brahman.

- **Different:** Buddhism does not support the caste system or believe that a person must cycle through the caste system in order to reach nirvana. Hinduism remained an Indian religion, while Buddhism spread to other nations.

Map Extension

Ask students to use the map on page 51 to answer the following questions:

- What geographical range did the Maurya Empire cover? (central western, or north part of bottom triangle)

- In which geographical direction did the Gupta Empire spread beyond the borders of India? (east)

- Which empire was larger? (Maurya)

- Which empire included the Ganges River within its borders? (Gupta)

Extension

Students interested in art may wish to create a mandala, or circular map of the cosmos, often used in Buddhism. Mandalas may be carved or painted of any material; some monks have been known to make them of colored sand. Buddhists use them as a meditation aid.

The Indian Subcontinent | 51

Picturing History

The photograph at the top of page 52 shows one of the pillars that Asoka erected with the laws of the Empire carved on it. Ask students to recall what other ruler had laws posted for the benefit of his subjects. (Hammurabi)

Pillars were also placed along the roads at famous sites related to Buddha's life and pilgrimage. Made of polished sandstone, they were as tall as 50 feet (15 m), weighing up to 50 tons (50,000 kg) each.

Time Box Extension

Ask students to calculate how much time elapsed between the founding of the Gupta and Maurya Empires. (644 years)

Picturing History

The mural shown at the bottom of page 52 is one of many from the caves at Ajanta, India. They depict life during the Gupta era. Ajanta is located in western India, about 62 miles (99 km) north of Aurangabad. Thirty temples are carved into the sides of a crescent-shaped gorge. Some of the murals show scenes from the life of Buddha, while others depict life in towns or forests or at court. The artists remain anonymous.

Indian Subcontinent, 2500 B.C.–A.D. 500

India and to other places to preach Buddhist teachings. Missionaries go out to preach to and convert people to their religion.

Missionaries often went along on trading expeditions. The Maurya Empire was part of a large trade network that reached from the Pacific Ocean to Southwest Asia and the Mediterranean. The Empire grew wealthy under Asoka and later rulers. Asoka is considered one of India's greatest rulers.

Asoka had rules carved on pillars.

The Golden Age of the Gupta

The Maurya Empire lasted only 50 years after Asoka died. The period between 186 B.C. and A.D. 320 was marked by invasions and warfare. Nomads from Central Asia overran parts of the subcontinent. Rival Indian kingdoms fought for power. In the year 320, a new Indian dynasty, the Gupta, rose to power in northern India. It lasted until the end of the 400s.

Unlike the Maurya, the Gupta were Hindus, not Buddhists. Like Asoka, the Gupta rulers encouraged trade. Their trade network spread to include China and Southeast Asia as well as the Mediterranean. Their rule is known as the "Golden Age of the Gupta." The name honors the important contributions made during this time. The Arabic number system was

Time Box

324 B.C.
Maurya Empire founded

A.D. 320
Gupta Dynasty founded

Murals at the Caves of Ajanta show life during the Gupta period.

52 Chapter 4

Extension

In 1983, the cave paintings at Ajanta were designated as a United Nations Educational, Scientific, and Cultural Organization (UNESCO) World Heritage Site. Ask students to find out more about this program and about how the sites are chosen using library resources or the Internet.

developed. When Arab scholars adopted the system in the A.D. 800s, its use spread to Europe. Discoveries in one world region often spread to other places.

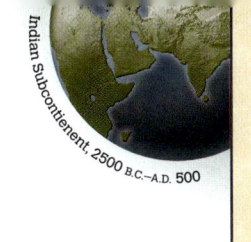

Achievements of Maurya and Gupta Empires

- smallpox vaccination
- medical advances such as surgery and setting of broken bones
- Stupa, a large dome-shaped shrine
- Arabic number system
- idea of zero (0)
- decimal system
- mapped the stars and planets
- discovered that Earth was a sphere, rotated on its axis, revolved around the sun

Putting It All Together

To review this lesson, write five questions and answers using important information from this lesson. Read an answer to your partner. He or she has to give you the question. Take turns giving answers and questions.

From the *Arthashastra*

The *Arthashastra* was written during the rule of Chandragupta who founded the Maurya dynasty around 300 B.C. The *Arthashastra* is considered a major work of political policy. The following explains the duties of a ruler.

"[The ruler] should facilitate mining operations. He should encourage manufacturers. He should help exploitation of forest wealth. . . . He should construct highways both on land and on water. He should plan markets. He should build dikes for water. . . .

The ruler should maintain adolescents, the aged, the diseased, and the orphans. He should also provide livelihood to deserted women . . . and protection for children born to them . . . .

He should protect cultivation from heavy taxes, slave labor and severe penalties, herds of cattle from cattle lifters, wild animals, . . . and diseases. . . .

He should not only conserve existing forests, buildings, and mines, but also develop new ones."

reading for understanding

Which of the duties listed relate to businesses?

Which of the duties listed relate to making people's lives better?

Are any of the duties similar to things that government does in the United States? If yes, list them.

Chart Extension

Students may wish to use library resources or the Internet to further explore Indian architecture or medical advances.

Putting It All Together

Students' questions and answers will vary but should include information about Buddhism and the Gupta and Maurya Empires.

Reading for Understanding

1 The first two items deal with businesses.

2 The final three items deal with making people's lives better.

3 Yes; lists may include assisting mining and forestry, building highways and dams and other public works, assisting disadvantaged people, and caring for those who have no one to help.

Extension

Ask students to compare and contrast the *Arthashastra* with the rules from Hammurabi's Code, found on page 22.

The Indian Subcontinent

Chapter Review

1. Students' choices and headlines will vary. Possible choices are Buddha, Hinduism, Asoka, Aryan invasion, caste system, meditation.

2. Check to see that students have added India to their world maps.

   PLEASE NOTE: The world map being created by students will be used throughout this book.

Chapter Summary

- The Indian **subcontinent** is part of the continent of Asia. Its northern **plains** are home to the Indus and Ganges River Valleys. The Deccan **Plateau** is in the south.
- **Monsoons** greatly affect the climate of the subcontinent.
- The earliest civilization was in the Indus River Valley. Two important sites were Harappa and Mohenjo-Daro.
- Aryans from Central Asia invaded the subcontinent around 1500 B.C. They brought with them the Sanskrit language, their belief in Brahma, and the **caste** system. Their priests were called **Brahmans**.
- **Hinduism** and **Buddhism** are two world religions that began on the Indian subcontinent.
- Hindus believe that the goal for the **atman**, or soul, is union with Brahman. **Karma** and **dharma** guide Hindus on this journey toward **reincarnation**.
- Hinduism reinforced the caste system and limited social **mobility**.
- Much of what we know about Siddhartha Gautama, the Buddha, comes from **tradition**. He was the son of a **rajah** and gave up his life as a prince to find the answer for human suffering. He found his answer through **meditation**.
- The basic principles of Buddhism are found in the Four Noble Truths and the Eightfold Path.
- Buddhists believe in reincarnation and union with the universe in **nirvana**.
- Asoka of the Maurya **dynasty** converted to Buddhism. He sent **missionaries** to preach and convert people.

Chapter Review

1. Choose five people, ideas, or events from this chapter. Write a two-line headline for each one.

2. Add the geographic features of the Indian subcontinent to the world map that you began at the beginning of the chapter. Be sure to add to the map's key.

Novel Connections

Below is a list of books that relate to the time period covered in this chapter. The numbers in parentheses indicate the related Thematic Strands of the National Council for the Social Studies (NCSS).

Sherab Chodzin, Alexandra Kohn. *The Wisdom of the Crows and Other Buddhist Tales.* Ten Speed Press, 1998. (I, V)

J.E.B.Gray. *Tales from India.* Oxford University Press, 2001. (I, V)

Uma Krishnaswami. *Broken Tusk: Stories of the Hindu God Ganesha.* Linnet Books, 1996. (I, V)

James B. Robinson. *Hinduism.* Chelsea House Publishers, 2004. (I)

Vijay Singh. *The River Goddess: A Hindu Tale.* The Creative Company, 1997. (I, V)

Skill Builder

Outlining Information

An outline is like the skeleton of a piece of writing. It lists the basic information in the piece. Making an outline is a good way to organize information when you study. To make an outline, look for the main idea—the most important information—in a section. Then look for the details that support it.

An outline has a standard format of levels, letters, and numerals. Each level is indented.

I. Main ideas are listed with Roman numerals.
    A. The most important details are listed with capital letters.
        1. Less important details are listed with Arabic numerals.

An outline for part of Lesson 1 looks like this:

> I. Civilizations along the Indus and Ganges Rivers
>   A. Geography of the Indian subcontinent
>   1. Deccan Plateau—high, flat land
>   2. Monsoons—winter and summer
>   B. The first civilization
>   1. Mohenjo-Daro developed around 2500 B.C.
>   2. Economy based on farming
>   C. The impact of Aryan invaders

This outline makes it easy to answer the question, "What influenced the development of civilizations along the Indus and Ganges Rivers?"

Complete the following outlining activities.

1. Outline "Basic Beliefs of Hinduism," pages 47–48.

2. Outline Lesson 3. Use each subheading in the lesson as a main idea. Your outline will have Roman numerals I through III for main ideas. The number of other lines in your outline will depend on how many supporting details you list.

The Indian Subcontinent 55

Skill Builder

1. Outlines will vary. Possible outline:

   I. Deities of Hinduism
      A. Brahma
      B. Shiva
      C. Vishnu

   II. Beliefs of Hinduism
      A. Brahman is supreme and eternal spirit
      B. Goal of every soul is to become part of Brahman
      C. Karma determines soul's next life

2. Student outlines will vary, but should include key concepts and supporting details.

Classroom Discussion

Discuss with students some of the broader topics covered in this chapter.

- How do conquering cultures impose their ideas on the civilizations they conquer?
- What effects do geography and climate have on a region's history?
- How can religion affect a society?

The Indian Subcontinent 55

Chapter Summary
Refer to page 68 for a summary of Chapter 5.

Related Transparencies

T-1 World Map

T-2 Outline World Map

T-4 Silk Road

T-18 Three-Column Chart

T-19 Venn Diagram

Key Blacklines

Primary Source—
The Analects of Confucius

CD Extension

Encourage students to use the reading comprehension, vocabulary reinforcement, and interactive timeline activities on the student CD.

Picturing History

The terra cotta soldiers, shown on page 56, represent only a fraction of those buried with Emperor Qin Shihuangdi. Chinese peasants found the burial site while digging a well. The first formal excavation was in 1974, when archaeologists found 6,000 figures. Two years later, a second site yielded 1,400 warriors and horses. A third pit, found in 1980, is the smallest, with six warriors, a chariot, and a few weapons. As one who had survived three assassination attempts, Qin Shihuangdi wanted to be well protected in the afterlife. The soldiers and their horses were meant to be lifelike.

Chapter 5
EARLY CHINESE CIVILIZATIONS
(1750 B.C.– A.D. 200)

Getting Focused

Skim this chapter to predict what you will be learning.
- Read the lesson titles and subheadings.
- Look at the illustrations and read the captions.
- Examine the maps.
- Review the vocabulary words and terms.

What do you know about China and the Chinese people? Make a list of things you know. Then look through this chapter at the illustrations and headings. What questions do they raise in your mind about Chinese civilizations? Write at least three questions about early China that you want answered by the end of the chapter. Be sure to add China to the world map you began in Chapter 4.

Picturing History, continued

Expressions, costumes, height, hair styles, and gestures differ among the figures. Even the horses are posed differently.

Pre-Reading Discussion

1 Discuss with students how people in the United States gain political power. Broaden the discussion by including other government systems, such as monarchies and dictatorships. Tell students that they are about to learn the system of government by which China was governed for millennia.

2 Ask students to identify reasons to overthrow a government. Have them link this idea to the American Revolution. Explain that they will read about the Chinese theory for changing dynasties.

LESSON 1

The First Chinese Civilizations

Thinking on Your Own

Read the Focus Your Reading questions and the vocabulary words. Write the vocabulary words in your notebook. Discuss the possible meanings with a partner. As you read, write the meanings next to the words. Then use each word in a sentence that shows the word's meaning.

Like early civilizations in Mesopotamia, Egypt, and the Indian subcontinent, the first civilization in China began in a river valley. The Huang He Valley is in eastern China. It was here that farming began in China. Like the Tigris, Euphrates, Nile, and Indus Rivers, the Huang He River flooded. When the river returned to its banks, it left rich soil behind.

Like other people, the Chinese had to learn to build dikes to control the river. They also learned to dig irrigation systems to water their fields. Every few years, the floods of the Huang He were very destructive. There was so much water that the dikes could not hold back the river. The river roared out of the dikes and over the land. Thousands of people and farm animals drowned. Houses, tools, and crops were destroyed. The Chinese began to call the Huang He the "river of sorrows."

focus your reading

How is early Chinese civilization similar to early civilizations in other world regions?

Why are the Xia and Shang Dynasties important?

What was the Mandate of Heaven?

What was the traditional Chinese family like?

vocabulary

ancestor worship
mandate
dynastic cycle
filial piety
extended family

Early Chinese Civilizations | 57

Lesson Summary
The lesson explores early Chinese civilizations. Farming began in eastern China along the Huang He Valley.

The Xia Dynasty began about 2200 B.C. Some 500 years later, the Shang Dynasty began. In 1045 B.C., the Zhou Dynasty began as a rebellion against the Shang. The Zhou believed they had a mandate from heaven to rule and that all emperors gained their power through divine right.

Lesson Objective
Students will learn about the early settlements and dynasties of China. They will also learn about the family as the foundation of Chinese society.

Focus Your Reading Answers

1 Like other places in the world, China developed first in river valleys where the soil was fertile and water was abundant. The Chinese also learned to control the rivers through dikes and to irrigate their fields.

2 The Xia and Shang Dynasties were the first ruling dynasties. They were both farming economies with knowledge of bronze work. The Shang developed a writing system and the practice of ancestor worship.

3 The Mandate of Heaven was the Zhou explanation for their overthrow of the Shang Dynasty. They believed their power to rule came as a command from the deities. The people had the right to rebel when rulers did not act in their best interests.

4 Traditional Chinese family life was based on filial piety. Each family member had both a responsibility and a duty to every other family member.

Lesson Vocabulary
Introduce each of the following vocabulary terms.

Explain that *ancestors* are family members from the past. The practice of *ancestor worship* was a way to honor the dead and to provide for them in their new life. Offering sacrifices to bring good luck became part of *ancestor worship* for centuries.

Point out that *mandate* and *command* are synonyms. The emperors believed that they had a *mandate* from heaven to rule.

The rise, rule, and fall of a dynasty is the *dynastic cycle*. This *dynastic cycle* occurred over tens or hundreds of years.

In traditional Chinese society, *filial piety* was extremely important. *Filial piety* refers to the duty each family member had to one another. An *extended family* was composed of several generations, headed by the oldest male. The *extended family* could include uncles, aunts, and cousins.

Early Chinese Civilizations | 57

Map Extension

Ask students to use the map on page 58 to answer the following questions:

- Which dynasty was the smallest geographically? (the Xia Dynasty)
- Which dynasty had the most coastline? (the Shang Dynasty)
- In what direction(s) did the Zhou Dynasty spread farther than the others? (north and south)

Time Box Extension

Ask students to calculate which dynasty ruled the longest.

Picturing History

Have students look at the photograph on page 58. The tip of the elephant's trunk is comprised of a crouching tiger and a phoenix head. The bronze vessel was probably used for rituals. Food and drinking containers were used in both state rituals and ancestor worship. Archaeologists believe that only the royal family and the aristocracy could use bronze vessels. The Shang were known for using wine in their rituals. To distance themselves from this practice, the Zhou produced more food containers and fewer wine vessels.

The First Dynasties: Xia and Shang

The earliest Chinese dynasty was the Xia (SYAH), which began around 2200 B.C. It was a prehistoric civilization, as there is no written record. What is known about the Xia comes from the work of archaeologists. The Xia built their civilization in the Huang He region. The economy was based on farming. However, at least some of the people lived in cities. The Xia knew how to make bronze tools. Archeologists have also found pottery and large tombs.

Legend says that Tang, the leader of the Shang (SHAHNG) people, overthrew the last Xia ruler. Tang established the Shang Dynasty around 1750 B.C. Like the Xia, the Shang were farmers. But many people lived in large, walled cities. Like the Xia, the Shang knew how to make bronze.

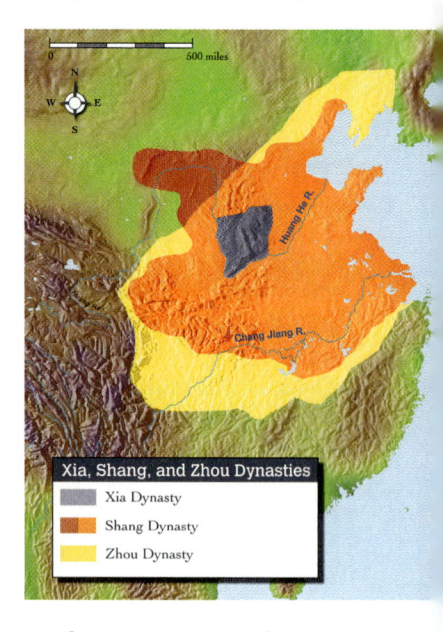

The Shang left their impact on future generations of Chinese in two important ways. It was the Shang who developed a writing system for the Chinese language. The Shang also began what is called **ancestor worship**. Ancestors are members of a family who have lived and died. Like other early people, the Shang believed in life after death. They buried the dead with things that the person might need in the afterlife. The Shang also believed that the dead could either help the living or bring them bad luck. As a result, the living

This bronze elephant represented the trustworthy and peaceful Shang government.

Time Box

c. 2200–1750 B.C.
Xia Dynasty

c. 1750–1122 B.C.
Shang Dynasty

1045–256 B.C.
Zhou Dynasty

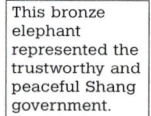

Extension

Ask students to find out more about the lost method of casting bronze in wax. Many scholars believe this was the casting method used in early China. Have students make a poster to present their findings.

58 Chapter 5

began to offer sacrifices to their ancestors. This form of religious worship continued for thousands of years.

The Zhou Dynasty and the Mandate of Heaven

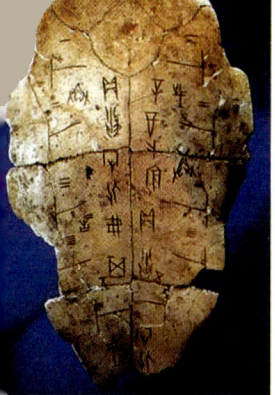

The Zhou (JOH) people rebelled against the Shang in 1045 B.C. The Zhou set up their own dynasty and ruled in central China.

To explain why they overthrew the Shang, the Zhou developed the principle of the **Mandate** of Heaven. A mandate is a command. The Zhou said that the deities in heaven ordered the Zhou to replace the Shang ruler. The Zhou used this principle to justify, or support, their overthrow of the Shang. According to the Mandate of Heaven, the king—and all later emperors— ruled by divine right. Their power came from the gods.

In time, the Chinese expanded the theory. Rulers did not always act in the best interests of the people. Then the Mandate of Heaven gave the people the right to rebel against their ruler. The result was the development of the **dynastic cycle**. This is the rise, rule, and then fall of a dynasty over a number of years. Over time, the Mandate of Heaven became the basis for the way the Chinese changed their rulers.

Chinese Writing

Written Chinese first developed during the Shang Dynasty. English is based on a 26-letter alphabet. To read English, a person has to learn those 26 letters and their 43 phonetic sounds. Chinese is based on characters, not letters. Each character stands for a picture of something or an idea. There are thousands of characters in Chinese. An elementary school student knows at least 1,500 characters.

Translation: Studying old history helps in the learning of new ideas.

stop and think

The Chinese language uses characters or groups of characters to make words. With a partner, think of six words that you could make by drawing pictures. Three of the words should be persons, places, or things. Three should be ideas. Draw your characters and under each one write its meaning in English.

Picturing History

To consult with the spirits of ancestors, the Shang rulers used oracle bones such as those pictured on page 59. A tortoise shell or ox bone was heated until it cracked. Then, the cracks were interpreted as giving a sign from an ancestor. Sometimes, as in the tortoise shell shown, the question and its answer were then carved on the bone.

Picturing History

The Chinese language has more than 40,000 characters. Learning the art of Chinese calligraphy requires years of practice. Each brush stroke must be made in a certain style and order. Elaborate rituals and accessories were developed for this fine art, including brushes, brush washers, and brush rests, as well as inks and artists' seals. Students may be interested in the contemporary uses of calligraphy. Ask them to bring to class samples they have seen on cards, invitations, and calendars.

Stop and Think

Students' characters and words will vary, but at least three should represent nouns and three should depict ideas.

Chart Extension

Ask students to read over the chart. Then ask them to compare and contrast this cycle with the history of dynasties of Egypt they have already studied.

Picturing History

Draw students' attention to the separation of men and women in the posed, formal photograph on page 60. Three generations are represented in the photograph. Ask students how this relates to the traditional structure of Chinese family life.

Putting It All Together

Students' paragraphs will vary. However, they should include both comparisons and contrasts between modern families and ancient Chinese families.

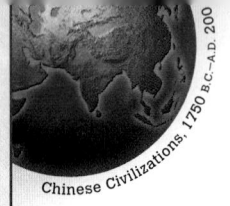

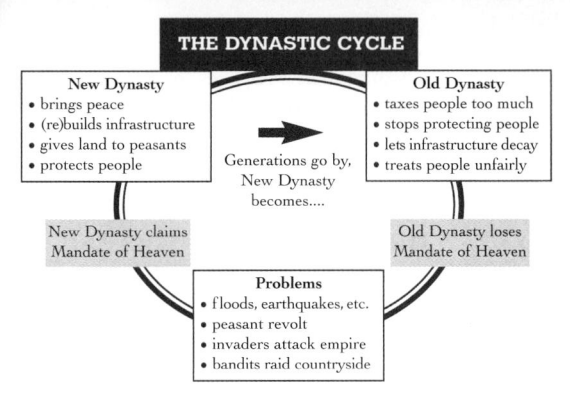

Chinese Civilizations, 1750 B.C.–A.D. 200

THE DYNASTIC CYCLE

New Dynasty	Old Dynasty
• brings peace	• taxes people too much
• (re)builds infrastructure	• stops protecting people
• gives land to peasants	• lets infrastructure decay
• protects people	• treats people unfairly

Generations go by, New Dynasty becomes....

New Dynasty claims Mandate of Heaven

Old Dynasty loses Mandate of Heaven

Problems
• floods, earthquakes, etc.
• peasant revolt
• invaders attack empire
• bandits raid countryside

The Importance of the Family in China

The family was the basic unit of Chinese society and the most important. Each member of a family had a duty and responsibility to every other member. This duty was known as **filial piety**. It governed the relationships among family members. Sons and daughters were to obey their parents. Parents were to obey their parents.

All family members were to obey the oldest male of the family. He was the head of the **extended family**. An extended family contains all the related members of a family—grandparents, parents, children, aunts, uncles, and cousins. The oldest male member of an extended Chinese family might have been a great-great-grandfather.

Filial piety governed life in the extended family.

Putting It All Together

The extended family was an important part of Chinese life. Discuss the importance of the extended family with a partner. Then write a paragraph to compare and contrast the extended family in ancient China to your modern family.

Picturing History

The image on page 61 depicts Confucius and his disciples. Confucius's sayings were written down and preserved in *The Analects*. After the Han Dynasty (207 B.C.–A.D. 220) adopted Confucianism as the state religion, *The Analects* became the basis for education.

LESSON 2

Chinese Philosophies

Thinking on Your Own

To help you study this lesson, create a three-column chart. Label the columns "Confucianism," "Daoism," and "Legalism." As you read, take bulleted notes about each of these Chinese philosophies.

By A.D. 100, Buddhism had spread to China. Over the next 300 years, many Chinese adopted Buddhism. Buddhism in turn adopted teachings of the Chinese. One of the features that it adopted was filial piety. By then, filial piety had become an important part of a Chinese philosophy known as **Confucianism**.

Philosophy is the search for knowledge about the world. It studies the natural world, human behavior, and thought. Philosophy is not the same as **religion**. Religion is the belief in and worship of a divine or superhuman power. Judaism, Hinduism, and Buddhism are religions. Confucianism was a philosophy.

focus your reading
What are the Five Constant Relationships?
What was the lasting effect of Confucianism?
How is Daoism different from Legalism?

vocabulary
Confucianism   civil service
philosophy   Daoism
religion   Legalism

The Teachings of Confucius

Confucianism was based on the teachings of Confucius. He was a wandering scholar who lived from 551 to 479 B.C. Confucius tried to interest the rulers of local Chinese states in his ideas. He never succeeded with the rulers. But his ideas impressed other Chinese.

Confucius and some of his followers

Lesson Vocabulary

Discuss each of the vocabulary terms with students.

Confucianism is based on the teachings of Confucius. Although not a *religion*, *Confucianism* does teach moral conduct.

The search for knowledge about the world is called *philosophy*. *Confucianism* is a *philosophy* that emphasizes harmony in relationships. *Daoism* is a *philosophy* based on living in harmony with nature. *Daoism* refers to the word *dao*, which means "way." *Legalism* was the *philosophy* that emphasized the need for strict laws and harsh punishment to keep order in society. *Legalism* was based on the teachings of Hanfeizi.

Religion is the belief in and worship of a supreme being. Buddhism became a major *religion* of China.

Those who work for the government are in the *civil service*. *Civil service* exams were given in China for 2,000 years.

Lesson Summary

The philosophy of Confucianism took hold during the fifth century B.C. Confucius wanted to bring harmony through the Five Constant Relationships. Confucianist ideas came to influence the Chinese government in its civil service exams.

Daoism, based on the teachings of Laozi, emphasized achieving harmony by being in nature. The word *dao* means "way."

Legalism taught that people were naturally bad and needed to be controlled. During the 200s B.C., Hanfeizi developed this teaching.

Lesson Objective

Students will learn about the philosophies that developed in early Chinese civilizations.

Focus Your Reading Answers

1 The Five Constant Relationships are parent and child, husband and wife, older brother or sister and younger brother or sister, friend and friend, ruler and subject.

2 The most lasting effect of Confucianism was the civil service examination system, which lasted for 2,000 years.

3 Daoism believes that less government is desirable. Legalism believes that more government is needed to control people who are naturally wicked.

Early Chinese Civilizations | 61

Stop and Think

Students' paragraphs will vary but should take a position and support it with specific examples from the text and their own experiences.

Chart Extension

Ask students to investigate an achievement, such as papermaking, that involves a process with steps to be followed. Then have them present a speech to the class explaining the steps. Ask students to create flowcharts or other visuals to explain the process.

Extensions

1 Like other moral teachers, Confucius had a golden rule, which permeated all his scriptures. "Do not do to others what you do not wish to be done to you." Discuss with students the relationship of this statement to the idea of harmony between people.

2 Confucianism supported the idea of the Mandate of Heaven. Government officials who had been trained in this philosophy traveled throughout the country, looking for signs. They reported to the emperor what they had seen and experienced: weather, state of crops, the mood of the people. This allowed the emperor to assess how his reign was going.

Chinese Civilizations, 1750 B.C.–A.D. 200

A group of students began to gather around him. They collected his teachings and began to teach others.

Confucius was not interested in studying spiritual or religious questions. He wanted to bring harmony—peace and order—to this world. Filial piety played an important role in his plan for maintaining harmony. Confucius taught that duty to the family and the community was more important than a person's own needs and wants. Confucius illustrated his idea of duty with the Five Constant Relationships:

- parent and child
- husband and wife
- older brother or sister and younger brother or sister
- friend and friend
- ruler and subject

Achievements of the Ancient Chinese

- how to make paper—around A.D. 100. This knowledge spread to India in the 700s. It then spread to Europe in the 1100s.
- how to grow silk worms and weave silk cloth
- iron blades for plows to break up hard-packed dirt
- wheelbarrow
- compass—a device to find direction
- new ways to rig sails on ships so ships could sail against the wind
- rudder—a device to steer ships
- acupuncture—a way to treat disease using needles

Except for friendship, each relationship involved one person with authority over the other. However, friendship was between equals unless there was an age difference. Then, the older person was considered superior to the younger person. In the other relationships, the older person or person of higher rank was superior. Men were always on a higher level than women.

Confucius taught that the higher ranking person had a loving responsibility to care for the lesser person. The lesser person, in turn, had a duty to give loving obedience to the higher person. If everyone lived by his or her duty, then harmony would rule the family and the community.

Influence of Confucianism

Confucius thought the ruler of China was like the head of a family. All Chinese owed the ruler loving obedience. In turn, the ruler was responsible to heaven for the well-being of his subjects. The ruler must provide peace and order so the people might become wealthy.

62 | Chapter 5

Picturing History

The complementary forces of Yin and Yang are pictured in the symbol on page 63. Note that each has the "seed" of the opposite inside, shown by the small circles.

Traditionally, Yin stands for all that is female, passive, soft, cold, and below. Yang stands for male, active, hard, hot, and above.

---

stop and think

Choose one of the five relationships that Confucius listed. Do you think Confucius was right about how to create a good relationship between these two people? Talk over your ideas with a partner. Then write two or three paragraphs to explain why you agree or disagree.

If the ruler failed, heaven would allow his subjects to overthrow him.

The ruler had to be of good moral character and be an example to his subjects. This was also true of the officials who ran the government under the ruler. Confucius believed that public officials had to be moral and well-educated. Their only goal was the well-being of the people.

In time, Confucianist ideals came to control China's government. During the Han Dynasty, the rulers set up a school to train men who wanted to do government jobs. They had to pass a test known as a **civil service** examination. Civil servants work for the government. This system was the way public officials were chosen in China for 2,000 years.

The Yin Yang symbol represents an ideal of balance of the forces in nature.

Daoism and Legalism

Between 500 and 200 B.C., two other important philosophies developed in China. One was **Daoism** and the other was **Legalism**.

The name Daoism comes from the word *dao* meaning "the way." Daoism is based on the teachings of Laozi (LOW•DZUH). He probably lived at the same time as Confucius. Laozi taught that the way to happiness was to live in harmony with nature. One could not control it nor describe it. A person simply had to "be" in nature. In terms of government, a good ruler was one who did little.

Legalism was very different from both Confucianism and Daoism. It began with the teachings of Hanfeizi (HAHN•FAY•DZEE) who lived in the 200s B.C. Legalists believed that people were naturally bad. A strong ruler, a long list of laws, and harsh punishments were necessary. This was the only way to bring order to society.

Putting It All Together

Do you agree or disagree with the Legalists' viewpoint about people and government? To answer the question, talk with a partner. Then write a paragraph explaining your ideas about Legalism.

Early Chinese Civilizations

Picturing History

Until the Republic of China was formed in 1912, Confucianism provided the basis of training for government officials. The illustration at the top of page 63 shows people taking a civil service exam. To assist those preparing for the exams, Han emperor Wu Di founded a university in 124 B.C. Few people passed the exams, however, which required the candidate to memorize the 431,286 words of the classics of Confucianism. Those who did well entered the most rewarded and profitable career in China—civil service. In some cases, passing the top examinations led to marrying a princess. Most civil servants worked at the local level, inspecting schools, providing against famine, enforcing the law, and judging those brought to trial for breaking it.

Putting It All Together

Students' paragraphs will vary but should discuss ideas about Legalism's viewpoints on people and government.

Extension

The rank of civil servant was expressed in the clothing, jewelry, and emblems that civil servants were permitted to wear. Have students interested in fashion design research the different styles and their meanings. Suggest that students extend the project by comparing it to contemporary instances of dress that convey distinctions in rank, such as in the military or academia.

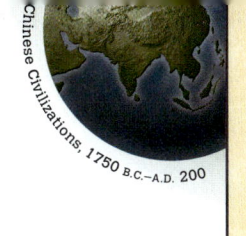

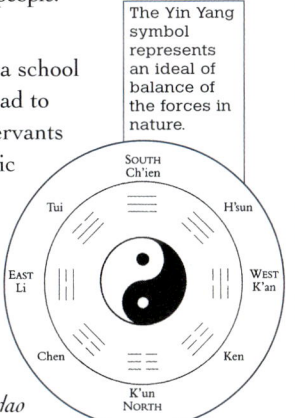

Picturing History

Few facts are known about Laozi, pictured at the bottom of page 63. One legend states that he was a scholar who rode an ox. At a border post, he was asked what his teachings were. He wrote the *Tao-te-Ching* and then disappeared.

Early Chinese Civilizations

Lesson Summary

The Qin Dynasty, known as the Warring States Period, began after the Zhou rulers, when powerful warlords fought for control. Qin Shihuangdi proclaimed himself the first emperor. He instituted a centralized government, complete with bureaucracy. Under his leadership, the Great Wall was built with forced peasant labor to protect the northern border.

As a result of the forced labor and heavy taxes, the peasants revolted. After defeating the Qin, the peasant Liu Bang adopted the name Han Gaozu, beginning the Han Dynasty. The Han ruled for over 300 years, continuing the governmental policies of the Qin, but adopting Confucianism. Under the Han, the Empire grew in both numbers and land.

The Silk Road was China's overland route to trade with Europe and Central Asia. The Chinese also set up sea routes for international trade.

Lesson Objective

Students will learn about the Qin and Han Dynasties of China.

Focus Your Reading Answers

1 Qin Shihuangdi was hated because of the high taxes and forced labor that his building projects demanded.

2 The long-term effects of the Han Dynasty include the civil service exam, the adoption of Confucianism, and growth in terms of land and population.

LESSON 3

The Rise and Fall of Dynasties

Thinking on Your Own

Create a Venn diagram to help you remember the differences and similarities between the Qin and Han Dynasties. Label the part where the two circles overlap "Similarities." Label the left circle "Qin." Label the right circle "Han." As you study the lesson, complete the diagram.

The Zhou had seized power of a large part of China by 1045 B.C. However, local chiefs known as **warlords** ruled states within the empire. By the 400s B.C., these warlords had seriously weakened the power of the Zhou rulers. The warlords fought one another for power and territory. As time went on, more and more wars broke out among these local chiefs.

focus your reading

Why was Qin Shihuangdi hated?

What were the long-term effects of the Han Dynasty?

vocabulary

warlords   bureaucrats
emperor   censors
centralized government

The period from the 400s to the 200s B.C. is known as the Warring States Period. That is the reason that Confucius tried to get the warlords to accept his ideas. He wanted to bring peace and stability to the empire.

A battle between Chinese warlords

Qin Dynasty

Confucius was unsuccessful in his effort to change the ideas of the warlords. The Qin were more successful with their iron swords. By 221 B.C., the people of the Qin state had won control of most of China. The Qin ruler, Qin Shihuangdi (CHIN SHUR•HWONG•DEE), declared himself China's first **emperor**.

64 Chapter 5

Lesson Vocabulary

Discuss each of the vocabulary terms with students.

Warlords were local chieftains. The *warlords* fought for control of land and power.

An *emperor* is a single, powerful ruler over an empire. Qin Shihuangdi declared himself the first *emperor* of China.

A *centralized government* is one in which power is in one place, not in the hands of local chieftains. Qin Shihuangdi set up China's first *centralized government*. Government officials who enforce that government's rules are *bureaucrats*. The local provinces of China were ruled by *bureaucrats*. Qin Shihuangdi also set up a censorate, a system of *censors*, who were to check up on the *bureaucrats*.

64 Chapter 5

For the first time, China had a single **centralized government**. Before Qin Shihuangdi, local lords ruled their own states. The new emperor removed the local lords. He divided China into provinces and counties. **Bureaucrats** were appointed to oversee the new regions. A bureaucrat is a government official who enforces the rules of the government. Under the Zhou Dynasty, government positions had been passed down from father to son. Qin Shihuangdi ended this practice. He also set up the censorate. The members of this department were known as **censors**. Their job was to check up on the bureaucrats.

Qin Shihuangdi established an army to keep order and to protect China. A system of roads was built to make it easier to move troops quickly from place to place. One area that needed protection was the northern frontier. The Xiongnu (SYEN•NOO) were threatening the region. They were nomadic herders who raised sheep, cattle, and goats. They were also fierce fighters. To keep them out of China, Qin Shihuangdi had the Great Wall built across the northern region.

The Great Wall was one of the reasons that the peasants turned against the Qin Dynasty. The wall was built with the forced labor of peasants. It was also an expensive project. Qin Shihuangdi placed heavy taxes on his subjects to pay for the wall and for his armies.

Time Box

c. 400–221 B.C.
Warring States Period

221–206 B.C.
Qin Dynasty

202 B.C.– A.D. 220
Han Dynasty

The Great Wall of China

Han Dynasty

The leader of the peasant revolt against the Qin was Liu Bang (LYOH•BONG). He was a peasant himself. His victory over the Qin gave him great power. He took the name Han Gaozu.

...ring History

...ng was fierce among the seven warring ...in China. One of these battles is shown in ...cture on page 64. At one battle in 260 B.C., ...than 500,000 soldiers died. Sun Zi wrote ...st military handbook, *The Art of War*, ...g this time. The invention of the crossbow, ...ime prior to 450 B.C., made chariot warfare ...te. Small Mongolian ponies were used in ...until 101 B.C., when Emperor Wu Di ...ed larger horses from Central Asia.

Time Box Extension

Ask students to determine how long each period lasted. (Warring States Period–179 years; Qin Dynasty–15 years; Han Dynasty–422 years) Which time period lasted the longest? (the Han Dynasty)

Map Extension

Ask students to use the map on page 65 to answer the following questions:

- What border was the Great Wall designed to protect? (the northern border)
- Which empire expanded farther west? (the Han Empire)
- Which seas formed borders for the Qin Empire? (Yellow, East China, and South China)

Picturing History

Construction of the Great Wall began in 221 B.C. About 300,000 men were used to build the original section. A portion of the Great Wall is shown in the photograph on page 65. The wall was not completed until A.D. 1500. It is about 1,500 miles long (2,414 km) and is made of many different kinds of materials, ranging from tamped earth to granite. The wall is 15 to 30 feet wide (4.6m to 9m) and 15 to 50 feet tall (4.6m to 15m), with guard towers interspersed along it. A Chinese myth states that every stone of the wall stands for a man's life that was lost during the building. It remains the world's longest structure.

Extension

Have students explore the construction of the Great Wall or other building projects of the first dynasties. Allow time for students to report their findings to the class.

Early Chinese Civilizations

Picturing History

Have students look at the photograph on page 66. Explain that since the pre-Shang era, carving jade has been one of the great arts of China. Jade was thought to have magical attributes and was connected with immortality. In addition to its familiar green color, jade may also be brown or gray. Polishing renders jade satiny smooth.

Extension

Suggest that students use the library or Internet resources to investigate jade's use in jewelry and beauty-related tools in ancient China, such as combs and makeup boxes.

Stop and Think

Students' lists and reasons will vary but should be supported with facts.

Bio Facts

- Born 259 B.C.
- His name means "the first Qin emperor."
- At age thirteen, ascended to the throne in 246 B.C.
- Created a single monetary system.
- Built a system of roads.
- Began the Great Wall of China.
- Ordered his chief minister to burn all books except the memoirs of Qin Shihuangdi.
- Died in 210 B.C.

Chinese Civilizations, 1750 B.C.–A.D. 200

(HAHN GOW•DZOO) and declared himself the first Han emperor. The Han Dynasty lasted for 400 years. For more than 300 years, China was peaceful and prosperous under the Han.

Han Gaozu kept the government structure that Qin Shihuangdi had set up. China remained divided into provinces and counties. Han Gaozu also adopted the Qin's use of appointed bureaucrats. Over time, the Han developed a civil service exam to find the best qualified civil servants. Han rulers set up a school to train candidates for government work. The students learned Confucianism and Chinese history and law.

Han Gaozu replaced the harsh laws and punishments of the first emperor. Qin Shihuangdi had forbidden the teaching of Confucianism. Han Gaozu adopted Confucianism. The Five Constant Relationships supported peace and order in Chinese society. They also strengthened the position of the emperor.

During the Han Dynasty, the population of China tripled. It went from 20 million people to 60 million. The empire also grew in land area. Han armies extended the empire north, south, and west.

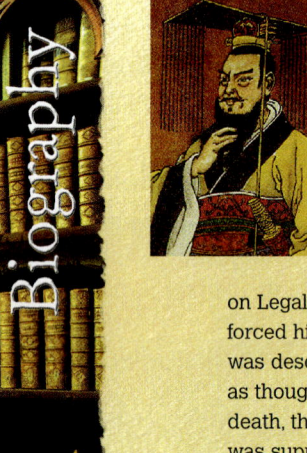

Piece of carved jade from the Han Dynasty

stop and think

Make a list of the things that Qin Shihuangdi did as emperor. Decide if they helped China become strong (S) or harmed (H) it. Write "S" or "H" next to each item on your list. Share and explain your list with a partner.

Biography

Qin Shihuangdi

Before he became emperor, Qin Shihuangdi's name was Zh[eng] Zheng. *Shihuangdi* means First Emperor. He declared hims[elf] the First Emperor of the Qin, or Chin. This is how the name "China" began.

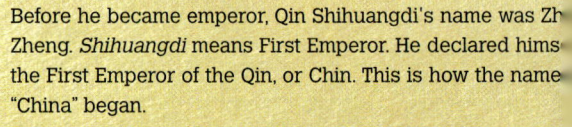

Calling himself emperor is just one example of Qin Shihuangdi's boasting. He also claimed that his dynasty wo[uld] last for 10,000 generations—about 250,000 years.

Qin Shihuangdi was a ruthless emperor. He based his ru[le] on Legalism. He governed with harsh laws and severe punishments. He forced his subjects to pay high taxes and to work on his building projects. [He] was described as having "the heart of a tiger and a wolf . . . he punished [men] as though he were afraid he would never get around to them all." After his death, the peasants rebelled against the next Qin emperor. The dynasty th[at] was supposed to last 250,000 years lasted only 11 years.

Biography Extension

Like many rulers, Qin Shihuangdi felt books were dangerous. Totalitarian systems rely on mental conformity and do not encourage intellectual curiosity or introspection. In 213 B.C., all Confucianist books were burned, with the exception of one copy kept in the state library. At that time, the chief minister proclaimed, "No one is to use the past to discredit the present." Books on oracles, medicine, and agriculture were not burned. The ban on books was lifted in 191 B.C. during the Han Dynasty.

Have students use library resources or the Internet to research other examples of book burnings throughout history. Suggest that they create timelines or a world map to pinpoint the instances. Display students' work in the classroom.

---

66 | Chapter 5

By A.D. 170, Han control over China was slipping. There were peasant revolts over living conditions. Rival military leaders fought for power. In 220, a rebel general seized power. However, his rule did not last. For the next 400 years, China was the scene of civil wars and invasions by nomadic people from the north.

The Silk Road and Sea Routes

Beginning around 200 B.C., China became part of the international trade network. Chinese merchants traded along land routes and sea routes. Their ships sailed throughout Southeast Asia and into the Indian Ocean. The land route became known as the Silk Road. This was because China's most important trade good on this route was silk. The Silk Road stretched 4,000 miles from eastern China to the Roman Empire.

Besides silk, Chinese merchants traded spices, tea, and porcelain—a type of fine pottery. Ivory, cotton cloth, pepper, and gems flowed east and west from Indian merchants. Roman merchants sent woolen and linen cloth, glass, and gems to the east.

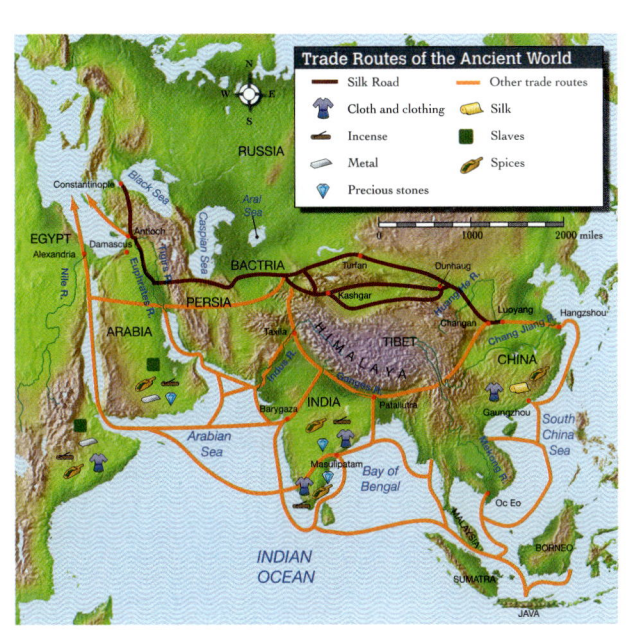

Putting It All Together

Review the Venn diagram you filled in as you read this lesson. Write two or three paragraphs to explain how the Qin and Han Dynasties were the same and how they were different.

Early Chinese Civilizations | 67

Map Extension

Ask students to use the map on page 67 to answer the following questions:

- What was the final western stop of the Silk Road? (Constantinople)
- What trade goods did China obtain from Arabia? (slaves, spices, metal, incense, precious stones)
- Through which bodies of water did other trade routes pass? (South China Sea, Bay of Bengal, Arabian Sea, Indian Ocean)

Extension

Travel through the desert along the Silk Road was possible only because of Bactrian camels. These two-humped camels could carry people as well as trade goods. In addition, they could anticipate sandstorms and locate underwater springs. They could even run, as well as walk, over the desert sands. Museums have many examples of pottery models of camels from the Tang Dynasty (A.D. 618–A.D. 907).

Putting It All Together

Paragraphs will vary but may include the following details

Qin Dynasty

- begun by a powerful warlord
- set up centralized government and bureaucrats
- opposed Confucianist ideas
- created public works using peasant labor
- lasted 15 years
- ended in power struggles

Han Dynasty

- begun by a peasant who led a revolt
- continued system of centralized government and bureaucrats
- accepted Confucianist ideas
- lasted more than 400 years
- ended in power struggles

Early Chinese Civilizations | 67

Chapter Review

1. Students' questions and answers will vary but should reflect the information and details provided in the text.

2. Headlines will vary; possible responses include

   (a) Qin Victor Against Zhou

   (b) Mandate of Heaven Explains Dynastic Order

   (c) Confucius Presents Relationships as Basis of Harmony

   (d) Traders Battle Desert Climate in Hope of Riches

Chapter Summary

- During the Shang Dynasty, the Chinese developed a writing system based on characters, not letters. The Shang also practiced **ancestor worship**.
- The Zhou overthrew the Shang ruler.
- The **Mandate** of Heaven explains the **dynastic cycle** that developed in China.
- The family was the basic unit of Chinese society. The **extended family** included all related family members. Each family member had a duty and responsibility to every other family member. This duty was known as **filial piety**.
- During the early period of Chinese history, three important **philosophies** developed: **Confucianism**, **Daoism**, and **Legalism**. A philosophy is different from a **religion**.
- After the Zhou were overthrown, China entered the Warring States Period. Rival **warlords** fought for power.
- Qin Shihuangdi united and expanded China. He declared himself China's first **emperor**. He set up a **centralized government** and used **bureaucrats** to run it. **Censors** made sure that officials did their jobs.
- Qin Shihuangdi began the building of the Great Wall of China.
- The Qin Dynasty was overthrown by the Han. The Han adopted Confucianism. They kept the idea of appointed civil servants and set up **civil service** exams.
- Trade became important under the Han. Many trade goods flowed back and forth along the Silk Road.

Chapter Review

1. Review the questions that you wrote at the beginning of the chapter. Talk with a partner about your questions and possible answers. Then write an answer for each question.

2. Imagine you are a headline writer for a Chinese newspaper. Write a two-line headline for each of the following: (a) the overthrow of the Zhou, (b) the Mandate of Heaven, (c) the teachings of Confucius, (d) a trading trip on the Silk Road.

Novel Connections

Below is a list of books that relate to the time period covered in this chapter. The numbers in parentheses indicate the related Thematic Strands of the National Council for the Social Studies (NCSS).

George Beshore. *Science in Ancient China.* Franklin Watts, 1998. (VIII)

Cyril Birch, Rosamund Fowler. *Tales from China (Oxford Myths and Legends).* Oxford University Press, 2000. (I, III)

Lee Fang. *The Ch'i-lin Purse: A Collection of Ancient Chinese Stories.* Farrar, Straus and Giroux, 1997. (I, III)

Leonard Everett Fisher. *The Great Wall of China (Aladdin Picture Books).* Aladdin, 1995. (I, III, VIII)

Eleanor Hall. *Ancient Chinese Dynasties.* Greenhaven Press, 2000. (I, VI, X)

Jane O'Connor. *The Emperor's Silent Army: Terra cotta Warriors of Ancient China.* Viking Books, 2002. (I, III, VI)

Virginia Schomp. *The Ancient Chinese.* Franklin Watts, 2004. (I, II, III)

Suzanne Williams, Andrea Fong. *Made in China.* Pacific View Press, 1997. (I, VIII)

Skill Builder

Using Special-Purpose Maps

There are many kinds of maps. There are road maps, historical maps, land-use maps, natural-resources maps, and the list goes on. Most of the maps in this book are historical maps.

To read and use the information on the map, follow these steps:

1. Read the title of the map to find out what it is about.
2. Look at the map to see what colors and symbols are used.
3. Match the colors and symbols to the map key. This explains what the colors and symbols represent.
4. Read the map scale. This tells you the distance between places shown on the map.

Skill Builder

1. Qin and Han Empires; Xia, Shang, and Zhou Dynasties
2. a solid black line with regularly spaced marks
3. The yellow region on the map at the right represents the Zhou Empire.
4. about 1,000 miles (1,609 km)

1. What is the title of each map?
2. What symbol is used to show the Great Wall?
3. How do you know which area was ruled by the Zhou?
4. What is the greatest distance from east to west that the Shang ruled?

Early Chinese Civilizations

Classroom Discussion

Discuss with students some of the broader topics covered in this chapter.

- How should people in power govern?
- How can a philosophy shape a government?
- What are the benefits and problems of a centralized government with a bureaucracy?
- In what ways does trade enrich a culture, beyond the wealth from buying and selling goods?

Early Chinese Civilizations

Chapter 6
Ancient Greek City-States
(1750–133 B.C.)

Chapter Summary
Refer to page 84 for a summary of Chapter 6.

Related Transparencies

T-1 World Map

T-2 Outline World Map

T-5 Hellenistic World

T-18 Three-Column Chart

Key Blacklines

Biography—Homer

CD Extension

Encourage students to use the reading comprehension, vocabulary reinforcement, and interactive timeline activities on the student CD.

Picturing History

The photo on page 70 shows the Parthenon, located at the highest part of the Acropolis in Athens. Built between 447 and 432 B.C., the Parthenon was a temple dedicated to Athena. The citizens of Athens felt they were under the protection of this goddess of war and wisdom. They worshiped her and honored her every year with a festival called the Panathenia.

Getting Focused

Skim this chapter to predict what you will be learning.
- Read the lesson titles and subheadings.
- Look at the illustrations and read the captions.
- Examine the maps.
- Review the vocabulary words and terms.

All the civilizations that you have studied so far had one thing in common. They all developed in river valleys. Ancient Greece, however, developed on a mountainous peninsula and on many rocky islands. How do you think its geography affected the way ancient Greece developed? Write a brief paragraph to predict how geography affected the development of ancient Greek civilization. As you read the chapter, check your prediction. Remember to add Greece to your world map.

Extension

Ask students to research efforts to restore the Parthenon, or other ancient Greek sites, using library resources or the Internet. Have them create a poster to show their findings.

Pre-Reading Discussion

1 Ask students to identify some of the different forms of national, state, or local government with which they already are familiar. Tell them that in this lesson they will learn about forms of government in ancient Greece.

2 Discuss with students what they believe should be the proper qualifications to be allowed to vote. Encourage them to note the standards of ancient Greece as they read and then compare them to those in the United States today.

LESSON 1

The Development of Greek City-States

Thinking on Your Own

Create a three-column chart to compare and contrast Sparta and Athens. Label the first column "Categories." Write topics in this column, such as "Government" and "Role of Women." Label the other columns "Sparta" and "Athens." Fill in the columns as you read the lesson.

Much of the Greek peninsula and nearby islands are mountainous. In some areas, river valleys cut through the mountains. Small, low plains dot the region. At some time in the ancient past, groups of people settled in these valleys and plains. The mountains kept these groups separate from one another. Over time, people living in the groups developed independent, self-governing city-states.

Many Greeks earned their living from the sea. They became expert sailors. Their trading network spread the length and width of the Mediterranean Sea. Eventually, people moved from Greece to set up colonies in other parts of the Mediterranean. Merchants moved to the new colonies to start trading businesses. Other Greeks went to find better farmland. Between 1100 B.C. and 750 B.C., people left Greece to escape invaders.

focus your reading

What forms of government were developed by the Greek city-states?

What was life like for Spartans?

Why is Athenian democracy called limited democracy?

vocabulary

polis
agora
aristocrats
oligarchy
tyrants
democracy
ephors
helots

Lesson Summary

The lesson offers a look at the Greek city-states, particularly Sparta and Athens. Greece's early settlements became independent city-states.

The center of a Greek city-state, the polis, was built around a hill. The acropolis, with temples and public buildings, was at the top of the hill.

Sparta became a military state with harsh laws. Women were expected to take responsibility while men were away fighting. Daily government was carried out by a council of five men called ephors. Citizens, defined as native-born men over the age of thirty, were allowed to vote. Sparta remained isolated from the rest of the world.

Athens began an experiment in limited democracy in 512 B.C. Athens became an important trade center.

Lesson Objective

Students will learn about the development of Greek city-states.

Focus Your Reading Answers

1 The Greeks developed monarchies, oligarchies, and democracies.

2 Life for Spartans was harsh and disciplined. Boys trained to be soldiers. Women were to be physically strong. They enjoyed more responsibility than was often allowed in other ancient societies. In this military state, the only job was that of a soldier.

3 Public officials were elected by the members of the assembly. Women, slaves, and foreign residents could not vote.

on Vocabulary

uce each of the following vocabulary terms to students.

was a Greek city-state. Athens was a *polis*. Tell students that words such as *metropolis* come is root.

en space in each Greek city was known as the *agora*. The *agora* was both a market area and a or meetings.

ats were the wealthy landowners. Some *aristocrats* were able to seize power. An *oligarchy* is the state by a few people. In Greece, the members of the *oligarchy* were elected by other ats and ruled only for a short time.

t was one man who gained power and ruled alone. During the 500s B.C., *tyrants* ruled

cracy offers people a say in how their state is run. The *ephors* were the council of five men who wer in Sparta. *Ephors* managed the government on a day-to-day basis.

vere people who had been captured in war and enslaved. The *helots* did the work of farming ta.

Ancient Greek City-States

Greek City-States

The Greek city-state was called a **polis**. It was both a place and a governing body. The English word *politics* comes from the Greek word *polis*. City-states were built around a hill. At the top of the hill was an area called the acropolis. Temples and public buildings were built there. The rest of the city was built below the acropolis on flat land. One area of the city was kept as open space. It was called the **agora**. Citizens assembled there for meetings and used it as a marketplace. Over time, the area surrounding the city came under the control of the city-state.

The earliest city-states were monarchies ruled by kings. Some men became wealthy because of the amount of land they owned. Their wealth gained them power. In some city-states, these **aristocrats** were able to overthrow the king and set up rule by **oligarchy**. An oligarchy is a state that is ruled by a few people. Generally, the rulers of the oligarchy were elected by other aristocrats and ruled only for a certain period of time. When their terms ended, another group was elected.

Ancient Greek City-States, 1750–133 B.C.

The Minoan civilization developed on the island of Crete. It was ruled by a king and its economy was based on trade. The details of Minoan paintings tell much about their lives. The Minoans were probably conquered by Mycenaen people from the Greek mainland.

Mycenae was made up of a number of independent royal centers. Each was ruled by a king who lived in a walled palace-fort on a hill. The people lived in scattered settlements around the forts. The Mycenaen civilization was based on trade. They traded gold, bronze daggers, beads, and pottery. Mycenae collapsed because of warfare among rival kings and invaders from the north.

The next 350 years is called the Dark Ages because few records have been found. *The Iliad*, however, may be rooted in truth. It is an epic poem by Homer about the Trojan War. Archaeologists have not been able to prove or disprove its story. The Greeks won the war by hiding soldiers in a huge wooden horse that was sent to Troy as a gift. The Trojans wheeled the horse inside their city walls. At night, Greek soldiers crawled out of the horse and seized the city. They burned it to the ground.

The Erechtheion on the Acropolis in Athens, Greece

72 Chapter 6

Time Box

2800–1450 B.C.
Minoan civilization

1600–1100 B.C.
Mycenaen civilization

1100–750 B.C.
Dark Ages

Time Box Extensions

Which of the three periods lasted the longest? (Minoan) the shortest? (Dark Ages)

What civilizations were developing in other parts of the world in the same time period? (Egypt, China, Indus, Nubia)

Picturing History

The gold mask in the middle of the box on page 72 was once thought to be of Agamemnon, who, according to legend, was king of Mycenae during the Trojan War. Later studies have proven that it is not, but it is still often called the Mask of Agamemnon. It is considered an outstanding example of Mycenaen artistry.

Picturing History

The site of ancient Troy, (origin of the Trojan horse, pictured at the bottom of the box on page 72), located in modern Turkey, was discovered in 1870. German archaeologist Heinrich Schliemann found nine cities built atop one another on that site. He had spent several years searching for the location of Troy, finally finding it using Homer's directions in the *Iliad*. Archaeologists and historians are still not sure that this site is the real Troy, or even if Troy actually existed.

Picturing History

The photo at the bottom right of page 72 shows the caryatids of the Erechtheion. The Erechtheion was a small temple built on the acropolis in Athens. These were sculptures of women (rather than just columns) that held up the roof of the porch. Today, the original sculptures, with the exception of one that remains on the Erechtheion, are in a museum in Athens. Plaster casts from the original are installed on the temple today.

Extensions

1 Have students read paraphrases or summaries of the story of the Trojan horse. Then ask them to compare the written story to any depictions they have seen in movies.

2 Students may wish to investigate what is known about the blind poet Homer, who wrote the *Iliad*. Have them share their findings with the class by using the Student Presentation Builder on the student CD.

stop and think

Greece and its colonies had large resources of silver, gold, iron, and timber. How would these help the Greeks become successful traders? Talk over possible answers with a partner. Then write a paragraph to answer the question.

The 500s B.C. marked the rise of **tyrants**. A tyrant was not always a cruel ruler, as the word means today. In ancient Greece, a tyrant was a government ruled by one man. Rule by tyrants was the first step toward democratic rule, as they were often caring and fair rulers. In some cities like Athens, tyrants made important reforms to help the poor. But overall, Greeks turned away from absolute **rule** and toward **democracy**. They wanted a say in how they were governed.

Sparta: The Military Polis

Over time, Sparta and Athens became the most important city-states in Greece. During the 700s B.C., Sparta became a military polis. Harsh laws governed all parts of Spartans' lives. Boys were trained from childhood to be soldiers. At age seven, they were sent to live in barracks. Discipline was severe and punishments were harsh. At age twenty, Spartan men became soldiers and could marry.

Sparta

The Greek historian Xenophon describes one way Spartan boys prepared to become soldiers.

"Instead of softening their feet with shoe or sandal, . . . [they went] barefoot. This habit . . . enabled them to scale heights more easily and clamber down precipices with less danger. In fact, with his feet so trained the young Spartan would leap and spring and run faster unshod than another [in shoes]. . . .

Spartan boys were given little food. They were expected to steal more. This was to train them to find food when they were fighting. The Greek historian Plutarch describes the process.

'[Spartan youths were required to steal . . .], which they did by creeping into the gardens, or . . . into the eating houses; if they were taken in the act, they were whipped without mercy, for thieving so poorly and awkwardly. They stole, too, all other meat they could lay their hands on, looking out and watching all opportunities, when people were asleep or more careless than usual. If they were caught, they were not only punished with whipping, but hunger, too.'"

reading for understanding

What were Spartan boys able to do easily without shoes?

Why were boys whipped when they were caught stealing?

What do you think about the reason for teaching Spartan boys to steal food?

Ancient Greek City-States, 1750–133 B.C.

Stop and Think

Students' paragraphs will differ but may mention that other countries might want gold, silver, iron, and wood. These natural resources also helped the Greeks to produce desirable goods such as vases, goblets, and knives for trade.

Reading for Understanding

1 Spartan boys could climb mountains, leap, spring, and run faster without shoes.

2 They were whipped for being so bad at stealing as to get caught.

3 Students' answers will vary but may suggest that although the reasoning makes some sense, it would be better to feed an army than risk having soldiers weak from hunger.

Extension

Sparta and Athens were rivals. During the Peloponnesian War, 431–404 B.C., they fought for dominance of the region. Each city-state was supported by others. Sparta finally won, but all the city-states that had taken part in the conflict were weak from loss of lives and money.

Map Extension

Ask students to use the map on page 71 to answer the following questions:

- What does the map indicate about the landforms of Greece? (Greece is mostly mountainous.)
- What body of water would you cross to get from Athens to Troy? (Aegean Sea)
- On what island is Knossos located? (Crete)

Ancient Greek City-States | 73

Picturing History

Every Greek town had a section where the potters worked. The vase on page 74 is an example of the black-on-red pottery that was popular during the sixth century B.C. It was first produced in Corinth. Potters used metal or bone tools to cut the details of the illustration. Different shapes of vessels were used for different purposes. This one, known as an amphora, was used to hold liquids such as oil, wine, or water. The graceful shape continues to be popular with contemporary potters and glassmakers.

Picturing History

The painting at the bottom of page 74 depicts the right to free speech that began in ancient Athens. An Athenian man is addressing a crowd of men and women, probably at the agora. Explain to students that this is not a realistic depiction. Men did not wear laurel wreaths or carry large shields in public. The temple-like buildings would be on the hill, not in the flat area.

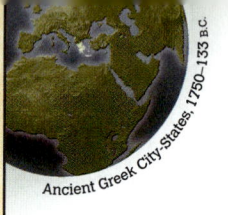

Ancient Greek City-States, 1750–133 B.C.

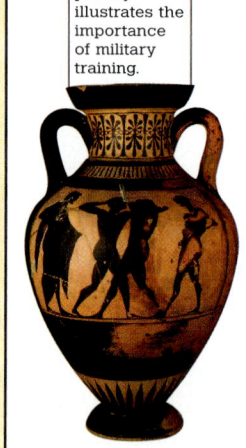

Spartan pottery illustrates the importance of military training.

Women and girls also had roles in this military state. Their job was to marry and have strong, healthy children. As a result, women, too, had to take part in vigorous exercise. Because husbands lived in barracks for many years, Spartan women had more authority and responsibility than women in many cultures.

Sparta's government and army were headed by two kings. However, the real power lay with a council of five men called **ephors**. These men managed the government on a daily basis. There was also a council of elders made up of the two kings and 28 citizens over the age of sixty. There was an assembly of citizens who voted on issues put before them by the council of elders. The assembly was not allowed to discuss the issues, only to vote. Only native-born men thirty years of age and older were citizens.

The only job for a Spartan citizen was soldier. All other work such as farming was done by **helots**. These were people captured in battle and enslaved.

To protect its way of life, Sparta cut itself off from the rest of the world. Travel was forbidden. Visitors from the outside were not welcome. The study of literature, the arts, and philosophy was not encouraged. New ideas could be dangerous.

Athens: An Experiment in Limited Democracy

The earliest government of Athens was a monarchy. In the 700s B.C., an oligarchy of aristocrats replaced the king. Nine members of the wealthiest families in Athens made up this ruling council. An assembly of citizens elected the nine oligarchs who served for a certain period of time. Otherwise, the assembly had little control over the government.

Between 560 B.C. and 510 B.C., tyrants ruled Athens. By 512 B.C., Cleisthenes had the support of enough Athenians to gain control of the government.

Democracy was an important aspect of Athenian life.

Chapter 6

Extension

The Greeks were known for their skills in discourse and argumentation. Have students find out more about the various styles of debate popular at the time. Allow them the opportunity to share their findings with the class, perhaps in a creative demonstration of the techniques.

He reorganized Athens' government. Cleisthenes is regarded as the founder of Athenian democracy. Native-born Athenian women were citizens, but they could not vote. Slaves and foreign residents were not citizens.

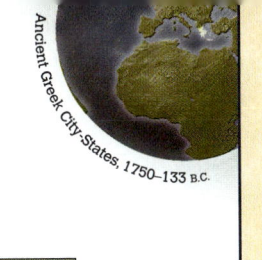

Government Set Up by Cleisthenes

Government Body	Members	Duties
Assembly	• all male citizens of Athens, eighteen years of age and older	• debate and pass laws • elect public officals • decide all matters of war and foreign policy
Council of 500	• 500 citizens chosen by lottery to serve for one year—50 from each of the ten tribes that made up Athens city-state and surrounding area	• prepare laws for debate by the Assembly • carry out decisions of the Assembly
Law Court	• 6,000 citizens chosen by lottery from the Assembly	• serve as judge and jury for criminal and civil trials
Board of Generals	• ten generals elected by the Assembly	• advise the Assembly • lead the army and navy

Most families in Athens could afford a slave or two. Many worked in homes doing cooking and cleaning. The enslaved were also used for farm work. By the 400s B.C., Athens was an important trading center. It grew much of its own food, but also imported grain in large amounts. Some of its trade goods were wine and olive oil. Slave labor was used to manufacture these goods.

Slaves often worked in Athenian homes.

Putting It All Together

Imagine you are a Spartan in 507 B.C. An Athenian visits your family and talks about the government of Athens. How could this be dangerous for the rulers of Sparta? Talk about it with a partner. Then write a paragraph to explain how learning about the government in Athens might be dangerous. Use examples from the lesson to support your opinion.

Ancient Greek City-States | 75

Chart Extension

Have students work in pairs to create flash cards with the information presented in the second and third columns of the chart. They can use the cards to drill the facts prior to a test or quiz. Students should be able to identify the government body with which each fact is associated.

Picturing History

The section of pottery pictured on page 75 shows slaves serving in a wealthy household. Slaves, who were generally prisoners of war or kidnapped, were sold in the agora. At a time when soldiers earned a drachma a day, slaves were sold for 150 to 300 drachmas. Slaves were branded; their children belonged to the master. Slaves might work in households like those shown here, as field hands, or in the silver mines. A few slaves were tutors to the sons of the wealthy. Those who worked for the government were given a small salary and permitted to marry.

Putting It All Together

Students' paragraphs will differ but may suggest that ideas about a more democratic form of government could spark rebellion or dissatisfaction over Sparta's military rule.

...uring History

...xample of red-on-black pottery shown on page 75 depicts the shift that occurred ...ttery around 500 B.C. The Athenians developed the technique of leaving the ...es of red clay visible, but painting the background with a clay solution that ...d black when the clay was fired. The drawing skills were even finer than those ...e black-on-red pottery. Greek potters today still use these ancient techniques.

Ancient Greek City-States | 75

Lesson Summary

During the classical era, from about 500 to 338 B.C., the Greeks made great strides in the arts and sciences. While Athens grew in power, it also fought two wars.

The first war was with Persia. Against the odds, Athens defeated Persia. Later, it formed the Delian League to regain control of Greek colonies.

The reign of Pericles was notable for its achievements in reforms for the poor as well as in the arts. The Parthenon and other public works buildings offered jobs for the poor.

Athens fought Sparta and its allies in the Peloponnesian War for 26 years.

Herodotus, considered the first Western historian, chronicled both wars. Homer produced the epics the *Iliad* and the *Odyssey*, and dramatists wrote comedies and tragedies.

Lesson Objective

Students will learn about the wars with Persia and between Sparta and Athens, as well as of the leadership of Pericles and Greece's cultural achievements.

Focus Your Reading Answers

1 The leaders of Athens had the treasury of the Delian League moved to Athens. They then used the money from the treasury to rebuild Athens.

2 Pericles expanded the rights of Athenians by allowing citizens who did not own property to hold office.

3 The various city-states divided into allies of either Athens or Sparta.

4 The Greeks gave the world great poetry, drama, sculpture, and architecture.

LESSON 2
Classical Greece

Ancient Greek City-States, 1750–133 B.C.

Thinking on Your Own

Create two columns in your notebook. Title one "War with Persia," and the other "The Peloponnesian War." As you read, fill in the columns with key information about each war and its effect on ancient Greece.

Between about 500 B.C. and 338 B.C., the Greeks developed what is called **classical** Greek civilization. They made great contributions to the arts and sciences. Also during this period, Athens increased its power and fought two long and costly wars.

focus your reading

How did the leaders of Athens use the Persian Wars to benefit Athens?

How did Pericles expand Athenian democracy?

What effect did the Peloponnesian War have on the Greek city-states?

What contributions did classical Greece make to world culture?

vocabulary

classical	blockade
allies	tragedy
plague	comedy

War with Persia

By the mid-500s B.C., Persia had taken control of the Greek colonies of Iona in what is now Turkey. The war between Persia and Greece began over the control of these colonies. In 499 B.C., the Athenian navy helped the Ionian colonies to rebel. The Persians crushed the revolt.

Darius, the Persian king, was angered that Athens had sent ships to help the rebels. In 490 B.C., he sent the Persian army to destroy Athens. The smaller Athenian army met the Persians on the plain of Marathon. In a deadly battle, the Athenians defeated the Persians.

Wars were a common theme of Greek pottery.

Lesson Vocabulary

Discuss each of the vocabulary terms with students.

The *classical* age of Greek civilization was the age of its greatest cultural achievements, between 500 and 338 B.C.

Countries that join together in war to fight a common enemy are *allies*. Both Sparta and Athens had *allies* during the Peloponnesian War.

A *plague* is a deadly disease. During the war with Sparta, a *plague* broke out in Athens and one-third of the population died.

A *blockade* is a shutting of ports or cities to outside deliveries so that no food, fuel, or other resources can get through. The Persians *blockaded* Athens during the Peloponnesian War. (Examples to help students understand the concept include the British *blockade* of Boston during the Revolutionary War and the Soviet Union's *blockade* of West Berlin during the Cold War.)

A Greek *tragedy* addressed the rights of the individual and themes of good and evil. Some Greek *tragedies* are still performed. A *comedy* is a humorous play. Greek *comedies* criticized society using humor. Politicians were often a target of a Greek *comedy*.

76 Chapter 6

Pheidippides
...ed after
...asping out
...e news of
...thens'
...ctory after
...e Battle of
...arathon.

In 480 B.C., Darius' son Xerxes ordered the Persian army and navy to go to war against Athens again. In 479 B.C., the Athenian army and its **allies** defeated the Persians at Plataea.

The following year, Athens formed the Delian League, or alliance, with other Greek city-states. The purpose of this alliance was to take back control of the Greek colonies from Persia. In time, the League was successful.

The Age of Pericles

Athens reached its greatest glory in the years between the Persian Wars and the Peloponnesian War. This period in Greek history is often called the Age of Pericles.

Pericles was a general of the board of generals and a forceful public speaker. His position gave him great influence over public policy. Although an aristocrat, Pericles focused on the poor in guiding reforms. Reforms were passed that helped poor citizens participate more fully in Athens' government. Citizens who did not own property were allowed to hold public office. In addition, those who served on juries and held office were paid for their time. Pericles was also a supporter of the arts. It was during this period that the Parthenon was built. It and other public works projects gave jobs to the poor.

Stone relief depicts democracy crowning the people of Athens.

Ancient Greek City-States 77

Picturing History

In the illustration of an engraving at the top of page 77, Pheidippides is shown dying after he has run 25 miles to bring the news of the Athenian victory over the Persians at Marathon. Point out to students the reaction of people in the background to the news of victory, despite the plight of the runner.

Marathon was about 25 miles from Athens. This long-distance run is the origin of contemporary marathon races. The Olympic marathon in 2004 followed Pheidippides' route as much as possible.

After the Persian War, the Athenians built a treasury at Delphi to house the Persian spoils. The treasury was also built as an offering to Apollo, showing the close relationship of politics and religion in ancient Greece.

Picturing History

The piece of Greek pottery at the bottom of page 76 depicts a war scene and demonstrates the Greek love of symmetry. Note the use of shields, an innovation that led to the success against the Persians at Marathon.

...nsion

...rds of the Persian Wars come from
...dotus, the "Father of History." According
...erodotus, the Athenians sent Pheidippides
...arta to ask for help against the Persians.
...dippides ran 150 miles in two days. But his
...not the only feat. After winning the battle,
...thenians began to fear that their
...fended city would be easy prey for the
...ans. They headed back to Athens at once,
...ing before the Persians. It took eight hours
...arch back; the sail from Marathon to
...ns usually took 12 to 14 hours. The
...ans, seeing that the Athenian army had
...ed, sailed back to Persia.

Picturing History

The stone relief at the bottom of page 77 is from the agora in Athens. It depicts the personification of democracy crowning the people of Athens.

Ask students why this caption is not completely true. (The *people* of Athens would include women and slaves, as well as landowners.)

Ancient Greek City-States 77

> **Picturing History**
>
> Draw students' attention to the photograph of the Parthenon today on page 78. Tell them that the Parthenon had 46 columns. Dedicated to the goddess Athena, it housed a statue of her, 38 feet tall, carved by Phidias. He also carved many of the marble friezes and other statuary. Athena's robe and shield were made of gold. The gold itself weighed more than a ton. The statue disappeared early in the Parthenon's history. Today, what remains of its many sculptures and friezes are in museums in Athens and throughout the world. A few plaster copies of the original sculptures have been placed on the Parthenon.

> **Extension**
>
> Have students research the story of the marble statues and friezes that once decorated the Parthenon. Tell them to find out the role Lord Elgin of Britain played in salvaging them. Ask students to decide who they think is right in the dispute between Greece and the British Museum as to who owns the marbles. Hold a debate on the issue.

The Parthenon was constructed in Athens between 447 B.C. and 432 B.C.

One of the greatest glories of Athens at this time was its government system. Under Cleisthenes, Athens had become a direct democracy. Citizens took part in governing Athens directly. The Athenian Assembly met every 10 days to discuss and vote on issues. All 43,000 citizens did not show up for each meeting, but the meetings were held and citizens could attend. Today, we would call Athens a limited democracy because women and slaves could not vote.

The Peloponnesian War

While the Delian League was freeing Greek colonies, Athens was using the League to create an empire. Athens' leaders held the major positions of power in the League. As a result, they were able to move the League's treasury to Athens. Each city-state contributed money to the treasury, which was to be used for the League's expenses. Instead, the leaders of Athens used the money to rebuild their city. If a city-state tried to leave the League, Athens sent soldiers to stop it.

Athens' power soon divided the Greek city-states into allies and enemies. Sparta was its chief rival. With its own allies, Sparta formed the Peloponnesian League. In 431 B.C., Sparta and Athens and their respective allies went to war.

> **Time Box**
>
> 499 B.C.
> Uprising of Greek colonies in Persian Empire
>
> 490–479 B.C.
> Persian Wars against Greek city-states
>
> 461–429 B.C.
> Age of Pericles
>
> 431–405 B.C.
> Peloponnesian War

> **Time Box Extension**
>
> Ask students to develop a symbol for each event in the Time Box. They can associate the symbol with the time period, which will help them recall the facts for a quiz or test.

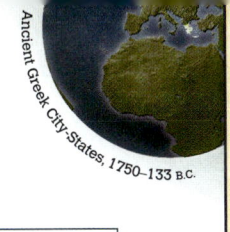

Mural depicting the Peloponnesian War

Athenian leaders decided to keep its army within the city's walls and wait out the Spartans. The Spartans were stronger fighters. Spartan soldiers surrounded the city and waited for two years. In the second year, a **plague**, or deadly disease, broke out in Athens. About a third of Athens' population died. However, the conflict continued.

In 405 B.C., Persia joined with Sparta to destroy Athens' navy. They also **blockaded** Athens' port. Food and other supplies could no longer reach Athens. The city finally surrendered in 404 B.C. As a result of its defeat, Athens lost its empire. It was no longer a powerful force in Greek affairs. Other city-states fought Athens and one another for power. The Greek mainland was torn by conflict for the next 100 years.

stop and think

How did the desire for power and territory cause both the Persian Wars and the Peloponnesian War? Write down some notes to answer this question. Share your ideas with a partner. Then write two or three paragraphs to answer the question.

Cultural Achievements of Classical Greece

Since the earliest times, the Greeks had composed stories and poetry and made artworks. The Age of Pericles marked the peak of ancient Greek culture. One of the most important contributions of classical Greece to Western civilization was the development of written history. History is the study of past events in an organized way. Herodotus, who lived from about 484 B.C. to 425 B.C., is considered the first Western historian. He traveled widely to interview eyewitnesses to events.

Picturing History

Draw students' attention to the mural at the top of page 79. It is an idealized drawing of a battle during the Peloponnesian War. Ask students what advantages horses and chariots gave an army.

Stop and Think

Students' paragraphs will vary but may mention that both wars were the result of the desire for more territory. Athens' defense of the Ionian colonies against the Persians contributed to the Persian War. Athens' desire to control more land in Greece led to Sparta's decision to fight the Peloponnesian War.

Chart Extension

Divide the class into three groups, assigning each group one of the three philosophers to research. Allow students time to prepare the material they find. Then have them present the information to the class.

Picturing History

Greek drama and tragedy are depicted in the modern masks on page 80. Tragedy is always dark and grim, while comedy is light and happy.

Extension

The four major Greek dramatists of the fifth century B.C. were Sophocles, Euripides, Aristophanes, and Aeschylus.

Dramas were performed in celebrations of Dionysus, the god of wine, illusion, fertility, and new life. The theaters of the time resembled modern sports stadiums in their seating capacity. One estimate is that some 17,000 people could see a performance at the theater in Athens.

Suggest that students interested in drama find out more about these dramatists and the works of theirs that have survived and are still performed today.

Ancient Greek City-States, 1750–133 B.C.

Greek literature began with Homer's two epics about the fall of Troy—the *Iliad* and the *Odyssey*. The ancient Greeks are also known for their development of drama. Greek **tragedies** dealt with themes such as good and evil and the rights of individuals. Some of these plays are still performed today. Greek **comedies** used humor to criticize society, especially politicians. The ancient Greeks, like the ancient Chinese, were also interested in understanding the universe and humans' place in it. Greek philosophers such as Socrates, Plato, and Aristotle developed ideas about the world.

Masks depicting tragedy and comedy

Important Greek Philosophers

Philosopher	Teachings	Lasting Contributions
Socrates, c. 470–399 B.C.	• "The Unexamined life is not worth living." • He used questions to get people to think about issues.	• Teaching by asking questions is known as the Socratic method. It is still used today in schools and colleges.
Plato, c. 427–347 B.C.	• Reality is made up of ideal, eternal Forms. • The ideal government would have three groups: philosopher-king as ruler, soldiers to protect the people, and workers (all other men and women). • Men and women should be treated equally.	• *The Republic* is Plato's writings about the ideal government.
Aristotle, 384–322 B.C.	• He rejected Plato's concept of ideal Forms. • Analysis, observation, and investigation are needed to answer questions about life and human nature. • Based on his research, he found monarchy, aristocracy, and constitutional government to be the best ways to govern people. • Constitutional government was the best form to use.	• Aristotle's work on government and other areas such as astronomy, biology, and physics influenced Western thinking until the A.D. 1600s.

Putting It All Together

This lesson discusses many events. Create a timeline to put the dates and events in sequence. Share your timeline with a partner. Ask questions about when one event happened in relation to another. Was it earlier, later, or at the same time?

Putting It All Together

Students' timelines will vary but should include the major events of the lesson. Possible events include the information in the Time Box on page 78.

LESSON 3

Alexander the Great and Hellenism

Ancient Greek City-States, 1750–133 B.C.

Thinking on Your Own

Read the Focus Your Reading questions. Then write three more questions you have about the lesson. Share your questions with a partner and answer all the questions as you read.

The Peloponnesian War greatly weakened all the Greek city-states, not just Athens. Over the next 60 years, the city-states fought one another for more power. They were further weakened by almost constant conflict.

King Philip II of Macedonia took advantage of the conflict. Macedonia is located to the north of Greece. Philip ruled Macedonia from 359 B.C. to 336 B.C. He formed alliances with some Greek city-states by using bribery and threats of force. Athens would not agree, however. It formed an alliance with the city-state of Thebes instead. In 338 B.C., Philip's army defeated Athens and Thebes. Philip then seized control of all Greece. Philip's next plan was to **conquer** the Persian Empire. However, he was assassinated before he could attack.

focus your reading

How did Philip II gain control of Greece?

How large was Alexander's empire?

What is Hellenism?

vocabulary

conquer   Hellenism

Alexander's Army on the March

Philip's son Alexander became king at age twenty. He had been well trained by his father to be a soldier and a general. Alexander was also a student of the great philosopher Aristotle. In 334 B.C., Alexander launched an invasion of the

Ancient Greek City-States 81

Lesson Summary

The conquests of Alexander spread Greek civilization across several regions of the world. Alexander came to power in Macedonia after the death of his father. At only twenty, he commanded an army that was stopped only by the prospect of fighting troops mounted on India's elephants.

As Alexander conquered each area, he set up his own government headed by Greeks. Thus, the Greek language and culture spread, as did architecture and the arts.

Lesson Objective

Students will learn about the conquests of Alexander the Great and the subsequent spread of Hellenic ideals.

Focus Your Reading Answers

1 Philip formed alliances with some city-states. When Athens would not agree to an alliance, Philip defeated Athens and Thebes, an ally of Athens, and took control of all of Greece.

2 Alexander's empire stretched from Greece to the edge of India and included Arabia and North Africa.

3 Hellenism is the adopting of Greek culture and language in the lands that Alexander conquered.

Lesson Vocabulary

Discuss each of the vocabulary terms with students.

To *conquer* is to defeat. Philip II planned to *conquer* the Persian Empire. Alexander *conquered* many countries.

Hellenism is the adoption of Greek culture and language in the lands that Alexander *conquered*. Under Alexander's policy of *Hellenism*, Greeks were placed in positions of leadership. The word is a derivation of a Greek word that means "to imitate the Greek."

Picturing History

Philip of Macedonia, pictured on page 81, was Alexander's father. Philip provided for his son's education in every regard. Not only did Alexander learn the techniques of war, but he also was tutored by Aristotle.

Ancient Greek City-States 81

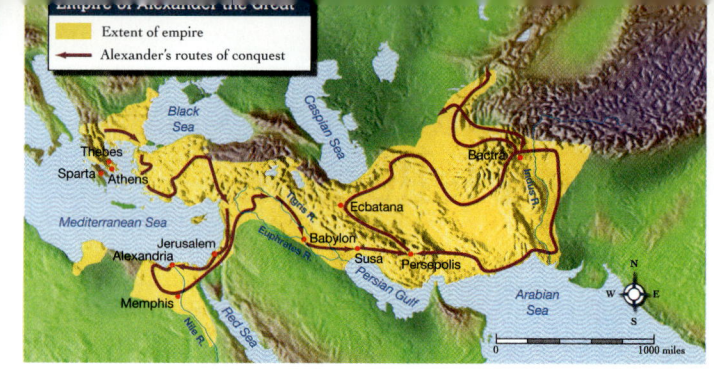

Map Extension

Ask students to use the map on page 82 to answer the following questions:

- In what general direction did Alexander's army march? (east)
- Across which major rivers did the army travel? (the Nile, the Tigris, the Euphrates, the Indus)
- At what point did the army stop its conquest? (at the edge of India, just past the Indus River)

Picturing History

The mosaic at the bottom of page 82 depicts Alexander and his famous horse, Bucephalus. As Alexander's power grew, he was so fond of his horse that he demanded that both he and his horse be worshiped as gods. Legend says that Bucephalus was a horse that no one could tame or ride. When Alexander was still a youngster, he was the only person able to tame the horse. The mosaic was found in the House of the Faun in Pompeii.

Stop and Think

Students' lists will vary but should include the names of specific mountains, rivers, and deserts.

Persian Empire. He led Macedonian and Greek forces into battle.

Between 334 and 326 B.C., Alexander brought under his control all or part of what are the modern nations of Iran, Egypt, Syria, Lebanon, Israel, Turkey, Iraq, Pakistan, Afghanistan, Turkmenistan, Uzbekistan, and Kazakhstan. In 326 B.C., Alexander led his army across the Indus River into India. Fighting Indian soldiers who were on war elephants, combined with being away from home for a long time, was too much for his troops. They refused to continue. Alexander agreed to turn back.

Alexander died three years later from a fever. His empire was split among four generals. One general took Macedonia and Greece and set up his own kingdom. The glory of Greece was dimmed but not dead. Greek culture continued to influence other cultures and to be influenced by them.

Time Box

359–336 B.C.
Rule of Philip II as king of Macedonia

336–323 B.C.
Rule of Alexander the Great

Alexander the Great in battle

stop and think

Locate the world map at the end of this book. With a partner, figure out where Alexander's military campaigns took him. Use the information in your textbook to help you. What obstacles did his army face? Make a bulleted list of geographic obstacles.

Hellenistic World

Hellenism was the adoption of the Greek language and culture by the peoples that Alexander conquered. His march across Southwest Asia and into North Africa and South Asia left

Time Box Extension

Ask students to determine how long each king ruled. (Philip II–23 years; Alexander–13 years)

Which king ruled longer? (Philip II)

82   Chapter 6

its mark. Alexander's army spread the Greek language and Greek ideas wherever it went. The result was the Hellenistic Era.

As each area was conquered, Alexander set up his own government to oversee it. He put Greeks in positions of power. The kings who followed him continued this practice. Only Greeks were allowed to govern, and Greek was the language of the government. In time, non-Greeks were able to gain government jobs. However, they, too, had to use the Greek language in their work.

Alexander also set up new settlements in the areas he conquered. They were settled by Greeks from the mainland. This practice of sending Greeks to settle in conquered territory continued after his death. Some of the colonists were soldiers. Most were ordinary citizens. They did all the jobs that a city needed—merchant, farmer, artisan, actor, architect, and so on.

The temples and other public buildings in these new cities were based on the plans of Greek architects. Statues and wall paintings looked like ones in Athens or Corinth. The colonists held religious festivals and sporting contests as though they were in Greece. Over time, local people picked up Greek styles and customs. Greek colonists, in turn, picked up local ideas. The result was a vast merging, or blending, of Greek, Persian, Egyptian, and Indian cultures.

Hellenistic kings spent money on architecture and sculptures such as Winged Victory.

Achievements of the Hellenistic Era

Mathematics and Science

- Pythagoras figured out how to find the sides of a right triangle—Pythagorean theorem.
- Euclid developed the basic principles of geometry.
- Archimedes determined the value of *pi*, which is used in geometry. He also invented the pulley.
- Eratosthenes determined that the earth was a sphere and figured out its circumference.
- Aristarchus determined that the earth rotated on its axis and orbited the sun.

Putting It All Together

Write two-line headlines for each of the following: (1) Philip's taking control of Greece, (2) Alexander's plan to invade the Persian Empire, (3) Alexander's death, (4) the Hellenistic Era.

Ancient Greek City-States | 83

Picturing History

The statue *Winged Victory* on page 83 depicts a common motif in Greek statuary. *Winged Victory*, also known as Athena Nike, appeared in several locations, including the Parthenon. This manifestation of the goddess is her role as goddess of victory in battle.

Map Extension

Ask students to use the map on page 83 to answer the following questions:

- What continents did the reach of Hellenism include? (Africa, Asia, Europe)
- What was the approximate east-west distance of the extent of Hellenism? (about 1,000 miles)
- What bodies of water touched on the land affected by Hellenism? (Mediterranean Sea, Black Sea, Red Sea, Persian Gulf, Nile River, Tigris River, Euphrates River)

Chart Extension

Invite students who are interested in mathematics and science to use library resources or the Internet to investigate one of the achievements listed in the chart. Allow time for a report to the class.

---

ng It All Together

ts' headlines will vary. Possible answers are

ip of Macedonia Conquers Greece!
sian Empire Next

xander Completes Father's Vision
ves to Conquer Persian Empire

xander Dead at 33
er Ends Life in India

ek Ideas Spread
lenism Triumphs Throughout Empire

Ancient Greek City-States | 83

Chapter Review

1. Students' paragraphs will vary. Possible topics are:

    (a) Athenian navy victorious
    Persia defeated

    (b) Athens surrenders
    Peloponnesian League gains power

    (c) Assembly to meet weekly
    Direct democracy gains hold

    (d) Socrates' teaching methods win favor
    Art of question directs learning

    (e) Alexander continues conquest
    Goal is India

2. Students' slogans or logos will vary but should incorporate key concepts and terms related to life in Athens.

Chapter Summary

- The basic unit of Greek government was the **polis**, or city-state. It had two levels: the acropolis, or hilltop, and the **agora**, or open market and assembly place.
- In general, city-states went through four stages of political development: monarchy, **oligarchy** made up of **aristocrats**, rule by **tyrants**, and **democracy**.
- Sparta was a military city-state. Its male citizens were trained to be soldiers. All other work was done by **helots**, or enslaved peoples. Five men called **ephors** ran the city.
- The years between 500 B.C. and 338 B.C. are known as the **classical** period in Greek history. The three great Greek philosophers—Socrates, Plato, and Aristotle—lived during this period. Dramas of **tragedy** and **comedy** developed as well.
- Athens and its **allies** defeated Persia in a series of wars.
- Athens and Sparta and their allies fought one another in the Peloponnesian War. Athens' loss was partly due to a **blockade** of the city and a **plague** that wiped out many of its citizens.
- Philip II of Macedonia **conquered** the Greek city-states. His son Alexander the Great joined Greek and Macedonian forces to seize the Persian Empire.
- After Alexander's death, the new rulers continued his policies. Greek influence, or **Hellenism**, spread throughout the regions.

Chapter Review

1. Write lead newspaper paragraphs for each of the following: (a) Persian Wars, (b) Peloponnesian War, (c) Cleisthenes' reforms, (d) Socrates, (e) Alexander the Great. Be sure to include *who*, *what*, *where*, *why* and *when*.

2. You want to attract residents to Athens. With a partner, design a logo or write a slogan about Athenian democracy. A slogan is a phrase or sentence that describes the most important point about a product.

Novel Connections

Below is a list of books that relate to the time period covered in this chapter. The numbers in parentheses indicate the related Thematic Strands of the National Council for the Social Studies (NCSS).

Padraic Colum. *The Adventures of Odysseus and The Tale of Troy*. Dover Publications, 2004. (I, III, V, IX)

Priscilla Galloway. *Courtesan's Daughter*. Random House Children's Books, 2002. (I, III)

Sheldon Oberman. *Island of the Minotaur: The Greek Myths of Ancient Crete*. Interlink Publishing Group, 2003. (I, II, VI)

Jennifer T. Roberts. *Ancient Greek World*. Oxford University Press, 2004. (I, III, IX, X)

Kelly Trumble. *The Library of Alexandria*. Clarion Books, 2004. (I, II, III, IX)

Susan Zannos. *The Life and Times of Socrates (Biography from Ancient Civilizations* series). Mitchell Lane Publishers, 2004. (I, III, IV, IX, X)

Skill Builder

How to Write a Persuasive Essay

An essay is a composition of several paragraphs. An essay may explain or describe something. An essay can also attempt to persuade the reader. This is a persuasive essay.

To write a persuasive essay, you must do some work before you begin writing.

- First, decide what you think about the issue. For example, suppose the issue is whether the United Nations should send peacekeepers to a particular region. What might happen if the peacekeepers are sent? If they are not sent? What might be the long-term results?
- Write notes about your ideas as you think about the issue.

Now you can start the writing process.

- Review the notes you wrote. Cross out ideas that do not fit your point of view. Add ideas that support your viewpoint.
- Put your ideas in the order that you will use them in your essay. Do not rewrite your ideas. Number them so you can find each one when you are ready to use it.
- Write your topic sentence. This should contain your viewpoint. This viewpoint is the main idea of your essay.
- Add other paragraphs that support your viewpoint with more evidence. Each paragraph should include one piece of evidence that supports your viewpoint.
- End with a strong concluding paragraph. Restate your point of view. Briefly restate your strongest evidence.

1. Think of an issue in your school. (a) State the issue in a sentence. (b) What is your point of view about the issue? Follow the steps above to decide on your viewpoint. (c) Write an essay to persuade someone else to adopt your viewpoint.

2. Sparta trained its male citizens to be soldiers. It was their only job. Foreigners and slaves did every other kind of work. Was this a practical and efficient way to set up a society? Write a persuasive essay to answer this question.

Skill Builder

1. Students' essays will vary but should include a specific issue and point of view, a topic sentence, supporting evidence and details, and a concluding paragraph.

2. Students' essays will vary but should include a specific issue and point of view, a topic sentence, supporting evidence and details, and a concluding paragraph.

Classroom Discussion

Discuss with students some of the broader topics covered in this chapter.

- What are the advantages and disadvantages of each type of governmental system?
- What effect does war have on the economies of the nations involved?
- What are some of the ways that ideas spread from one culture to another today?
- Imagine that we are living in the classical age of the United States. What might future societies consider to be our major accomplishments?

Chapter Summary
Refer to page 102 for a summary of Chapter 7.

Related Transparencies

T-1 World Map

T-2 Outline World Map

T-19 Venn Diagram

T-20 Concept Web

Key Blacklines

Primary Source—Roman Houses

CD Extension

Encourage students to use the reading comprehension, vocabulary reinforcement, and interactive timeline activities on the student CD.

Getting Focused

Students' lists will vary but may include the ideas of a strong central government, a shared culture and language, and love of and loyalty to one's country.

Chapter 7 ANCIENT ROME

(500 B.C.–A.D. 500)

Getting Focused

Skim this chapter to predict what you will be learning.
- Read the lesson titles and subheadings.
- Look at the illustrations and read the captions.
- Examine the maps.
- Review the vocabulary words and terms.

The Roman Empire was one of the world's largest empires. Many different groups lived under its rule. You have studied several empires in this book. Based o what you know, what do you think helped to keep the Roman Empire together? List your ideas. As you study chapter, check your list. Add to or cross out ideas. Also, remember to add Italy to the world map you are makir

Picturing History

The photograph on page 86 is of the Pont du Gard, an aqueduct built by the Romans in what is now southern France. Throughout the Empire, soldiers built aqueducts to bring clean water down from the hills to the cities. The three-story bridge was built to carry an aqueduct over a gorge. The water flowed through a covered channel along the top. This aqueduct ended in a reservoir after about 30 miles (50 km). It supplied the city of Nîmes with 22,000 tons of water daily. Most of the aqueduct is still standing today.

Pre-Reading Discussion

1 Review with students the organization of the United States federal government. Tell them that they will read about the example that the founding fathers followed in designing the government. Ask them to watch for the information as they read.

2 Discuss with students the challenges geography presents to maintaining a unified nation or empire, as well as to expansion. Tell them that in this chapter they will learn about various geographical factors that influenced the growth and decline of the Roman Empire.

LESSON 1

The Roman Republic

Thinking on Your Own

Look at the lesson subheadings. Use these to create an outline for the lesson in your notebook. As you read the lesson, fill in the outline.

Italy is a peninsula that extends out into the Mediterranean Sea. The Roman Republic began along the banks of the Tiber River in Italy. The river runs through the plain of Latium, which is about halfway down the west side of the peninsula. A peninsula is a piece of land that is surrounded on three sides by water.

Sometime around 1500 to 1000 B.C., people began moving into the Italian peninsula from the north. Some were Latins who settled on the plain of Latium. The plain takes its name from these people. By 800 B.C., they had set up small villages on seven hills along the Tiber River.

Around 650 B.C., Etruscans moved into Latium from the north. They seized control of much of central Italy. They turned the seven villages into the city of Rome. The Etruscan state was a monarchy. In 509 B.C., the Romans overthrew the Etruscan king. Romans considered this act the beginning of their nation.

focus your reading

How was Rome founded?

How was the government of the Roman Republic organized?

How did the Republic gain control of the Mediterranean region?

Why was Rome able to keep the territory it conquered?

vocabulary

republic
patrician
plebeian
consuls
diplomacy
Roman Confederation

Lesson Summary

Early Latin settlers reached the Italian peninsula between 1500 and 1000 B.C. The Etruscans founded Rome by combining seven Latin villages into one city. Romans set up a republic, governed mainly by patricians. Eventually the plebeians gained rights to office as well. Rome extended its Empire from present-day Spain to Turkey. To maintain control of North Africa, Rome fought three Punic Wars against the city of Carthage. The Roman Confederation was a group of alliances between Rome and other city-states.

Lesson Objective

Students will learn about the early days of Rome and the Roman Republic.

Focus Your Reading Answers

1 Rome was founded by people from farther north who moved into the Italian peninsula. They set up villages on Rome's hills. After overthrowing the Etruscans in 509 B.C., the Romans set up their own government.

2 The Roman Republic set up a system of citizens electing representatives.

3 By conquering city-states and making alliances, Rome gained control of the Italian peninsula. The army's conquests extended to present-day Spain in the west and what is now Turkey in the east.

4 Rome extended comparative peace among the city-states. It granted citizenship and its privileges to conquered people.

---

on Vocabulary

ice each of the following vocabulary terms. Discuss with students words that are derived e Latin words.

lic is a form of government in which citizens are governed by representatives they elected. omans preferred a *republic* to a democracy, such as Athens had. Words that are derived e Latin word and used today are *republican* and *public*.

ricians were the wealthy landowning class of Rome. *Patricians* made up the majority of the Senate. Merchants, craftworkers, small landowners, and farmers made up the *plebeians*. excluded from the Senate, the *plebeians* set up their own assembly in 471 B.C.

suls headed the Roman government. The *consuls* were elected by the Centuriate Assembly. rds *consult*, *consultation*, and *consular* come from the Latin word *consul*.

cy is one of the ways that Rome gained control of the Mediterranean. The use of *diplomacy* alternative to war. *Diplomats* and *diplomatic* are derivatives.

man Confederation involved alliances between Rome and other regions of Italy. The *Roman ation* granted trade rights to member states.

Ancient Rome 87

Picturing History

The Etruscan mural at the bottom of page 87 is most likely a fresco. While the plaster was still wet, fresco painters hurried to complete their designs. Once the plaster dried, it would not absorb paint. Many of the frescoes survive today, their colors still vivid.

Extension

Ask students with an interest in art to use library resources or the Internet to find out more about frescoes. Allow time for them to report their findings to the class.

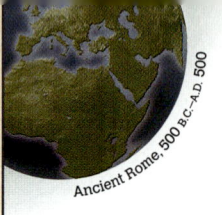

Ancient Rome, 500 B.C.–A.D. 500

The Government of Rome

Instead of a monarchy, the Romans set up a **republic**. In a republic, citizens elect representatives to govern. This is different from the democracy that Athens developed. In Athens, citizens voted directly in their Assembly on running the government.

At first, **patricians** decided who would govern Rome. Patricians were wealthy landowners and were the most important social class in the Republic. They were also the soldiers of the Roman army. The small landowners, farmers, craftworkers, and merchants, who were known as **plebeians**, had little say in deciding who would govern. Both patricians and plebeians were citizens. For much of the history of the Republic, patricians and plebeians clashed for political power.

The government was headed by two **consuls**. Until the 300s B.C., the office of consul was open only to patricians. They were elected by the Centuriate Assembly, which the patricians controlled. The consuls issued laws and orders and could veto each other's decisions. They did not have to send their laws to the Senate for a vote, although they could.

The Senate was also made up mostly of patricians. The Senate's duties included seeing that the laws and orders of the consuls were carried out and advising the consuls on issues.

In time, the plebeians gained a larger voice in Roman government. In 471 B.C., they won the right to set up their own assembly called the Council of Plebs. The council passed laws for plebeians. By 409 B.C., plebeians had gained the right to hold public office. Before this, only patricians could be elected to office. However, unlike Athens, Rome did not pay its officeholders. This meant that plebeians were less likely to serve in government. After 287 B.C., the Assembly of the People, which included all male citizens, could make laws that all Romans had to obey.

Rome's location was ideal because it was near the sea but far enough away from it to avoid pirates.

Government Office/Body	Members	Duties
Consul (509 B.C.)	• two citizens elected by the Centuriate Assembly • until the 300s B.C., office of consul open only to patricians	• issue laws and orders with or without sending them to the Senate for a vote • veto each other's decisions • command the army
Dictator	• appointed by the consuls and the Senate • hold power for six months	• rule during an emergency • hold absolute power
Praetor (197 B.C.)	• six male citizens • elected	• second in power to the consuls • act as judge in civil cases
Senate (509 B.C.)	• around 300 members, including former office holders • mostly patricians	• see that the laws and orders of the consuls are carried out • advise the consuls
Centuriate Assembly (509 B.C.)	• army of Rome • patrician majority in the assembly	• elect consuls and praetors • pass laws
Council of the Plebs (471 B.C.)	• all male plebeians	• elect 10 tribunes to represent plebeians' issues • pass laws for plebeians • after 287 B.C., pass laws for all Romans
Assembly of the People (447 B.C.)	• all male citizens of Rome	• at first, only proposed laws • after 287 B.C., pass laws for all Romans

The Roman Army on the March

The Romans gradually extended their control over Italy and the Mediterranean. By 261 B.C., the entire Italian peninsula was under Roman control. Rome had conquered some city-states and made alliances with others. By 146 B.C., the Roman army had gone far beyond Italy. It had reached as far west as what is today Spain. By 129 B.C., the army had taken control of the Greek peninsula to the east. Farther east it had seized territory in what is today Turkey. By 44 B.C., Rome controlled the Mediterranean.

The three Punic Wars were fought between Rome and Carthage. Carthage was an important trading rival in North Africa. By the 200s B.C., Carthage had set up colonies in Spain and on islands in the Mediterranean near the Italian peninsula. This was threatening to Rome. In 264 B.C., Rome attacked the Carthaginian colony in Sicily, beginning the First Punic War. It took 23 years, but the Romans defeated the Carthaginian navy and seized Sicily. This was the first of Rome's foreign territories, or provinces. As a result of these wars, Rome also controlled an area in North Africa.

Chart Extensions

1 Have students take on roles of offices or bodies of the Roman government. Two people can be consul, one dictator, and so forth. Have students explain their duties to the class. The four large groups can be represented by four small groups of students. You may also wish to have students switch groups/roles.

2 The terms *patrician* and *plebeian* continue to be used in English. Challenge students to learn not only the meanings but the connotations of these words.

3 The plebeians gained the right to elect tribunes to share in the making of laws. The tribunes could block a measure the Senate introduced by calling out, "Veto," which is Latin for "I forbid it."

Map Extension

Ask students to use the map on page 90 to answer the following questions:

- Which city was farther from Rome, Athens or Carthage? (Athens)
- Was Britain part of the Roman Republic? (no)
- What natural barriers stopped the Romans in at least four places? (mountains)

Time Box Extensions

Ask students to determine the length of each of the Punic Wars. Calculating B.C. dates can be difficult for students, and they may need additional instruction to find the correct answers. (First Punic War—23 years; Second Punic War—16 years; Third Punic War—3 years)

Ask students to determine how many years passed between the start of the First Punic War and the end of the Third Punic War. (118 years)

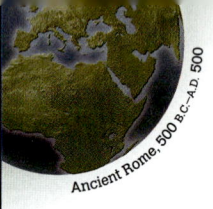

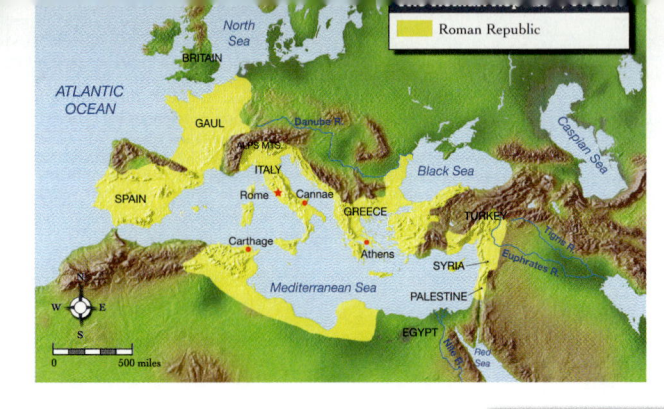

Ancient Rome, 500 B.C.–A.D. 500

Twenty-three years after the end of the First Punic War, the Carthaginian general Hannibal invaded Italy. Hannibal had been only six when Rome defeated Carthage the first time. Hannibal decided on an overland route to surprise the Romans. Carthaginian ships carried 46,000 soldiers, horses, and battle elephants to Spain. Hannibal then marched his army across what is today France and over the Alps mountains.

At Cannae, the Roman and Carthaginian armies faced off. By the end of the battle, almost 40,000 Roman soldiers had died or been wounded. Those who were left retreated. Hannibal and his remaining soldiers continued to harass the Italian peninsula. Rome had not finished the fight, however. Its generals put together another army and invaded Spain. The Romans defeated the Carthaginian colonies there and then sailed to North Africa. They took the war to the walls of Carthage itself. Hannibal and his army hastily returned from Italy, but the Romans overwhelmed them.

As a result of its victory, Rome added Spain to its provinces. Rome also allowed Carthage to remain. This was a mistake. In 149 B.C., a third war broke out between Rome and Carthage. This time Rome destroyed and burned Carthage so

Time Box

Roman Conquests

264–241 B.C.
  First Punic War; Rome won

218–202 B.C.
  Second Punic War; Rome won

149–146 B.C.
  Third Punic War; Rome won

148–146 B.C.
  Controlled Macedonia and Greece

129 B.C.
  Seized territory in Asia

44 B.C.
  Controlled Mediterranean region

90 Chapter 7

that it could never threaten Rome again. Its citizens were sold into slavery. The area was renamed Africa and became another Roman province.

Reasons for Rome's Success

Rome used both force and **diplomacy** in gaining control of the Mediterranean. The **Roman Confederation** is an example of its use of diplomacy. This example also helps explain why Rome was able to keep control for centuries.

The Roman Confederation set up a series of alliances between Rome and other areas in Italy. In return for loyalty, member city-states could run their own governments. They also received many benefits from their relationship with Rome:

1. Rome ended the rivalry among city-states on the peninsula. The result was a period of peace and prosperity.
2. Rome granted citizenship to member city-states. This gave them special privileges in the Roman Republic.
3. Member city-states were granted trading rights with Rome. The road system that Rome built throughout Italy helped the spread of trade.
4. In return, member city-states had to provide soldiers for the Roman army. However, Rome did not require that the city-states pay to support the army.

Putting It All Together

Create a concept web to describe the Roman Republic. At the center draw a large circle and label it "Roman Republic." Then add lines and smaller circles for each of the important subtopics: "Government," "Wars," and "Reasons for Success." To fill in the concept web, draw more lines and smaller circles and fill with additional information.

> **stop and think**
>
> Create a chart to compare and contrast Carthage and Rome. Work with a partner to fill in details. Then write a short paragraph explaining the similarities and differences.

The Appian Way, built in the 300s B.C., was the first major Roman road.

Stop and Think

Students' charts and paragraphs will vary but may include the following points:

- Rome had a larger army.
- Rome refused to be defeated.
- Carthage had determined generals and elephants.
- Hannibal had the advantage of a surprise overland strategy.
- Carthage had a strong navy.

Picturing History

The Appian Way, shown at the bottom of page 91, was built of paving stones fit together so well that they did not need mortar. The surface was designed for the ease and comfort of both chariot wheels and soldiers' feet. Milestones, 6 to 13 feet high, were engraved with the distance from point to point. The Appian Way was part of the network of 60,000 miles (96,500 km) that connected Rome and southern Italy.

Putting It All Together

Students' concept webs will vary but may include the following ideas:

- Government: republic, two consuls, Senate, Centuriate Assembly, Council of the Plebs, Assembly of the People
- Wars: conquests of Italy, Greece, Turkey; three Punic Wars against Carthage
- Reasons for Success: Pax Romana; diplomacy exemplified in Roman Confederation

Ancient Rome

Lesson Summary

After a series of civil wars, three leaders formed a triumvirate. Julius Caesar gained supreme power, but was assassinated. A second triumvirate formed but Octavian became the sole ruler. This was the end of the Republic and the beginning of the Empire.

The Empire expanded and brought the ideas of a law code to other nations. This time of relative peace was known as the Pax Romana, which lasted more than 100 years.

Roman men had the power in their families. Slavery was common. The Romans adopted and adapted Greek ideas and culture.

Lesson Objective

Students will learn about the political structure, expansion, and culture of the Roman Empire.

Focus Your Reading Answers

1 After a series of riots and rebellions, a group of three generals, the First Triumvirate, took power. Caesar ultimately gained control after civil wars and became a dictator. A Second Triumvirate did not last, and Octavian took power in 31 B.C. This event marked the end of the Republic.

2 The emperors were interested in expanding the Empire and in maintaining the Pax Romana.

3 Roman life borrowed from the Greeks, adapting their gods, literature, sculpture, and architecture. Slavery was common; slaves worked in households and on building projects for the Empire.

92 Chapter 7

LESSON 2

Politics and Society

Ancient Rome, 500 B.C.–A.D. 500

Thinking on Your Own

As you read this lesson, make a timeline of important dates and events. This will help you remember the sequence, or order, in which events happened.

Over time, the government of the Republic changed. The plebeians had gained many rights. However, these rights came to mean little. By the 100s B.C., the real power lay with wealthy patricians in the Senate. The result was a growing gap between rich and poor.

Reformers attempted to help the poor but had little support in the Senate. Meanwhile, there were riots among the poor and rebellions among slaves. Ambitious generals took advantage of the uncertain times. They used the armies they commanded to fight one another for power. The result was a series of civil wars between 82 and 31 B.C.

Roman slaves at work are depicted in this mosaic.

focus your reading

What caused the end of the Roman Republic and the rise of the Empire?

What kind of rulers were the Roman emperors?

What was Roman life like during the Empire?

vocabulary

successor gladiators
hereditary adopted
Pax Romana adapted

The Rise of the Empire: The First Triumvirate

In 60 B.C., three rival forces joined together—Julius Caesar, Pompey, and Crassus, the richest man in Rome. They formed the First Triumvirate, or an alliance of three people. By using their combined political power, they had Caesar elected consul. The three then took command of armies in different regions. In 53 B.C., Crassus was killed in battle. Then Pompey turned against Caesar. Prompted by Pompey, the Senate tried to force Caesar to give up his command.

92 Chapter 7

Lesson Vocabulary

Discuss each of the vocabulary terms with students. Discuss with students the root words and derivatives.

A *successor* is one who comes after. Augustus began the practice of emperors choosing a *successor*. The word comes from the Latin *success*. Other derivatives are *successful* and *successfully*.

If something is *hereditary*, it is passed down within a family. The emperor's title became *hereditary*. Words we derive from the Latin are *heritage* and *inherit*.

The *Pax Romana* was the century of peace and prosperity from A.D. 96 to 180. People, ideas, and trade goods moved freely during the *Pax Romana*.

The *gladiators* fought in Roman arenas as public amusement. Many *gladiators* were slaves captured in war. If something is *adopted*, it is taken as belonging to oneself. The Romans *adopted* much of Greek culture. Things that are *adapted* are changed. The Romans also *adapted* what they borrowed from the Greeks.

Caesar and his army had just fought and won much of Gaul—modern-day France. Instead of returning alone, a victorious Caesar marched his army to Rome. A civil war with Pompey's troops broke out. Caesar defeated Pompey and became dictator in 45 B.C. Caesar attempted a series of reforms, including taking land from the wealthy and giving it to veterans of his army. He also put the jobless to work on public building projects. In an effort to reduce the Senate's power, Caesar enlarged the Senate to 900 members. Angered by his actions, a group of senators killed him in 44 B.C.

The Second Triumvirate

Allies of Caesar formed the Second Triumvirate after his death. Caesar's nephew Octavian joined with Mark Antony, who had been consul with Caesar in 44 B.C., and Lepidus, who had been an officer under Caesar's command. The Second Triumvirate lasted only a short time. By 37 B.C., Octavian and Antony had defeated Lepidus. They split the Roman territory into two regions. Octavian ruled the western part and Antony ruled the eastern part.

Tiberius and Gaius Gracchus

Gracchus brothers, Tiberius (163–133 B.C.) and Gaius -121 B.C.), belonged to one of the most important cian families in Rome. However, they chose to work on lf of the poor. They saw the declining number of small ers as the basis of the Republic's problems. The ion was to give public land to small farmers who had heir land. However, much of the public land was dy divided among senators.

133 B.C., Tiberius was elected a tribune. He made a proposal to the Council of s to redistribute land. The Council passed the law and the government began ng over land to people without land. However, Tiberius had made enemies ng the senators. When he tried to run for a second term, he and 300 orters were killed in an election riot.

123 and 122 B.C., Gaius was elected tribune. Like his brother, he wanted public given to the poor. He also sponsored a program to buy grain and sell it to the at a reduced price. His ideas cost him re-election in 121 B.C. The Senate then pted to repeal, or undo, his reforms. Riots broke out and he was killed. Some of his supporters were executed.

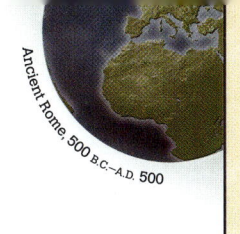

Picturing History

In 46 B.C., Julius Caesar, pictured at the top of page 93, was an emperor who brought change to Rome. One of the things he did was institute the Julian calendar, devised by Sosigenes, a mathematician. The calendar had 365 days, divided into 12 months. Like modern western calendars, it added a leap day every four years. To make the calendar work, 67 days were added during what became known as the Year of Confusion.

Biography Extension

The Gracchus brothers wanted to enforce existing laws about the amount of land that could legally be owned. Roman law set the limit at 500 acres, plus 250 acres for each of as many as two sons, for a total of 1,000 acres. Some senators, however, held vast estates. Their increasing use of slave labor also harmed the landless farm workers who were replaced by slaves.

Bio Facts

Tiberius Sempronius Gracchus

- Born 163 B.C.
- Son of a Roman aristocrat. His mother was the daughter of the man who conquered Hannibal.
- Natural talent in public speaking was enhanced by his Greek education.
- Military service was in Carthage and Spain.
- Elected tribune in 133 B.C. and proposed land reforms unpopular with the aristocracy.
- Angered by his decision to seek reelection, a group of senators started a riot in which Tiberius was clubbed to death.

Gaius Sempronius Gracchus

- Born 154 B.C.
- Protested against a senator accused in his brother's death.
- Enforced the land laws his brother had passed.
- Served in the military before becoming a quaestor, a magistrate's position associated with financial matters.
- Elected a tribune twice, beginning in 123 B.C.
- Spent two months in Carthage, North Africa, setting up a colony of 6,000.
- Committed suicide during a massacre of the area to which he had retired.

Ancient Rome

Stop and Think

Students' answers will vary but may include the following points:

- A desire for power is often shown through military campaigns. Caesar was a conquering general who could gain power through the loyalty of his troops.
- Pompey tried to gain power through influencing the Senate after turning on Caesar following the death of Crassus.
- Octavian's rivalry with both Lepidus and Antony led to his seizing power.

Map Extension

Ask students to use the map on page 94 to answer the following questions:

- What major city was added to the Empire during Trajan's expansion? (Babylon)
- Which rivers provided a natural barrier on the north? (Rhine and Danube Rivers)
- In what two directions did the Roman Empire grow under Trajan? (farther east into Armenia and southwest to Mauritania on the North African coast)

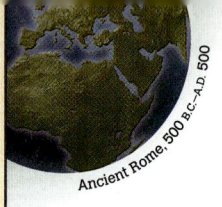

But there was to be no peace between the rivals. In 31 B.C., Octavian defeated Antony and seized power for himself. Octavian was given the title "Caesar Augustus," meaning "honored one." The year 31 B.C. marks the end of the Republic and the beginning of the Empire.

Augustus changed the way leaders were chosen. The Senate and the Centuriate Assembly had elected two consuls yearly. Augustus established a new system. The emperor would choose his **successor** from his own family. The title of emperor would be **hereditary**. It would be passed down from one man to another within a family. No longer would a man have to earn the right to be elected. The Senate would never again be so powerful.

Expansion and Peace

Under Augustus and later emperors, Rome continued to expand its borders. Emperor Claudius, who ruled from A.D. 41 to 54, added Britain to the Empire. He also granted Roman citizenship to people in the Roman provinces. The Empire reached its largest territory under Emperor Trajan, who ruled from 98 to 117.

One of the greatest achievements of the Roman Empire was the **Pax Romana**. This is the name given to about 100 years of peace and prosperity. It began with Emperor Nerva in 96 and ended in 180 with the death of Emperor Marcus Aurelius. During this time, people, trade goods, and ideas moved freely back and forth along the Empire's trading network. The peace ended with another civil war. The next 300 years saw periods of war and peace and a slow decline of Roman power.

One of the most important and lasting

stop and think

Julius Caesar, Pomp[ey], and Octavian were ambitious men. How did they use their ambition to gain power? Talk over y[our] ideas with a partne[r]. Then write a bullete[d] list of ideas to expla[in] how ambition cause[d] these men to act in [a] certain way.

Extension

Have students interested in military science, architecture, or sculpture use the library or Internet resources to find out about Trajan's Column. Trajan's Column stands in Rome today. Ask students to explain to the class how this column helps us know more about military life in the first century.

Picturing History

The mosaic on page 92 shows slaves at work. Mosaics depicted not only historic events but also everyday life.

94 Chapter 7

Achievements of the Romans

dome
first to use concrete for large buildings
improved on design of Etruscan arch
improved on Greek designs for columns
aqueduct, a bridge-like structure to carry water great distances
roads and bridges — The Roman Empire was connected by 50,000 miles of roads.

contributions of the Roman Empire was its law code. As Rome extended its rule beyond the borders of Italy, it developed the Law of Nations. Among its basic principles were (1) people are innocent until proved guilty and (2) people may defend themselves before a judge. In the early 200s, Roman judges put together law books for use by judges in all parts of the Empire.

Roman Society and Culture

Under the Republic, the father and husband had absolute authority in the family. Over time, this changed and women gained more freedom.

Upper-class boys and girls were taught to read and write. In addition, boys learned Roman law and moral principles. For girls, education ended when they got married. Most girls married between the ages of 12 and 14. By law, boys could marry at 14 but were usually older.

Romans enslaved people that they captured in war. Slaves were used for entertainment in Roman arenas. Trained as **gladiators**, they fought each other to the death while Romans cheered. Most slaves, however, labored on farms or on public building projects. They are the ones who built the Roman roads, bridges, aqueducts, temples, and arenas.

The Romans borrowed much from Greek civilization. Greek styles in sculpture and architecture were **adopted** by the Romans and **adapted**, or changed, to make them their own. In literature, the Romans borrowed Greek ideas, too. The poet Virgil wrote the *Aeneid* to give Romans the same kind of epic story as the Greeks had in the *Odyssey*. The Roman historian Livy wrote a 142-volume history of Rome.

Putting It All Together

At the beginning of this lesson you began creating a timeline of events. Use this timeline to develop a short essay about the Roman Empire. Select several key events and use them as the main ideas of your essay.

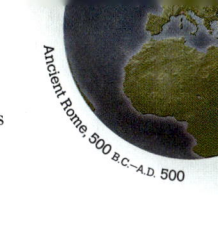

Hadrian's Wall marked the northern boundary of the Roman Empire in Britain.

Chart Extension

Divide the class into six small groups. Assign each group one of the achievements of the Romans. Have group members do research to learn more about the assigned achievement. Give each group time to make a presentation to the rest of the class using pictures, maps, and drawings.

Picturing History

Hadrian's Wall, pictured on page 95, extended about 75 miles (118 km) along Britain's northern border. In A.D. 122, Hadrian commanded the 20-foot-high wall be built to defend against Scotland's Caledonians, who had not been conquered. Legionnaires built the wall, and auxiliaries guarded it from within the 14 forts placed at intervals along the wall. Parts of the wall remain standing today.

Putting It All Together

Students' timelines and essays will vary but may include the following events:

- 100s B.C. Senate holds real power
- 82–31 B.C. civil wars
- 60 B.C. First Triumvirate
- 45 B.C. Caesar becomes dictator
- 44 B.C. Second Triumvirate
- 37 B.C. Octavian and Antony rule
- 31 B.C. Octavian becomes sole ruler; Republic ends and Empire begins
- 41–54 B.C. Claudius rules, adds Britain to Empire
- A.D. 98–117 Empire reaches its greatest size under Trajan
- A.D. 96–180 Pax Romana

Lesson Summary

The Empire gradually declined over centuries. The causes were economic, social, political, and military. The economic causes involved the loss of population due to civil wars, plague, and invasions. Taxes continued to be high to feed and entertain the poor who fled to the cities when they lost their land because of those same taxes.

The social causes included the loss of adherence to the traditional Roman values of duty and loyalty.

The division of the Empire into east and west for more efficient rule was one political cause of the fall of the Empire.

The invasion of many different tribes at many points of the Empire led to further decline, until the Empire collapsed in 476.

Lesson Objective

Students will learn about the causes of the end of the Roman Empire.

Focus Your Reading Answers

1 Taxes were high to meet the expenses of government and the military. People died of plague, so there were fewer people to pay taxes. When farmers lost their land, they moved to cities, where they were given food and free admission to the circuses. This added to the Empire's expenses, so taxes grew higher; more farmers lost land, and the spiral continued downward.

Ancient Rome, 500 B.C.–A.D. 500

LESSON 3

The Fall of the Roman Empire

Thinking on Your Own

Create a table with four columns. Label the table "Causes for the Fall of the Roman Empire." Label the columns "Military," "Political," "Social," and "Economic." As you read the lesson, fill in the columns with information about the decline of the Empire.

The decline and fall of the Roman Empire in the west took place over a long period of time. It was more a gradual loss of its power over the centuries than a quick collapse in a few decades. There were many reasons for the slow loss of Rome's power: economic, social, political, and military. All of these reasons mixed together to create trouble for the Empire.

focus your reading

How did the tax policies of the emperors weaken the Empire?

Why did the lack of traditional values weaken the Empire?

How did political problems weaken the Empire?

How did nomadic people weaken the Empire?

vocabulary

plague   values

Economic Causes

As the Roman Empire expanded, so did its expenses. The new provinces had to be governed, and this meant new public officials. Roman soldiers had to keep the newly conquered people from rebelling. To pay these expenses, emperors imposed high taxes.

At the same time, the population of the Empire was declining. Civil wars, invasions by nomadic people, and **plague** killed many people. Plague is a deadly disease that spreads quickly. As a result, there were fewer people to pay taxes. More and more small farmers lost their lands when they could not pay their debts or their taxes. Toward the end of the Empire, they moved to cities.

The Colosseum in Rome was the site of "bread and circuses."

Focus Your Reading Answers, continued

2 Traditional Roman values such as loyalty and duty became less important. The army was composed not of citizen-soldiers, but of men who joined for pay. They consequently felt less loyal. Local people gradually replaced Romans as rulers. Wealthy families became more interested in simply increasing their wealth than in serving the Empire.

3 Political problems weakened the Empire by splitting the power between east and west. Constantinople became wealthy, even as Rome and the western part of the Empire declined. Civil wars weakened the Empire by costing money and lives.

4 Foreign invaders slowly took control of the edges of the Empire, defeating Romans and settling on territories in Britain, North Africa, and Spain. Ultimately, nomadic tribes from Gaul and Asia invaded Rome. After several attempts in A.D. 476, the Visigoths succeeded in capturing Rome, and Odoacer declared himself king.

96 Chapter 7

To keep the poor and jobless in the cities from rebelling, emperors began to give out food. They also arranged entertainment for city residents. This practice of giving food and entertainment came to be known as "bread and circuses." All this free food and entertainment cost money. The result was higher taxes, which meant more farmers became landless, and so the cycle continued.

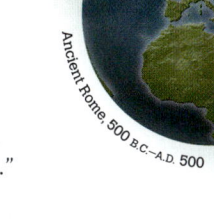

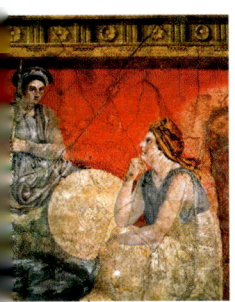

Social Causes

Loyalty and duty to one another and to the government had been two important **values**—or principles—of the early Republic. Over the centuries, such values became less important.

For example, the Roman army had once been made up of citizen soldiers. After the 200s, many soldiers were non-Romans. They worked for pay, not out of loyalty to the Empire. As new provinces joined the Empire, many local officials remained in place. This meant that in many provinces, there were few Romans in the government. In time, even the emperor was a non-Roman.

The lack of traditional values was also evident among the wealthy. With increased trade, wealthy patrician families became wealthier. Eventually the men of these families became less interested in providing leadership for the government. They were more interested in leading lives of luxury and idleness.

Upper-class women in ancient Rome had slaves do their work.

Political Causes

By the time of Emperor Diocletian, the Empire had become too large to rule efficiently. In 293, he divided it into an eastern and a western empire. He ruled the eastern part. Constantine succeeded him in 312. By 324, Constantine had become the sole ruler. However, he did not rule from Rome. He built a new capital in what is today Turkey. His city, Constantinople, became the gateway to trade with Asia. It grew wealthy while the western part of the Empire became poorer and weaker.

stop and think
Romans valued loyalty and duty to one another. What do these values mean? Write a definition of each value and give an example for each one. Share your ideas with a partner and revise your definition if needed.

Ancient Rome, 500 B.C.–A.D. 500

Picturing History
The picture of the mosaic on page 97 depicts a slave working in a wealthy Roman household with her mistress.

Slaves cleaned, cooked, took care of the children, and, in some cases, educated the children of the wealthy classes.

Stop and Think
Students' definitions will vary.

Lesson Vocabulary
Discuss each of the vocabulary terms with students.

A *plague* is a fast-spreading, deadly disease. *Plague* caused the population decline of the Empire.

Another word for *values* is principles. Two *values* of traditional Rome were duty and loyalty.

Ancient Rome 97

Picturing History
The emperor Vespasian came to power in A.D. 69 following an eighteen-month period in which four emperors had died. To ensure his own safety, Vespasian decided to build something for the people to enjoy. The Colosseum, shown at the bottom of page 96, was built on the site of Nero's hated Golden House, of which few rooms have survived. The Colosseum opened the year after Vespasian's death, in A.D. 80.

Extension
Ask students to find out ways, such as the entry and seating, in which modern sports stadiums follow practices used in the Colosseum. Have students present their findings by using the Student Presentation Builder on the student CD.

Ancient Rome 97

Picturing History

The Emperor Constantine, shown on page 98, came to power in the midst of early fourth-century intrigue. A group of four rulers tried to hold the Empire together after Diocletian abdicated. Constantine grew stronger while in Gaul and Britain. Constantine's troops proclaimed their loyalty to him. In 313, he marched his troops to Rome. There he defeated Maxentius, who drowned in the river after falling off Milvian Bridge. Constantine thus became sole ruler of the western part of the Empire. In 322, he defeated his brother-in-law Licinius, ruler of the eastern part of the Empire and chief rival, becoming sole emperor until his death in 337.

Map Extension

Ask students to use the map on page 98 to answer the following questions:

- Which tribes attacked Britain? (Angles/Saxons)
- Which tribe attacked from the east? (the Huns)
- What region did the Franks attack? (Gaul)

Putting It All Together

Students' T-charts will vary but should include facts relating to economic, societal, political, and military events and outcomes.

Ancient Rome, 500 B.C.–A.D. 500

Civil war also weakened the Empire. Between 235 and 284, Rome had 22 emperors. The civil wars that raged during the later years of the Empire had serious results. First, the civil wars cost the government precious tax money. Second, they killed thousands of soldiers that could have been better used against the Empire's outside enemies. Third, they left the borders open to those enemies.

Military Causes

Beginning in the A.D. 200s, Germanic peoples from the north and east migrated into the Empire. Among the first nomadic invaders were Visigoths from around the Black Sea. They moved south and west through much of the Roman Empire, settling on land from Greece to Spain. In the 400s, the Vandals moved west across the Empire to Spain. Then they took their campaign into the Roman provinces in North Africa. From there they sailed to Italy and invaded Rome in 455.

Other invaders of the 400s were the Angles and Saxons from what is today Germany. They crossed the North Sea to invade Britain and defeat the Roman army.

Perhaps the fiercest invaders were not Germanic peoples, but the Huns from Central Asia. Between 441 and 450, they swept into Gaul, Italy, and Greece under their leader Attila. Unlike the Germanic peoples, the Huns did not stay.

The final blow came from the Visigoths. In 410, they had invaded Rome. In 476, Odoacer overthrew the emperor and proclaimed himself king. This event marks the end of the Roman Empire.

Emperor Constantine

Invasions of the Roman Empire, 200 to 500
Western Roman Empire — Vandals — Franks — Angles/Saxons
Eastern Roman Empire — Huns — Visigoths

Putting It All Together

Create a T-chart to show the events and outcomes for the decline and fall of the Roman Empire. Fill in your chart. Share it with a partner to make sure that you listed all the reasons.

Extension

Alaric was the Visigoth king who invaded Rome in 410. He had been a volunteer in the Roman army, rising to the level of commander. He left the army to become king. Because he was a Christian, he prevented his invading army from abusing the women, stealing Christian objects, or destroying churches. This command saved Rome from complete destruction during three days of burning and pillaging. Have students use library resources or the Internet to research objects that were saved, such as busts of emperors, buildings, mosaics, and the like. Have them create a poster to explain their objects to the class.

Chapter 7

LESSON 4

The Rise and Spread of Christianity

Ancient Rome, 500 B.C.–A.D. 500

Thinking on Your Own

Look at the subheadings in this lesson. Turn each into a question. Write the questions in your notebook. Write the answers as you read the lesson.

The Roman government supported an official state religion. It centered on the worship of various male and female deities. The Romans borrowed many of their deities from the people they conquered. For example, the chief Roman god was Jupiter, the god of thunder and the skies. He was similar to Zeus, the chief god of the Greeks.

focus your reading

What was the central message of Jesus' teachings?

Why were early Christians persecuted by the Romans?

Why did Christianity appeal to so many people?

vocabulary

messiah
Gospels
apostles
persecute
martyrs
tolerance
charity

The Romans allowed the people they conquered to keep their own religions. As a result, the Jews in Judaea continued to practice Judaism after the Roman conquest. Many Jews were awaiting the coming of the **messiah**, the one sent by God to lead the Jews to freedom. He would fulfill the promise made to the Jewish people by God.

Jesus and His Teachings

Some Jews believed that a man named Jesus, a humble carpenter's son from Nazareth, was the messiah. Jesus began preaching around the age of 30. Most of what we know about him comes from the **Gospels**. These records of Jesus' life and teachings were written by four of his closest followers, who were known as **apostles**. The Gospels make up the first four

Ancient Rome | 99

Lesson Summary

The official state religion of Rome supported worship of many gods. The Roman government also practiced tolerance toward the religions of conquered people.

To many people, Jesus seemed to be the messiah. The records of his life make up the first four books of the New Testament. Jesus' teachings were rooted in the Judaic religion.

Jesus' apostles spread his teachings throughout the Empire, despite some persecution and martyrdom. The religion spread because of its appeal to the poor, its similarity to ideas of Greek philosophy, and its offer of a caring community.

Lesson Objective

Students will learn about the beginnings of Christianity and its broad appeal.

Focus Your Reading Answers

1 Love of God and each other was a central teaching of Jesus, who also taught his followers to help others. His teaching built on the Jewish law.

2 The early Christians were considered disloyal because they did not worship the emperor or Roman gods.

3 Christianity appealed to people for three main reasons. Jesus' message was attractive to the poor and the persecuted. His ideas also were familiar to people, because they resembled those of Greek philosophers. People feel a need to be part of a group, and Christianity offered community.

Lesson Vocabulary

Discuss each of the vocabulary terms with students. Discuss with students words we use today that are derived from the Latin.

A *messiah* is a person sent by God to be a deliverer. The Jewish people were waiting for a *messiah* when Jesus began teaching. A *Gospel* is a written record of Jesus' life. The Christian Bible has four *Gospels*. The *apostles* were Jesus' closest followers. One of the *apostles* betrayed Jesus. The *martyrs* were people who were killed because of their faith. The *martyrs* often met their deaths in the Colosseum.

Tolerance is the willingness to put up with something. The Edict of Milan made religious *tolerance* the official policy of the Roman Empire. A lack of *toleration* can lead to *persecution*. To *persecute* is to harass over a long period of time. Religious and ethnic groups are often the victims of *persecution*.

Charity originally meant kindness to others. Jesus preached the need for *charity*.

Ancient Rome | 99

Picturing History

The illustration at the top of page 100 depicts a miracle recounted in the Gospel of Luke, chapter 5. Jesus told some professional fishermen, including Peter, whose boat he had been using as a platform from which to teach, to go out and let down their nets for a great catch of fish. Peter told Jesus that they had struggled all night and caught nothing. However, when they obeyed and let down the nets, there were so many fish that the boat nearly sank. Peter and his partners, James and John, then left everything to follow Jesus.

Picturing History

Saint Peter, pictured at left on page 100, is shown carrying a large key, a symbol of his authority. In Matthew's Gospel (chapter 16, verse 18), Jesus tells Peter that he has been given the keys of the kingdom of heaven. This is the origin of the popular idea that Peter is heaven's gatekeeper. The key's design incorporates both a cross and a trefoil, the symbol of the Trinity.

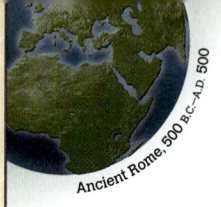

Ancient Rome, 500 B.C.–A.D. 500

books of the New Testament of the Christian Bible.

Jesus' message was based on the teachings of Judaism. He preached belief in one God and obedience to the Ten Commandments. But he also added new ideas. Love of God and love of one another were central to his message. He taught that people should help one another. If people fulfilled their duty, then the Kingdom of Heaven would appear on Earth.

Jesus' teachings attracted large crowds wherever he went. In time, he came to the attention of Roman officials. They feared he might lead the Jews in a revolt. Finally, one of Jesus' apostles, Judas, betrayed him to the authorities. Jesus was arrested, tried, and crucified. His followers declared that Jesus had risen from the dead and ascended into heaven.

Followers of Jesus believe he performed miracles

St. Peter

The Beginning of the Christian Church

The apostles spread the message of Jesus. At first, they continued his work among the Jews in Judaea. Within a short time, however, they moved throughout the Roman Empire spreading Jesus' word and converting non-Jews. Jesus became known as the Christ from the Greek word meaning "anointed one, the messiah."

At first, Christians attracted little attention from Roman officials. However, during the reign of Emperor Nero from 54 to 68, the policy changed. The government began to **persecute** Christians. The Romans thought they were disloyal. Many Christians, known as **martyrs**, met horrible deaths from torture. During the next two centuries there were fewer persecutions.

The Christian Church continued to grow and make converts. One of the most important was the Roman Emperor Constantine. In 313, by the Edict of Milan, he made **tolerance** of Christianity the official policy of the Roman Empire. Then in 381, Theodosius the Great made Christianity the official religion of the Roman Empire.

100 Chapter 7

Picturing History

Jupiter, shown at the top of page 99, was the main Roman god and Juno's husband. He was in charge of weather, light, and the sky, as well as of the state.

Juno, pictured below him on page 99, was the queen of heaven. She was goddess of women, marriage, childbirth, and light.

Extension

Invite students who are interested in mythology to prepare a visual aid showing the Greek and Roman pantheon. Ask them to show how the Romans adopted or adapted Greek gods.

---

100 Chapter 7

stop and think

Create a concept web that explains the beginnings of Christianity. Include names and important events. Share your web with a partner.

Spread of Christianity

Even while Christians were being persecuted, many people converted to Christianity. Once the persecutions ended, Christianity spread quickly. The system of Roman roads, the Roman trading network, and the size of the Empire itself helped Christian missionaries spread the word.

The appeal of Christianity was based on three main causes. First, the message of Jesus attracted the poor and the persecuted. Jesus preached **charity**, or kindness to one another, on Earth and promised equality and a better life after death.

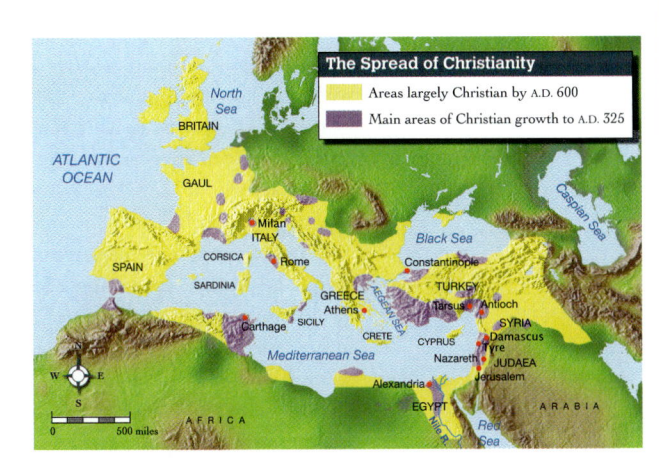

Second, some of the teachings were similar to the ideas of Plato and other Greek philosophers. They appealed to educated people because they were already familiar with the ideas.

Third, people have a need to belong to groups. The Christian Church offered a way to fill this need. Christians built a sense of community by worshiping together and by working together to help the poor and sick.

Putting It All Together

Write a short essay about the beginning and spread of Christianity. Use details from the questions and answers you wrote at the beginning of this lesson, as well as the information from your concept web.

Ancient Rome 101

Stop and Think

Students' concept webs will vary but may include the following ideas:

- Jesus of Nazareth begins preaching at age 30.
- Jesus is betrayed and crucified.
- Apostles move throughout Empire making converts.
- Persecution of Christians under Nero, A.D. 54–68.
- Constantine makes tolerance the official policy of Rome with the Edict of Milan in 313.
- Theodosius the Great makes Christianity the official religion of the Roman Empire, 381.

Map Extension

Ask students to use the map on page 101 to answer the following questions:

- How far west had Christianity spread by A.D. 600? (Spain and Britain)
- Which city on the map represents the Christian city farthest south? (Alexandria, in Egypt)
- Where were the largest areas of growth up to A.D. 325? (eastern shores of Mediterranean, North Africa)
- What direction did Christianity spread from Jerusalem? (north, south, west)

Putting It All Together

Essays will vary but should include information from the chapter about the early years of Christianity.

Extension

Christians found the Greek philosophies of the Stoics and the Platonists helpful in expressing their faith. Stoics taught adherence to a universal law as the path to reason. They stressed the virtues of justice, self-control, courage, and moral insight. They also criticized the religion of their time, which did not seem to call people to a life of virtue. Both Plato and his teacher, Socrates, believed in a perfect and unchangeable supreme being. They taught a world of unchanging truth. They also believed the soul was immortal. Christians adapted these ideas as they tried to communicate their message.

Chapter Review

1 Students' headlines will vary. Possible responses include:

(a) Romans Overthrow Etruscans!
New Nation Begins!

(b) Plebeians Set Up Own Council
Council to Pass Laws for Plebeians

(c) Romans Defeat Carthage
Expand Provinces into North Africa

(d) Civil War Ends!
Octavian Rules as Caesar Augustus

2 Students' speeches will vary but should be in support of Tiberius Gracchus' land policy reforms.

Chapter Summary

- The Romans set up a **republic**. **Patricians** and **plebeians** fought for political power.
- Two **consuls** ran the government of Rome. The Senate ensured that the laws and orders of the consuls were carried out.
- Rome used **diplomacy** and force to extend its power. An example of its diplomacy was the **Roman Confederation**.
- For a time, Julius Caesar took control as a dictator. He was killed by opponents in the Senate.
- The **Pax Romana** was a period of peace.
- Romans **adopted** many ideas from the cultures they conquered and **adapted** them to their needs. **Gladiators** were used for entertainment.
- Power was taken away from the Senate and emperors chose their own **successors**. The title of emperor was **hereditary**.
- The decline and fall of the Roman Empire took place over many years. The major reasons were military, political, social (**values**), and economic.
- The **plague** killed many in the Empire.
- Jesus was considered the **messiah** by some Jews. Much of what we know about Jesus comes from the **Gospels**. His teachings about **charity** and **tolerance** for one another attracted many people.
- The **apostles** and other followers spread Jesus' teachings. For a time, Christians were **persecuted** by the government. Many died as **martyrs**.

Chapter Review

1 Write two-line headlines to describe (a) the end of Etruscan rule, (b) right of the plebeians to hold office, (c) Punic Wars, and (d) end of the Republic.

2 Imagine you are a senator who supports Tiberius Gracchus' land proposal. Write a speech asking your fellow senators to vote for the proposal.

Novel Connections

Below is a list of books that relate to the time period covered in this chapter. The numbers in parentheses indicate the related Thematic Strands of the National Council for the Social Studies (NCSS).

Peter Chrisp. *The Colosseum*. Raintree Steck-Vaughn, 1997. (I, III, V, IX)

Simon James. *Ancient Rome*. Rev. ed. DK Publishing, 2004. (I, III, VIII)

Rita J. Markel. *Your Travel Guide to Ancient Rome*. Lerner Publications Company, 2004. (I, II, III, VIII, IX)

Marissa Moss. *Galen: My Life in Imperial Rome*. Harcourt, 2002. (I, III, V, VI)

Richard Watkins. *Gladiator*. Houghton Mifflin Company, 1997. (I, III, VI, IX)

Henry Winterfeld. *Detectives in Togas*. Harcourt, 2002. (I, III)

Skill Builder

Analyzing Cause and Effect

The cause is what makes something happen. The effect is what happens—or the outcome of the cause. For example:

The rivalry between Rome and Carthage resulted in the Punic Wars.

        Cause: rivalry   Effect: Punic Wars

It is easy to identify the cause and the effect in this sentence because the verb *resulted* signals the relationship between rivalry and Punic Wars. The word *because* in the last sentence is another cause-and-effect signal word. But in this case, the cause and the effect are not easy to identify.

Cause: the verb *resulted* signals the relationship   Effect: easy to identify the cause and effect in this sentence

The concept webs you created in this chapter are one way to determine cause-and-effect relationships. Another way is to use a flowchart. Sometimes the effect of one event is the cause of another. Then your flowchart would look like this:

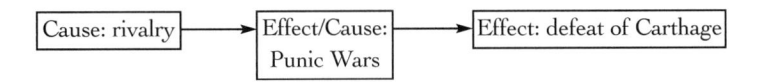

| Cause: rivalry | → | Effect/Cause: Punic Wars | → | Effect: defeat of Carthage |

Use the information about the decline and fall of the Roman Empire to complete these activities.

1. Write a sentence for each of the three Punic Wars. Explain the cause and effect for each war.

2. Write three sentences describing three cause-and-effect relationships that weakened the Roman Empire. Create a cause-and-effect flowchart for each one.

3. Write sentences explaining three causes of the appeal of Christianity. Create a flowchart to show the causes and effect.

Ancient Rome

Classroom Discussion

Discuss with students some of the broader topics covered in this chapter.

- What should qualify a person to hold political office?
- How can nations work together, as the Roman Confederation did, for the good of all the nations?
- What are some steps we could take to prevent a person's ambition from overruling democratic principles?
- In what ways do cultures today share and adapt ideas?

Skill Builder

1. Sentences will vary. Possible answers:
   First Punic War
   Rivalry for trade led Rome to conquer its first foreign territories.
   Second Punic War
   Revenge caused Rome to expand its territory.
   Third Punic War
   Out of revenge, Rome took over Carthage.

2. Sentences and flowcharts will vary. Possible sentences:
   Sentence 1: Civil wars caused increased taxes, deaths, and open borders, which in turn caused a weakening of the Empire.

   Cause: civil wars
   Effect/Cause: taxes, deaths, borders left open
   Effect: weakened Empire

   Sentence 2: Invading tribes caused a loss of territory and thus a decline in the Empire.

   Cause: invading tribes
   Effect/Cause: territory lost
   Effect: decline of Empire

   Sentence 3: The loss of farmland caused people to move to the cities to receive free food, which increased taxes.

   Cause: people losing farmland
   Effect/Cause: many more come to cities and are given free food
   Effect: taxes increase to feed and entertain the poor

3. Possible answers:
   Causes:
   - Many in cities were poor.
   - People had time for reading.
   - People needed to belong to groups.
   Effect: Christianity spread quickly.

Ancient Rome

Unit Objectives

After studying this unit, students will be able to

- summarize the major events of the Byzantine Empire and their relationship to the founding of Russia
- describe the beginning and spread of Islam
- compare and contrast the civilizations of Africa
- explain the rise and fall of empires in Central and South America
- identify the cultures of China, Japan, Korea, and India

Unit 3 focuses on world civilizations before, during, and after the medieval age.

Chapter 8, The Byzantine Empire, examines the Christian empire in present-day Turkey and the beginnings of Russia.

Chapter 9, Islam and Muslim Civilizations, discusses the revelations given to Muhammad and the growth of the Islamic Empire.

Chapter 10, Civilizations of Africa, explores the kingdoms of Africa.

Chapter 11, The Americas, presents the development of the Mayan, Inca, and Aztec civilizations.

Chapter 12, The Spread of Cultures in Asia, describes the worlds of China, Japan, Korea, and India.

Getting Started

Ask a volunteer to read aloud the information on page 104. Ask students to write in their notebooks a list of all the proper nouns in the paragraphs. As they read Unit 3, ask them to use the list to take notes about the important people, places, and events discussed.

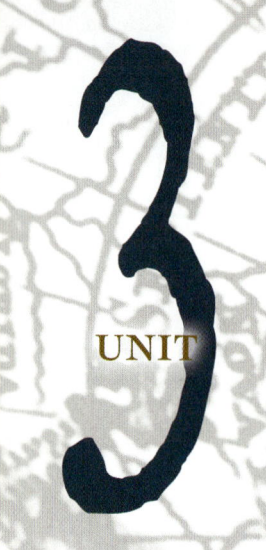

UNIT 3
LATER WORLD CIVILIZATIONS

After the fall of the Roman Empire, new empires and kingdoms rose and fell in Europe. The Roman Empire in the East, known as the Byzantine Empire, continued for another thousand years. Kingdoms and empires also began and ended in other parts of the world. In West Africa, mighty empires grew up along trade routes. China spread its influence east to Korea and Japan while continuing to trade with Europe. Mongols, a fierce warrior people from Central Asia, swept across China and seized power for a time.

During the 600s, the prophet Muhammad began to preach a new religion, Islam. In less than a century, his followers spread Islam throughout the Arabian Peninsula and were moving throughout the Mediterranean region.

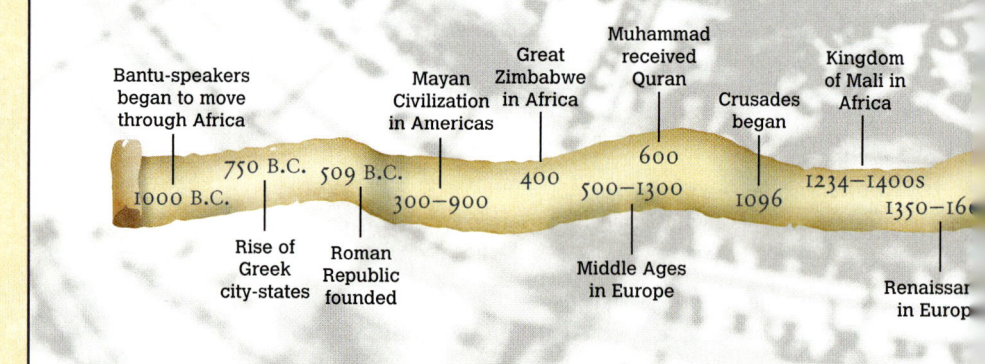

Timeline:
- 1000 B.C. — Bantu-speakers began to move through Africa
- 750 B.C. — Rise of Greek city-states
- 509 B.C. — Roman Republic founded
- 300–900 — Mayan Civilization in Americas
- 400 — Great Zimbabwe in Africa
- 500–1300 — Middle Ages in Europe
- 600 — Muhammad received Quran
- 1096 — Crusades began
- 1234–1400s — Kingdom of Mali in Africa
- 1350–16.. — Renaissance in Europe

Timeline Extension

Ask students to use the timeline to preview each chapter in the unit. Then have them answer the following questions:

- Did Columbus sail to the Americas before or after the Renaissance began in Europe?
- Which lasted longer, the Mayan civilization in the Americas or the Mogul Empire in India?
- How much time elapsed between the founding of Great Zimbabwe and the Kingdom of Mali?
- In what year did Muhammad receive the Quran text?

104 Unit 3

How did the West African kingdoms become wealthy?

How do the Five Pillars of Islam guide the life of Muslims?

How did the Incas rule over their vast empire?

Collage Answers

1 West African kingdoms became wealthy through trading in salt and gold.

2 The Five Pillars of Islam guide the lives of Muslims by offering concrete external observances to follow.

3 The Incas ruled over their empire with a system of regents, roads, and runners.

Collage Extension

Use the images and questions on page 105 to preview the unit. Ask students to imagine what the questions and pictures suggest they will learn about later world civilizations.

Timeline

- Aztec Empire Mexico: 25–1521
- Yi Dynasty in Korea: 1392–1910
- Inca Empire in South America: 1438–1535
- Ottomans conquered Constantinople: 1453
- Columbus sailed to Americas: 1492
- Mogul Empire in India: 1526–1857
- Reformation in Europe: 1517–1600
- Iroquois League: c.1570
- Tokugawa Shogunate in Japan: 1603–1867
- Korea became tribute state of China: 1630–1895

Picturing History

The images on page 105 represent people and places that will be discussed in Unit 3.

1 The top image is a picture of the rounded huts that are typical of a West African village. This one is in modern-day Timbuktu.

2 This image shows a Muslim muezzin (crier) calling people to pray.

3 The photograph is of the Incan site Machu Picchu. This ancient city was built high in the Andes Mountains.

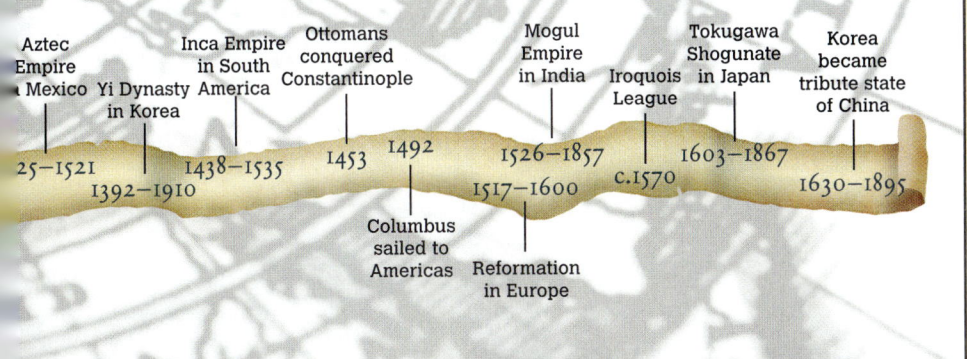

Measuring Time

Explain to students that Chapter 8 focuses on the Byzantine Empire, the eastern continuation of the Roman Empire. The events of that era appear on page 104 of the timeline.

Chapter 9 examines the development and growth of Islam. The events of that time are also on page 104.

Chapter 10 discusses African civilizations. The events that marked that period are on page 104 of the timeline.

Chapter 11 describes the Native-American civilizations. The events of that era are on pages 104 and 105 of the timeline.

Chapter 12 examines the growth of cultures in Asia. The events surrounding that growth are recorded on page 105 of the timeline.

Later World Civilizations

Chapter 8

THE BYZANTINE EMPIRE

(330–1618)

Getting Focused

Skim this chapter to predict what you will be learning
- Read the lesson titles and subheadings.
- Look at the illustrations and read the captions.
- Examine the maps.
- Review the vocabulary words and terms.

This chapter is about the Byzantine Empire and its neighboring areas. Create a concept web with "Byzantine Empire" in the center. As you read, add notes about Constantine, Justinian, religion, daily life, and the development of Russia. Remember to add the Byzantine Empire and Russia to the world map you began in Chapter 4.

Chapter Summary
Refer to page 116 for a summary of Chapter 8.

Related Transparencies

T-1 World Map
T-2 Outline World Map
T-18 Three-Column Chart
T-19 Venn Diagram

Key Blacklines

Primary Source—A Portrait of the Emperor Justinian

CD Extension

Encourage students to use the reading comprehension, vocabulary reinforcement, and interactive timeline activities on the student CD.

Getting Focused

Throughout the reading of the chapter, have students work together in pairs or small groups to check their concept webs.

Picturing History

Hagia Sophia has been a Christian church and a Muslim mosque and is now a museum. Point out to students that the minarets at the corners date from when the building was a mosque. The minarets were the towers from which people were called to prayer five times per day.

Pre-Reading Discussion

1 Ask students what city they would choose to be the capital of the nation in place of Washington, D.C. Talk with them about their choices and the implications of those choices for both the present and new capital cities.

2 Have students imagine that they do not have a written language. Ask them to figure out some of the steps that would be needed to create a written language.

106 Chapter 8

LESSON 1

The Byzantine Empire— Successor to Rome

Thinking on Your Own

Create an outline as you read this lesson. The outline will include the Roman numerals I, II, III, and IV—one for each subheading. Be sure to include important facts and details.

Constantine was the Roman emperor from A.D. 306–337. He granted freedom of worship to Christians. Constantine himself had converted to Christianity. Before this time, both Christians and Jews were often persecuted for believing in only one God. He also moved the capital in 330 to Byzantium, which he renamed Constantinople.

The original name of the town survived because the Empire itself was called Byzantine.

focus your reading

Why did Constantine choose Byzantium as the new capital?

What did Justinian accomplish for the Empire?

What were the reasons that Constantinople became an important trade center?

Explain the argument that took place over the use of icons.

vocabulary

aqueducts   Orthodox
civil law   textiles
customs duties   mosaics
schism   icons

Constantine's New Capital

Constantine decided to move the capital of the Roman Empire. He moved the capital away from the city of Rome because Germanic people frequently attacked the city. Constantine also wanted to keep track of the rival Sassanid Empire in Persia. The site of the new capital was located further to the east than Rome.

Lesson Summary
Constantine granted religious freedom throughout the Roman Empire. He built a new capital in Byzantium, which he renamed Constantinople.

The Empire grew under Justinian, who began to rule in 527. Justinian codified Roman law.

The Great Schism of 1054 divided the Christian Church into Roman Catholic (Western) and Eastern Orthodox branches.

Lesson Objective
Students will learn about the growth of Constantinople as the "New Rome" and its contributions.

Focus Your Reading Answers

1 Constantine chose Byzantium as the new capital because Rome was increasingly under attack from Germanic tribes. Byzantium also offered a closer view of Persia, which was thought likely to rebel against imperial rule.

2 Justinian developed a code of laws that became the basis for European laws for centuries. He also rebuilt the city of Constantinople after the Nika Riot. He built the church known as Hagia Sophia, as well as aqueducts for the city.

3 Constantinople became a center of trade because of its location on the Silk Road and at the crossroads of trade routes. Goods passing through the city created wealth for the city.

4 Church leaders argued over whether the icons were being worshiped. Some of them believed in the prohibitions against images that was part of the Jewish religion. They destroyed many of the icons.

Lesson Vocabulary

Introduce each of the following vocabulary terms. Many of the words contain roots that could be used to build new words: *aquifers, civil disobedience,* and so on.

The Romans built *aqueducts* to carry water to cities. Justinian had *aqueducts* built for Constantinople. *Civil law* governs the daily rules of society. Justinian also collected Roman *civil law* and codified it. *Customs duties* are taxes. Constantinople grew rich by collecting *customs duties* on goods passing through the city.

A *schism* is a division. The Great *Schism* in the Christian Church occurred in 1054. If something is *orthodox*, it is according to religious doctrine. The Eastern *Orthodox* Church began in 1054. *Unorthodox* means "not conforming to established forms and doctrines." An *unorthodox* church does not follow religious doctrine.

Textile is another word for fabric. The Byzantine Empire was known for its *textile* industry. *Mosaics* are designs or pictures made of bits of colored glass. Many churches in the Byzantine Empire were decorated with *mosaics*. *Icons* are images representing God, saints, or stories in the Bible.

Picturing History

The photograph of the interior of Hagia Sophia, on page 108, shows its beauty. In the words of a contemporary historian, the effect of the gold and marble made it seem as if the building was not "illuminated from outside by the sun, rather that the radiance was created from within itself." The building was dedicated in December 537. Alluding to the wealthy king of Israel who built Israel's grand first temple, Justinian at the dedication supposedly said quietly, "Solomon, I have surpassed you."

Extension

One of the most notable of the mosaics in Hagia Sophia is located above the south door of the narthex, or foyer, of the church. Made probably in the tenth century, it depicts Mary and the child Jesus in the center of the mosaic. To their left is Justinian, offering a model of Hagia Sophia. Constantine, on their right, holds out a model of the city he built. The mosaic emphasizes Constantine and Justinian as co-creators of the Empire.

Time Box Extension

Ask students to calculate the length of time from Constantine's moving of the capital to the collapse of Rome. Discuss whether they believe the Empire could have survived after Rome's falling to the Visigoths if the capital had not been moved.

Byzantine Empire, 330–1618

Byzantium was a fishing village and market town when Constantine decided to make it his capital. It was located in a strategic position on a peninsula. The location made the city easy to defend against invading armies. The city also had a natural harbor known as the Golden Horn. The town offered the chance to control sea traffic in the Mediterranean and Black Seas. Constantine had new walls built to enlarge the city, which he named Constantinople after himself. To fill the new capital, Constantine offered free grain to people who came to live there.

Like many emperors, Constantine loved to build. To his new capital, he added palaces, churches, two theaters, a university, and four courts of law. In addition, he brought statues and art from other places in the empire. He called Constantinople the "New Rome." Rome itself fell to invading Germanic people in 476.

Time Box

320 Constantinople becomes the Roman capital
476 Rome falls to the Visigoths
527 Justinian becomes emperor
532–537 Justinian rebuilds Hagia Sophia
1054 The Great Schism divides the Church

Hagia Sophia built as Christian place of worship and later became Muslim mosque

The Empire Expands

Several emperors ruled after Constantine's death. One of the greatest was Justinian. He became emperor in 527. Under the rule of Justinian, the Empire grew to its largest extent.

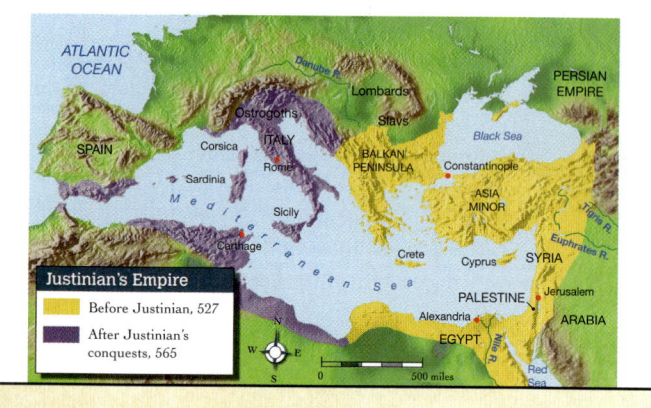

Justinian's Empire
- Before Justinian, 527
- After Justinian's conquests, 565

108 Chapter 8

Picturing History

Constantine's mother, Helen, was a Christian, while his father worshiped the Unconquered Sun. Before his Battle at Milvian Bridge, Constantine, shown at the bottom left of page 107, claimed to have dreamed of a cross of light over the sun, an ambiguous symbol combining the faiths of his parents. (The effect is of the two Greek letters *chi* and *rho*, which are the beginning letters of *Christ*.) Constantine said he had been commanded to use that emblem on his army's shields. After his victory, other armies feared the emblem. Constantine's own faith remains a subject of debate. He never renounced his worship of the Unconquered Sun and was not baptized (the official rite to enter the Christian Church) until on his deathbed.

However, not everyone approved of his reign. In 532, a protest broke out during a chariot race at the hippodrome, or the circus. It was called the Nika Riot—*nika* is the Greek word meaning "to conquer." That was the word that people shouted during the fighting. Rioters set fire to buildings and crowned a new emperor. When Justinian decided to fight rather than to run away, thousands of rioters were killed. Justinian won the battle and rebuilt Constantinople. He added 25 churches as well as bridges and **aqueducts**, which supplied the city with water.

Justinian is perhaps best known for codifying—or standardizing—Roman laws. The original laws had been added to for centuries. Justinian reviewed the laws and simplified them. These **civil law** codes influenced the laws in many parts of Western Europe.

Daily Life in the Byzantine Empire

For most of its existence, Constantinople was the largest city in Europe. Nearly one million people lived there. The population relied on farmers to supply the grain they needed. These farmers were often free peasants who worked on their own land. There was also a class of citizens who owned large amounts of land. Although the peasants there were not slaves, they

Justinian's Code

When Justinian reviewed all of Roman law, he divided it into 7 sections, containing a total of 50 chapters. The code covered matters such as contracts, property and inheritance laws, slavery, marriage, child guardians, and wills.

Here are some of the laws in Justinian's code:

- Women cannot adopt children after they have lost their own children without the permission of the emperor.
- Males at puberty and females at a marriageable age receive appointed curators until they are 25. Curators are people who protect the interests of those they serve.
- If someone is captured in war and is made a slave, then escapes, that person is again free when he is with his own people.
- If you find a precious stone or gem along the seashore, it is yours.

The Byzantine Empire 109

Picturing History

The drawing on page 109 suggests that the Byzantines had not only superior firepower but also more elaborate ships. Greek fire traveled across water, then ignited and burned the ships. One battle against Greek fire was all most enemies needed to face. On at least one occasion, the enemy forces returned to port, refusing to leave for fear of the new weapon.

Text Box Extension

Discuss the implications of the laws with students. You may want to draw on their general knowledge of slavery in the United States to contrast the laws about runaway slaves, particularly after the passage of the Fugitive Slave Act.

Extension

To compile the code, Justinian gathered a group of lawyers. The code was presented as Roman law, but in reality, Justinian reshaped the law for a Christian monarchy. He drafted most of the laws relating to religion and the Church. Justinian's ideas were expressed in a statue of the emperor outside Hagia Sophia. Seated on a horse, Justinian held an orb topped by a cross. This indicated his belief in the sacred source of his power, which was universal.

Map Extension

Ask students to use the map on page 108 to answer the following questions:

- What areas were added to the Empire after Justinian's conquests of 565? (Italy, Corsica, Sardinia, Sicily, southern Spain, and a strip along the North African coast)
- How could you describe the east-west distance of the Empire after the conquests? (Justinian doubled the total east-west distance.)
- From what direction would the Ostrogoths most likely invade the Empire? (from the north)

The Byzantine Empire 109

Picturing History

From the fifth to the thirteenth centuries, the population of Constantinople was close to one million people. Wealthy estate owners and peasant farmers, such as those pictured near the top of page 110, were key to keeping the food supply that the Empire needed. Free citizens of the capital were granted six loaves of bread daily.

Bio Facts

- Theodora was born c. 497.
- Her father worked at the Hippodrome (circus) in Constantinople as a bear keeper.
- Justinian raised her to the rank of patrician before marrying her.
- She and Justinian were wed in 525.
- She is mentioned in nearly all of the laws passed during her era.
- She died of cancer or gangrene on June 28, 548.

Byzantine Empire, 330–1618

were bound to the land and could not leave. Some of these peasants were sharecroppers. Part of their harvest went to the owner of the land. Very few of the sharecroppers could ever earn enough money to buy their own land.

Farming w important the econc of the Byzantine Empire.

Constantinople was an important trade center. The city was the crossroads of trade going both north-south and east-west. Its gold coin, the *bezant*, was the standard form of money for traders from the 500s to the 1200s.

Many people in Byzantine society could read and write. In 425, a school of higher learning in philosophy, medicine, and law was established by Theodosius II. The school, known as

Biography

Empress Theodora

Imagine a love so great that it changed the law. Before he became the emperor, Justinian fell in love with Theodora. She was a wool spinner who had been an actress. However, Roman law did not allow government officials to marry actresses. Justinian had the law changed so that he could marry Theodora.

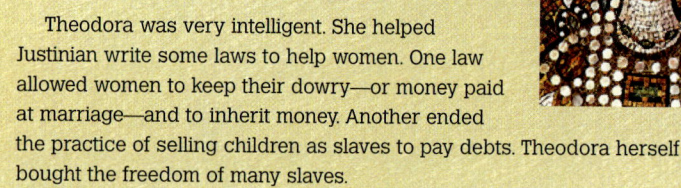

Theodora was very intelligent. She helped Justinian write some laws to help women. One law allowed women to keep their dowry—or money paid at marriage—and to inherit money. Another ended the practice of selling children as slaves to pay debts. Theodora herself bought the freedom of many slaves.

During the Nika Riot, Theodora encouraged Justinian not to run away. S said, "For a king, death is better than dethronement and exile."

Theodora also met with foreign diplomats who came to court. She took part in Councils of State as well. She died of cancer in 548. Justinian ruled alone for almost 20 more years. No major laws were passed after her deat

Biography Extension

The mosaic of Theodora, shown on page 110, is part of a panel in the church of San Vitale in Ravenna, Italy. Located on the south wall of the sanctuary, it faces a similar mosaic of Justinian on the north wall. Much of what we know about Theodora comes from a text known as *The Secret History*. Some historians are suspicious of this work, fearing Procopius, its Christian writer, had a grudge against both Theodora and Justinian. Procopius had served as secretary to the general Belisarius, who had served in the army Justinian had led before becoming emperor. Theodora later had Belisarius removed from command. Thus, some of the more lurid details of Theodora's life before her marriage to Justinian may be exaggerated.

Chapter 8

Constantinople University, lasted for more than one thousand years. Greek literature was also studied and valued. Many of the manuscripts—or written works—we now have are Byzantine copies of Greek works.

> **stop and think**
>
> In the Byzantine Empire, some peasant farmers were able to plant on their own land. Why might they work harder on farms that they owned? Work with a partner to develop a bulleted list of five reasons.

The city was also part of the famous Silk Road. The road was used by traders to transport goods between Asia and Europe. All of the goods that came through the city were subject to taxes. These taxes, called **customs duties**, helped make the city rich. In addition, artisans in Constantinople bought goods and added to their value. For example, they made jewelry out of raw gems from India and dyed wool from Europe. Then they resold these items to make a profit.

After Justinian's death, the Byzantine Empire began to weaken. It lost territory that had originally been part of the Roman Empire. Land that had been reclaimed by Justinian was soon lost to other growing powers. The Empire continued until the mid-fifteenth century, however, when it was conquered by the Turks. They renamed the capital city Istanbul. The church of Hagia Sophia became a center of Islamic worship. The influence of the Empire is still felt in nations such as Greece, Serbia, Russia, and Turkey.

Religion and Art of the Byzantine Empire

Just as there were political tensions between the capitals of Rome and Constantinople, disagreements over religion also occurred. Two groups formed within the Christian Church, and they argued over beliefs and practices. Some of these, such as whether a priest should have a beard, seem less important to us now.

There was also disagreement about the power of Rome over the Eastern churches. The pope claimed to rule over all the Christian churches. Not surprisingly, the head of the Church at Constantinople, called a patriarch, disagreed. In 1054, the pope and the patriarch broke their relationship. This was known as the Great **Schism**. The Eastern church became known as the

---

Stop and Think

Students' lists may vary but could include the following ideas:

- If the peasants were able to farm their own land, they would be able to make a profit. This, in turn, would benefit their families.

- They may also have taken pride in owning their own farms, usually considered a mark of success.

- They may have been able to enlist the help of family members, including children too young to work on estates, and thus been able to plant more seeds and gain a greater yield.

- Working their own land meant they did not need to travel to work and could spend energy tending their own crops rather than using time and energy walking or riding to the fields owned by others.

- They would be working to be able to pass down the land through the family.

Extension

In 425, the government endowed 31 chairs for professors in Constantinople. The number of those who taught in Latin, which was the official language of law, was nearly as great as those who taught in Greek, the language of the people. The curriculum focused on practical skills that officials needed to rise in the bureaucracy. Only one philosophy course was taught, in contrast to the emphasis on philosophy at older institutions such as those in Alexandria, Athens, and Antioch.

Extension

Contemporary cellist Yo-Yo Ma founded the Silk Road Project to encourage greater sharing by artists of both Eastern and Western traditions. Ask students who are interested in music to use library resources or the Internet to find out more about the project and report their findings to the class.

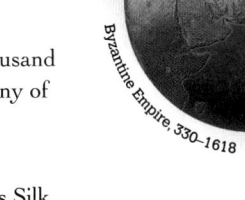

Picturing History

At the top of page 112, women are shown weaving on a loom. The seated woman to the right is spinning wool so that the woman on the left can weave it. Even today, textiles from Middle Eastern countries are prized for their craftsmanship and quality.

Picturing History

The icon of Mary and Jesus, at the left on page 112, demonstrates some of the common features of icons. The tradition did not call for creativity; rather, certain elements were repeated in all icons. For example, the three stars on Mary's robe indicate the belief that she was a virgin before and after the birth of Jesus. Mary is often pictured wearing red, the color that symbolizes humanity, while icons of the adult Jesus often show him wearing blue, the color of divinity.

Putting It All Together

Students' opinions will vary. Venn diagrams may include the following ideas

Hammurabi
- deals with crimes committed and proper punishment
- punishments were severe

Justinian
- deals with daily life of the family
- concern for children

Both
- tried to make the law clear to subjects
- took existing laws and put them in order

Byzantine Empire, 330–1618

Eastern **Orthodox** Church. The Western church was the Roman Catholic Church. The split continues to this day.

Istanbul was well known as a center for artisans. People worked in gold and silver, made glassware, and wove **textiles**. The textile, or fabric, industry grew even more when silkworms were illegally imported from China. Soon, silk from Constantinople was known for its high quality.

Along with their magnificent architecture, the Byzantines are well known for **mosaics** and **icons**. The Romans made mosaics from bits of marble. Beginning around 330, the Byzantines began decorating the floors, ceilings, and domes of their churches with pictures made of bits of colored glass.

Religious icons—or pictures of religious figures—could be painted on wood or made of mosaics. The Church had arguments about whether icons should be allowed. Some people were afraid that the icons were being worshiped instead of God. Others believed it was wrong to make any image of God, as was written in the Ten Commandments. Islam, which was becoming important in the East, did not allow images either. Many of the icons were burned or painted over. The church finally agreed in 843 to allow icons as long as they were not worshiped.

Textiles were woven by women

Religion was often the focus of intricate mosaics.

Achievements of the Byzantine Empire
- street lights
- table forks
- gunpowder
- silk making
- Justinian's code of law
- mosaics
- icons
- architecture

Putting It All Together

Look back at the laws of Hammurabi's Code in Chapter 2. Use a Venn diagram to compare the laws of Hammurabi with the laws of Justinian. Under which ruler would you prefer to live? Write a short paragraph supporting your decision with facts and details.

112 Chapter 8

Chart Extension

Ask interested students to use library resources or the Internet to learn more about the achievements of the Byzantine Empire. Allow time for them to share their findings with the class.

Map Extension

Ask students to use the map on page 113 to answer the following questions:

- What river route did the Vikings use to reach the Caspian Sea? (the Volga River)
- What major city was located on the Black Sea? (Constantinople)
- What sea did the Vikings have to cross when leaving Scandinavia? (the Baltic Sea)

LESSON 2

The Rise of Russia

Byzantine Empire, 330–1618

Thinking on Your Own

Create a T-chart in your notebook. Label the left column "Invaders and Leaders" and the right column "Details." As you read, make a list of all the different countries that invaded Russia and the leaders involved. In the right column, take bulleted notes about each invasion and leader. Share your list with a partner.

The Byzantine Empire continued to influence other nearby lands. The land we know as Russia was settled by nomadic people from eastern Europe around A.D. 500. These people, originally from central Asia, were known as Slavs. Later, Vikings explored Russia. They came from what is now Scandinavia. They set up trade routes along some of the major rivers of Russia.

focus your reading

What groups of people first settled in Russia?

Explain the contributions Cyril and Methodius made to Russia.

What were some of the contributions of the Byzantine Empire to Russia?

Discuss the importance of the Golden Horde.

vocabulary

principalities   tribute
feudal   horde

The Mission to the Slavs

Two brothers from Greece, Cyril and Methodius, went to the Slavic people as missionaries in the ninth century. The Slavs, who settled in the region northwest of Kiev, had no system of writing. Cyril and Methodius developed the Cyrillic alphabet. It allowed the people to learn how to read and write.

Viking Trade Routes
- Extent of Kievan Rus
- Viking trade routes

Lesson Vocabulary

Discuss each of the vocabulary terms with students.

Principalities are territories ruled by powerful princes. Slavs formed the *principalities* that became Kievan Rus.

In a *feudal* system there is a powerful ruler to whom everyone owes honor and loyalty. The Russians adopted the *feudal* system from the Byzantines.

Tribute is a synonym for taxes. Batu Khan demanded *tribute* from conquered people.

A *horde* is a political division, similar to a *principality*. The Golden *Horde* was the region ruled by the Mongols. The word has come to mean a large crowd.

Lesson Summary

Slavic nomads from eastern Europe first settled in Russia around A.D. 500. They were followed by Vikings from Finland, who set up trade routes.

Cyril and Methodius, brothers from Greece, came to Russia to teach the people about Christianity. They developed the Cyrillic alphabet to be able to translate the Bible into the language of the people.

Kiev was a major city north of Constantinople. It was the center of Kievan Rus, ruled in the ninth and tenth centuries by Vikings.

Mongol invaders arrived in 1223, led by a grandson of Genghis Khan. Batu Khan led an empire known as the Golden Horde. He demanded and received tribute.

Lesson Objective

Students will learn about the beginnings of Russia and its relationship to the Byzantine Empire.

Focus Your Reading Answers

1 The first settlers of Russia were Slavic people.

2 Cyril and Methodius devised an alphabet and translated the Bible. They also converted many people to Christianity.

3 Byzantine contributions included the feudal system, the idea of a written code of laws, and influence on architecture.

4 The Golden Horde was an area that stretched from the Caspian and Black Seas to western Siberia's plains. It was ruled by Genghis Khan's grandson Batu, who invaded Russia.

The Byzantine Empire

Picturing History

The icon of Cyril and Methodius holding a scroll of the Cyrillic alphabet, shown on page 114, demonstrates one of the features of icons. Subjects are nearly always shown facing the viewer, because the saints are regarded as being fully present to the viewer. The halo indicates holiness. Both brothers are shown wearing bishops' mitres (hats); Cyril died shortly after being consecrated as a bishop.

Map Extension

Ask students to use the map on page 114 to answer the following questions:

- What were the two major cities in Russia? (Novgorod, Kiev)
- Did early Russia extend to the Caspian Sea? (no)
- What was the approximate north-south distance of early Russia? (about 750 miles, or 1,200 km)

The Greek alphabet influenced the Cyrillic one, which is still used in Russia today.

The Cyrillic alphabet represents the sounds of Slavic languages more accurately than the Greek alphabet could. After the brothers created this alphabet, they translated the Bible into the Slavic language.

Kievan Rus

During the ninth and tenth centuries, the Slavs began forming territories ruled by powerful princes. These territories were called **principalities**. A group of them banded together as a confederation called Kievan Rus. Kiev, located north of Constantinople, was their major city. The Dnieper River and the Black Sea connect the two cities.

The rulers of the Kievan Rus were Vikings. The Vikings used the rivers as trade routes for slaves, amber, and furs. They also raided the Byzantine Empire. In 862, Rurik became a prince of Novgorod, a city farther north of Kiev. It may be that his clan name, Rus, is where Russia got its name. Oleg, who followed Rurik as prince, enlarged the rule to include more land. Rurik's descendants ruled over Russia until 1598.

Kiev became very rich through its trade with Constantinople and other regions. By the eleventh century, Kiev was reported to have 400 churches and eight large market centers. Nearly 30,000 people lived in Kiev by the early twelfth century.

Vladimir I was the ruler of Kievan Rus from 980 until 1015. In 988, he converted to Christianity. One legend says that he sent people to observe other religions. The group was most impressed with the beauty of worship in Hagia Sophia. This was the start of the Russian Orthodox religion. Kiev's Saint Sofia was built in 1037 to rival Hagia Sophia.

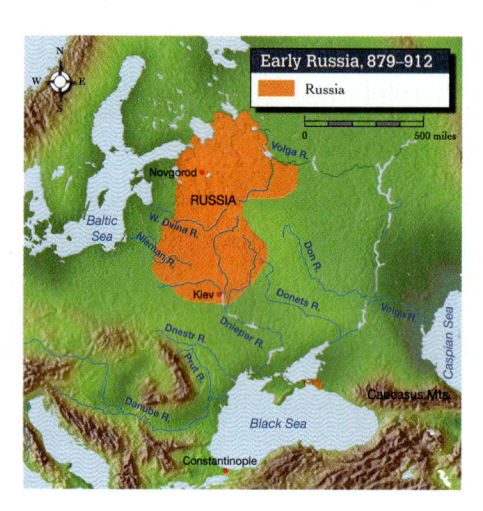

stop and think

Religion played an important role in people's lives during this time period. How did religion influence the development of Russia? Create a bulleted list of ideas and share them with a partner. Then add to your list.

Vladimir I also adopted the **feudal** system—a form of government used throughout the Byzantine Empire. The Kievan Rus had been ruled by clans. In a feudal system there is a powerful ruler to whom everyone owes honor and loyalty. Like the Byzantines, the Rus developed a written code of laws. Eventually, the Rus claimed that the city of Moscow was the Third Rome.

The Golden Horde

East of Kievan Rus was a tribe known as Mongols. The Mongols were originally from an area known as Mongolia in East Asia. These men were fierce fighters and were becoming more powerful. They were especially known for their skill with archery and horses. Genghis Khan, who ruled from 1206–1227, led an Asian army against Russia in 1223.

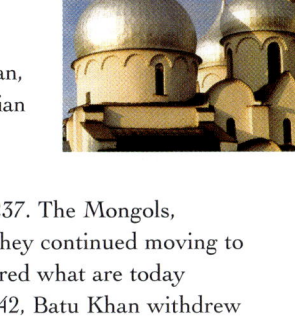

Gold and silver domes crown the cathedral of St. Sofia.

One of Khan's grandsons, Batu Khan, led an invasion of Russia in 1237. The Mongols, however, did not remain in Russia. They continued moving to the southwest and eventually conquered what are today Poland, Hungary, and Austria. In 1242, Batu Khan withdrew his armies from Europe. However, they still demanded military service from the people and **tribute**, or taxes. Batu ruled over an area that stretched from the Caspian and Black Seas to western Siberia's plains. It was known as the Golden Horde. A **horde** was the name for a political division, similar to a principality. It has come to mean "a large crowd."

Putting It All Together

Work with a partner to create a timeline of events in early Russian history. Include invasions, leaders, and other important events. Use the notes you took at the beginning of this lesson to help you develop your timeline.

The Byzantine Empire 115

Stop and Think

Students' responses will vary. Possible answers:

- Cyril and Methodius came to teach Christianity and developed an alphabet.
- Vladimir I converted to Christianity.
- The beauty of Hagia Sophia prompted the Russians to build their own beautiful churches.

Picturing History

Point out to students the onion-shaped domes of St. Sophia, pictured on page 115. The shape is characteristic of Russian domes. Byzantine domes are more shallow. One theory suggests that the onion shape allowed the roofs to shed snow more easily.

Putting It All Together

Events on timelines will vary but may include

- 500   Eastern Slavic peoples moved into Ukraine
- 700s Vikings moved into Slavs' land
- 863   Missionaries Cyril and Methodius converted eastern Slavs
- 900   Oleg founded Kievan Rus
- 988   Vladimir I converted to Christianity
- 1169 Civil wars ended the first Russian state
- 1200s Mongols invaded Russia

Extension

The Eastern Orthodox Church encompasses a number of national churches. These include the Russian Orthodox as well as the Greek, Serbian, Romanian, and Armenian churches. Have interested students research these sects and present their findings to the class.

The Byzantine Empire 115

Chapter Review

1 Students' cartoon storyboards will vary but should contain the facts of one of the narratives within the chapter.

2 News articles will vary but should include at least five vocabulary words from the chapter.

Chapter Summary

- Constantine moved the capital of the Empire from Rome to Byzantium, which he renamed Constantinople.
- Justinian created a summary of Rome's **civil laws**.
- Justinian rebuilt the church of Hagia Sophia, one of the oldest churches in the world. He also added **aqueducts** to Constantinople.
- The Byzantine Empire was known for its **mosaics** and **icons**.
- Constantinople was an important trade center and farming region. **Customs duties** helped the city become wealthy. Artisans created beautiful objects, including silk **textiles**.
- Disagreements between Rome and Constantinople led to a split in the Christian Church known as the Great **Schism**. The Roman Catholic Church became the Western church. The Eastern church is known as the **Orthodox** Church.
- The Byzantine Empire ended in the mid-fourteenth century with the Turks' victory.
- Viking and Eastern Slavic people settled in Russia.
- Missionaries Methodius and Cyril developed an alphabet for the Russians and translated the Bible.
- Strong rulers led **principalities** in Russia.
- Russians adopted many Byzantine ways of life, including the **feudal** system.
- Mongol invaders attacked Russia and demanded **tribute** money. They ruled an area known as the Golden **Horde**.

Chapter Review

1 Choose one of the events of the chapter and retell the story using cartoon storyboards.

2 Write a news article about something from the chapter, using at least five of the vocabulary words.

Novel Connections

Below is a list of books that relate to the time period covered in this chapter. The numbers in parentheses indicate the related Thematic Strands of the National Council for the Social Studies (NCSS).

Tracy Barrett. *Anna of Byzantium.* Laurel Leaf Books, 2000. (III, VI)

James A. Corrick. *The Byzantine Empire.* Gale Group, 1997. (I, II, III, V)

Denise Dersin, editor. *What Life Was Like Amid Splendor and Intrigue: Byzantine Empire, A.D. 330–1453.* Time-Life Books, 1998. (V, VI)

Elsa Marston. *The Byzantine Empire.* Benchmark Books, 2002. (I, II, III, V)

Tim McNeese. *Siege of Constantinople: April 6–May 29, 1453.* Chelsea House Publishers, 2003. (V, VI)

Jill Paton Walsh. *Emperor's Winding Sheet.* Farrar, Straus and Giroux, 1992. (I, III, V, VI)

Skill Builder

Analyzing Special-Purpose Maps

Maps can do more than tell you about the geography of an area. Some maps have special purposes. When reading a special-purpose map, be sure to:

- Read the titles carefully to determine what they can teach you.
- Look at the key for helpful symbols and colors used.
- Examine the map's scale, which tells you how to measure distances.

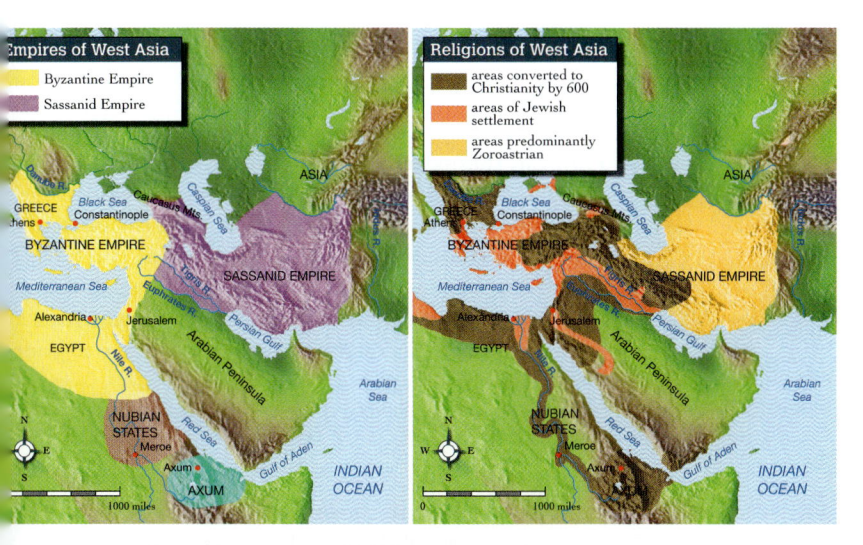

Use the maps to answer the following questions:

1. What different information does each map contain?
2. Which map would you use to find out where Jewish settlements were located in West Asia?
3. Where was the Zoroastrian religion strongest?
4. How far south did the Byzantine Empire spread?
5. What seas did the Byzantine Empire touch?

Skill Builder

1. The map on the left is of the Empires of West Asia. The one on the right is of Religions of West Asia.
2. To locate Jewish settlements look on the Religions of West Asia map.
3. The Zoroastrian religion was strongest in the Sasanid Empire and eastward.
4. The Byzantine Empire spread into Egypt and down the Nile to the border of the Nubian states.
5. The Byzantine Empire touched the Mediterranean, Black, and Red Seas.

Classroom Discussion

Discuss with students some of the broader topics covered in this chapter.

- What makes a city great?
- How can trade enrich a nation or an empire?
- What are some ways in which nations borrow ideas from other nations?
- What trade issues are in the news today?

Chapter 9: Islam and Muslim Civilizations

(622–1699)

Chapter Summary
Refer to page 130 for a summary of Chapter 9.

Related Transparencies
- T-1 World Map
- T-2 Outline World Map
- T-18 Three-Column Chart
- T-20 Concept Web

Key Blacklines
Biography—Harun al-Rashid

CD Extension
Encourage students to use the reading comprehension, vocabulary reinforcement, and interactive timeline activities on the student CD.

Getting Focused
Students' concept webs will differ. You may wish to lead a class discussion after students have worked with partners to see how much agreement exists. You can also discuss with students injustices that exist in the world today, and which people and organizations work to eliminate injustice. Then tell students they are about to study a major event in world history that continues to affect society around the world.

Getting Focused

Skim this chapter to predict what you will be learning.
- Read the lesson titles and subheadings.
- Look at the illustrations and read the captions.
- Examine the maps.
- Review the vocabulary words.

What changes have you seen in your school this year? How did these changes happen? Did one person make the change? A group? Make a concept web with "effective ways to bring about change" in the center. Write your observations about the changes you have seen. Also write your ideas about ways to bring about change. Then discuss and compare your ideas with a partner. Remember to add the Islamic Empire to your world map.

Picturing History
The Dome of the Rock, shown on page 118, was built as a tribute to Muhammad after his death. It is Islam's third-most holy site. It is not a mosque, but a site to commemorate events believed to have occurred there. Muslims believe that in 619, Muhammad visited Paradise from this location, returning with the instruction of daily prayer.

The Dome of the Rock is located in Jerusalem, Israel, on Mount Moriah, which was earlier associated with Abraham and the site of Solomon's temple. Thus, the location remains holy to both Jews and Christians. Built by the Umayyad, the Dome of the Rock was completed around 692.

Pre-Reading Discussion

1. Discuss with students some current world events that involve disputes over land or resources. students that they are about to of another era with the same disputes.

2. See if students can identify physical characteristics of various types of buildings. What have observed about restaurants or government buildings, for example (bright signs, recognizable logos, U.S. flag flying)

LESSON 1

The Beginnings of Islam

Thinking on Your Own

What do you already know about the history and practice of Islam? What would you like to know? Create a K-W-L chart. In the first column, list "What I Know." In the second column, list "What I Want to Know." In the third column, list "What I Learned." Fill in the first two columns as you skim the lesson and the last column as you read the chapter.

Most of the major religions of the world began with the thoughts and teachings of one person. In some areas of the world these men are called prophets. Judaism began in 2000 B.C. with the Mesopotamian leader, Abraham. Christianity appeared around A.D. 0 with Jesus of Nazareth. Islam's beginnings are traced to Muhammad Ibn Abdallah in A.D. 620. Like the others, Muhammad was a simple man who cared about the people of his country.

focus your reading

Why was Muhammad concerned about the Arabic society of his day?

Why did Muhammad and his followers go to Madinah?

Describe the conflict that divided the followers of Islam.

vocabulary

Quran
boycott
monotheists
caravans
hajj
caliphs

The Life of the Prophet Muhammad

When he was forty years old, an Arab merchant named Muhammad Ibn Abdallah heard a voice that changed his life. Muhammad was in a cave on Mount Hira outside Makkah (Mecca). Makkah is located in what is now the western part of Saudi Arabia. Muhammad usually went there during the month of Ramadan to fast and pray.

Lesson Summary

In 610, a merchant named Muhammad was praying when an angel revealed the scripture that would become the Quran. The people of Makkah placed a boycott on him and his followers, who left Makkah for Madinah.

Muhammad gave women rights they did not have in other cultures at the time. He also worked for peace until forced to go to war.

After Muhammad's death, the people were ruled by caliphs. A split arose because some Muslims believed that only those men directly descended from Ali, Muhammad's cousin and son-in-law, should be caliphs. Others believed that anyone from Muhammad's clan was allowed. These two factions became the Shia and Sunni Muslims.

Lesson Objective

Students will learn about Muhammad's founding of Islam and its early history.

Focus Your Reading Answers

1 Muhammad was concerned because people were mistreating slaves and children, worshiping many gods, and concentrating on making money rather than practicing the traditional Arabic values.

2 Muhammad and his followers went to Madinah to escape persecution.

3 Followers of Islam were divided over who should rule the Muslims. The Shia Muslims believed that only descendants of Ali, Muhammad's son-in-law and cousin, should rule. The Sunni Muslims felt that anyone from Muhammad's clan who followed the way of Islam was qualified.

Vocabulary

...ce each of the following vocabulary terms.

...*ran* (KUH-RAHN) is the Muslim holy book. The text of the *Quran* was not written down ...ter Muhammad's death. The *Quran* is to Muslims what the Bible is to Christians, and the ...s to followers of Judaism. *Caliphs* are ruling deputies in the Muslim world. The four ...guided *caliphs* followed Muhammad in leading the people.

...that a *boycott* is a refusal to buy or sell goods from certain groups or individuals. A two-...*cott* against the followers of Islam created poverty for some.

...*ists* are people who worship only one God. Muslims, Jews, and Christians are all ...*ists*.

...s are groups of people traveling together, usually for trade. *Caravans* were often robbed by ...s of other clans.

...*j* is the pilgrimage that Muslims make to Makkah. In 628, Muhammad went on a *hajj* to ...eace between warring clans.

Islam and Muslim Civilizations 119

Picturing History

Mount Hira is shown on page 120. It is located near the city of Makkah (Mecca) in modern-day Saudi Arabia. It is still a holy site to Muslims.

Time Box Extension

Ask students to determine how long Muhammad lived between receiving the Quran and his death. (22 years) Have them look back at Chapter 7 and determine how long Jesus preached.

Text Box Extension

Ask students what they observe about the Five Pillars of Islam. Make the point that Islam is outer-directed; nearly all of these rules involve external observances of religion. Muslim piety is defined as active and as giving to those in need.

Islam and Muslim Civilizations, 622–1699

Muhammad was worried about the Arabian people. They were more concerned with making money than with traditional Arabic values such as caring for one another. They sometimes mistreated slaves and children. They were also worshiping many gods instead of the one true God, Allah. At the shrine known as the Kaaba, there were 360 pagan gods. The Kaaba was thought to have been built by Adam. It was associated with a meeting of Abraham (Ibrahim) and his son Ishmael (Ismail), who was considered the father of Arab tribes.

According to legend, an angel appeared to Muhammad in the cave. The angel carried a scroll which he commanded Muhammad to read. Like most of his tribe, Muhammad could not read or write. The angel insisted he recite the words on the scroll. Muhammad recited words that are now part of the **Quran** (KUH•RAHN). The Quran is the sacred scriptures of Islam.

Muhammad doubted the source of his experience. For two years he told no one except his wife, Khadija, and a few close friends. Over the next several years, Muhammad received the full text of the Quran.

At that time, people were used to memorizing large pieces of literature. They trusted their memories more than they did written words. The text of the Quran was not written down until after the prophet's death. Muhammad became unpopular in Makkah because he spoke out against injustice. The ruling clan placed a **boycott** on Muhammad's tribe. No one would sell them food. This boycott lasted for two years.

Time Box

610
The prophet Muhammad receives the first parts of the Quran (Koran) in Makkah (Mecca). The Quran will become the holy book of Islam.

622
Muhammad and 70 families of his followers go to Madinah (Medina).

632
Muhammad dies.

638
Muslims capture Jerusalem, which becomes the third holiest Muslim city after Makkah and Madinah.

The Five Pillars of Islam

These five rules are required of all devout followers of Islam:
1. Believe in Allah as the only God.
2. Pray five times a day.
3. Give to the poor.
4. Fast during Ramadan.
5. Go to Makkah on pilgrimage.

The prophet Muhammad would retreat to a cave in Mount Hira to meditate.

In 622, a group of 70 families who believed the words Muhammad preached left Makkah to settle in Yathrib, in what is now western Saudi Arabia. They renamed Yathrib, Madinah (Medina). They became known as the Muslim—the followers of Islam. Such a move was a major decision. The people were leaving their old tribal loyalties, not just changing locations. They were giving their first loyalty to the ideals of Islam rather than to blood ties. This move was so important that the Islamic calendar considers it Year 1.

Muhammad did not at first think he was founding a new religion. He thought he was a Christian or Jewish prophet. He respected both Jews and Christians. They were also **monotheists** and "people of the Book." He had prayers on Friday nights, as the Jewish people did, and called for a fast on their Day of Atonement. However, the Jews did not believe Muhammad was a prophet. They did not accept his version of their scriptures.

Muhammad finally realized that the Muslims were not going to be a part of the Jewish faith. He had his followers switch the direction of their prayers away from Jerusalem and toward Makkah.

Muhammad's Ideals

Perhaps because he had been orphaned by the age of six, Muhammad was very concerned about helping others. He was interested in the equality of women. The Quran addresses both women and men and sees them as equally responsible before Allah. Muhammad mended his own clothes, helped with household tasks, and consulted his wives for advice. Islam also allowed women to divorce and to inherit property.

> **stop and think**
>
> Think about how Islam was different than other religions of the time. Make a bulleted list of how Muhammad's ideas and beliefs set Islam apart from other religions.

> **Picturing History**
>
> Madinah (Medina), pictured on page 121, is the location of Muhammad's tomb and a mosque enclosing that tomb. September 20, 622, the date when Muhammad arrived in the city from Makkah, marks the beginning of the Muslim calendar. The word *Madinah* means "city," and by extension, "city of the prophet." It was the capital of the caliphate from 622 until 661. In 683, the Umayyad sacked it, and its importance declined.

Stop and Think
Students' answers will vary but may include the following ideas:

- The worship of one God set Islam apart from the Arabic tribes, though not from Judaism and Christianity.
- In the Quran, Islam had a code that defined all aspects of life.
- The calendar was different.
- The gains for women were greater than in other religions of the time.
- Islam demanded pilgrimage as one of the Five Pillars.

the death of his parents, Muhammad was raised by an uncle. This same uncle ...ed a job for him on the caravan operated by a widow, Kadijah, whom ...mmad later married. Ali, who became Muhammad's son-in-law and later the ... of the Shia/Sunni controversy, was the son of this uncle.

...mmad's nickname as a teenager was Al-Amin, "the Truthful." He was also ... as a kind young man who loved children and animals.

Picturing History

The text of the Quran, shown at the top of page 122, is believed to be holy. The word *Quran* means "reading." Simply reading the Quran is considered an act of worship. The Quran is divided into 114 *suras*, or chapters. Each sura is subdivided into verses. Before touching the text, readers must ritually cleanse themselves. According to tradition, Muhammad commended the "beauty of handwriting . . . for it is one of the keys of man's daily bread." Calligraphy was described as a "spiritual geometry."

Extension

The Quran doesn't say much about art but does value the written word. Thus, mosques and other buildings are decorated with calligraphy texts from the Quran rather than with human or animal images.

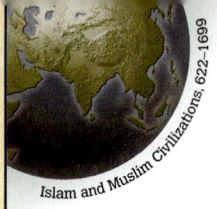

Islam and Muslim Civilizations, 622–1699

The Qu[ran] is the h[oly] book o[f] Islam.

This was hundreds of years before nations in Europe allowed these rights.

Muhammad was interested in peace. Arabic tribes had long been at war over the scarce resources of the desert region. The raiding of **caravans** was customary. Caravans were groups of people who traveled together. Strict rules governed the practice. For example, if your tribe or clan had made a treaty with another tribe, you could not raid that tribe's caravans. The battles that occurred after the Muslims went to Madinah were necessary. If the Muslims did not win the battles, they would be killed and the faith of Islam would die. The rule of the desert was to kill or be killed.

Muhammad tried to end the warfare by going on a **hajj**, or pilgrimage to Makkah, in 628. The hajj was a long-standing custom in the region. People came to Makkah to the Kaaba to worship. There were rules that forbade warfare or any killing. The pilgrimage was successful and led to a treaty between the ruling tribe of Makkah and the Muslim.

People were impressed with Muhammad's courage and his attempts at peace. More and more people converted to Islam. In 630, when the ruling tribe of Makkah broke the treaty, Muhammad led an army of ten thousand against the city. The people of Makkah knew they could not defeat the Muslim. They opened the city gates and surrendered.

Terms to Know

imam	leader of a Muslim congregation
Islam	surrender to God's will
jihad	effort, struggle
mosque	Muslim holy building
Muslim	one who accepts the teachings of Islam
Ramadan	month of fasting
salat	ritual prayer made five times a day
zakat	gifts to the poor

Extension

Have students who are interested in art use library resources or the Internet to learn more about calligraphy, not only in Islam, but in other settings. Suggest they present their findings to the class using visual aids.

Term Box Extension

Be sure to pronounce all the words so that students can say them correctly.

Pilgrims in Makkah circle the Kaaba, a sacred black stone covered by a beautiful cloth.

The Spread of Islam

By the time of Muhammad's death in 632, most of the Arabian tribes had become converts or allies of the Muslim. Four men who were relatives or friends to Muhammad ruled during the next thirty years. They were known as **caliphs**, or deputies. They did not claim to be prophets, but they guided the community in Muslim beliefs. As a group, they were known as the *Rashidun*, or the "rightly guided" caliphs.

The Rightly Guided Caliphs

	Abu Bakr	Umar	Uthman	Ali
Relationship to Muhammad	• father-in-law	• friend	• son-in-law • member of the Umayyad family	• first cousin • son-in-law
Career	• merchant	• merchant	• merchant	• soldier • writer
Caliphate	• 632–634	• 634–644	• 644–656	• 656–661
Achievements as Caliph	• spread Islam to all of Arabia • restored peace after death of Muhammad • created code of conduct in war • compiled Quran verses	• spread Islam to Syria, Egypt, and Persia • redesigned government • held a census • made taxes more fair • built roads and canals • aided poor	• spread Islam into Afghanistan and eastern Mediterranean • organized a navy • improved the government • built more roads, bridges, and canals • distributed text of the Quran	• reformed tax collection and other government systems • spent most of caliphate battling Mu'awiyah, the governor of Syria

Picturing History

The city of Makkah is located in Saudi Arabia. Makkah during the hajj, shown at the top of page 123, quickly fills with some two million pilgrims for two weeks annually. Part of their worship includes walking counterclockwise around the Kaaba seven times, while reciting prayers to Allah. The city prepares extra food, water, lodging, transportation, and restroom facilities for all these visitors. To accommodate the influx, the city was redeveloped during the oil boom of the 1970s.

Extension

Finding water for two million pilgrims in a desert city is not a problem any longer. Have students interested in science and engineering use library resources or the Internet to investigate Makkah's Red Sea desalination program for its water supply. Have students present their findings to the class by using the Student Presentation Builder on the student CD.

Chart Extension

Have students use the chart to compare the achievements of each caliph. Ask them to note similar activities; for example, both Umar and Uthman were involved in building roads and canals.

Chart Extension

Have students in pairs discuss which aspects of Allah they think were most important in the early days of Islam.

Putting It All Together

Students' paragraphs will vary but may include information from concept webs, the Stop and Think activity, and the following points:

- Arab tribes no longer worshiped many gods.
- The united empire spread.
- Arabs could agree on basic ways to live because of the rules in the Quran.
- The calendar changed and the importance of cities shifted.

Map Extension

Ask students to use the map on page 125 to answer the following questions:

- In what directions did Islam spread under the rightly guided caliphs? (north and southwest)
- How far east did Islam spread under the Umayyad caliphs? (to the Indus River)
- What city was the farthest west? (Córdoba)

Islam and Muslim Civilizations, 622–1699

Under the Rashidun, the Muslim Empire expanded. The Persian and Byzantine Empires had been fighting one another for many years. Their armies and resources were exhausted. Their lands came under Muslim control.

Each of the last three caliphs was assassinated. When Ali, who was Muhammad's cousin and son-in-law, was killed, the Muslim became divided. Some people believed that only Ali's descendants should rule. These people were known as the supporters of Ali, the *Shiah i-Ali*. The term was contracted to Shia or Shiite. At that time, people felt that the spirit and wisdom of one person could be passed on to his or her descendants.

Another group believed that Muhammad's successors did not need to be his direct descendants. Following the way of Muhammad and being from his clan was enough. The way of Islam was called the *Sunna*. These people became known as the Sunni Muslims.

One of the clans, the Umayyad, refused to recognize Ali as ruler. They believed his clan had something to do with the murder of one of the earlier caliphs. The conflict did not lead to war, however. Muslims refused to fight against other Muslims. A group of judges decided who would be the next leader. They chose Mu'awiyah, the governor of Syria, as the leader. He was the choice of the Sunnis.

The split between Shia and Sunni Muslims continues to the present. Sunni Muslims make up the majority of Muslims around the world.

The Names of Allah

The Quran gives 99 names to describe Allah, including:

The Guide	The Merciful
The Mighty	The Protector
The Creator	The Majestic
The Provider	The All Knowing
The Great One	The Judge

Putting It All Together

Look at the concept web that you made at the beginning of this chapter. Using what you have learned in this lesson and your bulleted notes from Stop and Think, write a paragraph that explains how Muhammad tried to bring about change.

Lesson Vocabulary

Discuss each of the vocabulary terms with students.

The *crusades* were efforts by Christian Europeans to regain the Holy Land from Muslims. The first of the *crusades* began in 1096. The *crusaders* were the men who went on the *crusades*. These were often kings, princes, and noblemen.

A *chieftain* rules over a group of people. Osman was a *chieftain* over a Turkish tribe. A monetary payment of conquered people is also known as a *tribute*. Balkan rulers paid *tribute* to the Ottoman Empire.

An *astrolabe* is an instrument sailors use to determine their position at sea. Muslim scientists improved the *astrolabe*.

Calligraphy is beautiful, decorative writing. Islam favors *calligraphy* in decorating its mosques. Ask students about the meaning of the term *graph*. Point out that *to graph* means "to write."

The towers at the corners of mosques are called *minarets*. From the *minarets*, the call to prayer is given five times a day.

LESSON 2

Empires and Legacies

Thinking on Your Own

What are some of the problems that come with having a large empire? Make a list and then work with a partner to see how your lists compare. Based on what you know about the Roman Empire, write a paragraph predicting what you think will happen to the Islamic Empire.

The Islamic Empire was a vast region. It was difficult to rule. Different problems confronted people in very different regions. Communication and transportation networks were slow. Eventually, the Empire broke apart.

focus your reading

Explain why the capital of the Islamic Empire was moved to Damascus, Baghdad, and Cairo.

What event caused Europe to see Islam as a world power?

What were the Safavid and Ottoman Empires?

Discuss some of the contributions of Islam to the world.

vocabulary

crusades
chieftain
tribute
astrolabe
calligraphy
minarets

Dynasties and Crusades

The Umayyad Dynasty, which included fourteen caliphs, lasted from 661 until 750. These rulers moved the capital to Damascus in Syria. Under the Umayyad, Islam continued to expand. The Empire reached as far west as Spain, where the Muslim conquests ended in 732. In addition to gaining the eastern and southern parts of the old Roman Empire, the Muslims moved northwest into central

The Spread of Islam
- At Muhammad's death, 632
- Under Rightly Guided Caliphs, 661
- Under Umayyad Caliphs, 750

Lesson Summary

The Umayyad Dynasty expanded the Islamic Empire west into Spain and in the Middle East.

The Abbasid Dynasty followed. Parts of the Empire began breaking away. Christians in Byzantium appealed to European nations for help. The crusades were launched to regain holy sites. The Mongols invaded the Empire.

The Safavid and Ottoman Empires were the strongest. The Safavids ruled Persia; disagreements led to the hatred between Sunni and Shia Muslims.

The Ottoman Empire ruled from western Turkey. They captured Byzantium in 1453 and changed its name to Istanbul. The Ottomans became a world power.

Islamic contributions to art and science include literature, architecture, and calligraphy, as well as improvements to the astrolabe and advances in medicine, chemistry, and mathematics.

Lesson Objective

Students will learn about the spread of Islam and its cultural contributions.

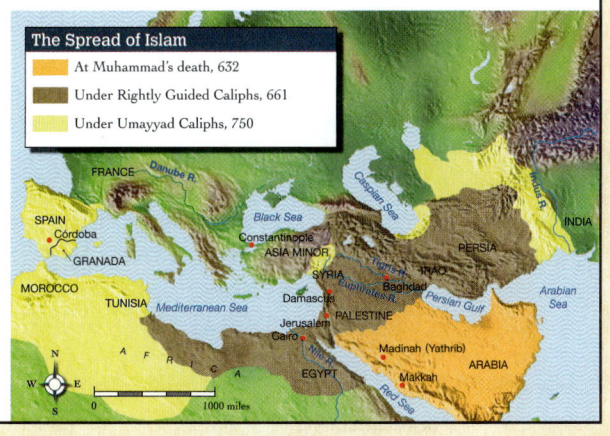

Focus Your Reading Answers

1 The capital moved to Damascus and Baghdad because those were the major cities of the dynasties in power. The capital moved to Cairo after the Mongols destroyed Baghdad.

2 The capture of Constantinople caused Europe to see Islam as a world power.

3 The Safavid Empire was founded by a group of extremist Shia Muslims. They ruled an area in southwest Asia known as Persia. The Ottoman Empire was founded by a member of a Turkish nomadic tribe. The Ottomans gained territory in Europe and captured Constantinople.

4 Some of Islam's contributions include translations of Greek works, as well as advances in mathematics, medicine, and chemistry. Muslim scientists improved the astrolabe. Calligraphers, writers, and architects added to the beauty of the world.

Picturing History

The mosque at Córdoba, Spain, pictured at the top of page 126, is considered to be one of the most beautiful buildings in the world. It was built in the late eighth century and enlarged over the following two centuries. The mosque has 19 aisles and 850 columns. In the tenth century, Córdoba was the capital of the al-Andalus region. It had free Islamic schools, a library of 400,000 books, and 10 miles (16 km) of publicly lighted roads.

Time Box Extension

Ask students to compare the length of the Umayyad Dynasty with the length of time between the Ottoman Empire's conquest of Constantinople and attack of Vienna.

Picturing History

The dancing Sufi, pictured at the bottom of page 126, represents the most mystical branch of Islam. The Sufis, who come from both Sunni and Shia traditions, emerged in a search for a more personal relationship with Allah. The word *suf* means "wool" and refers to the simple wool robes the Sufis used to wear. Sufis use dancing, drumming, and singing to bring them closer to Allah.

The Great Mosque at Cordoba is an example of Islamic architecture in Spain.

Asia and east into Persia and Mesopotamia.

In 750, a descendant of Muhammad's uncle founded a new dynasty, the Abbasid. The Abbasid Dynasty was the result of a revolution and the massacre of more than 70 Umayyad leaders. The leaders were killed by an Abbasid general while they were attending a banquet. The new Abbasid capital was Baghdad—the capital of modern-day Iraq. Located on the Tigris River, it was a crossroads for caravan travel.

Time Box

661–750 Umayyad Dynasty
1096 Crusades begin
1258 Mongols invade Baghdad
1453 Ottomans conquer Constantinople
1683 Ottomans attack Vienna

This was a time of peace within the Empire. Warriors had been the ideal citizens during the Umayyad Dynasty. Now, judges and merchants were respected. During the ninth century, the caliphs supported writers and artists.

Different parts of the Empire soon began to break away. Spain, Egypt, and Morocco on the African north coast each formed independent dynasties. The Seljuk Turks grew stronger, eventually taking over Baghdad in 1055. They defeated the Byzantine army. Then the Byzantine Empire asked the governments of Europe for help.

Beginning in 1096, the Christian nations of Europe mounted a series of **crusades** against the Turks. The Christians wanted to regain control of the holy sites under Muslim control. They had limited success.

A powerful Muslim ruler, Saladin, invaded Jerusalem in 1187. His army destroyed the Christian forces there. Saladin allowed Christian worship to continue and did not massacre the Christian invaders.

The Mongols of China and central Asia posed a greater threat to the Islamic Empire. In 1258, an invading force destroyed Baghdad after sweeping through Persia and Mesopotamia. Cairo, a city in Egypt, then became the new center of Islam.

126 Chapter 9

Extension

Have interested students use library resources or the Internet to find out more about the presence and influence of Islam in Spain. Allow time for them to share their findings with the class.

The Safavid Empire

The Islamic Empire became divided geographically. Two of the most successful empires were the Safavid and Ottoman Empires.

From 1500 until 1722, the Safavids ruled in Persia, now known as Iran, in southwest Asia. Their name comes from a leading brotherhood among Islam, the Safawiyya. The term means "red heads." They were called this because of the red caps they wore. The Safavids had originally been Sunni. During the fifteenth century, however, they became extremist Shia. They fought against the Ottomans to gain territory. The hatred between Sunni and Shia Muslims dates from this era.

The Poetry of Rumi

Sufis were the religous mystics of Sunni Islam. cused on close personal relationships with hey were also known for their ecstatic dancing anting.

i was a poet who composed as he danced. In wing poem, Rumi imagines the call of Allah to mad.

reading for understanding

Discuss the descriptive images used by Rumi.

What does God encourage Muhammad to do?

ho Wraps Himself

ed the Prophet Muhammad Muzzammil,
ne Who Wraps Himself,"
id,
out from under your cloak, you so fond
ing and running away.
over your face.
ld is a reeling, drunken body, and you
intelligent head.
de the candle
r clarity. Stand up and burn through
ght, my prince.
your light
t lion is held captive by a rabbit!

Be the captain of the ship,
Mustafa, my chosen one,
  my expert guide.
Look how the caravan of civilization
Has been ambushed.
Fools are everywhere in charge.
Do not practice solitude like Jesus. Be *in*
  the assembly,
  and take charge of it.
As the bearded griffin,
  the *Humay*, lives on Mt. Quf because he's
  native to it,
  so you should live most naturally out in public
  and be a communal teacher of souls."

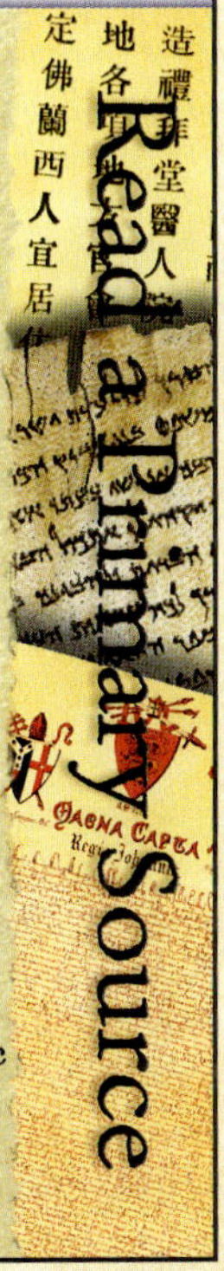

Map Extension

Ask students to use the map on page 127 to answer the following questions:

- Which bodies of water did the Safavid Empire touch? (Caspian Sea, Persian Gulf, Arabian Sea)
- Which direction was the Ottoman Empire from the Safavid Empire? (west)

Reading for Understanding

1 Read the poem aloud, asking students to listen for descriptive images that Rumi uses, such as the "candle of . . . clarity" and "the caravan of civilization."

2 God encourages Muhammad to

- come out from under his cloak
- stand proud
- be a leader
- be part of the people

Extension

Jalal ad-Din ar-Rumi taught at a religious school in Konya, in Anatolia, also known as Rum, which is how he received his name. After meeting Shams al-Din, a holy man of Islam who was later killed, Rumi turned to poetry. He wrote some 30,000 verses, as well as other thoughts. His influence on the cultural life of Turkey is enormous. Thousands still visit his mausoleum, the Green Dome, which is now a museum in Konya.

Map Extension

Ask students to use the map on page 128 to answer the following questions:

- Around which major city did the Ottoman Empire begin? (Constantinople/Istanbul)

- How would you describe the advance of the Ottoman Empire by 1481? (It expanded in all directions, forming a sort of circle around the old empire.)

- By 1683, what was the greatest west-east distance of the Empire? (around 4,000 miles or 6,437 km)

- Did the Ottoman Empire include Spain? (no)

Picturing History

The photograph at the center, left, on page 128 shows Muslim students. Because it is important for Muslims to know the Quran in Arabic, children, sometimes as young as four years of age, are taught to read and memorize texts from the Quran in that language. In some countries, the Bismillah ceremony, when a child can first read the Quran in Arabic, is celebrated together with family and friends. Covering the head is a way to show respect for the text.

The Ottoman Empire

In the early fourteenth century, Osman, a Turkish tribal **chieftain**—or leader—founded a principality in western Turkey. The empire he built is called Osmanli in the Turkish language. It is known in English as the Ottoman Empire. This empire grew from a Turkish nomadic tribe. Members of the tribe fled after the Mongol invasion destroyed Seljuk rule.

Islamic scholars made many contributions in science, literature, and architecture.

Osman and his son moved into Europe. Rulers in the Balkans of Eastern Europe paid **tribute**—or monetary payment—to them each year. The Ottomans fought against many European powers, gaining and losing territory. As a result of the development of cannons, the design of forts and other military buildings changed. Battle formations also changed.

Using this new military technology, the Ottomans captured Constantinople in 1453. They changed the city's name to Istanbul. It became the capital of the Ottoman Empire for the next 469 years.

The Empire continued to grow. Everyone except the Safavids in Iran saw the Ottomans as the heirs to the caliphs.

Under Süleyman the Magnificent, the Ottomans became a world power. However, after his death, the Empire declined. Taxing farmers, using slaves for the army, and keeping a large army all contributed to the decay.

stop and think

Discuss with a partner the contributions of the Muslim rulers and scholars. Then write a bulleted list of the ten most important contributions by Muslim rulers and scholars. Add to your list as you finish reading the lesson.

Stop and Think

Students' lists will vary but may include the following discoveries and works.

- respect for judges and merchants
- science
- literature
- architecture
- astrolabe
- chemistry
- medicine

Islamic Science and Art

Islamic scholars had translations of texts from Greek and Indian sources. From these, they developed an interest in astronomy and astrology. Knowledge of medicine came from Persian Christians, one of whom became a court physician. Other medical knowledge came from Jewish physicians.

During the early ninth century, one of the caliphs founded the "House of Wisdom." Here, Muslim and Christian scholars translated scientific and literary works from Greek into Arabic. Through their efforts, the learning of ancient cultures was preserved and later passed to Europe.

Islam also made great advances in mathematics. They invented algebra and borrowed the Hindu number symbols of 0 to 9. Today we call these symbols Arabic numerals. Muslim scientists improved the **astrolabe**. Sailors used the astrolabe to figure out their position at sea based on the location of the stars. Using the astrolabe to measure distances, Muslims discovered that the earth was round. The Arabs also pioneered work in chemistry and medicine. They were the first to learn that blood moves to and from the heart.

Muslims are also known for their literature and their **calligraphy**. *Calligraphy* means "beautiful writing." Because Islam forbids images in worship, calligraphers decorated mosques with verses from the Quran. Calligraphy was also used on books, carpets, and porcelain.

Because it became important to be able to study the Quran, schools were established and many people learned to read and write. Muslim writers created books of history, poetry, biography, and stories such as *The Arabian Nights*.

The Muslims built beautiful mosques and other buildings. The mosques have **minarets**, or towers, from which to call the faithful to prayer.

Putting It All Together

Make a Venn diagram comparing the Ottoman and Safavid Empires. List at least three distinct differences between the empires and three similarities.

early [astr]olabe

Minarets are towers from which people are summoned to *salat*, or prayer.

Picturing History

The minarets of the mosque pictured at the bottom of page 129 indicate immediately that the building is a house of worship. Although in ancient times a person stood in the towers to call people to prayer five times a day, in most modern countries the call is now conveyed through a loudspeaker system.

Picturing History

The Arabs improved the astrolabe, a Greek invention pictured at the left on page 129. The astrolabe was used to determine latitude, based on the angle of the pole star or sun above the horizon.

Putting It All Together
Possible answers:

Ottoman Empire
- arose in fourteenth century
- covered Turkey and parts of Europe
- used latest military technology

Safavid Empire
- began in sixteenth century
- covered Persia, which is present-day Iran
- included Sunni, then Shia Muslims

Both
- fought to gain territory
- were Muslim empires
- eventually declined

[Exte]nsion

[Suley]man was called the Magnificent by [Europ]eans; however, his own people [called] him the Lawgiver. His court was [notabl]e at the time for advancing people [based] on merit and ability. During his [long] reign (1520–1566), Süleyman [more] than doubled the amount of land he [ruled.] He was a brilliant military [strate]gist, personally leading 13 army [campa]igns. He followed the example set [by his] grandfather in supporting [archit]ecture and the arts. Mosques, [religio]us schools, bridges, and public [baths] were some of the construction [projec]ts of his reign.

Extension

Invite interested students to read one of the tales from *The Arabian Nights* and to present it to the class as a radio play, a reader's theater, or a dramatic presentation.

Islam and Muslim Civilizations

Chapter Review

1. Students' illustrations will vary but should depict an event from Muhammad's life.

2. Essays will vary but should focus on the importance of one of the empires discussed in the chapter.

3. Flowcharts will vary but should show the expansion in territory of the Islamic Empire.

Chapter Summary

- Muhammad had a series of revelations. People were angry and called for a **boycott** against his clan.
- Muhammad's followers were **monotheists** who worshiped Allah and followed the **Quran**.
- Muhammad tried to make peace among the tribes who raided each other's **caravans**. A treaty was created after Muhammad went on a **hajj**.
- After Muhammad's death, the community was led by a series of four **caliphs**.
- Sunni and Shia Muslims disagreed over who had a right to rule.
- Beginning in 1096, European nations sponsored **crusades** to try to regain Christian holy sites.
- Mongols invaded the Islamic world in the thirteenth century.
- The Ottoman Empire, led by **chieftains**, expanded into Europe. In 1453, Ottomans conquered Constantinople, which they renamed Istanbul. Conquered people paid **tribute** to the Ottoman rulers.
- Muslim scientists made advances in science and medicine, including using the **astrolabe** to determine the size of Earth.
- The **calligraphy** of Islamic artists is a way to decorate without using images.
- Islamic mosques are easily identified by their prayer towers, or **minarets**.

Chapter Review

1. Choose one event from Muhammad's life and illustrate it. You may use any artistic style to depict the event.

2. Write a three-paragraph essay explaining the importance of one of the empires discussed in the chapter.

3. Create a flowchart that illustrates the changes that took place in the Islamic Empire.

Novel Connections

Below is a list of books that relate to the time period covered in this chapter. The numbers in parentheses indicate the related Thematic Strands of the National Council for the Social Studies (NCSS).

George W. Beshore. *Science in Early Islamic Culture*. Scholastic Library Publishing, 1998. (I, VIII, IX)

Phyllis Corzine. *The Islamic Empire*. Thomson Gale, 2004. (I, V, VI)

David Macauley. *Mosque*. Lorraine Books/Houghton Mifflin Company, 2004. (I, III, V, VIII)

Elsa Marston. *Muhammad of Mecca: Prophet of Islam*. Scholastic Library Publishing, 2000. (I, III)

Batul Salazar, Philip Wilkinson. *Islam*. DK Publishing, Inc., 2002. (I, V, IX)

Kim Whitehead, Khaled Abou El Fadl (Editor). *Islam: The Basics (Introducing Islam* series). Mason Crest Publishers, 2003. (I, V, IX)

Bernard Wolf. *Coming to America: A Muslim Family's Story*. Lee and Low Books, 2004. (I, III)

Skill Builder

Reading a Circle Graph

Graphs represent data visually. They condense large amounts of information so that people understand it more easily. Graphs often show relationships. For example, a circle graph represents parts of a whole as percentages. To read a graph, follow these steps:

- Read the title of the graph so you know what it is about.
- Look at the labels of each segment.
- Study the colors and patterns used and compare them with the key.
- Compare the parts of the circle to find the relationships and draw conclusions.

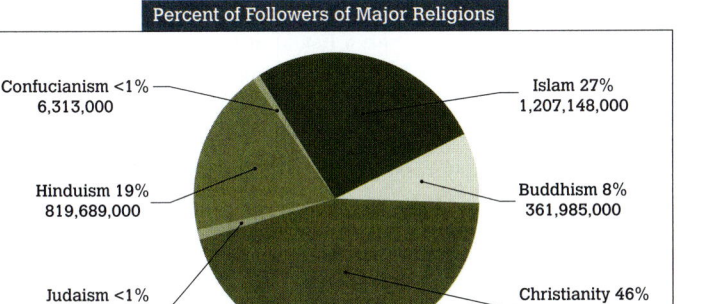

Percent of Followers of Major Religions

- Confucianism <1% — 6,313,000
- Islam 27% — 1,207,148,000
- Hinduism 19% — 819,689,000
- Buddhism 8% — 361,985,000
- Judaism <1% — 14,484,000
- Christianity 46% — 2,019,052,000

Use the circle graph above to answer the following questions:

1. Which religion has the largest percentage of followers? What is the percentage?
2. What percentage of people follow Islam?
3. Do Hindus or Buddhists represent a larger portion of the whole?
4. How could you state the percentage of Jewish followers in relation to Confucian followers?

Skill Builder

1. Christianity; 46 percent
2. 27 percent
3. Hindus
4. They are equal in percent, though there are more Jewish followers than Confucian followers.

Classroom Discussion

Discuss with students some of the broader topics covered in this chapter.

- What are some ways that scarce land and resources can be divided fairly?
- In what ways do the arts of a civilization define it?
- How can different religious groups learn to get along with each other?
- How can one person make a difference in the world?

Chapter 10

CIVILIZATIONS OF AFRICA

(750 B.C.–A.D. 1570)

Chapter Summary
Refer to page 146 for a summary of Chapter 10.

Related Transparencies
T-1 World Map
T-2 Outline World Map
T-6 Bantu Migrations

Key Blacklines
Biography–King Afonso

CD Extension
Encourage students to use the reading comprehension, vocabulary reinforcement, and interactive timeline activities on the student CD.

Picturing History
Thatched mud houses, pictured on page 132, are typical structures in some parts of Africa.

Getting Focused
The contents of students' lists and charts will differ. You may wish to divide the class into small groups after each student has made the first list. Working together as a group could make sorting lists and creating a chart more manageable, especially for students who have trouble following directions for multistep projects, as well as those whose first language is not English. Make a copy of each group's list for each member of the

Getting Focused

Skim this chapter to predict what you will be learning.
• Read the lesson titles and subheadings.
• Look at the illustrations and read the captions.
• Examine the maps.
• Review the vocabulary words and terms.

Make a four column chart. Label the columns "Geography," "People," "Places," and "Events." Then make a list of at least five things that you know about Africa. They might be facts about geography or about famous African people, places, or events. Review your list with a partner and add them to your chart. As you read the chapter, add at least twenty new facts to the chart. Be sure to find facts for each column. Remember to add Africa to your world map.

Getting Focused, continued
group, and have them individually add facts as they read the chapter. An alternative is to develop a class list on the board and have students copy the list as the basis of their working list.

Pre-Reading Discussion

1 Discuss with students the basis of your local economy. Tell them that they are about to learn of the economic foundations of several African kingdoms and states.

2 Ask students to identify several now-common items that were once considered precious and expensive (for example, all spices and silk). Tell them that they are about to learn of one such item, salt.

LESSON 1

The Bantu Migrations

Thinking on Your Own

Examine the subheadings and illustrations in this lesson. Write four questions in your notebook that you would like answered by studying this lesson. After you finish reading the lesson, answer the questions.

The African continent has many different **environments**. A region's environment includes all the outside factors that influence the development of a people. Among these factors are the physical geography and the climate where the people live. Climate is the weather that a place has over a long period of time. It is important to learn about the geography of Africa in order to understand the different kingdoms and empires that developed there.

focus your reading

Explain the land and climate zones in Africa.

Who are the Bantu-speakers?

Why did the Bantu-speakers migrate throughout Africa?

Describe African society during the Bantu migration.

vocabulary

environment
vegetation
savanna
rain forest
slash-and-burn
ethnic group
river basin

Geography of the African Continent

Africa has bands, or zones, of different kinds of climates and vegetation. **Vegetation** includes grasses, plants, bushes, and trees. The desert zones include the Sahara in the north and the smaller Kalahari in the south. Together, they make up about 40 percent of the African continent. Beginning in ancient times, traders set up a network to link sub-Saharan Africa with the Mediterranean region. Sub-Saharan Africa includes the regions located south of the Sahara Desert. Traders moved back and forth across the Sahara on camels.

Olokon was a sea god to the people of the Ife Kingdom.

Civilizations of Africa 133

Lesson Summary

Africa's climate zones include rain forest, savanna, mild zone, and desert.

Bantu-speakers are related by language group, not by ethnicity. More than 60 million Africans speak one of the Bantu languages.

The Bantu-speakers moved from the area around the Niger River into the Congo River basin and then farther east. Archaeologists suspect that the Bantu-speaking people moved because of population pressures. As they moved into different climate areas, they adapted to different lifestyles. Large empires developed in central and southern Africa from the mixture of native people and Bantu-speakers.

Lesson Objective

Students will learn about the Bantu-speaking people and their migration throughout Africa.

Focus Your Reading Answers

1 The land zones of Africa are desert, rain forest, and savanna. The climate is hot and dry with mild zones in the north and south of the continent.

2 Bantu-speakers are a group that share a common language family, one of more than 500 Bantu languages and dialects.

3 Bantu-speakers probably moved because of increased population putting pressure on the resources of a region.

4 African society centered in the village, which in turn was made up of a lineage group.

Lesson Vocabulary

Introduce each of the following vocabulary terms to students.

Explain that the *environment* includes all the outside factors that influence a group of people. The *environment* includes climate and physical geography.

The trees, bushes, plants, and grasses of an area are its *vegetation*. The *vegetation* of Africa includes the many plants of the *rain forest*. A *rain forest* is an area that is very hot and receives a lot of rain. A *savanna* is an area of grasslands with a few bushes. Africa's *savanna* makes up about 40 percent of its land.

Cutting trees and then burning them to clear land for farming is called *slash-and-burn* method.

An *ethnic group* is a group of people sharing the same culture. The Bantu-speaking people were not an *ethnic group*.

The area that a river runs through is called the *river basin*. The Bantu moved into the Congo *River basin*, perhaps as early as 1000 B.C.

Civilizations of Africa 133

Map Extension

Ask students to use the map on page 134 to answer the following questions:

- Through which region does the Tropic of Cancer pass? (desert)
- Which climates are part of Madagascar? (rain forest and savanna)
- What mountains are near the northern mild zone? (Atlas Mts.)

Picturing History

The savanna, shown at the bottom left on page 134, stretches through 27 modern African nations. It does not receive enough rain to support trees, even though during the rainy season (from May to November), the savanna receives 15 to 25 inches of rain each month. However, the remainder of the year is dry season, during which only about four inches of rain falls.

The African rain forest, pictured at the bottom right on page 134, is second in size only to South America's rain forest. More than 9 million acres of forest were lost annually between 1990 and 1995. Logging, overgrazing, civil unrest, clearing for farming, and the need for firewood and charcoal have all contributed to this loss. Africa is losing rain forest at an annual rate of .7 percent. Some fear that most of central Africa's rain forest will disappear within 20 years.

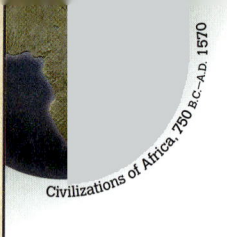

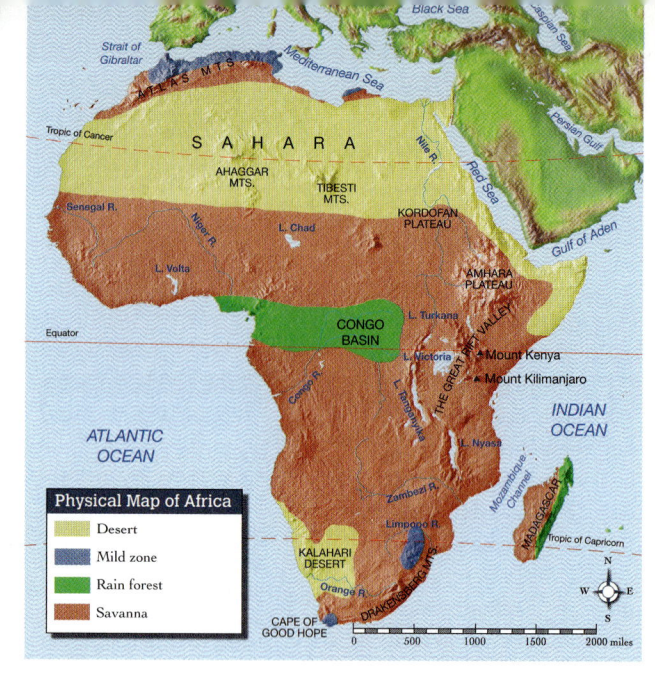

Civilizations of Africa, 750 B.C.–A.D. 1570

Physical Map of Africa
- Desert
- Mild zone
- Rain forest
- Savanna

Another large area is the **savanna**. This is a region of grasslands with small trees and bushes scattered here and there. Usually it rains enough in the savanna for farming and herding. However, a stretch of dry years without rain results in droughts and famine. Beginning in the 500s, wealthy kingdoms and empires developed in the savanna region of West Africa. Their wealth came from trade.

About 10 percent of the African continent is **rain forest**. This is the area bordering the equator. The region is very hot and receives a great amount of rain. As a result, vegetation is thick, but some farming has been possible since early times. Africans developed the **slash-and-burn** method to clear the forest. They would cut down trees and plants and then burn them to open land for planting crops.

Africa's geography includes savanna (left) and rain forest (right).

134

Extension

Many rain forest plants are known to have healing properties. Invite students interested in medicine or in plants to use library resources or the Internet to research the uses of rain forest plants and the need for efforts for rain forest preservation. Have them present their findings to the class by using the Student Presentation Builder on the student CD.

Extension

The Serengeti Plains are home to 45 mammal species, nearly 500 species of birds, and more than 50 kinds of acacia tree. The Serengeti has the world's largest diversity of hoofed mammals, including zebra, buffalo, rhinoceros, wildebeest, and antelope. Encourage students to learn more about this vast and important ecosystem using library resources or the Internet.

stop and think

Write a description of the various climates of the African continent. Use as many directions in your description as you can. Besides east, west, north, and south, try to use the intermediate directions northeast, northwest, southeast, and southwest. Share your description with a partner. Quiz one another on the climate zones of Africa.

Both the far northern region and the southern tip of the continent have areas with mild, rainy winters and hot, dry summers. In the north, this region is along the Mediterranean Sea.

Bantu-Speaking People

The Bantu-speaking people are not an **ethnic group**, like Italians, Chinese, Serbians, or Hispanics. An ethnic group shares the same culture. Bantu-speakers belong to many ethnic groups. What they have in common is their language family, or group of languages. There are over 300 Bantu languages or dialects. Today, over 180 million Africans speak a Bantu language.

The Bantu on the Move

Historians think that the first Bantu-speakers lived in what is today the nation of Cameroon. Bantu-speakers were farmers who moved and settled in small family groups. They lived in the region around the Niger River. Possibly as early as 1000 B.C., the Bantu began to move south into the Congo River basin. A **river basin** is a large area that includes a major river and its tributaries. Sometime around 500 B.C., Bantu-speakers also moved east. Over time, they spread throughout central Africa. By the 1200s, the Bantu were in much of southern Africa.

Archaeologists think that two events made it possible for Bantu-speakers to move out from the area of the Niger River. First was the discovery of iron-making. Someone figured out how to make iron into axes and hoes. With iron axes, men could cut down trees, and with iron hoes they could farm. Second, a trade network linked the Niger River area with the east coast. Traders along this route brought yams

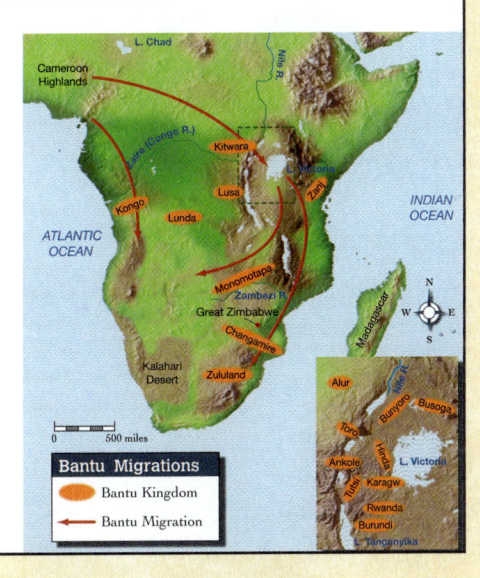

Civilizations of Africa, 750 B.C.–A.D. 1570

Stop and Think

Students' descriptions will vary. Possible response: Most of the northern third of the continent is desert. A small section to the northwest is savanna, sandwiched between the desert and the mild zone along the Mediterranean. Most of the sub-Saharan region is savanna. The Congo River basin, northwest of Lake Victoria, is rain forest. Other small mild zones are located south of the Limpopo River and at the Cape of Good Hope. The Kalahari Desert is in the southwest section of the continent, near the Tropic of Capricorn. The island of Madagascar, to the east of the continent, is divided between savanna to the west and rain forest to the east.

Map Extension

Ask students to use the map on page 135 to answer the following questions:

- Where did the Bantu migrations originate? (Cameroon Highlands)
- Which direction is the Kalahari Desert from the Zambezi River? (southwest)
- Using the inset map, which settlement is farthest north? (Alur)
- What lake supported many Bantu kingdoms? (Lake Victoria)

Picturing History

The Ife bronze, shown at the bottom of page 133, is of the sea god, Olokon. Point out the holes in the face. Decorations were placed in them during special celebrations.

Civilizations of Africa | 135

Picturing History

The carving shown at the top left on page 136 depicts scenes of Congo life. It shows a family at work on their farm.

The mask at the bottom left was probably used in religious ceremonies. Masks were believed to give shamans powers they did not otherwise have.

The statue to the right is of King Mishe miShyaang maMbul Kuba of the Bushoong people. The Bushoong, who lived in what is modern-day Congo, were part of the larger Kuba ethnic group. There have been 21 successive rulers since King Shyaang's rule in the sixteenth century.

Putting It All Together
Possible answer: Cameroon, Congo, Democratic Republic of Congo, Central African Republic, Chad, Sudan, Uganda, Kenya, Tanzania, Mozambique, Swaziland, Zambia, Zimbabwe, Botswana

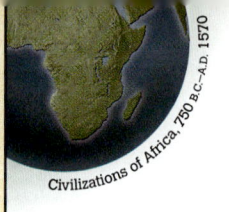

---

and bananas from Malaysia in Southeast Asia. These crops were especially suited to growing in hot, wet climates.

But why did the Bantu move? Archaeologists think that the population in the Niger River area was growing too large. The pressure of too many people caused some family groups to move to a new place. Over time, the population increased in the new area. Again, some families would decide to leave and look for a new place to settle. This cycle was repeated until Bantu-speakers had migrated to southern Africa. This movement took place over hundreds of years.

The environments were different in new areas where the Bantu settled. As a result, their previous ways of life did not always work in the new region. The Bantu-speakers had to adapt. For example, as the Bantu moved out of the rain forest and into the savanna, some gave up farming. They took up herding cattle. Other Bantu-speakers still farmed but with different crops. In East Africa, Bantu-speakers became part of a trade network that reached across the Indian Ocean.

Often the migrants learned new skills and how to grow new foods from people already living in the new areas. For the most part, the mixing of Bantu-speakers with native populations was peaceful. In many areas in central and southern Africa, large states and empires developed from the mixing of Bantu-speakers with others.

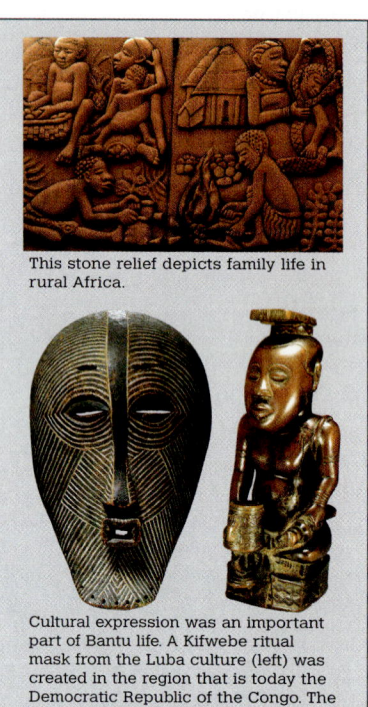

This stone relief depicts family life in rural Africa.

Cultural expression was an important part of Bantu life. A Kifwebe ritual mask from the Luba culture (left) was created in the region that is today the Democratic Republic of the Congo. The Ndop carving of King Mishe miShyaan maMbul Kuba was created in Zaire.

Putting It All Together
Use a modern political map of Africa to trace the migration of the Bantu-speakers. Work with a partner to make a list of all the modern nations that the Bantu moved through and the places in which they settled.

Lesson Vocabulary
Discuss each of the vocabulary terms with students.

A synonym for cement is *mortar*. The buildings in Great Zimbabwe were made of stone placed without *mortar*.

Lesser nobles are called *vassals*. Matope's *vassals* were part of his family and allies.

People who do business between traders are known as *intermediaries*. East African goods traveled to China through *intermediaries*.

Swahili refers to both the customs and language of a group of mixed African-Arab descent. Today, *Swahili* is the most widely spoken language in East Africa.

LESSON 2

The Trading States of East Africa

Thinking on Your Own

As you read each section in this lesson, create a concept web of the people who lived in East Africa. Include important details, facts, and dates.

The history of East African cultures features the mixing of different people. Many, of course, were African. But others were from the Arabian Peninsula, India, Persia, and even Greece. Trade was an important factor in the development of East African kingdoms and states.

focus your reading

Why did Axum fight with its neighbors to the south?

Decide why Great Zimbabwe is famous. Explain your decision.

How did the Swahili culture develop?

vocabulary

mortar   intermediaries
vassals   Swahili

The Kingdom of Axum

Around 700 B.C., Arabs set up a colony in what is today the East African country of Ethiopia. This was about the same time that the Greeks started colonies in Asia. Like the Greeks, the Arabs were interested in trade. By 300 B.C., Arabs and Africans had joined to create the rich trading kingdom of Axum.

The city of Adulis, located on the Red Sea, became the chief trading center of Axum. Trade goods from the interior of Africa passed through Adulis on their way to the Arabian Peninsula, the Mediterranean region, and Asia. Axum was part of a trade network that reached as far as India. The monsoon winds made it possible for early trading ships to sail across the Indian Ocean. African trade goods included ivory, slaves, and spices. Cloth, wine, and olive oil were among the goods imported by Axum's traders.

The barter system was replaced by shells, trinkets, and eventually, coins.

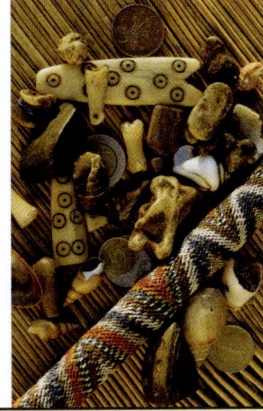

Focus Your Reading Answers

1 Axum fought with its southern neighbors over the trade in ivory and slaves.

2 Great Zimbabwe is famous as a building site. Structures such as a fort, a palace, towers, and fences are made with stone that did not need mortar to fit together.

3 The Swahili culture developed as a result of intermarriage between African and Arab people.

Picturing History

The collection of items shown on page 137 was found in Salcombe Bay in England, near Devon. Divers recovered them from a sunken ship. The gold came from mines near Timbuktu and Gao. These coins are from the sixteenth and seventeenth centuries.

Lesson Summary

Arabs and Africans joined together to create Axum around 300 B.C. in what is now Ethiopia. Adulis became its chief trading city, part of a network that reached as far as India. In A.D. 300, Axum defeated its chief trading rival, Kush. Shortly thereafter, Christianity became the official religion. Axum received help from Portugal against trading enemies in the south but split into smaller kingdoms in the sixteenth century.

Zimbabwe was a large settlement of stone buildings on a major trade route. The Shona took power in the area and defeated other groups. Matope enlarged the kingdom and set up the Monomotapa Empire, using a feudal system. Vassals governed the provinces of the empire. The Portuguese eventually defeated the empire.

Cities on Africa's East Coast, such as Zanzibar, Kilwa, and Mombassa, became independent city-states. They were wealthy through trade. Arab merchants acted as intermediaries for goods going as far as China.

The mixture of Arab and African cultures and people led to the Swahili language, which today is the most widely spoken language in East Africa. For hundreds of years, Arab city-states fought the Portuguese for control of the East Coast.

Lesson Objective

Students will learn about the major trading states of East Africa: Axum, Zimbabwe, and Swahili city-states.

Civilizations of Africa

Picturing History

The church shown on page 138 is one of 11 stone churches built by King Lalibela in Ethiopia during the twelfth century. According to legend, he was following instructions he received from God during a visit to heaven while in a coma. A UNESCO World Heritage site, it remains a living community where 450 monks, 250 deacons, 350 priests, and 400 students live. It is about 500 miles (700 km) from Ethiopia's capital, Addis Ababa. An Eastern Orthodox Christian pilgrimage site, this town of about 10,000 sometimes has 20,000 to 50,000 visitors, especially during religious holidays. Efforts are under way to preserve and restore the site.

Extension

Axum, now a part of Ethiopia, is also famous for its stelae, the carved monuments that marked the tombs of royalty during the fourth and fifth centuries. The tallest one still standing is 75 feet high (22.86 m), made from a single piece of granite that was quarried about two miles from the site. The largest, now fallen, was the size of a 13-story building and weighed 700 tons. The stelae are the largest decorated stones cut by humans.

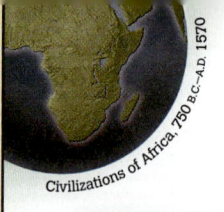

In A.D. 300, Axum defeated the kingdom of Kush, which was its trading rival. The king at the time was Ezana. In 324, he converted to Christianity and made Christianity the official religion of Axum.

A church built from solid rock in Lalibela, Ethiopia

Beginning in the 1100s, conflict broke out between Axum and the Muslim trading states to the south. The issue was control of the slave and ivory trade. The Muslim city-states were trying to take over the trade from Axum. Fighting occurred over the next few centuries. By the 1500s, Axum was a trading partner with, and an ally of, Portugal. It appealed to Portugal for help. In 1543, the allies defeated their southern rivals. Axum, however, split into several kingdoms. It was not until the 1880s that it would come together again as one nation, Ethiopia.

The Zimbabwe Region

Some Bantu-speakers moved east and then south along the eastern coast of Africa. The earliest Bantu-speakers were in the area by 400. Later groups came between 900 and 1500.

One of the places they settled came to be called Zimbabwe. The word means "great stone houses." It refers to the huge stone buildings that were built over many centuries. There are a number of these ruins, but the largest is known as Great Zimbabwe. It has a palace, towers, a fort, and fences all made from pieces of stone. The stones were laid one on top of another without any **mortar**, or cement, to keep them together. Archaeologists believe that Great Zimbabwe was the center of a huge trading kingdom. Zimbabwe was on the trade route that linked the interior of Africa with the East Coast and beyond to Asia. Zimbabwe's major export was gold.

By the early 1400s, the Shona, a Bantu-speaking clan, had seized power in the region and driven out other groups. The leader Mutota, and later his son Matope, gained control over their rivals. All traders traveling through their territory had to pay a tax on their goods.

Matope further enlarged his lands and set up the Monomotapa Empire. He developed a feudal system of government. Under feudalism, lesser nobles called **vassals** owed loyalty, service, and sometimes a yearly payment of money to a higher noble or king. Matope's vassals were relatives and allies. He divided the Empire into provinces, each governed by a vassal.

In the 1500s, the Monomotapa rulers began to lose power to the Portuguese. The Portuguese were slowly moving into the interior of East Africa from cities along the coast. They were looking for the gold mines that supplied the gold trade. In the 1620s, the forces of the Monomotapa king were defeated by the Portuguese.

stop and think

Write three important facts that you learned about Axum and three important facts about the Zimbabwe region. Turn the facts into questions. Take turns with a partner asking and answering questions.

Trading City-States

The trade from the interior passed through a few cities on the east coast of Africa on its way to Arabia or India. Eventually, coastal cities such as Kilwa, Mombassa, and Zanzibar became independent states with their own rulers, governments, and armed forces.

At one time or another, Persian, Arab, Indonesian, and Indian traders all settled in the cities along Africa's east coast. However, by 1000, Arab merchants had become the most important to the economy. They grew wealthy from international trade. They lived luxurious lives in huge houses with rugs from Persia and porcelain from China. They wore silk clothes from Asia and jewels set in gold. Their diets included coffee and fruits from the Arabian Peninsula.

Picturing History

Great Zimbabwe had three distinct areas of settlement. The walls of Great Zimbabwe, shown on page 139, are more than 30 feet (10 m) high and 16 feet (5 m) thick. Each new row of stones was set back a bit farther so that the wall sloped slightly. Some of the artifacts found at the site include goods imported from China and India, instruments used to make fine jewelry, and tools for smelting iron, copper, and gold.

Extension

Karl Mauch, a German explorer, discovered the ruins of Great Zimbabwe in 1871. Like many people of his time, Mauch believed Africans were an inferior race. He and other archaeologists assumed that the city must have been built by more northern people, perhaps Egyptians or Phoenicians. It took many years for Europeans to admit that civilizations south of the Sahara were capable of this achievement.

Stop and Think

Students' facts and questions will vary but should be about Axum and Zimbabwe.

Axum: Adulis was chief trading center; Christianity was the official religion; Axum was trading partner with Portugal

Zimbabwe: huge trading center; developed feudal system; defeated by Portuguese

Map Extension

Ask students to use the map on page 140 to answer the following questions:

- Where was Axum in relation to the Swahili settlements? (north)
- From the Gulf of Aden, through what body of water did traders pass to reach Cairo? (Red Sea)
- Which Swahili settlement was farthest north? (Mogadishu)
- About how many miles along the coast did the Swahili settlements extend? (about 2,000 miles)

Picturing History

The sails on the ship pictured on page 140 are known as lateen sails. They allowed ships to sail against the wind as well as before it. Lateen sails may have been used in the Mediterranean by the second century A.D., perhaps borrowed from the people of the Persian Gulf or Egypt.

The wealth of the merchants was built on trade in iron ore, ivory, slaves, and gold from the interior of Africa. The merchants exchanged these for their own luxuries, and other trade goods such as cloth, glass, and metal goods for customers in the interior. Through **intermediaries**, or middlemen, trade goods flowed back and forth between East Africa and India, Malaysia, Indonesia, and China.

In time, the population of the city-states began to change. Bantu-speaking Africans and Arabs mixed and intermarried. Many Africans converted to Islam. New customs and a new language called **Swahili** developed. Swahili means "people of the coast" in Arabic. Today, Swahili is the most widely spoken language in East Africa. It is the official language of the modern nations of Kenya and Tanzania.

The arrival of the Portuguese brought an end to centuries of relatively peaceful trade. The Portuguese were determined to take control of the East Coast trade. Beginning in 1505, the Portuguese fought the Arab city-states for power. For the next 300 years, conflict between Arabs and Portuguese on the East Coast was common.

The dhows used today are very similar to ancient Arabian trading ships.

Putting It All Together

Rivalry over trade caused conflict throughout East Africa. Create a cause-and-effect flowchart for conflict in each of the three kingdoms or regions described in this lesson. Be sure to indicate the cause and the result of each conflict. Share your flowchart with a partner and review the cause-and-effect relationships.

Putting It All Together
Cause-and-effect flowcharts will vary. Possible response:

Axum
Cause: control of slave and ivory trade
Effect: Axum fought Muslim trading states to south, enlisted help of Portugal

Zimbabwe
Cause: Portuguese were looking for gold mines
Effect: Portuguese defeated Monomotapa king

Swahili
Cause: Portuguese determined to take control of trade on East Coast
Effect: Portuguese fought Arab city-states for 300 years

LESSON 3

West African Kingdoms

Thinking on Your Own

As you study this lesson, create a table in your notebook to help you remember information about the three important kingdoms in West Africa. Use the following categories for your table: "Name of Kingdom," "Dates," "Location," "Trade Goods," and "Key Facts."

Between 500 and the late 1500s, three important **kingdoms**—or areas governed by a monarch—rose and fell in the savanna region of West Africa. Each one was based on trans-Saharan trade. Trade goods passed north to south and east to west along a series of trade routes. The network joined West Africa with the Mediterranean region and the Arabian Peninsula.

focus your reading

How did Ghana become wealthy?

Why is Mansa Musa remembered?

Explain how Songhai became so powerful.

vocabulary

kingdoms scholars
merchants rebel
Berbers

Gold, ivory, slaves, leather goods, cattle, sheep, and jewelry were sent north along the trade routes. Salt, cloth, wheat, dried fruit, horses, and metal goods were shipped south. Muslim **merchants**—or businessmen—slowly took control of the trade. They bought trade goods from West African traders. The merchants then sold these goods to **Berbers**, or desert nomads, who ran camel caravans across the Sahara. The Berbers sold the goods to merchants in North Africa. These merchants either sold the goods there or to other traders who carried them farther east, even to the Arabian Peninsula. Like the goods that traveled along the Silk Road, each time the goods were resold, they became a little more expensive.

Camel caravans are still used as a means of transporting goods.

Lesson Summary

Three major West African kingdoms existed between A.D. 500 and the 1500s. They were based on trans-Saharan trade.

Muslim merchants bought goods from West African traders, then sold them to nomads who sold them to merchants in North Africa.

Ghana traded salt and gold. Ghana declined and was eventually conquered by the Mali ruler Sundiata.

Mali's wealth was also based on taxes from trade. Mali's kings were Muslim and so were supposed to make a pilgrimage to Makkah. Mansa Musa distributed gold freely during his pilgrimage. He returned with architects and scholars, building the capital of Timbuktu into a major learning center.

Songhai, centered in Gao, increased in territory and in control of the gold and salt trade. Sunni Ali and Askia Muhammad expanded the kingdom. Songhai's glory faded after an invasion by Morocco.

Lesson Objective

Students will learn about the kingdoms of Ghana, Mali, and Songhai.

on Vocabulary

s each of the vocabulary terms with students.

ms are regions ruled by a king or queen. Several *kingdoms* arose and declined in Africa's savanna.

sspeople are also known as *merchants*. Muslim *merchants* controlled trade in Africa.

nomads were called *Berbers*. The *Berbers* guided camel caravans across the to sell goods to North African *merchants*.

s are those who study and are interested in learning. Islamic *scholars* came to following the arrival of *merchants*.

are people, groups of people, or states that fight against a custom or a ment.

Focus Your Reading Answers

1 Ghana became wealthy through its gold, which was traded for salt, and from taxes on trade goods.

2 Mansa Musa is remembered for his wealth, his pilgrimage to Makkah, and building Timbuktu.

3 Songhai became powerful through controlling trade, especially in gold and salt.

Civilizations of Africa 141

Map Extension

Ask students to use the map on page 142 to answer the following questions:

- What was the farthest eastern city on the trade route? (Makkah)
- Which city on the Mediterranean Sea was farthest north? (Tunis)
- Kukya was part of what kingdom? (Songhai)
- Which trade route had the greatest distance between cities? (Bussa to Cairo)

Stop and Think

Students' responses will vary but should reflect an understanding of imports, exports, and expenses related to doing business.

Extension

Salt is still mined in Africa. In its unrefined state, it is solid. Blocks of it are about one foot long with a grainy, rough texture. A trip to the salt mines with a camel caravan takes just over two weeks. The camels bring back four bars of salt each; the bars were worth about $8 each in the late 1990s. Even though salt can be found in more accessible locations, the way of life for salt traders has not changed. Have students do research on the life of salt traders today using library resources or the Internet. Have them make a poster to show their findings.

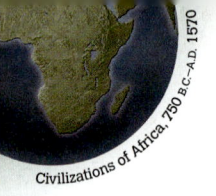

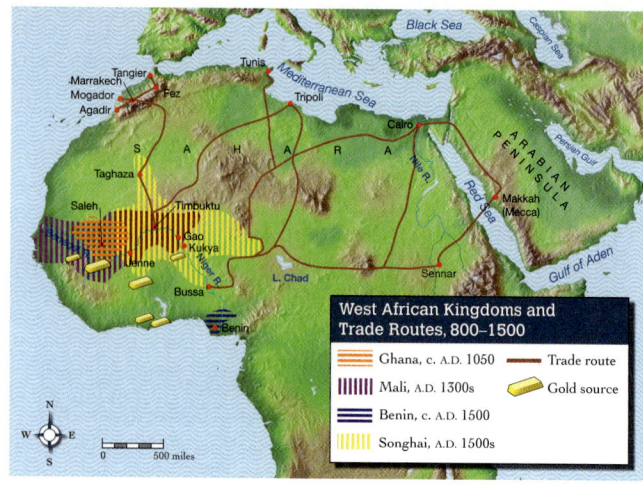

West African Kingdoms and Trade Routes, 800–1500

- Ghana, c. A.D. 1050
- Mali, A.D. 1300s
- Benin, c. 1500
- Songhai, A.D. 1500s
- Trade route
- Gold source

The Kingdom of Ghana

The first of the great West African kingdoms was Ghana. The kingdom reached into parts of what are today Mauritania, Mali, Senegal, and Guinea. Most of the people were farmers, but the wealth of the kingdom came from trading gold.

Ghana was located near a huge gold field. Ghanians mined the gold and traded it for goods from North Africa and beyond. Another important trade good was salt. Ghana had gold; North Africa had salt. The kings taxed the salt coming into the kingdom and the gold going out. They grew wealthy from the taxes placed on trade.

Beginning in the 600s, Islam became a major influence in West Africa. Invading armies spread Islam among the people they conquered. Muslim merchants also spread Islam. As merchants began to settle in market towns and cities, Islamic **scholars** followed them. The scholars soon began teaching about Islam. City dwellers, including the advisers to

stop and think

Imagine that you are an Arab merchant living in Ghana. What would you import that the people of Ghana wanted? What would you export for sale outside of Ghana to help pay for your imports? What other expenses would you have? Work with a partner to develop a list of imports, exports, and expenses.

Picturing History

Camels, which were known as "ships of the desert" and were ideal for caravan travel, are pictured at the bottom of page 141. Camels perspire very little and do not pant. They are the only mammals capable of raising their body temperature tolerance level to avoid losing water through perspiring. Camels' feet have leathery pads that spread, preventing them from sinking into the sand. Camels can go without food or water for 5 to 7 days. They can drink as much as 21 gallons (100 liters) in ten minutes, storing water in their bloodstream. A working camel puts in about 25 years of service, working six to eight months a year, carrying several hundred pounds and covering 25 miles (40 km) a day.

Ghana's kings, became Muslims. West Africans living in farming villages, however, did not convert to Islam. They tended to continue practicing their traditional religions.

Ghana began a slow decline in the 1100s. The kingdom never recovered from invasions by Islamic armies from North Africa. Rebellious states began to break away from the kingdom. The final blow came in 1240 when King Sundiata of Mali conquered what was left of the "land of gold," as Ghana was known.

The Kingdom of Mali

According to the *Epic of Sundiata*, Sumanguru, the ruler of the Kingdom of Kaniaga, seized power over part of the Kingdom of Ghana. In an effort to increase his power, Sumanguru invaded Mali and killed 11 princes who were the older brothers of Prince Sundiata Keita. When he grew to manhood, Sundiata Keita avenged the death of his brothers by killing Sumanguru. Like Sumanguru, Sundiata Keita then went on his own campaign to enlarge Mali. Over time, Mali spread its rule as far west as the Atlantic coast and as far east as what is today Niger.

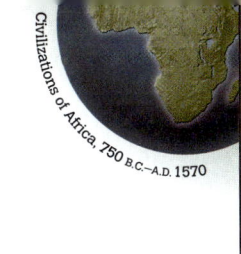

The burnt-brick mosque in Timbuktu, Mali

Most people in Mali were farmers who lived in villages. However, Mali's wealth was built on the gold and salt trade. The kings of Mali taxed all goods being exported and imported. They also collected taxes from their own people.

The kings of Mali became Muslims. Muslims are supposed to make a pilgrimage to Makkah (MECCA) once in their lifetime. Mansa Musa, who ruled from 1312 to 1337, made a

Picturing History

The Great Mosque at Timbuktu, pictured on page 143, was built following Mansa Musa's pilgrimage to Makkah in 1324. At its height, Timbuktu, the "pearl of the desert," had 180 Koranic schools as well as other places of higher education. The population may have reached 40,000–50,000 during the sixteenth century.

Extension

Chronicles from the Arab world and southern Europe commented on Mansa Musa's pilgrimage until the sixteenth century. His image even appeared on two maps from the fourteenth century.

> **Time Box Extension**
>
> Have students make bar graphs to show which kingdom lasted the longest.

> **Picturing History**
>
> The brass figure shown on page 144 depicts a Nigerian Edo bodyguard of the king. Plaques such as this were used on wooden pillars in the Oba's palaces. The Oba, or king, was believed to be a descendant of god. Craftworkers in Benin still create objects for use in rituals and ceremonies.

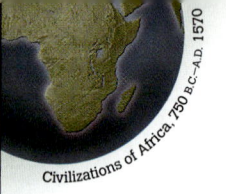

Civilizations of Africa, 750 B.C.–A.D. 1570

pilgrimage like no other. In 1324, he brought together 60,000 people for his trip across Africa and the Arabian Peninsula. Among them were 12,000 slaves. Of these slaves, 500 carried staffs, or walking sticks, made of gold. Eighty camels carried 300 pounds of gold each. Because of Mansa Musa's lavish spending and generosity in giving away so much gold on his trip, the price of gold fell sharply. It took 12 years for the price to rise to where it had been in 1324.

The great Islamic cities that Mansa Musa visited made an impression on him. He brought back architects and Islamic scholars to Timbuktu, the capital of Mali. He had mosques, palaces, and schools built. Timbuktu became the center of Islamic learning in West Africa.

Time Box
500–1240
Kingdom of Ghana
1234–1400s
Kingdom of Mali
1450–1600s
Kingdom of Songhai

Plaque of a Nigerian Edo bodyguard from the sixteenth century

Shortly after Mansa Musa died, Berbers from North Africa invaded Mali. At the same time, **rebel** states fought for power. Rebels often fight against a government and try to gain power. In 1359, Timbuktu and Gao broke away. Mali quickly lost its importance.

The Kingdom of Songhai

The city of Gao eventually became the trading center for the Songhai Kingdom. In 1464, Songhai's leader, Sunni Ali, set out to conquer more territory. But he was not interested in territory for the sake of expansion. He wanted the regions around Timbuktu and Jenne in order to gain control of the salt and gold trade.

After Sunni Ali's death, fighting broke out over who would rule. His son lost the struggle to Muhammad Ture. In 1493, Ture took command and changed his name to Askia Muhammad. Like Sunni Ali, he extended the borders of Songhai. Askia Muhammad also divided the kingdom into provinces managed by governors. He continued the practice of collecting taxes on all goods entering and leaving the kingdom.

> **Extension**
>
> The conflict after Sunni Ali's death was as much religious as it was political. Sunni Ali represented the tribal religions and had oppressed Timbuktu's Muslim holy men. The dynasty that Askia Muhammad founded stood for Islamic values.

A devout Muslim, Askia Muhammad also made an impressive pilgrimage to Makkah. He supported the building of mosques and schools and attempted to convert everyone in Songhai to Islam. Islamic principles became the basis of the court system and of social reforms.

Askia Muhammad's rule was a period of peace and prosperity. However, fighting among rivals and the invasion by the sultan of Morocco's army put an end to Songhai. By 1600, the glory of Songhai had faded like that of Ghana and Mali before it.

Putting It All Together

This lesson uses the comparison-and-contrast signal word *like* several times. Find three examples and write them in your notebook. Then review the information in the table that you created as you read this lesson. Write five comparison-and-contrast sentences using information from the table. Share your sentences with a partner.

Visit to Timbuktu

the early 1500s, Leo Africanus, a visitor m Morocco, described Timbuktu. The owing is an excerpt from his writings. *rbary* refers to North Africa, which was erwhelmingly Muslim by this time.

Here are many shops of tificers and merchants, pecially of such as weave linen d cotton cloth. And hither do e Barbary merchants bring the th of Europe.... The habitants... are exceedingly h.... Here are many wells ntaining most sweet water.... Corn, cattle, milk, and butter in s region yields in great abundance.... The inhabitants are ople of a gentle and cheerful disposition.... Here are great store doctors, judges, priests, and other learned men, that are untifully maintained at the king's cost and charges. And hither brought diverse manuscripts or written books out of Barbary, ich are sold for more than any other merchandise."

reading for understanding

Based on this reading and information from the lesson, how do you think the king gets money to pay for doctors and other services?

What does the high price of manuscripts and books tell you about the people of Timbuktu?

Describe Timbuktu in one sentence.

Extension

Originally from Morocco, Leo Africanus traveled throughout North Africa. Returning from a trip to Egypt, he was captured into slavery by Christian pirates. He was given to Pope Leo X as a gift. The Pope freed him and persuaded him to become a Christian. He learned Italian and Latin and taught Arabic. He wrote *Descriptions of Africa* in about 1526. Eventually he was able to return to North Africa, where he may have resumed Islamic beliefs.

Putting It All Together
Possible answers:

Like the goods that traveled along the Silk Road, each time goods were resold, they became a little more expensive.

Like Sumanguru, Sundiata Keita then went on his own campaign to enlarge Mali.

Mansa Musa made a pilgrimage like no other.

Like Sunni Ali, Askia Muhammad extended Songhai's borders.

The glory of Songhai faded like that of Ghana and Mali.

Mali's wealth, like that of Ghana, was built on the gold and salt trade.

Like Mansa Musa, Askia Muhammad made a pilgrimage to Makkah.

Reading for Understanding

1 The king gets money from the gold and salt trade.

2 They valued learning and the written word.

3 Timbuktu is a prosperous city that emphasizes education.

Civilizations of Africa

Chapter Review

1 Students' essays will vary. Possible points:

Similarities
- based on trade, especially of gold and salt
- eventually conquered by more powerful groups
- became Muslim

Differences:
- Mali was known for its education, especially in Timbuktu.
- In Songhai, Muslim principles became the basis for social reform and the court system.

2 Students' headlines will vary; possible responses include:
(a) Bantu-speakers Arrive in Congo River Basin! Long Journey from Cameroon Highlands Ends Here
(b) Europeans Arrive in Coastal Towns; Increased Trade Their Goal
(c) Palace Completed at Great Zimbabwe; Years of Building Result in Masterpiece
(d) African Ruler Arrives in Makkah; Generous Alms Given All Along the Pilgrimage
(e) Askia Muhammad Wins Power Struggle; Claims Muslim Values Will Shape Society

Chapter Summary

Civilizations of Africa, 750 B.C.–A.D. 1570

- Africa has many different **environments**. They include desert, **savanna**, and **rain forest**. Africans developed **slash-and-burn** agriculture to clear **vegetation**.
- Bantu is a language family, not an **ethnic group**.
- Bantu-speakers migrated into the Congo **River basin** around 1000 B.C.
- The buildings of Great Zimbabwe were made without using **mortar**.
- The Monomotapa kingdom was based on feudalism. The king made his relatives and allies **vassals**.
- Trade goods flowed through **intermediaries** along the network that linked the interior of East Africa, the East African city-states, India, Malaysia, Indonesia, and China.
- East African city-states were a mix of Bantu-speaking Africans, Arabs, Persians, and Indians. Arab **merchants** became economically important. Over time a new culture and language called **Swahili** developed.
- The **kingdoms** of Ghana, Mali, and Songhai developed in the savanna region of West Africa.
- Islam became an important influence in West Africa. Islamic **scholars** helped make the city of Timbuktu a center of Islamic learning.
- **Berbers** ran camel caravans across the Sahara and sold goods in North Africa.
- **Rebels** fought for power in Mali.

Chapter Review

1 Use the table you created in Lesson 3 as the basis for an essay about the differences and similarities among the three West African kingdoms.

2 Write two-line headlines for (a) the migration of Bantu-speakers into the Congo basin, (b) the arrival of the Portuguese in East Africa, (c) the completion of the palace in Great Zimbabwe, (d) Mansa Musa's arrival in Makkah, (e) Askia Muhammad as ruler of Songhai.

Novel Connections

Below is a list of books that relate to the time period covered in this chapter. The numbers in parentheses indicate the related Thematic Strands of the National Council for the Social Studies (NCSS).

James Haskins, Kathleen Benson. *African Beginnings.* Lothrop, Lee, and Shepard Books, 1998. (I, III, V, X)

Joseph Lemosalai Lekuton. *Facing the Lion: Growing Up Maasai on the African Savanna.* National Geographic Society, 2004. (I, III, IV, IX)

Patricia McKissack. *The Royal Kingdoms of Ghana, Mali, and Songhay: Life in Medieval Africa.* Gulliver Books, 2001. (I, III, VI)

Sean Sheehan. *Great African Kingdoms.* Raintree Steck-Vaughn, 1999. (I, III, V, X)

Veronique Tadjo. *Talking Drums: A Selection of Poems from Africa South of the Sahara.* Bloomsbury USA, 2004. (I, IX)

Skill Builder

Summarizing and Paraphrasing

A summary is a short description of something. For example, if a classmate asks you what happened on a TV show the night before, you explain the important points but leave out most of the details. You make it short. In other words, you summarize the show.

When you write a report, you often need to paraphrase what you have read. When you paraphrase, be careful not to write word-for-word what you have read. Use your own words and keep the important details as well as the main idea. A paraphrase may be about the same length as the original. Read the following paragraph from Lesson 2:

> The arrival of the Portuguese brought an end to centuries of relatively peaceful trade. The Portuguese were determined to take control of the East Coast trade. Beginning in 1505, the Portuguese fought the Arab city-states for power. For the next 300 years, conflict between Arabs and Portuguese on the East Coast was common.

The following is a paraphrase of that paragraph. It restates the main fact and important details in different words.

> The Portuguese wanted to control trade along the east coast of Africa. They started their campaign to take it over by fighting Arab city-states in 1505. For 300 years the Portuguese and Arabs fought on the East Coast.

Summarizing—a short restatement of the main idea

Paraphrasing—restating a passage in your own words, including the main idea and details

Complete the following activities.

1. Paraphrase paragraphs 2 and 3 under the subheading "The Geography of the African Continent."

2. Reread the section "The Kingdom of Ghana." Find the main idea of each paragraph. Then write a summary of "The Kingdom of Ghana."

Civilizations of Africa

Skill Builder

1. Answers will vary. Possible response: The savanna covers an equally large region. The area has bushes and small trees among the grasslands. There is usually enough rain to herd and farm. Droughts and famine come after a time of no rain. In the West African savanna, rich empires and kingdoms developed from the 500s onward. They were rich because of trade.

   The rain forest covers about one-tenth of Africa. It is just north and south of the equator. It gets a lot of rain and is very hot. Since early times, farming has been possible, even though the plant growth is thick. To make room for farming, Africans started a slash-and-burn policy in the forests. To make room for crops, they cut the trees and plants down and burn them.

2. Ghana was the first great West African kingdom. Its wealth was built on trade and taxes. Islam spread to West Africa through conquest and merchants. Scholars also came to teach Islam and converted city dwellers. Ghana began declining after Islamic armies invaded from North Africa. Sundiata, king of Mali, conquered Ghana in 1240.

Classroom Discussion

Discuss with students some of the broader topics covered in this chapter.

- What effect does climate have in determining a civilization's progress?
- How do feudalistic societies function?
- What are the dangers of building a society on trade?
- In what ways was African society a melting pot?

Chapter Summary
Refer to page 160 for a summary of Chapter 11.

Related Transparencies

T-1 World Map

T-2 Outline World Map

T-19 Venn Diagram

Key Blacklines

Primary Source–The Aztec Tribute System

CD Extension

Encourage students to use the reading comprehension, vocabulary reinforcement, and interactive timeline activities on the student CD.

Getting Focused
After students have made a list of topics, invite them to share. Make a class list; as each topic is covered in the chapter, put a check mark next to the topic. If there are topics that are not covered, invite interested students to use library resources or the Internet to enhance the chapter content. Allow time for students to share their findings with the class.

Chapter 11 THE AMERICAS

(1400 B.C.–A.D. 1570)

Getting Focused

Skim this chapter to predict what you will be learning.
- Read the lesson titles and subheadings.
- Look at the illustrations and read the captions.
- Examine the maps.
- Review the vocabulary words.

This chapter is about Native Americans. Based on your knowledge of how people moved from place to place and how civilizations developed, what do you think this chapter will tell you about Native American Predict the topics or categories of information that yo think it will discuss. Make a list of the topics that you think you will learn about Native Americans. Rememb to add North and South America to your world map.

Picturing History

Machu Picchu, shown at the bottom of page 148, was the home of Incan rulers. Located in the Urubamba River canyon cloud forest at 8,000 feet (2,438 m) above sea level, it was hidden until 1911, when Yale professor Hiram Bingham found the ruined city. Machu Picchu ("manly peak") had about 200 buildings, which were built to incorporate existing landforms. Rocks became sculptures and stone channels became fountains. Another Incan capital has recently been located, also in the Andes Mountains. Excavation of Vilcabamba is currently under way.

Pre-Reading Discussion

1 Ask students to share what they know about contemporary farming practices. Tell them that they are going to read about ancient techniques of raising and gathering food.

2 Discuss with students technological changes, such as personal computers, cell phones, and PDAs, that they have seen. How have these changes affected the way they live? Tell them that they are going to read about cultures in the midst of big changes.

LESSON 1

Cultures of Central and South America

Thinking on Your Own

Chapter 1 presented the six characteristics of a civilization. Make a table with four columns. In the first column, list the six characteristics. Label the other columns "Mayan," "Aztec," and "Incan." As you read the lesson, fill in each column with facts.

The first humans arrived in the Americas thousands of years ago. Archaeologists disagree on exactly when the first migrants came and where they came from. However, they have found no evidence dating earlier than about 12,000 to 15,000 years ago. During the last Ice Age many people crossed a **land bridge** that connected North America to Asia. As the ice melted, the land bridge was slowly covered by water. Today, this area is the Bering Strait. Some archaeologists think that early Americans came from Europe, Africa, or the South Pacific.

focus your reading

Summarize how North and South America became populated by the first Americans.

What happened to Mayan civilization in the Yucatán?

How did the Aztec rule their empire?

Explain how the Inca ruled their empire.

vocabulary

land bridge
Yucatán Peninsula
ceremonial centers
overfarmed
prophecy
commoners
quipu
terraced

Early Americans

The first Americans migrated in small groups across the continents. It took thousands of years, but they spread from the Arctic to the southern tip of South America. Wherever they settled, the first Americans had to adapt to their environment.

The Americas 149

Lesson Summary

Humans arrived in the Americas at least 12,000 to 15,000 years ago. Early Americans were hunters and gatherers.

The Mayan civilization was the largest in Mexico and Central America. The Mayans had a very structured society with rulers at the top.

The Aztec arrived in the Valley of Mexico during the 1200s. Their empire was based on city-states that the Aztec conquered. The Aztec were conquered by the Spanish.

The Inca Empire began in Peru. Local rulers remained in power. The Inca did not want tribute as much as labor for building projects or to maintain lands belonging to the empire or to the gods. The Spanish also conquered the Inca.

Lesson Objective

Students will learn about the Native-American cultures of Middle and South America.

Focus Your Reading Answers

1 Experts think that humans crossed a land bridge at the Bering Strait from Asia. Other theories suggest Africa, Europe, or the South Pacific as sources for the first Americans.

2 The Mayans left their settlements in the Yucatán. Some people think they may have overfarmed the land and needed somewhere else to grow their food.

3 The Aztec Empire was ruled through city-states with local rulers who owed allegiance and tribute to the king.

4 The Inca Empire was composed of four provinces. Local rulers owed loyalty and labor to the emperor.

Lesson Vocabulary

Introduce each of the following vocabulary terms to students.

Explain that a *land bridge* is a narrow strip of land connecting larger areas. Some people think Asian nomads crossed a *land bridge* over the Bering Strait.

The *Yucatán Peninsula* is located in Mexico between the Gulf of Mexico and the Caribbean Sea. Mayan civilization was centered in the *Yucatán Peninsula*. *Ceremonial centers* are places where religious ceremonies took place. The Mayans built *ceremonial centers*, not cities. Land that has been farmed until the nutrients are gone from the soil has been *overfarmed*. Some archaeologists believe that the Mayans *overfarmed* their land.

A *prophecy* is a prediction. The Aztec had a *prophecy* telling them where to build their city. *Commoners* were those Aztec who owned property and were not slaves or nobles. The *commoners* were the largest group in Aztec society. A *quipu* was a set of colored, knotted strings to keep Incan records. Government officials learned to use the *quipu* to keep track of tax payments. A *terraced* mountain is cut out like steps. The Inca used *terraced* land and irrigation systems to farm.

The Americas 149

Map Extension

Ask students to use the map on page 150 to answer the following questions:

- Which of the civilizations did **not** extend to the Pacific Ocean? (Olmec)
- Which civilization was farthest west? (Aztec)
- What was the greatest north-south distance of any of the civilizations, and which one? (about 700 miles (1,127 km), Mayan)

Picturing History

The Olmec head shown on page 150 was carved from basalt rock. In each of their three main ceremonial centers, the Olmec placed carved heads of their gods or rulers. The largest head is about 10 feet (3 m) tall. The Olmec had no wheels or draft animals. They would have quarried the rock, floated it on rafts to the destination, hauled it to the building site, and positioned it for the sculptor. Archaeologists estimate that each sculpture required the work of perhaps 1,000 laborers.

The Americas, 1400 B.C.–A.D. 1570

Civilizations in Mexico and Central America, 900 B.C.–A.D. 1500
- Olmec heartland
- Aztec civilization
- Mayan civilization

The first Americans were hunters and gatherers. They followed wild herds of big game like mastodons and mammoths. As the big-game herds died out, the men turned to hunting bison and smaller game like rabbits and deer. To add to their diet, the women gathered plants, nuts, and berries, and dug roots.

Some hunters and gatherers in Mexico and South America learned to domesticate plants and began growing food crops. This Neolithic revolution, as historians call it, had far-reaching effects. Farming produced a surplus of food, which freed some people to become craftworkers, full-time soldiers, and priests. In the Western Hemisphere, as well as in Europe and Asia, it made living in villages year-round possible. From that, came cities and civilization.

Mayan Civilization

The largest civilization in Mexico and Central America was the Mayan. Much of it was centered on the **Yucatán Peninsula** in what is today Mexico. The area is mainly rain forest.

The Mayan civilization reached its height between 300 and 900. Like the Olmec, the Mayans did not build cities. They built large religious centers, known as **ceremonial centers**. The centers had temples dedicated to the deities and palaces for the ruler and other nobles. There were also huge ball courts and marketplaces. Each center and its nearby villages made up an independent city-state. Rival city-states often warred against each other.

The temples were several stories high and were built in the shape of pyramids. However, the tops

The first civilization in Mexico and Central America was the Olmec. It developed in the rain forest along the Gulf of Mexico. Instead of cities, the Olmec built large religious centers. People lived in nearby villages. They came to the centers to worship in huge pyramid-shaped temples. This is one of the 40-ton carved heads that stood in the centers.

Extension

The name *Olmec* means "rubber people." It is a designation, made by archaeologists, based on the rubber trees that grew near the three major ceremonial centers of the Olmec. The first, on the site now known as San Lorenzo, began around 1200 B.C. Olmec civilization declined around 100 B.C.

were flat. Priests carried out human sacrifice on this flat space. The Mayans believed that they had to make sacrifices to the gods in order to satisfy them. If the gods were not happy, they would cause harm. Players on the losing side in a ball game were sacrificed. Enemies captured in battle were also sacrificed. Sometimes battles were fought just to get prisoners for sacrifice.

The ruler and his family were at the highest level of Mayan society. Below them were other nobles, and priests. Some nobles ran the government and collected taxes. Others were warriors who led soldiers into battle. Below this class were a small number of craftworkers, merchants, and traders. Like other early civilizations, most Mayans were farmers. They lived in villages outside the centers. Their chief crops were beans, corn, and squash. Mayan society also included slaves.

The Mayans developed a form of hieroglyphic writing and a very accurate calendar. Because the Mayan economy was based on farming, the calendar was very important. Mayans used the calendar to know when to plant their crops each year.

Sometime around 900, the Mayans left their centers in the Yucatán. Archaeologists do not know why but offer several reasons. The Mayans may have **overfarmed** their land. As a result, they migrated in search of new land. Enemies may have invaded their territory. Farmers may have rebelled under the burden of high taxes. Today, descendants of the Mayans live in Guatemala, the Yucatán Peninsula, and northern Mexico.

The Aztec Empire

During the 1200s, the Aztec migrated from the northwest into the Valley of Mexico. They were pushed out of their homeland by groups moving south. In 1325, the Aztec settled on islands in Lake Texcoco. There they built the city of Tenochtitlán (tay•NAWCH•teet•LAWN). In time it became the capital of a huge empire.

Time Box

00–900
 Mayan Civilization

325–1521
 Aztec Empire

438–1535
 Inca Empire

Montezuma (c. 1466–1520) was the Aztec ruler when the Spanish arrived.

The Americas 151

Extensions

The Lacandones, who live in Chiapas, Mexico, are the direct descendants of the Mayans. They continue to speak the Mayan language, live by farming, and wear traditional Mayan clothing.

Invite students interested in careers in food service to use library resources or the Internet to find out more about the Aztec emperor's food, especially chocolate. Have students present their findings to the class by using the Student Presentation Builder on the student CD. They may also want to design a presentation comparing chocolate consumption in the Aztec era with that currently in the United States. You may wish to show a clip from the 2000 film *Chocolat*.

Picturing History

The statue of a ball player at the top of page 151 may indicate the importance of games to Mayan civilizations. One game, known as *tlachtli*, was played on a rectangular court. Two vertical stone rings were placed high on the walls of the long sides. The object of the game was to pass the 8–10-inch rubber ball through one of the rings. Each team had seven players. The players used only knees, shoulders, or hips, as in modern soccer. The team that committed the fewest fouls was the winning team.

Picturing History

The image at the bottom of page 151 is of Montezuma. Montezuma was the Aztec ruler at the time of the Spanish invasion in 1519. Led by Hernán Cortés, the Spanish force of several hundred soldiers was at first welcomed by Montezuma. Aztec legend said that one day, a light-faced god would return to Mexico. They thought Cortés might be that god. After a battle in which Cortés escaped from the Aztec, he returned with both his soldiers and thousands of Native Americans and defeated the Aztec. He tricked Montezuma into thinking he would be freed, but the Spanish killed him.

The Americas 151

Picturing History

The photograph on page 152 shows an ancient Aztec site in modern-day Mexico City. Cortés and his soldiers destroyed the Aztec city. Today, Zócalo Square in Mexico City is located on about the same site as the sacred center of Tenochtitlán.

Extension

Have students examine the Mexican flag. The seal on Mexico's flag includes the eagle and rattlesnake atop a rock. The prickly pear cactus represents the human heart. On the left are oak branches to symbolize strength; to the right are laurel branches, signifying victory. The eagle symbol is taken from an ancient Aztec legend.

Stop and Think

Diagrams should include:

Aztec: Kings, writing system, tribute from conquered people

Inca: Emperors, labor from conquered people

Same: built cities, created empires, hierarchical social structure, developed irrigation systems, ended by Spanish, developed a calendar, practiced human sacrifice

The Americas, 1400 B.C.–A.D. 1570

The Empire was made up of city-states that the Aztecs had conquered. At the top of the Empire was the Aztec king in Tenochtitlán. The states were ruled by local leaders. Each state paid a yearly fee or tax, known as tribute, to the king. As long as the states paid their tribute, they were left in peace. If they tried to revolt, Aztec warriors would be sent to put a brutal end to the rebellion. By the time the Spanish arrived in 1519, the Aztec ruled approximately 5 million people.

Like the Mayans, the Aztec practiced human sacrifice. They believed it was necessary in order to keep the world from being destroyed. According to the Aztec religion, four worlds had already been destroyed by fighting between good and evil. It was only by making human sacrifice to Huitzilopochtli (wee•tsee•loh•POHKT•lee), the god of the sun and war, that the end of the fifth world—the current world—could be prevented. Wars were sometimes fought just to take prisoners for sacrifice.

Aztec Society

Aztec society was divided into social and economic classes. At the top were the monarch and his family. Next were nobles, which included priests, government officials, war chiefs, and wealthy merchants. The largest group were the **commoners**. This group included everyone who was not a noble or a slave, and who owned property. Small merchants, craftworkers, and farmers were commoners. Farmers were the largest section in this group. Below commoners were farm laborers. Slaves were at the bottom of the group.

Similar to the Mayan, the Aztecs developed a form of hieroglyphic writing and a calendar. They built palaces and huge pyramid-like temples. The tops of

Aztec legends explain why they chose their island home. Huitzilopochtli, the god of war, had made a **prophecy**. He said that they should settle down where they came upon a certain sign. The sign was an eagle sitting on a cactus that was growing out of rock. The word *Tenochtitlán* means "place of the cactus in the rock." The Spanish destroyed Tenochtitlán (above) in 1521 and built Mexico City over it. The eagle and cactus can be seen on the flag of Mexico.

stop and think

Create a Venn diagram to compare and contrast the Aztec and Inca Empires. Work with a partner to fill in the details.

Extensions

In 1524, the first Franciscan monks from Spain arrived. The priests learned the Náhuatl language and preserved some of the Aztec story. They became advocates for those Aztec whom the Spaniards were mistreating. They also taught the Catholic faith, although some questioned the sincerity of those Native Americans who converted. Nevertheless, the first bishop of Mexico claimed to have demolished 20,000 idols and 500 temples in five years.

Aztec pyramids were also flat for conducting human sacrifices and other ceremonies.

The end of the Aztec Empire came in 1521. Tribute states and the Spanish joined together to overthrow the Aztec king.

The Inca Empire

The Inca began as a small group in the mountains of Peru. Their center was Cuzco, a city 11,000 feet above sea level. Beginning with the rule of Pachacuti (pah•cha•KOO•tee) in 1438, the Inca set out to conquer surrounding groups. By 1527, the Inca had spread their rule over a vast area.

The Inca Empire was divided into four provinces. As soon as a group was conquered, their land was taken over by the government. Some of it was given back to the people. Some land was turned over to the Empire, and some was given to

Map Extension

Ask students to use the map on page 153 to answer the following questions:

- What formed a natural barrier to the east of the Inca Empire? (Andes Mountains)
- What can you say about the location of major Incan cities? (They were central or north-central and located comparatively near the ocean or Lake Titicaca.)
- At its widest east-west point, how much distance did the empire cover? (about 500 miles)

Pachacuti (?–1471)

Pachacuti became the ruler of the Inca in 1438. His name means "reformer of the world." Under his leadership, the Inca began the conquest of their neighbors. Like the Romans, Pachacuti used both force of arms and alliances to enlarge his empire. He managed the new parts of the empire with a mix of local rulers and his own appointed officials. Later emperors followed his system of government.

Pachacuti used the wealth from his empire to beautify his capital. Huge stone palaces and temples replaced mud buildings. It is possible that he designed his grand capital himself.

Bio Facts

- Date of birth is unknown.
- Name as a warrior was Cusi Inca Yupanqui.
- Ruled 1438–1471.
- Developed a form of ancestor cult; mummies of dead leaders were taken to ceremonies and houses of the living.
- Rebuilt Cuzco.
- Built Machu Picchu of white granite as a home and a ceremonial center.
- Compared to Philip II of Macedonia, father of Alexander the Great, for his swift expansion of the empire.
- Died 1471.

Biography Extension

Most of the Incan forts and cities were built on the steep slopes and highlands of the Andes Mountains. The skill of the builders continues to amaze contemporary researchers. Blocks of stone, each weighing several tons, were fitted together so tightly that not so much as a knife blade fits between them. The homes of commoners were also made of stone, with thatched roofs. This was accomplished without knowledge of the wheel. Have students use library resources or the Internet to research the building accomplishments of Pachacuti, including how they were financed, constructed, etc. Have students create a poster to show their findings.

The Americas

Picturing History

The Spanish print at the bottom right of page 154 depicts a man using a quipu. Reading the quipu required a special education. Ask students to identify professions today that are based on special knowledge of recordkeeping.

Picturing History

Inca gold work was very intricate. The medallion on page 154 has figures made of colored stone, and small gold balls surround the outside.

Chart Extension

Ask students to use library resources or the Internet to find out more about the role of women in Mesoamerica. Have students present their findings on posters.

The Americas, 1400 B.C.–A.D. 1570

the sun god. The lands for the sun god supported the priests who took care of the temples and conducted religious ceremonies.

Local rulers could remain in power as long as they were loyal to the emperor. The Inca did not demand tribute in gold or other goods from conquered people. Instead, the Inca required labor. Whole communities had to spend several weeks each year working on lands given to the Empire or to the sun god. They also had to work on building projects.

The Inca had several ways to ensure the loyalty of conquered people. Quechua (KEH•chuh•wuh), the language of the Inca, was taught to new people. The Inca sent Quechua-speaking colonists to live among a newly conquered group. Sometimes the Inca uprooted a new group. They were sent to live in an area where the people had been part of the Empire for a longer period of time. A road system kept Cuzco in touch with all parts of the Empire. Like the Roman system of roads, the Incan roads enabled the government to quickly send troops to troublespots. The Empire had 24,000 miles of criss-crossing roads.

Like the Aztec, the Inca believed that the sun was the chief deity. The Inca called their sun god Inti, and the Temple of

Role of Women in Mesoamerica

Empire	Role
Mayan	• take care of the home • take care of the children
Aztec	• could inherit property • could make legal contracts • take care of the home • take care of the children
Inca	• could inherit property • could own property • work the fields • take care of the home • take care of the children

The Inca produced intricate pieces of gold.

A 16- Span- print an In and quip-

154 Chapter 11

Extensions

1 Have students interested in military affairs use library resources or the Internet to research the Spanish conquests of the Aztec and Inca Empires. Ask them to develop a table showing comparisons and contrasts.

2 Students interested in theater may wish to read, view, or enact a scene from *The Royal Hunt of the Sun* by Sir Peter Shaffer, perhaps best known for his works *Amadeus* and *Equus*. *The Royal Hunt of the Sun* is a fictionalized version of the relationship between the Spanish conqueror Francisco Pizarro and the Incan ruler Atahuallpa.

the Sun in Cuzco was the center of Incan religion. Emperors were considered descendants of the sun god. They were mummified like Egyptian pharaohs and their mummies were worshiped.

Incan Society

The social and economic structure of the Inca Empire was similar to other early civilizations. The ruler and family were at the top. Below them were nobles and priests. Below them were merchants and craft workers. Most Inca were farmers who lived near their fields.

The Inca did not develop a writing system. Instead they used **quipu** (KEE•poo), knotted and colored strings to keep records. Special government officials were taught to use quipu. These officials could keep track of tax payments and similar information by knotting different strings. For example, the first string showed thousands. The second string showed hundreds. The third and fourth strings showed tens and ones. Suppose a farmer paid 1,200 bushels of grain in taxes. The official would tie one knot on the thousands string and two knots on the hundreds string. It is also possible that the quipu recorded dates and important events in Inca history.

The Inca also developed a calendar and a way to farm in the mountains. Look at the photo of Machu Picchu at the beginning of this chapter. The sides of the mountain were **terraced**, or cut out like steps. The Inca farmed each level of the terrace. The Inca also developed an irrigation system to bring water to their fields high in the mountains.

Like the Aztec, the Inca Empire ended when the Spanish came. Incan swords were no match for Spanish guns and horses.

Incan quipu

Putting It All Together

Imagine you are an Incan tax collector. Work with a partner to draw a picture of a quipu to record the following tax payments in bushels of grain: (a) 141, (b) 1,322 (c) 2,535.

Picturing History

The quipu, shown on page 155, was used to record anything that could be expressed numerically: the number of men who went to war, those who died, birth and mortality rates by month, and so on. The different colors of yarn stood for different kinds of things counted. Animals, weapons, textiles, and population each had a different color yarn.

Putting It All Together

(a) 141: one knot in the second string, four knots in the third string, and one knot in the fourth string

(b) 1,322: one knot in the first string, three knots in the second string, two knots in the third string, and two knots in the fourth string

(c) 2,535: two knots in the first string, five knots in the second string, three knots in the third string, and five knots in the fourth string

The Americas 155

Extension

Like many other ancient civilizations, the Inca had professional historian-storytellers whose job it was to recall things that could not be counted. Memorized speeches and poems were passed down from father to son. Great events were turned into poems that could be taught to and memorized by children or sung at feasts.

Lesson Summary
In what is now the southwestern United States, the ancestral Puebloans (formerly called the Anasazi) lived around A.D. 100 to the late 1200s. They left the area, possibly due to prolonged drought.

The Plains people lived in central North America. They included the Mound Builders, whose burial mounds continue to be studied. When the Plains people domesticated horses, brought by the Spanish, their way of life changed. Plains people were forced onto reservations when settlers expanded westward in the 1800s.

In the Eastern Woodlands, the Iroquois people formed a league with four other tribes to ensure peace. The league had a representative form of government and gave women power.

Lesson Objective
Students will learn about some of the cultures of North American groups.

Focus Your Reading Answers
1 The ancestral Puebloan people abandoned their area, possibly because of drought.

2 The arrival of the Spanish affected the Native Americans on the Plains because they brought horses. The horses changed the way buffalo were hunted.

3 The Iroquois League is important because there were groups working together, the government was representative, and women were included.

The Americas, 1400 B.C.–A.D. 1570

LESSON 2
North American Cultures

Thinking on Your Own
What do you already know about Native North Americans? Make a list of at least five facts that you know about Native Americans. To refresh your memory, look through the lesson. Read the subheadings and the captions. Look at the illustrations. Then write your list.

Experts think that about 70 million people lived in the Americas when Christopher Columbus sailed west in 1492. Of these, about 5 million lived in what would become the United States. There were various cultural regions, each with many different groups. This lesson includes **representative groups** in three of the regions. Representative groups are ones that have many characteristics in common with other groups.

focus your reading

What happened to the ancestral Puebloan culture?

Describe how the coming of the Spanish affected the culture of Native Americans on the Plains?

Why is the Iroquois League considered important?

vocabulary

representative groups
plateau
hides
tepees
reservation
sachem

The Ancestral Puebloans of the Southwest

More than 800 rooms were part of the ancestral Puebloan dwellings at Pueblo Bonito.

The ancestral Puebloans (Anasazi) are just one of the groups that lived in the area of modern day Arizona, New Mexico, Colorado, and Utah. The ancestral Puebloans began to develop their unique way of life around A.D. 100. They turned from hunting and gathering to farming. The area is very hot and dry for much of the year. However, if

Lesson Vocabulary
Discuss each of the vocabulary terms with students.

Representative groups have many characteristics in common with other groups. The Mandan are used as a *representative group* for the Plains people.

A *plateau* is a region of high and mostly flat land.

The cured skins of animals are the *hides*. Native Americans of the Plains used *hides* for clothing and shelter. Cone-shaped homes made of *hides* were called *tepees*. Plains people lived in *tepees*.

Reservations were lands set aside for Native Americans. Most Native Americans lived on *reservations* after 1890.

The chief of the Mohawk was a *sachem*. Hiawatha was a *sachem* who worked to develop the Iroquois League.

156 Chapter 11

rains came in the spring and midsummer, they brought occasional flash flooding. The ancestral Puebloans figured out how to use the rain water to irrigate their fields.

Around 900, ancestral Puebloan settlements began to grow in size. To fit the increasing population, the ancestral Puebloans developed an apartment-building style of housing. One of the largest settlements was Pueblo Bonito in northwestern New Mexico. From its ruins, archaeologists can tell that its 800 rooms housed more than 1,000 people. In Mesa Verde, part of modern day Colorado, the ancestral Puebloans built their houses into the sides of cliffs. They farmed on the **plateau** on top of the mountain.

In the 1200s, the ancestral Puebloans began to abandon their stone buildings and move out of the area. No one knows for sure why. One possible reason is the drought that lasted from 1276 to 1299. At about the same time, Navajos and Apaches began moving into the area. They may have pushed out the ancestral Puebloans.

It was the descendants of the ancestral Puebloans that the Spanish met in the Southwest in the 1500s. The Spanish called them Pueblo Indians because they lived in villages. *Pueblo* means "village" in Spanish.

Plains Peoples

The earliest people on the Plains were hunters and gatherers. Some, like the Mandan along the Missouri River, became farmers and traders. But many of the descendants of the first Plains people continued to hunt bison and gather wild foods until the late 1800s—but with one big change. The change came about when the

The Americas, 1400 B.C.–A.D. 1570

Between 1000 B.C. and the A.D. 1200s, people known as Mound Builders lived in the area from the Great Lakes to the Gulf of Mexico. They are called Mound Builders because they built huge mounds of earth (top). Some mounds were tombs. Others, like the Great Serpent Mound (bottom), were shaped like animals. Most Mound Builders were farmers, but a few were traders. Trade goods from as far away as Mexico have been found in the mounds. Over time, cities developed. One of the largest was Cahokia, in what is today Illinois. When the Spanish came, they met Natchez Native Americans, who were descendants of the Mound Builders.

stop and think

Create a Venn diagram to compare and contrast the ancestral Puebloans and the Plains people. Work with a partner to list information in each part of the two circles.

Picturing History

The ancestral Puebloan cliff dwelling, shown at the bottom of page 156, shows Pueblo Bonito in Chaco Canyon, a ten-mile area in northwestern New Mexico. Some archaeologists believe that this large complex was a ceremonial center. During the tenth and eleventh centuries, it was expanded seven times. It became the largest of the ancestral Puebloan planned communities.

Stop and Think

Venn diagrams will vary. Possible responses:

Ancestral Puebloans
- lived in apartment buildings on plateaus in southwest
- irrigated the land to grow crops
- moved from area, perhaps because of drought

Plains People
- lived in tepees on Great Plains
- followed the buffalo; were hunters and gatherers
- moved onto reservations because of settlers

Both
- adapted to the environment around them

The Americas 157

Extension

Suggest to students interested in art that they use library resources or the Internet to locate paintings by George Catlin. His work gives a view into Native-American life in the nineteenth century. They may wish to share examples of the paintings with the class.

Picturing History

The images on page 157 depict views of mounds in the settlement at Cahokia, Illinois. Of the more than 100 mounds at the site, the largest was the Monks Mound. It covered about the same area as 25 football fields, and it had a base larger than that of Egypt's Great Pyramid.

The Americas 157

Picturing History

The tepee shown on page 158 was a Plains home. For nomadic people, it was the perfect home: lightweight and portable. Native Americans often decorated the hides used in the tepee. The art might depict bravery in battle or patterns associated with a particular family. The patterns could be seen at a distance, making it easier for families to recognize their homes.

Map Extension

Ask students to use the map on page 158 to answer the following questions:

- In what region did the Nez Perce live? (Plateau)
- Which cultures would be most affected by the Hudson River? (the Iroquois League)
- Near what rivers was Mesa Verde? (Rio Grande, Colorado)
- Which two tribes lived farthest north? (Haida, Inuit)

Spanish brought horses to the Americas. Some horses escaped from the Spanish in Mexico and the U.S. Southwest. Other horses were stolen by Native Americans. Native Americans traded horses until they reached the Plains in the early 1700s.

Instead of hunting bison on foot, the Plains people began hunting on horseback. With horses they could kill more bison and go longer distances on the hunt. The bison was central to the Plains' way of life. It provided meat for food and **hides** for making clothes. The people also used hides to cover the sides of their cone-shaped homes called **tepees**. Because they moved often, Plains people sewed bags from bison hides to carry their belongings.

The Plains' way of life stayed much the same until the 1800s. Then settlers from the East Coast of the United States began to move onto the Plains. A series of Plains Wars in the

Animal hides were u to cove tepees.

Cultural Regions of North America, 4000 B.C.—A.D. 1500

Extension

Students interested in Native-American rights may wish to use library resources or the Internet to investigate early efforts to help Native Americans. Students may want to learn about writer Helen Hunt Jackson, who used her skills to protest the treatment of Native Americans following the battle of Wounded Knee. Students can also investigate the policy of assimilation expressed in the Dawes Act of 1887.

158 Chapter 11

mid-1800s killed many Native Americans. By 1890, those who were left were forced to live on **reservations**.

The Iroquois of the Eastern Woodlands

Before Europeans came to North America, about half of what is today the United States was forest. It is known as the Eastern Woodlands. In general, Native Americans in the region combined hunting and farming. They lived in villages and towns, sometimes surrounded by high walls made of logs. The walls were needed to keep out invaders.

The Iroquois lived in the Eastern Woodlands in parts of present-day New York, Pennsylvania, and Canada. Like other languages, Iroquois is a language family. There were several tribes, or groups, who spoke this language.

About 1570, Deganawida, an elder chief, tried to end the constant warfare among the Iroquois. Hiawatha, a **sachem**, or chief, of the Mohawk, joined him. Together, they enlisted the chiefs of five nations, or groups of people, in New York to form the Iroquois League. The five nations—Mohawk, Oneida, Onondaga, Cayuga, and Seneca—elected representatives to a Grand Council. The purpose of the council was to find solutions to problems and prevent warfare.

Women were very important in the government of the Iroquois nations. The women members of each clan in a nation chose a clan mother. The clan mothers then chose the 50 representatives to the Grand Council. A clan mother could remove a representative if she did not approve of his voting.

The Iroquois League was still in existence when the British began to settle the east coast. It did not help the five nations much in their dealings with the colonists. The Iroquois were caught in wars with the colonists and between the British and French for control of land.

The longhouse provided shelter for Eastern Woodland people.

Putting It All Together

Add to the list of facts you began writing at the start of this lesson. Compare your facts with a partner. Then use your facts to write a comparison and contrast paragraph about two of the Native-American groups you read about in this lesson.

Picturing History

The longhouse, shown on page 159, is a typical dwelling for Eastern Woodland groups. Several were built together to form a village. Each longhouse could hold as many as 24 families, generally from the same clan. They were usually about 18 feet (5.5 m) wide and anywhere from 40 to 200 feet (12 m to 61 m) long. There were two entrances, and holes were left in the roof to allow smoke out and sunlight in.

Putting It All Together

Students' paragraphs will vary but should compare and contrast any two Native-American groups discussed in the lesson.

Chapter Review

1 Students' tables will vary but should include information on the Mayan, Aztec, and Inca civilizations.
   Location:
   Mayan—Yucatán
   Aztec—Mexico
   Inca—South America
   Dates:
   Mayan—A.D. 300–900
   Aztec—A.D. 1325–1521
   Inca—A.D. 1438–1535
   Government:
   all three monarchies
   Religion:
   all many gods; human sacrifice
   Social and Economic Classes:
   Mayan—ruler; nobles and priests; craftworkers, merchants, and traders; farmers; slaves
   Aztec—king; nobles, priests, government officials, wealthy merchants; commoners; farm workers; slaves
   Inca—similar to Mayan and Aztec
   Achievements:
   Mayan—large buildings, writing, calendar
   Aztec—large buildings, writing, calendar
   Inca—roads, large buildings, calendar, terraced farming

2 Students' descriptions will vary but should be related to the information in Lesson 1.

3 Students' descriptions will vary but should concern a cultural region from Lesson 2.

Chapter Summary

- Experts think the first Americans came across a **land bridge** from Asia 12,000 to 15,000 years ago.
- The Mayan civilization developed in the **Yucatán Peninsula**. The Mayans developed **ceremonial centers**.
- **Overfarming** the land may have been one of the reasons the Mayans left their homes around A.D. 900.
- The Aztec built their capital, Tenochtitlán, on an island in Lake Texcoco because of a **prophecy**.
- The Aztec Empire was made up of conquered people. Most people were **commoners**.
- The Inca Empire began in the mountains of Peru.
- The Inca used **quipu** to record information. The Inca also developed a calendar and a system of farming that used **terracing** on mountainsides.
- The ancestral Puebloans, Plains people, and Iroquois are **representative groups** of North American cultures.
- The ancestral Puebloans farmed on a **plateau**.
- Plains people ate bison meat and used bison **hides** for clothing and **tepee** covers. By the end of the 1800s, Plains people were forced onto **reservations**.
- The chiefs, or **sachems**, of five Iroquois nations formed the Iroquois League.

Chapter Review

1 Make a table to compare and contrast information about the Mayans, Aztec, and Inca. For topics, use "Location," "Dates," "Government," "Religion," "Social and Economic Classes," "Roles of Men and Women," and "Achievements."

2 Imagine you are a farmer living outside a Mayan center. You have just come back from market day in the city. Write a description of the city. Use the information in Lesson 1 to give you ideas.

3 Choose a cultural region from Lesson 2. Describe life in this region prior to the arrival of Christopher Columbus in 1492.

Skill Builder

Drawing Conclusions

Suppose you come home from school to find a pillow torn apart on the living room floor. The stuffing has been pulled out, and small pieces of it are everywhere. As you set down your backpack, your dog runs up to you. She is covered with pieces of the pillow's stuffing. You know that you were the last person to leave that morning. No one has been at home since you left for school. You think about this information and conclude, based on the facts, that your dog shredded the pillow. This process is called drawing a conclusion.

You can also apply the skill of drawing conclusions to your schoolwork. Suppose you had to answer the following question: Why did early people migrate?

To draw a conclusion:

- Gather information about the topic. In this case, re-read the information about the Bantu in Chapter 10 and about the first Americans in this chapter.
- Write down any other facts you know about the topic.
- Draw a conclusion based on the information you gathered.

   Early people migrated for different reasons. Hunters and gatherers followed herds wherever they went. Farmers moved when the land wore out. Others moved when there were too many people in a place and they could not get enough food.

Answer the following questions by drawing conclusions.

1. Why do you think so many different Native-American cultures developed in North America?

2. Tribute states in the Aztec Empire became allies of the Spanish. They helped overthrow the Aztec king. Why do you think the tribute states joined the Spanish?

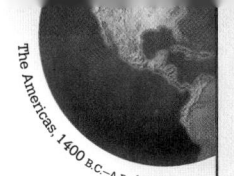

The Americas | 161

Skill Builder

1. Students' responses may vary. Possible response:

   The different cultures developed based on the climate and geography of the region each Native-American group lived in.

2. Possible response: Tribute states may have hoped that life under the Spanish would be better than under the Aztec, who imposed high tribute and took people as slaves.

Classroom Discussion

Discuss with students some of the broader topics covered in this chapter.

- How does a culture's art and architecture reflect the greater society?
- What are some contemporary examples of people adapting to different environments?

Novel Connections

Below is a list of books that relate to the time period covered in this chapter. The numbers in parentheses indicate the related Thematic Strands of the National Council for the Social Studies (NCSS).

Dale Anderson. *Anasazi Culture at Mesa Verde*. Gareth Stevens Audio, 2003. (I, III, V, VIII)

Elizabeth Baquedano. *Eyewitness: Aztec, Inca and Maya*. DK Publishing, Inc., 2000. (I, V, VI, IX)

Fern G. Brown. *American Indian Science: A New Look at Old Cultures*. Twenty-first Century Books, 1997. (I, VIII, IX)

Emory Dean Keoke, Kay Marie Porterfield. *American Indian Contributions to the World*. Facts on File, Incorporated, 2005. (I, VIII, IX, X)

Ted Lewin. *Lost City: The Discovery of Machu Picchu*. Philomel, 2003. (I, VIII)

Sue Nicholson. *Aztecs and Incas: A Guide to the Pre-Colonized Americas in 1504*. Houghton Mifflin Company, 2000. (I, III, V, VI)

The Americas | 161

Chapter Summary
Refer to page 178 for a summary of Chapter 12.

Related Transparencies

T-1 World Map

T-2 Outline World Map

T-6 Sui, Tang, Song Empires

T-20 Concept Web

Key Blacklines

Biography—Matsuo Basho

CD Extension

Encourage students to use the reading comprehension, vocabulary reinforcement, and interactive timeline activities on the student CD.

Getting Focused

Students will choose different illustrations to describe but should include the country of origin and a description of the picture, as well as a reason they selected it. You may wish to pair students and have them try to guess one another's choices based on the descriptions given.

Chapter 12
THE SPREAD OF CULTURES IN ASIA
(500–1650)

Getting Focused

Skim this chapter to predict what you will be learning.
- Read the lesson titles and subheadings.
- Look at the illustrations and read the captions.
- Examine the maps.
- Review the vocabulary words and terms.

This chapter discusses China, Japan, Korea, and India. Look through the chapter and choose one picture to describe from each lesson. In your descriptions, state what country the picture represents, what the picture shows, and why you chose this picture to write about. Be sure to use interesting words to describe what you Remember to add Japan and Korea to your world ma

Picturing History

The Grand Canal, shown on page 162, was completed in the sixth century. Emperor Yang Di had it built to transport soldiers and grain. It covered 1,500 miles (2,500 km). To celebrate the canal's opening, Yang Di's boat led a procession of boats said to have stretched for 62 miles (100 km). In 1411, Song Li, an engineer for the Ming Dynasty, improved the system. It was straightened, dredged, and widened between 1958 and 1964 to make it possible for large barges to travel the entire length of the canal.

Pre-Reading Discussion

1 Discuss with students the changes in power that they have witnessed in their lifetimes, both in the United States and around the globe. Tell them that this chapter will highlight several changes of power in Asia.

2 Ask students to identify some of the qualities that make good soldiers. Tell them that in this chapter they will learn about the famous Japanese samurai, the professional soldier.

LESSON 1

New Dynasties in China

Thinking on Your Own

As you read this lesson, create a timeline in your notebook. Include dates and facts for the five dynasties discussed in this lesson.

In A.D. 581, the Sui Dynasty brought order to China. With the collapse of the Han Dynasty in 220, the Chinese people had endured more than 300 years of civil war. The Sui rulers reunified the Empire. Among their lasting contributions was the building of the Grand Canal, which made it easier to ship rice from the south of China to the north.

focus your reading

Explain why the Tang and Song Dynasties are called Golden Ages.

How was the Yuan Dynasty similar to earlier dynasties?

Summarize how Yong Le attempted to restore China's greatness.

vocabulary

corrupt   fleet
monk   voyage

Time Box

581–618
  Sui (SWAY) Dynasty
618–907
  Tang (TAHNG) Dynasty
960–1279
  Song (SOHNG) Dynasty
1279–1368
  Yuan (YOO•AHN) Dynasty
1368–1644
  Ming (MING) Dynasty

The Tang and Song Dynasties

The Tang and Song Dynasties ruled during what are called Golden Ages in Chinese history. China was prosperous during these periods and extended its influence into new lands. These periods were also times of great cultural achievements.

The leaders of the Tang Dynasty expanded the area of Chinese rule and influence in Asia. The Tang Empire extended from the Pacific Ocean to

The Spread of Cultures in Asia | 163

Lesson Summary

The Sui Dynasty restored order to China after 300 years of civil war. It was overthrown by the Tang Dynasty.

Both dynasties experienced prosperity and were times of great cultural advances. The Song Dynasty followed.

The Mongols invaded from the north, replacing the Song Dynasty with the Yuan Dynasty. Under Genghis Khan, order was restored in China. The government was overthrown by a revolution, leading to the Ming Dynasty.

The Imperial City was the great building project of the Ming. Under Emperor Yong Le, a fleet of Chinese ships made seven exploratory voyages to Southeast Asia, India, and the Arabian Peninsula.

The Manchus came in from the north and set up the Qing Dynasty after a peasant revolt.

Lesson Objective

Students will learn about the Tang, Song, and Yuan Dynasties of China.

Focus Your Reading Answers

1 During the Tang and Song Dynasties, China prospered and extended its influence, as well as made great cultural contributions.

2 The Yuan Dynasty resembled earlier dynasties because it was prosperous, tried to extend territory, and had corrupt leaders.

3 Yong Le attempted to restore the country's greatness by retaking control of Vietnam, expanding trade and exploration, building the Imperial City, and strengthening the Great Wall.

Lesson Vocabulary

Introduce each of the following vocabulary terms to students.

Explain that *corrupt* is a synonym for spoiled or decayed. *Corrupt* government helped destroy the Yuan Dynasty.

A *monk* is a holy man. A Buddhist *monk* led a revolt against the Mongols.

A *fleet* is a group of ships. The Chinese *fleet* made seven trips of exploration under Yong Le. A *voyage* is a trip. Zheng He led the *voyage* of 62 ships that explored Southeast Asia, India, and the Arabian Peninsula.

The Spread of Cultures in Asia | 163

Time Box Extension

Discuss the Time Box on page 163 with students. Ask students to make bar graphs showing the time spans of the five dynasties.

Stop and Think

Students' definitions will vary but may suggest that a Golden Age is a time of achievement and prosperity.

Map Extension

Ask students to use the map on page 164 to answer the following questions:

- Which two cities did the Grand Canal connect? (Beijing and Hangzhou)
- Which earlier empire did the Tang Empire include? (Sui)
- Which empire covered the most territory? (Song)

Tibet. Tang armies conquered the Tibetan people. Through trade, China's influence later spread east into Korea, Japan, and Southeast Asia.

Tang and Song emperors tried to end corruption in government. They restored the ancient civil service system to fill government posts. Office seekers had to pass a civil service exam based on Confucian teachings. That kept powerful officials from appointing their relatives to offices.

The Tang and Song Dynasties brought prosperity to China. They limited the power of the wealthy landowners, taking land from them to give to the peasants. The growing trade with other nations also created business for merchants and craftspeople. As a result, the population of China's cities grew rapidly.

The Tang and Song Dynasties were periods of cultural advances. Among the most important was the invention of printing. It began with woodblock printing on paper in Tang China, in

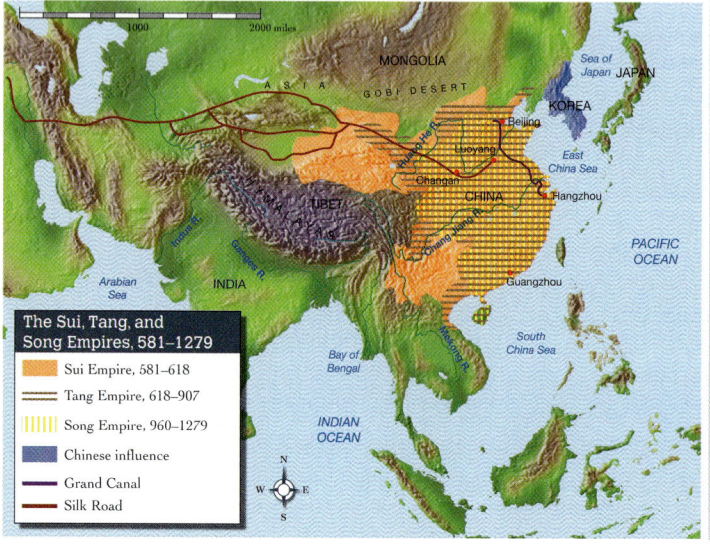

stop and think

The Tang and Song Dynasties were Golden Ages. What do you think this phrase means? Write a definition for *Golden Age*. Share your definition with a partner. Combine your ideas and write one definition for the phrase.

The Sui, Tang, and Song Empires, 581–1279
- Sui Empire, 581–618
- Tang Empire, 618–907
- Song Empire, 960–1279
- Chinese influence
- Grand Canal
- Silk Road

Chinese artists usua[lly] painted scenes of na[ture]. If people were in a s[cene] they were usually s[mall]. What was importan[t was] the grandeur of nat[ure]. However, people, ho[rses], camels, and other a[nimals] were often the subj[ects of] statues by Tang and [Song] artists. Brightly col[ored] statues offer a view [of] how people looked [and] what they did durin[g the] Tang and Song per[iods].

164 Chapter 12

Extension

Have students with an interest in art use library resources or the Internet to find out more about Chinese painting, particularly its interrelationship with calligraphy and poetry, known collectively as the three perfections.

Picturing History

The Chinese painting shown on page 164 reflects the ideals of Song painter Guo Xi, who believed that paintings should portray the harmonious relationship of heaven and Earth.

The rider pictured in the illustration below indicates the importance of horses. They had been brought to China in the early second century B.C. from what is now East Uzbekistan.

164 Chapter 12

Chinese Inventions, 600s to 1200s

Dynasty	Invention	Importance
Tang	gunpowder	• first used in fireworks • used in guns and cannons by the 1200s
Tang	woodblock printing	• invented printing 700 years before the European printing press
Tang	porcelain	• improved the production method • became valuable trade good under the Ming
Tang	steel	• developed process 900 years before Europeans • used for swords and farm tools
Song	movable type	• improved woodblock printing

the early 700s. Each page was carved in wood. By about the year 1000, printers of Song China had created moveable type. This allowed a printer to use the same type to print many different books.

As in earlier dynasties, peasant unrest over taxes helped to weaken Tang power. In 907, rebels overthrew the emperor. A series of civil wars followed. By 960, a general of the Song

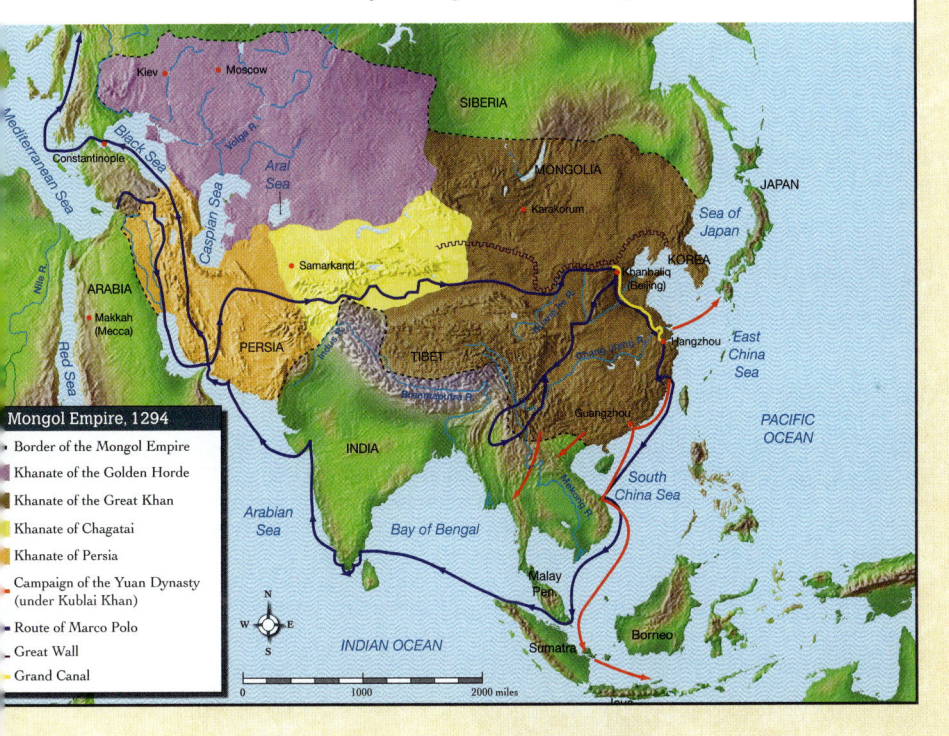

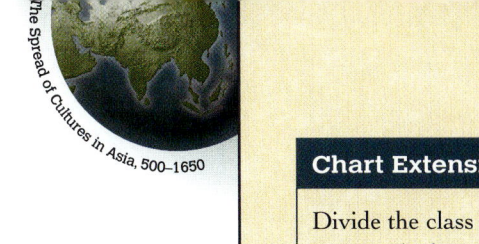

Mongol Empire, 1294
- Border of the Mongol Empire
- Khanate of the Golden Horde
- Khanate of the Great Khan
- Khanate of Chagatai
- Khanate of Persia
- Campaign of the Yuan Dynasty (under Kublai Khan)
- Route of Marco Polo
- Great Wall
- Grand Canal

Chart Extension

Divide the class into five groups. Assign each group one of the inventions listed in the chart. Ask them to use library resources or the Internet to find out more information. Have students present their findings to the class by using the Student Presentation Builder on the student CD.

Map Extension

Ask students to use the map on page 165 to answer the following questions:

- Did Marco Polo visit Samarkand? (no)
- Which major cities were a part of the Khanate of the Golden Horde? (Moscow and Kiev)
- To what khanate did Korea belong? (Khanate of the Great Khan)
- How far south did the campaign of the Yuan Dynasty go? (Java)

Extension

You may wish to bring in and display examples of various kinds and grades of china, so that students can see and feel the difference in the more delicate porcelain.

The Spread of Cultures in Asia

Picturing History

The Mongols, pictured on page 166, were known for their fierceness in battle and their skill at military tactics. Each horseman was able to fire three or four arrows at once from horseback. Their skills, however, were of little use in the attempt to conquer hilly, tropical regions where siege warfare and cavalry charges had little effect.

Extension

Have students interested in leadership or management study the lives and tactics of Genghis and Kublai Khan. Allow time for them to share their findings with the class.

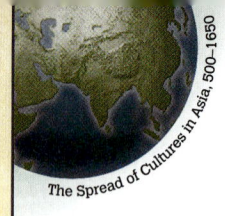

The Spread of Cultures in Asia, 500–1650

clan was strong enough to declare himself emperor.

The Song were unable to hold the Tang Empire together. Attacks by rebel groups within the Empire resulted in the loss of territory. In 1215, the Mongols began their conquest of China.

Mongol Invaders: The Yuan Dynasty

Under Genghis Khan (JEHN•GUHS KAHN), the Mongols roared into China in 1215 and conquered the northern section of the country. When Genghis Khan died in 1227, his empire was divided among his four sons into territories known as khanates. In 1279, Kublai Khan, one of his grandsons, overthrew the Song Dynasty. With the support of his army, Kublai Khan then declared himself ruler of China.

Kublai (KOO•BLUH) Khan took a Chinese name for his dynasty, Yuan (YOO•AHN). He followed a policy similar to

Read a Primary Source

The Travels of Marco Polo

Marco Polo was a trader who found his way to Beijing. Polo spent 20 years in China and may have worked for Kublai Khan. When Polo returned to Italy, he wrote about what he had seen in *The Travels of Marco Polo*.

"There are within the city ten principal squares or market places, besides innumerable shops along the streets. Each side of these squares is half a mile in length, and in front of them is the main street, forty paces in width and running in a straig[ht] line from one end of the city to the other. It is crossed by many lo[w] convenient bridges. These market squares are four miles from each other. Parallel to the main street, but on the opposite side of the squ[are] runs a very large canal. On the nearer bank of this stand large stone warehouses provided for merchants who arrive from India and othe[r] parts with their goods and effects. They are thus situated convenien[tly] close to the market squares. In each of these, three days in every we[ek] from forty to fifty thousand persons come to the markets and suppl[y] them with every article that could be desired."

reading for understandi[ng]

Why might a resident of Hangz[hou] think he or she was in paradise?

Marco Polo sometimes exaggera[ted] what he saw, especially number[s]. What in this excerpt might be exaggerated?

Why do you think Polo might h[ave] exaggerated what he saw?

Reading for Understanding

1 The city's grandeur, charm, and beauty could lead one to imagine oneself in paradise.

2 The idea that 40,000–50,000 people were coming to the markets might be an exaggeration.

3 Polo wanted to impress his European readers with the lands he saw and his own bravery in traveling to them.

Chapter 12

Genghis Khan's. Both allowed the conquered Chinese bureaucrats to remain in place at the local level. Higher level jobs, however, were filled by Mongols. Separate laws governed Chinese and Mongols in the Empire. The Chinese were also required to pay tribute to their Mongol rulers. No Chinese could serve in the army.

Kublai Khan re-established law and order in China. He had roads built and revived trade along the Silk Road. Arabs, Russians, Italians, and other traders made their way to Chinese cities. China prospered under his rule.

However, Kublai Khan was not satisfied with the size of his empire. He sent troops into Southeast Asia and Japan. They were successful only in conquering Vietnam.

Later Yuan emperors could not keep peace and order. Like earlier emperors, later emperors were **corrupt** themselves, or allowed others to take bribes and misuse their power. Peasants were angered by heavy taxes that were used for military campaigns. In 1368, Zhu Yuanzhang, a Buddhist **monk**, or holy man, led an army of peasants against the Mongols. The peasants succeeded in toppling the Yuan Dynasty. Zhu changed his name to Ming Hong Wu and took the title Emperor of China. The Ming Dynasty was born.

The Ming Dynasty

Ming Hong Wu was succeeded as emperor by his son Yong Le in 1398. Yong Le set about restoring China's greatness. Since the days of Kublai Khan, China had lost control of Vietnam. Yong Le sent an army to retake it. He had the Great Wall strengthened. He also built the Imperial City. This is a walled city—which still stands—within the capital city of Beijing. Beautiful gardens, great courtyards, and flowing waterways fill the Imperial City. The emperor's palace and government offices were there. Yong Le built the Imperial City to send a message about the wealth and power of the emperor.

During Yong Le's rule, **fleets** of Chinese ships made

Picturing History

The Imperial City in Beijing, shown on page 167, is now known as the Forbidden City. As the home of China's emperors for almost 500 years, it was not open to common people. Thus, it was "forbidden."

Extension

Have students who are interested in travel use library resources or the Internet to put together a travel brochure for China during one of the dynasties mentioned in the lesson. Make copies for the class as a study guide.

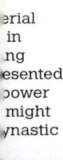

> **Map Extension**
>
> Ask students to use the map on page 168 to answer the following questions:
>
> - Did Zheng He travel south of the equator? If so, where? (yes; Java, Sumatra, cities along east African coast such as Malindi and Mombasa)
>
> - What cities on the Red Sea did Zheng He visit? (Makkah, Jeddah, and Aden)
>
> - From Calicut, sailing west, what was the next port Zheng He would have come to? (Hormuz)

Putting It All Together

Students' timelines should include the dates shown in the Time Box on page 163. Their choice of important facts will vary.

The Spread of Cultures in Asia, 500–1650

seven trips to explore Southeast Asia, India, and the Arabian Peninsula. Zheng He (JUNG HUH), a trusted official, led the expeditions. About 28,000 sailors, merchants, and soldiers sailed on 62 ships for the first **voyage**, or trip. The largest ship was 440 feet long. The average ship weighed 1,500 tons. One hundred years later, the average length of the first Portuguese ships to reach Asia was only 60 feet. Those ships averaged about 300 tons. Chinese naval technology was far more advanced than that of European nations at the time. The voyages ended after Yong Le's death. Historians are not sure why but offer some theories.

Confucianism was a strong influence on the Chinese. Confucianism honored tradition and the way that things had always been done. The voyages of exploration brought new goods and ideas back to China. These new ideas might upset tradition. As a result, government officials may have convinced the new emperor to end the voyages. It is also possible that the cost of the voyages was a factor. In time, the Ming limited how far Chinese ships could travel beyond China. The Chinese had decided that their ways were the best and everyone else's were inferior.

Like other Chinese dynasties, the Ming Dynasty slowly weakened. The final blow came in 1644 from a peasant revolt that overthrew it. The Manchus, who lived north of the Great Wall, saw an opportunity. They swept into China, conquered it, and set up the Qing (CHING) Dynasty.

Voyages of Zheng He
— Exploration routes of Zheng He's fleet

Putting It All Together

Complete your timeline of Chinese dynasties. Write down the names, dates, and three important facts about each dynasty. With a partner create a visual timeline like the ones that introduce each unit in this book. You will need to plan ahead to figure out how much space each dynasty will take on your sheet of paper.

168   Chapter 12

> **Extension**
>
> Ask students who are interested in sailing to use library resources or the Internet to find out more about Zheng He's travels and the ships he commanded. Allow time for students to present their findings to the class.

> **Extension**
>
> Have students interested in mythology use library resources or the Internet to find out more about the myth of Amaterasu and the continuing impact of this founding tale on Japanese culture. Even today's ruler, Emperor Akihito, is descended from the Yamato clan.

LESSON 2

Japan and Korea

Thinking on Your Own

As you read this lesson, create an outline to help you study. Use the titles of the subheadings for the Roman numerals I, II, and III. Compare your outline with a partner. Fill in the information as you read.

Japan is an **archipelago**, or chain of many islands. Since early times, most Japanese have lived on the four largest islands. Examine the map on the next page to see where Japan is in relation to China and Korea.

Rule by Emperor and Powerful Families

People settled in Japan as early as 3000 B.C. By the first couple of centuries A.D., the Japanese were living in **clans**. Clans are small groups of related people. Most clan members were farmers. However, there was a small number of wealthy members, or **aristocrats**, in each clan. The leader, or chief, of each clan was an aristocrat.

By A.D. 500, one clan, the Yamato, had gained power over the other clans. The leader of the Yamato became emperor of Japan and also high priest of **Shinto**, their religion. The Yamato claimed that the emperor was descended from Amaterasu, the female god of the sun. From the Yamato until 1945, the Japanese emperor was worshiped as a god.

The emperor may have come from the Yamato clan, but other clans remained powerful. By the 700s, the Fujiwara family had

focus your reading

How did the Fujiwara gain power?

Discuss how the Japanese feudal system worked.

In what ways did the Chinese influence Korea?

vocabulary

archipelago	daimyo
clan	samurai
aristocrat	ronin
Shinto	hostage system
imperial	tenant farmers
shogun	

The Spread of Cultures in Asia | 169

Lesson Summary
From among the ancient Japanese clans headed by an aristocrat, the Yamato gained power. The head of the clan became both Emperor of Japan and head of the Shinto religion.

Other clans remained powerful, resulting in civil war during the 1100s. Minamoto Yoritomo ended the civil war and became shogun. Japan developed a feudal system.

Korea is a peninsula off southeastern China. China influenced Korea in the areas of religion, writing, and pottery. Korea tried to break away from Chinese control; it was independent for about 250 years before again becoming a tribute state of China.

Lesson Objective
Students will learn about the role of clans and feudalism in Japan and the influence of China on Korea.

Focus Your Reading Answers
1 The Fujiwara gained power by putting family members in top government positions and by marrying into the imperial family.

2 The Japanese feudal system was headed by the emperor, a figurehead. The daimyo traded loyalty and service to the shogun. The samurai fought for the daimyo or shogun, as did the ronin. Next came craftspeople and traders, with merchants at the bottom.

3 The Chinese influenced Korea through colonists, Buddhist missionaries, and the visits of Korean scholars and officials to China. Korea adapted the Chinese writing system and pottery techniques.

Lesson Vocabulary
Discuss each of the vocabulary terms with students.

An *archipelago* is a chain of islands. Japan is really an *archipelago*.

A *clan* is a group of families. Most *clan* members in Japan were farmers. An *aristocrat* was a wealthy person. The chief of each *clan* was an *aristocrat*.

Shinto was the religion of Japan. The Emperor of Japan was also the high priest of *Shinto*. Something that is *imperial* is related to the empire. By marrying into the *imperial* family, the Fujiwara were able to control the emperor. A *shogun* was a military leader. The *shogun* had the real power in Japan.

The *hostage system* in Japan meant that when a *daimyo*, the head of a wealthy family, left the capital, his family stayed behind with the *shogun*. The *hostage system* ensured that *daimyo* remained loyal to the *shogun*. *Samurai* were professional soldiers in Japanese society who fought for a particular *daimyo*. *Ronins* were professional soldiers who fought for any *daimyo*. The *tenant farmers* worked land they did not own. Instead, *tenant farmers* paid rent to wealthy landowners.

The Spread of Cultures in Asia | 169

Picturing History

The Buddhist temple pictured on page 170 is located in Kyoto and is known as the Golden Pavilion. Originally built in the late fourteenth century as a country villa by a retired shogun, it became a Zen temple in 1422. Destroyed in a fire in 1950 and rebuilt five years later, it is decorated with gold leaf. It has been declared a national treasure.

Time Box Extension

Have students reorder the events of the Time Box on page 170 so that they represent spans of years from least to greatest. (Order should be Civil wars, Kamakura, Ashikaga, Tokugawa.)

Map Extension

Ask students to use the map on page 170 to answer the following questions:

- What bodies of water border the Korean peninsula? (Sea of Japan, Korea Strait, Yellow Sea)
- On which island is Mt. Fuji located? (Hunshu)
- Which island is farthest north? (Hokkaido)
- About how many miles separate the Japanese islands farthest apart? (about 1,000 miles)

---

become so powerful that the Yamato ruled in name only. The Fujiwara held the real power. Power was gained in two ways. They filled top government jobs with family members. In these positions, the Fujiwara could determine government policy. The Fujiwara also married into the **imperial** family. Family relationships made it easier to control the emperor.

Eventually, the Yamato and the Fujiwara ignored what was happening in the provinces. Various emperors had tried to centralize the empire's government. However, wealthy families in the provinces worked against the reforms. They saw the reforms as ways to limit their power, and they were right. As a result, the families weakened centralization however they could. In time, these wealthy families became powerful enough to challenge the Fujiwara and each other. The result was civil war by the 1100s.

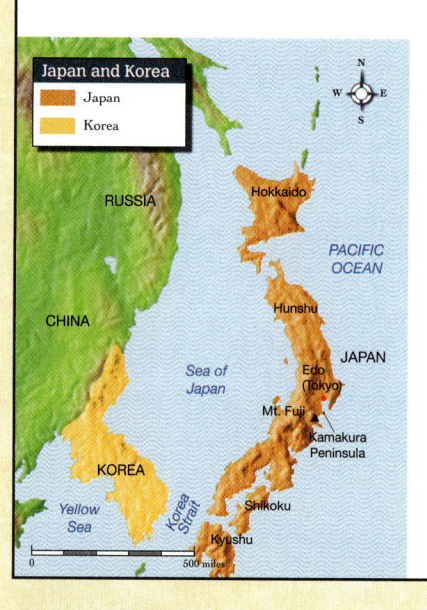

Time Box

1192–1333 Kamakura Shogunate
1333–1477 Ashikaga Shogunate
1467–1603 Civil wars
1603–1868 Tokugawa Shogunate

Rule by Shogunate

In 1192, Minamoto Yoritomo used alliances and force to end the civil war. He kept the emperor as a figurehead. However, Yoritomo took the title of **shogun**, meaning military commander. The new government structure was called a Shogunate. The real power lay with the shogun.

Yoritomo called his shogunate Kamakura, and it lasted for about 140 years. It ended after a Mongol invasion in 1281. The bloodshed and destruction that followed the invasion weakened the Kamakura. In 1333, it was toppled by the Ashikaga.

Extension

One of the most famous people of the Fujiwara clan is Murasaki Shikibu. Author of the Japanese classic *The Tale of Genji*, she is considered one of the first modern novelists. Because both her mother and older sister died when Murasaki was a child, her father decided to raise her himself, against the tradition of the time. He gave his daughter an education in Chinese literature and language that was generally reserved for boys. Following the death of her husband a few years after they were married, Murasaki became an attendant to the Empress Akiko. That position led to further insights about life at court, which enliven her novel. She also left a diary and more than 100 poems.

Chapter 12

Japanese Feudal Society

Emperor
- figurehead

Shogun
- held real power

Daimyo
- wealthy landowners
- vassals of the shogun

Samurai
- nobles and soldiers
- vassals of the shogun or daimyo

Ronin
- soldiers for hire

Peasants and Craftworkers
- most Japanese
- served higher classes

Merchants
- lowest class

Under the first two shogunates, Japan became a feudal society. The emperor was at the top. However, the real connection was between the shogun and the **daimyo** (DY•mee•OH). These were the heads of wealthy families. They owed the shogun loyalty and service in exchange for land. Under them were their vassals and **samurai**, or professional soldiers. Soldiers who would fight for any daimyo were called **ronin**. Next came peasants, farmers, and craftworkers. At the bottom of Japanese society were merchants. Making money by selling the work of others was looked down upon. Confucianism was the influence behind this idea.

In the mid-1400s, civil war broke out between rival daimyo. The Ashikaga Shogunate lost control of the country. It was not until 1603 that a daimyo was powerful enough to end the conflict. In that year, Tokugawa Ieyasu (tok•kuh•GAH•wah ee•YAH•soo) declared himself shogun and founded the Tokugawa Shogunate.

Among the first acts of Ieyasu was limiting the power of the daimyo. The shogun used a **hostage system** to achieve this goal. He forced the daimyo and their families to live at the royal court, or palace, in Edo—present-day Tokyo. If a daimyo left Edo to visit his lands in the provinces, his family had to stay behind.

Another factor that changed the feudal system was the economy. Up to the time of the Tokugawa, Japan's economy was based on farming. Beginning in the 1600s, manufacturing and trade became more and more important. One reason was the coming of Europeans and the opening of trade with Europe.

The feudal system also changed because the Tokugawa

Samurai wore colorful armor made of steel strips. The strips were covered with silk to hold them together. Samurai were supposed to live by a code of behavior called *bushido*. The word means "way of the warrior." Loyalty, unquestioning obedience to one's lord, courage, and honor were valued. If a samurai did not follow the code, he was expected to kill himself with his sword.

Chart Extension

Have students working in pairs make flash cards for each member of Japanese feudal society. In addition to the name and definition of the class, the cards should also include symbols that students design to help them remember each person and his or her role.

Picturing History

Traditionally, young samurai, like the one shown on page 171, lived in their lord's castle or in barracks in their lord's town, away from their own families. Samurai schools began in the 1100s as a place to further the education begun by the mothers, who taught their sons the feats of samurai ancestors and the way of Bushido. The young samurai began training in astronomy, math, and martial arts around the age of ten. Some of them became soldiers as young as sixteen.

Picturing History

Minamoto Yoritomo (1147–1199), pictured on page 171, was a Japanese warrior who founded the first shogunate. This feudal form of government lasted nearly 700 years. Yoritomo was a member of the Minamoto family, a powerful military clan. The Minamoto clan remained in power until 1219, when the line died. It was replaced by the Hojo. The shogunate set the pattern for governmental structure in Japan until the Meiji Restoration of 1868.

Extension

During the Tokugawa era, popular literature began to appear. Students interested in literature may wish to explore the work of poet Matsuo Basho and his influence on haiku. Encourage students interested in drama to use library resources or the Internet to research Kabuki theater and its influence on modern theater, even in the West.

Stop and Think

Students' paragraphs will vary, but their choices should be supported by reasons and facts from the lesson.

Picturing History

The large bell pictured on page 172 is part of a Buddhist temple. Bells were sounded to demarcate periods of the day. Note the monks in the background.

The Spread of Cultures in Asia, 500–1650

Shogunate was a time of peace. People could concentrate on earning a living. As a result, there was little warfare for samurai. Instead of professional soldiers, they became government officials and security guards.

Only the peasant farmers continued to suffer. Many lost their land because they could not pay their taxes. They became **tenant farmers**, paying rent to wealthy landowners. During the 265 years of the Tokugawa Shogunate, there were almost 7,000 peasant revolts. None managed to topple the shogunate.

stop and think

Imagine that you are a diamyo during the Tokugawa Shogunate. You have decided to make a gift of gold to a powerful person who can help you keep the land you hold. To which of the following would you make the gift: the emperor, the shogun, your favorite samurai, a peasant farmer, or a merchant? Write a paragraph to explain why you chose that person.

Korea and Chinese Influences

Korea developed on a peninsula that juts out from southeastern China. As a result of its closeness to China, Korea was strongly influenced by Chinese ideas.

The Han had seized control of northern Korea in 109 B.C. When the Han Dynasty collapsed in A.D. 220, Korea slipped from China's control. However, no single ruler rose up to unite the Koreans. Instead, three rival kingdoms fought for power until 668. By then the Tang Dynasty was in power in China and wanted to retake Korea. The Tang made an alliance with Silla, the smallest of the three kingdoms. China would help Silla defeat the other kingdoms. In exchange, Silla would agree to make Korea a tribute state of China.

The Silla Dynasty ruled Korea until 918. As in China, peasant revolts weakened the ruling dynasty. A new dynasty, the Koryo, was able to seize control. In 1231, the Mongols launched a successful invasion of Korea. They remained in Korea until the 1350s. It was around this time that their dynasty, the Yuan, collapsed in China.

Buddhism spread to Korea in the 300s.

In 1392, Yi Song-gye, a general, reunited Korea and founded the Yi Dynasty. Under the Yi, Korea remained an independent kingdom for almost 250 years. In the 1630s, the Ming ruler of China sent an army to subdue

---

Extension

Students with an interest in astronomy may wish to investigate Cheomseongdae, the world's first observatory. Built in the mid-600s, it was located in the capital of the Silla kingdom, Gyeongju.

Korea takes its name from the Koryo Dynasty, which Wang Geon established in 918 as peasants rebelled and aristocrats chipped away at the king's power. Silla was breaking apart. The last Silla king formally surrendered to Wang in 935. Wang also married a Silla woman from the royal family.

Chapter 12

Korea. Once again Korea became a tribute state of China. However, the Yi were allowed to remain in power. The Yi continued to rule until 1910.

During the Han occupation of Korea, Chinese colonists were sent to settle among the native people. These colonists were the first to bring Chinese ideas to Korea. Chinese influence increased when Chinese missionaries began traveling to Korea around 300. They came spreading the teachings of Buddha. Many Koreans converted to Buddhism. Around this time, the Chinese writing system was introduced into Korea.

When Korea became a tribute state of China, Korean officials, scholars, and merchants regularly visited China. They brought back news about everything from how the rich Chinese dressed to how they decorated their palaces. Scholars carried back Chinese paintings and books for Korean students. Confucianism was taught in Korean universities. When Yi became emperor, he based his government on Confucian principles.

Because Korea was under Chinese authority, there was a continuing peace between China and Korea. As a result, merchants grew wealthy from trade between the two kingdoms. Korean merchants were able to buy and then sell at home goods such as Chinese silk. They were also able to sell Korean trade goods to Chinese merchants for resale to Chinese customers.

The Koreans did not simply imitate what they got from the Chinese. They adapted it to their own needs and skills. For example, Koreans learned to make pottery from the Chinese. However, Korean craftworkers used what they learned to develop their own style of pottery.

Time Box

668–918
  Silla Dynasty
918–1392
  Koryo Dynasty
1231–1350s
  Mongol occupation
1392–1910
  Yi Dynasty
1630s–1895
  Tribute state of China

Putting It All Together

Create a concept web to show China's influence on Korea. Label the central circle "China's Influence." Draw smaller circles for each way that China influenced Korea. Add details from the lesson and share your web with a partner.

The Spread of Cultures in Asia

Time Box Extension

To emphasize the influence of the Chinese, ask students to make a timeline that merges the events of the Lesson 1 Time Box on page 163 with the events listed in the Time Box on page 173. Suggest that they use a different color for each country.

Picturing History

The porcelain vase pictured on page 173 is an example of celadon pottery. Note the engravings and the shape of the vase. Ask students to compare the vase with the Greek amphora pictured on page 74.

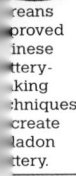

Putting It All Together

Students' webs will vary. Possible response includes Buddhism, writing system, pottery, Confucianism, and government.

Extension

During the Koryo Dynasty, artists perfected the art of inlaid designs in celadon porcelain. The complete works of Buddhist teaching were printed using more than 81,000 woodblocks.

Lesson Summary

India was divided among local Hindu rulers until the 1200s, when an Islamic conqueror, the sultan of Ghur, consolidated power. He founded the Sultanate of Delhi, which was ultimately conquered by Mongol and Turk invaders who destroyed Delhi and left. Muslim rulers kept a wall between Hindus and Muslims.

The Moguls returned in the 1500s and set up their own empire. Some emperors, such as Akbar, were wise and tolerant. Others, such as his great-grandson Aurangzeb, strictly enforced Muslim policies. There were occasional revolts, but none was capable of overthrowing the Moguls until the British arrived. The British seized control of India in 1857.

Lesson Objective

Students will learn about the empires of India and their influence on religious life in that country.

Focus Your Reading Answers

1 An Arab army under the sultan of Ghur invaded India. The army defeated Hindu warriors and spread Islam across the northern part of India. The Sultanate of Delhi was founded in that city in 1206.

2 Many people converted to Islam during the Sultanate of Delhi.

3 Akbar was a more tolerant ruler. He made sure that taxes were fair and developed a policy of religious tolerance. Aurangzeb, his great-grandson, ended the toleration and reinstituted the tax on Hindus.

LESSON 3

A Series of Empires in India

Thinking on Your Own

As you read this lesson, keep a list of events in the order in which they occurred. If a date is given, write the date, too.

The Gupta Dynasty in India began to weaken in the 400s. Rival groups fought for power, as they had in China when dynasties fell. For about the next 700 years, India was divided among a number of local Hindu rulers.

focus your reading

How was the Sultanate of Delhi founded?

Explain what lasting impact the Delhi Sultanate had on India.

Compare how Akbar's policies differed from those of Aurangzeb.

vocabulary

sultan   loot
rajputs   toleration
sultanate   suttee

Delhi Sultanate

In the early 1200s, things changed in India. An Arab army under the **sultan**, or ruler, of Ghur invaded India. Hindu warriors, known as **rajputs**, fought the invaders but were defeated. The sultan's army extended Islamic rule across the northern plain of India. In 1206, the sultan founded the **Sultanate** of Delhi, based in the city of Delhi. A sultanate is an area ruled by a Sultan. In the 1300s, the Sultanate added the Deccan Plateau to its territory.

Over time the Sultanate's hold on its territory weakened. By 1398, the Sultanate could not defend its Empire from an army of Mongols and Turks. Timur-i Lang (TEE•MOOR•YEE LAHNG), sometimes called Tamerlane, and his forces invaded India from the northwest. They robbed, burned, and killed as they moved across northern India. Even the city of Delhi came under their control. Delhi was left a smoking ruin. Supposedly

174 Chapter 12

Lesson Vocabulary

Discuss each of the vocabulary terms with students.

A *sultan* is a ruler. The *sultan* of Ghur invaded India.

A *sultanate* is an area ruled by a *sultan*. The *Sultanate* of Delhi was founded in 1206. Hindu warriors were called *rajputs*. The *rajputs* could not defeat the Arab army. *Toleration* means "putting up with." Akbar had a policy of religious *toleration*.

Suttee is the custom of burning a widow with her husband's body. The practice of *suttee* was forbidden under Aurangzeb. The material gains of a conquering army are called *loot*. The Mongols who destroyed Delhi took their *loot* and left.

174 Chapter 12

Time Box

1206–1526
 Sultanate of Delhi
1526–1757
 Mogul Empire

not even a bird stirred in the city for months.

Timur and his forces did not stay to set up an empire in India. They took their **loot** and rode west. The city of Delhi was rebuilt, but it was no longer the center of a prosperous empire. Local rulers carved up large parts of India for themselves.

Muslim Influences on Indian Society

Under the Delhi Sultanate, India became part of a vast network that stretched from Southeast Asia to Europe. The sultans, however, were not interested in understanding or adopting Indian customs and traditions. The sultans created a division between their Muslim subjects and their Hindu subjects. The Hindu were a conquered people. The Muslims meant to keep it that way.

But Muslim rulers also wanted to convert Hindus to Islam. Some early sultans persecuted Hindus and destroyed their temples. A heavy tax was placed on non-Muslims. This was an effort to get Hindus to convert. The Delhi Sultanate was strongest in northern India, and most converts were made there. Hindus converted for many reasons. One reason, of course, was that some people truly came to believe in Allah. Others converted because of the equality that Islam offered.

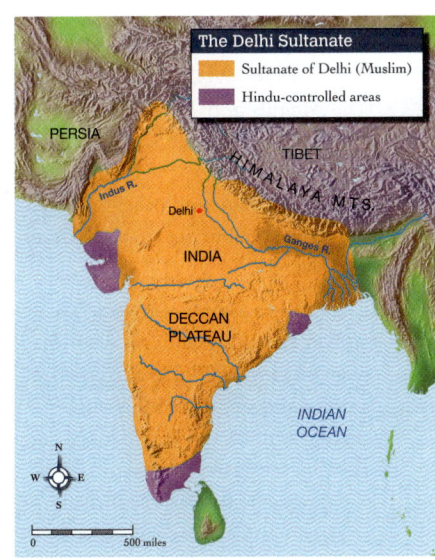

The Spread of Cultures in Asia, 500–1650

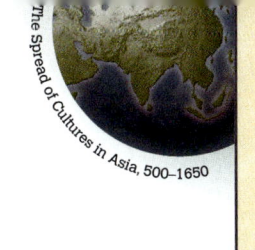

Map Extension

Ask students to use the map on page 175 to answer the following questions:

- Where were the areas of Hindu control in India? (southern tip, a small patch on both east and west coasts)

- About how many miles separated the east and west areas of Hindu control? (about 750 miles)

- What religion was practiced in the city of Delhi? (Islam)

The Delhi Sultanate
- Sultanate of Delhi (Muslim)
- Hindu-controlled areas

Extension

Delhi was chosen as the capital on the basis of its strategic importance. It controlled the access to the Punjab from the Ganges Valley. The sultans of Delhi had an army of 300,000 in the fourteenth century. Even an army of this size could not protect them, however; 19 of the 35 sultans of Delhi were assassinated.

Extension

Timur-i Lang means "Timur the Lame." His contemporaries called him this because of his limp. He was a conqueror, not an administrator, spending most of his life in battle. In his final illness, as he prepared to invade China, he had himself carried on a litter.

Chart Extension

Suggest to students that they make flash cards of each of the characteristics of the two major religions. Working in pairs, they can then quiz each other to review for a test.

Stop and Think

Students' responses may vary. Possible response:
added Deccan Plateau to conquered land; treated Hindus as a conquered people, with persecution, taxes, and rules; led to many Hindu converts

Picturing History

The illustration on page 176 is of a wedding feast in Turkey from 1562. Have students note the detail and use of color. Also note that there are no faces on the people in the painting.

The Spread of Cultures in Asia, 500–1650

Hinduism and Islam

Hinduism	Islam
• polytheistic, belief in many deities • many sacred books • caste system • priests • belief in cows as sacred animals • music as part of religious ceremonies	• monotheistic, belief in one God—Allah • one sacred book, the Quran • equality of all people • no priests • viewed cows as food • music in religious ceremonies was offensive to Allah

stop and think

Create a concept web to list the effects of the Delhi Sultanate. Label the large circle "Sultanate of Delhi." Draw a smaller circle for each effect that the Sultanate caused. Draw lines to connect the smaller circles to the large one.

There was no caste system in Islam. Some Indian merchants probably converted so they could more easily tap into the Muslim trade network. Some Hindus converted in order to marry a Muslim. Some people, of course, converted so they would not have to pay the nonbelievers' tax.

There were a number of differences between Islam and Hinduism. The differences were not just in religious ideas. There were also cultural differences, such as the use of music.

Ultimately, the sultans relaxed their opposition to Hinduism. Hindus were free to worship their deities as long as they paid the nonbelievers' tax. A vast number of people remained Hindus.

The Mogul Empire

The Moguls and Turks returned to India in the 1500s. In 1526, Babur led a combined Turkish and Mogul force. They easily defeated what was left of the Delhi Sultanate and other small kingdoms. Babur set up the Mogul Empire.

The most famous emperor was Akbar, Babur's grandson, who ruled from 1556 to 1605. He expanded the empire and set up an efficient organization to run it. He made sure that the tax system that supported the government was fair. Akbar understood that the tension between

A wedding feast in 1562

176 Chapter 12

Extension

Akbar took power in 1556, after an argument with a powerful man at court. Akbar threw the man out the window, dragged him back inside from the courtyard, and threw him out the window again to make sure he was dead.

176 Chapter 12

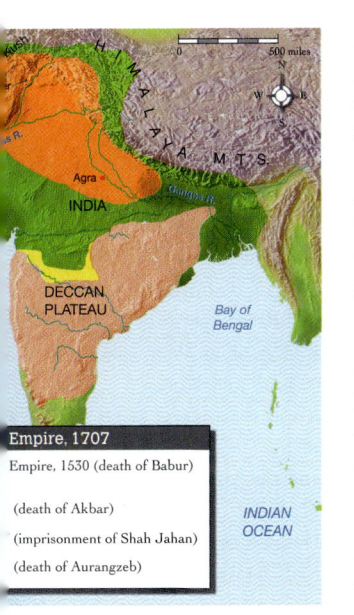

Islam and Hinduism created problems in the Empire. He ordered a policy of religious **toleration**. He married a Hindu and appointed Hindus to lower-level government positions. Top-level positions went to Muslims. The tax on non-Muslims was ended.

Not all of Akbar's successors followed his policies. In 1658, Aurangzeb, Akbar's great-grandson, seized power from his father, Shah Jahan. Aurangzeb ended religious toleration and began the persecution of Hindus. The nonbelievers' tax was reinstated. No new Hindu temples could be built. **Suttee**, burning a widow with the body of her deceased husband, was forbidden. Gambling and drinking, both banned under Islam, were also forbidden.

These actions resulted in a number of rebellions against Mogul emperors. However, no revolt succeeded in overthrowing the Empire. The Mogul Empire lasted until 1757 when Great Britain seized power. The first British traders had arrived in India in the 1600s.

The Taj Mahal (above) was built by Shah Jahan, the fifth Mogul emperor, as a tribute to his wife Mumtaz Mahal. The complex took 22 years to build and was completed in 1648.

Emperor Akbar (below) symbolically passes the crown from his son, Shah Jahan, to his grandson.

Putting It All Together

Imagine that you are a Hindu living in Delhi in 1757 when the British gained control of India. Write a letter to the new British governor asking for better treatment of the Hindus. Explain how India's Muslim leaders have treated your family during the past two hundred years.

The Spread of Cultures in Asia 177

Map Extension

Ask students to use the map on page 177 to answer the following questions:

- When did the Khyber Pass become part of the Mogul Empire? (by 1530)
- What area was the last to be added to the empire? (Deccan Plateau)
- How would you describe the Mogul acquisitions up to 1605? (Land was conquered in a circle all around the original empire.)
- Did the empire reach the Arabian Sea before 1605? (no)

Picturing History

The Taj Mahal, pictured on page 177, is considered to be one of the most beautiful buildings in the world. Prince Khurrum, whose nickname, Shah Jahan, means "King of the World," had it constructed as a memorial to his beloved wife, Mumtaz Mahal (Chosen One of the Palace). She died after giving birth to their fourteenth child.

The bottom image shows Emperor Akbar passing the crown from his grandson, Shah Jahan, to his great-grandson.

Putting It All Together
Students' letters will vary but should include specific details about Hindu life in India, and how Muslim treatment is unfair. Letters should follow proper format including a salutation, body, and closing.

Extension
Have interested students use library resources or the Internet to find out more about suttee, which continues to be practiced in some areas of the world.

The Spread of Cultures in Asia 177

Chapter Review

1 Students' choices of topics, headlines, and paragraphs will vary but should be based on chapter events and people.

2 Students' choices of people and questions will vary but should be based on chapter content.

Chapter Summary

- The Tang and Song Dynasties are known as the Golden Ages in China.
- Mongols invaded China in 1215. Kublai Khan founded the Yuan Dynasty. Later emperors were **corrupt**.
- In 1368, a **monk** and his followers overthrew the Yuan and founded the Ming Dynasty. Yong Le built the **Imperial** City. A **fleet** of his ships made **voyages** to explore Southeast Asia, India, and the Arabian Peninsula.
- Japan is an **archipelago** close to China and Korea.
- The early Japanese lived in clans and most were farmers. There were a few **aristocrats**.
- The Yamato **clan** gained power and the Yamato leader declared himself emperor and high priest of **Shinto**.
- Japan became a feudal society. The real power was with the **shogun**. The highest vassals were the **daimyo**. They were followed by the **samurai** and **ronin**. Most Japanese were **tenant farmers**.
- Tokugawa used a **hostage system** to control the daimyo.
- The **Sultan** of Ghur invaded India and defeated **rajputs**. He founded the **Sultanate** of Delhi and introduced Islam into India. Timur later invaded India, **looted**, and left a badly weakened Delhi Sultanate.
- In 1526, Babur set up the Mogul Empire. His grandson Akbar adopted religious **toleration**. A later emperor, Aurangzeb, banned **suttee**.

Chapter Review

1 Work with a partner to decide on topics and headlines for four newspaper articles about people and events in Chapter 12. Then write an introductory paragraph for each that includes *who, what, when, where,* and *why.*

2 Play "Who am I?" with a partner. Choose five people discussed in this chapter. Write three or four sentences to describe each person. End your descriptions with the question "Who am I?" Take turns quizzing each other.

Novel Connections

Below is a list of books that relate to the time period covered in this chapter. The numbers in parentheses indicate the related Thematic Strands of the National Council for the Social Studies (NCSS).

Lloyd Alexander. *Iron Ring*. Puffin, 1999. (I, III, IV)

Kara Dalkey. *Little Sister*. Harcourt, 1996. (I, III, IV)

May Holdsworth. *Women of the Tang Dynasty*. Odyssey Publications, Ltd., 1999. (I, IV, V, VI)

Lensey Namioka. *Samurai and the Long-Nosed Devils*. Charles E. Tuttle Co., Inc., 2004. (I, III, IV)

Katherine Paterson. *Of Nightingales That Weep*. HarperCollins, 1989. (I, III, IV, V)

Jon Scieszka. *Sam Samurai (The Time Warp Trio)*, Vol. 10. Puffin, 2002. (I, II, IX)

Skill Builder

Analyzing Sequence Using a Flowchart

Sequence is the order in which events happen. *Chronology* is another word for *sequence*. A timeline is one way to arrange the sequence of events. You can see that one thing happened before or after another from the location of events on the timeline. Making a timeline as you read can help you understand sequence more easily.

A writer does not always use dates to describe sequence. Sometimes a writer uses signal words. Some words that signal sequence are:

| first, second, third . . . | first . . . last | before | after |
| now | earlier | later | next | then |

Sometimes you have to figure out sequence without any timeline or any signal words. A flowchart can help you. Start with the first event and fill in each event in the order in which it happened. A flowchart of the invasion of India by Timur looks like the following:

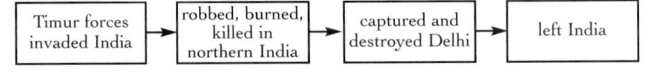

Timur forces invaded India → robbed, burned, killed in northern India → captured and destroyed Delhi → left India

The flowchart presents the main ideas. Details are left out. Making a flowchart can help you identify and remember the most important information.

Complete the following activities:

1. In Lesson 1 of this chapter you created a timeline. Use your timeline to create a flowchart of events. Share your flowchart with a partner. Quiz each other on when events happened in relation to each other. Use some of the signal words to ask your questions.

2. Create a flowchart to show the order of events under the Ming Dynasty.

3. Create a flowchart to show the chronology of events in India. Use your list of events from Lesson 3.

The Spread of Cultures in Asia | 179

Skill Builder

1. Students' flowcharts and questions will vary but should reflect events in the chapter.

2. Students' flowcharts will vary but should depict order of events in the Ming Dynasty. Possible response includes Yong Le builds Imperial City, sends Zheng He on voyages; next emperor ends these voyages; peasant revolt; Manchu invaders.

3. Students' flowcharts will vary but should show the chronology of events in India. Possible response includes Gupta Dynasty falls; sultan of Ghur conquers India; Sultanate of Delhi founded and expands to Deccan Plateau; Tamerlane invades and destroys Delhi; Babur sets up Mogul Empire; Akbar follows policy of religious toleration, which his great-grandson revokes; British traders arrive; Great Britain seizes power.

Classroom Discussion

Discuss with students some of the broader topics covered in this chapter.

- How do citizens today show loyalty to the government and their leaders?
- How can people begin to find common ground in different religions?
- What are the dangers and difficulties of conquering another land?

Unit Objectives

After studying this unit, students will be able to

- explain the religious, economic, and political structure of medieval Europe
- discuss the changes brought about by the Renaissance and Reformation
- describe the voyages of discovery undertaken by Europeans and their results for both conquering and conquered nations

Unit 4 focuses on the beginnings of the global age.

Chapter 13, Medieval Europe, examines feudalism and manorialism, the influence of the Church, and the growth of capitalism.

Chapter 14, Renaissance and Reformation, explores the way new discoveries and new doctrines affected Europe.

Chapter 15, Age of European Explorations, discusses the European voyages of discovery and their results.

Getting Started

Write the word *global* on the board. Ask students to add words that they have heard described as *global*. (network, communication, warming, etc.) Ask them what must be true for something to really be global. Have a student read aloud the title of the unit and the two paragraphs that follow it on page 180. Ask students to devote a page in their notebooks to creating a list of the global effects of this era.

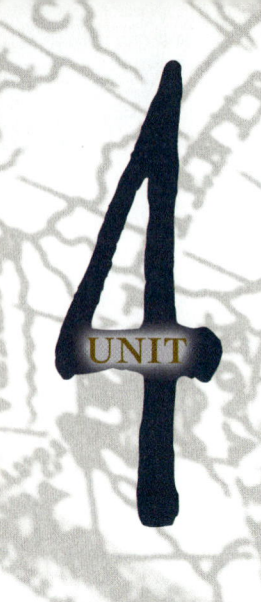

UNIT 4

THE GLOBAL AGE

The end of the Roman Empire in the West barely affected most people. They looked to their local landowners for protection and a way to earn a living. The Catholic Church remained a governing force in people's lives. But change was creeping across Western Europe.

By the 1500s, change came more rapidly—and not just to Western Europe. Europeans began to search out routes to rich trading nations in Asia. By accident, they bumped into the Americas. The race was on among European nations to establish colonies and gain riches.

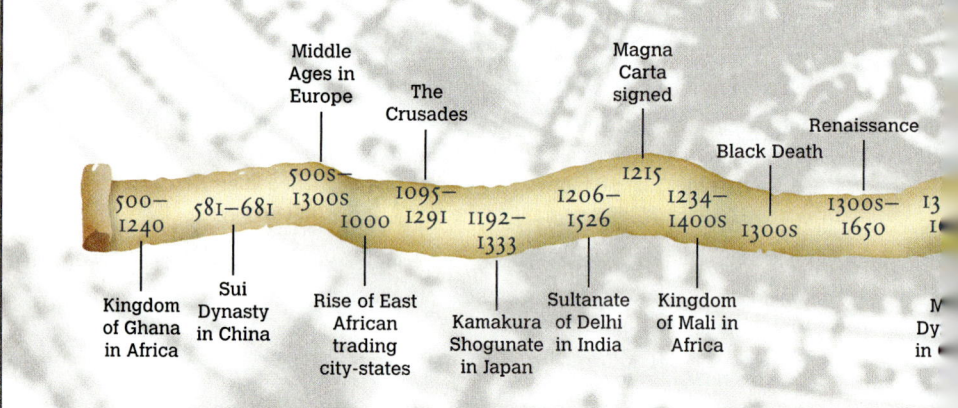

Timeline:
- Kingdom of Ghana in Africa: 500–1240
- Sui Dynasty in China: 581–681
- Middle Ages in Europe: 500s–1300s
- Rise of East African trading city-states: 1000
- The Crusades: 1095–1291
- Kamakura Shogunate in Japan: 1192–1333
- Sultanate of Delhi in India: 1206–1526
- Magna Carta signed: 1215
- Kingdom of Mali in Africa: 1234–1400s
- Black Death: 1300s
- Renaissance: 1300s–1650

Timeline Extension

Ask students to use the timeline to preview each chapter in the unit. Then have them answer the following questions:

- Which African kingdom occurred first, Mali, Songhai, or Ghana?
- When did the Crusades take place?

Measuring Time

Explain to students that Chapter 13 focuses on the society of medieval Europe. The events of that era appear on page 180 of the timeline. Chapter 14 examines the Renaissance and Reformation. The events that marked those eras are on both pages of the timeline. Chapter 15 discusses the early European explorations and their results. The events of that time are on page 181 of the timeline.

Why is the Renaissance considered a turning point in world history?

What was life like on the medieval manor?

How did European voyages of exploration and trade affect non-Europeans?

Collage Answers

1 The self-sufficient life of a medieval manor centered on obedience to and production for the lord of the manor. Serfs, who belonged to the land, paid for the use of the land and mill with crops. Nobles had complete control of their serfs.

2 The Renaissance is considered a turning point in history because it affected education and the way that people viewed life. The Renaissance emphasized current life and thus human achievement, rather than the life hereafter.

3 European voyages of exploration and trade affected non-Europeans by bringing diseases for which they had no immunity, taking their riches for the conquering country, forcing conversions to Christianity, and introducing new crops and animals.

Timeline

- 1420 — First Portuguese voyage along African coast
- 1450–1600s — Kingdom of Songhai in Africa
- 1492 — Christopher Columbus sailed west
- 1517 — Martin Luther's 95 Theses
- 1526–1857 — Mogul Empire in India
- 1534 — Church of England founded
- 1536 — John Calvin created theocracy in Geneva, Switzerland
- 1545 — Beginning of the Catholic Reformation
- 1603–1867 — Tokugawa Shogunate in Japan

Collage Extension

Use the images and questions on page 181 to preview the unit. Discuss what the questions and pictures suggest about life during the medieval period, Renaissance, and Reformation.

Picturing History

The images on page 181 represent people and places that will be discussed in Unit 4.

1 The top image is of an illuminated manuscript that describes the harvest on a medieval manor.

2 This is a reproduction of the *Mona Lisa*, one of Leonardo da Vinci's most famous works.

3 The full lateen sails of a caravel allowed global exploration. This is a sketch of a caravel under full sail.

The Global Age 181

Chapter 13

MEDIEVAL EUROPE

(500–1300)

Chapter Summary
Refer to page 198 for a summary of Chapter 13.

Related Transparencies

T-18 Three-Column Chart

T-19 Venn Diagram

T-20 Concept Web

Key Blacklines

Biography–Charlemagne

CD Extension

Encourage students to use the reading comprehension, vocabulary reinforcement, and interactive timeline activities on the student CD.

Getting Focused

You may wish to place students in small groups of mixed abilities. Each group can be responsible for one KWL Chart, which will be more inclusive than any single student's chart would be.

Picturing History

The haystacks shown on page 182 have been gathered as they would have been when the medieval citadel of Carcassonne in the background was a thriving place. Suggest that students interested in agriculture find out more about medieval techniques of farming.

Getting Focused

Skim this chapter to predict what you will be learning.
- Read the lesson titles and subheadings.
- Look at the illustrations and read the captions.
- Examine the maps.
- Review the vocabulary words and terms.

In your notebook create a KWL Chart. Title the first column "What I Know." Title the second column "What I Want to Know," and the third column "What I Learned." Fill in the first two columns as you preview the chapter. Fill in the last column after you complete your reading.

Pre-Reading Discussion

1 Discuss with students some of the basic liberties taken for granted in a democracy. Tell them that in this chapter they will study one of the foundational documents of liberty.

2 Ask students to identify the steps a person goes through today to prepare for a career. Identify the length of time required. Tell students they are about to learn of medieval job-training programs.

LESSON 1

Feudalism and Manorialism

Medieval Europe, 500–1300

Thinking on Your Own

Examine the pictures and captions in the lesson. Choose two pictures to write about. Describe how the people are dressed and what they are doing in each picture. Use words that will help your reader imagine the pictures. Also, use the vocabulary words.

In the early 700s, Muslims were on the march in Europe. When they invaded France, Charles Martel led an army of Franks against them. In 732, at the Battle of Tours, the Franks defeated the Muslim army. The Muslims were pushed back into Spain where they ruled until the late 1400s. By 800, Charles Martel's grandson Charlemagne had begun to put together an empire. His armies seized land in what are today France, Germany, and Italy. At the same time, Vikings were moving south from Norway and Sweden. They were threatening coastal cities in Britain and France.

focus your reading

How did European feudalism work?

Compare feudalism and manorialism.

Explain why the Roman Catholic Church was so important in the lives of Europeans.

vocabulary

fiefs
chivalry
manor
parish
bishop
archbishop
cardinal
pope

Beginning in the 400s, Germanic invaders set up small kingdoms in England to take the place of Roman authority. In the 800s, a single Anglo-Saxon kingdom gained power over the others. In 1066, England fell to Norman invaders from France. Their leader, William the Conqueror, seized the throne.

Charlemagne

Lesson Summary

The threat of a Muslim-controlled Europe ended in 732 at the Battle of Tours. Defeated by the Franks, Muslims retreated to Spain and remained there. Charlemagne ruled over a European empire, while Viking tribes pushed south into England. The Anglo-Saxons were conquered by William of Normandy, who brought the system of feudalism.

Feudalism is a political system. Manorialism was the economic system of medieval times.

The Roman Catholic Church also maintained a hierarchy of power, from the pope, who was at times more important than the monarch, to the local priest. The Church was the most stable element of society.

Lesson Objective

Students will learn about the development of feudalism and manorialism, as well as the role of the Roman Catholic Church in medieval times.

Focus Your Reading Answers

1 Feudalism was a system of loyalty and land rights. The monarch granted land to the nobles, who owed service as a result. The nobles parceled land to knights, who fought in battle in return.

2 Manorialism was the economic system, with serfs farming the land for the nobles and for themselves. Feudalism was a political system.

3 The Church was the most stable part of society. In addition, it offered people hope for a better life after death.

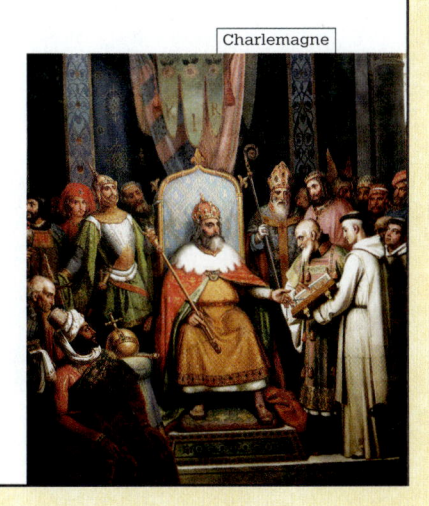

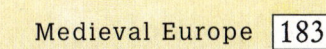

Lesson Vocabulary

Introduce each of the following vocabulary terms to students.

Explain that *fiefs* were grants of land. The monarch gave *fiefs* to loyal nobles. *Chivalry* was the code of behavior that knights followed. The code of *chivalry* gave women a place of special honor.

The *manor* was the house and lands on which the nobles lived. During the early Middle Ages, most Europeans lived on a *manor*.

A *parish* was the local level of the Church. The people in a *parish* were its parishioners. The *bishop* was the priest in charge of the whole diocese. The duty of a *bishop* was to care for all Christians in the diocese, especially the priests. The *archbishop* was the head of a province, which was a collection of dioceses. The *archbishop* also cared for all the *bishops* in the diocese. A *cardinal* was above the rest of the clergy. The *cardinals* were so named because of the red hats they wore. The highest rank of the Church was the *pope*. The *pope* had so much power that even emperors feared him.

Medieval Europe 183

Picturing History

The illustration on page 183 shows Charlemagne receiving the monk Alcuin, possibly an emissary from Pope Leo III.

Pope Leo III crowned Charlemagne on Christmas Day, 800. The pope was grateful for Charlemagne's help in repelling foreign invaders. In addition to his skills in battle, Charlemagne was a patron of the arts and a lawmaker.

Chart Extension

You may wish to have students compare the chart of feudal society on page 184 with some of the other social pyramids throughout the chapters studied thus far. For example, how does the feudal system compare with Egypt's social pyramid? with India's caste system? with Japanese feudalism?

Picturing History

The illustration on page 184 shows a medieval battle. The king, in simple clothes, but with a crown, is giving orders to his knights.

Feudalism

During the Middle Ages—the period between the fall of the Roman Empire and the Renaissance—Europeans began to use the political system called feudalism. It provided protection for people and a new way to organize governments. Feudalism also developed in the Byzantine Empire in eastern Europe, in the Monomotapa Empire in Africa, and among the Japanese.

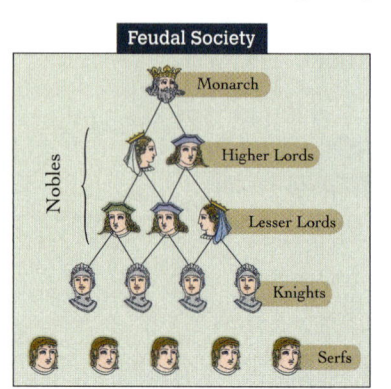

At the top of the feudal system was the monarch, or chief lord. All of the land belonged to him. He gave land to nobles who were loyal to him. The land grants, or gifts of land, were called **fiefs**. The nobles were vassals of the monarch, but they were lords to those below them in society. In return for land, the nobles owed the monarch loyalty. In time of war, they had to raise an army of knights and soldiers to defend the monarch. The nobles also made a yearly payment to the monarch for the use of their land.

Below the nobles were knights. They, in turn, were vassals of the nobles. The knights received land from the nobles and owed them loyalty in return. The knights had to defend their lord and his lands against attack. They also owed their lords annual payments for the land.

A medieval king giving orders during a battle.

Extension

The royal court was a means of displaying power and status. At court the monarch settled disputes, collected taxes, heard grievances, and made laws. There were banquets and entertainments, such as mock battles known as tourneys. Knights charged one another as the king and his court looked on. Once unhorsed, the knights continued fighting on foot. These jousts were a way to keep the noblemen at court, where the monarch could make sure no rebellion was being mounted.

Serfs were the lowest class in European society. They owed both loyalty and labor to the nobles, their lords. In addition, serfs had to pay yearly rent to their lords.

Over time, a code of behavior known as **chivalry** developed among the nobles and knights. Knights were supposed to be loyal, brave, and honorable. They were to treat prisoners well and defend women, children, the sick, and the elderly. Women were given a special place of honor in chivalry, but they lacked many of the rights that men had.

Manorialism

Manorialism was Europe's economic system during the Middle Ages. Most Europeans in the early Middle Ages farmed and lived on **manors**. These were the estates, or large landholdings, of the nobles. The manors were the nobles' fiefs from the monarch.

Very wealthy nobles, like dukes, might live in a castle. At times, the knights who served the noble lived there, too. However, the typical noble and his family lived in a large house on their manor. Serfs lived in a village on the manor. The village included a church and a mill for grinding grain.

Nobles kept about one-third to one-half of their manor's land for themselves. In return for protection, the serfs worked the lord's land about three days out of every week. The serfs worked the rest of the land in return for an annual payment. Women as well as men worked in the fields.

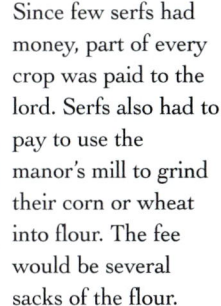

Since few serfs had money, part of every crop was paid to the lord. Serfs also had to pay to use the manor's mill to grind their corn or wheat into flour. The fee would be several sacks of the flour.

> **stop and think**
>
> Feudalism was the political system of the Middle Ages. Manorialism was the economic system. Explain how these systems worked together in medieval society. Write down your ideas. Talk with a partner to test your ideas. Then write one or two paragraphs to explain how feudalism and manorialism were related.

Medieval Europe | 185

Picturing History

Have students study the picture on page 185.

Glass was expensive and rare during the Middle Ages, used only in palaces or churches. This home probably relied on a cheaper material for windows. To allow light, merchants and nobles used panes made from horn. The horns of animals were softened in water for months, unwound, split, and polished to translucence. Although they did admit light, panes made of horn were nearly impossible to see through.

Stop and Think

Students' paragraphs will vary but may include the idea that large gifts of land to the nobles provided an adequate space for manorialism to flourish. Most citizens in an area were tied in some way to the manor. Feudalism was based on a system of loyalty and exchange. Certain people received land from those above them in return for their loyalty.

Extension

Students with an interest in literature may wish to examine some of the writings of the Middle Ages, such as the *Chanson de Roland* and *Sir Gawain and the Green Knight*. Others might look at the poetry written by Chrêtien de Troyes. Alternatively, invite a colleague from the English department to discuss the poetry of the Middle Ages and bring examples to class.

Medieval Europe | 185

Picturing History

Medieval cathedrals, such as Notre Dame, shown on page 186, were built in a new architectural style known as Gothic. The Abbey of St. Denis, built in 1140 near Paris, was the first to use this style. By incorporating the use of flying buttresses, which were outer structures that supported the weight of the roof, the cathedrals could soar ever higher. In Beauvais, France, one choir roof reached 157 feet (48 m). The image on the right is from a painting called *Adoration of the Kings* attributed to Simone Martini and others. The drawing at the bottom is of the interior of a building at Oxford University in England.

Medieval Europe, 500–1300

The lord had absolute control over the serfs on his manor. This control maintained law and order. The noble held his own court to try serfs accused of crimes. He also sentenced those who were convicted and saw that the punishment was carried out. If a serf wanted to leave the manor for any reason, the lord had to give permission. If a lord lost his manor, the serfs as well as the land became the property of the new lord. The new lord could not throw serfs off their land. Unlike slaves, serfs could not be bought and sold.

Roman Catholic Church

In the early Middle Ages, the Roman Catholic Church contributed to the stability of Western European society. Nobles and monarchs came and went, but the Church remained. Except for Muslims in Spain and groups of Jews, everyone in Western Europe was a member of the Roman Catholic Church.

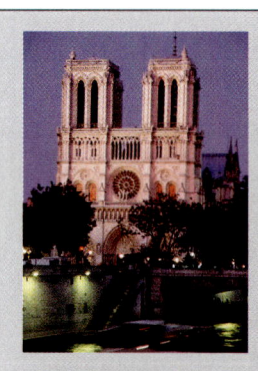

Religion and learning were important during the Middle Ages. Cathedrals such as Notre Dame in Paris were constructed (above left). Religious figures were often the subject of paintings (above right). Oxford University was a center for learning (bottom).

Church teachings helped people accept the hardships of their life on Earth. It also taught the common people to obey the rulers. The Church taught that the soul was more important than the body. People endured cruel lords, unjust laws, and poor living conditions. They believed that such hardships would earn them entry to heaven. As a result, the Middle Ages was not a time of rebellions and revolutions.

Since the days of the first Christians, the Church had grown in size and organization. At the local

186 Chapter 13

Extension

Have students with an interest in architecture use library resources or the Internet to discover how the use of flying buttresses changed the churches of medieval Europe. Have them present their findings to the class by using the Student Presentation Builder on the student CD.

level were parishioners who made up a **parish**. A priest led the parish in prayer and offered Mass, the central part of Catholic worship. A group of parishes made up a diocese. The diocese was headed by a **bishop**. A group of dioceses was called a province and was headed by an **archbishop**. **Cardinals** were above bishops and archbishops. The head of the Church was the **pope**.

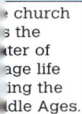

Because of the chaos in Europe in the early Middle Ages, the position of the pope grew in importance. At times, the pope was more important than any monarch. For example, in the late 1000s, conflict broke out between Pope Gregory VII and the emperor of Germany, Henry IV. The emperor was appointing unapproved men to Church positions. The pope forced the emperor to travel to Italy and do penance, or ask for forgiveness, for his actions. The emperor was barefoot and dressed in a burlap robe. The pope kept him waiting for three days in the cold before he would receive him. Making the emperor wait represented the power of the Church.

Putting It All Together

Using the information in this lesson, write a paragraph that explains how feudalism, manorialism, and the Roman Catholic Church worked together to maintain an orderly, but unequal, society. Share your paragraph with a partner.

Picturing History

The illustration on page 187 depicts the visit of a bishop to a local church. Point out to students the clothes of the priests and upper-class worshipers.

Putting It All Together
Students' paragraphs will vary but should show an understanding of each system.

Lesson Summary

The Crusades were an effort to end Muslim control of the Holy Land and the warfare among European states. Although the Muslims lost territory, they regained the Holy Land by the end of the Crusades.

Trade increased by the 1000s. The bartering system became outmoded and was replaced by a money economy. The growth of trade led to the development of banking and to the growth of capitalism. A further consequence was the spread of the bubonic plague.

Cities received charters from the lords who needed money and sold the rights to towns around them. Craftworkers came to the cities and established guilds and standard training in their crafts.

The development of cities and towns led to a middle class made up of craftworkers, traders, and merchants.

Lesson Objective

Students will learn about the Crusades and their effects on Europe, including increased trade, the growth of cities, and the development of a middle class.

Focus Your Reading Answers

1 The Muslims lost and then regained land. Europeans began searching for a sea route to Asia. Italian trading cities grew wealthy.

2 The merchants built new cities near a lord's castle for protection. The towns grew as craftworkers were drawn there.

3 As the middle class grew larger and more prosperous, they gained power.

188 Chapter 13

Medieval Europe, 500–1300

LESSON **2**

Changing Times

Thinking on Your Own

Create a concept web in your notebook. Label the center circle "Changing Times." In the surrounding circles, include information that explains how life was changing for people in Europe during the Middle Ages. As you read, fill in your web. Try to include all of the vocabulary words and terms in your circles.

By 1050, Europe was changing. Invasions had ended for the most part. Feudal monarchs were beginning to gain greater power over their nobles. Trade was increasing. Because of the growing trade networks, towns were growing in size and number. One important influence in this period was the Crusades.

focus your reading

How did the Crusades affect Europe and the Holy Land?

Why did trade cause the growth of cities?

What characteristics did the new middle class share?

vocabulary

crusade
Holy Land
unintended consequences
barter
money economy
capitalism
bubonic plague
charters
guild
journeyman
tenant farmers
middle class

The Crusades

The Christian rulers of Europe organized **crusades** to recapture the **Holy Land** from the Muslims. The Holy Land was the name that Christians gave Jerusalem and the parts of Palestine where Jesus had lived. In 1071, Seljuk Turks, who were Muslims, seized the Holy Land. They also threatened the Byzantine Empire. Byzantine Emperor Alexius I asked Pope Urban II for help in fighting the Turks.

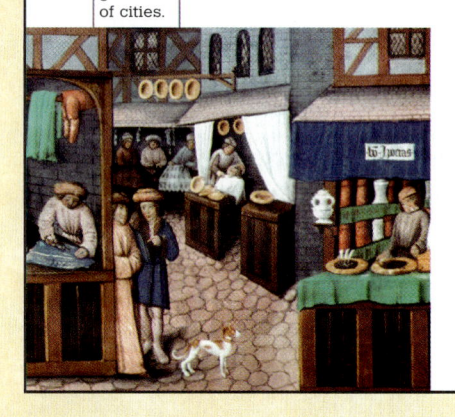

Merchant trade led to the growth of cities.

Lesson Vocabulary

Discuss each of the vocabulary terms with students.

The *Holy Land* was the name given to parts of Palestine and to Jerusalem. Christians wanted to free the *Holy Land* from Muslim control.

A *crusade* is a great military campaign. Pope Urban II called for the first *crusade* in 1095.

Unplanned effects are also known as *unintended consequences*. Some of the *unintended consequences* of the Crusades included the increase of Asian luxury goods in Europe and a desire to travel.

To *barter* is to exchange goods or services. The *barter* system was used until the later Middle Ages. A *money economy*, based on gold or silver coinage, resulted from the growth of trade networks. The economic system of *capitalism* is based on private ownership and profit. The growth of trade fueled *capitalism*.

The *bubonic plague* was an epidemic also known as the Black Death. Nearly half of all Europeans died from the *bubonic plague*.

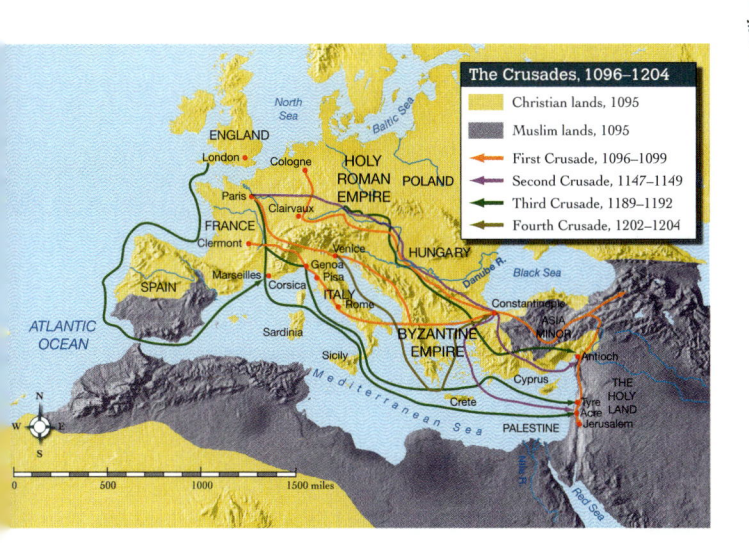

The Crusades, 1096–1204
- Christian lands, 1095
- Muslim lands, 1095
- First Crusade, 1096–1099
- Second Crusade, 1147–1149
- Third Crusade, 1189–1192
- Fourth Crusade, 1202–1204

The Roman Catholic Church and the Byzantine Church had recently split. However, the pope thought that a crusade, or great campaign, might heal the split between the two churches. A crusade was also a way to stop the constant warfare among Europeans. In 1095, Urban II called for a great crusade against the Turks. The pope promised forgiveness of sins and everlasting salvation to those who died fighting the Muslims. In all, there were eight Crusades. The early Crusades established a European foothold in the Middle East. The final four Crusades resulted in the loss of all the territory that had been gained in the first four. By 1291, the Muslims were again in control of the Holy Land.

The importance of the Crusades lies in their **unintended consequences**, or unplanned effects. Italian trading cities became wealthy from the Crusades. Their ships carried Crusaders to Southwest Asia and brought back loads of luxury goods for sale. Europeans also began to look for a sea route to Asia. An interest in travel and seeing faraway places developed. Persecution of Jews intensified. Muslims were attacked as unbelievers, and so were Jews.

> **stop and think**
>
> As you read this lesson, make a list of five or six of the most important changes that took place in Europe from 1050 to about 1350. You should complete this list by the end of the lesson.

Medieval Europe 189

Vocabulary, continued

...were documents that spelled out rights. Towns had *charters* that they received ...werful lords.

...ere organizations of craftworkers or merchants that formed for economic ...on. *Guilds* set prices and working hours. After being an apprentice for seven ...person became a *journeyman*. A *journeyman* could work for wages but not yet ...ild.

...rmers pay the owners of land money for use of the land. In medieval Europe, ...rfs became *tenant farmers*.

...*ldle class* was composed of traders, craftworkers, and merchants. The *middle* ...d a position between the nobles and the farmers.

Picturing History

The woman in the red head covering shown on page 188 was a merchant. In medieval times, women were active in trade and in crafts. They sometimes learned trades from their fathers or husbands. Women were not permitted to be members of most guilds. Although women did nearly all the silk weaving in London, they were not permitted to form a guild.

Map Extension

Ask students to use the map on page 189 to answer the following questions:

- From which countries did the Crusades begin? (England, France, Holy Roman Empire)
- To which city did the Second Crusade go? (Acre)
- Which Crusade began from the farthest point west? (Third)
- Which Crusade passed through Rome? (First)

Stop and Think

Students' lists will differ. Possible responses include

- interest in travel and exploration
- growth of wealthy Italian trading cities
- luxury goods from Asia reach Europe
- split of the Catholic Church
- persecution of Muslims and Jews

Medieval Europe 189

Map Extension

Ask students to use the map on page 190 to answer the following questions:

- What was the farthest northern point of the trade routes? (Bergen)
- Which city would have been the last eastern stop before heading on to China or India? (Baghdad)
- Did any of the trade routes go across the Caspian Sea? (no)
- About how far apart were Barcelona and Constantinople? (about 1,500 miles)

Increasing Trade

The vast trading network of the Roman Empire began to fall apart with the decline of the Empire. Most people during the early Middle Ages were farmers living on manors. For the most part, they made whatever they needed or they did without. However, trade never completely disappeared. As invasions ended and local warfare among nobles died down, trade increased.

There were always a few towns scattered here and there in a region. London in England and Paris in France had once been Roman towns. There were towns in Spain, Italy, and the Germanic states, also.

By the 1000s, the trade network had grown greatly. Italian city-states, such as Venice and Genoa, were building fleets of merchant ships. These ships sailed back and forth between the Byzantine Empire and Italy. They were loaded with goods from China, the Arabian Peninsula, and even Africa. Towns in northern Europe also became trading centers.

Also by the 1000s, some of the towns had become the site of yearly trade fairs. Merchants from as far away as Italy traveled to France to sell goods such as silks and spices from

Extension

During the medieval period, universities developed in the great cities of Italy, France, and England. Europe's first universities began in Salerno and Bologna, Italy. Nine additional Italian universities began during the thirteenth through fifteenth centuries. The University of Paris began between 1150 and 1170. Oxford University in England began in 1167–1168.

190 Chapter 13

China and cotton from India. Among the goods that they bought were wool cloth and crockery from Flanders—an area in modern Belgium and France—and furs from Russia.

Until the later Middle Ages, the **barter** system, or exchange, was used for business. The growth of trade networks and the specialization of trade made barter impractical. Merchants wanted gold or silver coins. This was the beginning of the **money economy**.

Increased trade brought about another change in the way people did business. Merchants began to borrow money to pay for trading voyages. Once they sold the goods their traders bought in Constantinople or Flanders, they could repay the loan. The banking business developed to finance these deals.

The growth of trade also fueled the growth of **capitalism**. This is an economic system based on the private ownership of production for the purpose of making a profit. Besides repaying the loan, a smart merchant could also make a profit.

The development of both the money economy and capitalism were unintended consequences of global trade. Another unintended effect was the spread of the **bubonic plague**, or Black Death. It was carried by infected fleas that lived on rats. The rats traveled on ships beween European ports and cities in Asia. People became ill after they were bitten by infected fleas. Between 1348 and 1353, some 38 million out of 75 million, or about half of all Europeans, died from the plague.

The plague, or Black Death, was carried by infected fleas that lived on rats.

Picturing History

The etching on page 191 depicts victims of the plague. Students who are interested in science or medicine may wish to investigate the plague further using library resources or the Internet.

Extension

Moneylenders in Italy did business on benches, also called banks. The wealth they generated due to interest on loans built great cities such as Genoa, Florence, Siena, and Venice.

Shakespeare's play *The Merchant of Venice* depicts the fortunes of a Jewish moneylender in that city. Interested students may wish to read or watch the play.

Map Extension

Ask students to use the map on page 192 to answer the following questions:

- In what year did the plague reach Novgorod? (1353)
- In which year did the plague spread over the most territory? (1348)
- What town was seriously affected by the plague in 1350? (Lübeck)
- In 1349, which town was totally or partially spared? (Nuremberg)

Picturing History

Medieval towns, as depicted on page 192, were often walled. These walls were as much as 33 feet (10 m) thick. The walls served as protection from criminals. They also made certain that merchants had to come in through a gate and pay a toll to do business in the town. The gates were opened at dawn and were locked at sunset.

Chart Extension

Discuss with students the rights of towns. Which of these rights seem most relevant to life in cities today? Which are no longer needed?

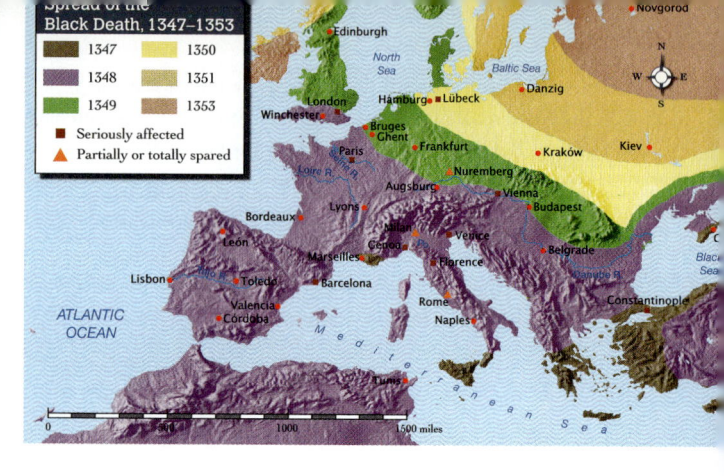

The Rise of Cities

Another outcome of the growth of trade was the growth of cities. These cities were often the sites of trade fairs. Sometimes a group of merchants built a new settlement. Often they chose a place near a castle. The merchants arranged with the lord of the castle to provide protection—for a fee. As the towns and cities grew, the population became more diverse.

Often, lords found themselves in need of money. They found an unusual way to get it. They sold rights to the towns in their territory. In exchange for money, the towns received **charters** spelling out their rights.

Medieval towns and cities grew and prospered.

Typical Rights of Tow[ns]

- Townspeople could elect l[...]
- Townspeople could manag[e] government of the town.
- Townspeople had their ow[n] law courts.
- Townspeople could buy a[nd] sell property.
- Townspeople were free fr[om] military service to the lord[.]
- If a runaway serf lived a y[ear] and a day in the town, the serf would be a free perso[n.]

Guilds

Craftworkers were drawn to the new towns because merchants needed goods to sell. Craftworkers set up shop and began to make products. Over time, craftworkers developed **guilds**. A guild was an organization of merchants or craftworkers who banded together to protect their economic interests. The purpose of the guilds was to set standards for the quality of work produced by its members. Guilds also set working hours and prices for goods.

Extension

A single industry might require several guilds. For example, cloth-making used the services of those who cleaned and compacted the cloth (fullers and walkers), those who brushed it (carders), those who trimmed it (shearmen), those who colored it (dyers), and those who wove it (weavers).

The guilds trained young people to become masters, or highly skilled workers, in a craft. Women as well as men could become master craftworkers. The first step was to become an apprentice. At ten years of age, a boy or girl entered an apprenticeship with a master craftworker. The apprentice worked for the master for seven years without pay. While doing whatever work was needed in the shop, the young person learned the skills of the craft.

At the end of seven years, the apprentice became a **journeyman**. He or she was allowed to work for wages but was not yet a guild member. To become a member, the journeyman had to create a masterpiece. This was a piece of work that the journeyman considered his or her best. Guild members would then decide if the journeyman was good enough to become a master.

Rise of the Middle Class

The rise of towns and cities was a major reason for the decline of manorialism and feudal society. Because lords needed money, they began to require money from their serfs instead of payments of crops. In this case, serfs became **tenant farmers**. Other nobles chose to keep all the land for themselves. They hired former serfs as laborers to work the land. By the 1300s, the manorial system had ended in Western Europe.

In feudal society, there were two classes: lords, or nobles, and serfs. Now there was a new social and economic class between nobles and farmers. The development of towns and cities resulted in the birth of a **middle class**. It was made up of merchants, traders, and craftworkers.

The nobles looked down on the middle class because they made their living by selling goods and services. Farmers looked up to the middle class because they wanted to be one of them. The middle class eventually grew in size, wealth, and power.

Putting It All Together

Review the list of important changes that you have made while reading this lesson. Compare your list with that of a partner and make a second list that you can both agree upon.

Fabric being weighed by a member of the Guild of Wool Merchants

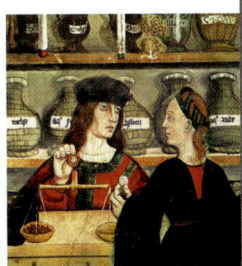

Merchants were often middle class members of their villages.

Medieval Europe | 193

Picturing History

Point out to students the different styles of clothing worn by the merchants and their customers in the illustrations on page 193. Remind students that clothing signified station in life during the Middle Ages. Ask them to deduce what they can about the people in the illustrations based on the clothing they are wearing.

Putting It All Together

Students' lists will vary. Have students share lists with a partner.

Extension

The journeyman's title had nothing to do with travel. The French word for "day" is *journée*. A journeyman could work for a daily wage, which an apprentice did not receive.

Medieval Europe | 193

Lesson Summary

England and France developed as nation-states during the medieval period.

William the Conqueror instituted a feudal system. Monarchs who followed him set up a bureaucracy to run the government and a circuit court system.

Nobles forced King John to sign the Magna Carta in 1215. The document guaranteed rights, first to the nobles and then to all Englishmen. The development of Parliament replaced the Great Council.

In France, Hugh Capet was elected king. He also strengthened the power of the monarchy.

Lesson Objective

Students will learn about the nation-states that developed in England and France.

Focus Your Reading Answers

1 The Magna Carta is important because it guarantees basic rights and limits the power of the monarchy.

2 The English Parliament became powerful by using its ability to approve taxes to make the monarch accept its demands.

3 Capetians gained power by being elected from among the feudal lords. Then the monarch made the position hereditary, increased the land under royal control, taxed, outlawed war between nobles, created an army run by monarch-appointed generals, and set up a bureaucracy made up of the middle class rather than nobles to run the country.

LESSON 3

Medieval Europe, 500–1300

The Beginning of Nation-States

Thinking on Your Own

Read the Focus Your Reading questions. As you read the lesson, take bulleted notes to help you answer the questions. When you have finished reading the lesson, review your notes with a partner. Check to make sure you listed all the important points in your notes.

The development of the **nation-state**, a large area of land ruled by a single government, did not happen at the same time in all of Europe. France and England developed as nation-states during the late Middle Ages. A single German nation did not exist until 1871.

The English Monarchy

William the Conqueror and his forces invaded England in 1066. They were from Normandy, a region in northern France. Their Viking ancestors had invaded France in the 900s and settled in the area that became known as Normandy.

William was the Duke of Normandy. His forces were made up of his Norman vassals and their knights and foot soldiers. Once he had conquered Anglo-Saxon England, William rewarded his Norman vassals with fiefs in England. He took the lands from the Anglo-Saxon lords he had defeated. In doing this, William was taking land from his enemies and

focus your reading

Explain why the Magna Carta is so important.

How did the English Parliament become so powerful?

Summarize how the Capetians gained and kept power.

vocabulary

nation-state
circuit courts
Magna Carta
rule of law
Parliament
representative government

Lesson Vocabulary

Discuss each of the vocabulary terms with students.

Large areas of land ruled by a single government are *nation-states*. During the late Middle Ages, France and England developed as *nation-states*.

England's royal court system was called the *circuit courts*. Judges rode from town to town in a *circuit*, trying cases.

The *Magna Carta* was the "great charter" of England. The *Magna Carta* guaranteed rights to the nobles and eventually to all citizens.

The *rule of law* was the idea that England would be governed according to laws. The monarch was not above the *rule of law*. *Parliament* was the group that replaced the Great Council. Knights, representatives from each town, the nobles, and clergy made up *Parliament*. A *representative government* is one that provides a *representative* for each group. England's *representative government* began with *Parliament*.

putting it into the hands of his loyal followers.

But William and his successors were aware that these same Norman vassals were possible rivals. Future English monarchs set up a paid bureaucracy to run the government. The monarchs also set up a royal court system, called the **circuit courts**, and a single set of laws for everyone. Judges rode from place to place on a regular circuit, or route, to try cases. This made it possible for all subjects everywhere in the kingdom to use the courts. Cases were heard by a jury of peers, not simply by a judge.

As a result of these actions, the power of the nobles was weakened. In 1215, a group of nobles rebelled. They forced King John to sign the **Magna Carta**, or "Great Charter." Most of the

The Magna Carta, 1215

The Magna Carta set out the basic rights of the English people. The document influenced the development of the government of the United States and of other nations. The following are some of the 63 articles in the Magna Carta.

We have . . . granted to all the freemen of our Kingdom, for us and our heirs forever, all the underwritten Liberties, to be enjoyed and held by them and by their heirs, from us and from our heirs.

No tax . . . shall be imposed in our kingdom, unless by the common council of our kingdom. . . .

[T]he City of London shall have all its ancient liberties. . . . Furthermore, we will and grant that all other Cities, Burghs, and Towns, and Ports, should have all their liberties. . . .

No free-man shall be seized, or imprisoned, or dispossessed . . . nor will we condemn him, nor shall we commit him to prison, excepting by the legal judgment of his peers, or by the laws of the land.

To none shall we sell, to none will we deny, to none will we delay right or justice.

reading for understanding

Which article guarantees the right to a trial?

Which article do you think was the basis of the American colonists' cry of "no taxation without representation"?

Explain in a paragraph what Article 1 means.

Picturing History

The signing of the Magna Carta by King John is depicted on page 195. The document grew out of some long-standing, specific grievances of the nobles against the monarchy. For example, three paragraphs deal with the royal forest, another three concern debt, one is about merchants, and another about London.

Reading for Understanding

1 Article 39 guarantees the right to a trial.

2 Article 12 is the basis for "no taxation without representation."

3 Students' paragraphs will vary but may suggest that the importance of the document lies in promising these rights and liberties to descendants forever.

Extension

Ask students who are interested in American government to research the connections between the Magna Carta and the ideas of the founding fathers of the United States. Have them share their findings with the class by using the Student Presentation Builder on the student CD.

Medieval Europe

Stop and Think

Students' lists and evaluations will vary. Possible answers include

- set up a bureaucracy to rule: probably hurt common people
- set up circuit courts: probably helped common people

Picturing History

The seal shown on page 196 is on the Magna Carta. It illustrates the practice of both signing and sealing a document. Monarchs and nobles had seals, as did merchants. Signatures could be forged, but seals were less likely to be copied.

Picturing History

The photograph on page 196 is a modern view of the British Houses of Parliament in London, England. The clock on the tower on the right side of the picture is called "Big Ben" although "Big Ben" is actually the bell inside the tower.

Medieval Europe, 500–1300

articles of the Magna Carta applied only to the nobles. However, the rights and liberties began to be applied to all English citizens. The Magna Carta established the **rule of law**. England was to be governed according to laws. The document stated that the monarch was not above the law. Unlike the French monarch, the English ruler did not gain absolute power over his or her subjects.

King John seal from Magna Carta

The Power of Parliament

According to the Magna Carta, the English monarch was supposed to be advised by the Great Council of nobles and bishops. Beginning in the 1200s, the Council was replaced by a larger assembly, or group, called **Parliament**. Two knights from each county and two representatives from each town joined the nobles and clergy. This was the beginning of **representative government** in England. Later, Parliament gathered in two groups: the House of Lords and the House of Commons.

British Parliament

Parliament had two duties: to set taxes and to pass laws to govern England. According to the Magna Carta, the Great Council had to approve taxes. Parliament took over this power and began to use it against the monarchs. By threatening not to enact taxes, Parliament could force the English monarchs to agree to its demands.

stop and think

List the actions English monarchs took to limit the power of their nobles. Did these actions help ordinary English people—that is, everyone who was not a noble? Work with a partner to decide if these actions helped, hurt, or had no effect on ordinary English people.

The French Monarchy

Charlemagne founded the Frankish Empire in what today includes the countries of Germany, France, northern Spain, and most of Italy. After his death, his sons fought over the

196 | Chapter 13

Extension

Invite students interested in contemporary history to find out how Parliament operates in Great Britain today. Allow time for them to share their findings with the class.

Empire. In 843, his grandsons divided the Empire rather than fight over it. Modern France developed from the western part of the Empire.

The last of Charlemagne's descendants in the western kingdom died in 987. The feudal lords of the kingdom chose a new king from among themselves. The man they selected was Hugh Capet, the Count of Paris. He founded the Capetian Dynasty of French rulers. They remained in power until the late 1700s when the French Revolution ended the monarchy.

Hugh Capet did not have large landholdings, nor did he have a huge army of knights and foot soldiers. But he was smart and so were his descendants. First, Capet made the position of monarch hereditary. Instead of selecting a lord to be king, the crown would pass from father to son.

Second, the Capetians increased the amount of land under royal control. Loss of their land lessened the power of the nobles. Additional land increased the wealth of the monarchy. Third, taxes were collected from the people. Fourth, war between nobles was outlawed. Fifth, an army was organized and led by generals appointed by the king. Sixth, like the English monarchs, the French kings set up a large and efficient bureaucracy to run the country. The bureaucrats came from the middle class, not from the nobility. Their only loyalty was to the monarch.

Over the centuries, through actions such as these, the Capetians were able to strengthen their rule. By the late 1600s, the power of the French kings—for good or bad—had become absolute, or all-powerful.

Putting It All Together

France and England developed two different forms of government. In England, Parliament held a great deal of power. In France, the king held all the power. With a partner, create a Venn diagram to show the similarities and differences between the two governments.

Picturing History

The French king pictured on page 197 is Hugh Capet.

Extension

Electing Hugh Capet to be the French king was not a revolution. The Archbishop of Rheims convinced the Frankish electors that the only descendant of Charlemagne who could claim the throne wasn't fit to rule. Hugh's grandfather, great uncle, and uncle had all been kings, though not of Charlemagne's dynasty. To assure the peaceful succession of his son Robert to the throne, Hugh had him crowned less than six months after his own coronation. Hugh ruled until his death nine years later.

Putting It All Together

Students' diagrams will vary. Possible responses:

England: royal court system guaranteed single set of laws for all; Magna Carta decreed rule of law; monarchy did not hold absolute power; Parliament served as beginning of representative government

France: monarchy made hereditary; brought more land under royal control to lessen power of nobles and increase monarch's wealth; monarchs had absolute power

Both: monarchy set up bureaucracy to run government

Chapter Review

1 Students' letters will vary but should include the selection of a craft to learn and reasons why it is of interest.

2 Headlines will vary; possible responses include:
   (a) Crusaders Prepare to Leave/Recapturing Holy Land the Goal
   (b) Plague Devastates Europe/Mass Graves Become Ordinary
   (c) Local Lord Gives Town New Charter/New Rights Spelled Out
   (d) William Invades England/Crowned King of England Redistributes Land

Students' paragraphs will vary.

Chapter Summary

Medieval Europe, 500–1300

- The monarch gave **fiefs** to the nobles.
- **Chivalry** developed to guide the behavior of knights.
- Nobles, knights, and serfs lived on **manors**.
- **Bishops**, **archbishops**, and **cardinals** all reported to the **pope**. Local communities were called **parishes**.
- European Christians went on eight **crusades** to the **Holy Land**. The crusades had many **unintended consequences**.
- In the early Middle Ages, business was done by **barter**. The increase in trade resulted in the development of the **money economy** and **capitalism**.
- **Bubonic plague** spread quickly throughout Europe.
- In exchange for a money payment to a local lord, a town received a **charter** guaranteeing certain rights.
- Craftworkers organized **guilds**. **Journeymen** were highly-skilled workers.
- By the 1300s, **tenant farmers** and hired farm laborers replaced serfs.
- By the end of the Middle Ages, a new **middle class** and **nation-states** had developed.
- Early English monarchs set up a paid bureaucracy, a **circuit court** system, and trial by jury. The **Magna Carta** established the **rule of law** in England.
- **Parliament** developed in the 1200s. It began **representative government** in England.

Chapter Review

1 Imagine it is time to become an apprentice and learn a craft. What would you like to learn to do? Write a letter to a master craftworker asking to become his or her apprentice. Explain why you want to learn that craft.

2 Write two-line headlines for the following: (a) the Crusades, (b) the bubonic plague, (c) a new town charter, (d) William, Duke of Normandy, being crowned the English king. Then write a lead paragraph for each headline.

Novel Connections

Below is a list of books that relate to the time period covered in this chapter. The numbers in parentheses indicate the related Thematic Strands of the National Council for the Social Studies (NCSS).

Simon Adams. *Castles and Forts* (*Kingfisher Knowledge* series). Houghton Mifflin Company, 2003. (I, II, III)

Polly Schoyer Brooks. *Queen Eleanor: Independent Spirit of the Medieval World.* Houghton Mifflin Company, 1999. (I, III, V, VI)

Karen Cushman. *Matilda Bone.* Random House Children's Books, 2002. (I, III, VIII)

Priscilla Galloway. *Archers, Alchemists, and 98 Other Medieval Jobs You Might Have Loved or Loathed.* Annick Press, Limited, 2003. (I, II, III, V, VI)

Sylvie Weil. *My Guardian Angel.* Scholastic, Inc., 2004. (I, III, VI, IX)

Skill Builder

Synthesizing Information

To *synthesize* means "to bring together separate pieces or parts." Suppose you want to go to the movies. There are two movies playing and you cannot decide which one to see. You ask four friends who have seen one movie or the other. You think about all the information you have gathered. You then make your decision. You have synthesized the information you gathered.

Writing a research report requires you to synthesize information from different sources.

> To synthesize information, follow these steps:
>
> 1 Choose the sources you will need to use.
>
> 2 Find the main idea and supporting details for the information you find.
>
> 3 Look for links between the information.
>
> 4 Put the information together based on those links.

Complete the following activities.

1. Lesson 2 in Chapter 12 and Lesson 1 in this chapter discuss feudalism. Work through Steps 2 and 3 to compare feudalism in Europe to feudalism in Japan. To help you, create a table or Venn diagram comparing feudalism in Europe and Japan. Use information in the two lessons to fill in the table.

2. Use the table or Venn diagram to write a three- or four-paragraph essay about feudalism in Europe and Japan.

Medieval Europe | 199

Skill Builder

1 Students' tables or diagrams will vary. Possible responses:
Japanese feudalism: based on relationship between shogun and daimyo; daimyo owed loyalty and military service in exchange for land; daimyo had samurai or ronin to fight for him; feudalism ended because of increased importance of trade and manufacturing and because of decline of wars in Tokugawa Shogunate.
European feudalism: monarch granted land to nobles, who owed him loyalty and a fighting force; nobles paid monarch annually for use of land; system was replicated between nobles and knights.

2 Students' essays will vary but should be based on information noted in activity 1 above, from Chapter 12, Lesson 2, and from Chapter 13, Lesson 1.

Classroom Discussion

Discuss with students some of the broader topics covered in this chapter.

- How are trade, prosperity, and the growth of cities related?
- What are the benefits and problems of capitalism?
- In what ways should people be trained for work?

Medieval Europe | 199

Chapter 14

RENAISSANCE AND REFORMATION

(1300–1650)

Chapter Summary
Refer to page 214 for a summary of Chapter 14.

Related Transparencies
T-1 World Map
T-18 Three-Column Chart

Key Blacklines
Primary Source—From *The Prince*

DVD Extension
Encourage students to use the reading comprehension, vocabulary reinforcement, and interactive timeline activities on the student DVD.

Getting Focused
Encourage students to show in their T-charts how one effect can become the cause in the next cause-effect chain. For example, interest in Greek and Roman work led to humanism, which then became the cause of new literature written in the vernacular languages.

Pre-Reading Discussion
Discuss with students their ideas about what makes a great piece of art, regardless of the medium. Tell them that they are about to study a period noted for the beautiful works its artists produced.

Getting Focused

Skim this chapter to predict what you will be learning.
• Read the lesson titles and subheadings.
• Look at the illustrations and read the captions.
• Examine the maps.
• Review the vocabulary words and terms.

The 1300s to around 1650 was a time of great change in western Europe. As you read this chapter, create a T-chart to keep track of the changes that occurred and the causes and effects of those changes. On the left side of the chart, list the cause of the change. List the effect, or result, of the change on the right side of the chart.

Picturing History
The city of Venice, pictured on page 200, was an independent republic during the Renaissance. Northern Italy was composed of several self-governed city-states. Some, such as Milan, were headed by a single family and known as duchies. Florence was a republic, with elected leaders. The papal states were in the center of Italy; the kingdom of Naples took up most of the southern part of modern Italy. Each state had its own area of specialization. Venice was noted for its glass.

Extension
Students with an interest in engineering or city planning may wish to investigate current efforts to save Venice, which is sinking. The Italian government plans to install 78 huge dams on the floor of the Adriatic Sea. Their purpose would be to block high-tide surges, which damage historic structures and the lagoon ecosystem. The plan is known as the Moses Project.

LESSON 1

The Renaissance

Thinking on Your Own

Outline this lesson in your notebook. Use the subheadings for Roman numerals I, II, and III. Be sure to organize information on the outline in descending order of importance. The more important the detail, the higher it belongs on the outline.

The **Renaissance** began in Italian city-states around 1300. The word *renaissance* means rebirth. It describes the spirit of curiosity and adventure that developed after the Middle Ages. By the late 1400s, the Renaissance had expanded into northern Europe.

The Renaissance started in Italy for two reasons. First, the Roman Empire had begun on the Italian peninsula. A major feature of the Renaissance was an interest in ancient Roman culture. Second, Italian city-states were growing rich from trade. Wealthy Italian citizens could support the cultural developments of the Renaissance.

focus your reading

Discuss the three key characteristics of the Renaissance.

Why was the invention of the printing press so important?

How did the lives of European women change during the Renaissance?

vocabulary

Renaissance
monasteries
scholarship
humanism
patrons
vernacular language
nuclear families

The Spirit of the Renaissance

The Renaissance had three major characteristics. First was an interest in the ideas of the ancient Greeks and Romans. Many people from the north and east migrated into western Europe beginning in the 200s. Invasions helped cause the fall of the Roman Empire. Education suffered in the centuries after the end of the Empire. If it had not been for monks in **monasteries**,

Renaissance and Reformation | 201

Lesson Summary

Around 1300, a rebirth in interest of the arts and antiquity, known as the Renaissance, began in Italy. The wealth of Italian trade cities funded artists.

Interest in the ideas of Greece and Rome led to the development of humanism, which emphasized the duty one had to improve life in the present, rather than simply await a glorious future.

Johann Gutenberg's printing press increased the availability and affordability of books and helped to spread new ideas.

The growth of towns and cities and the rise of the middle class also led to changes in family life. The nuclear family became the norm, instead of clans or tribes.

Lesson Objective

Students will learn about the development and effects of the Renaissance in Europe.

Focus Your Reading Answers

1. Three characteristics of the Renaissance were an interest in the ideas of the ancient Greeks and Romans, development of humanism, and belief in individual achievement.

2. Books became more affordable, ideas were spread more rapidly, and the use of the vernacular languages increased.

3. Women's lives changed little. The age for both women and men to marry increased. Some women became craftworkers or worked as servants. Daughters of the wealthy were privately educated.

---

on Vocabulary

uce each of the following vocabulary terms to students.

n that the *Renaissance* was a time of cultural rebirth. The *Renaissance* began in Italy and throughout Europe. *Monasteries* were places where monks lived and worked. *Monasteries* preserve learning. *Scholarship* is the knowledge that comes from study. The monks helped e Greek and Roman *scholarship*.

nphasis on present, earthly existence rather than a future, heavenly one is known as sm. *Humanism* emphasized poetry, philosophy, and history. People who supported the arts nown as *patrons*. *Patrons* were sometimes painted by the artists whom they supported.

mmon language of the people is called the *vernacular language*. The printing press helped the use of the *vernacular language*.

es consisting of a father, mother, and children are *nuclear families*. Living in *nuclear families* of in clans or extended families became more common during the *Renaissance*.

Picturing History

City officials feared that the dome of Il Duomo in Florence, Italy, pictured on page 202, would collapse without buttresses or framework. There are two domes, however, and the one inside makes the outer, visible dome sturdy. Brunelleschi wanted the interior of the dome to be gilt. Lorenzo de' Medici preferred mosaics. The dome was eventually painted with frescoes of the Last Judgment.

Picturing History

Petrarch, depicted on page 202, attempted to blend the learning of classical cultures with Christianity. At his father's behest, he studied law but left it to pursue literature and writing verse, biographies, dialogues with great figures of the past, and letters. His search for great literature of the past led to his most important discovery, the letters of Cicero, the Roman orator.

Renaissance and Reformation, 1300–1650

the works of the ancient Greeks and Romans would have been lost. The monks copied the works to study and preserve them. Islamic scholars in Spain and elsewhere also recorded much of the early Greek and Roman **scholarship**.

In the early 1300s, Italians began to rediscover the works of ancient Greek and Roman authors. The ideas of these early thinkers began to influence Italian writers and artists. As a result, a new intellectual movement known as **humanism** developed. Scholars turned to the study of poetry, philosophy, and history rather than to spiritual matters. Instead of using religious themes, many artists began to paint everyday subjects. Some painted portraits of their **patrons**. These were wealthy people who supported artists with money.

How people viewed life on Earth began to change as a result of humanism. Philosophers and writers began to stress the importance of life on Earth instead of a future life in heaven. This was a second major feature of the Renaissance. The teachings of the Roman Catholic Church promised people a better life in heaven. This promise helped the people of the Middle Ages to endure their terrible living conditions. Humanism prompted a change. Humanist thinkers called on the educated and the wealthy to take an active role in their communities. They had a duty to work for the good of the city and state.

The belief in individual achievement was a third major characteristic of the Renaissance. The Renaissance was a time of progress, or great change. As more things improved, people's belief in the ability of humans to make more changes and improve more things grew. Anything might change; anything might happen.

Architect Filippo Brunelleschi built Il Duomo in Florence. It is modeled after the dome of the Pantheon in Rome.

Petra[rch] is kno[wn] as the found[er of] huma[nism]

Time Box

1517
Martin Luther nails 95 theses to door of chur[ch] in Witttenberg

1521
Pope excommunicates Luther

1534
Henry VIII and Parliament create Chu[rch] of England

1536
John Calvin invited to make Geneva, Switzerla[nd] a model city

1545
Council of Trent

202 Chapter 14

Picturing History

Shown on page 203 is an illuminated manuscript page from Gutenberg's Bible, a two-volume work of more than 1,200 pages. It was the beginning of printed books. By 1500, more than 1,000 printing workshops were busy in Europe, primarily in Italy and Germany. Gutenberg's workshop could produce about 300 sheets daily. Illustrations were still drawn and colored by hand, however. Soon works that were not religious spread as well. The greater availability of books encouraged literacy.

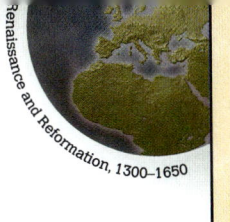

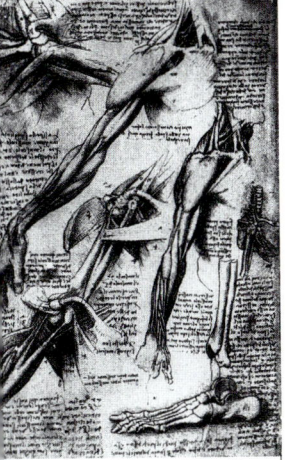

Michelangelo's painting on the ceiling of the Sistine Chapel (top left), Raphael's Madonna and Child, and DaVinci's drawings are examples of the great artists of the Renaissance.

The Printing Press

One of the most important inventions of the Renaissance was the printing press. The Chinese invented movable type during the Song Dynasty. Around 1455, Johann Gutenberg in Germany used movable type to print the first book in Europe. It was a copy of the Bible. Within 50 years, Europe had over one thousand printers. Almost 40,000 books were in print. Many were about religious topics. The writings of Martin Luther were quickly printed and widely shared. Without the printing press, his ideas would never have reached so many people.

The invention of the printing press made books more affordable. In addition, the printing press made copies of books available quickly. It took years for a monk to make one copy of the Bible by hand.

The printing press spread Protestant teachings and it also spread the use of the **vernacular language**. This is the language of ordinary people. At that time, highly educated people like scholars and lawyers wrote to one another in Latin. However, with the invention of the printing press, writers began to use the language spoken in their region, such as Italian or French.

Two of the most popular and important writers of the period were Dante, who wrote *Divine Comedy* in Italian, and Geoffrey

> **stop and think**
>
> List the three characteristics of the Renaissance. Write down ideas that you could use to explain each characteristic. Use your notes to explain the characteristics to a partner.

Johann Gutenberg produced the first printed book—the Bible—in 1455.

Extension

Michelangelo, DaVinci, and Raphael all knew and influenced one another. Michelangelo and DaVinci were rivals, their acrimony rooted in Michelangelo's mocking DaVinci over an unfinished work in Milan. While Michelangelo painted the Sistine Chapel's ceiling, Raphael worked on three rooms within the Vatican Palace. Raphael also borrowed DaVinci's technique of pyramidal composition.

Leonardo DaVinci was interested in many things. Divide the class into groups to research his interests and contributions in topics such as flight, drawing, painting, sculpture, architecture, and the study of optics. Have students present their findings to the class by using the Student Presentation Builder on the student DVD.

Picturing History

The ceiling of the Sistine Chapel, a panel of which is pictured at the top left of page 203, required more than four years of work. Michelangelo worked on the ceiling frescoes from a standing position on a special scaffold he designed. He dismissed his helpers, feeling their work was not up to his standards. He was locked in and refused to allow visitors. The famous *Creation of Adam* is one of nine central panels on the ceiling that tell the Bible stories of creation and Noah.

Many of Leonardo DaVinci's drawings, shown on page 203, were concerned with the muscle and bone structure of human anatomy. DaVinci also studied plant anatomy, giving his drawings of plants a realistic style that was new at the time.

The work of Raphael, shown at the top right of page 203, is only one of several renditions of the Virgin and Child, a popular topic during the Renaissance. Pope Julius II commissioned Raphael to paint frescoes in three rooms of the papal apartments. The first room he completed, known as the Room of the Signature, established his reputation. Perhaps the most well-known element of that room was *The School of Athens*, a fresco depicting literary heroes of both classical and Christian eras.

Stop and Think

Students' choices of three characteristics and explanations will vary but should reflect lesson content.

Renaissance and Reformation

Putting It All Together

Students' paragraphs will vary but should present reasons for the importance of printed books.

Picturing History

The portrait of a noblewoman on page 204 demonstrates the luxurious fabrics and jewels available to the wealthy. Increased trade with Asia made luxury goods, such as silk, accessible.

Extension

One of the more remarkable educated women of the time was Christine de Pizan. She is considered to be one of the first professional women writers. Venetian-born, she grew up and lived in Paris, where she may have been a book copyist, one of the few profitable jobs open to women. As a young widow, she began writing poetry about her grief. She is best known for her defense of women's intelligence in an age when women were considered inferior to men in every way.

Chaucer, author of the *Canterbury Tales* in English. Dante's work takes readers on a journey through hell, purgatory, and heaven. Chaucer wrote about a collection of pilgrims on their way to a holy place in England.

Renaissance Society

The Renaissance brought about a number of changes in western European society. Towns and cities were growing in size and number. Serfdom was ending, and many farm workers were moving to the new urban centers. A new middle class of merchants and craftworkers was developing as well. However, as much as 30 to 40 percent of the urban population still lived in poverty.

As people moved to towns and cities, the organization of the family changed. Instead of living in extended families as people had on manors, townspeople began to live in **nuclear families**. A household contained only a father, a mother, and their children. The age when people married also increased. By the 1500s, Europeans did not marry until their late twenties.

Women's chief duties were to raise children and take care of the house. Farm women still worked in the fields at harvest time. Women in towns and cities were able to find work as servants for wealthy families. Women were also employed in crafts such as spinning and weaving.

Because reading the Bible was important in Protestantism, girls were taught to read. However, Protestantism reaffirmed the lesser place of women in the family. Women were to bear and raise Christian children while obeying their husbands in all things.

Upper-cl... Renaissa... women w... often we... educated since the... had serv... to do the... work.

Putting It All Together

The invention of the printing press caused an increase in the number of books that were written and printed. Write a paragraph that explains the importance of printed books.

204 Chapter 14

Picturing History

Martin Luther, depicted on page 205, first entered an Augustinian monastery when he was nearly twenty-two, opposing the wishes of his father, who intended for him to have a career in law. Luther's superiors decided first that he should be a priest, then that he should teach Scripture at the University of Wittenberg. It was during his preparation to teach Saint Paul's Epistle to the Romans that Luther formulated his ideas on justification by faith alone.

LESSON 2

Martin Luther and the Protestant Reformation

Thinking on Your Own

As you read this lesson, create a cause-and-effect flowchart of Martin Luther's actions. Share your chart with a partner. Then create a flowchart for John Calvin's actions.

The Renaissance was not the only movement in Western Europe during this time period. The **Protestant Reformation** began as a way to protest against and reform practices of the Roman Catholic Church. Once begun, the Reformation had many unintended consequences.

Martin Luther and Lutheranism

Martin Luther was a Roman Catholic monk and professor in Wittenberg, Germany. He was disturbed by certain teachings of the Catholic Church, in particular the practice of selling **indulgences**. An indulgence frees a person from all or part of the punishment for sins. A monk in Wittenberg named Johann Tetzel was taking money in exchange for indulgences.

In 1517, Luther put together a list of 95 **theses**, or arguments, against the misuse of indulgences. He nailed the list to the front door of the church in Wittenberg. This act marks the

focus your reading

What ideas of the Roman Catholic Church did Martin Luther oppose?

What happened in German states as a result of Luther's teachings?

Explain how Calvinism became so important.

vocabulary

Protestant Reformation
indulgences
theses
salvation
excommunicated
Lutheranism
predestination
theocracy

Martin Luther

Lesson Summary

The Protestant Reformation in Western Europe began with Martin Luther's posting 95 theses on the door of the church in Wittenberg. After being excommunicated, Luther began his own church.

The new church led to conflict within the German states and to a prolonged war to be free of the rule of the Holy Roman Emperor.

Another reformer was John Calvin of Geneva, Switzerland. He agreed with Luther on justification by faith alone, but added the idea of predestination, that is, God determining a soul's eternal destiny. Calvin organized a theocracy in Geneva, a model widely studied in Europe. From Calvinism came the Presbyterian and Puritan religions.

Lesson Objective

Students will learn about the beginnings of the Protestant Reformation through the work of Martin Luther and John Calvin.

Focus Your Reading Answers

1 Luther opposed the sale of indulgences and the need for the pope and bishops to interpret God's word rather than having people read the Bible for themselves.

2 The teachings of Luther led to civil war among the German states and attempts to dissolve the Holy Roman Empire.

3 Calvinism became important because Geneva, Switzerland, was a theocracy. Rulers from all over Europe came to view this experiment in government and took it back to their own lands.

sson Vocabulary

cuss each of the vocabulary terms with students.

Protestant Reformation was initially the attempt to protest against and reform the Roman holic Church. The *Protestant Reformation* began with the protests of Martin Luther.

lgences were documents that guaranteed freedom from punishment of sins. The sale of *lgences* was the practice that most angered Luther. Arguments are also called *theses*. Luther ed 95 *theses* on the door of the church in Wittenberg. Entrance to heaven is called *salvation*. her believed that good works could not earn *salvation*. To be *excommunicated* is to be put out church. The pope *excommunicated* Luther for his radical ideas.

teachings of Martin Luther became known as *Lutheranism*. *Lutheranism* taught that people d and should read the Bible for themselves.

idea that God predetermines who will be saved and who will be damned is called *stination*. Calvin preached *predestination* in Switzerland. A *theocracy* is government ruled by ious leaders. Calvin headed a *theocracy* in Geneva.

Renaissance and Reformation | 205

> **Picturing History**
>
> The stained glass window shown on page 206 was only one of the many glories of Roman Catholic cathedrals. However, the common people sometimes resented this beauty, which came at a high price. Tetzel's sale of indulgences was one way Pope Leo X hoped to raise enough money to complete the Basilica of Saint Peter. Ironically, this treasured symbol of Roman Catholicism led to the Church's fracturing.

> **Picturing History**
>
> The etching, shown on page 206, of a Lutheran worship service demonstrates the contrast with the rich décor of Roman Catholic places of worship. Lutheranism was tied to German peasant uprisings against the excesses of the Church's wealth, so it is not surprising that Lutheran churches were simple at first.

beginning of the Protestant Reformation. Luther's document was printed and was distributed throughout Germany. It won many supporters.

By 1520, Luther was calling on the German princes to break with the authority of the pope in Rome. Luther urged them to set up their own German church. This new church would be based on two teachings that Luther considered central.

First, faith in God alone is all that is needed for **salvation**, or entrance into heaven. The Roman Catholic Church teaches that people need to believe in God and do good works. Luther rejected good works as a way to earn salvation. He preached that humans cannot earn salvation. God alone grants salvation to a person who has faith. Luther's teaching became known as "justification by faith alone."

Second, the Bible is the only source of God's word and religious truth. Luther believed that the pope and other members of the church's hierarchy, such as bishops, were unnecessary. He stressed the need for people to read the Bible. This increased the demand for Bibles in vernacular languages.

In 1521, the pope **excommunicated** Martin Luther. He was no longer a Roman Catholic. Luther continued to spread his teachings and to attract followers. His ideas became known as **Lutheranism**.

Lutheran churches were simple in design.

Art, such as stained glass windows, is one item Protestants wanted removed from churches.

Political Consequences

Many German princes cared less about Luther's religious teachings than they did about their own power. Over the centuries, the Roman Catholic Church had gained a great deal of power across Europe. The German princes saw Luther's

> **Extension**
>
> Luther first wrote 97 theses to be debated in formal academic style at the University of Wittenberg. These opposed some theological beliefs. No one was very excited about the document; Luther expected a similar reaction to his 95 theses. However, because he attacked the sale of indulgences and the notion of profit in religion, these writings challenged both the Church and the secular rulers.
>
> After being condemned as a heretic, Luther went into hiding for several years. He had every reason to expect to be burned at the stake, as another reformer, John Huss, had been. During his time in exile, Luther began translating the Bible into German. It eventually required 12 years to complete.
>
> Interested students may wish to investigate the life and influence of Katherine Von Bora, whom Luther married in 1525 after leaving the Roman Catholic Church and with whom he had six children. Allow time for students to present their findings to the class.

> **stop and think**
>
> Germans were not the only people who were forced to practice a religion chosen by their ruler. In many nations for many centuries, rulers chose their people's religion. With a partner, make a list of at least three reasons to either support or oppose this practice. Then write two or three paragraphs to explain why you support or oppose the practice.

invitation as a way to do away with the pope's power over them. They also saw it as a way to do away with the Holy Roman Emperor.

For centuries, Germany had been divided into several hundred small states ruled by princes. Ruling over them was the Holy Roman Emperor. The present emperor, Charles V, tried to force the Lutheran princes to abandon Lutheranism and become Catholics again. In the 1530s and 1540s, a series of wars broke out between Catholic and Lutheran princes. Charles and his allies were not strong enough to defeat the Lutheran princes. In 1555, he had to agree to the Peace of Augsberg.

The peace treaty allowed the German princes to choose which religion they would practice. However, their subjects were not given the same choice. They had to accept whatever religion their ruler chose.

John Calvin and Calvinism

John Calvin was a Roman Catholic who was born and educated in France. As an intellectual, he was disturbed by certain practices of the Church. In 1536, Calvin published *Institutes of the Christian Religion*. This work set out his ideas about Protestantism.

Like Luther, Calvin believed in justification by faith alone. However, Calvin went further than Luther. John Calvin preached **predestination**. According to Calvin, God determines who will be saved and who will be damned to hell forever.

John Calvin in Geneva, Switzerland

> **Stop and Think**
>
> Students' reasons will vary as they support or oppose the idea of a ruler decreeing the religion to be practiced in a nation. Paragraphs should be organized with logical support.

> **Picturing History**
>
> John Calvin, shown on page 207 speaking to the leaders of Geneva, Switzerland, was important as one who systematized theology. Trained in law, he applied calm logic to his analysis of doctrine and was determined to break with the Roman Catholic Church.

Renaissance and Reformation 207

> **Extension**
>
> The first printing of the *Institutes of the Christian Religion* sold out in nine months. Written in Latin and therefore accessible to all educated Europeans, the book was six chapters and 516 pages long. It was bound in a size small enough to fit in the wide pockets popular at the time, and so could circulate secretly. Calvin continued to expand and revise this treatise. The final edition, published before his death, was four volumes containing 80 chapters.

Renaissance and Reformation 207

Picturing History

The picture on page 208 shows John Calvin in Geneva. People from all over Europe came to see Calvin's theocracy in action.

Extension

Calvin intended to lead the life of a scholar. He was on his way to Strasbourg, a Protestant city, when he had to detour through Geneva. Intending to stay only one day, he was convinced to remain and assist the city in its Protestant reforms. However, because of the severity of Calvin's interpretations, he was banned from Geneva. Finally able to complete his trip to Strasbourg, there he wrote a French liturgy and translated hymns and psalms into French. He also married. After three years, he was invited by Geneva's new government to return.

Putting It All Together

Students' laws will vary but should be designed to promote hard work, thrift, and honesty.

In 1536, leaders in Geneva, Switzerland, invited Calvin to help them make their city into a model Christian community. Calvin organized a **theocracy**—a government run by religious leaders. A group known as the Consistory enforced morality. Misbehavior like dancing, playing cards, and swearing resulted in punishment. Hard work, honesty, and thrift were highly valued. Over time, Calvinists came to view these virtues as the sign of being saved by God.

John Calvin in St. Peter's Cathedral, Geneva

Religious leaders from across Europe traveled to Geneva to see Calvinism in practice. They took Calvin's ideas back to their people. Calvinism soon spread to Germany, France, England, Scotland, and the Netherlands. Calvinism had greater influence in Europe than Lutheranism. Puritanism and Presbyterianism developed from Calvinism.

Putting It All Together

Imagine you are a member of the Consistory. You want to promote hard work, honesty, and thrift. Work with a partner to write three laws that would encourage these values and discourage their opposites: laziness, dishonesty, and foolish spending of money.

Picturing History

Henry VIII, shown on page 209, was a Renaissance man himself. He spoke four languages, played the lute, and both sang and composed music. He was also a patron of Italian military engineers, craftworkers, and artists.

Extension

You may wish to show all or part of the film version of Robert Bolt's historical play, *A Man for All Seasons*, based on the life of Sir Thomas More. Although one of Henry VIII's most valued counselors, he was beheaded when he refused to acknowledge the king's right to a divorce.

LESSON 3

The Influence of the Reformation

Thinking on Your Own

Examine the paintings in this lesson. Choose one to describe. Begin by writing a list of five words or phrases about the painting. Consider what is happening in the painting, who is in the painting, what colors are used, and how the painting makes you feel. Then use these words and phrases to write a one-paragraph description of the painting.

The Protestant Reformation began as an effort to reform practices of the Roman Catholic Church. Reform became mixed with political ambition in Germany. In England, politics was the major force that caused the end of the Roman Catholic Church and the creation of the Church of England.

focus your reading

Why was the Church of England created?

What were the results of the Catholic Reformation?

Explain why religious persecution increased during the Reformation.

vocabulary

annulled   Inquisition
doctrines   heretics
decrees   reconquista

Henry VIII and the Church of England

King Henry VIII had been a strong defender of the Catholic Church when the Reformation began. He even wrote a book defending the Church. However, by the 1530s, Henry had a problem of his own to solve. To ensure that the English throne would stay in his family, he needed a male heir. His wife, Catherine of Aragon, had produced a daughter, Mary, but no son. Henry wished to have his marriage **annulled** in order to marry Anne Boleyn. An annulment would mean that the marriage had never taken place as far as the Church was concerned. There was no divorce in the Roman Catholic faith.

Henry VIII

Lesson Summary

The reforms of the Church became entwined with political considerations, particularly in England. There, Henry VIII broke with the Catholic Church, which refused to annul his first marriage. As a result, the Anglican Church was created with the king as the head. Henry enriched himself in the process, as well as obtaining divorces. Henry's daughter, the famed Elizabeth I, changed some practices of the new church.

Catholics responded by reforming the Church through the actions of the Council of Trent and by persecuting heretics, which included Jews and Muslims. The Inquisition, particularly in Spain, was noted for its cruelty toward those not in accord with the teachings of the Catholic Church.

Lesson Objective

Students will learn about the impact of the Reformation in England, within the Roman Catholic Church, and during the Inquisition.

Focus Your Reading Answers

1 Henry VIII broke with the Roman Catholic Church over the issue of annulling his marriage so that he could marry Anne Boleyn.

2 The Council of Trent stopped the selling of indulgences, reaffirmed the authority of the pope, and led to a greater emphasis on the pope's spiritual role, rather than on his power and wealth.

3 Religious persecution increased because of the Inquisition, which tried heretics.

Lesson Vocabulary

Discuss each of the vocabulary terms with students.

If something is *annulled*, it is treated as if it never occurred. Henry VIII wanted his first marriage *annulled*.

Doctrines are religious teachings. Despite founding a new church, Henry VIII made few changes in the *doctrines* of the church. *Decrees* are orders. The Council of Trent issued several *decrees*.

The *Inquisition* was a Roman Catholic organization designed to find those whose beliefs were not in accord with official teachings. The *Inquisition* used torture, especially in Spain, to get *heretics* to confess. *Heretics* believed in ideas not approved by the Catholic Church. *Heretics* could be punished in a wide range of ways, from fines to death.

The *reconquista* was the Spanish reconquering of land that the Muslims held. Spanish nobles began the *reconquista* during the 800s.

Renaissance and Reformation

Picturing History

Canterbury Cathedral, shown on page 210, became the focus of English Christianity. It had been a pilgrimage site for centuries since the death of Thomas Becket, who opposed Henry II, as Thomas More would oppose Henry VIII. In 1538, Henry VIII plundered Becket's shrine, part of his dissolution of Catholic lands and holdings.

Bio Facts

- Born 1533, Anne Boleyn's daughter.
- Declared illegitimate by Parliament in 1536 so that Jane Seymour's son had a clear path to the throne.
- Imprisoned in the Tower of London and at Woodstock.
- Faced the threat of the Spanish Armada in 1588; it was defeated by a storm and by her powerful naval commanders: Drake, Hawkins, Howard, and Frobisher.
- Survived the rebellion of Catholic Mary Stuart, Queen of Scots, whom she ultimately had imprisoned and killed.
- Died 1603.

Biography Extension

There are many fine plays and films about Elizabeth I, who was a complex woman and who enjoyed a long reign. Suggest that students interested in theater view at least two of these films and write reviews or discuss for the class the different portrayals of Elizabeth that they present.

The pope refused to grant an annulment. Henry then asked the Archbishop of Canterbury, the highest Church official in England, for an annulment. The archbishop, Thomas Cranmer, granted it in 1533. Anne and Henry were married and Anne produced a child—a girl, Elizabeth. When Henry tired of Anne, he took another wife, Jane Seymour. They had a son, Edward. In all, Henry had six wives.

In addition to marrying Anne Boleyn, Henry set up a new church. In 1534, he asked Parliament for and was granted the Act of Supremacy. This law created the Church of England with the monarch as head. The Church of England is also known as the Anglican Church. Henry closed all monasteries and took away all the land and buildings of the Roman Catholic Church. He kept some for himself and sold others to loyal followers among the nobility and wealthy middle class.

Many riches from Canterbury Cathedral were taken by Henry VIII.

Biography

Elizabeth I (1558–1603)

Elizabeth took the throne after the deaths of her half-brother Edward and half-sister Mary. Edward was only ten when he became king. His advisors attempted to tighten Protestant control of the nation. When Mary became queen, she attempted to return England to Roman Catholicism. Her harsh policies turned many English against her and in favor of Protestantism.

Elizabeth ruled for 45 years. Her primary goal was to make England a rich and powerful nation. She also set about making England a Protestant nation. She cared less about religious doctrine than she did about power. She saw Protestantism as a way to unify the nation and strengthen her power. Anyone who opposed her—Catholic or Protestant—was persecuted.

The religious wars that raged on the European continent did not affect Engla[nd]. Elizabeth was able to keep her subjects from fighting one another over religious differences. By the time she died, England was the most powerful nation in Euro[pe]. Her subjects mourned her as "Good Queen Bess."

Extension

Two of the world's great writers, an English playwright and a Spanish novelist, were working during the same period of time. William Shakespeare, born in 1564, wrote more than 30 plays that have survived, as well as sonnets. He was not only a playwright but also an actor and a managing partner in a troupe of actors patronized by King James I. He became the first playwright whose works had enough popular appeal to be printed and sold in his lifetime. He was buried on April 25, 1616, two days after Miguel de Cervantes was buried in Spain.

Born in 1547, Cervantes had been a soldier who fought in Italy and was captured and imprisoned for five years in Algiers. He later took a job in Sevilla, where he requisitioned olive oil and wheat for the Spanish Armada. Cervantes' greatest work was *Don Quixote*, considered the first modern novel.

stop and think

What characteristic did Henry and Elizabeth share? Discuss the question with a partner. When you come to an agreement, write a sentence that states the characteristic. Then make a bulleted list of the facts that support your conclusion.

However, Henry made little change in religious **doctrines**, or teachings. With the exception of the authority of the pope, religious teachings were much the same in the Church of England as they were in the Roman Catholic Church. It was Henry's daughter Elizabeth who changed religious doctrines. Among other changes, priests were allowed to marry. The Church of England adopted the Calvinist doctrine of predestination. English replaced Latin in church services.

The Catholic Reformation

By the 1600s, the number of people who followed the teachings of Protestantism had increased dramatically. The Roman Catholic Church did not ignore what was happening. Many Church leaders recognized the truth in some of the complaints about Church practices. The Church had clearly strayed from the simple spiritual message of Jesus.

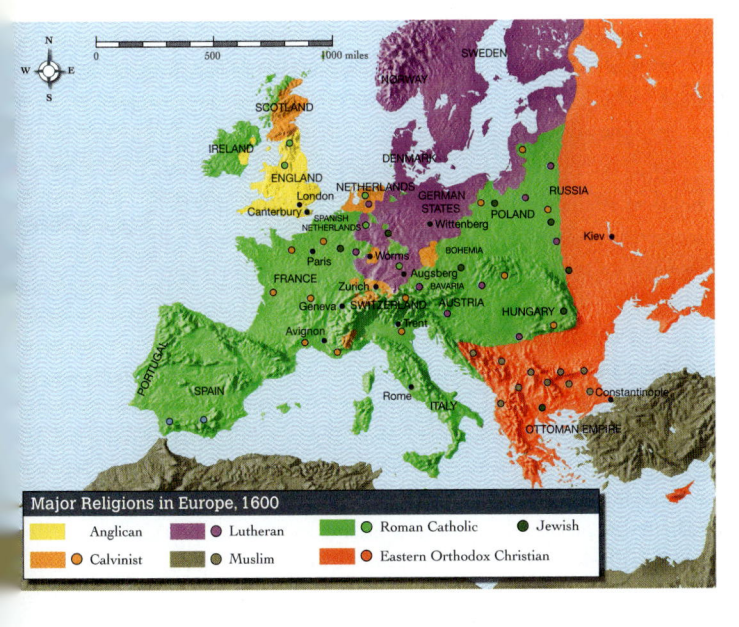

Stop and Think

Students' choices of characteristics will vary but should be supported by facts.

Map Extension

Ask students to use the map on page 211 to answer the following questions:

- What regions of Europe were Lutheran? (German states, Norway, Sweden, Denmark)

- Which religion covered the most territory in Europe? (Roman Catholic)

- What religion was practiced in London? (Anglican)

Renaissance and Reformation 211

Extension

After supporting the marriage of Henry VIII and Anne Boleyn, Thomas Cranmer became the future Queen Elizabeth's godfather. He also annulled Henry's marriage to Anne, aided in the king's divorce of Anne of Cleves, and warned Henry about Catherine Howard, who became Henry's fifth wife. He also sponsored a translation of the Bible into English and wrote the first *Book of Common Prayer*, which is used in Anglican worship. In his final years, Cranmer was condemned for treason and heresy and removed from the archbishopric. He signed recantations, but later renounced them. When burned at the stake, he put his right hand into the flames first, since he had recanted by that hand.

Renaissance and Reformation 211

Picturing History

The Council of Trent, pictured in the painting on page 212, is often said to have lasted from 1545 to 1563. However, during those years, it was often in recess. Few religious officials actually attended. When the Council, known within the Church as the nineteenth ecumenical council, first convened, only 31 prelates were there. At the last session, the number had grown to 213, still not many for all of Catholic Europe.

The Catholic Reformation set about renewing the spirit of the Church and returning it to its mission. In 1545, Pope Paul III called the Council of Trent. This committee of Church leaders met until 1563 and issued a number of **decrees**, or orders, to clarify Church teachings and reform its practices. Four of the decrees were:

- Luther's doctrine of faith without good works was rejected.
- Calvin's doctrine of predestination was rejected.
- The selling of indulgences was forbidden.
- The authority of the pope was reaffirmed.

After the Council of Trent, popes played less of a role in political affairs. At times, earlier popes had competed with monarchs and emperors for wealth and power. Later popes focused on their role as the spiritual leaders of Catholics.

Persecution and Inquisition

In the Middle Ages, the Catholic Church had set up a tribunal called the **Inquisition** to find **heretics**. These are people who believe in religious ideas that are not approved by the Church. The goal of the Inquisition was to bring people back to Catholicism. Anyone who refused to give up his or her wrong beliefs was punished by a fine, a prison sentence, and usually the loss of his or her property. Later, torture was added

---

Extension

The Council of Trent instituted both reforms within Catholicism and reactions against Protestantism. Among the reforms were the founding of seminaries to train men for the ministry; repudiating the custom of priests holding more than one office; declaring that bishops must live in their dioceses; and encouraging the study of Thomas Aquinas, whose theology became normative. To counter the effects of the Protestant movement, the Council affirmed that salvation was a combination of good works and grace; that there are seven sacraments; that the Vulgate, the Latin translation of the Bible, was authoritative on doctrine; and that the role of tradition is equal to the Scriptures.

to the questioning process. If a person refused to confess, he or she could be tortured. Execution became the final punishment. In the 1540s, the Inquisition was used to find Protestants in Italy.

Perhaps the most brutal use of the Inquisition was in Spain. In the 700s, Muslims had conquered large parts of Spain. They allowed Jews and Catholics to practice their religions in peace. Beginning in the 800s, Spanish nobles fought the Muslims and slowly forced them out of Spain. This was known as the **reconquista**.

By 1492, the armies of Spain's King Ferdinand and Queen Isabella had defeated the last of the Muslim strongholds in Spain. The monarchs were determined to unify their new nation. They ordered all Jews and Muslims to convert to Catholicism or leave. Forcing everyone to practice one religion was one way to unify the nation. The monarchs set up an Inquisition to make sure that everyone obeyed. It investigated Jews and Muslims who had converted to Catholicism but were suspected of practicing their old religions in private.

Putting It All Together

"Religion may be used as a cover for political actions." Find three examples in this lesson that support this statement. List them in your notebook. Share them with a partner and discuss how each political act was done in the name of religion but really disguised a grab for power.

Picturing History

The Spanish Inquisition, depicted on page 213, was notable for its fierceness. It was as much political as religious, as were so many of the movements during the age. Pope Sixtus IV issued a papal decree in 1478 setting up the Inquisition to deal with the Jews and converted Jews in Spain. He later realized his error in giving away his power to a secret organization that did not permit any appeals to Rome.

Extension

The year 1492 was remarkable in Spain for more than one reason. That year, Tomas de Torquemada, who, as first inquisitor general, had begun an anti-Jewish propaganda campaign, persuaded Queen Isabella to expel all the Jews who refused baptism. The "brain drain" created by the loss of perhaps 170,000 people left Spain vulnerable to German and Italian bankers.

Putting It All Together
Students' examples and their discussions will vary but should be based on events in the lesson.

Chapter Review

1 (a) Gutenberg Develops Printing Press/Books More Widely Available
(b) Luther Nails Roman Catholics with 95 Theses/Calvin Establishes Theocracy in Geneva
(c) Pope Calls Council of Trent/Group Determines True Doctrine of Church
(d) Inquisition Seeks to Punish Heretics/Spain Most Fierce

2 Possible responses:
- Printing changed life by creating new jobs and new tools for doing those jobs.
- The increased number of books made them available to more people.
- Desire for literacy increased.
- Ideas became more widely spread.

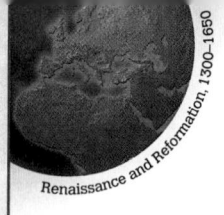

Chapter Summary

- The **Renaissance** began in Italy in the 1300s.
- The Renaissance had three major characteristics: ancient Greek and Roman ideas, which gave rise to **humanism**; the importance of life on Earth rather than on a future life in heaven; and a belief in individual achievement.
- Monks in **monasteries** helped preserve early **scholarship**.
- **Patrons** supported artists who painted everyday objects.
- The invention of the printing press spread Protestant teachings and the use of **vernacular languages**.
- People lived as **nuclear families**.
- The **Protestant Reformation** was a way to protest and reform practices of the Catholic Church, such as selling **indulgences**. Martin Luther's 95 **theses** marked the beginning of the Reformation.
- Luther taught that faith alone is all that is necessary for **salvation**. This **doctrine** is known as "justification by faith alone." Luther was **excommunicated**. His new ideas were called **Lutheranism**.
- John Calvin adopted Luther's teachings and added **predestination**. He set up a **theocracy** in Geneva.
- Henry VIII wanted his marriage **annulled**. The pope refused, so Parliament created the Church of England.
- Council of Trent **decrees** clarified Church teachings.
- The **Inquisition** found **heretics** in the Catholic Church. A **reconquista** gained Spanish lands back from Muslim rulers.

Chapter Review

1 Write two-line headlines for each of the following: (a) invention of the printing press, (b) Protestant Reformation, (c) Council of Trent, (d) Inquisition.

2 The invention of the printing press was as revolutionary in the 1400s as the invention of the computer was in the 1900s. With a partner think of all the ways that the printing press could have changed life in the 1400s. Write a bulleted list of the changes.

Novel Connections

Below is a list of books that relate to the time period covered in this chapter. The numbers in parentheses indicate the related Thematic Strands of the National Council for the Social Studies (NCSS).

Elizabeth Borton de Trevino. *I, Juan de Pareja.* Farrar, Straus and Giroux, 1984. (I, III, IX)

Louise Hawes. *The Vanishing Point: A Story of Lavinia Fontana.* Houghton Mifflin Company, 2004. (I, III, IX)

Carolyn Meyer. *Patience, Princess Catherine.* Harcourt, 2004. (I, VI, IX)

Donna Jo Napoli. *Daughter of Venice.* Bantam Doubleday Dell Books for Young Readers, 2003. (I, III, IV, V)

Jane Yolen, Robert J. Harris. *Queen's Own Fool.* Penguin Putnam Books for Young Readers, 2001. (I, III, VI)

Skill Builder

Fact and Opinion

The following sentence is a fact. It states specific information that could be proved to be true or false through additional research.

In the 700s, Muslims had conquered large parts of Spain.

The following sentence is an opinion. It represents the author's personal belief about the Spanish Inquisition. The author provides no evidence to support this statement.

Perhaps the most brutal use of the Inquisition was in Spain.

A fact is a statement	An opinion
• of specific information	• is what a person thinks or feels
• that can be proved true or false	• cannot be proved true or false

Signal words and phrases can help you decide if a statement is a fact or an opinion.

Signals for statements of fact include
- the use of specific people, places, events, and dates

Signals for statements of opinion include
- words such as *none, no one, every, always, never, perhaps, probably, maybe, excellent, greatest, best, worst, bad, good, poor*
- phrases such as *I think, I believe, in my opinion, in my judgment, as far as I am concerned*

Decide whether each of the following is a statement of fact or of opinion. Explain how you decided.

1. Luther nailed his 95 theses to the church door in 1517.
2. The Renaissance had the greatest artists that ever lived.
3. Wealthy Italians supported the artists of the Renaissance.
4. All the wealthiest people in Europe lived in Italy.
5. The 1300s began a period of great change in Europe.

Skill Builder
Students' explanations of their decisions will vary but should show logic.

1. Fact
2. Opinion
3. Fact
4. Opinion
5. Fact

Classroom Discussion

Discuss with students some of the broader topics covered in this chapter.

- How can artists best be supported and encouraged?
- How can governments make sure that religion and politics remain separate?
- What are some effective ways to protest against injustice, whether in the church or the political scene?

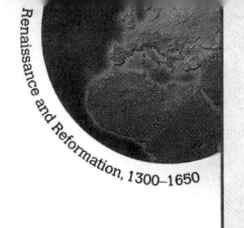

Chapter 15
AGE OF EUROPEAN EXPLORATIONS
(1415–1800)

Chapter Summary
Refer to page 236 for a summary of Chapter 15.

Related Transparencies

T-1 World Map

T-7 Trade Routes of Asia

T-8 Spanish America

T-19 Venn Diagram

Key Blacklines

Biography — Charlemagne

CD Extension

Encourage students to use the reading comprehension, vocabulary reinforcement, and interactive timeline activities on the student CD.

Getting Focused

You may wish to have students change partners several times so that all students can review the earlier civilizations and fix them firmly in their minds. Before a quiz or test, consider dividing the class into teams and playing games to review the ideas.

Getting Focused

Skim this chapter to predict what you will be learning.
- Read the lesson titles and subheadings.
- Look at the illustrations and read the captions.
- Examine the maps.
- Review the vocabulary words and terms.

Every continent in the world except Antarctica is discussed in this chapter. You have been making a world map. By now some part of every continent should be colored in. Make a list of each region that you have added to the map. Next to each region on your list add the name of the earliest human civilization in that region and its dates. With a partner, quiz each other on where the civilizations began and how long ago each one existed.

Picturing History

Columbus' three ships, shown in the sketch on page 216, sailed from Spain in August 1492, with a crew of 90 men. Columbus had a letter from King Ferdinand to the Grand Khan of China. A man on his ship could speak both Hebrew and Arabic; Columbus expected these languages to help them communicate once they reached China. These languages did not help with the Taino natives he found on the island he named San Salvador, in what are now the Caribbean islands.

Pre-Reading Discussion

1 Discuss with students current U.S. exports and imports, using almanacs or other sources to locate key facts and figures. Consider graphing the data to start the discussion.

2 Ask students to look around the room and quickly jot a list of items that they think were not made in the United States. Use this exercise as a way to talk about global interdependence.

216 Chapter 15

LESSON 1

New European Trade Routes

European Explorations, 1415–1800

Thinking on Your Own

Turn each subheading in this lesson into a question. Write them in your notebook. As you study each section of the lesson, write the answers to the questions.

The Renaissance was marked by a spirit of adventure and curiosity. This spirit was the result of a number of influences. In turn, it created an outcome of huge importance: the beginning of the **global age**. During the 1400s, for the first time, Europeans had direct contact with Africans, Asians, and by the end of the century, Americans.

focus your reading

Discuss what prompted Europeans to explore the world.

What successes did the Portuguese have in their voyages of exploration?

What European nations set up trading routes in Asia?

vocabulary

global age   astrolabe
compass   cargo

The Time Is Right

A number of developments took place that made the 1400s the right time for the global age to begin. The first development, or influence, was the Crusades. Large numbers of Europeans went to the Holy Land to fight the Muslims. Their travels showed them the marvels of other places. When they returned home, they told stories of what they had seen. The ships that returned from the Holy Land carried luxury goods like spices and silks. These goods were sold in European markets. Marco Polo's journal also told Europeans about life outside Europe.

But it was more than excitement about new lands that moved Europeans. For many, it was riches. Merchants in northern and western Europe wanted to sell goods like silks and spices without having to pay Arab and Italian merchants. Goods from Asia

Age of European Explorations

Lesson Summary

Worldwide exploration began in the fifteenth century. Prince Henry encouraged Portuguese sailors to explore the African coast and beyond. The Portuguese began trading in gold and slaves. They were the first to round the Cape of Good Hope (Africa) and the first to reach India. They eventually gained control of the spice trade.

Lesson Objective

Students will learn about early explorations, particularly those of the Portuguese.

Focus Your Reading Answers

1 Europeans began exploring the world because of curiosity about faraway places and the hope of riches. In addition, technology had advanced far enough to allow exploration.

2 Portuguese successes included establishing a trading network in West Africa, being the first nation to round the Cape of Good Hope, and arriving first in India.

3 European nations with trading networks in Asia included Portugal, England, Spain, France, and the Netherlands.

Lesson Vocabulary

Introduce each of the following vocabulary terms to students.

Explain that a *global age* is one in which all civilizations can be in contact with the others around the world. The first *global age* began during the 1400s.

A *compass* is an instrument that tells direction. The *compass* was one of the innovations that made European exploration possible. *Astrolabe* is explained in Chapter 9 Lesson 2 on page 129.

The goods carried in a ship or plane are its *cargo*. The *cargo* of spices that Vasco da Gama brought back to Europe repaid him 60 times.

Extension

Arab traders tried to protect their monopoly on spices by disguising both the location and cultivation of those spices. One story claimed that cinnamon grew in glens that were also home to poisonous snakes. Another spice, cassia, was said to be protected by winged animals as it grew in shallow lakes.

Age of European Explorations

Picturing History

The image on page 218 is a compass. Ask students to note the elaborate face of the compass and the gold case. The use of a compass aided fifteenth-century explorations.

Time Box Extension

Have students look at the Time Box on page 219 and answer the following questions:

- How many years were there between Dias' voyage and the founding of Quebec? (120 years)
- What three nations had permanent settlements in the New World by 1608? (Spain, England, France)

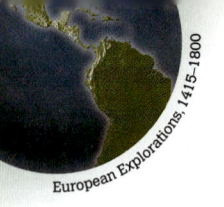

European Explorations, 1415–1800

traveled through either Southwest Asia or the Ottoman Empire. In both regions, they were sold to Arab merchants, who moved the goods along the trade routes to Europe. Merchants in the Italian city-states usually bought them. It took a long time for goods to reach merchants in northern and western Europe.

Each time the goods changed hands, the price went up. Each merchant took a share of the profits. If merchants in Portugal, England, or the Netherlands could buy goods direct from merchants in India, China, or Southeast Asia, the prices would be cheaper. The Europeans could then make more money. But to get to Asia, the merchants had to sail around Africa. No one had ever done that before.

Even if Europeans had wanted to explore beyond Europe by sea before the 1400s, they would not have been able to get very far. The technology that would allow them to make long sea voyages had not been invented in Europe. Four innovations made European exploration possible: accurate maps, the **compass**, the **astrolabe**, and a new type of triangular sail called the lateen sail. This new sail design allowed ships to sail into the wind.

The fourth reason that caused Europeans to want to explore new lands was to bring religion to nonbelievers. Specifically, Europeans wanted to bring and expand the influence of Christianity. Spreading Christianity became an important factor in exploration in most regions around the world.

Europeans learned the use of the compass (above) and astrolabe from the Arab traders.

Europeans also learned a new design of triangular sails from Arabs that resulted in the development of the caravel, a small, more easily maneuverable ship that could hold cannon and more cargo. The sails made it possible to sail farther out to sea.

Prince Henry and Portuguese Explorers

Beginning in 1420, the first Europeans to explore along Africa's west coast were the Portuguese. Prince Henry, the son of Portugal's king, encouraged Portuguese sea captains to make these voyages. He wanted Portugal to become rich from the spice trade. Prince Henry, known as Henry the Navigator, even set up a school that taught skills related to sailing.

The first trips were short voyages along the west coast of Africa. The captains were trying to determine the size of the African continent. Wherever they stopped, the captains

218 Chapter 15

Extension

Students interested in culinary careers may wish to investigate the use of spices as preservatives and flavorings. They may create displays of the most commonly available spices, or those of a particular culture, or provide samples for the class. (If so, be aware of the possibility of allergies.) Have students present their findings to the class by using the Student Presentation Builder on the student CD.

Map Extension

Ask students to use the map on page 219 to answer the following questions:

- Which nation claimed the trade center farthest east? (Spain)
- Which European power controlled Calcutta? (England)
- What areas did the French control? (Calicut, Pondicherry, Melaka, Batavia (Jakarta))

Time Box

1488
Dias rounds tip of South Africa

1487
da Gama sails to India

1492
Columbus sails to the Americas

1564
first permanent Spanish settlement in North America at St. Augustine

1607
first permanent English settlement in North America at Jamestown

1608
first permanent French settlement in North America at Quebec

---

established trading posts. This was the beginning of Portugal's trading empire in Africa. One of the goods they traded for was gold. They tapped into the existing gold network in West Africa. The Portuguese also began to take enslaved Africans back to Portugal to use as servants.

Portuguese sea captains continued their explorations long after Prince Henry's death. In 1488, Bartholomeu Dias finally rounded the southern tip of Africa. The Portuguese named the area the Cape of Good Hope. The wealth of the spice trade was almost in their hands.

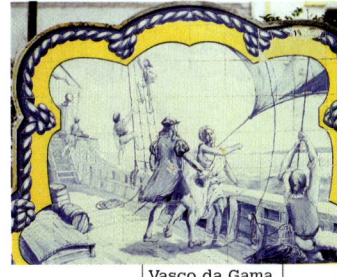

Vasco da Gama in Calicut, India

In 1497, Vasco da Gama set out to become the first Portuguese explorer to actually make the trip to India. He sailed south around the Cape of Good Hope and then across the Indian Ocean to southern India. He filled his ship with spices and set sail for Portugal. The round-trip took two years. His **cargo** of spices sold for 60 times the cost of his trip.

European Explorations, 1415–1800

European Trade Routes, 1700
Areas controlled by: England, Portugal, France, Spain, Netherlands — Trade route

stop and think

Why did European nations send out voyages of exploration in the 1400s? Check your ideas with a partner. Then write a paragraph to explain your reasoning.

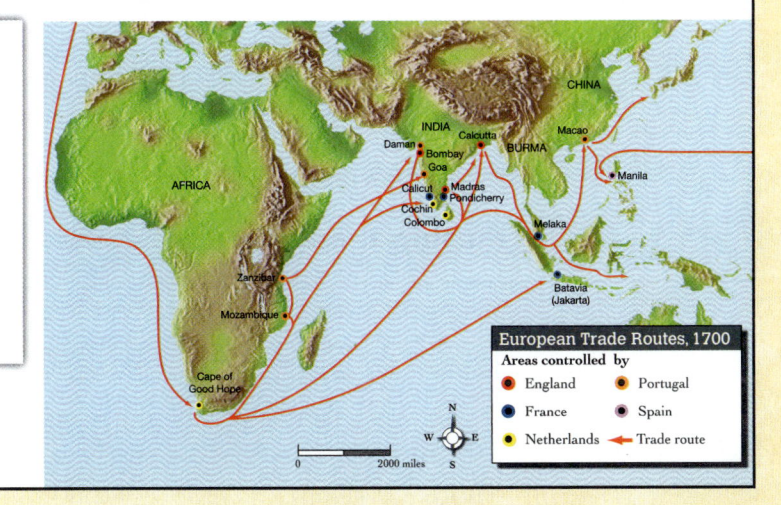

Picturing History

Vasco da Gama, shown in the illustration on page 219, set sail from Lisbon, Portugal, on July 8, 1497, with four ships, one of them in his brother's command. They rounded the Cape of Good Hope on November 22, arriving at Calicut, India, in May of the following year. By the time they returned to Lisbon in summer 1499, only 55 of the 170 original crew members remained. Most had died of scurvy, a common fate for seafarers of the time. Da Gama returned to India in 1502. Both trips brought him wealth and honor. In 1524, he was sent as viceroy to India to reform the colonial government, but he died a few months later.

Extension

Prince Henry was only twenty-one when he fought in a campaign in which the Portuguese captured Morocco's fort, Cueta. It was across the Strait of Gibraltar from Portugal. Henry's time in Cueta sparked the beginning of a lifelong interest in the African continent. Henry established a small court near the port of Lagos on Portugal's southwest tip. There, scholars pioneered work in astronomy, mapmaking, ship design, and navigation. Henry spent most of his fortune on these explorations and projects, dying in debt.

Extension

King John II of Portugal, disappointed in earlier voyages that failed to find the southernmost point of Africa, sent Bartolomeu Dias and three ships to do so. Dias rounded the Cape of Good Hope, but did not see it until the ships were on their way back to Portugal. Dias also joined da Gama's 1497 voyage for part of the journey. He was part of Cabral's fleet, which sighted Brazil. When that voyage reached the Cape of Good Hope, Dias was lost at sea.

Stop and Think

Students' paragraphs will vary but should be supported with reasons from the lesson. Ideas might include: Marco Polo's journal, stories of the Crusaders, excitement about new lands, rich goods, inventions, and the desire to bring religion to non-believers.

Age of European Explorations | 219

Picturing History

Afonso de Albuquerque, pictured on page 220, had a distinguished military career in Africa before being sent to India. Albuquerque built the first Portuguese fort in Asia and established a trading post in 1503. He returned to Lisbon, Portugal, then explored Africa's east coast, building a fortress near the mouth of the Red Sea, designed to cut off Arab trade with India. Sent back to India in 1508, he conquered Goa, a Muslim stronghold, in 1510. It remained in Portuguese hands until 1961. The victory over the Muslims enabled Hindu rulers to accept the Portuguese presence in India. During the next five years, which were his last, Albuquerque conquered Malacca, explored the coasts of Arabia and Abyssinia, and conquered Calicut.

Putting It All Together

Students' paragraphs will vary but should describe two events from the lesson. Possible topics are rounding the Cape of Good Hope, explorations of da Gama and Dias, and founding of colonies in Asia.

Trading in India, Southeast Asia, and China

Europeans were able to reach India to purchase spices, but India was not the source of the spices. Muslim merchants in India bought them from other merchants farther to the east. Many of the spices came from the Melaka islands in the East Indies. Europeans called these islands the "Spice Islands."

The Portuguese set out to gain control of the spice trade. First, they destroyed Muslim and Indian shipping along the coast of India. Then the Portuguese moved farther east and seized the Strait of Melaka in what is today Malaysia. By controlling this waterway, they could keep other Europeans out of the area. Finally, the Portuguese forced the ruler of the Spice Islands to sell them all its spices. In their dealings with the people of Asia, the Portuguese set the model for how Europeans dealt with non-Europeans. They used guns and cannon to get what they wanted.

In the meantime, the Portuguese tried to expand their trade with China. However, in 1535 China limited European traders to two ports. The Portuguese and other Europeans also failed in Japan. The Japanese, like the Chinese, thought the Europeans were uncivilized. Their trade goods had little appeal to either the Chinese or Japanese people. The rulers of China and Japan feared that the Europeans would use their weapons to seize land. Also, the missionaries who came with the traders raised suspicion among the rulers.

In time, more powerful European nations seized Portugal's trading empire in Asia. In 1595, the Netherlands began a campaign to capture Portuguese trading posts in the East Indies. The Dutch were able to end Portuguese control and also to keep France and England out of the East Indies.

Afonso de Albuquerque, governor and commander of the Portuguese empire in Asia, gained control of Melaka, on the Malay Peninsula, in 1511.

Putting It All Together

Choose two events described in this lesson and write a paragraph about each event. Exchange your paragraphs with a partner. Review each other's paragraphs to see if you can make them more interesting by adding action words.

Map Extension

Ask students to use the map on page 221 to answer the following questions:

- On which voyage did Columbus go farthest west? (fourth)
- Which voyage took place between 1493 and 1496? (second)
- How could you describe the third voyage using compass directions? (They took a more southerly route before turning west, landing in South America.)
- Where did three of the voyages stop before going farther west? (Canary Islands)

LESSON 2

Sailing West to Go East

Thinking on Your Own

Write the name *Christopher Columbus* in your notebook. List at least five facts that you know about him. Discuss these with a partner. As you read this lesson, add five new facts to your list.

While the Portuguese were exploring the African coast, the Spanish were busy fighting Muslims. The armies of King Ferdinand and Queen Isabella drove the last Muslim invaders out of Spain in 1492. When Christopher Columbus came to them asking for help, the time was right. The Spanish were ready to think about an **overseas** empire.

focus your reading

Explain why Columbus wanted to sail west to find Asia.

How did the Spanish conquer the Aztec Empire?

Summarize how the Spanish conquered the Inca Empire.

vocabulary

overseas
Line of Demarcation
conquistadores

Columbus and the Spanish Monarchs

Columbus' plan was to sail west to go east. He believed that he could reach Asia and the East Indies by sailing west. For many centuries, common people believed the earth was flat. If a ship sailed too far, it would fall off the edge. By the 1400s, educated people knew that this was not true. However, they could only estimate the true size of the earth. They did not know how far west the East Indies were located.

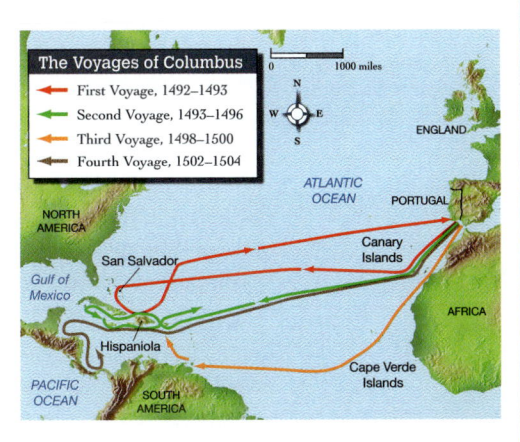

The Voyages of Columbus
- First Voyage, 1492–1493
- Second Voyage, 1493–1496
- Third Voyage, 1498–1500
- Fourth Voyage, 1502–1504

Age of European Explorations 221

Lesson Summary

King Ferdinand and Queen Isabella supported Columbus as he sailed west to find the East Indies. Instead, Columbus found Hispaniola and Cuba. Spain and Portugal divided the New World between them.

Hernán Cortés overthrew the Aztec Empire in Central America.

Francisco Pizarro conquered the Inca Empire in the Andes of South America.

Lesson Objective

Students will learn about the Spanish explorations and conquests in the Caribbean and Latin America.

Focus Your Reading Answers

1 Columbus thought he could reach Asia faster by sailing west, not realizing there were two continents in his path.

2 The Spanish conquered the Aztec Empire with trickery and guns.

3 The Spanish conquered the Inca Empire by trickery and by taking advantage of the civil war going on at the time.

Lesson Vocabulary

Discuss each of the vocabulary terms with students.

If something is *overseas*, it is across the sea or abroad. The Spanish were ready to consider an *overseas* empire when Columbus came to court.

The *Line of Demarcation* divided the so-called New World between Spain and Portugal. The 1494 Treaty of Tordesillas established the *Line of Demarcation*.

The Spanish word for conquerers is *conquistadores*. Cortés and Pizarro were *conquistadores*.

Age of European Explorations 221

Picturing History

Ferdinand and Isabella of Spain, depicted on page 222, were typical rulers of their time, believing that the people Columbus had encountered were now their subjects. Fifty years after Columbus first landed on Hispaniola, their grandson, King Charles I, decreed that Indians could not be enslaved, thus inadvertently beginning the importation of African slaves.

Stop and Think

Students' essays will vary but should include the search for riches, the desire for empires, and the desire to spread religion.

European Explorations, 1415-1800

For years, Columbus tried to persuade the rulers of Portugal and then Spain to finance his plan. When he tried again in 1492, Queen Isabella agreed. He persuaded her by telling her of the riches that would come to Spain. Perhaps more important to her, however, were the non-Europeans that could be converted to Catholicism.

Columbus and 90 sailors set sail in three caravels on August 3, 1492. They found land slightly more than two months later, on October 12. However, the land they found was not Asia; it was the islands of Hispaniola and Cuba. Columbus returned three more times to the Caribbean looking for the Asian mainland. Because he thought he had reached the East Indies, he called the people he met *Indios*, or Indians.

Ferdinand and Isabella of Spain funded the voyages of Columbus in 1492.

stop and think

The phrase "for God, glory, and gold" is sometimes used to describe why Europeans set out to find new lands. What information in this lesson supports the reasons given in this phrase? Check your ideas with a partner. Then write a three-paragraph essay to explain the phrase.

It did not take long for Spain and other nations to realize Columbus' mistake. He had not found Asia. He had found two unknown continents that Europeans called the *New World*. The Spanish and the Portuguese, who had discovered what is now Brazil, decided that the wealth and people of these continents belonged to them. To prevent disputes between the two nations, Pope Alexander VI divided the New World in 1494. The Treaty of Tordesillas established the **Line of Demarcation** at 38° west longitude. It separated Spanish lands from Portuguese lands. Everything west of the line belonged to Spain; everything east of the line belonged to Portugal.

Overthrowing the Aztec Empire

By 1515, the Spanish controlled most of the islands in the Caribbean. From their base in Cuba, they set out to explore the mainland of Central America. One of the first conquerors, or **conquistadores**, was Hernán Cortés.

In 1519, Cortés, 500 soldiers, some horses, and a few cannon landed on the Yucatán Peninsula. They began a march inland. Early on their journey, they met Malinche, an Aztec

---

Extension

Suggest to interested students that they use library resources or the Internet to find out more about the ways in which the cultures of Brazil (Portuguese influence) and the rest of South America (Spanish influence) are alike and different. Ask them to create a Venn diagram or other visual to share their findings with the class.

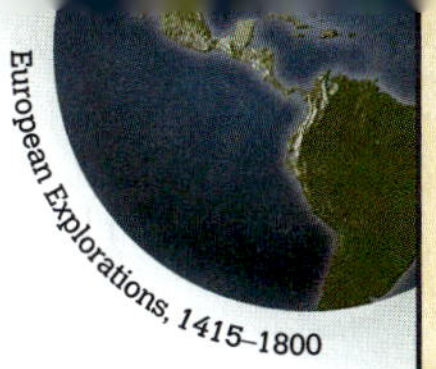

who had been captured by Mayans. Cortés took Malinche along as interpreter.

While Cortés continued his march to the city of Tenochtitlán, the Aztec ruler, Montezuma, waited. He had learned that the Spanish were on their way, and he was fearful. According to an ancient prophecy, a white god, Quetzalcoatl, had once lived among the Aztec. He had returned home, but would one day come back. When he did, the Aztec Empire would end.

Montezuma decided to welcome the Spanish. He showered them with food and riches. He gave them a palace where they could live. In a short time, however, Cortés tricked Montezuma into becoming his prisoner. Cortés and the Spanish were then in control of the city. In 1520, the Aztec rebelled against the Spanish. Montezuma died in the fighting. The Spanish fled Tenochtitlán.

A Spanish Attack

...records of the Aztecs and Incas were destroyed by the Spanish. A few survived. ...following excerpt is from an Aztec description of a battle to capture Tenochtitlán.

"...n one occasion, four Spanish ...alrymen entered the market ...e. They rode through it in a ...t circle, stabbing and killing ...y of our warriors and ...mpling everything under their ...ses' hooves. This was the first ...e the Spaniards had entered ...market place, and our warriors ...e taken by surprise. . . .

...was at this time that the ...niards set fire to the temple ... burned it to the ground. ...flames and smoke leaped high into the air with a terrible roar. ...people wept when they saw their temple on fire. . . .

...e battle lasted for many hours and extended to almost every ...er of the market place."

reading for understanding

Why were the Aztecs taken by surprise?

Why do you think the Spanish burned the temple?

Discuss why fighting on horseback was an advantage to the Spanish.

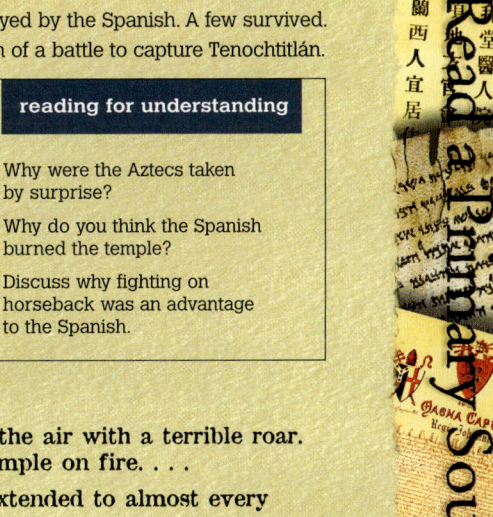

European Explorations, 1415–1800

Picturing History

The Aztec codex on page 223 pictures a conversation about the Spanish invaders. Their arrival seemed to Montezuma just one of many signs, including a comet, that pointed to the fulfillment of a prophecy. Trying to forestall trouble, Montezuma sent gifts, including a costume of Quetzalcoatl, to Cortés. Quetzalcoatl was the god of lightning and thunder. In response, Cortés first placed the emissaries in chains, then had a cannon fired that destroyed a tree on the shore. Two of the Aztec fainted, believing they had witnessed the god's power.

Extension

The Aztec considered the Spanish invasion a fulfillment of an ancient prophecy of their empire's end and were uncertain what to do. Cortés tricked Montezuma, the leader, into becoming a prisoner; he later killed the ruler.

Reading for Understanding

1 The Spanish had not entered the market place before.

2 The Spanish may have burned the temple to assert the strength of their God and to destroy the worship of what they considered false gods.

3 From horseback, the soldiers could strike harder and were harder to hit. The hooves of the horses could also be used as weapons.

Age of European Explorations

Picturing History

Atahualpa, shown on page 224, was apparently his father's favorite son, although illegitimate. Atahualpa ruled the northern part of the Inca Empire from Quito when his father died in 1527. Civil war with his older half-brother led to problems economically. Still, when Pizarro demanded gold, the emperor's subjects filled a room with gold and silver objects. When melted down into ingots and bullion, the treasure weighed 24 tons.

Pizarro followed the example of Cortés, taking Atahualpa prisoner. The Spanish gained much gold from these conquests.

Putting It All Together

Students' diagrams and paragraphs will vary but may suggest that in both cases the Spanish used trickery and firepower to achieve their conquests.

The following year Cortés returned with more soldiers. Reinforcements had been sent from Cuba. The new Spanish force, fully equipped with horses and guns, defeated the Aztec. They destroyed Tenochtitlán and built Mexico City in its place. The Aztecs' temple was replaced by a Catholic Church.

Overthrowing the Inca Empire

During the 1520s, the Spanish moved throughout Central America. They took land and began building settlements. Native Americans were considered subjects of Spain but had no rights. As the Spanish moved farther south, they heard stories of a rich kingdom somewhere in the Andes Mountains. This was the Empire of the Inca.

Francisco Pizarro, another conquistador, set out to find the Inca. In 1531, he reached the Incan capital of Cuzco. He had only 180 soldiers with him, but they were enough. The Empire was torn by civil war. Rival forces of Atahualpa and Huascar, half-brothers, were fighting for power over the Empire.

Atahualpa asked Pizarro for help in defeating Huascar. Instead, Pizarro made Atahualpa his prisoner. To save himself, Atahualpa arranged for enough gold and silver to fill two rooms to be given to Pizarro. Atahualpa also had to arrange for the murder of Huascar. Rather than set Atahualpa free, Pizarro seized the ransom. He then had Atahualpa tried, convicted, and executed for Huascar's death.

The Inca were leaderless. Without a ruler, the Empire began to fall apart. Pizarro seized much of the territory and its vast wealth of gold and silver for Spain.

Putting It All Together

What did the Spanish overthrow of the Aztec and Inca Empires have in common? Create a Venn diagram to decide whether the Spanish tactics were the same or different against the two empires. Work with a partner to complete the diagram. Then write a paragraph that explains the tactics of the Spanish.

Atahualpa

Extension

Spain created the Viceroyalty of New Grenada in 1739 and the Viceroyalty of the Rio de la Plata in 1776. These new viceroyalties stripped territory from Peru, which was among the most valuable Spanish colonies because of the silver mines. Lima, the capital, was a wealthy city for the Spanish ruling class. The Andes Mountains made communication and government difficult, however. After a series of uprisings, Peru declared independence in 1821, capturing the viceroy and his generals in 1824. Present-day Peru and Chile, all that was left of the viceroy of Peru, became independent nations.

LESSON 3

Colonizing Central and South America

European Explorations, 1415–1800

Thinking on Your Own

What do you know about the Spanish in the Americas? Create a T-chart. Label one side "Spanish Government." Label the other side "Spanish Society." List at least three facts on each side of your chart. As you read the lesson, add to your chart.

The Spanish quickly expanded their territory in the Americas. By the mid-1500s, they claimed Mexico and much of Central and South America. They were also moving north into what would become the United States. How would the Spanish control this vast new territory? How would they govern it?

focus your reading

How did Spain govern its colonies in the Americas?

Explain how the encomienda affected Native Americans and Africans.

How was Spanish society organized in the colonies?

vocabulary

viceroyalties   creoles
encomienda   mestizos
immunity   mulattos
peninsulares

Governing Spanish America

The Spanish decided to set up colonies. The Spanish monarchs encouraged their citizens to sail to the Americas and build settlements. The more wealth the colonies created, the wealthier the monarchs became. Part of every shipment of gold, silver, and other goods from the colonies went to the monarchs.

To govern Spanish America, Spain set up **viceroyalties**. Each viceroyalty was an area governed by a viceroy—or a governor who represented the monarch. By 1535, there were two viceroyalties: the Viceroyalty of New Spain and the Viceroyalty of Peru. In the 1700s, the latter was split into three units.

Lesson Summary

The Spanish set up colonies in the New World, which were governed by viceroyalties. Although converting the Native Americans to Christianity was an objective, the Spanish also used them as slaves in the encomienda system. Efforts to help the Native Americans led to the importing of African slaves to work on sugar plantations.

Spanish society in the New World was headed by the peninsulares, followed by creoles, the Spanish descendants of the original colonists, with mestizos and mulattos at the bottom. Native Americans and Africans were outside the system.

The Spanish created beautiful capital cities such as Lima, Peru, and Mexico City, Mexico.

Lesson Objective

Students will learn about the Spanish colonization of Central and South America.

Focus Your Reading Answers

1 Spain governed its colonies in the Americas by a system of viceroyalties. Governors who represented the monarch were placed in charge of New Spain and Peru.

2 Encomienda led to the death of many Native Americans who were worked to death in the mines, fields, or private homes. It also led to the importing of Africans for labor after a priest urged kinder treatment for the Native Americans.

3 From top to bottom, Spanish society was organized into peninsulares, creoles, mestizos, and mulattos, with Native Americans and enslaved Africans outside the system.

Lesson Vocabulary

Discuss each of the vocabulary terms with students.

Viceroyalties are areas governed by a representative of the monarch. Spain set up the *viceroyalties* of New Spain and Peru.

The system of *encomienda* allowed the Spanish to enslave Native Americans. Queen Isabella granted Spanish colonists *encomienda*.

An *immunity* to a disease means you are protected from it. The Native Americans had no *immunity* against diseases the Spanish brought.

Native-born Spanish sent to run the colonies were called *peninsulares*. The *peninsulares* were at the head of the social classes. The descendants of the original Spanish settlers were *creoles*. Creoles had little power but owned mines, plantations, and businesses. Children of Spanish and Native Americans were *mestizos*. Mestizos were part of the lowest social class. Children of Spanish and Africans were called *mulattos*. Mulattos also were part of the lowest social class.

Age of European Explorations   225

Picturing History

Sugar plantations, such as the one pictured on page 226, formed a major part of the economy of Cuba and Hispaniola for centuries. In colonial days, both enslaved Native Americans and Africans worked the plantations.

Extension

Ask students with an interest in medicine to use library resources or the Internet to find out more about smallpox, which killed many of the peoples of the New World. Have them report on the vaccine developed and the current status of smallpox.

Stop and Think

Students' essays will vary but should give reasons that support the statement "two wrongs don't make a right" as it applies to enslaving Africans.

Converting Native Americans to Christianity, however, remained an important goal. Missionaries came with the colonists to Christianize Native Americans. They burned native books and tore down native temples and statues. Their mission was to turn Native Americans into Spaniards. Native Americans were to give up their native dress, customs, language, and religion.

Enslaving Native Americans and Africans

When colonists began settling the islands in the Caribbean, Queen Isabella granted them **encomienda**. This was the right to demand labor from Native Americans living on the land. The queen had intended to protect Native Americans. However, the colonists used the encomienda to enslave them. When the Spanish discovered gold and silver in Peru and Mexico, the Spanish forced Native Americans to work in their mines.

Slaves working on a sugar plantation on the island of Hispaniola

The Spanish worked hundreds of thousands of Native Americans to death. Hundreds of thousands more starved to death. European diseases caused even more deaths. Native Americans had no **immunity** to diseases such as smallpox and measles. The island of Hispaniola is an example. Experts believe that 250,000 Native Americans lived on the island when Christopher Columbus landed there in 1492. By 1538, only 500 Native Americans remained. Experts estimate that between 1519 and 1630, some 24 million Native Americans died in Central Mexico alone.

In an effort to save Native Americans, Bartolomé de Las Casas, a priest, urged using Africans as workers. As early as 1518, a few Africans had been shipped to the Caribbean. The Spanish replaced Native American

stop and think

"Two wrongs don't make a right" is an o... saying. Write an essa... of two or three paragraphs to suppo... the idea of the sayin... Use the enslaving of Africans to save Native Americans as your example. Ask a partner to read your essay and suggest ways to make it stronger and clearer...

226 Chapter 15

Extension

Bartolomé de Las Casas left his native Spain for Hispaniola in 1502. After taking part in several expeditions, he received an encomienda. After being ordained as a Dominican priest in 1512 or 1513, perhaps the first person in America to be received into holy orders, he began evangelizing the Native Americans. In 1515, he returned to Spain to plead the cause of the Native Americans, having given his encomienda back to the governor of Cuba. For the rest of his long life, he traveled back and forth from New Spain to old Spain, serving as court advisor and writing several important works detailing the harsh treatment of Native Americans.

laborers on sugar plantations. After 1542, the Spanish were forbidden to enslave Native Americans. As a result, the trans-Atlantic trade in enslaved Africans became big business for the Spanish—and later for the English. It is estimated that at least 10 million Africans came to the Americas in chains. Perhaps twice that many died on the journey.

Society in Spanish America

The most important posts in colonial government were held by **peninsulares**. These were native-born Spanish who were sent from Spain, which was a peninsula, to run the colonies. They consisted of a very small number of people, but they made up the highest social class.

The next social class were **creoles**. Their ancestors had been the original Spanish colonists. Creoles usually owned plantations, mines, and trading businesses. They had little power in the colonies.

Mestizos were descended from Spanish and Native Americans. **Mulattos** had ancestors who were Spanish and African. The two groups made up the lowest social classes. Native Americans and enslaved Africans were below the social system.

The big cities of Spanish America such as Mexico City and Lima, Peru, were designed like European cities. They had wide avenues and huge churches and government buildings. The homes of the wealthy were decorated with beautiful furniture and paintings. Universities were built to educate young men of the upper classes. Wealthy young women were educated at home or by Catholic nuns at local convents. Spanish influence could be seen in all aspects of daily life.

The adobe mission in Picuria Pueblo, New Mexico, shows the blending of Spanish and Native American cultures.

Putting It All Together

Create a diagram to illustrate the social system in Spanish America. Work with a partner to decide on the shape of the diagram. Include the details about government and society from the T-chart you created.

Age of European Explorations

Picturing History

The New Mexican adobe mission, shown in the photograph on page 227, is an example of Spanish colonial architecture. This Baroque style sometimes mixed with indigenous styles. In the twentieth century, the mission churches of New Mexico became inspirations for the painter Georgia O'Keeffe.

Picturing History

Quito is one of the premier sites of Spanish colonial architecture, as demonstrated by La Compania, the church shown on page 227. Quito is the oldest capital of South America; its old town became a UNESCO World Heritage Site in 1978. Quito was also the site of the first art school in South America, established in 1552. The art school supported a religious art movement in Quito. Baroque in style, its huge altars are covered with gold leaf.

Extension

One of the most famous Catholic nuns was the seventeenth century's Sor Juana Inés de la Cruz, a brilliant Mexican who entered the convent of San Jerónimo at eighteen years of age to dedicate her life to learning. She had already begged to be disguised as a boy so she could study at the University of Mexico, where she learned Latin. Noted for her poetry and defense of women's ability to learn, she gave up her scholarly work and devoted herself to the poor and to her religious duties. She died during an epidemic, nursing the nuns of her convent.

Putting It All Together

Students' diagrams will vary but should include the following information:

from the top level of society to the bottom—peninsulares, creoles, mestizos, and mulattos, with Native Americans and enslaved Africans outside the system

Age of European Explorations

Lesson Summary

European nations wanted a share in the North American continent. The Spanish claimed land in Florida, Texas, and California. The area now called Canada was known as New France. It was a region of fur trappers and traders. For a short time, Dutch and Swedish colonies existed in parts of what are now New York, New Jersey, Connecticut, and Delaware. These, along with other colonies along the eastern seaboard, became English colonies. Most English colonies were either proprietary or royal. The colonists drove Native Americans from their land through several wars.

Lesson Objective

Students will learn about the European colonies in North America.

Focus Your Reading Answers

1 Spanish settlements were mostly forts or missions, with few families. Missions housed priests and the Native Americans who were forced to work for them.

2 Most people in New France made a livelihood by trapping or trading furs.

3 Sweden and the Netherlands lost their colonies in North America because they lacked strong armies. The Dutch took over the Swedish settlements and were in turn overtaken by the English.

4 The English settlers hoped for gold, religious freedom, or land to farm.

LESSON 4

Colonizing North America

European Explorations, 1415–1800

Thinking on Your Own

Create a concept web to help you remember information about the colonization of North America. Label the large circle "Colonizing North America." Add a circle for each European nation that built colonies in North America. Add smaller circles for the most important information about the colonies.

By the 1500s, European nations were competing for land and power in Europe. As their explorers found "new" lands, European monarchs often transferred their rivalry to these parts of the globe. For example, Queen Elizabeth I made Francis Drake a knight for sailing around the world. He and the crew of his ship *Golden Hind* chased down Spanish treasure ships on their way back to Spain from the Americas. The English seized the Spanish cargoes of gold and silver. To the English, Drake was a hero. To the Spanish, he was a pirate.

focus your reading

Describe the Spanish settlements in what is today the United States.

How did people make their living in New France?

How did Sweden and the Netherlands lose their colonies in North America?

Explain why people came to the English colonies.

vocabulary

mission
joint-stock company
proprietary colonies
royal colonies

This rivalry among European nations was behind the desire to claim territory and set up colonies in the Americas. It was not only the Spanish and Portuguese who wanted to build empires. The French, English, Dutch, and Swedes also claimed land in North America.

228 Chapter 15

Lesson Vocabulary

Discuss each of the vocabulary terms with students.

A *mission* was a place where priests lived. The original goal of the *mission* was to convert Native Americans to Christianity.

A *joint-stock company* was one in which groups of English merchants funded voyages and settlements in North America, hoping for a return on their investment. Jamestown was a *joint-stock* venture. *Proprietary colonies* were owned by private companies or individuals. About half of the colonies were *proprietary colonies*. Colonies belonging to the English monarch were *royal colonies*. The *royal colonies* made up the rest of the 13 colonies.

New Spain

By 1513, Spanish explorers were moving into what is today the United States. In that year, Juan Ponce de Leon explored Florida. The first permanent Spanish settlement was built in Florida in 1564. St. Augustine was settled to keep the French out of the area. In 1598, Spanish colonists moved into what is today the Southwest United States. In 1682, the Spanish built two **missions** and forts in Texas. By the mid-1700s, the Spanish also had settlements in modern day California, Arizona, and New Mexico.

Spanish priests, soldiers, and farmers played an important part in settling the Southwest. Many settlements were forts or missions. The missions housed a priest and Native Americans who had been converted to Catholicism. Spanish farmers in New Mexico settled next to Pueblo villages. At first, they fought for control. In time, they became good neighbors. Both had to protect their homes from raids by unfriendly Native American warriors from the Great Plains.

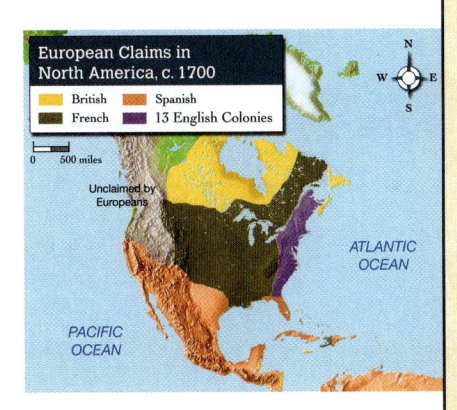

Trappers, Traders, and New France

The French attempted to build forts and claim territory all along the Atlantic coast. However, the Spanish drove them out.

In 1608, Samuel de Champlain founded Quebec in what is today Canada. By the late 1600s, the French had a line of trading settlements in New France from Canada all the way to the Gulf of Mexico. Most of the settlers were fur trappers and traders. They hunted animals like beaver for their fur or

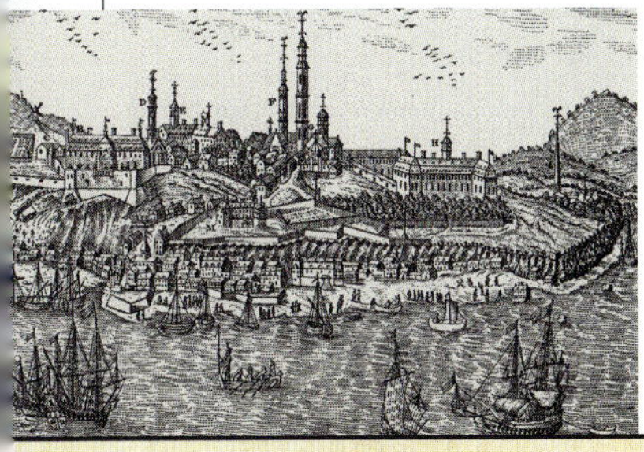

Age of European Explorations

Picturing History

St. Augustine, shown in an etching at the top of page 229, is widely acclaimed as the oldest continuous settlement in North America. St. Augustine was founded in 1565. In 1586, Francis Drake looted and burned the town. In 1672, the Spanish began to build Castillo de San Marcos, now the oldest masonry fort in the United States. Spain ceded Florida to Britain in 1763 as part of the Treaty of Paris. Twenty years later, it was returned to Spanish control and then given to the United States in 1819.

Map Extension

Ask students to use the map on page 229 to answer the following questions:

- What European power claimed the land just south of the 13 colonies? (Spain)

- Where was France's primary land claim? (central North America and the northeast of Canada)

- In what geographic region was land still unclaimed? (northwest North America)

- In addition to the 13 colonies, where else did Britain claim land? (Canada)

Picturing History

Quebec, depicted at the lower left on page 229, was a site of decisive battles in both the French and Indian War and the Revolutionary War.

Extension

Invite students interested in military strategy to use library resources or the Internet to find out about the Battle of Quebec during the French and Indian War. Allow time for them to report their findings to the class.

Age of European Explorations 229

Picturing History

In 1625, the Dutch founded New Amsterdam, shown on page 230, on Manhattan Island. The next year, Dutch West India Company representative Peter Minuit bought Manhattan with baubles worth about $24.00. That year, the Dutch built about 30 houses on the island. The first colonists were either indentured servants who had to work on farms owned by the Dutch West India Company or free citizens. The latter group received two years of free provisions and were able to own homesteads. To protect the settlement from Native American attacks, the Dutch walled the lower island. This is *the* wall of Wall Street, now the financial center of the United States.

Extension

Invite students to use library resources or the Internet to learn about the differences between Puritans and Pilgrims. Have them present their findings to the class, perhaps in a drama or a radio play.

---

traded with Native Americans for animal skins. The furs and skins were shipped to France where they sold for high prices.

New Netherlands and New Sweden

The Netherlands was a rich and powerful nation in Europe. They financed the exploration of North America. As a result, the Netherlands claimed a large part of what is today New York, Connecticut, New Jersey, and Delaware.

The Dutch founded trading posts along the Hudson River. They tried to take the Native American fur trade away from New France. The Dutch did not have a powerful army in the colony. In 1664, the English sailed several ships into the New Amsterdam harbor, what is now New York Harbor. They demanded that the Dutch surrender. With no way to defend itself, the colony gave up.

New Amsterdam during the 1600s

Sweden had also grown wealthy from trade. It sent colonists to settle along the Delaware River in what is today southern New Jersey. The Dutch seized the settlements in 1655. They, too, became English territory in 1664.

English Colonies

England's first permanent colony in North America was Jamestown, settled in 1607. A group of merchants set up a **joint-stock company** to pay for the voyage and the settlement. In return, they expected to make a fortune on the gold the colonists would find. However, there was no gold and many of the early colonists starved to death.

In 1620, a religious group known as Pilgrims settled Plymouth Colony. They fled religious persecution in England. Ten years later, another group of English Protestants, the Puritans, settled nearby. They came voluntarily to set up a community based on their Puritan religious views. They founded the Massachusetts Bay Colony, which was a church-state. Like the Pilgrims and Puritans, Quakers, Catholics, and Jews came to the colonies for religious freedom.

Extension

The English and Dutch each formed companies at the beginning of the seventeenth century to explore Asia and exploit the spice trade. Privately owned and funded as joint-stock companies, without government oversight, their charters gave these companies the right to buy, sell, construct trading posts, and even wage war if it were in the company's best interest. Their cheaper, faster, and more powerful ships gave them a military advantage, as well as an economic one, over other European nations. They realized huge profits. In one two-year voyage, an English ship began with 30,000 pounds sterlings' worth of silver and gold, returning with spices worth more than one million pounds sterling.

stop and think

The Spanish, French, Dutch, and English settlers in North America were not alike in how they treated the Native Americans. How and why were they different? With a partner, look for information to answer this question. Write a one-paragraph answer.

People came to the English colonies to make a better life for themselves. They looked for economic opportunities as farmers, fishers, and crafts people. Many people in the New England and Middle Colonies were the owners of small farms. However, a plantation system developed in the Southern Colonies. The climate and soil were well suited to growing crops like rice and indigo. Eventually, tobacco became a major crop. To work their plantations, owners began to import enslaved Africans. As a result, the colonies became part of the trans-Atlantic slave trade.

As more colonists immigrated, they wanted more land. The only way to get land was to push the Native Americans off. This resulted in a number of wars between colonists and Native Americans. By the 1700s, most Native Americans had been killed or forced west.

While taking away the freedom of Africans and killing Native Americans, the colonists were working to keep and enlarge their own rights. About half the colonies were **proprietary colonies**. They were owned by individuals or private companies. The other colonies were **royal colonies**. They belonged to the English monarch.

Putting It All Together

Play "Ten Questions" with a partner. Write ten questions and answers about the information in this lesson. Then take turns asking and answering the questions.

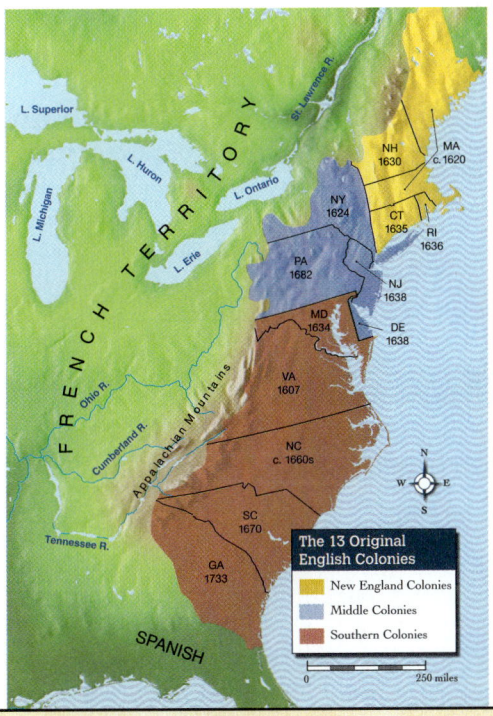

Extension

Joint-stock companies initiated the settlements of Virginia, Plymouth, and Massachusetts Bay. Proprietary colonies included Maryland and Pennsylvania. The remainder of the English colonies were royal colonies.

Stop and Think

Students' paragraphs will vary but should include

Spanish—enslaved the Native Americans, tried to convert them to Christianity

French—traded with Native Americans, tried to convert them to Christianity

Dutch—traded with Native Americans

English—fought with Native Americans

Map Extension

Ask students to use the map on page 231 to answer the following questions:

- Where were the New England colonies located geographically? (They were the farthest north.)
- In what group was Pennsylvania? (Middle Colonies)
- What natural barrier prevented further settlement to the west? (Appalachian Mountains)
- In which region were the largest colonies? (southern)

Putting It All Together

Students' questions and answers will vary but should relate to lesson content.

Age of European Explorations

Lesson Summary

Four major changes marked the effects of the first global age. The Columbian Exchange was the transfer of goods and ideas from the Old and New Worlds. Mercantilism was an economic theory stating that a nation's wealth was dependent on its gold and silver supplies. The death and dislocation of Native Americans due to wars and disease was a third change. Finally, the African slave trade affected colonies and home countries alike.

Lesson Objective

Students will learn about the results of European interaction with the New World.

Focus Your Reading Answers

1. The Columbian Exchange was the sharing of goods and ideas between Europe and the Americas.

2. The colonies sent raw materials to the home countries and became markets for the goods produced by the home countries.

3. Native Americans died in huge numbers because of European colonization. They were enslaved, worked to death, and exposed to diseases against which they had no immunity. They were forced to give up their lands.

4. Many areas of West Africa lost their youngest, strongest, and healthiest people to slavery, leaving no one to carry on the line. The importance of West Africa declined as new kingdoms near the coast became important. Individuals lived in fear and under threat; those who were enslaved faced a miserable life if they managed to survive the Middle Passage.

LESSON 5

The Effects of the First Global Age

European Explorations, 1415-1800

Thinking on Your Own

Look at the vocabulary words. Write them in your notebook. Write a definition for the words that you think you know. Then check the meaning as you read and rewrite your definitions.

The first global age began with Christopher Columbus' voyage in 1492. By the late 1700s, the interactions of Europeans with Asians, Africans, and Americans greatly changed the world. Four of the most important changes occurred between 1492 and 1800. These four changes affected all parts of the world.

focus your reading

What was the Columbian Exchange?

Explain how mercantilism affected European colonies.

What effects did European colonization have on Native Americans?

Summarize how the trans-Atlantic slave trade affected both African nations and individual Africans.

vocabulary

Columbian Exchange
mercantilism
favorable balance of trade
exports
imports
ethnocentric

Columbian Exchange

The **Columbian Exchange** is named for Christopher Columbus who began all the changes. It refers to the sharing of goods and ideas that began with Columbus' first voyage. The diagram on this page shows just some of the foods and animals that Europeans carried from region to region as they moved around the world. They also introduced their own ideas about religion, government, the arts, and language. The Spanish, for example, forced Native

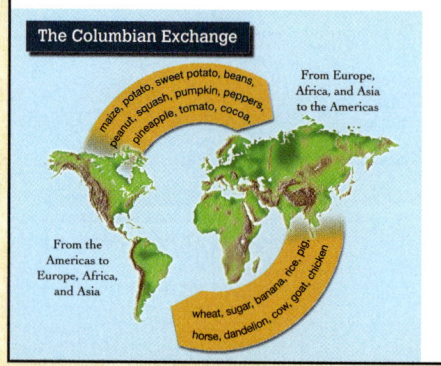

The Columbian Exchange

From Europe, Africa, and Asia to the Americas: maize, potato, sweet potato, beans, peanut, squash, pumpkin, peppers, pineapple, tomato, cocoa

From the Americas to Europe, Africa, and Asia: wheat, sugar, banana, rice, pig, horse, dandelion, cow, goat, chicken

Lesson Vocabulary

Discuss each of the vocabulary terms with students.

The sharing of goods and ideas between Europe and the Americas was known as the *Columbian Exchange*. The *Columbian Exchange* was named for Christopher Columbus. *Mercantilism* is the theory that a nation's wealth is based on how much gold and silver it has. *Mercantilism* played an important role in the relationship of colonies and home countries. A *favorable balance of trade* occurs when the value of a nation's *exports* is higher than the value of its *imports*. Having a *favorable balance of trade* is one way to keep gold and silver in the country. What a country sells to other nations is its *exports*. Raw materials were common *exports* from the colonies to the home countries. What a country buys from other nations is its *imports*. The colonies received *imports* from the home countries.

Europeans during the colonial period felt they were far superior to people in the rest of the world. This is called an *ethnocentric* view.

232 | Chapter 15

Americans to convert to Catholicism and learn Spanish. Native Americans had to give up their own religions and languages.

The exchange was not all one-sided, however. Europeans taught Native Americans how to make iron and copper. Native Americans taught Europeans how to farm unfamiliar land in unfamiliar climates. They also introduced Europeans to corn and tobacco. The early colonists would have starved without corn. It became the major part of their diets. Tobacco became the chief crop in Virginia Colony. Its farmers grew wealthy growing and selling tobacco to European markets.

Mercantilism

European governments encouraged global trade for their own reasons. Across Europe, governments adopted the policy of **mercantilism**. According to mercantilism, the wealth of a nation depends on how much gold and silver it has. One way to keep gold and silver in a country is to keep a **favorable balance of trade**. This occurs when the value of the goods that a nation **exports**, or sells to other nations, is greater than the value of the goods that it **imports**, or buys from other nations.

Dutch fur traders along the Hudson River

Colonies played an important role in mercantilism. Colonies provided their home countries with raw materials to be used for manufacturing. In return, colonies were markets for finished goods from their home countries. Home countries passed laws to keep their colonists from buying goods from other nations.

stop and think

With a partner, read the diagram about the Columbian Exchange. Choose two items from the diagram. Discuss how life in the United States would be different if these two items were not exchanged. Make notes as you discuss your ideas. Then write two paragraphs, one for each item, to explain how life would be different without it.

Picturing History

Founded in 1621, the Dutch West India Company, whose representative is depicted on page 233, existed to undermine the Spanish and Portuguese colonial empires in South America, the West Indies, and the west coast of Africa. Never terribly successful against its more powerful rivals, the Netherlands dissolved the company in 1794.

Stop and Think

Students' choices and paragraphs will vary but should involve two items from the Columbian Exchange diagram on page 232.

Age of European Explorations

Extension

Have students who are interested in economics use library resources or the Internet to investigate the current U.S. balance of trade. If possible, have them gather historic data and present the information in a graph showing the changes over the past 20 years.

Diagram Extension

Ask students to formulate generalizations about each side of the Columbian Exchange, shown on page 232. For example, Europe's contributions included animals, but the Americas' contributions included food items only.

Age of European Explorations

Picturing History

During King Philip's War, the effects of which are shown in the painting on page 234, the Native Americans were led by Metacom, whom the colonists called King Philip. The son of Massasoit, the chief who aided Pilgrim settlers, Metacom had seen his father's generosity ill rewarded and his brother Wamsutta, or Alexander, killed by the colonists, whether from poison or disease. Metacom hoped to forge an alliance to remove the colonists but could not prevail against the superior numbers and firepower of the colonists. Metacom was killed; his wife and son, along with many others, were sold into slavery in the West Indies.

European Explorations, 1415–1800

Native American Defeats

Interactions between Native Americans and Europeans resulted in the deaths of millions of Native Americans. Some experts estimate that 70 million Native Americans lived in the Americas when Christopher Columbus landed on Hispaniola in 1492. About 5 million lived in what is today the United States. Less than 400 years later, there were only 340,000 Native Americans in the United States.

European colonists throughout the Americas murdered, worked to death, and starved to death Native Americans. What European guns did not do, their diseases did. Europeans wanted Native-American labor, wealth, and lands. After the end of the encomienda, Spanish colonists could no longer enslave Native Americans. In various parts of Spanish America, Native Americans were forced to live at missions.

King Philip's War was fought between the Wampanoag and New England colonists in the 1670s.

English colonists had less concern for Christianizing Native Americans. They wanted Native American land and fought deadly wars to gain it. After the American Revolution, the new United States continued the policy of taking Native American land—usually at gunpoint.

The African Slave Trade

Many Europeans did not think that there was anything wrong in enslaving Africans. Slaves had been used by the ancient Egyptians, Greeks, Romans, and Gauls. Europeans thought of themselves as far superior to everyone else in the world. Africans' languages and customs were very different from European ways. Therefore, Africans must be greatly inferior to Europeans. This **ethnocentric** view developed because of the slave trade. It also made the slave trade possible. Otherwise, it would not be possible to enslave another person.

In addition to this attitude toward Africans, the slave trade had many other effects. First, slave raiders kidnapped the

234 Chapter 15

Extension

Students interested in the Native American wars may wish to use library resources or the Internet to find out more about the centuries of conflict. Suggest they use an illustrated timeline to present their findings to the class.

Extension

Students interested in the slave trade may wish to use the Internet or library sources to find out more about the *Amistad*. Have students present their findings to the class.

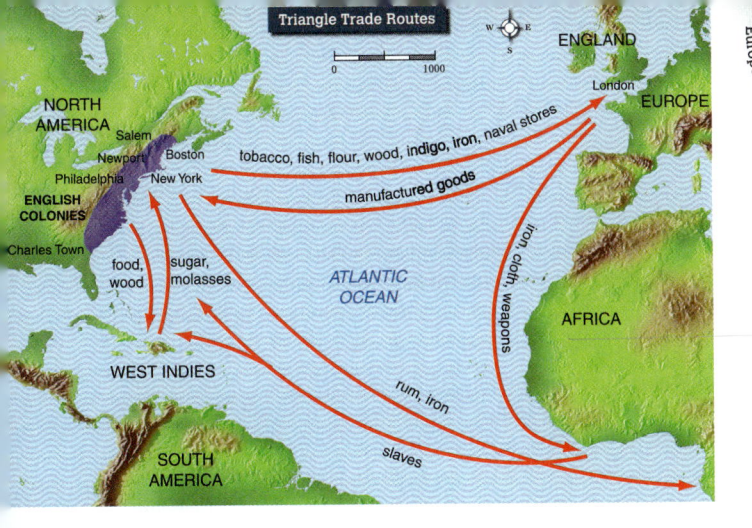

Triangle Trade Routes

A diagram of the cargo hold in a slave ship.

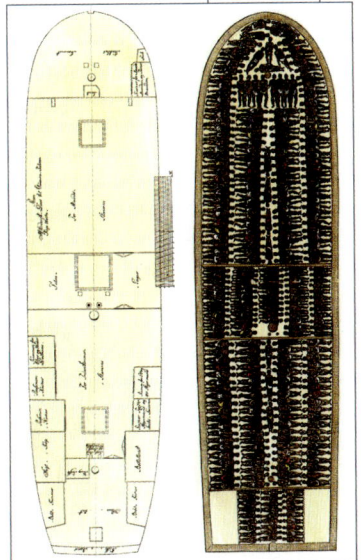

Tunnel slaves ships at House Slaves Goree and off coast Dakar.

youngest and healthiest Africans. This meant that large areas of West Africa were left without young people to have families.

Second, the empires of West Africa became less important. New kingdoms, closer to the coast, rose in importance. These kingdoms were based on trading people in exchange for guns.

Third, the more wealth a ruler had, the more he wanted. A cycle of warfare to gain captives to sell to slavers developed among many African kingdoms. People lived in a state of constant warfare and fear.

Putting It All Together

Imagine you have to teach about European actions either toward Native Americans or toward Africans. Choose one of the two. Make notes to help you explain what happened and why. Review Lessons 2, 3, and 4 if necessary. Present your ideas to a partner as though you were teaching. Ask if your presentation was clear and how you might make it clearer.

Picturing History

The diagram on page 235 depicts a slave ship used during the Middle Passage, the horrific journey across the Atlantic Ocean. The trip took between 21 and 90 days. Ships carried 150–600 people. To prevent a mutiny, male slaves were shackled to each other or to the deck. Still, between 1699 and 1845, there were at least 55 recorded accounts of mutiny. Slaves had an average of 6 feet by 16 inches for an individual space allotment. The death rate on the Middle Passage is estimated at 13 percent. Sharks followed the slave ships, having seen the Africans tossed overboard after succumbing to illness or starvation.

Map Extension

Ask students to use the map on page 235 to answer the following questions:

- Where did sugar come from? (West Indies)
- What goods went from the colonies to London? (tobacco, fish, flour, wood, indigo, iron, naval stores)
- What goods went from London to Africa? (iron, cloth, weapons)
- What did the colonies send to the West Indies? (wood, food)

Picturing History

Declared a World Heritage Site, the 88-acre Goree Island is a tourist destination for many, particularly those of African descent. One of its tunnels is shown on page 235. Some experts doubt that Goree Island was a major slave center and charge that it is being exploited for the tourist dollars it will bring the country of Senegal. Others estimate that some 40 million slaves went through the so-called door of no return.

Putting It All Together

Students' presentations will vary but should be based on European actions toward either Africans or Native Americans.

Chapter Review

1. Students' headlines will vary; possible responses include
   (a) Foreign Invaders Arrive/Strange Men with a Thirst for Gold
   (b) Prophecy Fulfilled?/White Men and Weapons Arrive
   (c) Foreigners March to Capital/Citizens Urged to Hide All Gold

2. Students' headlines will vary. Possible responses include
   (a) Columbus' Hunch Pays Off/Triumphs in Caribbean
   (b) Cortés Quests Gold/Natives Ready to Rebel
   (c) Pizarro Unstoppable/Troops Headed for Cuzco in Triumph

Chapter Summary

European Explorations, 1415–1800

- The first **global age** began with Christopher Columbus' voyage of exploration in 1492.
- Four factors caused Europeans to begin **overseas** exploration in the 1400s: the Crusades; the desire for riches from trade with Asia; inventions including better maps, the **compass**, the **astrolabe**, and a new type of sail; and the desire to expand Christianity.
- China and Japan limited **cargo** trade with Europeans.
- The Portuguese and Spanish divided the New World between them by the **Line of Demarcation**.
- **Conquistadores** set out to explore and conquer the Americas for Spain.
- Spain divided its territory into **viceroyalties** to govern.
- The **encomienda** gave Spanish landholders the right to the labor of Native Americans. Millions died from a lack of **immunity** to European diseases.
- Society in the Spanish colonies was made up of **peninsulares**, **creoles**, **mestizos**, and **mulattos**.
- The Spanish forced Native Americans to live at **missions** and convert to Spanish ways.
- **Joint-stock companies** paid the expenses to set up some **proprietary colonies**. Other colonies were **royal colonies**.
- The effects of the first global age included the **Columbian Exchange** and **mercantilism**. Mercantilism required a **favorable balance of trade** between **exports** and **imports**.
- The slave trade supported **ethnocentrism**.

Chapter Review

1. Imagine you are a Native American. Write two-line headlines for the following events: (a) Columbus lands in the Caribbean, (b) Cortés lands in Mexico, (c) Pizarro marches toward Cuzco.

2. Now write headlines for these events as though you were writing for a Spanish newspaper.

Novel Connections

Below is a list of books that relate to the time period covered in this chapter. The numbers in parentheses indicate the related Thematic Strands of the National Council for the Social Studies (NCSS).

Michael Cadnum. *Ship of Fire*. Viking Children's Books, 2004. (V)

Waldtraut Lewin. *Freedom Beyond the Sea*. Random House Children's Books, 2003. (I, IV, V)

Janet Taylor Lisle. *The Crying Rocks*. Jackson Books/Atheneum Books for Young Readers, 2004. (I, II, IV)

Virginia Schomp. *Around the World in . . . 1500*. Benchmark Books, 2004. (I, III, V, VI)

Michele Torrey. *To the Edge of the World*. Alfred A. Knopf, 2003. (I, VIII)

Stuart Waldman. *We Asked for Nothing: The Remarkable Journey of Cabeza de Vaca*. Mikaya Press, 2004. (I, II, VI)

Skill Builder

Analyzing a Line Graph

A line graph shows information about a topic over a period of time. Usually, the quantity, or amount, is listed along the left side, or vertical axis, of the graph. Time is shown along the bottom, or horizontal axis. A line on the graph shows the ups and downs of the amounts. Sometimes, a graph will have several lines. Each line stands for a separate item.

By reading a line graph, you can see a trend, or pattern, over time. Understanding a trend can help you decide if something is important. For example, a line graph shows increasing shipments of tobacco from Virginia to England between 1650 and 1700. You can decide that tobacco was becoming more and more important to the economy of Virginia.

To read a line graph:

- Read the title of the graph to see what it is about.
- Examine the vertical axis to determine the quantity.
- Examine the horizontal axis to determine the time period.
- Read the key for the graph.
- Examine the lines on the graph.

1 What is the title of the graph?

2 What do the lines represent?

3 When do imports become greater than exports?

4 What trends do the two lines show?

5 What conclusions can be drawn based on the information on the graph?

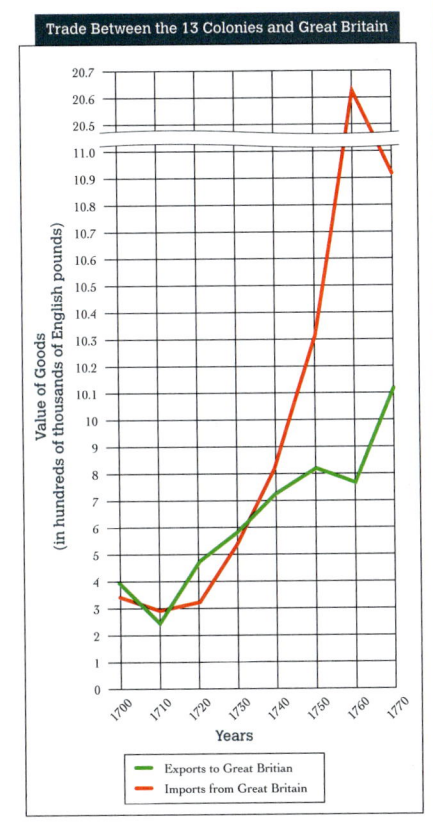

Skill Builder

1 Trade Between the 13 Colonies and Great Britain

2 Exports to Great Britain are in green; imports from Great Britain are in red.

3 About 1735, the imports become greater than the exports.

4 The colonies became increasingly dependent on goods from Great Britain. Although exports to Great Britain increased nearly every year from 1710 on, the level of imports rose more quickly.

5 The colonies were in an unfavorable balance of trade with Great Britain.

Age of European Explorations

Classroom Discussion

Discuss with students some of the broader topics covered in this chapter.

- What are some of the challenges of life in a global society?
- In what ways could descendants of Native Americans and African Americans be compensated for past injustices?
- What kinds of government best foster good trade relationships?

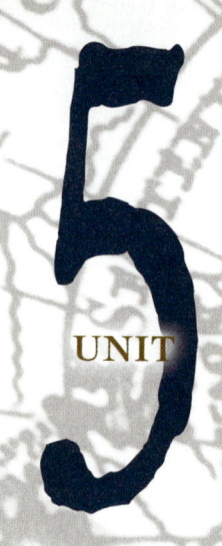

UNIT 5
MONARCHIES AND REVOLUTIONS

Unit Objectives

After studying this unit, students will be able to

- describe the political revolutions in England, the United States, France, and Latin America
- analyze the effects of the Industrial Revolution
- explain the revolution in thought after the Enlightenment

Unit 5 focuses on the revolutions in Britain, the United States, Latin America, and France and the impact of the Scientific and Industrial Revolutions.

Chapter 16, Political Revolutions, examines the political and scientific changes that took place during the seventeenth and early eighteenth centuries.

Chapter 17, Social Revolutions, explores the changes in society brought about by the Industrial Revolution.

The 1600s to the mid-1800s were a time of revolution. Some of the revolutions involved political change. For example, the French overthrew their king and set up a republic. The English replaced one king with another. At the same time, the English greatly limited the power of the monarchy. Across Spanish America, descendants of Spanish settlers fought Spanish armies in order to gain their independence.

The Agricultural and the Industrial revolutions were peaceful. However, their effects were dramatic and far-reaching. The two revolutions began in Europe and spread around the globe. The way people earned their living, and where and how they lived, would never be the same.

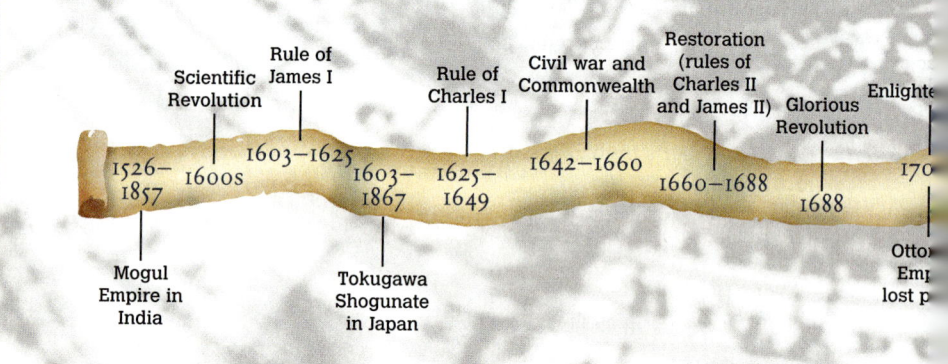

Timeline:
- 1526–1857 Mogul Empire in India
- 1600s Scientific Revolution
- 1603–1625 Rule of James I
- 1603–1867 Tokugawa Shogunate in Japan
- 1625–1649 Rule of Charles I
- 1642–1660 Civil war and Commonwealth
- 1660–1688 Restoration (rules of Charles II and James II)
- 1688 Glorious Revolution
- 170— Enlighte—
- Otto— Emp— lost p—

Getting Started

On the board, write the names of current monarchs; see if students can identify the group as a category. Then ask a student to read aloud the title of the unit and the two paragraphs that follow it on page 238. Ask students to suggest how the two nouns in the unit title are related. Encourage them to continue thinking about the relationship of monarchs and revolutions as they read Unit 5.

Timeline Extension

Ask students to use the timeline to preview each chapter in the unit. Then have them answer the following questions:

- How much time elapsed between the English colonies declaring independence and the beginning of the French Revolution?
- In what regions were wars of independence fought in the early 1800s?
- What era followed the Tokugawa Shogunate in Japan?
- When did the Glorious Revolution occur?

Measuring Time

Explain to students that Chapter 16 examines the political revolutions of England, the United States, Latin America, and France. The events of that era appear on both pages of the timeline. Chapter 17 looks at the impact of the Industrial Revolution. The events of that chapter are on page 239 of the timeline.

Why did the French overthrow the monarchy?

What changes did the Industrial Revolution bring about?

How did the English safeguard their rights?

Collage Answers

1 The French overthrew the monarchy because of the extravagant and callous lifestyle of the French monarchs. While the nation was on the verge of bankruptcy, Louis XVI led a luxurious life and disregarded the call for reform issued by the Estates-General.

2 The Industrial Revolution changed society by making production of goods a factory function, replacing cottage industry. Many people exchanged rural life for urban poverty and disease. Entrepreneurs with money to invest in the new technologies grew wealthy.

3 The English safeguarded their rights by increasing and upholding the rights of Parliament and law above the divine right of monarchs.

Collage Extension

Use the images and questions on page 239 to preview the unit. Ask students what contrasts the questions and pictures suggest about the age of revolution.

3 English colonies declared independence — 1776
Industrial Revolution began — 1780s
French Revolution began — 1789
Napoleon in power in France — 1799–1815
Urbanization in Europe and the United States — 1800–1850
Haiti declared independence — 1804
Wars of independence in Central and South America — 1810–1823
European nations began to colonize Africa — 1830
Meiji Restoration in Japan — 1868–1912

Picturing History

The images on page 239 represent people and places that will be discussed in Unit 5.

1 The top image is of the Hall of Mirrors in the Palace of Versailles. The palace is an example of the opulence of the kings of France.

2 Smoke and other pollutants from the Industrial Revolution blanket the English town of Liverpool in the early 1800s.

3 This is a painting of a session of the British Parliament in the 1700s.

Monarchies and Revolutions

Chapter Summary
Refer to page 262 for a summary of Chapter 16.

Related Transparencies

T-1 World Map

T-19 Venn Diagram

T-20 Concept Web

Key Blacklines

Primary Source—
Declaration of the Rights of Man and Citizen
Declaration of the Rights of Woman and Citizen

CD Extension

Encourage students to use the reading comprehension, vocabulary reinforcement, and interactive timeline activities on the student CD.

Getting Focused

Place students in three groups, assigning each group one of the situations in the Getting Focused questions. Extend the exercise by asking students to develop alternatives to the courses of action taken in the three situations.

Chapter 16 POLITICAL REVOLUTIONS

(1600-1815)

Getting Focused

Skim this chapter to predict what you will be learning.
- Read the lesson titles and subheadings.
- Look at the illustrations and read the captions.
- Examine the maps.
- Review the vocabulary words and terms.

The following actions are described in this chapter:
1) Oliver Cromwell's supporters tried King Charles I, convicted him of being a traitor, and had him beheaded
2) Colonists in Boston rebelled against unfair taxes.
3) Radical Jacobins in Paris arrested and executed thousands of their opponents. Could you defend any of these actions if you believed they advanced freedom and liberty? Discuss this question with a partner. Then write a short paragraph that explains your position.

Picturing History

The Palace of Versailles, shown on page 240, is the largest palace in France. Louis XIV, known as the Sun King, had the palace built because he envied the palace belonging to his superintendent of finances. From 1682 until the beginning of the French Revolution in 1789, it was the royal residence.

Construction went on during the 1700s; about 36,000 workers were involved in the project. The building could house 5,000 people. Now a national monument, it is both a museum and a seat of government offices. In the late 1980s, the French government financed a $70 million restoration. The largest such effort in Versailles' history, it involved more than 80 rooms.

Pre-Reading Discussion

1 Discuss with students any current world situations that involve political revolutions or the overthrowing of government. See if students can identify common causes or characteristics.

2 Ask students to give conditions under which they would support a regime change. Jot these down on a transparency. As you study the chapter, use the list to check each revolution for criteria that the students approve or to add new ideas.

LESSON 1

The Importance of the English Parliament

Thinking on Your Own

This lesson is about how the English gained additional rights. As you read about each event, create a time box. Include important dates and events.

The English people gained certain rights under the Magna Carta. Over the centuries, English monarchs did not give up or take away any more rights.

Monarchs versus Parliament

James I succeeded Elizabeth I on the throne of England. Many monarchs in Europe at that time, such as in France, believed that they ruled by **divine right**. Their right to rule came directly from God. The English monarchs had not adopted this idea until James I. He and his successor, Charles I, believed that the king's power to rule came from God and, therefore, was absolute. No one could question his decisions.

focus your reading

Why did James I and Charles I quarrel with Parliament?

Discuss the causes of the English civil war.

Why is the Glorious Revolution considered so important in English history?

vocabulary

divine right
traitor
commonwealth
military dictatorship
constitutional monarchy
Restoration
Glorious Revolution

Parliament was used to exercising its rights in the name of the English people. The king and Parliament soon clashed. James I lived a life of luxury. He needed more money than existing taxes provided. Parliament refused to pass new taxes. When James wanted to go to war, he also needed new taxes. He called Parliament into session and asked for more money. In order to get it, James I had to agree that the monarch

Political Revolutions 241

Lesson Summary
James I of England believed in rule by divine right. Both James and his heir, Charles I, needed Parliament's approval for taxes. Charles I was beheaded and Oliver Cromwell, a Puritan, ruled a military dictatorship. Shortly after Cromwell's death, Charles II returned to the throne in what was known as the Restoration. James II attempted to return England to Catholicism. Instead, some members of Parliament arranged to have James' eldest daughter, Mary, come to rule. This event is known as the Glorious Revolution.

Lesson Objective
Students will learn about the conflicts in Britain that led to a bloodless revolution.

Focus Your Reading Answers

1 James I and Charles I quarreled with Parliament over the issues of divine right and taxes. Only Parliament could grant power to tax, so the monarchs had to allow Parliament to meet.

2 The English civil war was rooted in religious arguments. Some Puritans believed that the Church of England was too much like the Catholic Church, and they wanted reforms. James and Charles persecuted Puritans and wanted the church to remain as it was. Charles sent soldiers to Parliament to arrest the Puritans, who escaped. Cromwell's forces defeated the king's army and convicted Charles, who was beheaded as a traitor.

3 The Glorious Revolution is important because it affirmed rule by Parliament, not by divine right of a monarch.

Lesson Vocabulary
Introduce each of the following vocabulary terms to students.

Explain that *divine right* is the idea that monarchs have the right to rule from God. English monarchs believed in *divine right*.

A *traitor* is one who is disloyal to a country or betrays that country to an enemy. Charles I was convicted as a *traitor*.

A *commonwealth* is a republic. Parliament declared England a *commonwealth* after Cromwell took power. A *military dictatorship* is rule by one person, backed by the armed forces. Cromwell set up a *military dictatorship*. A *constitutional monarchy* limits the power of the monarch by law.

Restoration means returning something to its original form. The *Restoration* in England happened when Charles II was brought back to rule.

The *Glorious Revolution* was the triumph of English law over *divine right*. William of Orange and Mary became rulers at the *Glorious Revolution*.

Political Revolutions 241

Picturing History

Parliament, shown in session on page 242, met by invitation of the monarch. In 1605, both Parliament and the king were nearly blown up in the so-called Gunpowder Plot, headed by a group of Catholic extremists. They placed barrels of gunpowder in underground storage beneath Parliament, planning to destroy both the Puritans and King James. The plot was discovered before the gunpowder was ignited. The leaders and several others were executed after the plot was discovered. Persecution against Catholics increased; many were imprisoned.

Picturing History

Oliver Cromwell, whose portrait appears at the bottom of page 242, was a member of the House of Commons and a comparatively wealthy man. Cromwell, who had become a Puritan only a few years before, led his cavalry, called Roundheads, into battle against Charles I. All of his soldiers were singing psalms as they went into battle.

---

could not make laws without the approval of Parliament.

In 1625, Charles I succeeded his father. By 1628, Charles I was badly in need of money and called Parliament into session. Before it would agree to new taxes, Parliament forced him to agree to the Petition of Right. This document added to the basic rights of the English people. Parliament alone had the right to impose taxes. Charles I got the money and promptly dismissed Parliament.

Parliament in the 1600s

The English Civil War

The troubles of James I, and especially of Charles I, were not just economic. The two kings also made enemies of the Puritans. They believed that the Church of England was still too much like the Roman Catholic Church.

Since Henry VIII, many large landowners and wealthy merchants had become Puritans. They were elected to the House of Commons and opposed James I and Charles I. Although Protestant, the two kings strongly supported the Church of England as it was. Both kings persecuted the Puritans.

In 1640, Charles called Parliament into session. He needed money for a war against Scotland. The Puritans were now in control of Parliament. Before giving Charles I the money, Parliament passed a law that the monarch could not dismiss Parliament unless it agreed. Charles I agreed. Once he got the money, he marched into Parliament with a unit of soldiers to arrest the Puritan leaders, but they escaped. The fight between Charles I and the Puritans exploded into civil warfare in 1642.

Oliver Cromwell

The leader of the Puritans was Oliver Cromwell. He pulled together an army of supporters known as Roundheads. Charles' supporters were known as Cavaliers. In 1646, Cromwell's forces defeated Charles' Cavaliers. Charles I surrendered and was tried, convicted, and beheaded as a **traitor** in 1649.

Extension

Charles convened and dismissed three Parliaments within the first four years of his 24-year reign. After an 11-year gap, during which Charles ruled by himself, he needed funds to support a war against Scotland. He called the Short Parliament in 1640, dissolving it to prevent discussion of issues of concern to the legislature. Only a year later, after Scottish rebels invaded England, Charles called what became known as the Long Parliament. This was the session that demanded it not be dismissed without its consent. When the king discovered that Parliament was forming its own militia, he gathered his troops and went into battle. At his trial before the House of Commons, Charles refused to defend himself, believing that the judges there had no legal right or power over him.

Cromwell seized control of the government. The House of Commons was allowed to remain. The House of Lords was abolished. The new Parliament ended the monarchy and declared England a republic, or **commonwealth**. A Council of State governed in place of the monarch. The members of the Council were chosen from the House of Commons. By 1653, Cromwell could not control his new Parliament. He dismissed it and the Council. In their place, he set up a **military dictatorship**. He ruled alone with support from the army.

Cromwell tried to turn England into a strict Puritan nation. However, most English people were satisfied with the Church of England. Most English people also did not want a republic. They wanted a **constitutional monarchy**. Under this system of government, the power of the monarch is limited by law.

The Glorious Revolution

The Commonwealth quickly fell apart after Cromwell's death in 1658. By 1660, Parliament had asked Charles' son to return as King Charles II. The period between 1660 and 1688 is known as the **Restoration** because the monarchy was brought back.

The Church of England was also restored as the nation's official religion. At the same time, Parliament passed laws limiting the rights of Catholics and Puritans. Charles II was a Protestant—at least in name. Charles also cancelled the laws against Catholics and Puritans.

When Charles died, his brother James II became king. He was a Catholic. In 1687, he granted freedom of worship to Catholics and Puritans. Some members of Parliament thought that James II meant to return England to Catholicism and also limit Parliament's power. These wealthy nobles, landowners, and merchants plotted against James.

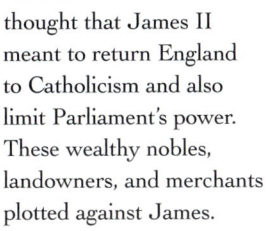

Men in the 1600s wore long hair. The Roundheads cut off their hair to distinguish them from Charles' supporters.

Charles' supporters were Cavaliers.

Charles II returned to London from exile 1660.

Political Revolutions | 243

stop and think

Write a summary of one section in this lesson. Share your summary with a partner. Ask your partner to make sure that you included all the most important ideas.

Picturing History

Roundheads and Cavaliers, shown on page 243, were distinguished by their clothing as well as by their hairstyles. Point out to students the more rich and ornate clothing style of the Cavaliers.

Stop and Think

Students' summaries will vary but should reflect a section of the lesson content, such as the English civil war, monarchs versus Parliament, or the Glorious Revolution.

Picturing History

Charles II, shown at the bottom left of page 243, returned to the throne almost by default. He had fled to Europe after Cromwell assumed power. Cromwell was offered the crown and refused it, hoping for a republic. After Cromwell's death, his son Richard ruled briefly before resigning, lacking his father's ability. On his deathbed, Charles II admitted to being a Catholic; under his brother James, Catholics were given powerful positions, and those who attended unauthorized worship were arrested.

Extension

Two of the greatest and most influential Puritan writers were John Bunyan and John Milton. Invite students interested in literature to find out more about these men using library resources or the Internet. Have them present their findings to the class by using the Student Presentation Builder on the student CD.

Political Revolutions | 243

Picturing History

William and Mary, depicted on page 244, followed a policy of religious tolerance. According to the English Bill of Rights, however, Roman Catholics were not permitted to rule. By mandating that monarchs be Anglican, Parliament dispelled the fear of a Catholic regaining the throne. This provision was an outgrowth not only of James II's open Roman Catholicism, but of the birth of his son to his Catholic queen, Mary.

Chart Extension

Discuss with students how these provisions of the English Bill of Rights affected both Parliament and the monarchy.

Putting It All Together

Flowcharts/timelines will vary. Possible response:

James I rules, 1508; Charles I rules, 1625; Charles calls Parliament, 1640; civil war begins, 1642; Cromwell's forces victorious, 1646; Charles I beheaded, 1649; Cromwell sets up a military dictatorship, 1653; Cromwell dies, 1658; Charles II restored, 1660; James II becomes king; Glorious Revolution, 1688.

William and Mary accepted Parliament's request for the English Bill of Rights

They negotiated with Mary, James' oldest daughter, and her husband, William, the Duke of Orange, to become king and queen. In 1688, William led 14,000 soldiers in an invasion of England. James II fled to France.

Before William and Mary could be crowned, however, Parliament forced them to sign the English Bill of Rights. The monarch now ruled by the power of Parliament, not God. This event became known as the **Glorious Revolution**.

English Bill of Rights

Parliament:
- alone had the right to make laws
- alone had the right to impose taxes
- had to agree to the suspension of any laws—the monarch could not act alone
- had to agree to maintain an army during peacetime
- was to meet yearly
- was guaranteed free elections

Citizens' rights that were confirmed included:
- the forbidding of large bail and fines
- the forbidding of cruel and unusual punishment
- the right to a jury trial

Putting It All Together

Create a sequence flowchart to help you remember when events happened in this lesson. Add a date to each event to turn it into a timeline. Share your flowchart/timeline with a partner. Take turns quizzing each other about time periods between events.

Picturing History

The earliest European telescopes, like the one shown on page 245, were made in Holland. At first, they could magnify items only three times. In 1609, Galileo created one that magnified 20 times. Using this telescope, he discovered Jupiter's satellites and noted that the moon's surface was mountainous rather than smooth.

LESSON 2

Scientific Revolution and Enlightenment

Thinking on Your Own

Progress was an important concept to people during the Enlightenment. They believed that the Scientific Revolution and Enlightenment thinking would bring progress to humankind. Write a list of five events from your lifetime or earlier in history that you think show progress. After you have written your list, write a sentence to explain why each event shows progress. As you read, add to your list of events and sentences.

In the 1600s, people began to question old ideas about the world around them. They used reason, or rational thinking, to look for new answers. This questioning spirit led to the Scientific Revolution and the Age of Reason, or the **Enlightenment**.

focus your reading

Summarize the controversy over the work of Copernicus, Kepler, and Galileo.

Why were the philosophes important?

Explain how Adam Smith affected economic thinking.

vocabulary

Enlightenment
scientific method
natural law
Scientific Revolution
natural rights
social contract
laissez-faire economics
philosophes

The Scientific Revolution

The modern study of science began in Europe in the 1600s. The systematic process for gathering and analyzing evidence is called the **scientific method**. Francis Bacon developed the idea.

Bacon called for scientists to develop theories, or hypotheses, and then test them in carefully designed experiments. The scientists would observe what happened during the experiments.

Political Revolutions 245

Lesson Summary

The Scientific Revolution, or Age of Enlightenment, occurred during the 1600s as people questioned old ideas.

Copernicus, Kepler, and Galileo alarmed some people with their idea that the sun did not revolve around Earth, but rather the opposite. John Locke and Adam Smith were two influential thinkers. Locke's ideas about government and the natural rights of people were widely spread and discussed. Adam Smith's ideas about laissez-faire economics have affected modern economics.

The French philosophes wanted to use reason for the benefit of society.

Lesson Objective

Students will learn about the Enlightenment's new ideas in science, economics, and literature.

Focus Your Reading Answers

1 Copernicus published a book that contradicted Ptolemy's theory that the sun revolved around Earth. Kepler extended Copernicus's ideas. Galileo's observations confirmed that Earth revolved around the sun.

2 The philosophes tried to improve society using reason. The ideas of Montesquieu, Voltaire, and Diderot influenced government, literature, and learning.

3 Adam Smith developed the idea of laissez-faire economics, which states that governments should leave the economy alone, letting supply and demand work freely.

Lesson Vocabulary

Discuss each of the vocabulary terms with students.

The *Enlightenment* was an age of scientific inquiry and reason. The *Enlightenment* began in the 1600s. The *scientific method* is a way to gather and analyze evidence. Francis Bacon developed the *scientific method*. The laws of nature are the basis of *natural law*. Scientists discovered *natural law* based on observing and experimenting. The *Scientific Revolution* was a period of rapid scientific discoveries and changes.

Natural rights are rights belonging to people by their nature as human beings. John Locke taught that *natural rights* included life, liberty, and the right to possession. *Social contract* exists between government and the people. *Social contract* was another of Locke's ideas.

The idea that government should do nothing to regulate the economy is known as *laissez-faire economics*. Adam Smith first developed the notion of *laissez-faire economics*. The French philosophers, or *philosophes*, wanted to use reason for the good of society. Voltaire was one of the *philosophes*.

Political Revolutions 245

Picturing History

Galileo, depicted at the left of page 246, was a mathematics professor at the University of Padua when he began making improvements to the telescope. Using his mathematical skills, he realized that to obtain a greater magnification, the telescope needed a strong concave lens and a weak convex lens. To get the lenses the correct strength, Galileo learned to grind them himself. He demonstrated the telescope to the Senate of Venice. From Venetian bell towers, senators gazed out on ships at sea. They clearly saw the military advantages of such a device.

Picturing History

Copernicus, shown at the bottom right of page 246, had his work approved by Pope Clement VII in 1530. This sort of precaution was necessary due to the Inquisition. The pope asked for a copy of Copernicus's complete manuscript, which was not available until 1543, the year of Copernicus's death.

Political Revolutions, 1600–1815

The results would either prove or disprove the theory. Through experimentation and observations, scientists would learn how things in nature such as the planets, weather, and plants worked. From their observations, scientists would be able to figure out the laws of nature, or **natural law**.

Using experiments and observation gave rise to the **Scientific Revolution**. Scientists were making so many discoveries and overturning so many ideas that it seemed like a revolution. Not everyone was happy with the changes.

Perhaps most alarming to many Europeans were the ideas of Nicholas Copernicus, Johannes Kepler, and Galileo Galilei. Each man's work built on the ideas of the other. They all investigated the relation between Earth and the other planets.

Ptolemy, a Greek astronomer in the A.D. 200s, developed the idea that the planets revolved around the earth. In 1543, Copernicus published a book disagreeing with this theory. He stated that all the planets, including the earth, revolve around the sun. The Catholic Church decided to accept Ptolemy's theory and taught that the earth was the center of the universe.

In the early 1600s, Kepler further developed Copernicus's theory. Around the same time, Galileo used the telescope to observe the sky. What he saw confirmed that the earth moved around the sun. He also developed some theories of his own. His work attracted the attention of many Europeans—including the Catholic Church. Galileo was tried and convicted of heresy by the Inquisition. He had to recant, or take back, his theory or be burned alive. He agreed to recant. However, as he left the court, he supposedly said under his breath, "The earth does move." Copernicus, Kepler, and Galileo, however, were correct. Their theories have been proved to be true.

Galileo demonstrates using a telescope in this fresco.

Nichola Copern develop theories about th univers

246 Chapter 16

Extension

Suggest that students find out more about Galileo's life and experiments by using library resources or the Internet. Those students who have an interest in mathematics or science will find many ideas to pursue. Other students may want to know more about Galileo's daughters, whom he placed in a convent, or about Galileo's trial before the Inquisition.

European Contributions to Science

Andreas Vesalius (1514–1564)	described the structures and organs of the human body
William Harvey (1578–1657)	described the heart and blood circulation system in humans
Anton van Leeuwenhoek (1632–1723)	discovered cells in living matter using a simple microscope
Isaac Newton (1642–1727)	developed the Universal Law of Gravitation; explained why planets orbit the sun
Joseph Priestly (1733–1804)	discovered oxygen
Antoine Lavoisier (1743–1794)	developed a system for naming chemical elements; considered the founder of modern chemistry
Edward Jenner (1749–1823)	discovered a vaccine for smallpox

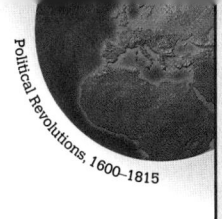

Enlightenment Thinkers

The Scientific Revolution influenced European philosophers as well as scientists. Philosophers tried to apply principles of rational thought to the study of human life. By using the scientific method and reason, they hoped to figure out ways to improve conditions for people.

One of the most important English philosophers was John Locke. He believed that people have certain **natural rights** that belong to them as human beings. Among these rights are life, liberty, and property, or belongings. Locke also believed that government is necessary to ensure that people keep those rights. However, the powers of government should be limited. According to Locke, a **social contract** exists between people and their government. If a government does not govern justly, the people have the right to overthrow that government.

Another important British thinker was Adam Smith. He developed the idea of **laissez-faire economics**. He believed that when it came to the economy, governments should do nothing. The natural forces in the economy, such as supply and demand, should be allowed freedom to work. That means the role of government is greatly limited. For example, Smith believed that government should protect its citizens from invasion by an enemy, but not from poverty.

stop and think

Examine the table "European Contributions to Science." How do you think these contributed to human progress? With a partner, choose two ideas. Discuss how each discovery or invention has made a difference to people over the centuries. Write two or three paragraphs to explain your ideas for each discovery or invention.

Political Revolutions | 247

Table Extension

The table offers a chance to challenge students to create devices to help them remember the inventors and their contributions. For example, *Jenner* and *smallpox* both have double letters; "OP" could stand for "oxygen/Priestly," and so on. Allow students to work in pairs, then share their results with the class. Remind students that these devices are meant to be helpful, so whatever works, even if it sounds crazy, is fine.

Stop and Think

Students' choices and paragraphs will vary but should be based on two of the contributions mentioned in the table on page 247.

Picturing History

Adam Smith, pictured on page 247, spent ten years writing his most famous book, *The Wealth of Nations*, which was published in 1776. Two years later, Smith went to Edinburgh to accept an appointment as commissioner of customs. He remained in that city until his death in 1790.

Extension

John Locke's father was a Puritan lawyer who, during the civil war, fought for Cromwell. Friends urged Locke to become a Church of England priest, but Locke turned his attention to science. He became one of the most noted medical practitioners of his time. Locke was suspected of disloyalty to the government for his association with the Earl of Shaftesbury, who had been indicted for high treason. For his own safety, Locke spent the five years prior to the Glorious Revolution in Holland.

Picturing History

The painting on page 248, Anicet Lemonnier's *Madame de Geoffrin's Salon*, depicts a group of people listening to one of Voltaire's plays being read. Voltaire's 1759 novella *Candide* continues to be popular in a musical version composed by Leonard Bernstein with playwright Lillian Hellman. The musical, later revised by Stephen Sondheim, became a hit on Broadway in 1973 and, in 1982, was added to the repertoire of the New York City Opera.

Putting It All Together

Students' choices of characters will vary but should be based on people mentioned in this lesson.

Extension

The *Encyclopedia* had 28 volumes; later, an additional seven volumes were added. The French Council of State suppressed several volumes of the work, which was also under attack from Jesuit censorship. Diderot persisted, obtaining permission for the volumes to be published. A revision, arranged topically rather than alphabetically, was published in 1782, but was not completed until 1832, the 50th anniversary of the first volume's publication.

Political Revolutions, 1600–1815

The Philosophes

A group of French philosophers, *philosophes* in French, also attempted to use reason for the good of society. Three **philosophes** stand out for their contributions.

Charles-Louis de Secondat, the Baron de Montesquieu, studied a number of European governments. In 1748, he published his findings. He greatly admired the English government. The English had created a separation of powers by having three branches of government: executive, legislative, and judicial. Each branch was to limit the power of the others through a system of checks and balances. Although Parliament was fast becoming the dominant branch of government, Montesquieu helped make the idea of a separation of powers popular. This idea influenced the future leaders of the United States of America.

French salons were a meeting place for the philosophes.

Another important philosophe was François-Marie Arouet, or Voltaire. He was a poet, novelist, and playwright as well as a philosophe. Some of his themes were the need for religious toleration, justice for all, free speech, and an end to the slave trade. He attacked corruption in government as well as in the Catholic Church. His enemies had him arrested and sent into exile where he continued to write.

Denis Diderot published the 28-volume *Encyclopedia*, or *Classified Dictionary of the Sciences, Arts, and Trades*. It took from 1751 to 1772 to complete and contains articles by important philosophes. It found customers among the French middle class, including doctors, lawyers, and teachers. The *Encyclopedia* was also translated into other languages and spread the ideas of the Enlightenment as far as the Americas.

Putting It All Together

Play "Who Am I?" with a partner. First, choose five people from this lesson. Then write two or three sentences to describe, or identify, each person. End each identification with the question "Who am I?" Take turns asking and answering the questions with a partner.

248 | Chapter 16

Extension

Nine colonies sent representatives to the Stamp Act Congress of 1765, which convened in New York City at the suggestion of James Otis. This moderate group originated the phrase "no taxation without representation." Merchants in New York City, Philadelphia, and Boston agreed not to import British goods until the Stamp Act was repealed. Rather than use the stamps, the courts also closed. British exports to the colonies declined by more than 300,000 pounds sterling, creating financial difficulties in England. London merchants called for a repeal of the act. Parliament voted to repeal the Stamp Act less than a year after it was instituted.

LESSON 3

The 13 English Colonies Rebel

Thinking on Your Own

What do you already know about the American Revolution? Write a bulleted list of 10 facts in your notebook. As you read this lesson, add new facts to your list.

The rivalry among European nations spilled over into their colonies around the world. In the 1750s, France and Great Britain were at war against each other in India and North America. When the French and Indian War was over, Great Britain controlled its 13 colonies in North America. It also controlled Canada and all French territory west of the Mississippi River. Great Britain also had won control of a large part of India from the French.

focus your reading

What were the causes of the American Revolution?

Explain how the British lost the American War for Independence.

The new United States government was based on what ideas?

vocabulary

possessions
mercantilism
revenue tax
federal system
ratify

The war and its new **possessions** put an economic strain on the British Empire. The need for money became a major problem between Britain and its 13 North American colonies.

Causes of the American Revolution

European countries operated under the policy of **mercantilism**. Colonies existed to make the home country rich. One way to do this was to make sure that trade with the colonies was regulated, or managed, to the home country's benefit. Before the Stamp Act, this was the purpose of taxes imposed on the colonies. The Stamp Tax was a different kind of tax. Its purpose was not to regulate trade, but to raise money. It was a **revenue tax**.

Political Revolutions 249

Lesson Summary

The British won a war against France but had spent great sums of money to do so. They wanted to gain revenue from the American colonies and instituted a stamp tax. The unpopularity of the tax led to disagreements, repeal of the tax, and ultimately to war. With the help of France, Spain, and the Netherlands (the Dutch Republic), the colonies defeated the British.

The Articles of Confederation provided a federal form of government. Power would be divided among three branches of government, with a system of checks and balances. The Constitution was adopted and a Bill of Rights added. The framers borrowed ideas from the Enlightenment and from the British form of government.

Lesson Objective

Students will learn about the causes and results of the American Revolution.

Focus Your Reading Answers

1 The American Revolution was caused by a series of taxes that the British imposed and by Britain's unwillingness to see the colonists' viewpoint.

2 The British lost the war due to George Washington's leadership and the help of European nations who sided against the British by supporting the colonists with aid and soldiers.

3 The new government was based on Montesquieu's ideas of three branches of government with checks and balances. It also included Locke's ideas about the natural rights of people and was based on many ideas in English law.

Lesson Vocabulary

Discuss each of the vocabulary terms with students.

Mercantilism refers to a policy prevalent in the 17th century, which held that a nation's prosperity depended upon a vast supply of silver and gold.

Lands controlled by a home country are its *possessions*. England's new *possessions* created economic strain for the empire. A *revenue tax* is meant to raise money. The stamp tax was a *revenue tax*.

In a *federal system*, power is shared among national, state, and local governments. The founding fathers set up a *federal system*.

To approve a document is to *ratify* it. At least nine states had to *ratify* the Constitution.

Political Revolutions 249

Picturing History

British soldiers, as depicted on page 250, wore red woolen coats and were called Lobsterbacks and Redcoats. They were hindered by their equipment as well as by their uniforms. Their boots weighed 12 pounds (5.5 kg). The 40-mile trip (67 km) from Fort Ticonderoga to Saratoga required two months, resulting in the loss of many men to American snipers.

Picturing History

The members of the Second Continental Congress, shown in the painting at the bottom of page 250, were divided for some time on the question of independence. Several representatives wanted to reconcile with the home country. Not until June 11, 1776, did Congress name a five-man committee to draft a statement of independence. On June 28, two days before the assigned deadline, Jefferson submitted the document, which continued to be debated in a room with the doors and windows shut, for fear of spies. When the vote was taken on the morning of July 2, no colony refused to vote for independence, although New York abstained.

Under this law, colonists had to pay a tax for all kinds of printed materials ranging from newspapers, playing cards, and wills to marriage licenses. An official stamp on the document proved that the tax had been paid.

The colonists reacted swiftly with loud cries of "No taxation without representation." Colonists claimed that only their own colonial legislatures could impose taxes on them. Parliament and the king rejected this idea. They claimed that Parliament represented all citizens including those in the colonies. Therefore, Parliament could impose taxes on the colonists.

Colonists reacted violently to the Stamp Tax. Parliament repealed the Stamp Act in 1766. However, it refused to agree with the colonists' view of taxation.

The disagreement flared again and again throughout the 1760s and early 1770s. By 1775, colonists were stockpiling weapons. The first shots of the American Revolution were fired at Lexington, Massachusetts, early on the morning of April 18. By summer, the Second Continental Congress had organized an army. The following summer, on July 4, 1776, the Congress adopted the Declaration of Independence. In writing this document, Thomas Jefferson used many ideas from John Locke about the social contract.

British uniforms were impractical for fighting the North American colonists.

The War of American Independence

The Americans had many disadvantages in their battle for independence from Great Britain. They faced the largest and strongest professional army and navy in the world. The American army was made up of untrained recruits who served for only short periods of time. Their navy never had more than a handful of ships.

The Americans also had advantages. The first and possibly greatest advantage was their leadership—men like George Washington,

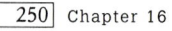

Extension

Students may wish to use library resources or the Internet to investigate the recent restoration project for the Declaration of Independence and the Bill of Rights. These documents are on display in Washington, D.C., at the National Archives.

Thomas Jefferson, Benjamin Franklin, and John Adams. Washington put together an army, chose good officers, and inspired his men to fight.

Benjamin Franklin negotiated with France to enter the war on the side of the United States. Spain and the Dutch Republic also joined against their old enemy, Great Britain. France sent soldiers and ships as well as money and supplies. With the help of the French navy, Washington was able to block Lord Cornwallis' retreat at Yorktown, Virginia. Cornwallis surrendered in October 1781. The war was over and a new nation emerged.

Setting Up the New Nation

The first written plan of government for the new nation was the Articles of Confederation. The states deliberately adopted a plan that did not create a strong central government. By 1787, however, it was clear that the Articles did not cover the many issues that came before the new government.

That summer, state delegates met in Philadelphia. Rather than revise the Articles, they wrote a new plan. The United States Constitution set up a **federal system**. Power was shared between a national, or central, government and the state governments. Among the powers given to the national government were the powers to establish an army, regulate trade, impose taxes, and create a national system of money.

The central government was divided into executive, legislative, and judicial branches. A system of checks and balances was developed so that no one branch of government could gain too much power over the others. The writers of the Constitution borrowed both ideas from Montesquieu, the French philosopher. Before the Constitution could go into effect, nine of the thirteen states had to **ratify**, or approve, the document. A number of Americans did not think that the Constitution went far enough. They wanted certain rights

Picturing History

The Battle of Saratoga, shown on page 251, was supposed to be a British victory. Three British armies—Burgoyne's, Howe's, and one from the west—were to meet and entrap the American army. The plan went awry; the western army never arrived, and Howe set off on other conquests. By the time the British army reached Saratoga, the Americans had fortified the site with cannons. When the Americans learned that the British army had arrived, farmers joined in. The American army outnumbered the British three to one. British casualties were four times those of the Americans.

Extension

Invite students to learn more about the roles of women in the Revolutionary War, including those who served in the colonial army dressed as men. Deborah Sampson, for example, served as a soldier for three years and was wounded twice. Allow time for students to share their findings with the class.

Picturing History

The cartoon on page 252 depicts the struggle to get nine colonies to ratify the Constitution. Students may wish to investigate the use of cartoons, humorous songs, and clever rhymes in the American Revolution.

Stop and Think

Students' headlines will vary. Possible responses:

(a) Stamp Act Passed/Colonies Declare No More Imports

(b) Shots at Lexington!/Weapons Stockpile Raided

(c) Congress Signs Declaration of Independence/States to Set Up New Government

(d) Washington Becomes Leader of Continental Army/Past Experience Most Valuable

(e) France Is with Us!/Victory at Saratoga Key

(f) Brits Going Home!/Cornwallis Surrenders at Yorktown

> The Ninth PILLAR erected!
> "The Ratification of the Conventions of nine States, shall be sufficient for the establishment of this Constitution, between the States so ratifying the same." Art. vii.
> INCIPIENT MAGNI PROCEDERE MENSES.
>
> From the Independent Chronicle and Universal Advertiser, Boston, Thursday June 26, 1788.

This political cartoon depicts the first nine states to ratify the U.S. Constitution and the t[wo] states tha[t] soon followed.

guaranteed by the Constitution. The battle over ratification was fierce in some states. Finally, an agreement was reached. If the Constitution was ratified, one of the first acts of the new Congress would be to add a Bill of Rights.

The Constitution was ratified in 1788 and the Bill of Rights was added. These first 10 amendments to the Constitution guarantee freedoms of religion, speech, press, assembly, and petition; the right to bear arms; freedom from housing soldiers against one's will; freedom from unlawful search and seizure; the right to a fair and speedy trial and to a trial by jury; and freedom from excessive bail, fines, and punishment.

Many of these rights are the same as Americans had as English colonists. These rights are also similar to the natural rights identified by philosophers of the Enlightenment. To many people in the 1700s, the American Revolution was the fulfillment of Enlightenment ideals.

Putting It All Together

Write an explanation of how the separation of powers and system of checks and balances works. Share your explanation with a partner. Then incorporate your notes with the bulleted notes you wrote at the start of this lesson to create a short essay about the outcomes of the American Revolution.

stop and think

Write two-line headlines for the following events: (a) passage of the Stamp Act, (b) Battle of Lexington, (c) Declaration of Independence, (d) Washington is made general of the army, (e) France becomes an ally, (f) Cornwallis surrenders. Share your headlines with a partner. Ask your partner to suggest words that could ma[ke] your headlines more interesting or excitin[g].

Putting It All Together

Students' explanations and essays will vary but should discuss separation of powers, checks and balances, and facts about the American Revolution.

Picturing History

The color engraving shown on page 253 depicts revolutionary women marching on the Palace of Versailles on October 5, 1789.

LESSON 4

Napoleon and the French Revolution

Thinking on Your Own

As you read this lesson, create a cause-and-effect flowchart for each event. Remember that a cause may have more than one effect, or result. A result may have more than one cause. Then write a paragraph about one cause-and-effect event.

Through the centuries, French monarchs kept a tight hold on their power. The one thing they did not control was their expenses. By 1789, France was on the verge of bankruptcy.

To raise taxes, King Louis XVI needed the agreement of the Estates-General—France's legislature. It was made up of three **Estates**, or groups. The First Estate was the **clergy**. The Second Estate was the nobility, who owned about a third of the nation's land and held all the high government posts. Everyone else was a commoner and made up the Third Estate. The First and Second Estates paid no taxes. France's entire tax burden fell on the poor Third Estate.

focus your reading

Explain what the National Assembly accomplished.

What was the sequence of events during the National Convention?

Why did Napoleon rule France for so short a time?

vocabulary

Estates
clergy
Napoleonic Code
nationalism

National Assembly

On May 5, 1789, the Estates-General met for the first time in 175 years. Each Estate met by itself and had one vote. Members of the Third Estate feared what would happen if this practice continued. Their attempts at reform would fail.

The Third Estate wanted the Estates-General to meet and count each member's vote individually. Because some members of the

Women march on the Palace of Versailles on October 5, 1789.

Lesson Vocabulary

Discuss each of the vocabulary terms with students.

Another word for groups within France's legislature is *Estates*. There were three *Estates*: *clergy*, nobility, and commoners.

The *clergy* are religious leaders. The *clergy* made up the First *Estate*.

The *Napoleonic Code* was a system of law reform. The *Napoleonic Code* was made up of seven law codes.

A strong feeling of loyalty for one's own culture is called *nationalism*. A spirit of *nationalism* grew across Europe because of French rule.

Lesson Summary

The first meeting of France's Estates-General in 1775 led to calls for reform. Although he would not get the money he needed in taxes, Louis XVI did not agree to them. In 1789, a mob began the revolution in Paris. The National Assembly, composed of members of the former Third Estate, approved a new constitution. During the chaos of rule by the Directory, Napoleon Bonaparte took power. He ended wars with other European powers, but new ones began in an effort to check his desire for an empire. Napoleon did reform and simplify France's law codes but claimed more and more power. European powers joined to defeat him.

Lesson Objective

Students will learn about the French Revolution and the rule of Napoleon.

Focus Your Reading Answers

1 The National Assembly wrote a constitution and a Declaration of the Rights of Man. It ended the privileges of the clergy and the nobility. The Catholic Church came under the government's rule.

2 During the three-year rule of the National Convention, the monarchy ended; Louis XVI was condemned and beheaded; the radical Jacobins began a Reign of Terror; and a new constitution was adopted.

3 All of the major European nations joined to defeat Napoleon, who had declared himself emperor and fought for power in Europe.

Political Revolutions | 253

Time Box Extension

Provide four different-colored index cards to each student. Ask them to select a color for each ruling group: monarchy, National Convention, Directory, and Napoleon. For each period of rule, have them write down specific dates and events. They can associate colors with events to enhance retention.

Chart Extension

Give students copies of the English Bill of Rights and the first ten amendments to the United States Constitution. Have them compare those documents with the Declaration of the Rights of Man, noting similarities and differences in a Venn diagram.

First and Second Estates had agreed on the need for reforms, all three Estates could force Louis XVI to agree to the changes. Only then would he get his money.

Louis refused to allow the three Estates to vote together. The Third Estate renamed itself the National Assembly and began work on a constitution. Louis locked the Assembly out of its meeting hall. Members simply moved to the palace tennis court. They took what is called the Tennis Court Oath. They swore they would not disband until they had written a new constitution.

Louis began secretly bringing in troops to drive out the Third Estate. They were saved when the people of Paris took to the streets in rebellion. On July 14, 1789, a mob destroyed the Bastille, a hated Paris prison. This day marks the beginning of the French Revolution.

The National Assembly eliminated privileges of the First and Second Estates. The Assembly approved the Declaration of the Rights of Man. Like the American Declaration of Independence, it stated the reasons for the Revolution.

In 1791, the National Assembly adopted a constitution for France. The powers of the monarchy were limited. The government was divided into three branches—executive, legislative, and judicial. Church property was taken by the government and sold. The government controlled the Catholic Church in France and paid the salaries of priests. The National Assembly disbanded and a new Legislative Assembly was elected.

National Convention

Fearing the French Revolution would spread to their nations, Prussia and Austria attacked France. They wanted to defeat France and restore

Declaration of the Rights of Man

- all men equal before the la
- right to liberty and proper
- right to hold public office a to elect others to public offi
- taxes based on ability to p
- religions to be tolerated

Time Box

1789
  French Revolution began
  Declaration of the Rights of Man
1791
  Constitution adopted
  Prussia and Austria attacked France
1792–1795
  National Convention governed France
  French Republic declared
1793
  Louis XVI executed
1795–1799
  Directory governed France
1799
  Directory overthrown; Napoleon seized power
1804
  Napoleon crowned himself emperor

Extension

Ask students to create a bar graph to represent the following data on the Estates:

First Estate: 100,000 members of the clergy

Second Estate: 400,000 nobles

Third Estate: 24 million serfs, free peasants, and city dwellers

Ask them to determine from the graph why Louis XVI was opposed to giving the Third Estate more than one vote.

Louis to absolute power. Mobs again took to the streets of Paris.

Radicals who wanted a republic opposed more moderate members of the Legislative Assembly. The radicals took advantage of the chaos in Paris and called for a National Convention to write a new constitution. The National Convention governed from 1792 to 1795. During this time, the monarchy was abolished. Louis was tried, convicted, and beheaded for treason.

The Jacobins, the most radical members of the Convention, seized power in 1793. They began what is called the Reign of Terror. Anyone suspected of opposing the Jacobins faced arrest and execution. The Terror lasted only one year, but thousands died.

In 1795, a new constitution established a legislature with two houses and an executive branch of five directors. The Directory governed France from 1795 to 1799. While the nation was living through political chaos, a young military officer, Napoleon Bonaparte, was winning victories on the battlefield. In 1799, he and a group of officers overthrew the Directory. Napoleon became the new ruler of France.

Rise and Fall of Napoleon

Napoleon soon agreed to a peace treaty to end the wars against France. France had already won control of a large part of North America. France also controlled the island of Haiti.

In 1803, France was once again at war with Great Britain. To raise money, Napoleon agreed to sell the Louisiana Territory to the United States for $15 million. At home, Napoleon restored order and the economy improved. Napoleon set up a centralized government managed by a professional bureaucracy.

One of Napoleon's most important reforms was the **Napoleonic Code**. This was actually seven law codes that replaced the many systems of law in France. At the same time, Napoleon took more and more power for himself. He ignored the freedom of the press guaranteed by the Revolution and shut down newspapers

Once emperor, Napoleon crowned his empress, Josephine.

Picturing History

Marie Antoinette is shown on page 255 about to be guillotined. She was hated because of her Austrian ancestry, her influence over Louis XVI, and her extravagance. At fifteen, she was married to Louis, then the sixteen-year-old prince, as part of a political alliance between Austria and France. In 1774, Louis became king of a country that was nearly bankrupt, a fact his queen did not understand. In 1789, the royal family was placed under guard in the palace. They tried to flee in 1791, dressed as commoners, but the ruse was discovered and they were turned back. Louis was put to death in January 1793. The following October, the Reign of Terror condemned the queen to die.

Picturing History

The painting at the bottom of page 255 shows Napoleon placing the imperial crown on Josephine's head. A brilliant strategist, Napoleon was a general at only twenty-four. He became consul for life in 1802 and emperor two years later.

Extension

Charles Dickens' novel *A Tale of Two Cities* vividly depicts the era of the French Revolution. You may wish to show clips from a film version or to obtain a retold or illustrated version of the book for those who would have difficulty reading the novel.

Political Revolutions | 255

Map Extension

Ask students to use the map on page 256 to answer the following questions:

- In what category on the key was the Kingdom of Naples? (nations ruled by members of Napoleon's family)

- How far east did Napoleon get in Russia? (Moscow)

- Was Prussia an ally of France? (yes)

- What generalization can you make about the location of the French Empire? (It was bounded on all sides by nations governed by someone in Napoleon's family.)

Stop and Think

Students' choices of events and explanations will vary but should be drawn from the Time Box on page 254.

Putting It All Together

Students' lists will vary but may include

- French Revolution of 1789
- Constitution of 1791
- French Republic formed
- Execution of Louis XVI
- Overthrow of Directory

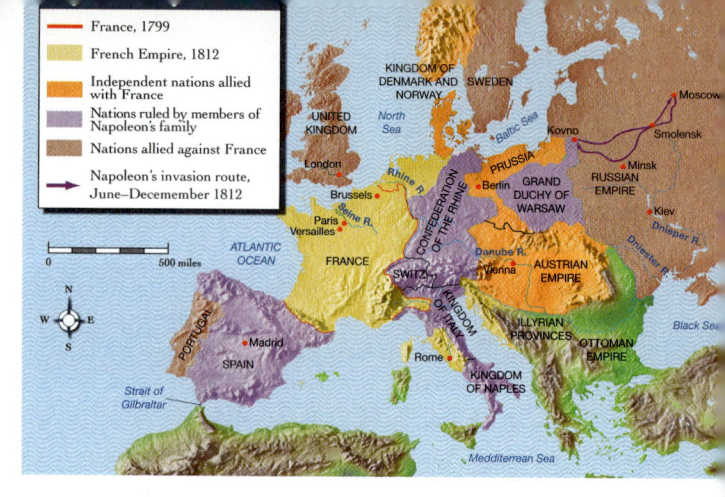

that opposed him. Napoleon was determined to create an empire in Europe. In 1804, Napoleon declared himself emperor. From 1805 until 1813, he led France into one war after another, including an invasion of Russia.

Europe's rulers joined forces against Napoleon. After more defeats, he was forced to step down in 1813 and was sent to the island of Elba in the Mediterranean. He escaped in 1815 and took command of another French army. Three months later, they fought a coalition of European armies at the Battle of Waterloo. Again, Napoleon was defeated. This time he was sent to Saint Helena Island in the South Atlantic where he died in 1821.

Napoleon wanted to spread the ideas of the French Revolution. In the nations that he conquered, he set up governments based on legal equality, economic opportunity, and religious toleration. He also stripped the clergy and nobility of their special privileges. Other nations may have welcomed the changes, but they did not like French rule. This resulted in a growing spirit of **nationalism** across Europe. Nationalism is a strong feeling of loyalty for one's own culture.

stop and think

Choose two events from the Time Box. Write an explanation of each event. Be sure to include any causes and effects. Share your explanation with a partner. Ask for suggestions about how to make it clearer.

Putting It All Together

Create a bulleted list of events that relate to Napoleon becoming emperor. Compare your list with a partner's and make needed corrections.

Extension

The Napoleonic Code affected not only France but also many of the law codes throughout Europe and Latin America. The code made all male citizens equal, but reversed some of the gains women had made during the Revolution, returning them to a subordinate position. The laws, which in some places remained in effect until the second half of the twentieth century, gave men control of property and children.

LESSON 5

Latin American Revolutions

Thinking on Your Own

As you read, create a table to keep track of the Latin American nations that won their independence. Your table should have three columns. The first column should list the name of the nation. Column 2 should list the date it became independent. Column 3 should briefly explain how it became independent.

The American Revolution was influenced by the ideas of the Enlightenment. The French Revolution was influenced by the American Revolution and the Enlightenment. All three influenced revolutions in Latin America in the early 1800s.

Society in Spanish America was divided among **peninsulares**, creoles, and mestizos. As the creole population grew in numbers and wealth, they wanted a say in government. However, a council in Spain made all the laws for the colonies. The council sent officials from Spain—the peninsulares—to see that the laws were carried out. The ideas of the Enlightenment and the success of the American and French revolutions inspired the creoles to act. However, the first uprising in Latin America did not take place among the Spanish.

focus your reading

How did Haiti gain its independence from France?

How was the Mexican revolution different from other revolts in Spanish America?

What was the sequence of events that led to the liberation of Spanish South America?

vocabulary

peninsulares
L'Ouverture

Uprising in Haiti

The French Revolution sparked a rebellion in the French colony of Saint Domingue in the Caribbean. The island colony had a population of about 500,000 enslaved people of color, about

Political Revolutions | 257

Lesson Vocabulary

Discuss each of the vocabulary terms with students.

Peninsulares is the name given to men who were sent from Spain to rule the colonies. They held the most important government posts and made up the highest social class.

L'Ouverture is a French word, meaning "opening." A leader of the Haitian rebellion took the name *L'Ouverture*.

Extension

Five different kingdoms existed on Ayiti when Columbus arrived. Ayiti was the local name for the island. He called the island Hispaniola, or Little Spain. The eastern part of the island was later called Santo Domingo. The western half of the island was deeded to the French in 1697. The French called their colony Saint-Domingue, and the Spanish side continued to be called Santo Domingo. After exhausting the soil by growing indigo, the planters switched to sugar cane, which was more profitable.

Lesson Summary

The ideas of the Enlightenment, as well as of the American and French Revolutions, inspired several leaders of Latin America. In Haiti, Toussaint L'Ouverture led a rebellion that freed the slaves and ended European control. In Mexico, creole priest Miguel Hidalgo led a call for rebellion. Mexico became a republic in 1823. Simón Bolívar and José San Martín liberated other countries in South America.

Lesson Objective

Students will learn about the nineteenth-century revolutions in Central and South America.

Focus Your Reading Answers

1 Haitians were inspired by the French Revolution. Toussaint L'Ouverture, a freed slave, led the nation in a battle to be free of French, Spanish, or British control. They resisted an invasion by Napoleon's troops. Haiti declared independence in 1804.

2 The Mexican revolution came after a creole priest led a rebellion. This priest and the one who took over the fight were not trained as soldiers, as were some of the leaders elsewhere in Spanish America.

3 Simón Bolívar and José San Martín studied in Europe, becoming convinced of the need for independence after reading the works of the Enlightenment. Bolívar freed Venezuela. José San Martín returned to Argentina and freed Lima and the remainder of Peru and Chile, with Bolívar's help.

Political Revolutions | 257

Picturing History

The French soldiers, pictured in battle on page 258, were part of a force of 25,000 soldiers sent to Haiti in 1802. Even though Toussaint L'Ouverture did not declare independence from France, the French, possibly with memories of the Reign of Terror fresh in their minds, were frightened. Many of the French citizens and slaves fled the island for New Orleans, helping to create that city's distinctive culture.

Bio Facts

- Born a slave about 1743.
- Legally freed in 1777.
- First fought for the Spanish in a war in 1793, then switched to the French side because they had freed their slaves.
- Helped to restore economy as lieutenant governor.
- 1799—the British withdrew from the island when he was governor-general.
- 1801—gained control of Santo Domingo and freed slaves there.
- Surrendered to the French in 1802 on condition that slavery not be restored.
- Died 1803.

Toussaint L'Ouverture and soldiers fight the French at the Ravine aux Couleuvres

32,000 French colonists, and another 24,000 free people of color. After learning of the "Declaration of the Rights of Man," the free people of color demanded citizenship. The wealthy French colonists resisted. The result was rebellion.

In 1794, the National Convention ended slavery in France's colonies. At the time, the French were fighting Spain and Great Britain to keep control of Saint Domingue. The rebels, under the control of François-Dominique Toussaint L'Ouverture, were allied with Spain. They switched sides and joined forces with the French. Together, they defeated France's enemies. As a reward, the French government made Toussaint governor-general for life of the colony.

François-Dominique Toussaint L'Ouverture (c. 1743–1803)

François-Dominique Toussaint was the son of enslaved plantation workers in the French colony of Saint Domingue. The plantation owner allowed Toussaint to learn to read. From books, he learned about the Enlightenment.

Toussaint joined the Haitian rebellion that broke out in 1791. His skills soon made him the rebel leader. He was given the name **L'Ouverture** because of his bravery in battle. The word *l'ouverture* means "opening." He once broke through an enemy line, allowing his forces to overwhelm the enemy.

After the rebellion, the French appointed him governor-general of the colony for life. When Napoleon attempted to restore slavery, Toussaint once again took to the battlefield. The French captured him. As he was taken to prison in France, he supposedly said:

"In overthrowing me, you have cut down in Haiti only the trunk of the tree of liberty. It will spring up again by the roots, for they are numerous and deep."

On January 1, 1804, Toussaint was proved right. On that day, Haiti declared its independence from France.

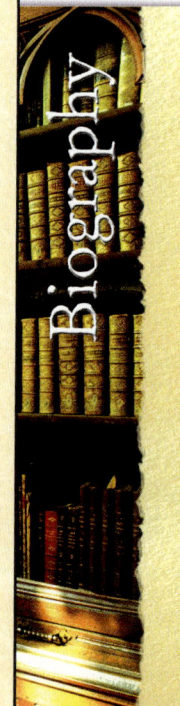

Biography Extension

No portraits were drawn of L'Ouverture during his lifetime. The first likenesses of him were produced early in the nineteenth century. An early portrait was made based on oral description. "[I]n person, Toussaint was of a manly form, above the middle stature, with a countenance bold and striking, yet full of the most prepossessing suavity. . . ." The image on this page is the one most commonly reproduced. French lithographer Nicolas Eustache Maurin created it in 1832.

Extension

Invite students to note similarities in the beginnings of Haiti and the United States. For example, both fought for independence at the end of the 1700s. Both had native populations wiped out by disease and overwork. The economies of both depended on African slaves.

Napoleon seized control of France in 1799. One of his goals was to create an American empire. His plan was to restore slavery and put French officials in control of Saint Domingue. Napoleon sent troops to invade the island and take control. The invasion failed. However, Toussaint was captured, shipped to France, and died there in prison. One of his former generals, Jean-Jacques Dessalines declared Saint Domingue independent on January 1, 1804. The new nation took the name Haiti, meaning "a higher place."

Mexican Independence

The Enlightenment and the French Revolution also influenced Mexico's fight for independence from Spain. Father Miguel Hidalgo, a creole, began the fight. The Enlightenment ideas of liberty and equality inspired him. On September 16, 1810, he rang the bell of his church and called on his people to rebel against the Spanish. Known as "El Grito de Dolores!" (the Cry of Dolores), his call to rebellion marks the beginning of the Mexican revolution.

Hidalgo's army numbered some 60,000 mestizos and Native Americans. Armed with clubs and knives, they marched toward Mexico City. The rebel army captured several provinces and set up a government. Land was returned to Native Americans, and slavery was ended.

Unfortunately, Hidalgo was not much of a general. In addition, the peninsulares and creoles were frightened of Hidalgo's policies. They did not want to give up their wealth and power to mestizos and Native Americans. The creoles and peninsulares wanted an end to the revolution and supported the Spanish government. Hidalgo's army was no match for well-trained and well-armed Spanish troops. In the fighting, Hidalgo was caught. He was later tried and executed.

But El Grito de Dolores did not die. Another priest, José Maria Morelos, a mestizo, took over the fight. By 1821, peninsulares and creoles decided to act for themselves. With their support, Agustín de Iturbide, a creole, came to power. He had the backing of rebels as well as the wealthy. His forces defeated the Spanish, and Mexico declared its independence. The following year, Iturbide proclaimed himself emperor.

Miguel Hidalgo

Picturing History

Miguel Hidalgo, shown on page 259, was a practical man. In addition to his pastoral duties, he taught the Native Americans Spanish; began brickmaking, pottery, and other small industries; and introduced new methods of farming to the Dolores parish. He had been in Dolores only two years when he called for a revolt against the Spanish, who, in addition to practicing slavery, imposing high taxes, and discriminating, had been destroying all attempts at independence.

Extension

Like his older mentor, Father Hidalgo, José Maria Morelos studied for the priesthood at the Colegio de San Nicolás. Although he held most of Mexico southwest of Mexico City, he could not retain power. He did, however, call a congress in 1813 to draft a constitution and begin a government. The congress had to move from place to place to avoid capture. When captured, Morelos was defrocked and, again like Hidalgo, shot as a traitor.

Map Extension

Ask students to use the map on page 260 to answer the following questions:

- Where were the remaining European colonies in South America located geographically? (northeast)
- When did Costa Rica gain its independence? (1821)
- What European powers still had colonies in the region? (Britain, the Netherlands, Spain, France)
- How many nations made up the United Provinces of Central America? (five)

He was overthrown in 1823, and Mexico became a republic with a government headed by a president.

Freeing Spanish South America

Simón Bolívar and José de San Martín were major figures in the fight for independence in Spanish South America. Both men were creoles and were sent by their families to study in Europe. While there, they read the works of the Enlightenment. They became convinced that the colonies must free themselves from Spanish rule.

Bolívar returned to his native Venezuela and spent 11 years fighting to free it. He finally succeeded in 1821. He was hailed as the "Liberator" and made president of the new republic of Gran Colombia.

Extension

The Battle of Carabobo, fought on June 24, 1821, was the decisive battle in Venezuela's war for independence. The battle lasted just over an hour. Venezuela's 7,500 troops, including hundreds of hired British soldiers, overpowered the 5,000 Spanish soldiers. The date is still celebrated in Venezuela.

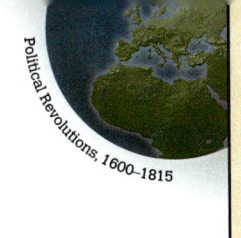

San Martín and his army crossing the Andes

In 1812, San Martín returned from Europe to what is today Argentina. Part of the area had already declared its independence from Spain. But Spanish forces remained in what are today Chile and Peru. San Martín believed that freedom was not safe as long as Spanish forces remained anywhere in South America. In January 1817, he put together an army of volunteers and marched them over the Andes. His strategy worked. He caught the Spanish by surprise and defeated a large Spanish force.

In 1821, San Martín set out to capture Lima, the capital of the Viceroyalty of Peru, and end Spanish control in South America. His forces took Lima, but the Spanish army retreated into the mountains. Bolívar and his army joined San Martín. The two men could not agree on tactics and San Martín withdrew. Bolívar's forces liberated the rest of Peru. By 1825, all that was left of the Spanish empire in the Americas were the islands of Cuba and Puerto Rico.

stop and think

What similarities and differences can you find between the fights for independence in Haiti and Mexico? Work with a partner to create a Venn diagram to show how they were alike and different. When you are finished, use the information to write three or four paragraphs explaining the differences and similarities.

Putting It All Together

With a partner examine a map of Central and South America. Chose one of the countries indicated. Use the library or the Internet to find out more about the struggle for independence. Create a concept web using the information from your research. Then write a short essay about the country's independence movement.

Political Revolutions | 261

Extension

Have students interested in further exploration of South American independence use library resources or the Internet to investigate Bernardo O'Higgins. The leader of Chile's quest for independence, he was the first national leader in all the Americas to abolish slavery of Africans. Ask students to find out about his connection to San Martín.

Picturing History

San Martín crossing the Andes is depicted on page 261. The Andes stretch along the western part of South America. Some of the highest mountains of the range are in Argentina, including the Aconcagua, which at 22,384 feet (6,823 m), is the highest mountain not only in the Andes but in the Western Hemisphere. Argentina has five mountains above 21,000 feet (6,400 m). San Martín's crossing was no easy task.

Stop and Think

Students' Venn diagrams and paragraphs will vary but may mention the following ideas:

Alike: both were against the Spanish; both were rooted in Enlightenment ideas and sparked by the French Revolution; both required more than ten years of effort.

Different: Mexico's fight was led by priests, not soldiers; in Mexico, slavery ended and land was returned to Native Americans; after independence, an emperor briefly ruled Mexico.

Putting It All Together

Students' choice of country, concept maps, and essays will vary but should focus on a nation in Central or South America.

Political Revolutions | 261

Chapter Review

1. Students' concept maps will vary but may include the nations of Britain, the United States, France, Haiti, Venezuela, Colombia, and Peru.

2. Students' concept webs and essays will vary but should focus on one of the revolutions described in the chapter.

Chapter Summary

- James I and Charles I introduced rule by **divine right**.
- Charles I was executed as a **traitor**. Oliver Cromwell set up a **commonwealth** and later a **military dictatorship**.
- The **Restoration** placed Charles II on the English throne. Concern over his Catholic faith resulted in the **Glorious Revolution**. The Bill of Rights set up a **constitutional monarchy**.
- The **Scientific Revolution** and the **Enlightenment** began during the 1600s. Philosophers used the **scientific method** to determine **natural law** and people's **natural rights**.
- John Locke wrote about the **social contract** between government and the governed. Adam Smith developed the theory of **laissez-faire economics**.
- Montesquieu, a **philosophe**, wrote about the separation of powers and checks and balances.
- England passed tax laws for their colonial **possessions**.
- European **mercantilism** relied on taxes. The 13 English colonies objected to **revenue taxes**.
- The **ratified** U.S. Constitution set up a **federal system**.
- The French Revolution began when the three **Estates** met and ended special privileges for the **clergy** and nobles.
- In 1799, Napoleon Bonaparte introduced the **Napoleonic Code**. Nations under his rule developed **nationalism**.
- Spanish **peninsulares** tried to maintain laws in Central and South America.
- Toussaint **L'Ouverture** led the rebellion in Haiti. Mexico rebelled against being a Spanish possession. San Martín and Bolívar became the liberators of Spanish Central and South America.

Chapter Summary

1. Create a concept map to show how many nations were influenced by the ideas of the Enlightenment.

2. Create a concept web for one of the revolutions described in this chapter. Use your web to write a short essay about the revolution.

Novel Connections

Below is a list of books that relate to the time period covered in this chapter. The numbers in parentheses indicate the related Thematic Strands of the National Council for the Social Studies (NCSS).

Jim Murphy. *An American Plague: The True and Terrifying Story of the Yellow Fever Epidemic of 1793*. Houghton Mifflin Company, 2003. (I, II, III, VIII)

Don Nardo. *Trial of Galileo*. Thomson Gale, 2004. (I, VI, VIII)

Baroness Orczy. *The Scarlet Pimpernel*. Sagebrush Education Resources, 1997. (I, V)

Ann Rinaldi. *Or Give Me Death: A Novel of Patrick Henry's Family*. Harcourt, 2003. (I, IV, X)

Katherine Sturtevant. *At the Sign of the Star*. Farrar, Straus and Giroux, 2000. (I, IV, VII)

Skill Builder

Analyzing Paintings and Photographs

Paintings and photographs can be valuable tools in studying the past. Some show us historical events such as Napoleon crowning his empress, Josephine. Such visual images show us who was there and what they were doing.

Paintings and photographs can also show us how people dressed and what they did for a living. Look through this textbook and find examples of these kinds of visual images.

Like all historical sources, visual images can be biased. A painter or photographer may arrange the subject of the picture in such a way as to favor his or her interpretation, or point of view. For example, the painter of the picture on page 243 included commoners and soldiers to emphasize the support of the English people for Charles II's return.

To analyze paintings and photographs:

1. Identify what is happening in the image.
2. Examine the details. Look at what is happening in the background and in the foreground. Look at the clothing or furniture. Look at the choice of colors an artist uses.
3. Identify the emotions or attitude the artist or photographer is trying to show.
4. Read the caption.
5. Identify the purpose in making the image.
6. Identify any bias in the image. Who is the artist or photographer? Do you know anything about him or her? What can you tell about the person's point of view?

Complete the following activities.

1. Examine the images on pages 244 and 255. Use the six steps listed above to analyze the images.

2. Choose one illustration from Chapter 16 and follow steps 1 through 6. Then write three paragraphs analyzing your choice.

Political Revolutions | 263

Skill Builder

1. Students' analyses will vary but should include the steps outlined on this page.

2. Students' choices of photographs and analytical paragraphs will vary but should include the steps outlined on this page.

Classroom Discussion

Discuss with students some of the broader topics covered in this chapter.

- What "natural rights" should be granted to all people?
- What are some of the current scientific revolutions?
- In what ways do the economic and political theories explained in this chapter continue to affect our lives?

Political Revolutions | 263

Chapter Summary
Refer to page 276 for a summary of Chapter 17.

Related Transparencies

T-1 World Map

T-9 European Industrial Centers

T-18 Three-Column Chart

T-19 Venn Diagram

Key Blacklines

Biography—Charles Dickens

CD Extension

Encourage students to use the reading comprehension, vocabulary reinforcement, and interactive timeline activities on the student CD.

Getting Focused
You may wish to extend the Getting Focused activity by asking students to determine how a modern industrial city is different from one in the early 1800s. (telephone wires and power lines; some attempts to control smoke pollution; superhighways)

Picturing History

Smoke billows over Sheffield, England, in 1884, the industrialized city in the painting on page 264. Due to the layers of dust and grime that characterized it during the Industrial Revolution, the entire West Midlands region of England is still known as the "Black Country."

Chapter 17 SOCIAL REVOLUTIONS
(1750–1910)

Getting Focused

Skim this chapter to predict what you will be learning
- Read the lesson titles and subheadings.
- Look at the illustrations and read the captions.
- Examine the maps.
- Review the vocabulary words and terms.

Before the Industrial Revolution, most people in Russ China, India, Europe, and the United States lived in r areas. Most made their living by farming. The develop of factories changed where people lived and what the did for a living.

Imagine that you are a farmer living on a small plot o land in England or Europe about the year 1800. You s more opportunity in the cities for yourself and your family. But you know life will be very different. Mak list of what you would expect to find in an industrial

Pre-Reading Discussion

1 Discuss with students some of the ways that industries are currently trying to prevent pollution.

2 Talk with students about contemporary instances of protest against sweatshop conditions and child labor abroad.

Extension

By 1851, so many industrial products existed that London hosted the Great Exhibition of Industry of All Nations in the newly built Crystal Palace. During the five and a half months of the exhibition, more than six million people attended. Of the more than 13,000 exhibitors, nearly half represented nations other than Britain. The United States sent 560 exhibits; France sent 1,760. The exhibition led to subsequent ones in Dublin, New York, Munich, Amsterdam, and India.

LESSON 1

The Industrial Revolution

Thinking on Your Own

You have read about a number of revolutions in this book: Neolithic, American, Scientific, and French. Now you will read about the Industrial Revolution. Look at the illustrations in this lesson and the subheadings. Then write a definition of "Industrial Revolution." Share your definition with a partner. As you read this lesson, add to or change your definition as needed.

Until 1800, most people in Western Europe and the United States lived on farms. The economies of these nations were based on farming, the making of goods by hand, and trading. During the **Industrial Revolution**, machines replaced hand tools in the manufacturing of goods. More and more people left their farms to work in factories. Within 100 years, many nations had become industrial giants.

focus your reading

Why did industrialization begin in Great Britain?

How was the factory system different from earlier ways of producing goods?

Explain how industrialization spread.

vocabulary

Industrial Revolution
natural resources
capital
textile
cottage industry
entrepreneur

Industrial Great Britain

The Industrial Revolution began in the 1780s in Great Britain. There were a number of reasons why it began there. Britain at that time had all the factors of production that were needed to succeed in changing from an agricultural to an industrial society. The country had the people needed to work in manufacturing. Britain also had valuable **natural resources**. It had the iron and coal needed to make machines and run steam engines. In addition, Britain had money to invest in railroads and

Social Revolutions, 1750–1910

Lesson Summary
During the 1780s, Great Britain became the birthplace of the Industrial Revolution, a time when machine-made goods became more prevalent than handmade goods.

The factory system replaced the cottage industry system, as people moved from doing one step of a process in their homes to operating machinery in factories.

Industrialization spread to the United States, Japan, and other European countries. Russia remained agricultural, as did European colonies in Africa, Asia, and Latin America.

Lesson Objective
Students will learn about the beginnings and spread of the Industrial Revolution, as well as some of the key inventions that made it possible.

Focus Your Reading Answers

1 Great Britain had all the factors of production needed to change from an agricultural to an industrial society. There were enough people and natural resources. There was also money to invest and there were markets for the finished goods, as well as new inventions and technology.

2 The factory system moved the work from private homes where people could work the hours they chose to large factories that could hold many machines. Skilled workers were not needed to run the machines.

3 Industrialization spread to continental Europe and then to the United States and Japan. Colonies in Africa, Asia, and Latin America were happy to continue selling raw materials to the home country.

Lesson Vocabulary
Introduce each of the following vocabulary terms to students.

Explain that the *Industrial Revolution* was a time when machines rather than hand tools were used to make goods. The *Industrial Revolution* began in Great Britain. *Natural resources* are resources from nature that can be useful to people. Iron and coal are examples of *natural resources*.

Money to invest in business is called *capital*. Wealthy people in Great Britain invested *capital* in railroads and factories. *Capital* is explained in detail in Chapter 13.

Textile is another word for "cloth." The *textile* industry was the first to industrialize. A *cottage industry* is one in which each of the steps of making something is done in different homes. Cloth-making had been a *cottage industry* before the *textile* mills were built.

Entrepreneurs are people who organize, operate, or assume risks for a new business. New England *entrepreneurs* invested in *textile* factories.

Social Revolutions

Picturing History

The woodcut on page 266 depicts child workers in a mine. The children are pushing up an incline a wagon loaded with coal. All work was done by hand; crouching miners used picks to dig the coal away from the walls. Before the tracks and coal cars were installed, women and children crawled on hands and knees with baskets to drag the coal to the surface of the mine. Tunnels ran into the coal mines, but they were generally not tall enough to allow workers to stand upright.

Extension

Have students interested in industrial safety use library resources or the Internet to find out more about precautions that have been instituted for coal miners since the nineteenth century. Have them present their findings to the class by using the Student Presentation Builder on the student CD.

Social Revolutions, 1750–1910

factories, as well as the markets where it could sell the manufactured goods.

By the 1780s, Britain had a surplus of food. That is, it had more food than was needed to feed the population. Farmers had learned ways to grow new crops, such as potatoes, and better ways to farm. Fewer farmers produced more food than ever before. This forced many farm laborers off the land. They were available to work in factories.

With more food to eat, people lived longer. They also had more children. Discoveries about what causes diseases and how they are spread were also important. Better sanitation and medical care were available. More people were able to avoid and survive disease. A large population meant there was a large number of workers available. All of these factors contributed to the development of the Industrial Revolution.

Great Britain had a large number of very wealthy people. Economic stability meant that people had the **capital**, or money, to invest in manufacturing. Investing in new businesses like factories was one way they could make huge profits on their money.

Children haul a coal wagon in Lancashire, England.

Manufacturing depended on natural resources. Great Britain had large amounts of two of the most important resources: coal and iron ore. It also had a colonial empire to supply other needed materials. India, for example, sent tons of raw cotton to England's new **textile**, or cloth-making, mills.

Factory owners needed markets for their products. Britain had a growing market at home and markets in its overseas colonies. In addition to supplying raw materials, Britain's colonies could buy the finished goods from Britain's factories.

Finally, Britain was the center of a revolution in technology. Inventors created new machines that made goods faster and cheaper than goods made by hand. The invention of the steam engine created a new source of energy and a revolution in transportation.

Inventions in transportation helped move raw materials and finished products more quickly. In 1807, Robert Fulton launched the first successful steamboat in the United States. Soon ships could sail around the world without waiting for the wind. Another American, Peter Cooper, took James Watt's steam engine and made the first successful steam locomotive.

1825 am gine in rlington, gland

Social Revolutions, 1750–1910

The Factory System

Before people worked in factories, they worked in their own homes or in workshops. Cloth was made in steps by different workers in their homes, or cottages. This was known as the **cottage industry** system. Raw cotton was delivered to the homes of spinners. They used a spinning wheel operated by a foot pedal to spin it into thread. The thread was then taken to weavers. Weavers worked on small, hand-operated looms to weave cloth. A merchant collected and sold the finished cloth and paid the workers.

A series of inventions in the late 1700s changed the textile industry. John Kay invented a flying shuttle that speeded up the weaving of cloth. To speed up the production of thread, James Hargreaves, in 1764, invented a new spinning machine. This spinning jenny spun several threads at the same time. Richard Arkwright invented a water-powered spinning frame that produced thread still more quickly and cheaply.

Factors of Production

Any industry or service must have some form of the factors of production in order to succeed.

- Land—includes natural resources
- Labor—people to do the work
- Capital—money to invest
- Enterprise—ability to combine the other three factors and create a business or service

stop and think

Create a table showing the reasons that industrialization began in Great Britain. Label the left side "Industrialization in Great Britain." In that column, list the various factors that you read about that led to industrialization. Label the right side "Examples." In that column, provide examples and details for each factor in the left column.

Chart Extension

Select industries or services in your community and have students analyze which factors of production each has available. Have students make a chart or graph to demonstrate similarities and differences among them.

Stop and Think

Students' tables may vary but should include most of the following:

Factors: surplus of people; economic stability and capital; natural resources; markets for finished goods; revolutionary new technologies

Examples: people were living longer because of enough food and better medical care; wealthy people were willing to invest capital into new businesses; Britain had coal and iron ore; markets both at home and in colonies; steam engine

Social Revolutions 267

Picturing History

Early steam locomotives, such as the one pictured on page 267, could not attain the speed of a horse. The first locomotive to do so was called the *Rocket*. Built by British inventor George Stephenson, it traveled at 30 miles an hour.

Extension

The nineteenth century was a time of many inventions. Have students use library resources or the Internet to find out more about the steam engine and its applications to ships and locomotives, as well as the invention of common implements, such as matches and can openers.

Social Revolutions 267

Picturing History

Children working in an English brickyard in the early nineteenth century are shown at the top of page 268. Working conditions were often dangerous and harsh. Employees received few breaks, working 12–14 hour days, six days a week. The National Labor Union, formed in the United States in the mid-1860s, demanded an eight-hour workday.

Picturing History

The illustration of the textile mill at the bottom of page 268 demonstrates that most of the workers were women and their supervisors were men. This mill was in Tewkesbury, England. Have students note the formal attire on the supervisors. Many girls from farming areas wanted a taste of city life before they married. Their income was also needed to support their families back home. Even though they earned about half of what men earned in the textile industry, it was more money than they could make as seamstresses or domestic servants.

Social Revolutions, 1750-1910

Eli Whitney invented the cotton gin in 1793. This machine greatly improved the cleaning of raw cotton. This led to an increase in cotton production.

In 1782, James Watt figured out how to use the steam engine to power machines. The next step was adding steam power to spinning and weaving machines. The steam engines used coal for fuel. In time, water-powered and steam-powered looms replaced the weavers' hand looms.

Machines powered by water and steam led to the factory system of production. Few old-time spinners could afford to buy these new machines. Building the dozens of spinning frames that could be run by a single water wheel or steam engine involved a large investment of money. This required a wealthy person or a group of investors. They also had to build the factory to provide a central location for the machines. As most of the early spinning factories used water as their power source, they were located along a stream or canal.

Factory owners hired workers to run the machines. They did not need skilled spinners or weavers. Workers with few skills could be trained in a short time to operate the machines. Because the machines were so large, they needed many workers to operate them. The owners even hired children to do the work. Now large numbers of workers were brought together in the factories. There, the workers ran endlessly whirring machines, turning out cotton cloth for world markets.

The Spread of Industrialization

By the mid-1800s, Great Britain was the leading industrial nation in the world. Its mines and factories turned out half the world's coal and manufactured goods. British technology spread to continental Europe and the United States.

The first nations in Europe to shift to the factory system of

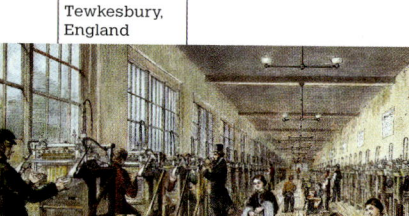

Children work in English brickyard

Robert Owen's textile mill in Tewkesbury, England

Extension

Some students in the class may already be working. Ask them to find out about the battles during the late nineteenth century to protect children who were working and current labor laws for young people. Allow time for them to report their findings to the class, perhaps as a skit.

268 | Chapter 17

European Industrial Centers, c. 1870

- Coal mining
- Iron ore deposits
- Major centers of industry

production were Belgium, Germany, and France. Germany and France, in particular, became highly industrialized nations in the 1800s. Japan also became industrialized. Russia, on the other hand, remained a rural country where most goods were made by hand.

The technology needed to start a textile industry reached the United States in the early 1800s. **Entrepreneurs** in New England invested in the first textile factories. Entrepreneurs are people who organize, operate, and assume the risk for a new business. Improvements in technology similar to what happened in the textile industry caused changes in other industries.

European nations were not interested in industrializing their colonies in Asia and Africa. The home countries wanted to keep their colonies as sources of raw materials and as markets for manufactured goods. Wealthy planters and mine owners in newly independent Latin American countries were happy to make their money selling raw materials to European businesses. Why risk money by building factories and starting new businesses?

Iron played a crucial role in the development of new machines.

Putting It All Together

Create a diagram to show how spinning and weaving went from a cottage industry to factory work. Work with a partner to figure out what to show on the diagram. Then decide how to illustrate your diagram.

Social Revolutions   269

Map Extension

Ask students to use the map on page 269 to answer the following questions:

- What can you say about Russia and Austria-Hungary, based on this map? (They were not major industrial centers.)
- Which nation had the most industrial cities? (Britain)
- Which nation had the largest single coal deposit area? (France)
- What resource did Sweden have? (iron ore deposits)

Picturing History

Ironworkers are shown in the painting on page 269. Have students speculate as to why the woman in the foreground might be there and why the foundry was located near the port.

Putting It All Together

Students' illustrated diagrams will vary but may include the following information: Making cloth was a multistep process done in homes. John Kay's flying shuttle sped up the weaving of cloth. James Hargreaves invented a spinning machine to improve the production of thread. Richard Awkwright's water-powered spinning frame produced thread even more cheaply and rapidly. Cotton production increased with the invention of the cotton gin. Steam- and water-powered looms replaced hand looms. Factory owners brought many large machines to a single spot and hired workers to run the machines.

Social Revolutions   269

Lesson Summary

Cities in Europe and the United States became increasingly urbanized as people moved to the cities in search of work. Many of them lived in tenements clustered in slums. Without basic sanitation or police protection, these were places of disease and crime. Working conditions were difficult and dangerous, particularly for women and children. No medical or unemployment benefits existed.

A middle class arose among the professionals, craftworkers, merchants, and shop owners. They often had at least one servant.

Lesson Objective

Students will learn about the growth of industrial cities and the rise of the middle class.

Focus Your Reading Answers

1. The first industrial cities were overcrowded and dirty. Many families crowded into tenements without running water. Because there was no sewage collection, disease spread quickly. There were no attempts to prevent or control fires or crime.

2. The working class generally did not get to take advantage of the benefits of the city that the rich enjoyed. Working hours were long, and conditions were dangerous and led to illness or accidents. Women and children worked, but at lower wages than men received.

3. The new middle class was composed of the financiers and managers of the new factories. They had large homes with yards and sometimes servants, which their wives managed. Children were trained to replicate their parents' roles.

270 | Chapter 17

Social Revolutions, 1750–1910

LESSON 2

Growth of Cities

Thinking on Your Own

Examine the illustrations in this lesson. From what you observe, what do you think life was like for people during this time? Write two paragraphs to describe life for the working class and the middle class.

Between 1800 and 1850, the population of cities in Europe and the United States grew rapidly. Workers needed to live close to factories and mills. At the same time, changes in farming meant that fewer farm workers were needed. People were being pushed out of rural areas. Some countries also suffered years of poor harvests, which drove even more farmers off the land. As a result, more people moved from rural areas to industrial cities.

focus your reading

Explain what the first industrial cities were like.

What was life like for the working class?

Describe the new middle class.

vocabulary

urbanization
slums
tenements
middle class

Industrial Cities

Between 1800 and 1850 there was a significant increase in the number and size of cities in Europe and the United States. This is called **urbanization**. For example, London's population grew from 1 million people in 1800 to 2.5 million in 1850.

The Krupp Steelworks in Essen, Germany

Living conditions in cities were terrible for workers. They gathered in neighborhoods near their work. These very poor, crowded neighborhoods became known as **slums**. People lived in five- and six-story wooden apartment buildings called **tenements**. Whole families crowded into tiny, two-room

Lesson Vocabulary

Discuss each of the vocabulary terms with students.

Urbanization is the increase of the size and number of cities in Europe and the United States. *Urbanization* took place during the early 1800s.

The crowded neighborhoods where the poor lived were called *slums*. Slums were often located near the factories where the working poor were employed. *Tenements* were the five- or six-story wooden apartment buildings where workers lived. Most *tenements* did not have running water or sewer systems.

The Industrial Revolution enlarged the *middle class*. The new factory owners and managers joined doctors, lawyers, craftworkers, and merchants.

apartments. People got their water from hand-operated pumps. There was no organized fire or police protection. Cities also had no garbage collection or sewer systems. Waste piled up in streets and alleys. Diseases spread quickly through these urban areas. It was not until the late 1800s that nations began to clean up their cities and pass laws that regulated tenements.

The Working Class

Cities may have offered work, but the work paid poorly. The work day was long and hard. Working conditions in the new factories and mills were dangerous.

Factories could be boiling hot in summer and freezing cold in winter. They lacked large windows to let in fresh air and furnaces to heat the rooms in winter. Dust in the air in textile factories sickened workers.

Men and women worked 12- to 16-hour days. However, women were typically paid 50 percent of what men were paid. Children, too, worked because their families needed the money. Most countries did not require all children to attend school in the early 1800s. After 1833 in Great Britain, children from ages 9 to 13 could work only 9-hour workdays. Children over the age of 13 could work 12 hours a day.

Tired workers were sometimes careless. Accidents could cost workers a finger, a hand, an eye, or even their life. There was no medical insurance to pay for medical care for injured workers. Until the late 1800s, there were no labor unions to demand shorter working hours and safe and healthful working conditions.

stop and think

Imagine you are living in a new industrial city. Plan a letter to the editor demanding that living conditions be improved for the working poor. Discuss your ideas with a partner. Then write a three- or four-paragraph letter stating what you think should be done and why.

Time Box

1780s
Industrial Revolution began in Great Britain

1800s (early)
Industrial Revolution spread to United States

1850s
Industrial Revolution spread to Germany, Belgium, and France

1920s
Industrial Revolution spread to Russia

Picturing History

Overcrowding was a problem in the cities, as shown in the painting of a London street on page 271. Overcrowding and unsanitary conditions led to crime and illness. *Harper's Weekly* stated of New York City in 1876, "From the nearly 200,000 tenement houses come 93 percent of the deaths and 90 percent of the crimes of our population."

Extension

Have students interested in social work use library resources or the Internet to investigate the work of late nineteenth-century reformers such as Jane Addams in Chicago and photographer Jacob Riis in New York.

Stop and Think

Students' letters will vary but should put forth reasons for improving living conditions for the working poor in the newly industrialized cities.

Picturing History

The painting on page 270 depicts the Krupp Steelworks in Essen, Germany, in the late nineteenth century. The smoke and stench from factories made city life unpleasant and unhealthy. A reporter from the *Chicago Times* wrote in 1880, "The river stinks. The air stinks. People's clothing, penetrated by the foul atmosphere, stinks. No other word expresses it so well as *stink*."

Time Box Extension

Have students determine the span of time between each of the first three entries in the Time Box and the spread of the Industrial Revolution to Russia. Review Russian history from Chapter 8 to help students explain the time lag.

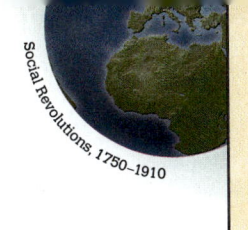

Reading for Understanding

1 Elizabeth worked for 13 hours every day.

2 He or she was hit with a strap.

3 Students' lists will vary but may include the following ideas:

- Children began working as young as six.
- They were expected to work a full day, as adults were.
- There were no breaks and only a 40-minute lunch period.
- Boys and girls who were late or didn't work hard enough were hit with a strap.

Extension

Students interested in literature may wish to use library resources or the Internet to find out more about the effect of an American, Rebecca Harding Davis articles and novels on the plight of millworkers. Her work, *Life In the Iron Mills* was published in The "Atlantic Monthly" in 1861.

Putting It All Together

Students' signs will vary but should indicate understanding of the difficulties faced by workers. Possible signs:

Eight-Hour Days for All!

Give the Children a Break!

The New Middle Class

Since the Middle Ages, there had been a **middle class** of craftworkers, merchants, shop owners, and professionals such as lawyers and doctors. The Industrial Revolution created new members of the middle class. These new members were the men who provided the money to build the new factories and the men who managed the new businesses.

Middle-class families lived around the central city of working-class neighborhoods. They had large, well-built, single-family homes with yards. Often, they had a servant or two. The wives did not work outside the home. Their job was to manage the servants, raise the children, and make a pleasant home for their husbands when they came home from work.

Putting It All Together

Imagine you are a member of a union in a textile mill. Work with a partner to design a sign to carry in a protest for better working conditions.

Factory Conditions

The following excerpt is from testimony by Elizabeth Bentley. She appeared in 1815 before a commission of the British Parliament that was looking into factory conditio[ns]

What time did you begin work at the factory?
When I was six years old.

What were the usual hours of labour?
From six in the morning till seven at night.

What time was allowed for meals?
Forty minutes at noon.

Had you any time to get your breakfast or drinking?
No, we had to get it as we could.

Suppose you flagged a little, or were late, what would they do?
Strap us.

And they are in the habit of strapping?
Yes.

Is the strap used so as to hurt excessively?
Yes, it is.... I have seen the overlooker go to the top end of room, where the little girls [wor] he has taken a strap, and a whi[p] in his mouth, and sometimes he got a chain and chained them, a[nd] strapped them all down the roo[m]

reading for understanding

How long was Elizabeth's workday

What happened if a worker was slow at his or her job?

Using the information in this reading, write a bulleted list of facts about child labor.

Picturing History

Karl Marx, whose photograph appears on page 273, lived in England after being forced to leave his native Germany and Paris because of his radical ideas. With Friedrich Engels, a textile manufacturer who paid Marx's bills, Marx co-authored works that profoundly influenced the events of the twentieth century. However, during his life, he experienced deep poverty and, at his death, a mere eight people came to hear Engels' funeral oration at Highgate Cemetery.

LESSON 3

Changes in Society

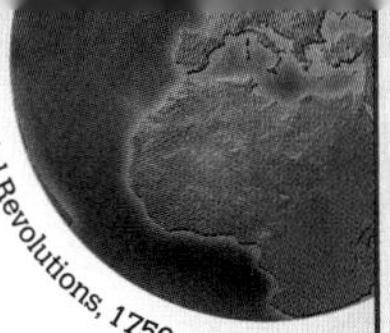

Thinking on Your Own

Look at the vocabulary words for this lesson. Write them in your notebook. Work with a partner to develop definitions. As you read, change the definitions if they are not correct.

The way people lived changed greatly during the Industrial Revolution. For the working classes, life became harder. For the wealthy and well-educated, it was a time for discovery. Discovery and invention often led to a better life for all classes.

focus your reading

Discuss the social philosophies that developed during the Industrial Revolution.

What did labor unions want to achieve?

Explain how some of the inventions of the nineteenth century changed the way people lived.

vocabulary

socialism
proletariat
Social Darwinism
labor union
strike
realism
invention

New Philosophies

New philosophies of life developed during the Industrial Revolution. Some people wanted to find ways to make conditions better for workers. Others thought that the poor were responsible for their own troubles.

Karl Marx

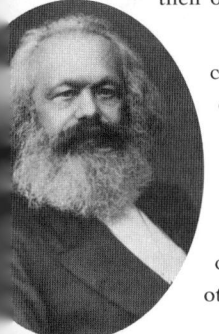

According to **socialism**, the ownership and control of the means of production and the distribution of the goods produced belongs to society. There is no private ownership of factories, railroads, or any other business. Under socialism, all members of society share in the work and the goods produced. There are no capitalists, or investors who make money while other people do the work.

Social Revolutions 273

Lesson Summary

New philosophies such as socialism and Social Darwinism fueled the activities of workers and business owners. Labor unions became common. Realism in literature depicted life as it really was.

Many scientists and inventors discovered and produced new technologies. Some of the most famous were inventors Alexander Graham Bell and Thomas Edison, and scientists Louis Pasteur and Marie and Pierre Curie.

Lesson Objective

Students will learn about the changes brought about by socialism, Social Darwinism, the growth of unions, and new discoveries in science.

Focus Your Reading Answers

1 Socialists believed that the people should have common ownership of the means of production and distribution of goods. Social Darwinism held that only the fittest survived, including among humans. Thus, the poor were poor because they lacked intelligence and were unfit to survive. This theory allowed business owners to ignore the problems of workers.

2 Labor unions wanted better working conditions, which included safety measures, protection of children, shorter hours, and fair wages for all.

3 The telephone allowed communication over long distances. The incandescent light bulb made it possible to work after dark and to be safer on city streets. Advances in medicine included a vaccine against rabies. New chemical elements were discovered.

Lesson Vocabulary

Discuss each of the vocabulary terms with students.

The theory that there should be common ownership of the means of production and distribution of goods is known as *socialism*. Karl Marx was one of the founders of *socialism*. The workers are the *proletariat*. Marx believed that the *proletariat* would overthrow the capitalists one day. *Social Darwinism* was Charles Darwin's theory of survival of the fittest, applied to people. Some people explained poverty through the lens of *Social Darwinism*. *Realism* is the idea of seeing the world as it really is. *Realism* affected literature and politics as well as science.

Groups of workers formed organizations called *labor unions* to protest working conditions. One goal of the *labor unions* was eliminating child labor. A *strike* is a work stoppage designed to make owners give in to demands of the workers. In Great Britain, *strikes* became a right after 1870.

An *invention* is a new device or process. The telephone and light bulb were *inventions* that made life easier.

Social Revolutions 273

Picturing History

Charles Darwin, shown on page 274, spent five years as an unpaid naturalist on the *Beagle*, which sailed around the globe. This was the formative event of Darwin's life. In studying fossils, geologic formations, and living plants and animals, Darwin formulated the questions that would lead to his famous and still controversial theories.

Stop and Think

Students' lists will vary but should reflect the realities of child labor.

Chart Extension

Have students make Venn diagrams to show the material in another form. Encourage students to work in teams to find out when each of the goals was accomplished.

Extension

In 1860 shoemakers in Lynn, Massachusetts, went on strike for better wages. Nearly 5,000 shoemakers, 800 of them women, marched in the streets. Strikes had been judged legal by the Massachusetts Supreme Court in 1842. The strike went on for two weeks.

Social Revolutions, 1750–1910

The most famous socialist was Karl Marx. In 1848, he published his ideas and beliefs in *The Communist Manifesto*. He predicted that the **proletariat**, or workers, would overthrow the capitalists. His philosophy gave rise to communism and the Russian Revolution in the 20th century.

Social Darwinism was a philosophy based on the ideas of Charles Darwin. Darwin's theory was that only the strongest and best adapted animals survived. In 1842, he wrote an essay called *Natural Selection*. In 1859, he wrote *On The Origin of Species by Means of Natural Selection*. Darwin, however, studied animals, not humans. Others took his work and adapted his ideas to humans. Social Darwinists said that, like animals, only the fittest—or the strongest and smartest—people grew wealthy. The poor were poor because they were stupid and lazy. Wealthy business owners used this argument to explain their rise to wealth and power. It also gave them a reason not to improve conditions for their workers.

Charles Darwin

Goals of United States Labor Unions 1850–1910

Knights of Labor
- eight-hour workday
- equal wages for women
- end child labor

American Federation of Labor
- eight-hour workday
- higher wages for working men
- safer working conditions
- benefits for injured workers

Women's Trade Union League
- eight-hour workday
- minimum wage
- end child labor

Rise of Labor Unions

The horrible working conditions in factories in the 1800s led to the development of **labor unions**. Groups of workers formed organizations to protest the conditions. They also wanted reforms like shorter working hours, age limits for working children, and safety measures.

The unions used **strikes**, or work stoppages, to pressure employers. They organized protests and marches to make their issues known. Unions won the right to strike in Great Britain in 1870. By 1900, trade unions in the rest of Western Europe and the United States had made progress.

stop and think

Imagine that you a ten-year-old child working in a textile factory. You can't d the things that wealthy children d With a partner, ma a list of those thin in one column lab "Wish." In the seco column label "Why Can't" and write th reasons that you c enjoy these things

Extensions

1 Have students interested in science use library resources or the Internet to investigate the ongoing research of the Charles Darwin Research Station, which is involved in conservation in the Galapagos Islands. Allow time for them to present their findings to the class.

2 Students interested in science may also want to investigate the ongoing debate between evolutionists and creationists, perhaps conducting a debate according to formal rules and using the arguments set forth by each side. Alternatively, they may wish to role-play William Jennings Bryan and Clarence Darrow in what is known as the "Scopes Monkey Trial."

Science and Literature

Realism, or the philosophy of seeing the world as it really is, influenced science, politics, literature, and the arts after 1850. A number of scientific discoveries and inventions took place. Writers such as Charles Dickens described the life of the urban poor in such novels as *Oliver Twist* and *David Copperfield*.

The rise of industrialism and **inventions** to make work easier and faster led to other discoveries. With leisure time created by machines doing work, people had more opportunity to read, think, and experiment. Inventors in the United States changed the way the world lived with their inventions. Alexander Graham Bell invented the telephone in 1876, which allowed people to talk with each other over distances. In 1879, Thomas Edison invented the incandescent light bulb. This was one of more than one thousand items he worked on.

In 1885, Louis Pasteur, a French scientist, developed a vaccine against rabies. Marie Curie, also a French scientist, working with her husband, Pierre, announced the discovery of new chemical elements in 1898. Working together, they had isolated polonium and radium.

Many more inventors around the world made machines and discoveries that changed the way of life of millions.

Putting It All Together

Make a concept web with "Scientific Discoveries" in the center. Draw lines to circles with inventions in them. Then write how each invention affected daily life in the new urban cities.

Alexander Graham Bell (1847–1922)

Thomas Edison (1847–1931)

Louis Pasteur (1822–1895)

Marie (1867–1934) and Pierre (1859–1906) Curie

Social Revolutions, 1750–1910

Picturing History

The photographs show, from top to bottom, Alexander Graham Bell, Thomas Alva Edison, Louis Pasteur, and Marie and Pierre Curie.

Both Bell's grandfather and father worked with human speech and taught the deaf. Bell's primary interest was in teaching the deaf. His telephone was inspired by a desire to help the hearing impaired. In February 1876, he applied for a patent a mere two hours before another inventor arrived at the Patent Office with a similar idea.

Edison's inventions made him famous by the age of thirty. Nearly deaf from an accident at twelve, he was largely self-educated. He set up what he termed an "invention factory" in New Jersey's Menlo Park in 1876. For five years he and his team of assistants patented a new invention almost monthly. By the time of his death, Edison had more than 1,000 patents.

Pasteur may be most associated with the process he invented to purify liquids, pasteurization. However, he also worked on preventing anthrax.

Marie and Pierre Curie shared the 1903 Nobel Prize in physics with Henri Bequerel. In 1911, Marie Curie won the Nobel Prize in chemistry for her work with radioactivity. The Curies' daughter Irene, with her husband, Frederic Joliot, received the 1935 Nobel Prize in chemistry.

Extension

Have students working in small groups make timelines of inventions, including those discussed in the chapter and others from the period. Encourage them to illustrate their timelines with photocopied illustrations of the invention or inventors or with original artwork. Post the timelines to help students recall important discoveries.

Putting It All Together

Students' concept webs will vary. Possible responses: the telephone made it possible to communicate with family and friends far away; electric lights allowed people to work or study after the sun went down and provided a crime deterrent in city streets; the discovery of radioactivity led to advances in medical treatments.

Social Revolutions

Chapter Review

1. Students' letters will vary but should discuss changes in the community due to industrialization and take a position as to whether it is good or bad for the lives of people there.

2. Students' paragraphs will vary but should include information from the chapter to support their position.

Chapter Summary

Social Revolutions, 1750–1910

- The **Industrial Revolution** began in the 1780s in Great Britain. It was made possible by the growth in population, the number of people with **capital** to invest, large supplies of **natural resources**, large markets for finished goods, and improvements in technology.
- Before the Industrial Revolution, **textiles** were made by a **cottage industry**.
- Belgium, Germany, and France soon industrialized. **Entrepreneurs** in New England invested in building textile factories.
- To find work, people moved to cities. The result was rapid **urbanization** of industrial nations.
- Workers lived in **slums** in five- and six-story **tenements**.
- A new group of business owners and managers developed in the **middle class** as a result of the Industrial Revolution.
- **Socialism** calls for the ownership and control of the means of production and distribution of goods to belong to society. Karl Marx believed that the **proletariat** in time would overthrow capitalists.
- The philosophy of **Social Darwinism** states that only the strongest and smartest people succeed.
- **Realism** describes life the way it really is.
- Working conditions for the working class were very hard, unsafe, and unhealthful.
- Workers organized **labor unions** and **strikes** to protest their problems.
- **Inventions** such as the light bulb and telephone changed peoples' lives.

Chapter Review

1. Imagine that you are a skilled textile spinner in the late 1780s. Write a letter to a friend about the changes taking place in your village as a result of the factory system. Is your life better or worse? Why?

2. Do you think the Social Darwinists were right or wrong? Write a paragraph or two defending your position. Use information from this chapter to support your argument.

Novel Connections

Below is a list of books that relate to the time period covered in this chapter. The numbers in parentheses indicate the related Thematic Strands of the National Council for the Social Studies (NCSS).

Catherine Gourley. *Society Sisters: Stories of Women Who Fought for Social Justice in America.* Lerner Publishing Group, 2003. (II, III, V, VI)

Judy L. Hasday. *Marie Curie: Pioneer on the Frontier of Radioactivity.* Enslow Publishers, Incorporated, 2004. (IV, VII, IX)

Dorothy Hoobler and Thomas Hoobler. *We Are Americans: Voices of the Immigrant Experience.* Scholastic, Inc., 2003. (II, III)

Anita Louise McCormick. *The Industrial Revolution in American History.* Enslow Publishers, Incorporated, 1998. (III, VII, VIII)

Jill Paton Walsh. *Chance Child.* Farrar, Straus and Giroux, 1991. (I, III, VI, VII)

Adam Woog. *A Sweatshop During the Industrial Revolution.* Thomson Gale, 2002. (VI, VII, VIII)

Skill Builder

Analyzing a Bar Graph

In Chapter 15, you learned that a line graph is a good way to show changes in statistics over time. A bar graph also shows data. It shows information for several nations or companies at a particular time.

Usually, the quantity, or amount, is listed along the left side, or vertical axis. The subjects are shown along the bottom, or horizontal axis. The time period is given in the title.

To read a bar graph, follow these steps:

1. Read the title of the graph to learn what it is about.
2. Examine the vertical axis to learn the quantity.
3. Examine the horizontal axis to learn the subjects.
4. Examine the bars to learn about the relationship between the subjects.

Use the graph to answer these questions.

1. What is the title of the graph?
2. What do the bars represent?
3. Which nation had the most railroad track in 1850?
4. Which nation had about 2,500 miles of track?
5. What can you infer about industrialization in these four countries?
6. How might the amount of railroad track influence a country's ability to industrialize?

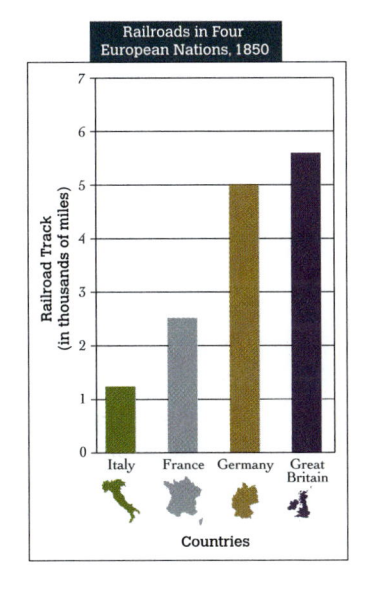

Skill Builder

1. The title is "Railroads in Four European Nations, 1850."
2. The bars represent railroad track in thousands of miles.
3. Great Britain had the most railroad track in 1850.
4. France had about 2,500 miles of track.
5. Based on the information from the chapter and the graph, students can infer that countries with more railroad track industrialized faster.
6. Countries with more railroad track may find it easier to industrialize, as goods can be shipped more efficiently.

Social Revolutions 277

Classroom Discussion

Discuss with students some of the broader topics covered in this chapter.

- How can successful entrepreneurs address social problems?
- What are some of the challenges that workers face today?
- In what ways has contemporary science affected politics and world events?

Unit Objectives

After studying this unit, students will be able to

- analyze the effects of nationalism in Europe
- identify the factors in and results of European colonization of Africa, Asia, and Latin America

Unit 6 focuses on the growth of independent nations in Europe and their colonial expansion.

Chapter 18, Nationalism in Europe, examines the role of nationalism in the independence movements in Italy and Germany.

Chapter 19, Imperialism and Modernization, explores the way European nations staked claims to land, markets, and resources in Africa, Asia, and Latin America.

Getting Started

Write a T-chart with the words *old* and *new* on the board. Ask students to identify some of the characteristics of nations they have studied thus far. Write their responses in the column for *old*. Ask students to make a copy of the T-chart in their notebooks and to fill out the *new* column as they read Unit 6. Then have a volunteer read aloud the two paragraphs on page 278.

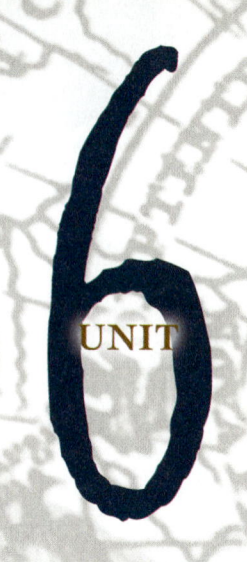

UNIT 6

A NEW AGE

The late 1800s was another time of important changes. In Europe, German and Italian nationalists were fighting to unify their countries. Their success had far-reaching resul[ts] in the 20th century.

Europeans also brought dramatic changes to other parts o[f] the world. European nations competed with one another [to] increase their power in Asia, Africa, and Latin America. Their goals were the same. They wanted more raw materi[als] for their growing industries at home and more overseas markets for their goods. The results were tragic for Asian[s,] Africans, and Latin Americans.

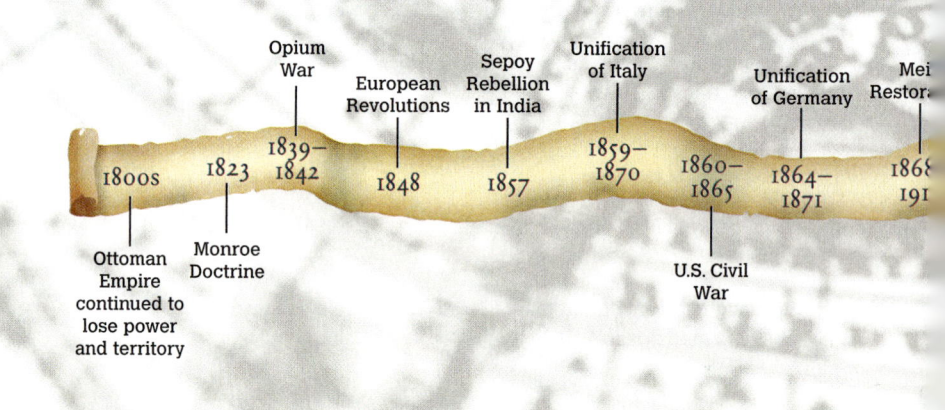

Timeline

- 1800s — Ottoman Empire continued to lose power and territory
- 1823 — Monroe Doctrine
- 1839–1842 — Opium War
- 1848 — European Revolutions
- 1857 — Sepoy Rebellion in India
- 1859–1870 — Unification of Italy
- 1860–1865 — U.S. Civil War
- 1864–1871 — Unification of Germany
- 1868–191[?] — Mei[ji] Restor[ation]

Measuring Time

Tell students that Chapter 18 discusses the growth of nationalism in Europe. The events of that era appear on page 278 of the timeline. Chapter 19 views European and Japanese imperialism and the attempts of Asian nations to modernize. Pages 278–279 of the timeline depict the events that marked this era.

Timeline Extension

Ask students to use the timeline to preview each chapter in the unit. Then have them answer the following questions:

- Which nation was first unified, Germany or Italy?
- When was Africa divided?
- What two rebellions took place in Asian countries? When and where did they occur?
- What three wars does the timeline show?

Who joined Garibaldi's Red Shirts to create an Italian nation?

What did Japanese officials hope to gain by modernizing their nation?

How did Great Britain win control of India?

Self-strengthening Movement in China — 1800s–1890s

Berlin Conference divided Africa — 1884

Sino-Japanese War — 1895

Open Door Policy in China — 1899

Cuba U.S. Protectorate — 1901–1934

Boxer Rebellion in China — 1900

Roosevelt Corollary — 1904

Japan annexed Korea — 1910

Chinese Republic was declared — 1911

Collage Answers

1 To create an Italian nation, a volunteer army of Sicilian patriots joined Garibaldi's Red Shirts.

2 By modernizing their nation, Japanese officials hoped to make the nation rich and strong.

3 Great Britain won control of India by defeating the French forces and the Mogul army and nationalizing their holdings in the East India Company.

Collage Extension

Use the images and questions on page 279 to preview the unit. Discuss what the questions and pictures suggest about this new age. What do the illustrations suggest were some of its characteristics?

Picturing History

The images on page 279 represent people and places that will be discussed in Unit 6.

1 This is a print of Garibaldi's Red Shirts fighting during the Italian Civil War.

2 A Japanese factory in the late 1800s is shown in this drawing.

3 Indian women served British families during the colonial era.

A New Age

Chapter Summary
Refer to page 290 for a summary of Chapter 18.

Related Transparencies

T-1 World Map

T-18 Three-Column Chart

T-20 Concept Web

Key Blacklines

Primary Source—from *Young Italy* by Giuseppe Mazzini

CD Extension

Encourage students to use the reading comprehension, vocabulary reinforcement, and interactive timeline activities on the student CD.

Getting Focused

Divide the class into seven small groups, assigning each group one of the categories of reasons listed as motivating people to work together to form a single nation. Ask the groups to look for specific examples of their category as they read the chapter. Have each group create a chart showing how their category applies to Germany and Italy.

Chapter 18
NATIONALISM IN EUROPE
(1815–1914)

Getting Focused

Skim this chapter to predict what you will be learning.
- Read the lesson titles and subheadings.
- Look at the illustrations and read the captions.
- Examine the maps.
- Review the vocabulary words and terms.

Until the late 1800s, Germany and Italy were not their own nations. Parts of each were ruled by princes, dukes, or other nobles. What would make people want to join together and become part of a large nation? Work with a partner to think of economic, geographic, political, religious, technological, societal, and cultural reasons.

Pre-Reading Discussion

1 Discuss with students some of the contemporary struggles of nations toward freedom. See if students can identify some common features.

2 Ask students to recall examples of nations striving for freedom in earlier time periods they have studied. Consider making a chart of the wars for independence or using flags on a world map to highlight these.

Picturing History

The battle on the barricades, shown in the painting on page 280, depicts the 1830 French uprising that resulted when Charles X suspended freedom of the press and dissolved the French legislature. That uprising and its social context became the seed for Victor Hugo's 1862 epic novel *Les Misérables*. That novel found worldwide readership. It was very popular in the United States; some Confederate soldiers referred to themselves as "Lee's Miserables." You may wish to show clips from a film version or play a sound recording of the popular musical to give students a feel for the time period.

LESSON 1

Conservatives in Control

Thinking on Your Own

Read the subheads in this lesson. As you read the lesson, create a sequence flowchart. Use the subheads to help remember the order in which events happened. Use as many vocabulary words as possible in your flowchart.

After defeating Napoleon I at Waterloo, the rulers of Europe wanted peace and stability. They hoped to prevent future wars, revolutions, and democratic change. At the Congress of Vienna, held in Vienna, Austria, in 1814, they agreed to restore power to Europe's royal families. These **conservatives** believed that the monarchy was the best form of government. They also wanted to maintain a **balance of power** between Europe's strongest nations. That is, they wanted Russia, the Austrian Empire, Prussia, France, and Great Britain to keep one another in check.

focus your reading

What caused the revolutions of 1848?

What part did Camillo di Cavour play in the unification of Italy?

Why was Giuseppe Garibaldi successful in helping to unify Italy?

vocabulary

conservatives
balance of power
liberals
nationalists
ethnic groups
appease
depose

Preventing Change

The leader of the conservatives was Prince Klemens Von Metternich of Austria. He wanted to keep **liberals** and **nationalists** from gaining power. Liberals wanted to protect people's civil liberties, including freedom of speech, press, and assembly. They believed that governments elected by the people

Nationalism in Europe 281

Lesson Summary

Conservatives who controlled the Congress of Vienna wanted a balance of power among the European nations. Austria's Prince Metternich spearheaded the movement toward conservatism. In 1848, many nations tried to gain independence from monarchical forms of government. In most cases, these uprisings failed.

Italy was unified into a single state after the mergers of smaller kingdoms. Cavour, Garibaldi, and King Victor Emmanuel were key in this process.

Lesson Objective

Students will learn about the Congress of Vienna and the unification of Italy.

Focus Your Reading Answers

1 The revolutions of 1848 were caused by nationalists who wanted to set up new nations based on ethnic groups.

2 Camillo di Cavour helped to unify Italy by freeing Italian territory from Austrian control and joining in a military alliance with Napoleon III.

3 Garibaldi successfully unified Italy with his Red Shirt volunteer army, which aided a revolt on Sicily, then moved on to battles on the mainland. They controlled all of Sicily within two months.

Lesson Vocabulary

Introduce each of the following vocabulary terms to students.

Explain that in this lesson those who believed that the monarchy was the best form of government were called *conservatives*. *Conservatives* at the Congress of Vienna agreed to restore power to the royal families of Europe.

The *balance of power* as used in this lesson is the idea that Europe's strongest nations would keep each other in check. The *balance of power* would prevent future wars. Those who wanted to protect people's civil liberties were called *liberals*. Prince Metternich of Austria did not want *liberals* to gain power. The *nationalists* believed that people owed loyalty to a nation rather than to a royal family. The *nationalists* were another group that Metternich distrusted. An *ethnic group* is a nationality. Some people believed that each *ethnic group* should have its own government.

To *appease* means "to calm or make someone content." Austria tried to *appease* the rebellious forces by removing Metternich as foreign minister. When someone is *deposed*, he or she is overthrown. Northern Italian *nationalists deposed* their rulers.

Nationalism in Europe 281

Picturing History

The Austrian army had already suppressed a revolt in Prague when it turned to the Vienna uprising, as pictured at the top of page 282. Radicals held the city for several months but were unable to keep their support in the face of unemployment and low wages, coupled with their demands to free the serfs. The uprising did accomplish the removal of Ferdinand I, who abdicated in favor of his son Francis Joseph.

Map Extension

Ask students to use the map on page 282 to answer the following questions:

- Were there uprisings in Spain between 1848 and 1849? (no)
- Which city in the two Sicilies was the site of an uprising? (Palermo)
- To what political state did Budapest belong? (Austrian Empire)
- In what French cities did uprisings occur? (Paris, Lyon)

Picturing History

The cartoon at the bottom of page 282 depicts the leaders of countries beset by revolution trying to make a clean sweep of the opposition. Have students look for familiar figures and symbols to identify what is happening. (For example, the Prussian with a broom is wearing a Christian cross.)

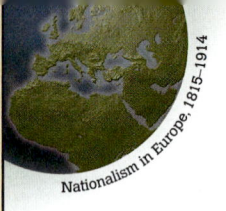

---

were best able to do this. Nationalists insisted that people owed loyalty to the nation, not to a king or royal family. They thought that each **ethnic group**, or nationality, should have its own government. Both liberals and nationalists were a threat to the existing order.

For several years, Metternich and the leaders of Europe managed to prevent change. In 1823, liberals in Spain tried to overthrow the monarchy. A French army crushed the uprising. Revolts also broke out in France, Belgium, and Italy. These, too, were put down by military force.

Many ethnic groups in the Austrian Empire wanted nations of their own. These groups included Croats, Czechs, Germans, Hungarians, Italians, Poles, Serbians, Slovaks, Slovenes, and Romanians. They were a serious problem to Metternich.

The year 1848 saw liberal and nationalist uprisings across Europe. In France, liberals overthrew the monarchy and set up the Second Republic. But the French soon replaced it with a Second Empire under Emperor Napoleon III—sometimes referred to as Louis-Napoleon. He was the nephew of Napoleon Bonaparte.

In Austria, Hungarian and Italian nationalists tried to set up new nations of their own. The Austrian government tried to **appease** the rebels by removing Metternich from his position as foreign minister. When that did not work, Austrian armies put down both uprisings.

Leaders of France, Prussia, and Austria tried to sweep away the revolutionaries in 1848.

Extension

Prince Metternich held a variety of diplomatic positions for Austria, including minister to France and minister of foreign affairs. By keeping Austria neutral in the Napoleonic conflicts for as long as possible, Metternich allowed that nation to build up armaments secretly. For his political and military expertise, Metternich was named prince. After being removed from his position as foreign minister, Metternich was appointed chancellor in 1821.

Unifying Italy

While nothing happened in the 1848 uprising, Italian nationalists did not give up their desire for a nation. Austria controlled a large section of what is now northern Italy in 1848. The rest of the peninsula was made up of small kingdoms. Here, conservatives finally met their match.

One of those kingdoms, Piedmont, was ruled by a king, Victor Emmanuel II. In 1852, he chose Camillo di Cavour as his prime minister. Cavour set about freeing Italian territory from Austrian control and uniting the peninsula.

Unification of Italy, 1859–1870
- Kingdom of Sardinia, 1858
- Added to Kingdom of Sardinia, 1859
- Italy, 1860
- Added to Italy, 1866
- Added to Italy, 1870

Cavour joined Emperor Napoleon III in a military alliance. In 1859, the armies of France and Piedmont went to war against Austria. The allies won the war. Examine the map of the unification of Italy from 1859 to 1870. Locate the territory that was added to the Kingdom of Piedmont after the war in 1859. In exchange for France's help, Cavour agreed to let France take the regions of Nice and Savoy.

Austria supported the governments of several northern Italian states. Nationalists in these states were inspired by Piedmont's success. They **deposed**, or overthrew, their rulers and joined their states with Piedmont.

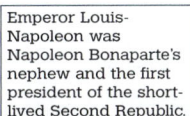

Emperor Louis-Napoleon was Napoleon Bonaparte's nephew and the first president of the short-lived Second Republic.

Map Extension

Ask students to use the map on page 283 to answer the following questions:

- Which state was added to Italy in 1866? (Venetia)
- Which state was added to the Kingdom of Sardinia in 1859? (Lombardy)

Picturing History

Emperor Louis-Napoleon, whose portrait appears on page 283, twice tried unsuccessfully to gain the throne of France after Napoleon II's death. After his first attempt, in 1836, he was sent to the United States but settled soon after in England. His second attempt, in 1840, led to his being sentenced to life in prison. He escaped after six years and again went to England. He returned to France during the 1848 revolt and was elected president. In 1851, knowing he could not be re-elected according to provisions of the constitution, he headed a military coup and declared a new constitution. Napoleon III was taken prisoner in 1870 during the Franco-Prussian War. The French defeat was part of the desire for revenge against Germany. Napoleon III once more fled to England where he died in 1873.

Extension

The Congress of Vienna, noted on page 281, began five months after Napoleon I first abdicated, completing its work just before his Hundred Days of power ended at Waterloo. Representatives from the five nations were the real decision-makers, even though other nations, such as Sweden and Portugal, attended. Still, most of the provisions of the Congress lasted for 40 years. Some historians believe the Congress held tensions in check until World War I.

Extension

Camillo di Cavour became interested in politics in 1830 after being sent to Genoa as a military engineer. In 1847, he founded a liberal newspaper that became the mouthpiece for the Italian national movement. In it, Cavour advocated reforms in industry and agriculture and called for railroads to unite the nation. Cavour's careful planning led to Victor Emmanuel II being proclaimed king of a united Italy, just as Cavour had hoped. Less than six months later, Cavour died.

Nationalism in Europe

Stop and Think

Students' letters will vary but should include persuasive reasons for an alliance between Napoleon III and Italy.

Picturing History

Garibaldi, shown on page 284 meeting with Italy's king, became a member of Young Italy while in the Kingdom of Piedmont's navy. Giuseppe Mazzini, the man who inspired the Italians to seek liberation from Austria, had formed this secret group. After the discovery of Garibaldi's plan to seize the frigate on which he was sailing to assist Genoa's struggle for freedom, Garibaldi escaped. He went first to France and then to South America. He participated in wars in Brazil and Uruguay. In Uruguay he formed and commanded the Italian legion and met the woman he would marry. When Mazzini's Roman Republic collapsed, Garibaldi fled. He spent part of his exile as a candlemaker in New York City. Returning to farm on the island of Caprera, he led 1,000 Red Shirts in 1860. After achieving victory, he handed Sicily and Naples to Victor Emmanuel II and returned to his island. He later served with the French in the Franco-Prussian War before his final retirement to Caprera.

Nationalism in Europe, 1815–1914

Garibaldi and His Red Shirts

Victor Emmanuel and Cavour had united most of northern Italy. In the south, Giuseppe Garibaldi was building support for a single Italy. Garibaldi was a strong nationalist. Unlike Cavour, he did not want to see Italy become a monarchy. He wanted an Italian republic.

By 1860, Garibaldi had pulled together a volunteer army of 1,000 patriots. They wore red shirts as their uniforms. As a result, they were known as Red Shirts. Garibaldi and his army aided a revolt on the island of Sicily. It was part of the Kingdom of the Two Sicilies, made up of Sicily and Naples. When they had freed the island, the Red Shirts took the fight back to the mainland. Within two months, they controlled the entire kingdom.

Garibaldi meeting Victor Emmanuel

Garibaldi turned over control of the kingdom to Victor Emmanuel. In exchange, the king and Cavour agreed to a constitutional monarchy to govern the new nation.

The regions of Venetia and the Papal States were not yet part of Italy. Austria gave up Venetia in 1866 after Austria lost the Austro-Prussian War. Italy had been an ally of Prussia in the war.

Italian forces invaded the Papal States in 1870. Emperor Napoleon III defended the states. After he removed his troops to fight Prussia in the Franco-Prussian War, the citizens of the Papal States voted to join the new nation of Italy. Rome became its capital.

Putting It All Together

Create a concept map to show how Italy became a nation. Label the large center circle "Unifying Italy." Then draw smaller circles for the different steps in the process. Work with a partner and be sure to include details from the lesson.

stop and think

Imagine you are Cavour. What would you say to Napoleon III to get his help in adding territory to Piedmont? List as many ideas as you can think of that would convince Napoleon III to help. Then use those ideas to write a persuasive letter to the emperor asking for France's support against Austria. Share your letter with a partner. Ask a partner for ideas to make your letter more persuasive.

King Emma...

284 Chapter 18

Picturing History

Victor Emmanuel, shown at the bottom of page 284, became monarch of the united kingdoms of Sardinia-Piedmont in 1849 when his father abdicated after being defeated by the Austrians. Not until 1861 did he reign over a united Italy. The two final states to join Italy were Venice in 1866 and the Papal States in 1871. That was the year that Victor Emmanuel II marched into Rome and made it his capital.

Putting It All Together

Students' concept maps will vary. Possible response: Cavour joined Napoleon III against Austria; northern Italian nationalists joined with Piedmont; Garibaldi and the Red Shirts liberated Sicily; Italy formed a constitutional monarchy; Venice and the Papal States joined the rest of Italy.

LESSON 2

The New Nation of Germany

Thinking on Your Own

As you read the lesson, take bulleted notes about Bismarck and his policies. Include information from his biography. Use the vocabulary words in your notes. After you have finished reading the lesson, think about the kind of man Bismarck must have been. Write one sentence that describes Bismarck's character. Use information from your notes to support your opinion.

In 1860, there was no single German nation. People who considered themselves German lived in Prussia, the Austrian Empire, and 39 small states ruled by princes, dukes, and kings. German nationalists were inspired by the success of Cavour in Italy. They began to look for ways to unify the many German states. The best choice to lead them seemed to be Prussia.

focus your reading

How did Otto von Bismarck enlarge the Prussian army?

How did William I become kaiser of a united Germany?

What policies did Bismarck adopt for governing the new German nation?

vocabulary

industrialize   kaiser
militarism   authoritarian
domination

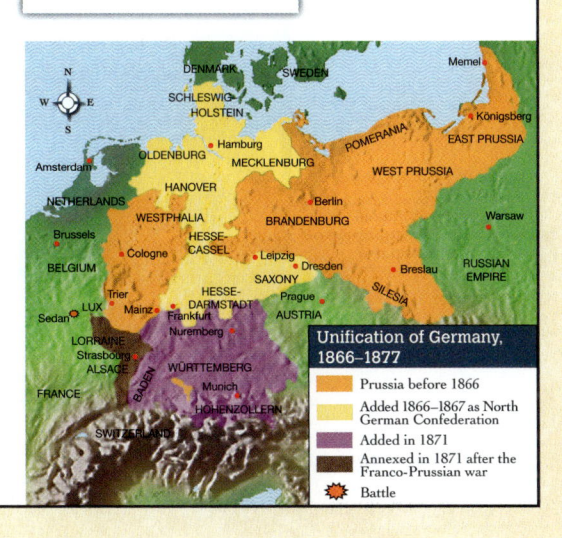

Prussia and Bismarck

Prussia in the early 1860s was large, wealthy, and rapidly **industrializing**—or developing a strong manufacturing sector. Prussia already had a leadership role among the other German states. It had put together a trade association that negotiated trade policies between the German states and other nations.

Unification of Germany, 1866–1877
- Prussia before 1866
- Added 1866–1867 as North German Confederation
- Added in 1871
- Annexed in 1871 after the Franco-Prussian war
- Battle

Lesson Summary

Inspired by Italy's success, German nationalists began to unify German states in 1860, beginning with Prussia. That state had already negotiated trade policies between the German states and other nations. Under the leadership of William I and Otto von Bismarck, who built up the Prussian army, Germany drove Austria from its lands. A North German Confederation resulted, under Prussian leadership. When the Prussians were victorious over Napoleon III in the Franco-Prussian War, grateful German states invited William to become kaiser. He and Bismarck focused on building a strong economy through industrializing.

Lesson Objective

Students will learn about the founding of Germany.

Focus Your Reading Answers

1 Otto von Bismarck enlarged the Prussian army, as William I desired, by using taxes.

2 William I became kaiser of a united Germany at the request of German states that were grateful for the defeat of the French in the Franco-Prussian War.

3 To govern the new German nation, the conservative Bismarck raised tariffs to protect manufacturing, strengthened the banking system, and granted certain benefits to workers to keep them from joining a new socialist party.

Lesson Vocabulary

Discuss each of the vocabulary terms with students.

Developing a strong manufacturing sector is called *industrializing*. The *industrializing* of Prussia began in the early 1860s.

Militarism is belief in the need for a strong military force. Both King William I and Bismarck believed in *militarism*. Another word for "control" is *domination*. The North German Confederation was under Prussia's *domination*.

The German word for "emperor" is *kaiser*. William I became the first *kaiser* of the German Empire. In an *authoritarian* government, the power is in the hands of one person. Germany under the *kaisers* was an *authoritarian* state.

Nationalism in Europe   285

Picturing History

The Prussian army, shown at the top of page 286, had suffered a terrible defeat at the hands of Napoleon in 1806. Less than a decade later, the army had recovered sufficiently to aid in that leader's final overthrow. Prussia's military might was fully restored under William I and Albrecht von Roon, his minister of war.

Picturing History

Emperor William I, depicted at the bottom of page 286, was not crowned king of Prussia until he was sixty-three years of age. As the second son of King Frederick William III, he took part in military campaigns. He was appointed regent for his mentally ill older brother, Frederick William IV, in 1858 and became king at Frederick's death. William became the head of the North German Confederation in 1866 after commanding a three-week battle against the Austrians.

Extension

Ask students to investigate the results of militarism in Europe in the nineteenth century. What had been the effects of military buildups in previous centuries? Have students present their findings to the class by using the Student Presentation Builder on the student CD.

Nationalism in Europe, 1815–1914

The Prussian army was well-disciplined, tough, and well-equipped.

What Prussia needed was someone to make unification happen. That person was Count Otto von Bismarck. In 1862, Bismarck was appointed prime minister by King William I of Prussia. Both men strongly believed in **militarism**. They supported having a strong military force.

The king had asked Parliament to raise taxes to increase the size of the army. The Prussian Parliament refused to go along with the king's proposal. Bismarck ignored the legislature. He moved forward with the king's plan to enlarge the Prussian army. If it would not vote him new taxes, he would use money from current taxes. Bismarck bled the national tax revenues to build up the army.

William I being crowned emperor

286 Chapter 18

Map Extension

Ask students to use the map on page 285 to answer the following questions:

- When was Munich added to Germany? (1871)
- What was the land called that was added during 1866–1867? (North German Confederation)
- Where was a major battle fought? (Sedan)
- What general descriptive statement can you make about Prussia before 1866? (It was divided into two sections, east and west, that were separated by other German states.)

286 Chapter 18

The Siege of Paris, 1870

Building the German Empire

Bismarck then set about using the army. He wanted to gain the regions of Schleswig and Holstein from Denmark. He also wanted to drive the Austrians from German territory. By 1866, the Prussian army had succeeded in achieving both goals. The following year, Schleswig and Holstein combined to form the North German Confederation. The new confederation was under Prussia's **domination**—or control. New areas were added to Prussia between 1864 and 1867.

At the same time the four southern German states entered into military alliances with Prussia. These states bordered France. Bismarck convinced them that France would try to take them over. Becoming allies of Prussia, he argued, would protect them.

There was some truth to Bismarck's claim about France. Or so he believed. He was convinced that France did not want a strong Germany as its neighbor. In 1870, Bismarck pushed France into declaring war on Prussia. The Franco-Prussian War lasted less than six months. The Prussian army invaded France and quickly captured the French army and Napoleon III. The citizens of Paris held out until January 1871, but they finally surrendered.

The German states celebrated their victory over France. In appreciation, they asked William I of Prussia to become **kaiser**,

stop and think
With a partner, create a flowchart to track the causes and effects that resulted in a united Germany. Include all key events, people, and dates from the lesson.

Picturing History
William I of Prussia commanded that nation's forces in the Franco-Prussian War. The battle for Paris is shown in the painting on page 287. The decisive victory occurred at Sedan in 1870. The southern German states that had joined with Prussia to defeat Napoleon III agreed to join the North German Federation. Thus, in 1871, the German Empire came into existence when William I was crowned emperor at Versailles.

Stop and Think
Students' flowcharts will vary but should include key events and people from the lesson. Possible response: 1862: Otto von Bismarck appointed prime minister and built up the Prussian army; 1866: Prussia drove Austrians from German territory and gained two regions from Denmark; 1867: North German Confederation formed; between 1864 and 1867: Germany added new states; 1870–1871: Franco-Prussian War, William I became kaiser; 1910: Germany was largest industrial nation in Europe.

Extension
William II was the last German emperor, ruling from 1888 until 1918. He was born with a crippled left arm but took as his motto "If I rest, I rust." Like his father, he believed in the divine right of kings. The grandson of England's Queen Victoria, as emperor he wanted to build a navy that would rival Britain's. This led to a military buildup among European powers. William II abdicated and went to the Netherlands at the end of World War I. When he died in 1941, Hitler gave him a military funeral.

Bio Facts
- Born 1815 at Schönhausen.
- Studied law and entered Prussian civil service.
- Served from 1847–1862 as representative at assembly of German Confederation and as ambassador to both Russia and France.
- Appointed chancellor and given rank of prince by Kaiser William I.
- Supported Germany's colonial efforts in the Pacific and in Africa.
- Forced to resign in 1890 so Kaiser William II could have absolute power.
- Died 1898 at Friedrichsruh.

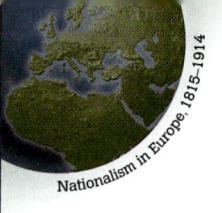

Nationalism in Europe, 1815–1914

or emperor, of a new German Empire. The coronation took place in the palace of Versailles, not far from Paris. German nationalists had achieved their dream. Led by Bismarck, they had created a single nation.

Building German Power at Home

The government of the new Germany had a constitution and a legislature with two houses. The upper house was appointed by the rulers of the German states. The lower house was elected by male citizens. The real power, however, lay with the kaiser—and with Bismarck.

When the constitution was written, Bismarck made sure that the legislature had little power. The heads of all government departments reported to the president of the upper house. The president was appointed by the kaiser. For nearly 20 years, William I and then William II appointed Bismarck to this post. The military and government bureaucracy reported to the kaiser, not to the legislature. In addition, foreign policy was controlled

Biography

Otto von Bismarck (1815–1898)

Otto von Bismarck is known in history as the "Iron Chancellor." This title comes from his first speech as prime minister to the Prussian Parliament. He said, "The great issues of the day will be decided by speeches and the resolutions of the majorities but by iron and blood."

Bismarck used the iron of weapons and the blood of soldie to build the German state. He was not educated to be a soldier. His university studies prepared him for work as a civil servant. He did not like the work and resigned. He returned home to manag his father's estate, but he was not content to remain in the country. Bism eventually joined the diplomatic service in the late 1840s and served Prussia until 1

In that year, Bismarck was called to Berlin to meet with William I. His views evide pleased the king who named Bismarck prime minister and later foreign minister. As reward for putting together the German Empire, he was appointed chancellor in 187

Once the German Empire was created, Bismarck kept the new nation out of war. He spent Germany's resources on building up the nation. His views clashed with th new kaiser, William II. The kaiser wanted Germany to play a larger role in world poli Bismarck was forced to step down in 1890.

Biography Extension

Napoleon III ruled France when Otto von Bismarck was Germany's ambassador. Challenge students to imagine a dialog between the two men on one of the issues of the day or to role-play a meeting between them.

288 Chapter 18

by the kaiser. The result was an **authoritarian** government. All power was in the hands of the ruler.

Although a nationalist, Bismarck became a strong conservative. He believed that people would not demand political rights if their basic needs were met. As a result, once Germany was united, Bismarck focused on the economy. Among Bismarck's actions was raising tariffs to protect German manufacturing. The banking system was also strengthened. A few laws were passed to aid workers. Workers who were too sick or injured to work were paid for six months. An old-age pension was set up for retired workers aged 70 and older. Bismarck's motive for these laws was to prevent workers from joining a new socialist political party.

By the end of the 1870s, Germany was the greatest industrial power in Europe. By 1910, it had surpassed Great Britain.

Germany, like Great Britain, had coal and iron resources to fuel industrialization. It also had a large population, so there were plenty of workers for the growing factories. Like Bismarck, wealthy business owners were conservatives. They supported strong government and militarism. By 1910, all these factors combined to make Germany the largest industrial nation in Europe.

Putting It All Together

Each paragraph under the subheading "Building German Power at Home" has a different topic. Draw four columns in your notebook. Label each column with the topic of one of the four paragraphs. Then list additional information about each topic in the correct column. Share your chart with a partner to make sure you have included all the important details about each topic.

Picturing History

Germany's industrialization, depicted in the painting on page 289, initially lagged behind that of France and Belgium, partly because of the competition among the German states. However, iron and coal production increased during the 1840s, and a railroad network began by the 1850s. Bismarck favored the development of heavy industry in order to strengthen Germany's military capacity.

Putting It All Together

Students' charts will vary but should include information from each paragraph of the section. Topics might be government, kaiser's power, Bismarck's actions, and German industrialization.

Chapter Review

1. Students' reasons and essays will vary. Possible responses include more protection and benefits for common people; greater pride in the nation; more opportunities for work and advancement.

2. Students' headlines will vary, possible responses include:
   (a) Revolts Across Europe/Armies Put Down Most Rebels
   (b) Napoleon III and Cavour Now Allies/Join Together Against Austria
   (c) Garibaldi Liberates Sicily/Red Shirts Victorious
   (d) Prussia Picks a Fight/France Not Prepared
   (e) William I New Emperor/Versailles Site of Coronation
   (f) Bismarck Out of Power/William II Wants Iron Chancellor Gone

Chapter Summary

- In 1848, a series of revolutions broke out in Europe. The first was in France. It resulted in Louis-Napoleon becoming emperor of the Second Republic.
- Major uprisings also took place in the Austrian Empire. To **appease** revolutionaries, the emperor made some changes.
- The 1800s saw disagreements between **conservatives** and **liberals** over the proper role of government. Conservatives tried to keep a **balance of power**.
- A spirit of nationalism inspired **ethnic groups** within the Austrian Empire to fight to have their own nations.
- In 1859, Camillo di Cavour was allied with France. Together, they defeated the Austrian Empire.
- **Nationalists** in other northern states on the Italian peninsula **deposed** their governments and united with the Kingdom of Piedmont.
- Giuseppe Garibaldi and his Red Shirts defeated the Kingdom of the Two Sicilies in southern Italy.
- Otto von Bismarck was a strong supporter of **militarism**.
- Bismarck set out to **dominate** territory from Denmark and to break Austria's control over German territory. He created a North German Confederation.
- The Franco-Prussian War lasted six months. William I was asked to become **kaiser**.
- The government of the new Germany was **authoritarian**. Its economy was based on **industrialization**. Germany soon became the largest industrial nation in Europe.

Chapter Review

1. Review your list of reasons why people would want to become part of a large nation. Choose three reasons and write a short essay explaining the reasons.

2. Write two-line headlines for each of the following: (a) 1848 revolutions, (b) alliance between Cavour and Napoleon III, (c) Garibaldi and the Red Shirts, (d) Franco-Prussian War, (e) crowning of William I, (f) firing of Bismarck.

Novel Connections

Below is a list of books that relate to the time period covered in this chapter. The numbers in parentheses indicate the related Thematic Strands of the National Council for the Social Studies (NCSS).

Eva Ibbotson. *The Star of Kazan.* Penguin Putnam Books for Young Readers, 2004. (I, IV)

Tom McGowen. *Frederick the Great, Bismarck, and the Building of the German Empire in World History.* Enslow Publishers, Incorporated, 2002. (V, VI)

Herman J. Viola, Susan Viola. *Giuseppe Garibaldi.* Chelsea House Publishers, 1987. (V, VI, X)

Skill Builder

Analyzing a Political Cartoon

Political cartoonists use the current events of their time as topics for their cartoons. As a result, political cartoons, like photographs and paintings, can be valuable tools to study history.

The goal of a political cartoonist is to make people think about an issue. However, a political cartoonist has a point of view. He or she may be for or against the issue and may want readers to agree with that point of view. The bias is usually easy to detect.

Political cartoonists use symbols and caricature to make their point. A symbol is a person or object that stands for something else. For example, a crown may represent Louis XVI in an 18th-century cartoon about the abuses of the French monarchy.

To analyze political cartoons:

1. Identify the characters and other images used in the cartoon.
2. Identify the topic of the cartoon. Determine what is happening and read all labels and writing.
3. Identify the opinion, or point of view, of the cartoonist.

Complete the following activities. You may need to review the biography of Bismarck.

1. (a) Who is the man putting on his hat? (b) Who is the man wearing the crown?
2. Why is the man leaving?
3. Who is the woman watching what is happening?
4. (a) What object is the man with the crown holding? (b) Why do you think the political cartoonist used this symbol?
5. (a) What is the man with the crown sitting on? (b) Why do you think the political cartoonist used this symbol?

Skill Builder

1. (a) The man putting on his hat is Otto von Bismarck.
   (b) The man wearing the crown is William II.
2. The man is leaving because he has been fired.
3. The woman is Germany personified, worried about the actions of William II.
4. (a) He is holding a puppet labeled *Socialism*.
   (b) The cartoonist may have used this symbol because socialism became more acceptable under William II.
5. (a) He is sitting on a throne made of weapons.
   (b) The cartoonist may have used this symbol because William II built up the German navy and army.

Classroom Discussion

Discuss with students some of the broader topics covered in this chapter.

- How can the unification of states or regions help the citizens of those areas? Look at Chapter 24 for ideas.
- What could be done in regions of the world that are still divided among ethnic groups? Look at the lesson on genocide in Chapter 24.
- In what ways could nations that are currently industrializing benefit from knowing about Germany's experience?

Nationalism in Europe

Chapter Summary
Refer to page 314 for a summary of Chapter 19.

Related Transparencies

T-1 World Map

T-10 Imperialism in Africa, 1914

T-18 Three-Column Chart

T-20 Concept Web

Key Blacklines

Primary Source—In Protest of the Opium Trade

CD Extension

Encourage students to use the reading comprehension, vocabulary reinforcement, and interactive timeline activities on the student CD.

Getting Focused

Students' lists and letters will vary but should provide reasons why European powers should leave. Extend the activity by discussing areas of the world that are still under the rule of a Western government, or discuss the recent movement in Hawaii to renounce statehood.

Chapter 19
Imperialism and Modernization
(1800–1914)

Getting Focused

Skim this chapter to predict what you will be learning.
- Read the lesson titles and subheadings.
- Look at the illustrations and read the captions.
- Examine the maps.
- Review the vocabulary words and terms.

Suppose you are the leader of a kingdom in Africa or Asia. A European government has sent troops to take over your country and officials to tell you how to run your government. You are angry and decide to write a letter to the European government explaining your position. What would you say? Work with a partner to create a list of reasons why the Europeans should leave. Use the list to write your letter.

Pre-Reading Discussion

1 Discuss with students some of the current struggles of nations in Africa and Asia to modernize.

2 Ask students to identify ways in which contemporary governments subsidize business and technological expansion.

Picturing History

For the British, life in India was luxurious, as the illustration on page 292 clearly shows. This British family is celebrating Christmas. The British passed the Permanent Settlement Act in 1793. The law was intended to ensure payment of taxes to the British. It mandated that landowners who did not pay the taxes on their land would forfeit the land, creating a class of landless peasants. In addition, laws were passed that prohibited Indians from holding high government positions. The gap between the British and the Indians widened.

LESSON 1

British Rule in India

Thinking on Your Own

Draw two columns in your notebook. Label the left column "Causes of Imperialism" and the right column "Facts and Examples." As you read, fill in the chart with causes. Then add facts and examples found in the lesson to explain each cause.

The Industrial Revolution speeded up the economic development of Europe and the United States. It also established the way industrial nations viewed their colonies. They began to see the colonies as markets for goods as well as sources of raw materials. The result was a new stage of **imperialism**. This activity took place in Africa, Asia, and Latin America.

focus your reading

What factors caused imperialism in the 19th century?

Explain how the British gained control of India.

How did the British rule India?

Summarize the Indian Nationalist Movement.

vocabulary

imperialism   racism
markets   sepoys
humanitarian   Westernize

For the first time, the United States began looking overseas for areas to colonize. At the same time, the U.S. wanted to keep Europeans out of the Americas. U.S. presidents in the late 1800s reminded Europeans of the Monroe Doctrine. This document was written in 1823 by President James Monroe. It declared the Western Hemisphere closed to further colonization by European nations. In reality, the U.S. used the Monroe Doctrine to control the Americas.

Causes of the New Imperialism

The major reason for European interest in imperialism was economic. The factories and mills of the Industrial Revolution required vast amounts of raw materials, like cotton. Regions in Africa, Asia, and Latin America had raw materials in abundance.

Imperialism and Modernization 293

Lesson Summary
The United States and Europe, in a search for raw materials and new markets, became involved in imperialism in Asia, Africa, and Latin America.

India became the first battleground of the European powers for colonies. Britain's East India Company defeated the French for control in the 1750s.

A group of upper-class Indians started the Indian Nationalist Congress in the late 1800s. Muslims formed their own organization in 1906, hoping for a separate state.

Lesson Objective
Students will learn about British rule in India during the 1800s.

Focus Your Reading Answers

1 Nineteenth-century imperialism was caused by economic concerns. Raw materials and new markets were needed because of the Industrial Revolution. Nationalism also played a role as European nations fought for power.

2 The British gained control of India by establishing trading posts and by defeating both the French and the Indians for control.

3 British rule of India was under the control of a viceroy appointed by Parliament. British officers held top positions in the civil service and the army.

4 The Indian Nationalist Movement was a group of upper-class Indians working to end imperial rule. They agreed that India needed to Westernize its economy and society. They were content with a gradual end to British rule.

Lesson Vocabulary
Introduce each of the following vocabulary terms to students.

Explain that *imperialism* is a government policy based on a home country building an empire. *Imperialism* took place in Asia, Africa, and Latin America.

Places to buy finished goods are known as *markets*. To Western business owners, Asia, Africa, and Latin America represented *markets* for their finished goods.

People desiring social reforms were also known as *humanitarians*. *Humanitarian* motives were part of *imperialism*. The belief that one race is better than another is known as *racism*. Racism and Social Darwinism were often linked.

The British called Indian soldiers *sepoys*. The *sepoys* objected to cartridges greased with animal fat that was forbidden by their religions.

To *Westernize* in the context of this lesson is to modernize. The Indian Nationalist Movement agreed on the need to *Westernize* India.

Imperialism and Modernization 293

> **Picturing History**
>
> The African women in the photograph on page 294 are carrying crops on their heads in the traditional fashion. Point out to students the railroad bed on which they are walking.

Once goods, such as cloth, were produced, European and U.S. business owners needed **markets**—people to whom they could sell the finished goods. European and U.S. business owners could sell their goods to their home countries. However, Africa, Asia, and Latin America represented huge new markets.

Setting up colonies ensured that the flow of raw materials to the home country continued. It also ensured that the home country controlled the sale of goods in the colonies.

In addition to economic reasons, a spirit of nationalism motivated imperialists. European nations were still competing with one another for power and wealth. This competition started the beginning of the global age. Setting up colonies was one way to show how one nation was more powerful and wealthy than another. The United States began to build an overseas empire for this reason.

The colonies provided raw materials for businesses in Europe and the United States.

Humanitarian reasons also moved some people to support imperialism. Humanitarians often thought that native people should be more like Europeans. Sometimes, humanitarians were helpful, like when medicine and education were provided. However, they often caused more harm than good. The main force behind humanitarianism was Social Darwinism. Social Darwinists believed that Western civilization—European and U.S.—was far superior to all other civilizations. As a result, they believed that whites had a responsibility to convert and educate native peoples. They thought that helping colonized people was the "white man's burden." This belief in Western superiority is a type of **racism**—the belief that one race is superior to another.

The East India Company and the Sepoy Rebellion

European nations first competed for colonies in India. In the 1600s, the British East India Company began trading in India and elsewhere in Asia. France also established trading posts in India. War broke out between the two nations in India in the 1750s. The British, under the command of Robert Clive, were victorious. The French were limited to a few small areas in southeastern India.

294 Chapter 19

> **Extension**
>
> The phrase "the white man's burden" comes from the title of a poem by Rudyard Kipling, a British writer of the late nineteenth century. Written after the United States' takeover of the Philippines, it exhorts the whites "[t]o serve your captives' need." The poem suggests that a large part of the burden is the need to act in a mature, unselfish manner, remembering the future judgment of history.

Clive was the head of the East India Company in India. His job was to increase the Company's wealth. To gain more trading rights, he fought the Indians as well as the French. In 1757, Clive's forces defeated a Mogul army at the Battle of Plassey. The East India Company slowly extended its rule across the Indian subcontinent.

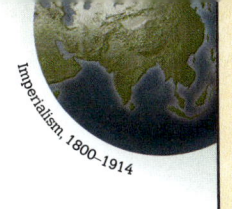

By the 1850s, more than 60 percent of India was under the control of the East India Company. The Company did make life better, in some ways, for some Indians. It set up schools, improved roads, and built railroads. It also kept peace between rival local leaders. At the same time, the Company grew more and more powerful and wealthy. Many of the officials of the Company, as well as other British merchants who went to India, made fortunes from Indian resources and labor.

Indian workers and British officials at the British East India Company.

The Company had its own army and forts to protect its property and British citizens. It also hired Indian soldiers known as **sepoys**. In 1857, the Company gave these soldiers new rifles. To load them, the soldiers had to bite off the end of the powder cartridges with their teeth. The cartridges were greased with fat either from cows, which were sacred to Hindus, or pigs, which Muslims were forbidden to eat.

When the sepoys refused to put the cartridges in their mouths, they were sent home without pay. They rebelled against this unfair treatment. British men, women, and children were slaughtered. It took a year for the British to

The Sepoy Rebellion was known as the First War of Independence by Indians.

Picturing History

The British East India Company, depicted in the illustration at the right of page 295, brought advances to India as well as hardship for Indians. The Company built a network of railroads to move goods. In 1853, the first steam locomotive left Bombay. Within less than 30 years, more than 9,000 miles (14,400 km) of track existed.

In this picture, dock workers in London are unloading tea from India.

Picturing History

The First War of Independence, illustrated at the bottom of page 295, occurred mainly in the northern part of India. The greased rifle cartridges were the final straw for the Indians, who feared that the British were undermining their society without regard for their culture. The British had abolished the custom of burning widows on funeral pyres, and they allowed widows to remarry. They also stopped infanticide and allowed people who became Christians to inherit property. In 1856, they passed an act that required sepoys to serve overseas. The introduction of Western medicine, religion, education, and technology seemed to both Muslims and Hindus as an attack on their way of life. After the struggle, the British reorganized the army using a two-to-one ratio of Indians to British soldiers.

Extension

Numerous films and television series have depicted life during the Raj. You may wish to show clips from one of these, such as *The Jewel in the Crown*, to give students a flavor for the class distinctions and the wealth of the British.

Imperialism and Modernization

Stop and Think
Students' paragraphs will vary but should express both the British and Indian points of view on the war of 1857.

Picturing History
The painting on page 296 shows the manner in which the British tried to recreate the life they had known in England. The wives of British officers and governors ruled over many household servants. Nearly the entire British population in India left Delhi to spend the hottest months at Shimla, the summer capital. By the early twentieth century, there were 1,400 European homes on the top of the hill in Shimla. The Viceregal Lodge, built in 1888, was the site of grand balls for hundreds of British.

regain control of the rebellious regions. The British, in turn, burned villages and slaughtered Indians. The British Parliament acted quickly. It ended the East India Company's control of India. Beginning in 1858, India was ruled directly by Parliament. It sent more British troops to India.

British Rule
Parliament appointed a viceroy to govern India. A civil service was set up with British officials in top positions. British officers also commanded the army. However, lower government posts were filled by Indians. Most soldiers were also Indians. Upper-class Indian families sent their sons to Great Britain for their education.

The effect of British rule on India was disastrous for most Indians. First, British manufacturers sent British-made cloth to India for sale. This destroyed the Indian textile industry because the imported cloth was cheaper. Second, the British collected taxes from Indians to keep the British army in India.

stop and think
The Indians call the uprising in 1857 the First War of Independence. The British call it the Sepoy Rebellion. These names represent opposite opinions about the same event. Write a paragraph from the viewpoint of a British citizen to justify the term *Sepoy Rebellion*. Then write a paragraph from the viewpoint of an Indian to justify the term *First War of Independence*. Share your writings with a partner. Discuss how you could make your arguments stronger.

Colonial British officers lived luxurious lives in India

Extension
Discuss with students the possible life of an upper-class Indian boy sent to England for an education. Ask students to imagine the sorts of things to which the boy would have to adjust. You may wish to explain that girls were long considered uneducable. Even today, women's literacy rate in India remains far below that of men. In 2001, male literacy was 75.3 percent, while female literacy was only 53.7 percent.

Trade increased between India and Europe when the Suez Canal opened in 1869.

This bankrupted some Indian farmers. Third, the British need for cotton moved many Indian farmers to grow cotton instead of food. As a result, famines in the late 1800s caused millions of deaths among India's poor.

The Indian Nationalist Movement

By the late 1800s, a small group of upper-class Indians was working to end imperial rule. They had learned about such Western ideas as democracy and freedom in their British schools. In 1885, they set up the Indian National Congress, or Congress Party. They expected a gradual end to British rule. They agreed with British ideas about modernizing—or **Westernizing**—the Indian economy and society. They also wanted a greater say in governing.

In 1906, Muslim nationalists broke away from the Congress Party. They set up their own All-India Muslim League. They were already talking about a separate Muslim nation once the British left.

Representatives at an early Indian National Congress meeting

Putting It All Together

Create a T-chart. On one side write "Benefits to Indians from British Rule." On the other side write "Costs to Indians." With a partner discuss whether the Indians were better off or worse off under the British.

Imperialism and Modernization

Picturing History

The painting at the top of page 297 portrays the interest shown in the Suez Canal. The first canal had been built by Egyptian pharaohs more than 4,000 years before the one shown opening in 1869. The Suez Canal cut more than 5,000 miles (8,046 km) off the journey from London to Bombay, reducing it to 7,250 miles (11,670 km). About twice the length of the Panama Canal, the Suez Canal is 101 miles (163 km) long. Even so, because it is built over flat terrain and does not require locks, it was easier to construct. A trip through the Suez Canal requires 12 to 18 hours for modern ships.

Picturing History

The Indian National Congress, members of which are shown in the photograph at the right on page 297, had been discussed for more than two decades before it officially formed. At first contented with resolving reforms, the group became increasingly radical as a result of the poverty that British policies brought to Indians. By the early twentieth century, the group began boycotting English goods as a political tool.

Putting It All Together

Students' T-charts will vary. Possible response:

Benefits: railroads, schools, better transportation

Costs: many became poor and lost land, lack of self-rule, textile industry ruined

Imperialism and Modernization

Lesson Summary

In 1884, European nations met in Berlin to divide Africa among themselves. Only Ethiopia and Liberia remained independent. The British used indirect rule in their colonies; the French favored direct rule and wanted to assimilate their subjects. Africans resisted the Europeans although they could not overcome the advantage of their superior military weapons.

Lesson Objective

Students will learn about the European rush to colonize African lands during the nineteenth century.

Focus Your Reading Answers

1 The African continent was divided among the nations of Europe at an 1884 conference in Berlin hosted by Otto von Bismarck.

2 The British followed one method, known as indirect rule, in which local Africans implemented decisions made by the British. Direct rule, in which a governor was appointed for a colony, was the French method.

3 Africans resisted European rule through military rebellions, such as those at Khartoum, West Africa, and East Africa. The Europeans, with superior weapons, always won.

Extension

Ask interested students to investigate the ongoing questions about the ivory trade. Suggest that they form sides and debate the issue in class.

298 | Chapter 19

LESSON 2

The Scramble for Africa

Imperialism, 1800–1914

Thinking on Your Own

Continue to fill in the "Causes of Imperialism" and "Facts and Examples" chart that you began in Lesson 1. Use as many vocabulary words as you can in your chart.

"The scramble for Africa" refers to the race among European nations to seize parts of the continent. In 1850, there were only a few small European colonies along the coasts of Africa. By 1914, Europeans had carved up the entire continent. Only Ethiopia and Liberia remained independent nations.

European nations viewed Africa much as they did other less-developed parts of the world. It was a source of ivory, copper, and other raw materials. They also saw Africa as a market for European goods. Europeans also wanted to stamp out the slave trade and bring Christianity to Africa. By 1850, most European nations had outlawed the African slave trade. But Arab and African traders still bought and sold slaves.

focus your reading
How was the African continent divided among European nations?
What were the different ways that Europeans ruled their colonies?
Describe how Africans resisted colonial rule.

vocabulary	
partition	assimilate
indirect rule	elite
direct rule	

Partitioning Africa

The first Europeans to move into the interior were explorers who mapped Africa's rivers, mountains, and plains. European missionaries soon followed. The goal of missionaries was to convert the native people to Christianity and to abolish slavery. As in India, local civilizations were considered inferior to Western culture. European merchants and settlers also moved into the African interior.

298 | Chapter 19

Lesson Vocabulary

Discuss each of the vocabulary terms with students.

To divide something is to *partition* it. Europe decided to *partition* Africa without consulting the African nations.

To rule allowing the colonials to carry out decisions made by the Europeans is called *indirect rule*. The British favored *indirect rule*. *Direct rule* involves an appointed governor from the major power. The French practiced *direct rule*.

To absorb something is to *assimilate* it. The French wanted the Africans in their colonies to *assimilate* French culture.

The upper class is the *elite*. *Elite* Africans were encouraged to send their sons to Europe to be educated.

Imperialism in Africa, 1914

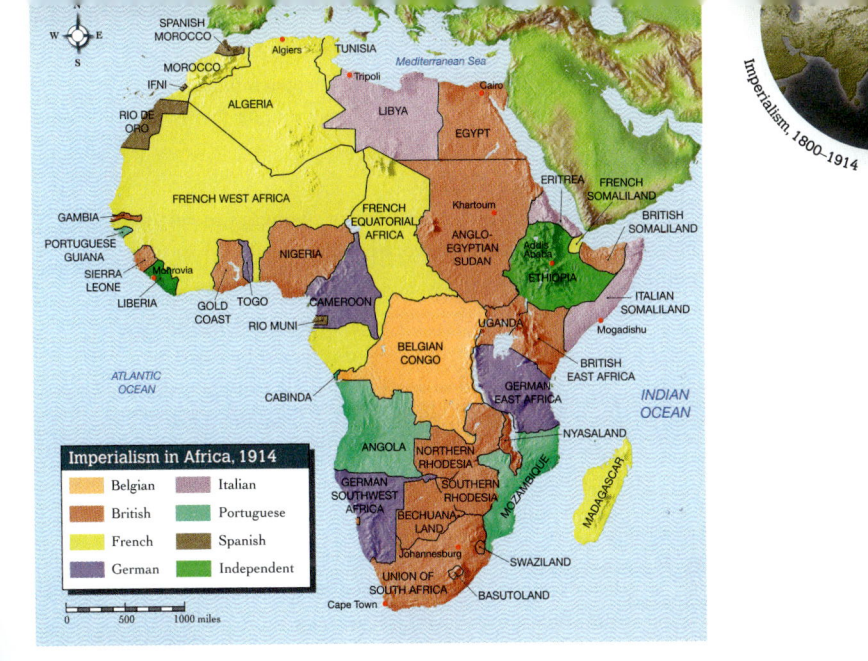

Legend:
- Belgian
- British
- French
- German
- Italian
- Portuguese
- Spanish
- Independent

Map Extension

Ask students to use the map on page 299 to answer the following questions:

- Where was French control most evident? (northwest part of Africa)
- Which European nation controlled Cameroon? (Germany)
- Where did Italy have control? (Libya, Eritrea, and Italian Somaliland)
- In what way are the British and Portuguese holdings alike? (They are separated rather than consolidated areas; Portuguese holdings are on east and west coasts, British holdings are on north and south coasts.)

stop and think

Write four statements about the information shown on the map on this page. Then turn your statements into questions. Take turns asking and answering questions with a partner.

Africans often resisted these groups. The Europeans then asked their home countries for military protection. Their governments sent troops with instructions to end the problem and build permanent forts. Once in Africa, the military was there to stay.

By the early 1880s, European nations were quarrelling among themselves over territory in Africa. In 1884, German Chancellor Otto von Bismarck called a conference in Berlin to **partition**—or divide up—the continent by formal treaty. Fourteen European nations and the United States were represented. Not one African nation or person was invited.

Germany and Great Britain agreed on the division of East Africa. King Leopold of Belgium personally took control of Central Africa. Portugal's claim to territory was also recognized. Some earlier claims of nations, such as those of France, were also

This cartoon from the late 1800s portrays European countries "carving up the African pie."

Stop and Think

Students' statements and questions will vary but should be based on the map at the top of page 299.

Picturing History

The cartoon on page 299 shows Africa being carved as a pie and eaten by a European imperialist. The helmet of the pie eater suggests a Prussian military man. Otto von Bismarck is likely the man carving the pie at the 1884 Berlin conference.

Imperialism and Modernization

Picturing History

The photograph at the left on page 300 shows an African slave in the Belgian Congo caught in a net and shackled. Before 1908, the Belgian Congo was known as the Congo Free State and was under the direct rule of Leopold II of Belgium, according to the agreements at the Berlin Conference. Natives of the Congo were assigned worker quotas to gather ivory, oil, and rubber. Hostage taking was a common way to meet forced labor quotas. Natives were mutilated as punishment. By 1908, outrage among Britain and other European nations forced Leopold to abdicate his power to the Belgian government.

Extension

Students who wish to understand more about the complex effect of slavery on Africa may wish to read or watch the Henry Louis Gates 2001 book/video *Wonders of the African World*. This travelog of his trip through Africa over ten months is filled with beautiful photographs that all can appreciate.

Imperialism, 1800–1914

The Belgian Congo was the most brutal of all colonial administrations.

recognized. Between 1885 and 1914, European nations continued to divide the African continent among themselves.

Colonial Rule

European nations mainly chose one of two ways to rule their new colonies. The British favored **indirect rule**. Most other nations used **direct rule**.

The British ruled through existing rulers and local officials. The British believed it would be easier to maintain law and order if the people were allowed to keep some of their traditions and customs. This included their political system. British officials, however, made all the decisions. Local African officials simply carried them out.

The French used direct rule. The government in France appointed a governor for each colony. Below him were a number of government officials. The highest levels were filled with men sent from France. Lower levels, down to the local villages, were filled by native Africans.

Biography

Menelik II (1844–1913)

Ethiopia remained independent while other African kingdoms were seized by Europeans. Why? The answer is Emperor Menelik II. He came to the throne of Ethiopia in 1889. By that time, France and Italy had set up colonies on Ethiopia's borders. He knew that to be free, his kingdom would need to modernize—and quickly.

Menelik began with education. He used European teachers to modernize the curriculum. He upgraded the Ethiopian army. He played Italy off against France to buy new weapons from both. He also strengthened ties with local leaders of different groups across Ethiopia.

In 1895, Italy went to war against Ethiopia. At the Battle of Adowa in 1896, the Ethiopians overwhelmingly defeated the invading Italians. Menelik led an army of 90,000 soldiers against a badly outnumbered Italian army. Italy was forced to sign a peace treaty recognizing Ethiopia's independence. Europe was shocked that an African nation had defeated a European power.

Bio Facts
- Born 1844.
- Held captive from 1855–1865.
- Spent 1868–1889 as a warrior, enlarging the kingdom's territory.
- Made emperor in 1889.
- Defeated outnumbered Italian army at Battle of Adowa, March 1, 1896.
- Suffered first in a series of strokes in 1906.
- Died in 1913 in Addis Ababa, Ethiopia's capital.

Biography Extension

Ask students to recall from Chapter 2 the rule of Israelite king Solomon, the son of David, who built the first capital. Menelik II, who was born Sahle Mariam, took his name to honor the legendary son of Solomon and the Queen of Sheba, Menelik I, considered a founder of Ethiopia.

The French wanted to **assimilate** their African subjects. The French government set out to introduce French culture, including its political system, to its colonies. The goal was to have Africans think and act like French men and women. As in India, the British and French encouraged the ruling **elite**—the upper class—to send their sons to school in Europe. These young men provided educated rulers and officials in later years. Most Africans, however, were little affected by assimilation.

African Resistance

The educated elite saw both the good and bad side of Westernization—the acceptance of Western culture. They learned about Western ideas like freedom and democracy. Yet, they saw how Western democracies refused to extend these rights to their colonies. By the early 1900s, groups of nationalists in many colonies were working for independence from imperialist rule.

In some areas, local groups fought European rule. In 1885, Muhammad Ahmad al-Mahdi and his followers crushed British forces led by General Charles Gordon at Khartoum in Sudan. The British ended the uprising 13 years later.

The Asante fought the British in West Africa and lost. Britain annexed the region in 1901. In East Africa, the Maji-Maji rebelled against the Germans in 1905 but were defeated. Each time, the superior weapons of the Europeans ended African defiance.

Putting It All Together

Why were Europeans able to carve up Africa so quickly? Make a bulleted list of reasons and share them with a partner. Then write an essay of two or three paragraphs to explain your reasons.

Imperialism and Modernization | 301

Picturing History

The battle at Khartoum, shown in the painting on page 301, led to the massacre of the entire British garrison, including its leader, Charles Gordon. He had been known as "Chinese Gordon" since his exploits in China, where he helped to end the Tai Ping Rebellion. This act so pleased the Chinese emperor that he gave Gordon a mandarin's peacock feather and yellow jacket. Gordon also served in the Crimean War, helped to map the upper Nile, and worked to end the slave trade in Sudan. The British forces sent to assist Gordon and his troops, who had been under siege for ten months, arrived two days after the fall of the garrison.

Extension

Muhammad Ahmad gave himself the title al-Mahdi, meaning "right-guided one." An Islamic mystic who believed he was to purify Islam, al-Mahdi was also a warrior who, within four years, pushed the Egyptians and British out of Sudan, capturing Khartoum. He led an Islamic state for six months in 1885 until his death.

Putting It All Together

Students' lists and essays will vary but should provide reasons for the European scramble over Africa. Possible reasons: the presence of military troops, the use of direct and indirect rule, and the assimilation of native peoples to European customs

Lesson Summary

The United States wanted Japan to resume contact with the Western world. In 1853, Commodore Matthew Perry entered Tokyo Bay with a list of demands. Recognizing that they could not defeat his cannons, the Japanese agreed when Perry returned several months later. The Meiji Restoration brought the emperor to power once more and ended the shogunate. Japan modernized and Westernized. The government subsidized new industries and began mandatory public education.

The Japanese also sought an empire, chiefly to gain natural resources. Japan defeated China and Russia, gaining Korea, Taiwan, and other islands.

Lesson Objective

Students will learn about the Meiji Restoration and the opening of Japan to the West.

Focus Your Reading Answers

1. The United States sent Commodore Matthew Perry and a fleet of warships to force Japan to begin diplomatic and trading relations. Knowing they could not overpower the cannons, the Japanese complied.

2. The Meiji Restoration ended the shogunate and feudalism, studied Western ideas, industrialized the nation, started public education, wrote a constitution, and established a legal system.

3. Japan's need for natural resources and space for its growing population prompted imperialist actions.

LESSON 3

Modernizing Japan

Thinking on Your Own

What do you think *modernizing* means? Examine the subheadings and illustrations in this lesson. Then write a three- or four-sentence definition of the word *modernizing*. Use examples from the subheads and illustrations to support your definition.

One Asian nation that was able to stay free of European control was Japan. It took the West as a model and modernized quickly. It learned Western ways so well that it became an imperialist power.

focus your reading

Explain how Japan was opened to outsiders in the 1850s.

What changes did the Meiji Restoration make in Japan?

Why did Japan become an imperialist power?

vocabulary

isolation
fleet
Meiji Restoration
subsidy

Opening to Western Influences

The Tokugawa Shogunate came to power in Japan in 1603. By the mid-1600s, it had closed off Japan to outsiders. It maintained diplomatic relations only with Korea. In the mid-1800s, however, the United States decided to force an end to Japan's **isolation**. The goal was to open trade with the island nation.

In 1853, Commodore Matthew Perry and a **fleet** of four U.S. warships sailed into Tokyo Bay. Perry presented a letter from President Millard Fillmore to the emperor. The letter demanded that Japan open diplomatic and trading relations with the United States. Perry and his fleet sailed out of the bay with a promise to return. Japanese officials debated the issue for six months. They determined that Japan could not win against the cannon power on Perry's warships.

Emperor Mutsuhito

Lesson Vocabulary

Discuss each of the vocabulary terms with students.

Anything in *isolation* is kept apart from others. The U.S. and European nations wanted to end Japan's *isolation*.

A *fleet* is a group of ships. Commodore Perry's *fleet* of warships convinced Japan to trade with the United States.

The *Meiji Restoration* was the period from 1868 to 1912, a time of power restored to the emperor. During the *Meiji Restoration*, Japan modernized and Westernized.

A *subsidy* is a government payment to a non-government entity. The Japanese government provided a *subsidy* program to help industrial growth.

302 | Chapter 19

At the end of the six months, Perry sailed back with a larger fleet of warships. The Japanese government reluctantly agreed to a treaty with the United States. Japan also was forced to sign similar treaties with the major European nations.

Meiji Restoration

Not all Japanese were pleased with the new agreements. But they came to realize that Japan could not defeat the westerners. In 1867, rival leaders forced the end of the Tokugawa Shogunate. They said they "restored" power to the emperor. The emperor, however, did not govern. As under the shoguns, the men who kept the emperor in power controlled the government.

The period from 1868 to 1912 is called the **Meiji Restoration**. The word Meiji means "enlightened rule." During this period, Japanese officials modernized and Westernized the nation. They made a careful and systematic study of Western technology and science, as well as political and economic ideas. They put an end to feudalism and made Japan an industrial nation.

The Meiji adopted a constitution modeled after Germany's. An executive branch was set up with a prime minister and cabinet who supposedly reported to the emperor. Real power, however, remained in the hands of a small group of

Imperialism, 1800–1914

Traditional Japanese values (top) were influenced by Western ideas (bottom) during the Meiji Restoration.

Commodore Perry arriving in Tokyo Bay 1853

Imperialism and Modernization 303

Picturing History

Commodore Perry arrived in Tokyo Bay in 1853, as the illustration at the top of page 303 depicts. Perry, the younger brother of the U.S. War of 1812 hero Oliver Hazard Perry, devoted his life to expanding the navy. In an early mission, Matthew Perry took freed slaves to the new nation of Liberia.

Extension

The knowledge that the Japanese had coal deposits was the incentive to open that nation for trade, since steam power relied on coal. Americans hoped to establish coaling stations as a way to cross the Pacific, since no ship could carry a sufficient amount of coal to make the journey without stopping. The mission to Japan was dangerous; previous unwanted visitors had faced jail, torture, or decapitation.

Picturing History

The two illustrations at the bottom of page 303 show the changes that Western influences brought to Japan. Have students look for similarities and differences in the two depictions.

Picturing History

Emperor Mutsuhito, shown on page 302, came to power at age fifteen. He chose the name *Meiji* (enlightened) to describe his leadership. Born in 1852, he was declared crown prince at age eight and came to power at the death of his father in 1867. He gained popularity by coming out of the seclusion typical of an emperor and making inspection trips around Japan.

Extension

The rule of Emperor Meiji began in 1867 and lasted for 45 years. The new emperor was fifteen years old when he took the throne. He moved the capital from Kyoto to Tokyo (known before his reign as Edo), which means "Eastern Capital." Under his leadership, a constitution was written in 1889 and a governing body, the Imperial Diet, began the following year. Meiji also sponsored modernization. Tokyo's streets soon filled with trolleys, wheeled vehicles, and electric lights.

Imperialism and Modernization 303

Picturing History

The Japanese factory shown on page 304 is an example of the *zaibatsu*, which were family-owned, private companies. One of the first such companies, which grew to be one of the largest, was Mitsubishi. These companies partnered with the government to finance Japan's modernization. In this print, women are working in a raw-silk reeling factory.

Extension

Have students investigate Japanese manufacturing today, perhaps by studying a successful global corporation such as Honda or Samsung. Ask students to learn about the history and processes of the company. Have them present their findings to the class by using the Student Presentation Builder on the student CD.

Imperialism, 1800-1914

Meiji officials. They selected the prime minister and cabinet. The constitution also established a legislature of two houses. The upper house was appointed by the emperor. The lower house was elected by male voters. The legislature had little power. Japan also adopted a legal system modeled after the French system.

Industrialization was an important part of the Meiji's plans for Japan. They realized that a farming economy would not make Japan a rich country and a strong state. To aid industrial growth, the government created a **subsidy** program. A subsidy is a payment by a government to nongovernment entities. The Japanese government provided money to help start new industries. By 1900, Japan was becoming a leading producer of silk cloth, steel, ships, and weapons.

To aid modernization, the Meiji used British expertise to build the first Japanese railroad and a telegraph system. Western-style banking and postal systems were also organized. Harbors and roads were improved. The Meiji also set up a modern army and navy. All men had to serve in the army for three years.

Modernization also included changes in society. The public education system was modeled on the U.S. system. All boys and girls were required to attend school for six years. Many of the subjects were the same as those studied by students in other countries. The schools also taught traditional Japanese values.

Japanese Imperialism

As an island nation, Japan faced many problems in trying to become an industrial power. Japan lacked many of the natural resources, such as coal, that were needed for industry. Gaining colonies would provide sources of raw materials. Colonies would also provide larger markets for Japanese goods.

Japanese factories made si cloth in late 180

stop and think

Create a concept web to show the changes that occurred in Japan as a result of the Meiji Restoration. Draw a large circle and label it "Meiji Restoration." Draw and label a smaller circle for each change caused by the Meiji. Connect the smaller circles to the large circle with lines.

304 | Chapter 19

Stop and Think
Students' concept webs will vary. Possible responses: more democratic government, industrialization, improved transportation and communication, public education

There was one additional roadblock. Although there are thousands of islands in the Japanese island chain, almost all the population lived on four islands. As Japan industrialized, the population grew. This meant more workers, but also a lack of living space. Moving some of the population to colonies would ease the strain of overpopulation.

In 1874, the Meiji made the decision to build an empire overseas. They seized the Ryukyu Islands off the coast of China. In 1895, Japan defeated China in the Sino-Japanese War and added Taiwan to its territory. In 1905, Japan and Russia went to war. Western nations were shocked at Japan's easy victory over Russia. No Asian nation had defeated a Western power before. Each time, Japan added territory to its empire.

In 1910, Japan was bold enough to make Korea part of its nation. It attempted to do in Korea what Western nations were doing in other parts of the world. Japan took most of Korea's wealth for itself. It imposed the Japanese language on Koreans and tried to stamp out their culture. The result was the development of a nationalist movement similar to those growing in other colonies.

Japanese Expansion, 1870–1918

Soldiers in the Russo-Japanese war, 1905

Putting It All Together

List the reasons why Japan became an imperial power. Share your list with a partner to make sure you included everything. Then write a short essay explaining the reasons and outcomes of Japanese imperialism.

Map Extension

Ask students to use the map on page 305 to answer the following questions:

- In which geographic directions did Japan's empire expand from the main islands? (west, north, and south)
- When did Taiwan become part of the Japanese Empire? (1895)
- What was the final nation gained in 1910? (Korea)
- South Sakhalin is nearest which Japanese island? (Hokkaido)

Picturing History

Japanese troops in the Russo-Japanese War are shown in the photograph on page 305. The skill of the Japanese army and navy produced land gain for Japan. As a result of the Sino-Japanese War, Japan gained Taiwan and part of Korea. From Russia, Japan gained control over both Korea and southern Manchuria. Such was the navy's accuracy that during the Russo-Japanese War, Admiral Togo and his men sank 35 of Russia's 38 ships.

Extension

The Japanese continue to face pressures created by overpopulation. Have students find current statistics, including population density figures. Ask them to locate cities in the United States with a density comparable to Tokyo's. Discuss with students the problems that overcrowding might cause.

Putting It All Together

Students' lists and essays will vary but may mention as reasons the need for natural resources, for markets, and land for a growing population. The outcomes included increased land for Japan and a new respect for an Asian nation that defeated a Western one.

Imperialism and Modernization

Lesson Summary
The Chinese experienced pressures from foreign nations in the 1800s. The United States forced the Open Door Policy.

China's internal pressures included food shortages due to a population explosion, plus widespread poverty. These contributed to the Tai Ping Rebellion, which led to reforms in the Qing government. Because of the introduction of Western ways and industrialization, the Boxer Rebellion tried to remove foreigners and their influence. After a period of several uprisings, the Chinese declared a republic, with Sun Yat-sen as their leader.

Lesson Objective
Students will learn about the internal and external pressures on China and the changes that resulted.

Focus Your Reading Answers
1 Foreign nations gained spheres of influence by treaties made after China fought and lost wars during the latter half of the nineteenth century.

2 The Qing Dynasty fell because of the external pressures from European powers and internal problems such as poverty and a refusal to accept modernization.

3 Sun Yat-sen called for a new government based on *Three Principles of the People*: nationalism, democracy, and economic well-being. He traveled to Europe and the United States, trying to win support. When rebels occupied China, Sun returned and was elected president of the first republic.

LESSON 4
European Powers and the Chinese Revolution

Thinking on Your Own
This lesson describes foreign pressures on China and its political changes over more than 80 years. As you read, create one timeline that shows both series of events.

The first Qing (CHING) emperor came to power in 1644. After ruling more than 200 years, the Dynasty might have collapsed without outside help. The Qing was so corrupt that in time, people would have overthrown it. However, the demands of foreign nations added to the problems of the Chinese government and weakened it even more.

The Empress Dowager Ci Xi ruled in the name of her son and nephew for almost 50 years and added to the problems of the Qing and China.

focus your reading
How did foreign nations gain spheres of influence?

Discuss the causes of the fall of the Qing Dynasty.

Describe the role Sun Yat-sen played in the founding of the Chinese Republic.

vocabulary
extraterritoriality
concessions
spheres of influence
self-strengthening

Foreign Pressures
By the early 1800s, British merchants were importing opium from India into China. The Chinese government demanded that the British government halt the opium trade. Opium is an addictive drug. The Chinese appealed to the morality of the British. However, the British government refused to stop the British East India Company. When the Chinese attempted to end the trade themselves in 1839, the British attacked several cities. This was the beginning of the three-year Opium War. The Chinese were not equipped to fight the modern British army and navy. In the end, the Chinese government backed down and signed the Treaty of Nanjing. The British opium trade continued.

Lesson Vocabulary
Discuss each of the vocabulary terms with students.

Allowing Westerners to live in treaty ports in their own sections and under their own laws is called *extraterritoriality*. At the end of the Opium War, China agreed to *extraterritoriality*.

Concessions are agreements that allow something that would not normally be permitted. Foreign nations usually won *concessions* from China by force.

Areas where only certain foreign nations had the right to trade with the Chinese were known as *spheres of influence*. The *spheres of influence* were usually the result of treaties after the five wars that China lost between 1842 and 1895.

The Qing began a series of reforms known as *self-strengthening*. *Self-strengthening* began as a result of the growing power of the warlords.

China agreed to

- repay Great Britain for its costs in the war
- open five treaty port cities to foreign trade
- allow Westerners to live in their own sections under their own laws in these treaty ports. This is known as **extraterritoriality**.
- give Great Britain the island of Hong Kong

The Opium War was only the beginning of foreign pressure on the Chinese government. Over the next 50 years, foreign nations won more **concessions** from China, usually by force. China fought and lost five wars between 1842 and 1895. As a result of unequal treaties, foreign nations were able to carve out **spheres of influence** for themselves. A sphere of influence was an area where only the foreign power had the right to trade with the Chinese. By 1912, foreign nations controlled more than 50 treaty ports and the areas around them.

The United States did not have its own sphere of influence. In 1899, John Hay, the U.S. secretary of state, played the foreign powers in China off against one another. He forced them to accept an Open Door Policy. All nations would have equal rights to trade in China. This made it easier for U.S. companies to do business in China.

Internal Pressures

At the same time the Chinese government was dealing with foreign nations, it was trying to deal with internal problems. China was suffering from a population explosion and food shortages. Officials in the bureaucracy could be easily bribed. The government could not collect enough tax revenue to cover its costs. Peasants and urban workers made up the majority of the population. They lived in terrible poverty.

Hong Kong was returned to the People's Republic in 1997.

Picturing History

The French-Chinese War, depicted at the top of page 307, was fought over the province of Tangking (North Vietnam). The Chinese fought five wars over land during the nineteenth century.

Picturing History

In 1997, Hong Kong ceased to be a British possession, as shown in the photograph at the bottom of page 307. Have students use library resources or the Internet to find out more about the success of the "one country, two systems" pledge by the People's Republic of China.

Extension

The Open Door Policy might have been interpreted as trying to preserve China from being carved up by foreign powers. Although the United States did not wish to make any land claims, it certainly wanted the right to trade anywhere in China and to exploit the resources of that vast nation. Secretary Hay simply wrote letters to the French, German, Italian, British, Russian, and Japanese governments announcing this new policy. Despite this correspondence and a second letter prompted by the Boxer Rebellion, the Open Door Policy was not formalized by treaty until the Washington Conference that followed World War I. It remained in force as part of American policy until the Communist victory of 1949.

Picturing History

The Empress Dowager Ci Xi, shown on page 306, ruled as regent first for her four-year-old son and then at his death at nineteen, for her four-year-old nephew. Even after her nephew became emperor, Ci Xi read all official government documents, thus retaining a measure of power. One of her acts was to use money that had been set aside to create a modern navy for China to rebuild Beijing's Summer Palace. When told in 1898 that her nephew, who had begun a program of reform, planned to take her prisoner, the Empress Dowager placed him under house arrest and ruled in his place until her death in 1908.

Stop and Think

Students' lists will vary. Possible responses:

External: Opium War, foreign powers demanding trade rights

Internal: population explosion, food shortage, poverty, Tai Ping Rebellion, outdated government system, Boxer Rebellion and its results

Picturing History

During the Boxer Rebellion, shown on page 308, northern Chinese protested Western technology, missionaries, and diplomats. Members of the Society of Righteous and Harmonious Fists practiced martial arts, which the British called shadow boxing, hence the name Boxers. The Society attracted not only peasants and craftworkers, but also scholars who staffed the Qing Dynasty. Diplomats from Germany and Japan were murdered. The foreign death toll during the Boxers' 56-day siege of Beijing was 250. Countless Chinese Christians were murdered as well. The Boxers also destroyed telegraph and electrical lines, and they burned churches and railway stations.

Imperialism, 1800–1914

The anger of the lower class erupted into open rebellion in 1850. The Tai Ping Rebellion lasted until 1864 when the Chinese government crushed it with foreign help. By that time, some 20 million Chinese had died in the uprising. Its leader was Hong Xiuquan (HOONG shee•OH•chew•an), who had converted to Christianity. He called for land reforms and equal treatment for women.

Qing officials realized that something had to be done to regain their power. By 1870, local warlords were challenging the central government. The Qing began a period of reform known as **self-strengthening**. The most radical reformers wanted to introduce democracy. However, they lost to Qing officials who wanted to keep the Confucian system of governing.

These officials accepted the need to introduce Western technology and science but nothing else. As a result, China began industrializing. Railroads, shipyards, weapons factories, and other types of factories were built. The army was modernized. However, the government continued to be based on Confucian values and the civil service system.

The final blow to the Qing Dynasty was the Boxer Rebellion. The Boxers were a secret society whose members swore to destroy foreigners. In 1900, they began killing foreigners across China, especially Christian missionaries. They trapped foreign residents in Beijing, China's capital. France, Germany, Great Britain, Japan, Russia, and the United States sent troops to rescue them. This ended the rebellion. Once again, China had to give up more treaty ports. It also had to make another huge payment to the foreign nations for their losses during the rebellion.

The Boxer Rebellion

The Founding of the Chinese Republic

The Boxer Rebellion frightened the Qing officials into action. The civil service examination system was ended. A new public

stop and think

As you read, make a list of the external and internal problems that China faced during the 1800s. At the end of this lesson, compare your list with that of a partner.

Extension

As reparation for the Boxer Rebellion, China was assessed 450 million ounces of silver, a payment equal to five years of the Qing government's income. The debt was not completely paid off until 1940. China was already paying Japan for its loss in the Sino-Japanese War. Ask students to imagine the financial consequences to China of this burden.

school system was adopted in its place. Women were allowed to attend school. A new national assembly was set up but had no law-making powers. Its role was to advise Qing officials. None of these changes, however, reached the peasants or urban workers.

One result of China's growing Westernization was the development of a middle class. Often the sons of these families were sent to study in the United States or Europe. They came back wanting to replace the emperor with a government based on Western principles. One of these young men was Sun Yat-sen. He called for a new government that adapted Western ideas to Chinese needs. He called his policy *Three Principles of the People*. His principles were nationalism, democracy, and livelihood—or economic well-being for everyone.

Throughout the early 1900s, various groups began uprisings but nothing came of them. Then in 1911, one uprising succeeded. Within months, the rebels held most of southern China. Sun, who had been in the United States, rushed back to China. A republic was declared, and Sun was elected president by his followers.

However, Sun's Nationalist party was not strong enough to seize control of China from local warlords. In 1912, Sun resigned in favor of Yuan Shigai (YOO•AHN SHUR•GIE). Yuan was himself a powerful warlord from northern China who promised to rule democratically. However, once in power, he had no interest in creating a democratic China. He wanted to set up his own dynasty and rule as emperor. Yuan was overthrown in 1916. Civil war and foreign invasions marked China's history until 1949. In that year, Mao Zedong finally unified China under a Communist government.

Putting It All Together

Create a chart with the following four columns: "Opium War," "Boxer Rebellion," "Treaty of Nanjing," and "Sun Yat-sen." Under each, list one or two ways imperialism influenced each topic. Then use your chart to write a paragraph explaining how imperialism influenced China.

Sun Yat-sen speaking at a gathering

Picturing History

The photograph on page 309 shows Sun Yat-sen presiding over the first Chinese parliament in 1912. Sent as a teenager to join an older brother with a business in Hawaii, Sun became interested in the West. Educated by British Anglicans, he became a Christian. He studied medicine and began a practice in Macao, a Portuguese colony, using his income to finance revolutionary activity. He became internationally known when he was imprisoned by the Chinese during a trip to Britain in 1896. Freed by the intervention of a British doctor with whom he had studied in China, Sun spent two years studying in European libraries and museums.

Extension

One of Sun's lieutenants, Chiang Kai-shek, served as head of a military academy established in 1924. He later led an expedition against the warlords to unify China. Opposed to communism, he fought against Mao Zedong and lost, retreating to Taiwan and establishing a Chinese government, the Republic of China, there.

Putting It All Together

Students' charts and paragraphs will vary. Possible response:

Opium War: British wanted to continue opium trade, and their army and navy were superior fighters; Boxer Rebellion: China gave up more ports and paid more reparations after losing the war; Treaty of Nanjing: granted extraterritoriality to Westerners, opened five port cities to foreign trade, gave Hong Kong to Britain; Sun Yat-sen: learned Western ideas that he tried to implement in China

LESSON 5

Imperialism in Latin America

Lesson Summary
Although nations in Latin America won independence, they were dependent on the U.S. and European nations for manufactured goods and for markets for their crops and raw materials.

As a result of the Mexican War of the 1840s, the United States gained land in North America. It also annexed Puerto Rico, declared Cuba a protectorate, and gained land for the Panama Canal.

President Theodore Roosevelt declared the Roosevelt Corollary in 1904. It promised that the U.S. would keep peace in the Western Hemisphere.

Lesson Objective
Students will learn about the imperialism of European nations and the United States in Latin America.

Focus Your Reading Answers

1. Latin American nations were farming nations. They depended on Europe and the United States for goods, such as machines and cloth.

2. After both the Mexican War and the Spanish-American War, the United States gained territory from Spain. The U.S. also aided a rebellion in Panama, gaining land for the Panama Canal.

3. The Roosevelt Corollary stated that the U.S. would keep peace and prevent wrongdoing in the Western Hemisphere. To keep European nations from invading the Dominican Republic to collect debts, Roosevelt insisted that the U.S. would collect the money. The U.S. remained in the Dominican Republic for nearly 40 years.

Thinking on Your Own

As you read this lesson, make an outline of the important points. Use Roman numerals I, II, and III for your subheadings. Include details under each Roman numeral in their order of importance, from most important to least important.

The independence movements in the 1800s ended Spanish and Portuguese rule in Central and South America. However, independence brought little political or social change to Latin Americans. A huge gap still existed between the rich upper class and the generally poor mestizos, mulattos, and blacks. The majority of wealth in the new nations remained in the hands of large landowners. These landowners were also the most politically powerful people in the new nations. They ran the national governments and saw that government policies favored their interests.

focus your reading

Explain how Latin American nations became economically dependent on the United States and European nations.

In what ways did the United States use force to gain territory in Latin America?

How was the Roosevelt Corollary used to intervene in Latin America?

vocabulary

economic imperialism
cash crops
protectorate
annex

Economic Imperialism

Once free of Spain and Portugal, the new nations adopted free-trade policies. Their major trading partners became Great Britain and the United States. British and U.S. investors also bought large amounts of farmland in some countries and ran plantations and ranches. During the Industrial Revolution, foreign investors also built factories to produce goods for local and overseas sale.

Lesson Vocabulary
Discuss each of the vocabulary terms with students.

Keeping Latin America dependent on Western nations for manufactured goods was known as *economic imperialism*. *Economic imperialism* was in the best interests of Europe and the United States.

Cash crops are those grown to be sold to others instead of being used by the farmers. Major *cash crops* of Latin America were wheat, sugar, bananas, cotton, and coffee.

A *protectorate* involves a more powerful nation taking control of a weaker, smaller one to protect it. Cuba was a United States *protectorate*.

To *annex* a country is to take control of it by force. The United States *annexed* Puerto Rico after the Spanish-American War.

However, Latin American nations did not become industrialized like the United States and European nations. They remained farming nations.

It was in the economic interests of the United States and European nations to keep Latin Americans dependent on them for manufactured goods. If Latin American nations industrialized, their trading partners would lose their markets. This Latin American dependence on the United States and European nations was a form of imperialism. It was **economic imperialism**. The buyers set the prices because Latin American producers had nowhere else to sell their crops and raw materials. As a result, foreign companies and investors made fortunes from Latin American resources and labor. Local landowners and business owners also grew rich from trade.

Latin American nations exported raw materials such as tobacco, wool, rubber, and silver. They also exported **cash crops** such as wheat, sugar, cotton, bananas, and coffee. Cash crops are crops grown to be sold to others rather than to be used by the farmer. In exchange, companies in Britain, the United States, and other European nations sold Latin Americans finished goods, such as cloth and machinery.

United States Intervention

The United States issued the Monroe Doctrine in 1823. Its purpose was to close the Americas to any future European colonization. Some European nations were considering sending troops to restore Spanish power over its former colonies. European nations did not think the new United States could stop them. However, Great Britain supported the goal of the Monroe Doctrine. The British navy was the strongest navy in the world, and no nation wanted to engage it in battle. As a result, nothing came of the idea of European intervention.

As it turned out, the United States took territory from a former Spanish colony. As a result of the Mexican War from 1846 to 1848, the United States gained what are the present

stop and think

To help you remember the information about economic imperialism, write a summary of this section. Share your summary with a partner. Ask your partner to make sure that you have included all the major points.

Picturing History

The photograph on page 311 shows workers on a banana plantation in the early twentieth century. The United States controlled the banana and coffee export trade through its United Fruit Company and the Standard Fruit and Steamship Company. Workers on the banana plantations were often brought from Jamaica and other islands in the Caribbean to Central American nations.

Stop and Think

Students' summaries will vary. Possible response: The new nations of Latin America became major trading partners of Great Britain and the United States. Wealthy investors bought land and built factories. Latin America remained agricultural. Britain and the United States practiced economic imperialism, keeping the Latin American nations dependent on them for manufactured goods. Latin America grew cash crops such as coffee and bananas, while industrialized nations sold them machinery and cloth.

Extension

Encourage students to look at a land-use map of Latin America. Have them identify which regions are still primarily agricultural and what crops grow in what areas.

Extension

To protect its interests in Latin America, the United States intervened in many Latin American nations. Have students use library resources or the Internet to investigate when and where these interventions occurred and what the result of each was.

Picturing History

Benito Juarez, pictured at the top of page 312, served as minister of justice and chief justice of Mexico's Supreme Court before his presidency. As minister of justice, he denied the army and the Church immunity to the law.

Picturing History

The workers on the Panama Canal, shown at the bottom of page 312, faced many dangers, most notably diseases such as malaria and yellow fever. Nearly 6,000 workers died as a result of disease. The canal cost the United States $352 million. When President Theodore Roosevelt visited the site in 1906, he was the first president to travel outside the U.S.

Map Extension

Ask students to use the map on page 312 to answer the following questions:

- What do you observe about the pattern of the railroad and the canal? (The railroad ran alongside the canal whenever possible.)
- How many locks are pictured on this map? (three)
- Near what city did the Caribbean side of the canal end? (Colón)

---

states of California, Nevada, Utah, and parts of Arizona, New Mexico, Colorado, and Wyoming. Texas, which had declared its independence from Mexico earlier, asked to join the United States. This had begun the war.

The United States gained more territory as a result of the Spanish-American War in 1898. The United States came to the aid of Cuban patriots trying to free their island from Spain. After the war, the United States made Cuba a **protectorate**. The United States set up a government for the island and declared that Cuba was under its protection. Cuba did not gain independence until 1934. The United States also **annexed** Puerto Rico after the war. Unlike Cuba, Puerto Rico became a territory of the United States. U.S. territories are directly governed by the United States. In 1917, U.S. citizenship was given to Puerto Ricans. In 1952, Puerto Rico became a commonwealth with its own governor and legislature. However, it continues a voluntary association with the United States.

By 1900, the United States also had political and economic interests in the Pacific. For example, it had recently annexed Hawaii and taken control of the Philippine Islands in the Pacific. The U.S. needed to be able to move its warships and merchant ships quickly from one coast to the other. The only way to do this was to build a canal through Central America. The best place seemed to be Panama, which was then part of Colombia. A French company had already started a canal there in 1881.

When there seemed no other way to gain control of the area, the United States aided a rebellion in Panama in 1903. President Theodore Roosevelt

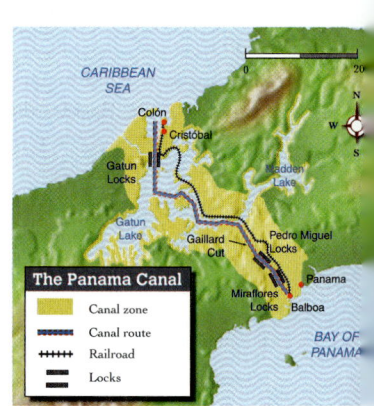

Benito Juarez, the son of Native-American peasants, served as president of Mexico from 1861–1865 and again from 1867–1872. He initiated many social reforms, including separation of Church and state, distribution of land to the poor, and universal public education.

Workers digging the Panama Canal

Extension

Students interested in medicine may wish to use library resources or the Internet to find out more about the fight against disease during the building of the Panama Canal. Suggest that they dramatize the discoveries of William Gorgas and present them to the class.

sent warships to threaten Colombia. Colombia had little choice and allowed the rebels to declare independence. The Panamanians gave the United States control of what became the Panama Canal Zone. The canal opened in 1914.

The Roosevelt Corollary

In 1904, Venezuelans could not repay debts to German and British businesses and investors. It looked as though these foreign governments might send troops to collect payment. President Roosevelt acted first. He announced in 1904 that the United States would police the Western Hemisphere. It would keep order and prevent wrongdoing. Great Britain, Germany, and Venezuela negotiated a settlement. President Roosevelt's policy is known as the Roosevelt Corollary to the Monroe Doctrine.

The United States used its self-appointed police powers the following year. Several European nations appeared ready to invade the Dominican Republic to collect its citizens' debts. Instead, Roosevelt insisted that the president of the Dominican Republic ask the United States to collect taxes. U.S. officials used the tax money to repay the foreign businesses and took a fee for the United States. The United States remained in the Dominican Republic until 1941.

Eventually, the U.S. government sent military forces into Cuba, Mexico, Guatemala, Honduras, Nicaragua, Panama, Colombia, and Haiti to protect U.S. interests. Sometimes they stayed for years. Besides the Dominican Republic, for example, U.S. forces remained in Haiti from 1915 to 1934. This action often gave rise to hard feelings against the United States.

The Roosevelt Corollary is often referred to as the "Big Stick" policy.

Putting It All Together

Create a concept map of U.S. intervention in Latin America. Include the use of the Roosevelt Corollary. Draw a large circle and label it "U.S. Intervention." Then draw smaller circles for each example. Draw lines to connect them to the large circle.

Chapter Review

1. Students' signs will vary. Possible response: Foreigners Go Home!

2. Students' lists of goals and newspaper articles will vary but should focus on nationalist goals in an African nation.

3. Students' letters to the editor will vary but should express opinions either for or against the United States' policy in Latin America at the beginning of the twentieth century.

Chapter Summary

Imperialism, 1800–1914

- Four factors contributed to **imperialism**: economics, nationalism, **humanitarianism**, and Social Darwinism. Social Darwinism led to **racism**.
- The British East India Company governed and attempted to **Westernize** India until the **Sepoy** Rebellion.
- European nations **partitioned** Africa in the 1880s.
- Imperialist powers used two methods to govern their colonies: **indirect rule** and **direct rule**. The British used indirect rule and the local ruling **elite**. The French used direct rule and attempted to **assimilate** their colonists.
- Japan's **isolation** ended when a **fleet** of U.S. warships arrived in 1853.
- The **Meiji Restoration** tried to Westernize and industrialize Japan by providing **subsidies**.
- Nations carved out **spheres of influence**. China also had to agree to **extraterritoriality** for foreign citizens. Foreign nations continued to demand **concessions** to Chinese **markets**.
- The **self-strengthening** movement resulted in some reforms in China in the late 1800s.
- **Economic imperialism** in Latin America led to exported raw materials and **cash crops** in exchange for manufactured goods.
- After the Spanish-American War, the United States made Cuba a **protectorate** and **annexed** Puerto Rico.
- The Roosevelt Corollary enhanced the Monroe Doctrine.

Chapter Review

1. Imagine you are going to a protest against European imperialism in your nation. Design a sign to carry.

2. Imagine you are founding a nationalist organization in an African nation. List the goals for your organization. Then write a newspaper article supporting your position.

3. Write a letter to the editor either for or against U.S. policy in Latin America in the early 1900s.

Novel Connections

Below is a list of books that relate to the time period covered in this chapter. The numbers in parentheses indicate the related Thematic Strands of the National Council for the Social Studies (NCSS).

Emily Crofford. *Born in the Year of Courage*. Lerner Publishing Group, 1991. (VI, VII, IX)

Ann Graham Gaines. *Commodore Perry Opens Japan to Trade in World History*. Enslow Publishers, Incorporated, 2000. (VI, VII, IX)

Fred L. Israel, ed. *Building the Panama Canal: Chronicles from National Geographic*. Chelsea House Publishers, 1999. (VI, VIII)

Betsy Harvey Kraft. *Theodore Roosevelt: Champion of the American Spirit*. Clarion Books, 2003. (III, IV)

Katherine Paterson. *Rebels of the Heavenly Kingdom*. Dutton, 1995. (IV, VI, X)

Laurence Yep. *Mountain Light*. Sagebrush Education Resources, 1997. (III, VI)

Skill Builder

Creating and Analyzing Tables

Tables are good tools to use to sort information. They provide a way to focus on just the important information about a subject. There are a number of tables in this textbook. You have also been asked to make tables as study aids. The following are some general steps for making tables.

How to Make a Table

Step	Process
1	Decide on the categories you need to use to sort the information.
2	Create the form for your table. You will need a column for each category and a row for each topic you want to include under each category. Suppose you want to create a table about the nations of Central America. The categories you want to include are "Nations," "Population," "Type of Government," "Exports," and "Imports." That means you will need five columns. Your topics are the seven nations in Central America. Your table will need seven rows.
3	Find the information to complete your table. Sometimes, you might not find information for every box in every row. A blank box is just as important as one with information. A blank box tells you that the topic is missing something that others in the same category have. For example, suppose one of the categories on your table was "Oil." If one of the nations did not have that box filled in, you would know that it lacked a major export that would bring it money.
4	Write a title for your table.

Complete the following activities to practice using tables.

1. Create a table about the development of independence in Africa. You will need information from the lesson on pages 298–301. Your table will need three columns. Make 10 rows and select 10 independent nations in modern Africa. The labels for your columns are "Modern Nation," "Colonial Name," "Imperial Power." Some modern nations may have been part of more than one colony. Check your table with a partner to make sure that you listed every modern nation.

2. Discuss the information on the table with a partner. For example, count the number of modern nations that were once French colonies. Name the nations that were once British colonies.

Skill Builder

1. Students' tables will vary.

2. Nineteen modern nations were French colonies; 15 were British colonies; two were shared between Britain and France; one was shared among Belgium, Britain, and France; one was shared among Germany, Britain, and France; one was shared between Italy and Britain; one was shared between Germany and Britain; one was shared between Germany and France.

Classroom Discussion

Discuss with students some of the broader topics covered in this chapter.

- How should modern industrialized nations assist nations that are still primarily agricultural?
- Can an agricultural nation survive in today's world?
- Are there conditions in which imperialism could be justified today?

Unit Objectives

After studying this unit, students will be able to

- summarize events leading to the Russian Revolution
- explain the causes, progress, and outcomes of the world wars
- describe the economic and political climate of the era between the wars

Unit 7 focuses on the first half of the twentieth century.

Chapter 20, World War I and the Russian Revolution, examines the events of World War I and the Russian Revolution.

Chapter 21, Between the Wars, explores the emergence of totalitarian governments in Italy, Germany, and the Soviet Union.

Chapter 22, World War II and the Cold War, discusses the events of World War II and the Cold War.

Getting Started

Using a large classroom map, place a sticker, flag, or marker on the areas of the world affected by the two major wars of the first part of the twentieth century. This will allow students to visualize why these were called world wars.

Have a student read aloud the title of the unit and the two paragraphs that follow on page 316. Ask students to identify Communist regimes that currently exist. Then draw their attention to the photographs on page 317. What do students think the photographs suggest about the era?

UNIT 7
THE WORLD AT WAR

For much of the 20th century, the world was at war. World War I began in 1914 and ended in 1919. World War II began 20 years later and ended in 1945. During the period between the wars, the Russians overthrew the czar. A worldwide depression occurred. Dictators came to power in Italy, Germany, and the Soviet Union. Japan continued its pursuit of an empire through military force.

The end of World War II laid the basis for the Cold War. It was a war of nerves and words between the United States and the Soviet Union. However, the Soviet Union supported Communist takeovers in Eastern Europe. In other world regions, the two superpowers took opposite sides in civil wars.

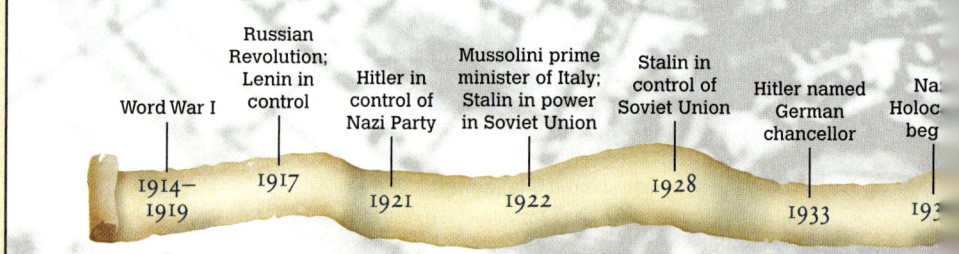

World War I	Russian Revolution; Lenin in control	Hitler in control of Nazi Party	Mussolini prime minister of Italy; Stalin in power in Soviet Union	Stalin in control of Soviet Union	Hitler named German chancellor	Nazi Holocaust begins
1914–1919	1917	1921	1922	1928	1933	193

Measuring Time

Explain to students that Chapter 20 focuses on the events of World War I. The major events of that era appear on page 316 of the timeline. Chapter 21 examines the rise of dictators and other events between the wars. The events that marked this brief interlude are also on page 316 of the timeline. Chapter 22 examines World War II. The events that marked that war and its immediate aftermath are on page 317 of the timeline.

Timeline Extension

Ask students to use the timeline to preview each chapter in the unit. Then have them answer the following questions:

- For how many years was Hitler in control of the Nazi Party before becoming chancellor of Germany?
- When did Great Britain and France declare war on Germany?
- How long did the Cold War last?
- Which conflict lasted longer, World War I or the Korean War?

What decisions made during World War II set the stage for the Cold War?

Why were Mussolini, Hitler, and Stalin able to come to power in the 1920s and 1930s?

How was World War I fought differently from earlier wars?

Collage Answers

1 The decisions made near the end of World War II set the stage for the Cold War. Boundaries were drawn for new nations without regarding the wishes of people who lived there. In addition, Germany was to be divided into military zones. After the war, Stalin backed out of his earlier promise to allow free elections in the nations of Eastern Europe.

2 Mussolini, Hitler, and Stalin came to power during the 1920s and 1930s in large part because of a worldwide economic depression. In the cases of Mussolini and Hitler, both men appealed to an earlier glorious age, promising to restore their nations to that period.

3 World War I was fought differently than previous wars had been. Airplanes were used for the first time. Poison gas and tanks were also introduced. Trench warfare became commonplace. Machine guns and submarines were also new weapons.

Timeline:
- 1939 — at Britain and France declared war on Germany
- 1940 — Germany invaded France
- 1941 — Japan bombed Pearl Harbor
- 1941–1975 — Vietnam War
- 1944 — D-Day Invasion
- 1945 — Atomic bombs dropped on Japan
- 1940s–1989 — Cold War
- 1950–1953 — Korean War
- 1959 — Cuban Revolution

Picturing History

The images on page 317 represent people and places that will be discussed in Unit 7.

1 This is a photograph of the Yalta Conference in 1945. Seated in the front are the leaders known as the Big Three: Winston Churchill of Britain, Franklin Delano Roosevelt of the United States, and Joseph Stalin of the Soviet Union. The photograph was taken at the conference, at which the men tried to envision a post-war world.

2 Adolf Hitler, at left, reviews troops in Germany.

3 Dogfights between airplanes were a new aspect of warfare in World War I.

Collage Extension

Use the images and questions on page 317 to preview the unit.

- What impression do the photographs give of the men responsible for the war's outcome?
- What increased dangers did new methods of warfare pose?

The World at War

Chapter Summary
Refer to page 334 for a summary of Chapter 20.

Related Transparencies

T-1 World Map

T-11 World War I Map

T-18 Three-Column Chart

T-20 Concept Web

Key Blacklines

Biography—Edith Cavell

CD Extension

Encourage students to use the reading comprehension, vocabulary reinforcement, and interactive timeline activities on the student CD.

Getting Focused

Extend the activity by placing students in small groups. Ask them to exchange charts and see if together they can find the answers they need by skimming different sections of the first two lessons.

Chapter 20
WORLD WAR I AND THE RUSSIAN REVOLUTION
(1914–1919)

Getting Focused

Skim this chapter to predict what you will be learning
- Read the lesson titles and subheadings.
- Look at the illustrations and read the captions.
- Examine the maps.
- Review the vocabulary words and terms.

Make a five-column chart in your notebook. Title the chart "World War I." Label the columns "What I Know "What I Want to Know," "What I Learned," "What I S Want to Know," and "How I Will Learn It." Before yo read, fill in the first two columns. As you read, fill in t third column.

Pre-Reading Discussion

1 Discuss with students some of the recent world conflicts in the news. Have students identify some of the weaponry and strategy that is being used. Tell them that new weapons used in World War I changed the way wars were conducted.

2 Ask students to identify the advantages and disadvantages of owning a business. Tell them that in Russia, an experiment in government ownership of businesses and land began in the early twentieth century.

Picturing History

The photograph on page 318 is of German soldiers who have dug a trench and set up their weapons to protect them from the advancing army. German troops, who felt that they were claiming territory, made elaborate trenches, some 30 feet (9 m) deep and lined with concrete to prevent collapse. Some German trenches even had carpeting, wallpaper, shuttered windows, and electricity. Most were more basic.

The Allies considered their dugouts temporary shelters. The dugouts had bunks and a table; the corrugated iron roofing didn't even protect the soldiers from rain.

LESSON 1

War Breaks Out in Europe

Thinking on Your Own

Kaiser William II, of Germany, believed that the way to end disagreements between nations was by war. Do you agree or disagree with him? Think of three reasons to support your opinion. Read this lesson and then review your position. Revise your ideas if you have changed your mind or have found stronger reasons.

European nations competed for territory and economic gain in Asia and Africa in the late 1800s. Tensions between European nations grew. Eventually, these tensions affected Europe.

focus your reading

Discuss the causes of World War I.

Explain how new weapons of war changed the fighting.

What events led to the U.S. joining the war?

vocabulary

Triple Alliance
Triple Entente
trench warfare
stalemate
neutral
armistice

World War I

In the early 1900s, the situation in Europe was extremely tense. Its industrial nations competed for trade, markets, and colonies. Rivalry between these great powers was fueled by intense feelings of nationalism.

Suspicious of one another, the nations of Europe formed defensive alliances. In 1882, Germany, Austria-Hungary, and Italy organized the **Triple Alliance**. In 1907, France, Great Britain, and Russia formed the **Triple Entente**. In the spirit of militarism, most alliance members built up large navies

World War I, 1914–1919

Lesson Summary

The nations of Europe were rivals for markets, trade, and colonies and were suspicious of one another. They formed defensive alliances in the late 1800s and early 1900s. They also built up armies and navies.

In Austria-Hungary, nationalistic feuding led to the assassination of Archduke Ferdinand and his wife, Sophia. Because of the alliances in place, all of Europe was soon at war.

The war was a stalemate along the Western Front, where both sides engaged in trench warfare, with very little land gained. After a prolonged attempt to remain neutral, the United States entered the war in 1917. A year later, an armistice was signed.

Lesson Objective

Students will learn about the European beginnings of World War I.

Focus Your Reading Answers

1 Rivalry among European states, coupled with fierce nationalism, led to a military buildup. Tensions in the Balkan states resulted in the assassination of Austria-Hungary's Archduke Ferdinand and his wife, Sophia. Because of alliances, soon all of Europe was at war.

2 New weapons of war changed the fighting in several ways. Airplanes could observe and bomb targets. Machine guns created trench warfare. Poison gas killed or disabled soldiers. Submarines halted Allied shipping.

3 The sinking of merchant and passenger ships by submarines and the discovery of the Zimmermann telegram led the U.S. into the war.

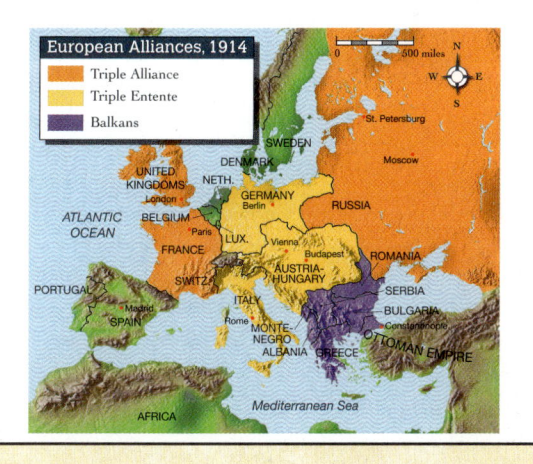

Lesson Vocabulary

Introduce each of the following vocabulary terms to students.

Explain that the *Triple Alliance* was the defensive allegiance among Italy, Germany, and Austria-Hungary. The *Triple Alliance* was formed in 1882. The nations of Russia, Great Britain, and France formed the *Triple Entente*. When Germany declared war on Russia, the rest of the *Triple Entente* nations also went to war.

Digging deep, protective ditches for soldiers to stand in is called *trench warfare*. *Trench warfare* was one reason the war dragged on for so long.

A *stalemate* occurs when neither side wins or loses. The Western Front was a *stalemate*.

A nation that takes neither side during a war is termed *neutral*. The United States was at first *neutral* during the war.

A cease fire is an *armistice*. The Allies signed an *armistice* on November 11, 1918.

World War I and the Russian Revolution | 319

Picturing History

The photograph on page 320 shows a happy moment for Archduke Ferdinand and his wife before tragedy struck. There were six assassins waiting along various points of the route planned for the Archduke that day. One of them threw a bomb that bounced off the canopy of Ferdinand's car and rolled under the car behind it, injuring two army officers when it went off. Later in the day, Ferdinand and Sophia went to visit them in the hospital. As they drove, their car made a wrong turn, and they encountered Gavrilo Princip, who was able to shoot from the running board of the open car. Princess Sophia was killed immediately; the Archduke died ten minutes later.

Stop and Think

Students' T-charts will vary. Possible answers:

Causes of World War I: defensive alliances; nationalism in the Ottoman Empire and Austria-Hungary; assassination of Archduke Ferdinand and his wife, Sophia

Details: nations in Europe aligned themselves with the Triple Alliance or the Triple Entente, pledging to help one another in war; series of uprisings in the Balkans, which became known as a powder keg; Austria declared war on Serbia; Russia, as Serbia's ally, began to ready for war; Germany declared war on Russia; Russia's ally France offered to help; Germans attacked France, invaded Belgium, brought England into the war

---

and well-equipped armies. They also made war plans that could be put into effect on short notice. Europe was becoming a region waiting to explode.

Ethnic nationalism in Austria-Hungary provided the spark. Many ethnic groups lived in larger nations, especially in Austria-Hungary and the Ottoman Empire. Once Italy and Germany were unified, these groups also wanted their own nations. The result was a series of uprisings. Russia supported the new nation of Serbia against Austria-Hungary. This added to tensions between the European alliances. Serbia was part of an area known as the Balkans. The area was now known as the "powder keg of Europe" because the situation there was so tense.

The immediate cause of World War I was the assassination of Archduke Francis Ferdinand of Austria-Hungary and his wife, Sophia. They were shot by Gavrilo Princip, a young Serbian nationalist. He was a member of a group called the Black Hand. The organization wanted Bosnia to become part of the new kingdom of Serbia. Bosnia was part of Austria-Hungary at the time.

Archduke Ferdinand and his wife leave the Sarajevo Senate on June 28, 1914, minutes before their assassination.

A Global War

During July and August, 1914, peace in Europe quickly fell apart. Austria blamed the Serbs for trying to break up its empire. It declared war against Serbia. Serbia's ally, Russia, then prepared its army for war. Fearing that Russia would attack it as well as Austria, Germany declared war on Russia. Russia was France's ally. When France offered to help Russia, Germany declared war against France. To attack France, Germany invaded neighboring Belgium. Belgium's ally, Britain, then declared war against Germany. Soon all of Europe was at war. As the war began, the Triple Alliance became known as the Central Powers. The Triple Entente became the Allies.

stop and think

Create a T-chart for the causes of World War I. Label the left column "Causes of World War I," and the right column "Details." As you read, add specific information about the causes. Share your T-chart with a partner.

Extension

Ask students who are interested in world politics to find out what alliances exist today. For example, what nations belong to the North Atlantic Treaty Organization (NATO) or the Southeast Asia Treaty Organization (SEATO)? Do these alliances resemble those of the early twentieth century? Have students present their findings to the class by using the Student Presentation Builder on the student CD.

Map Extension

Ask students to use the map on page 319 to answer the following questions:

- What strategic advantage did geography offer the Triple Alliance nations? (They could squeeze the Triple Entente nations from both east and west.)
- What alliance was Greece part of? (Balkans)
- The city of Rome was in the midst of a nation belonging to what alliance? (Triple Entente)

Trench warfare was a factor in the length of WWI.

Europe's leaders hoped the war would be over by Christmas, but it dragged on for four years. **Trench warfare** is one explanation. Each side dug trenches, or ditches, deep enough for a soldier to stand in. Both sides dug a line of trenches from the English Channel to Switzerland. The Western Front, or combat area in Western Europe, turned into a **stalemate**. Neither side was able to budge more than a few miles from this line for four years.

World War I Combatants

The Allies (Triple Entente)
Australia, Belgium, Brazil, Britain, Canada, China, Costa Rica, Cuba, France, Greece, Guatemala, Haiti, Honduras, India, Italy, Japan, Liberia, Montenegro, New Zealand, Nicaragua, Panama, Portugal, Romania, Russia, San Marino, Serbia, Siam, South Africa, United States

The Central Powers (Triple Alliance)
Austria-Hungary, Bulgaria, Germany, Ottoman Empire

On the Eastern Front, Germany and Austria-Hungary were more successful. Early in the war, they defeated Russia in several battles. The Russian army was poorly equipped. The Russians began retreating eastward in 1915. A revolution in 1917 ended Russia's role in the war.

In 1915, Italy left the Triple Alliance to join the war on the side of the Allies. An Italian army began an attack on Austro-Hungarian forces. Like Russia, Italy was badly defeated. Only the help of British and French troops saved Italy from being overrun.

Great Britain soon took the war to the Middle East. In 1916, the British aided a revolt by Arabs against the Ottoman Empire. Within two years, the empire of the Ottoman Turks had been greatly reduced. To fight its battles in the Middle East, Great Britain used colonial troops from India, Australia, and New Zealand. France used troops from its colony of Morocco in North Africa.

Picturing History

British soldiers are shown in this 1914 photograph on page 321. By December of that year, a line of trenches covering 400 miles (644 km) extended from the Belgian coast to the Swiss border. Soldiers typically rotated on and off the front, living for seven to ten days in trenches, then going on reserve duty, and finally heading for a rest, which included a bath and clean clothes.

Chart Extension

Have students use a map in the text or a large classroom map to locate each of the nations of the Triple Entente. Point out to students that this truly was a global war, as opposed to previous local wars. Ask them what factors helped make this possible. (Possible answers: improved communication and transportation, loyalty [or conscription] of colonies to home countries)

Extension

Ask students to imagine that they are from one of the colonies of France or Great Britain serving on the Western Front. Remind students that women also served as nurses, ambulance drivers, bakers, and laundresses. Have each of them write a journal entry or a letter to family or friends back in the colony, describing his or her day and the life he or she is leading.

Map Extension

Ask students to use the map on page 322 to answer the following questions:

- How far east did the Central Powers' army advance? (about 500 miles (805 km), into Russia)
- On what side did Morocco fight? (Allies)
- Near what major city was there trench warfare? (Paris)
- What position did Spain take in the war? (remained neutral)

Picturing History

The photo collage at the bottom of page 322 illustrates the changes in warfare that accompanied World War I. Machine guns could fire as many as 600 bullets per minute. Because machine guns were small and could be positioned quickly, they were harder for the enemy to destroy. German submarines were known as U-boats, short for *Unterseeboot*, or undersea boat. From February to December 1917, U-boats sank 2,966 Allied or neutral ships that were carrying soldiers, weapons, or food to Allied countries. One-fourth of all boats leaving Britain were sunk. Powered flight was just over ten years old when the war began. At first, military leaders didn't see how the planes, which had been used almost exclusively for civilian travel, could be of any use in the war. However, after Antony Fokker, who had a factory in Germany, invented a way

Picturing History, continued

to fire machine guns between the propellers, the war became airborne. During what became known as Bloody April, in 1917, 316 British airmen were killed. A new recruit's average flying life lasted only 17 hours.

In Asia, Japan used the war to further its own imperial interests. It seized German islands in the Pacific. These islands included the Marshalls, the Marianas, and Carolines. It also took control of German areas in China, including Kiaochow, on China's Shantung Peninsula.

But the war in Europe dragged on until 1917. A revolution in Russia caused that nation to leave the war. There was no longer any danger to Germany on its eastern border. Germany could send all its forces against the Western Front. They hoped to end the stalemate and seize all of France.

A New Kind of War

Several inventions changed the way World War I was fought.

- Airplanes were used first for observation and later for bombing enemy targets.
- Machine guns fired large numbers of bullets rapidly at advancing soldiers. They helped to create trench warfare.
- Poison gas sickened and killed thousands. Gas masks were the only protection.
- Submarines, known as German U-boats, crippled Allied shipping.

Extension

Students interested in aircraft or military strategy may wish to learn more about the famous fighter planes and aces of World War I. For example, the German Baron Manfred Von Richthofen, who shot down 80 pilots before his own death in 1918 behind Allied lines, was known as the Red Baron because of the color of his plane. British captain Albert Ball, who died in 1917, shot down 44 pilots.

The End of the European Stalemate

When the war broke out, President Woodrow Wilson asked Congress to declare the United States a **neutral** nation. It would take neither side in the war. However, events in Europe pushed the United States to enter the war in 1917. Those events included unrestricted submarine warfare and the Zimmermann telegram.

German U-boats torpedoed and sank both merchant and passenger ships. The United States had protested the policy in 1916 and Germany had stopped. However, in an effort to starve the British, the Germans restored the policy in 1917. President Wilson was furious. At the same time, the Zimmermann telegram became public. In it, Germany asked Mexico to enter the war on its side. In return, it promised that Mexico would receive Texas and the other territories it had lost to the United States in the 1800s.

In April 1917, the United States declared war on Germany. Within a year more than 1 million U.S. troops had arrived in Europe. They were in time to fight the final German advance. It began near Paris in April and lasted until September 1918.

By then it was clear that Germany could not win. It asked for peace. The Allies refused as long as the kaiser and his government remained in power. Uprisings began across Germany. The German people were tired of the misery of war. Without support, the kaiser stepped down. The Social Democrats, a political party, set up a German republic. The Allies agreed to an **armistice**, or cease fire. It was signed on November 11, 1918.

Putting It All Together

Create a timeline to track the sequence of events that led to the war, fighting the war, and the war's end. Review your timeline with a partner. Ask your partner if you have included all the important dates and events.

cannon workshop in Germany at the Krupp factory

The sale of war bonds helped morale on the home front and kept soldiers supplied.

Picturing History

The photograph at the left on page 323 shows the Krupp factory, where cannons were made. Krupp was the largest arms supplier in the world. The firm had been involved in Germany's move from an agricultural to a manufacturing nation.

Picturing History

The poster pictured at the bottom right on page 323 is an example of U.S. propaganda. Students interested in art may wish to use library resources or the Internet to find out more about artists who designed the posters. Howard Chandler Christy created this one in 1917. Fred Strothmann drew the one pictured on page 335. There were also official war artists, such as Britain's Paul Nash, sent to the front to paint the war.

Putting It All Together

Timelines will vary.

Possible response: Triple Alliance, 1882; Triple Entente, 1907; military buildup, uprisings in Balkans, assassination of Archduke Ferdinand, 1914; war declared, 1914; Russian retreat, 1915; Italy joins Allies, 1915; British-aided Arab revolt, 1916; Russian Revolution ends Russian participation in war, 1917; United States enters the war, April 1917; defeat of German advance, September 1918; armistice, November 11, 1918.

Extension

Have interested students use library resources or the Internet to find out more about the role of women in the war. Britain's Women's Land Army, for example, worked to increase food production during the war. Women also worked in laundries and bakeries, drove trucks and ambulances, and did nursing work.

Lesson Summary
The Paris Peace Conference tried to provide ways for ethnic groups to have homelands. Britain, France, and the United States differed in their goals for the conference. France and Britain wanted to humiliate Germany and ensure that the nation would be disarmed. Wilson longed for a just peace.

Wilson proposed a plan of Fourteen Points. He gave up some of them but insisted on a League of Nations to prevent another global war.

Lesson Objective
Students will learn about the Treaty of Versailles and its provisions.

Focus Your Reading Answers
1. The goals of the Big Three at the Paris Peace Conference differed. Great Britain and France wanted to disarm and humiliate Germany. Woodrow Wilson wanted to create a just peace and the League of Nations to prevent future wars.

2. The Treaty of Versailles changed the map of Europe by taking land from Germany, as well as Poland and Germany's colonies in Africa and Asia. Taking land from Russia and Austria-Hungary, the Treaty created Finland, Latvia, Estonia, Lithuania, Poland, Czechoslovakia, Austria, Hungary, and Yugoslavia.

3. The treaty determined that the Middle East and Africa were to be divided between England and France. Great Britain, France, and Belgium received control over Palestine, Iraq, Syria, and Lebanon.

LESSON 2

Making the Peace

Thinking on Your Own

As you read, create an outline of this lesson. Use the subheadings for Roman numerals I, II, and III. Be sure to include information in your outline in order of most important to least important. Use the vocabulary words in your outline.

By the end of the war, Austria-Hungary no longer existed. Like Germany, the people rebelled. Ethnic groups took advantage of the war to claim nationhood. The Austro-Hungarian Empire was divided into the Kingdom of Yugoslavia and the republics of Austria, Hungary, and Czechoslovakia. Other ethnic groups in Eastern Europe also demanded independence. Would they get it? The Ottoman Empire was no longer strong and powerful. What would the Allies do with it? What would happen to Germany's colonies in Africa?

focus your reading

Describe the goals of the Big Three at the Paris Peace Conference.

How did the Treaty of Versailles change the map of Europe?

Summarize how the Treaty of Versailles dealt with the Middle East and Africa.

vocabulary

League of Nations
reparations
demilitarized zone
mandate system

Prime Minister Bethlen of Hungary addresses the crowd during elections.

The war had been costly. Some 8.5 million people died. More than 17 million had been wounded. The regions where battles had been fought lay in ruins. National war debts had mounted into the millions. Who was going to pay for the rebuilding? Who was going to repay the war debts?

Lesson Vocabulary
Discuss each of the vocabulary terms with students.

The *League of Nations* was to be an international peacekeeping organization. Woodrow Wilson was the primary supporter of the *League of Nations*.

Damages paid because of war are *reparations*. Germany was assigned *reparations* of $30 million.

A *demilitarized zone* is an area where no weapons or fortifications are allowed. The land between Germany and France became a *demilitarized zone*.

The *mandate system* gave the *League of Nations* the task of setting up governments in former German territories. The *mandate system* failed because France and Great Britain did not help the new regions modernize or prepare for independence.

324 Chapter 20

Treaty of Versailles

The Paris Peace Conference that began in 1919 tried to answer these questions. Great Britain, France, and the United States were the major decision makers at the conference. They were called the Big Three. Germany was not allowed to take part in the negotiations. German representatives were called in at the end to sign the final treaty, called the Treaty of Versailles.

The Big Three disagreed about what the peace settlement should contain. David Lloyd George, prime minister of Great Britain, wanted to punish Germany. He wanted Germany to pay the entire cost of the war. Georges Clemenceau, premier of France, shared this goal. He also wanted to make sure that Germany could never threaten France again. Germany had to be disarmed.

Woodrow Wilson, the U.S. President, had a very different goal for the Paris Peace Conference. He proposed setting up an international peacekeeping organization to settle disagreements between nations. He called his idea the **League of Nations**. It was one of Fourteen Points that he wanted included in the peace treaty. These included such worthwhile goals as the end to secret treaties, freedom of the seas, and the right of self-determination—or the right of all people to govern themselves.

In the end, Wilson gave up a number of his Fourteen Points. However, he held firm to his idea of a League of Nations. The Allies finally accepted it. However, the U.S. Senate refused to ratify the Treaty of Versailles. Senators

Government officials left the Treaty of Versailles in the Hall of Mirrors.

Picturing History

The photograph on page 325 shows diplomats in the Hall of Mirrors at Versailles, working on the treaty that would end the war. Negotiations had nearly broken down several times before agreement was reached eight months after the armistice. Ironically, the German Empire had been proclaimed in that same hall just 48 years earlier.

Extension

As a boy growing up in the South after the Civil War, President Wilson had seen the power of hatred and desire for revenge after defeat. He toured the United States by train to raise support for membership in the League of Nations, speaking sometimes three and four times a day. The trip exhausted him; he nearly collapsed in Colorado, then suffered a stroke and never fully recovered. The Senate refused to ratify participation in the League of Nations, preferring a return to isolationism.

Picturing History

The Prime Minister of Hungary is shown on page 324 speaking to the crowd that has come to vote. Ask students to analyze the expressions and body language of the listeners and deduce how well Prime Minister Bethlen might do in the election.

Picturing History

Germans shown in the photograph on page 326 protest against being driven from Alsace-Lorraine. The region had belonged to France originally, becoming German territory by the Treaty of Frankfort in 1871. In World War II, it was retaken by the Germans and held from 1940–1944, then restored to France by French and American armies.

Stop and Think

Students' conclusions and summaries will vary. Possible response: The leaders of Britain and France won. Germany had to pay heavy reparations and lost land and prestige.

Thousands attend a demonstration to protest the loss of the Alsace-Lorraine region in Germany.

worried that membership in the League meant the United States was giving up its ability to act in its own interests. Without the United States, little came of Wilson's grand idea of a global peacekeeping organization.

The final Treaty of Versailles included the following:

1. Germany and Austria-Hungary had to admit guilt for starting the war.
2. Germany had to pay $30 million in **reparations**—or damages—to the Allies for their costs in the war.
3. The German army and navy were reduced in size. Its air force was disbanded.
4. An area between Germany and France was set up as a **demilitarized zone**. No weapons or fortifications, like trenches, were allowed in the area.
5. Germany had to return territory to France that it had taken in the Franco-Prussian War. It also lost land to the new nation of Poland.
6. German colonies in Africa and Asia were taken.

stop and think

President Wilson wanted a "just peace," a "peace without victory," that would n[ot] punish Germany and Austria. He did not want nations to have reason for another war. The leaders of France and Britain wanted revenge. Wh[o] won out in the final peace treaty? Discus[s] the terms of the treat[y] with a partner. Write your conclusion as a summary in your notebook.

326 | Chapter 20

Europe After World War I

New nations

Changes in Europe

The negotiators at the peace conference redrew the map of Eastern Europe. They took land from Germany, Austria-Hungary, and Russia. The redrawn map included the new, independent nations of Finland, Latvia, Estonia, Lithuania, Poland, Czechoslovakia, Austria, Hungary, and Yugoslavia.

Poland had once been an independent nation. However, 100 years before, Russia, Prussia, and Austria had divided it after a series of wars. Bosnian nationalists who started World War I got their wish. They were joined with Serbia and four other areas to become the nation of Yugoslavia. Yugoslavia also included large numbers of Croatians and Slovenes.

Map Extension

Ask students to use the map on page 327 to answer the following questions:

- How many new nations were created? (nine)
- Which new nation appears to be the largest in area? (Poland)
- What generalization can you make about the location of the new nations? (They were located in land between Germany and Russia, along with some Balkan states.)

The Fourteen Points

January 8, 1918, President Woodrow Wilson delivered a speech to a joint session of Congress. In it, he discussed Fourteen Points for reconstructing Europe at the end of World War I. Several of the points address broad topics such as abolishing secret treaties (Point I), freedom of the seas (Point II), arms reduction (Point IV), and the creation of a League of Nations (Point XIV).

Open covenants of peace, openly arrived at, after which there shall be no private international understanding of any kind but diplomacy shall proceed always frankly and in the public view.

Absolute freedom of navigation upon the seas, outside territorial waters, alike in peace and in war, except as the seas may be closed in whole or in part by international action for the enforcement of international covenants.

Adequate guarantees given and taken that national armaments will be reduced to the lowest point consistent with domestic safety.

A general association of nations must be formed under specific covenants for the purpose of affording mutual guarantees of political independence and territorial integrity to great and small states alike.

reading for understanding

Explain why a government may not support Point I.

How do countries today work to achieve the same goals listed in the Points?

What is the modern outcome of Point XIV?

Reading for Understanding

1 Governments sometimes like to determine treaties secretly.

2 Treaties exist to limit arms and to allow for open trade.

3 The outcome of Point XIV is the United Nations.

Extension

Many refugees from the war were able to return to old homelands with new names and new governments. Have students use library resources or the Internet to investigate the plight of persons displaced by war today. Allow time for students to share their findings with the class.

World War I and the Russian Revolution

| **Map Extension**

Ask students to use the map on page 328 to answer the following questions:

- How many new nations were created in the Middle East? (five)

- Which new nation received the smallest area of land? (Lebanon)

- What geographic disadvantage did Jordan have? (no coast, port, or access to seas)

Putting It All Together
Students' outlines and essays will vary but should reflect the lesson content.

I. Treaty of Versailles
   A. The goals of Britain and France
      1. Punish Germany
      2. Disarm Germany
   B. The goals of Wilson
      1. League of Nations
      2. Fourteen Points
   C. Final provisions of the Treaty of Paris
      1. Germany heavily fined
      2. Germany lost land in Europe, Asia, and Africa

II. Changes in Europe
   A. New nations created from Germany, Austria-Hungary, and Russia
   B. Ethnic minorities in most of the new nations

III. The Mandate System
   A. League of Nations to set up governments in former German lands
   B. System did not work as intended

This combining of different ethnic groups in a single nation had long-term consequences. Over centuries, different ethnic groups in Eastern Europe had migrated throughout the area. When the negotiators at the peace conference set new borders, they included ethnic minorities in most of the new nations. There was little the negotiators could do about it. Forcing these different groups to live within the same boundaries, however, would create problems in the future.

The Mandate System

World War I ended the Ottoman Empire. During the war, Great Britain had helped Arabs in the Middle East fight the Ottoman Turks. The Arabs had been promised independence if they supported the Allies.

After the war, the Allies went back on their promises. Instead of granting independence, they created the **mandate system**. Under the mandate system, members of the League of Nations were responsible for setting up governments in former German territories. The Ottoman Empire was broken up and divided between France and Great Britain. Supposedly, Great Britain and France were to help the mandates modernize. When the mandates were considered ready, they were to become independent nations. This did not happen. The mandates were supposed to be governed under the authority of the League of Nations. However, Great Britain and France treated them like their other colonies.

The system was also applied to former German colonies in Africa. Great Britain, France, and Belgium were given authority over Lebanon, Syria, Iraq, and Palestine.

Putting It All Together

Review the outline notes you took as you read this lesson. Work with a partner to make sure you included all the main ideas and key information. Use your notes to write a three paragraph essay about the Treaty of Versailles, changes in Europe, or the mandate system.

LESSON 3

Russian Revolution and Communism

Thinking on Your Own

As you read, create a cause-and-effect flowchart to show the causes of the Russian Revolution and its effects. List all the causes that led to the Russian Revolution. Then list all the events that happened as a result of the revolution.

Russia's entry into World War I drew attention to the nation's problems. Because of its lack of factories, soldiers went into battle without guns and supplies. Two million soldiers died and perhaps as many as six million more were wounded or captured. People on the **home front**—those not in the military—suffered from shortages of food and other goods.

focus your reading

Describe the sequence of events that brought about the Russian Revolution.

How did Lenin gain power?

Explain how Lenin turned Russia into a communist nation.

vocabulary

home front
serfs
emancipated
provisional
soviets
war communism
New Economic Policy

The Beginning of Revolution

Russia did not industrialize quickly, as many European nations did. By 1890, the Russian economy was still based on farming. However, in the 1890s the government began to work with foreign investors and Russian businessmen. New industries were started and industrial production began to grow. The need for workers caused people to begin moving from farms to cities.

Until 1861, Russian peasants, called **serfs**, could not become factory workers. They were the property of their landowners and could not move from one estate to another or to a town. This system of feudalism had ended in Western Europe in the Middle

World War I and the Russian Revolution 329

Lesson Summary

The serfs in Russia were freed in 1861. The Russian Revolution began with riots in 1917. The czar resigned; he and his family were later shot. A provisional government ruled until Lenin took power later in 1917.

Lenin and the Communists pulled out of World War I. Russia endured civil war until 1921. The Red Army was victorious and the government took control of nearly everything. Lenin introduced the New Economic Policy in 1921. When Lenin died in 1924, a power struggle within the Communist Party began. Joseph Stalin emerged as the leader.

Lesson Objective

Students will learn about the 1917 Russian Revolution and the beginnings of communism.

Focus Your Reading Answers

1 The Russian Revolution began as a result of uprisings among factory workers. On March 10, 1917, a strike crippled St. Petersburg. The czar was forced to resign; he and his family were killed in July 1918. Russia's legislature, the Duma, began writing a constitution for a republic, but also continued participation in World War I, angering the people.

2 Lenin gained power by promising to end Russia's involvement in the war and to give lands to the peasants and control of factories to the workers.

3 Lenin developed war communism, taking control of food supplies, banks, railroads, factories, and mines. After many people died because of famine, Lenin began the New Economic Policy.

Lesson Vocabulary

Discuss each of the vocabulary terms with students.

Those who were not in the armed forces were part of the *home front*. People on the *home front* suffered during the war because of food shortages.

Landless peasants were called *serfs*. The *serfs* were not allowed to become factory workers. Those who were freed were *emancipated*. Russia's czar finally *emancipated* the *serfs* in 1861.

Something that is temporary is *provisional*. After the czar resigned, the Duma set up a *provisional* government. Councils of workers, soldiers, and peasants formed *soviets*. Lenin and the Bolshevik Party influenced the *soviets*. Taking control of the means of production is known as *war communism*. *War communism* was intended to supply the needs of the military during World War I. The *New Economic Policy* was one of Lenin's plans to turn around the Russian economy. The *New Economic Policy* allowed some private ownership.

World War I and the Russian Revolution 329

Picturing History

The photograph on page 330 shows a demonstration in Petrograd in 1917. The women's protest was one of several that year. In October, Lenin gave the signal to storm the Winter Palace, which housed the provisional government. The signal was the firing of a shell from the *Aurora*. The battleship became an important symbol of the revolution. The Russians sank the ship during World War II to prevent German bombs from destroying it. The ship is now a museum.

Stop and Think

Students' lists and concept webs will vary but should include reasons for soldiers to act against their officers and the czar. Possible response: poor wages, loyalty to families, disgust with the czar's policies, losses from World War I

Ages. The czar finally **emancipated**, or freed, Russia's serfs in 1861. Most serfs continued to work on farms. Some of these former serfs, however, became the new urban working class in the 1890s. Just as in Western Europe and the United States, these workers lived and worked under terrible conditions. They were paid poorly, worked in unsafe factories, and lived in slums.

The Russian Revolution began among these workers in March 1917. Women workers in Petrograd—now St. Petersburg—began a protest. Some 10,000 women marched with shouts of "Peace and Bread." They and other workers called for a general strike on March 10. All factories in the city shut down. Czar Nicholas II ordered the army to fire their guns at the demonstrators. Many of the soldiers refused. The soldiers turned on the government and joined the demonstrators.

Women demonstrate in Petrograd in April 1917.

The Duma, or Russian legislature, met on March 12. It set up a **provisional**, or temporary, government and called for the czar to resign. Nicholas II had little choice and resigned. His abdication ended three centuries of Romanov rule. The former royal family was executed in July, 1918, by the Bolsheviks.

Once the czar was removed from power in 1917, the Duma began writing a constitution to create a Russian republic. It also continued Russian participation in World War I. The peasants and urban workers were angered by this decision. After three years, they wanted an end to the war.

In the meantime, socialists were organizing **soviets**. These were councils made up of workers, peasants, and soldiers. The soviets soon came under the influence of Vladimir I. Lenin and the Bolshevik Party.

stop and think

Why do you think the soldiers joined the marchers in March of 1917? Make a list of possible reasons. Discuss your list with a partner. Add to it or cross off ideas. Then use these ideas to create a concept web of ideas that answer the question.

Extension

Some students may be interested in exploring the story of Anna Anderson, the woman who claimed to be the czar's daughter Anastasia and to have survived when the rest of the czar's family was executed. Suggest that students use library resources or the Internet to determine the validity of her claims.

The Rise of Lenin and the Bolsheviks

As a young man, Vladimir I. Lenin read the writings of Karl Marx. By 1895, Lenin was trying to stir up revolution in Russia. The government arrested him and sent him to prison. On his release, he left the country. When the czar stepped down, Lenin returned to Russia.

The provisional government was losing control of the country. Russians were still dying on the battlefields. Shortages of food and other goods were worsening. Workers were rioting in the streets. The Bolsheviks promised to take Russia out of the war. They would seize land from large landowners and give it to the peasants. Capitalists would lose their factories. The workers would run them. The provisional government would be overthrown and the soviets would take control of the government.

Vladimir Lenin addresses a Moscow crowd in 1920.

In the November Revolution of 1917, Lenin and the Bolsheviks seized power. On November 6, they took over the building that housed the provisional government. Officials put up little resistance. On November 8, Lenin turned over the government to the All-Russian Congress of Soviets. A small group of officials called the Council of People's Commissars actually ran the government. Lenin was the leader of this group.

Picturing History

The photograph in the center of page 331 is of Vladimir Lenin. Lenin turned to Marxism after his older brother Nikolai was hanged for plotting to assassinate Czar Alexander III. He adopted the name Lenin after the Lena River, located in eastern Siberia, to which he had been exiled. After his death in 1924, Lenin's body was entombed in a glass coffin in Red Square. For decades, visitors came daily to honor him.

Extension

According to the March 1918 Treaty of Brest-Litovsk, Russia lost land in Poland, Finland, and the Baltic regions. The treaty, which was made with Germany, was nullified by the defeat of the Germans later that year, and much of the territory was restored. This initial loss of land, however, was seen as a betrayal of Russia and was one of the causes of the ensuing civil war.

> **Chart Extension**
>
> Divide the class into two groups to review the information in the chart on page 332. Have students in one group make a timeline showing the relationship of the three different revolutions. Ask students in the second group to locate on a world map where the three revolutions occurred and their areas of influence.

World War I, 1914–1919

The Bolsheviks changed their name to the Communist Party. They withdrew from World War I and made peace with Germany. They also determined to turn Russia into a communist state. However, not everyone agreed. A civil war broke out in 1918 and lasted until 1921.

Lenin's Red Army was opposed by the White Army, which supported the czar and landowners. Ethnic groups in areas ruled by Russia also opposed the communists. These groups were fighting for the freedom to set up independent nations. The Allies sent troops and supplies to aid the White Army. However, the communist forces defeated the White Army and the nationalist groups.

Comparison of Revolutions

Criteria	American Revolution	French Revolution	Russian Revolution
Was it a short-term success?	Yes. It freed the 13 English colonies from Great Britain.	Yes. It ended the French monarchy.	Yes. It ended the monarchy.
	Yes. It set up a government based on democratic ideas.	Yes. It set up principles of democracy.	No. It did not give Russians political, social, or religious freedoms.
Was it a long-term success?	Yes. Its ideas are still the basis of the U.S. government in the 21st century.	No. Several times during the 1800s, France returned to being a monarchy.	No. The communist system in Russia collapsed in the late 1980s and early 1990s.
		Yes. Since the late 1800s France has been a republic.	
Did it have influence?	Yes. It influenced the French revolution and the revolutions in Latin America.	Yes. It influenced the revolutions in Latin America.	Yes. It provided a model of communist government for in Eastern European nations and other parts of the world.
	Yes. It continues to influence the government of nations in the 21st century.		No. Eastern European nations rejected communism in the 1980s also.

Beginning of Communist Government

By the end of the civil war, Russia had a new centralized government and a single political party, the Communist Party. During the war, Lenin developed what he called **war communism**. In order to supply the Red Army, the government took over banks, mines, factories, railroads, and the food supply.

Chapter 20

> **Extension**
>
> Invite interested students to learn more about the American Relief Administration, which fed many in Russia during the years of famine. Herbert Hoover, future president of the United States, headed the agency.

Workers on a Ukrainian collective farm have dinner in the fields.

Picturing History

The photograph on page 333 shows Ukrainian workers at the Lenin's Way collective farm having dinner in the fields. Ukraine continues to be known for its sugar beets, one of the nation's top agricultural products.

However, war communism was not an effective way to govern. Two years of famine caused great hardship and millions of deaths. Industrial production slowed dramatically. Workers may have owned the factories according to communist theory, but in practice they worked for very low wages. Life in general had not improved under communism.

In order to turn the economy around, Lenin introduced his **New Economic Policy** (NEP) in 1921. Some private ownership was allowed. Peasants could keep some of what they raised and grew. They could use it themselves or sell it. Small factories were returned to private ownership. Small stores could also be privately owned. Wages were increased for factory workers.

Lenin died in 1924. Various Communist Party leaders fought among themselves for power. By 1928, Joseph Stalin was firmly in control of the Soviet Union, Russia's new name.

Putting It All Together

"Private ownership of farms, factories, and stores is good for a nation's economy." Discuss this statement with a partner and make a bulleted list of reasons that either support or argue against the statement. Then use your flowchart, concept web, and bulleted list to develop an outline for an essay about the Russian Revolution.

Putting It All Together
Students' lists will vary but should offer reasons for or against the statement in the text. Outlines will vary based on previous work with the flowchart and concept web, as well as with the list.

Chapter Review

1. Students' questions and answers will vary.

2. Students' charts and essays will vary but should be related to chapter content.

Chapter Summary

- Long-term causes of World War I were rivalry among European nations, a system of alliances, ethnic nationalism, and militarism.
- The **Triple Alliance** included Germany, Austria-Hungary, and Italy. The **Triple Entente** included Great Britain, France, and Russia.
- The immediate cause of World War I was the assassination of Archduke Francis Ferdinand.
- The United States remained **neutral** at the start of the war because of pressure on the **home front**.
- **Trench warfare** resulted in a **stalemate**. An **armistice** ended the war in 1918.
- President Wilson's Fourteen Points included a **League of Nations**. In the end, Germany had to pay large **reparations**. A **demilitarized zone** was set up between France and Germany.
- The Treaty of Versailles established a **mandate system** in the Middle East.
- In 1861, Russian **serfs** were **emancipated**.
- The Russian Revolution began in March 1917. The czar was forced out and the Duma set up a **provisional** government. A socialist government used the **soviets** and seized power in November 1917.
- Lenin developed **war communism** to take control of Russia's means of production during the civil war.
- After the war, Lenin announced his **New Economic Policy** (NEP) to increase economic development.

Chapter Review

1. With a partner, play a question-and-answer game. First, write ten answers with a question for each answer. Take turns giving answers and responding with questions.

2. Complete the last two columns of the chart you began at the start of the chapter. Select three topics from column four—topics that you still want to learn more about. After researching the topics, write a five-paragraph essay about your topics.

Novel Connections

Below is a list of books that relate to the time period covered in this chapter. The numbers in parentheses indicate the related Thematic Strands of the National Council for the Social Studies (NCSS).

Kathryn Lasky. *Night Journey.* Viking Juvenile, 2005. (I, III, IV)

Iain Lawrence. *Lord of the Nutcracker Men.* Random House Children's Books, 2001. (IV, VI, VIII)

Diana Preston. *Remember the Lusitania!* Walker & Company, 2003. (V, VI)

Gloria Whelan. *Angel on the Square.* HarperCollins Children's Books, 2003. (III, VI)

Karen Zeinert. *Those Extraordinary Women of World War I.* Lerner Publishing Group, 2001. (III, VIII)

Skill Builder

Analyzing Propaganda

Propaganda is the spreading of information, beliefs, and ideas to influence people for or against an issue or person. Propaganda does not always tell the whole truth and is usually biased. Bias is a strong feeling for or against a person or issue without facts to support that feeling.

Advertising is a form of propaganda. Advertisers want you to buy their products instead of their competitors' products.

To analyze propaganda:

1. Identify the topic of the cartoon, poster, ad, or writing.
2. Identify who is responsible for the piece—for example, a political candidate, a company, or the government.
3. Determine the message of the piece.
   Ask yourself: Does it present only one side? Does the picture or text exaggerate?

Nations also use propaganda to sell the public on an idea. For example, governments want to inspire their people to make sacrifices during wartime. They sometimes use propaganda against the enemy to do this. Posters were used by the U.S. government to raise money during World War I. Notice how the Germans are portrayed as blood thirsty, vicious Huns in the 1918 war bond poster. They have blood on their hands and bayonets as they seize control of Europe.

Complete the following activities.

1. What emotions is this poster designed to evoke? What impression does the looming figure provide to the viewer? In a time before television and the internet, why do you think the government relied on posters such as this?

2. With a partner, think of a TV commercial about one of your favorite products. List three ways it uses propaganda.

Skill Builder

1. Students' answers will vary. Possible response: The poster evokes threat and danger. The blood may symbolize the shed blood of the troops killed or injured already. The impression of the looming figure is that he is dangerous and determined. The government may have used graphic images such as these to shock people into action.

2. Students' answers will vary but should identify propaganda techniques used in a television commercial.

World War I and the Russian Revolution | 335

Classroom Discussion

Discuss with students some of the broader topics covered in this chapter.

- How can international organizations help to prevent war?
- How can the costs of war be recovered fairly?
- What are the best ways to improve economic development?
- In what ways can being neutral in a conflict be an advantage?

World War I and the Russian Revolution | 335

Chapter 21
BETWEEN THE WARS
(1919–1939)

Chapter Summary
Refer to page 348 for a summary of Chapter 21.

Related Transparencies
T-1 World Map
T-20 Venn Diagram

Key Blacklines
Biography—Mohandas Gandhi

CD Extension
Encourage students to use the reading comprehension, vocabulary reinforcement, and interactive timeline activities on the student CD.

Getting Focused
Students' lists will vary. You may wish to extend the activity by making a composite class list and posting it, then referring and adding to it as the various items come up during the study of the chapter.

Pre-Reading Discussion

1 Discuss with students contemporary dictators that they learn about in the news. Ask students to suggest how these people keep power.

2 Ask students to imagine that money has become worthless. How would their lives change? What hard decisions would they have to make?

Getting Focused

Skim this chapter to predict what you will be learning.
• Read the lesson titles and subheadings.
• Look at the illustrations and read the captions.
• Examine the maps.
• Review the vocabulary words and terms.

A totalitarian government is one that attempts to cont? the politics, economy, society, and culture of a nation. People's freedoms are limited. Between 1919 and 1939 three totalitarian governments emerged in Europe: Ita the Soviet Union, and Germany.

What freedoms would people lose under a totalitarian government? How would a government make people obey laws that take away their freedoms? Work with a partner to make a list of your ideas. As you read this chapter, check your list against what these government actually did.

Picturing History
The Austrian children pictured on page 336 were giving the "Heil, Hitler" salute as the dictator came to town in 1938. In March of that year, Hitler declared an *Anschluss,* or union, of Austria and Germany. Austrians generally favored this move. However, unifying the two nations violated the Treaty of Versailles. Also in 1938, Hitler took control of a border region of Czechoslovakia, the Sudeten. When he took over all of Czechoslovakia six months later, he ended hopes of "peace for our time," as British Prime Minister Neville Chamberlain had put it.

Time Box Extension
Have students create timelines using the dates on page 337 and add details from the previous chapter, such as Lenin's New Economic Policy in 1921.

LESSON 1

Totalitarianism in Italy

Thinking on Your Own

Make a list of the vocabulary words in your notebook. Then skim the chapter for more words that you do not know. Work with a partner to define each of the words on your list. Once you agree on a definition, write a sentence that shows the word's meaning. Then write a synonym for each of the words.

After World War I, people in Europe and the United States were tired of war. They were horrified at its costs in lives and damage. The League of Nations was created to ensure that a global war would never happen again. However, the League was doomed to fail. Its 40-member nations could not agree on policies, including how to stop aggressive nations. In addition, the United States never joined the League.

focus your reading

Explain how Mussolini gained power.

What is fascism?

How was the government set up under Mussolini?

vocabulary

depression fascism
inflation censor
Blackshirts corporate state
dictator

A major problem that nations also faced in the 1920s was a worldwide **depression**. A depression is a period of rising unemployment and low economic activity. It began in the early 1920s in Europe and spread around the world. By the early 1930s, the economy of the United States had also collapsed. The depression caused great hardship everywhere. Leaders in several countries promised to end the suffering by setting up totalitarian governments.

Time Box

1919
Fascist Party founded

1922
Mussolini named prime minister

1926
Mussolini declared himself *Il Duce*

Between the Wars 337

Lesson Summary
The world experienced an economic depression that began in Europe in the 1920s. Totalitarian governments promised to end the hardship. In Italy, Benito Mussolini tried to rebuild a Roman Empire. Mussolini built supporters into a group known as Blackshirts. They were anti-Communist and anti-Socialist. In 1922, Mussolini became prime minister and then dictator three years later. Italy became a Fascist state. Mussolini used censorship, terror, and propaganda to control Italy. He also headed the economy.

Lesson Objective
Students will learn about the rise of fascism in Italy under Benito Mussolini.

Focus Your Reading Answers

1 Mussolini gained power by using the economic problems of Italy and playing on people's fears and hopes for a new empire.

2 Fascism is an anti-Communist, anti-Socialist government headed by a dictator. Its philosophy is that the state is more important than the people.

3 The government under Mussolini banned all political parties other than the Fascist Party. Businesses were run by corporations, which Mussolini headed. Terrorism, censorship, and propaganda were widespread.

Lesson Vocabulary

Introduce each of the following vocabulary terms to students.

Explain that, as used in the economic sense, *depression* is a time of rising unemployment and low economic activity. During the 1920s, many nations faced a *depression*. A rapid increase in the price of goods is called *inflation*. Italy's economic troubles began with *inflation*. *Blackshirts* were Mussolini's supporters, named for the color of their shirts. The *Blackshirts* broke up meetings of Socialists.

A *dictatorship* occurs when one person has complete control of the government. Mussolini set up a *dictatorship* in Italy. A totalitarian government that is not Communist is *Fascist*. The state is more important than individuals in *fascism*. Forbidding the views of those who disagree with the government is to *censor* them. Mussolini *censored* the mass media in Italy.

A *corporate state* exists when workers are grouped by occupations, and those groups are called corporations. Mussolini headed a *corporate state* in Italy.

Between the Wars 337

The Rise of Mussolini

The first person to set up a totalitarian government was Benito Mussolini in Italy. He used the Treaty of Versailles and Italy's economic problems to gain power.

During World War I, Italy fought on the side of the Allies. At the end of the war, Italy wanted to annex land to its east along the Adriatic Sea. Instead, the Big Three—the United States, Great Britain, and France—gave the land to the new nation of Yugoslavia. This angered Italian nationalists. Mussolini appealed to them by promising to create a new Italian empire.

Like much of Europe, economic troubles began in Italy right after World War I. **Inflation** became a problem. Inflation is a rapid increase in the prices of goods. Prices rose but workers' wages did not. Workers called strikes to demand higher pay. Socialists preached an end to capitalism. Middle-class owners of businesses and large landowners feared socialism. They were worried about a Communist takeover of Italy. At that time, Communists were calling themselves Socialists.

Mussolini used the fears of the middle class. In 1919, he founded the Fascist Party. In the early 1920s, groups of his supporters known as **Blackshirts** broke up strikes and attacked Socialists' meetings and offices. By 1922, Mussolini had the support of a large portion of the middle class. In that year, Mussolini and his followers marched on Rome. Mussolini boldly demanded power from King Victor Emmanuel III. The king saw no choice and made him prime minister.

By 1925, Mussolini had set up a dictatorship. Under a dictatorship, a single person, the **dictator**, has complete

Fascist "March on Rome," 1922

Picturing History

Benito Mussolini, shown at the top of page 338, appealed to a time of former glory. The *fasces* in *fascist* referred to bound rods that were symbols of ancient Rome's power. Mussolini wanted a new Roman Empire, which he planned to build in North Africa. Italy invaded Ethiopia (then known as Abyssinia) in 1935 and later invaded Libya.

Picturing History

After the October 1922 "March on Rome," soldiers burned Socialist literature in the streets, as depicted in the photograph at the left on page 338. Some 30,000 Blackshirts marched on Rome, causing King Victor Emmanuel III to fear civil war and send for Mussolini, who had been waiting in Milan. At thirty-nine, Mussolini became the youngest prime minister of Italy.

Extension

Just as Woodrow Wilson had predicted, the League of Nations proved ineffectual in stopping the Italian conquest.

Although the League declared Italy an aggressor in Ethiopia in 1935, nothing was done. An arms embargo against Italy was not enforced, allowing Italy to gather armaments against the poorly equipped Ethiopians. Haile Selassie, exiled emperor of Ethiopia, spoke before the League. France and Britain recognized Italy's power in Ethiopia, although the Soviet Union and the United States refused to do so. Not until Italy entered World War II on Germany's side did Western democracies aid Ethiopia.

stop and think

As you read, create a cause-and-effect flowchart that illustrates how Mussolini came to power.

control of the government. Italy was still called a constitutional monarchy. Victor Emmanuel III was still king. However, Mussolini had taken control of the government for himself. He had elections fixed so that only his supporters were elected to office. He removed opponents from government jobs. By 1926, he was calling himself Il Duce, the leader. The king was only a figurehead.

Fascism

Mussolini's dictatorship was called **fascism**. The name came from his political party. Fascism is a totalitarian government that is not Communist. Fascists in the 1920s and 1930s were strong anti-Communists and anti-Socialists.

According to fascism, the state is more important than individuals. As a result, a Fascist nation has a strong central government. There is a single leader who is a dictator. The government controls the economy. Individuals and companies may own businesses and land. However, the government controls how the owners run them. Individuals have limited freedoms.

In a Fascist state, rival political parties are banned. The mass media—newspapers, radio, and movies—is **censored**. In this context, to censor means to forbid the communication of views that oppose the government. Police spies and terror are used to enforce government policies. Propaganda is another important tool in a Fascist state. It is used to brainwash people into believing what the government says. The way Mussolini governed Italy shows how a Fascist state works.

Mussolini in Power

As prime minister, Mussolini banned all political parties except the Fascist Party. The press, radio, and movies were

Benito Mussolini speaking to followers in 1930

Stop and Think

Cause-and-effect flowcharts will vary. Possible response:

Cause: land given to Yugoslavia;
Effect: promised to build new Italian empire.
Cause: inflation a problem;
Effect: founded Fascist Party.
Cause: Mussolini wanted power;
Effect: March on Rome and prime ministership.
Cause: set up dictatorship;
Effect: elections are fixed.

Picturing History

In 1930, Benito Mussolini, shown in the photograph on page 339, proved an inspiration for Adolf Hitler, who organized Germany on the Fascist pattern. The two men joined to form the Rome-Berlin Axis. Hitler, who had withdrawn Germany from the League of Nations in 1933, invaded the Rhineland in 1936 after Mussolini's successful conquest of Ethiopia and the lack of effective reprisals from the League.

Extension

Mussolini was known for his oratory. Have students use library resources or the Internet to investigate his background in journalism, which surely helped his command of words.

Between the Wars, 1919–1939

Picturing History

The photograph on page 340 shows Fascist youth standing at attention to greet Mussolini. About two-thirds of Italian young people were members of Fascist youth groups by 1939. The groups promoted military values and activity.

Picturing History

The hammer and sickle depicted on page 341 symbolized the Soviet Union. The symbol appeared not only on flags but also on public buildings.

---

censored. Nothing could be printed or said that opposed Mussolini's rule.

Terror became a weapon of the government. In 1926, Mussolini set up a secret police force to spy on people and create fear. Opponents were arrested and tortured. Some were sent into exile and others were killed.

To gain support, Mussolini used propaganda. The message was obedience to the government and dedication to the nation. One slogan was "Believe! Obey! Fight!" Another was "Mussolini Is Always Right." Propaganda urged women to stay at home and raise children. Men were told to be ready to fight for Italy. Children were enrolled in youth groups to learn Fascist philosophy. These youth groups were based on military principles. Children practiced marching like soldiers and learned discipline and obedience to their leaders.

A Fascist youth group on parade

Under Mussolini, the government controlled Italy's economy. He set up a **corporate state** in which workers were grouped by occupations. These groups were called *corporations*, and Mussolini headed them. He did not end capitalism as a Socialist would have. Rather, he used capitalism. The corporations, along with the Fascist Party, controlled how businesses and farms were run. The economy improved, but workers lost out. They could not strike and their wages remained low.

Mussolini was building a nation based on military discipline. He expected to use it to build a new Italian empire.

Putting It All Together

Create a T-chart. In the left column, list the characteristics of a Fascist nation. Then write examples from Mussolini's government for each characteristic. Work with a partner and compare your charts.

Putting It All Together
Students' T-charts will vary. Possible response:

Fascist nation: totalitarian; non-Communist; state more important than individual; strong central government; ruled by a dictator; government controlled economy; rival political parties banned; mass media censored; police spies, terror, propaganda
Mussolini's Italy: all political parties banned except Fascist Party; mass media censored; secret police, terrorism, propaganda; corporate state; businesses and farms controlled by corporations and Fascist Party

LESSON 2

Stalin and the Soviet Union

Thinking on Your Own

Italy under Mussolini and the Soviet Union under Stalin were totalitarian states, or nations. As you read this lesson, make a list of the characteristics of a totalitarian communist society.

Joseph Stalin came to power in the Soviet Union in the late 1920s. He survived a struggle with other Communist Party leaders after Lenin's death. Part of the struggle had been over how quickly to industrialize the nation. Lenin's New Economic Policy had improved the economy after the war. However, Stalin and his supporters wanted more improvements—and quickly. They wanted the Soviet Union to become a major industrial nation.

focus your reading

Discuss how the Five-Year Plans affected the Soviet economy.

At whom were Stalin's purges aimed?

Describe what life was like in the Soviet Union under communism.

vocabulary

Five-Year Plans
collectives
quotas
kulaks
purges

Stalin's Five-Year Plans

Once Stalin had defeated his rivals, he pushed through a series of **Five-Year Plans**. The Plans began in 1928. They were aimed at increasing industrial and agricultural production.

Industry was to focus on making steel, machines, weapons, and farm and transportation equipment. The transportation system was improved and expanded. New power plants were built. More money was put into mining and oil drilling.

To increase farm production, Stalin ended private ownership of farms. Farms were turned into **collectives**.

The Soviet symbol of the hammer and sickle. The hammer represented industrial workers, and the sickle, farm workers.

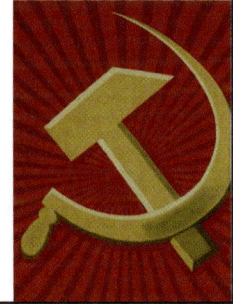

Lesson Vocabulary

Discuss each of the vocabulary terms with students.

Five-Year Plans were meant to increase factory and farm production. Stalin began the *Five-Year Plans* in 1928. *Collectives* were large farms made by combining the small farms of many peasants. Farm animals, tools, and supplies belonged to the *collectives*.

Set amounts are *quotas*. The Soviet government set prices and production *quotas*. Farm owners who did not want to be collectivized were called *kulaks*. The *kulaks* were sent to Siberian labor camps. Attempts to get rid of political opponents are *purges*. Millions of people died during Stalin's *purges*.

Lesson Summary

Stalin defeated his political rivals to become the head of the Soviet Union after Lenin's death. Wanting the Soviets to industrialize, he created a series of Five-Year Plans. Industries worked to produce machines, weapons, and steel. Farms were no longer privately owned. People who resisted were killed or sent to Siberian labor camps. Many starved. Stalin also began purges to eliminate his enemies.

In the Soviet Union, people had little money and few luxury goods. Most money went toward housing and food, which was bought only after standing in long lines. Stalin built a military state, using secret police and propaganda to achieve his ends.

Lesson Objective

Students will learn about the Soviet Union under Joseph Stalin.

Focus Your Reading Answers

1 The Five-Year Plans affected the Soviet economy by collectivizing farms and factories. The effort was a failure, with millions dying of starvation.

2 Stalin's purges were aimed at the resistance, especially the peasant landowners and anyone who opposed him politically.

3 Under communism, life in the Soviet Union was difficult. Food was scarce because Stalin exported it to buy equipment. Wages in factories were low, and there were few luxury goods available even if people could have afforded them.

Between the Wars

Picturing History

The photograph on page 342 shows women helping to thresh grain on a collective farm in the 1930s. The peasants resisted collectivization, in some cases killing their animals before allowing them to become state property. In 1930, they killed one-third of the pigs and one-fourth of the cattle, goats, and sheep of the nation. Agriculture moved backward, rather than forward, when experienced farmers were killed or sent to the labor camps. In Ukraine farmers were hardest hit, starving while accused of hiding grain from Stalin. In 1933 alone, five million peasants starved to death.

Stop and Think

Students' Venn diagrams will differ. Possible response:

Italian Fascism: corporate state

Soviet Communism: purges, collectivization, plans to modernize, banned religion

Both: totalitarian rulers, secret police and terror, propaganda, built strong military

These huge farms were made by combining the small farms of many peasant families. The collectives were to be run by groups of peasants. The peasants could keep their homes and a small plot of land on which to grow their own food. However, all farm animals, tools, and supplies belonged to the collective. The peasants were to manage and work the farms together. They would not be paid wages, but they would share in any profits. However, the government set prices and **quotas** for production. A quota is a set amount. Quotas regulated the amount of crops that each collective could produce.

The peasants, especially those who had owned their own farms, rebelled. They burned their fields or hid their crops after the harvest. They killed their farm animals and broke the new tractors and other tools the government had given them.

Stalin used force to end the resistance. He sent the **kulaks** to labor camps in Siberia, the coldest, farthest part of the Soviet Union. Kulaks were the farm owners who resisted collectivization. Stalin's policies and the resistance of peasants had a cost. Terrible famines occurred across the Soviet Union in 1932 and 1933. As many as 10 million peasants may have died.

Stalin's Purges

The persecution of the kulaks was just one of Stalin's **purges**. A purge is an attempt to get rid of political opponents. The period from 1934 to 1936 is called the Great Purge.

Stalin used his secret police to spy on and arrest those who disagreed with him. The accused were tried and sentenced to death or to a labor camp in Siberia. Perhaps 8 million people died because of the Great Purge.

Like Mussolini, Stalin used terror to make Soviets obey the government. He also used the Great Purge to

---

> **stop and think**
>
> Make a Venn diagram. Label the circles "Italian Fascism" and "Soviet Communism." Fill in the diagram with information about how the two governments were similar and different.

342 Chapter 21

Extension

Encourage students to read George Orwell's novel *Animal Farm*, which can be interpreted as a beast fable about life under Stalin. You may wish to show clips of the film to your students.

Students may also be interested in *The Gulag Archipelago*, written by Alexander Solzhenitsyn, the winner of the 1970 Nobel Prize in Literature, who survived one of the Siberian labor camps.

remove anyone from the Communist Party who might challenge his power. Those jobs were filled by young Communists who were grateful to Stalin and, therefore, loyal to him.

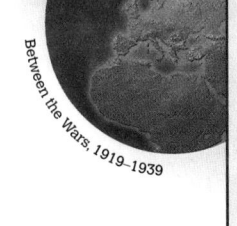

Life in Soviet Society

Stalin put few resources into producing consumer goods such as refrigerators, furniture, and cars. As a result, there were few luxuries for workers to buy. Additionally, they had little money to spend on anything except food and housing. Wages were low. Like that of earlier European and U.S. factory workers, housing was crowded. Living conditions were bad. Families often shared two- or three-room apartments. Food in the cities was in short supply. Women stood in long lines daily to buy food.

Stalin had achieved his goal of increasing food production. However, much of the food was exported. Stalin needed to sell huge amounts of food to other nations in order to buy goods needed for industry and the military. Like Mussolini and Hitler, Stalin was building a strong military.

Also like Mussolini and Hitler, Stalin used propaganda to promote his goals. Everywhere, Soviets saw and heard messages glorifying the Soviet Union. They were encouraged to work harder and to produce more. Stalin also encouraged nationalism and suspicion of Western nations. Religion was banned because it distracted people from loyalty to the government.

Time Box
1922
    Stalin elected leader of Communist Party
1928
    Five-Year Plans
1934
    Great Purge began

The shortage of food that began during the 1930s remained an issue for Soviet citizens into the 1980s.

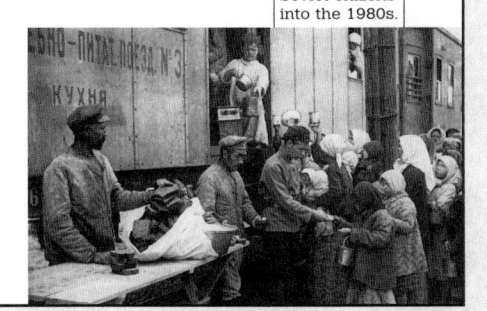

Putting It All Together

Why is the Soviet Union called a totalitarian nation? Review the list that you made as you read this lesson. Use it to write an essay of three or four paragraphs to answer the question. Ask a partner to review your essay. Ask for suggestions on how to make it clearer and more interesting.

Extension

"Stalin" was an alias that the Soviet leader adopted in 1912. It comes from the Russian word for steel, *stal*. It was not the first alias Stalin used. Arrested and exiled six times between 1902 and 1913, he chose a series of different names after escaping. Only in 1913, after the sixth arrest, did he fail to escape exile in Siberia. He was freed by the success of the 1917 revolution, which freed all political prisoners.

Picturing History

The 1936 photograph at the top of page 343 shows Leningrad workers at a turbine shop meeting to approve the first Purge. Almost half a million people were forced into labor camps, placed in prison, or killed during the purges in 1935–1936. The following three years were known as the Great Purge, during which Stalin had many of his political rivals killed. Lenin, who had been impressed by Stalin, nevertheless once said he was "too rough."

Picturing History

The photograph at the bottom of page 343 illustrates the continuing problem of food shortages in the Soviet Union. The famine was created by Stalin's insistence that the nation industrialize. When announcing the first Five-Year Plan, Stalin told the nation it was 50 to 100 years behind and must make up that distance in ten years.

Putting It All Together

Students' essays will vary but should support the idea that the Soviet Union was a totalitarian nation.

Between the Wars 343

Lesson Summary

The economic depression of the 1920s and 1930s hit Germany very hard. Adolf Hitler, who became head of the Nazi Party in Germany, promised to end the hardships and to rebuild Germany's military. He became chancellor and then dictator, using terror and propaganda to achieve his ends. Concentration camps were built for Jews, homosexuals, gypsies, and Roman Catholics. A rabid anti-Semite, Hitler tried to destroy the Jewish people. Jews were persecuted by means of acts of mass terror, such as *Kristallnacht*, and a series of laws.

Lesson Objective

Students will learn about the early years of Hitler's power and the Nazi persecutions.

Focus Your Reading Answers

1 Hitler gained absolute power in Germany by promising a return to former glory, an end to economic hardship, and a military buildup. He became head of the Nazi Party, then chancellor, then dictator.

2 Nazi policies included terror through concentration camps and the secret police. Propaganda encouraged people to accept the Nazi policies. The government controlled business. The military was strengthened, and public works gave people jobs.

3 Hitler persecuted the Jews in the following ways: Jews lost citizenship, were forced to wear a Star of David, and were forbidden to marry non-Jews. The Jews were not allowed to use public transportation, attend or teach in schools, or work in stores or hospitals. In addition, there was public violence, such as *Kristallnacht*.

344 | Chapter 21

LESSON 3

Hitler and Nazi Germany

Thinking on Your Own

As you read this lesson, take bulleted notes on the ways that Hitler gained and kept power. Title your notes "Hitler's Policies." When you finish the lesson, compare your notes with that of a partner. Add any new concepts to your list.

The conditions that helped Adolf Hitler take over Germany were similar to those that helped Mussolini. Germans were angered at their treatment by the Allies at the Paris Peace Conference. German nationalists wanted the land that was taken from them under the Treaty of Versailles. Germany was also suffering from the worldwide depression. However, the Allies insisted that Germany continue to pay the huge reparations called for by the treaty.

focus your reading

Describe how Hitler gained absolute power in Germany.

Explain the policies of the Nazi government.

List examples of the ways in which Hitler persecuted the Jews.

vocabulary

Nazi Party
concentration camp
anti-Semite
genocide

Inflation was so severe in Germany that money was used to light a stove.

Hitler's Rise to Power

After the war, many nationalist political parties were developing in Germany. Adolf Hitler joined one of them, the small National Socialist German Workers' Party. The name was eventually changed to the **Nazi Party**. By 1921, he headed the party. Two years later the party tried to overthrow the German government. Nothing came of the uprising, and Hitler was sent to jail.

After his prison term, Hitler set out to make the Nazis the most powerful political party in Germany. By 1929,

Lesson Vocabulary

Discuss each of the vocabulary terms with students.

The *Nazi Party* was the National Socialist German Workers' Party. Hitler became the head of the *Nazi Party*.

A *concentration camp* is a prison camp. People sent to a *concentration camp* either became laborers or were put to death.

A person who hates the Jewish people is an *anti-Semite*. The most famous *anti-Semite* was Adolf Hitler. To kill an entire ethnic group is *genocide*. Hitler practiced *genocide* against the Jews.

Adolf Hitler preparing to address a crowd

its membership had expanded from 27,000 to 178,000. Like Mussolini, Hitler appealed to nationalists. If Germans followed him, he promised to stop the payment of reparations. He would rebuild the German military. Germany would create a new empire. Like Mussolini, Hitler also appealed to business leaders and large landowners. He promised security from a Communist takeover and an end to the depression.

At the beginning of 1933, the president of the German Republic was forced to make Hitler chancellor. The Nazis had

Inflation in Germany

writer Ernest Hemingway and his wife Hadley spent September 19, 1922, in Kehl, many. In this excerpt, Hemingway describes how high prices were because of inflation.

[W]e changed some French money the railway station at Kehl. 10 francs I received 670 marks. francs amounted to about cents . . . The 90 cents lasted . . . a day of heavy spending and . . . had 120 marks left!

picked out five very good-king apples and gave the woman 0 mark note. . . . A very nice-king, white-bearded old gentleman us . . . and raised his hat.

ardon me . . . how much were apples?'

. . told him 12 marks.

. . . shook his head, 'I can't pay t is too much.'

reading for understanding

How many marks did Hemingway receive for 10 francs?

Why wasn't the man able to buy apples?

How do you think Germans felt about not being able to buy basics like food?

"With marks at 800 to a dollar, or 8 to a cent, . . . [p]eas were 18 marks a pound, beans 16 marks. . . . Kehl's best hotel . . . served a five-course . . . meal for 120 marks, which amounts to 15 cents in our money."

Picturing History

The photograph on page 345 shows Hitler before speaking to a crowd in 1934. He is climbing the stairs at Beckeberg between rows of Storm Troopers carrying swastika banners. Hitler was an expert manipulator. As early as the 1920s, he had photographs taken so that he could find the most effective gestures for public speaking. Banners, singing, parades, and lighting were all planned for effect. Before the news was broadcast on radio, a fanfare was played to heighten the excitement.

Reading for Understanding

1 He received 670 marks for 10 francs.

2 He said they cost too much.

3 The Germans were no doubt discouraged and humiliated at not being able to buy the basics of life.

Picturing History

The photograph on page 344 illustrates the worthlessness of German money, which was more valuable as fuel than as money. Although the collapse was official in late 1923, it began more than a year earlier when former Allies refused Germany permission to postpone paying reparations. By November 1923, a single loaf of bread cost more than 200 billion marks.

Extension

Encourage students interested in economics to compare and contrast the depression experience of Germany and other nations. Have them find out such things as gross national product, unemployment, and inflation rates. Have them present their findings to the class by using the Student Presentation Builder on the student CD.

Between the Wars

Stop and Think

Students' flowcharts will vary. Possible response: joined Nazi Party, became head of Nazi Party, tried to overthrow government, went to prison, expanded Nazi membership, became chancellor, became dictator

Picturing History

The photograph at the center of page 346 shows a parade of SS troops at a Nuremberg rally. Beginning in 1933, the Nazis held an annual rally in Nuremberg. The rallies demonstrated the power of both Hitler and the Nazis. In a fitting twist, the post-war trials of Nazi and Japanese leaders were held in Nuremberg.

Picturing History

A Nazi youth group is shown at the bottom of page 346. Hitler Youth was formed as the male youth division of the Nazis in 1926. There was also a League of German Girls. After 1936, all other youth groups disbanded, and joining Hitler Youth was mandatory for children ages ten to eighteen. In 1943, those over sixteen were called to fight. American journalist Dorothy Thompson visited one of the youth camps in 1934. She saw an enormous banner on the hillside, with a swastika and seven words: "You were born to die for Germany."

---

won a majority of seats in the German Parliament. Hitler acted quickly to cement his power. He had Parliament suspend the constitution. Hitler no longer needed the legislature to make laws. The law was whatever Hitler decided it was. With the support of the Nazi Party, Hitler created a dictatorship. Germans began calling him Der Fuhrer, or the leader.

The Nazi Government

By 1934, there was no one who could challenge Hitler. The only political party allowed in Germany was the Nazi Party. Labor unions were banned. Hitler used terror and propaganda to maintain control and achieve his policies. The Gestapo, his secret police, spied on possible enemies. Anyone who opposed Hitler's ideas could be sent to a **concentration camp**—a type of prison camp. This was the beginning of the persecution of Jews, homosexuals, gypsies, Roman Catholics, and others.

Hitler had promised to end the depression. Unlike Stalin, Hitler did not do away with private industry. But like Mussolini, he did control business and labor. The government set up massive public works projects to employ people. It also provided funding to private industry to create jobs. Hitler also stopped World War I reparation payments and set about re-arming Germany. Thousands of jobs were created to help build and equip the military.

A constant chorus of propaganda urged Germans to support the Third Reich. This was Hitler's name for the new German empire. Youth groups trained young men in military discipline and values. Like Mussolini, Hitler discouraged women from working outside the home.

SS troops in 1933

A Nazi youth group

346 Chapter 21

stop and think

Create a sequence flowchart to track how Hitler came to power. Share your flowchart with a partner. Ask your partner to check it to make sure it has all the events in order. Discuss which events caused other events.

Extension

Leni Riefenstahl was one of the photographers and filmmakers of Nazi Germany. Encourage students interested in film to use library resources or the Internet to find out more about her.

Jews were forced to wear a Star of David.

Anti-Semitism

Hitler was a fanatical **anti-Semite**. He hated Jews. Hitler had developed a theory that Germans were descended from a pure Aryan race. To Hitler, this was the master race, superior to all other races. Jews in Germany endangered the purity of the race. He also blamed the Jews for most of Germany's problems. In the beginning, Hitler wanted to drive all Jews from the country. Later, he turned to **genocide**, which is the murder of all members of an ethnic group.

In 1935, the Nuremberg Laws stripped German Jews of their German citizenship. Germans Jews could no longer marry non-Jewish Germans. German Jews were also forced to wear a yellow Star of David on their clothes to mark them as Jews.

The night of November 9, 1938, is known as Kristallnacht, the Night of Broken Glass. In Paris two days before, a young Jew had shot a German diplomat. He was taking revenge for violence against his parents in Germany. The Nazis used this as an excuse to attack Jews. Jewish businesses, homes, and synagogues were destroyed. Jews were beaten in the streets, and more than 100 Jews were murdered. After the violence, some 30,000 German-Jewish men were sent to concentration camps.

More persecution followed. German Jews could not ride public transportation. They could not attend or teach in German schools. They could not work in stores or in hospitals.

Time Box

1921
Hitler took over Nazi Party
1933
Hitler named chancellor of Germany
1935
Nuremberg Laws
1938
Kristallnacht

The aftermath of Kristallnacht

Putting It All Together

You have now read about three totalitarian dictators. With a partner create a table to compare and contrast them. Use the following categories or topics: "Country," "Date Came to Power," "Official Title," "Political Party," "Type of Government," and "Ways to Control the Nation."

Picturing History

The Jews in the photograph at the top of page 347 were wearing the Star of David that marked their ethnicity. After 1933, the star was required on shops owned by Jews. It was a way to boycott Jewish businesses, as well as an easy identifier for *Kristallnacht* violence.

Time Box Extension

Have students compare the dates in this Time Box with the ones in the Time Box on page 337 to compare the rise of Mussolini and Hitler.

Picturing History

The photograph at the bottom of page 347 shows the results of *Kristallnacht*. Point out to students the undamaged shop at the left of the picture, clearly owned by non-Jews. Synagogues were burned also, and any Jews in the streets were beaten. More than 7,000 stores owned by Jews were broken into and looted.

Putting It All Together

Students' tables will vary but should contain accurate information from the three nations studied.

Extension

Students should be encouraged to investigate the life of Anne Frank, the young Jewish girl whose diary has become a classic. You may wish to show clips from the film *The Diary of Anne Frank*, or direct students to a Web site about the Secret Annex, the building in Amsterdam in the Netherlands where Anne and her family hid from the Nazis.

Between the Wars, 1919–1939

Between the Wars

Chapter Review

1. Students' essays will vary but should compare and contrast Mussolini and Stalin, Stalin and Hitler, or Hitler and Mussolini.

2. Students' ideas about alternatives will vary. Possible responses include: remove Hitler from power; allow Jews to leave the Third Reich; protect and hide the Jewish people

3. Students' essays will vary but should discuss the governments formed under Mussolini, Stalin, and Hitler.

Chapter Summary

- Benito Mussolini in Italy, Joseph Stalin in the Soviet Union, and Adolf Hitler in Germany set up totalitarian governments. The worldwide **depression** and soaring **inflation** aided their rise to power.
- Mussolini used the **Blackshirts** to terrorize Socialists. He promised nationalists that he would create a new Italian empire. He established a **corporate state**.
- Mussolini set up a totalitarian government with himself as **dictator**. He governed Italy according to **fascism**. Newspapers, radio, and the movies were **censored**.
- Joseph Stalin replaced Lenin's NEP with a series of **Five-Year Plans**. The government set **quotas** for industrial and farm production. Peasants rebelled at the **collectivization** of their farms. To end their resistance, Stalin had **kulaks** sent to labor camps in Siberia.
- In the Great **Purge**, Stalin used the secret police to arrest those who disagreed with him or who might challenge him.
- Adolf Hitler led the **Nazi Party** to power in Germany.
- Once in power, Hitler banned labor unions and all political parties except the Nazi Party. Those who opposed him were sent to **concentration camps**.
- Hitler was a fanatical **anti-Semite**. He adopted a policy of **genocide** toward Jews. The Nuremberg Laws and Kristallnacht are two examples of his anti-Semitism.

Chapter Review

1. Review the table you created at the end of Lesson 3. Use the information to write an essay comparing and contrasting two of the following leaders: Mussolini, Stalin, and Hitler.

2. What could German non-Jews have done about the treatment of Jews? Discuss the question with a partner. Write your ideas in a paragraph.

3. Write a five-paragraph essay discussing the formation of governments under Mussolini, Stalin, and Hitler.

Novel Connections

Below is a list of books that relate to the time period covered in this chapter. The numbers in parentheses indicate the related Thematic Strands of the National Council for the Social Studies (NCSS).

Karen Levine. *Hana's Suitcase*. Albert Whitman & Company, 2003. (V, IX, X)

Sonia Levitin. *Room in the Heart*. Dutton Children's Books, 2003. (VI)

Robin Nelson and Jeremy Roberts. *Benito Mussolini*. Lerner Publishing Group, 2005. (V, VI)

Jerry Spinelli. *Milkweed*. Knopf Books for Young Readers/Random House Children's Books, 2003. (IV, V)

Gloria Whelan. *The Impossible Journey*. HarperCollins Children's Books, 2003. (I, III, VI)

Skill Builder

Identifying Point of View

A person's point of view is shaped by his or her family, religion, education, friends, and experiences. The time period in which a person lives is also important in determining what a person thinks about an event or another person.

For example, although British, French and Germans all fought in World War I, their experiences after the war led to different points of view. Many Germans believed that the Treaty of Versailles was unfair. Most British and French thought Germany should be punished.

To help in identifying a point of view, follow these steps:

1. Identify the author or the speaker's background.
2. Identify the argument, issue, or main idea.
3. Identify the facts and other information used to support the argument. Distinguish facts from opinions.
4. Examine the kinds of words and phrases that the author or speaker uses. Do they favor one side of the issue?
5. State the person's viewpoint in your own words.

Read and answer the questions about the excerpt below.

Bahithat al-Badiya lived from 1886 to 1918. She was an educated, upper-class woman who lived in Cairo, Egypt.

> **"Men say when we become educated we shall push them out of work. . . . But isn't it rather men who have pushed women out of work? Before, women used to spin and to weave cloth . . . but men invented machines for spinning and weaving. . . . I am not urging women to neglect their home and children to go out and become lawyers or judges or railway engineers. But if any of us wish to work in such professions our personal freedom should not be infringed."**

1 What do you know about the writer?

2 What point or argument is she making?

3 What information does she use?

4 Write a sentence stating the writer's point of view.

Skill Builder

1 The writer is an educated, upper-class Egyptian woman living during the late nineteenth and early twentieth centuries.

2 She is making the argument that women can be educated and that men have taken over jobs that traditionally were done by women.

3 She uses historical information and common sense.

4 Students' sentences will vary. Possible response: The writer believes that women should have the freedom to be educated and to work.

Classroom Discussion

Discuss with students some of the broader topics covered in this chapter.

- How can the power of dictators and totalitarian regimes be lessened?
- How can the international community better respond to atrocities such as genocide?
- What are the legitimate uses of media censorship?

Chapter 22
World War II and the Cold War
(1931–1955)

Chapter Summary
Refer to page 366 for a summary of Chapter 22.

Related Transparencies

T-1 World Map
T-11 World War II Map
T-18 Three-Column Chart
T-20 Concept Web

Key Blacklines

Primary Source—Visiting Hiroshima

CD Extension

Encourage students to use the reading comprehension, vocabulary reinforcement, and interactive timeline activities on the student CD.

Getting Focused

To extend the Getting Focused activity, have students rotate partners at the beginning of each lesson and update their K-W-L charts as they work through the chapter.

Pre-Reading Discussion

Ask students to identify some strategies for dealing with bullies. Tell them that they are going to read about nations that acted like bullies during World War II and the Cold War. These nations used military strength to gain control of smaller nations.

Getting Focused

Skim this chapter to predict what you will be learning.
- Read the lesson titles and subheadings.
- Look at the illustrations and read the captions.
- Examine the maps.
- Review the vocabulary words.

Make a World War II K-W-L chart with three columns your notebook. Label the columns: "What I Know," "What I Want to Know," and "What I Learned." After skimming the chapter, make a list of what you know about World War II in the first column. In the second column, list questions you have about World War II.

Picturing History

The photograph on page 350 shows American troops landing in Normandy on D-Day, June 6, 1944, to begin to battle the Germans. More than 100,000 British, Canadian, and American troops landed in northern France to begin regaining French soil. More troops landed the following day. Omaha Beach was the scene of heavy fighting, with 3,000 Allied forces killed.

Picturing History

Shown in the photo on page 351 are some of the nearly 300 two-man tanks that were part of a military parade honoring Hitler's forty-seventh birthday in 1936. Large and medium-sized tanks were also part of the parade, the largest held in Berlin since the end of World War I.

350 Chapter 22

LESSON 1

The Road to War

Thinking on Your Own

Take outline notes on the important information in this lesson. Use the dates on the timeline as the basis for your notes. Write down the date and the information from the timeline. Then list details from the text to help you remember why each event was important.

During the 1930s, Germany, Japan, and Italy prepared for war. Hitler and Mussolini were firmly in control of their nations. The emperor ruled Japan, but military leaders made most of the decisions. In each nation, these dictators wanted to build great empires. They were ready to use their armies and navies to do this.

focus your reading

Explain why Italy and Japan seized territory in the 1930s.

Describe how Germany took control of neighboring nations in the 1930s.

Why did Great Britain and France finally act to stop Hitler?

vocabulary

appeasement
Anschluss
blitzkrieg
isolationist

Japan and Italy on the March

Japan faced serious economic problems in the early 1930s. Like other industrial nations, it suffered from the Great Depression. But Japan had its own special problems. A small island nation, it lacked iron ore, oil, rubber, and other resources. It also needed markets beyond Japan for the goods it produced. The Japanese government decided to expand into Asia to get control of resources and to sell its goods.

Hitler salutes tanks in 1936 during the re-arming of Germany.

Lesson Vocabulary

Introduce each of the following vocabulary terms to students.

Explain that *appeasement* is giving in to the demands of a hostile group or person to keep peace. Great Britain followed a policy of *appeasement* in dealing with Hitler.

The union of Austria and Germany was known as *Anschluss*. *Anschluss* took place in 1938.

Blitzkrieg is a German word meaning "lightning war." The *blitzkrieg* against Poland began in 1939.

Isolationists did not want the United States to get involved in European struggles. The *isolationists* argued against involvement by using the statistics of cost and number of deaths during World War I.

Lesson Summary

Italy, Japan, and Germany all prepared for war during the 1930s. They were ready to use military might to enlarge their empires. Japan needed resources and markets. Italy conquered Ethiopia. The League of Nations protested but did nothing. Nor did it act when Hitler began a military buildup in Germany or sent an army into the Rhineland. Britain wanted to try appeasement rather than go to war again. Hitler annexed Austria and gained control of the Sudetenland, then seized Czechoslovakia. Italy, Germany, and Japan signed a defense pact. The Nazi-Soviet Non-Aggression Pact promised that the two nations would not fight one another. They moved together against Poland and conquered it. The United States wanted to stay out of Europe's problems.

Lesson Objective

Students will learn about events leading to World War II.

Focus Your Reading Answers

1 Both Italy and Japan were in need of more land and resources, as well as new markets.

2 Germany violated the Treaty of Versailles and ignored the League of Nations. In 1936, Hitler sent troops into the Rhineland, and nothing was done to stop him. The British policy of appeasement allowed him to annex Austria in 1938. British and French leaders gave part of Czechoslovakia to Germany in 1938; Hitler then seized the rest of that nation.

3 Hitler invaded Poland. As a result, Great Britain and France, which were allies of Poland, entered the war.

World War II and the Cold War

Picturing History

Nanjing was the capital of China between 1928 and 1937, and again from 1946 to 1949. Capturing it was a major goal of the Japanese forces, as shown on page 352. Chiang Kai-shek was attempting to avoid war with Japan so that he could concentrate Chinese forces against the Communists. Like Britain's Chamberlain, he was willing to try appeasement. In late 1936, Chiang formed a new, united front against the Japanese. Chiang refused to surrender to the Japanese after the capital fell, moving his government to Hankow and later to Chongqing. Ironically, as a young man, Chiang had spent three years training in and serving with the Japanese army. After World War II ended, Chiang resumed his fight against communism. When his army lost to Mao Zedong in 1949, he transferred his government to Taiwan, where he remained president until his death in 1975.

Stop and Think

Students' letters will vary but should explain how the aggression of Italy, Germany, and Japan threaten world peace and address concerns of preserving peace.

Japanese troops in Nanjing, China, in 1937

In 1931, Japanese troops took control of Manchuria, a region in northeastern China. The Japanese claimed that Chinese troops had attacked their railroad in that region. The Japanese had actually staged the attack themselves. They dressed up in Chinese army uniforms and raided their own railroad.

Chiang Kai-shek, the head of China's government, tried to limit the spread of Japanese power in China. He agreed to let Japan govern parts of northern China. However, by 1937, China and Japan were fighting a full-scale war.

In 1940, Japan moved farther south to the French colony of Indochina. The United States warned the Japanese that it would stop selling them oil and scrap iron if they did not retreat. Japan did not retreat.

The League of Nations had objected to each of Japan's invasions and seizures of territory. However, it had no power to force Japan to give up the territory. This also was true when Italy invaded Ethiopia in 1935.

Ethiopia had resisted European domination longer

Japanese Expansion 1933–1941
- Japanese territory, 1933
- Japanese acquisitions to November 1941

stop and think

Pretend that you are an American citizen living in 1937. Write a letter to the League of Nations pointing out how the actions of Germany, Italy, and Japan are a threat to world peace. What would you ask the League to do to preserve the peace?

Extension

The conquest of Nanjing was known as the Rape of Nanjing. Japanese soldiers raped thousands of Chinese women in that city during a two-month period. They also used an estimated 400,000 Chinese for bayonet practice and machine-gunned them into open graves. One-third of the homes in Nanjing were destroyed.

Map Extension

Ask students to use the map on page 352 to answer the following questions:

- Was the city of Chongqing part of Japan's conquest? (no)
- About how many miles north-south did the land Japan acquired on mainland China extend? (about 2,000 miles/3,220 km)
- In what direction did the Japanese expand their territory between 1933 and 1941? (southwest)

than any other African nation. But in 1936, the nation fell to Italy. Mussolini had finally conquered the kingdom that defeated Italy in 1896.

Germany on the March

In Germany, Adolph Hitler also decided to ignore the Treaty of Versailles and defy the League of Nations. By the terms of the treaty, Germany's air force was abolished and its army reduced in size. In 1935, Hitler began to create an air force and expand the army. The League of Nations did nothing to stop him.

The treaty also created a zone along Germany's border with France that the German army could not enter. This area along the Rhine River belonged to Germany, but it was demilitarized to help protect France. In 1936, Hitler sent a German army into the Rhineland. Again, the League did nothing.

France and Great Britain protested Hitler's re-arming of the Rhineland. France would have fought to force Germany to remove its soldiers but needed Great Britain's help. The British, however, would not fight. This was the beginning of Britain's policy of **appeasement**. Appeasement is giving in to the demands of a hostile person or group in order to keep peace.

Hitler was now convinced that Great Britain and France would not fight. His next goal was **Anschluss**, or union of Austria with Germany. Austria was a nation that Hitler wanted to control, in part because he had been born there. By 1938, the Nazis had become an important political party in Austria. Hitler warned the chancellor of Austria to appoint Nazis to government positions of power or Germany would invade Austria. The chancellor agreed to Hitler's demand. Later, when Hitler made further demands, the chancellor refused. Hitler sent troops and proclaimed Austria part of Germany.

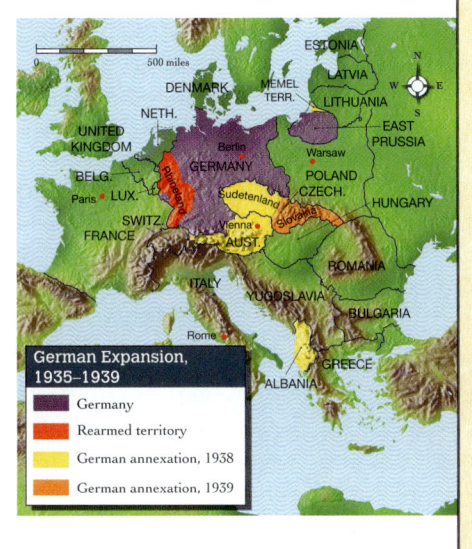

World War II 353

Map Extension

Ask students to use the map on page 353 to answer the following questions:

- When did Vienna become part of Germany? (1938)
- Which area was added in 1939? (Slovakia)
- What region was rearmed? (Rhineland)

Extension

Invite students interested in art to find a copy of Pablo Picasso's 1937 painting *Guernica*. Ask them to use library resources or the Internet to learn more about the events of Germany's assistance to the Spanish Civil War, including the massacre of Guernica. Have them present their findings to the class by using the Student Presentation Builder on the student CD.

World War II and the Cold War 353

Picturing History

The photograph on page 354 shows German tanks invading Poland. Although the Polish army attempted to defend that nation, they were fighting on horses, using lances against tanks. Stukas, dive-bombers that hit railroad lines and road intersections, accompanied the German tanks. Heavy bombing of both military and civilian targets reduced the capital of Warsaw to rubble. Soviet forces also invaded from the east.

Next on Hitler's list was Czechoslovakia. Czechoslovakia was created by the Treaty of Versailles. It had a number of ethnic groups within its borders. One large group was German. Many lived in a region called the Sudetenland. In 1938, Hitler demanded the return of the Sudetenland to Germany.

In 1938, British and French officials met with Hitler in Munich. At the Munich Conference, these officials again gave in to Hitler. They agreed that Hitler could take control of the Sudetenland. In return, Hitler promised that Germany would not take control of additional regions of Czechoslovakia. British Prime Minister Neville Chamberlain said the settlement had achieved "peace in our time." The following spring, Hitler seized the rest of Czechoslovakia.

WAR!

Hitler and Mussolini established an alliance between Germany and Italy in 1936. That same year, Germany and Japan signed a defense pact, or agreement. This set up the Rome-Berlin-Tokyo Axis. These three nations became known as the Axis Powers. Hitler signed his final alliance in August 1939 with Joseph Stalin. They agreed to the Nazi-Soviet Non-Aggression Pact. The pact stated that the two nations would not fight one another. In addition, the Soviet Union was promised part of Poland if conquered by Germany.

German panzer division rolling in Poland o Sept. 1, 1

Extension

Despite a desire to believe in the success of appeasement, the British government could see the war coming. Just one day before the blitzkrieg against Poland began, 1.5 million British children, accompanied by their teachers, were evacuated from major cities to the countryside. Have students interested in education or child care use library resources or the Internet to find out about this mass evacuation and its results. Allow time for them to report their findings to the class.

The Non-Aggression Pact left Hitler free to invade Poland. He had feared that Stalin would join with western European nations to resist an invasion of Poland. On September 1, 1939, Hitler launched his **blitzkrieg**, or lightning war, against Poland. The blitzkrieg included armored columns, known as panzer divisions, each containing about 300 tanks. They were accompanied by airplanes and support troops. The speed and efficiency of the blitzkrieg stunned Polish forces, who surrendered after only four weeks of fighting.

On September 3, 1939, Great Britain and France, which were Poland's allies, declared war on Germany. However, it was too late to help Poland. Hitler's modern army quickly overran the western section of the country. Stalin's forces attacked from the east. Within one month, Stalin and Hitler had divided Poland.

In the meantime, the United States decided not to join the fighting. **Isolationists** in the United States believed that the country should stay out of European problems. They defended their argument by pointing out the number of deaths and money spent during World War I. President Franklin Roosevelt, however, was determined to help the Allies— the British and French. British and French leaders had hoped to avoid war by agreeing to Hitler's demands. Instead, appeasement allowed Hitler to buy time. He used that time to build a mighty war machine.

Putting It All Together

With a partner, create a timeline of the steps Hitler took that ignored the Treaty of Versailles. Then write a brief paragraph in your notebook to explain what Britain, France, and the League of Nations might have done to stop Hitler.

Time Box

1931
Japan seized Manchuria

1936
Germany seized the Rhineland
Italy conquered Ethiopia
Italy and Germany created the Rome-Berlin Axis
Germany and Japan signed the Anti-Comintern Pact

1937
Japan seized much of eastern China

1938
Germany annexed Austria
Germany took over the Sudetenland from Czechoslovakia
Munich Conference

1939
Germany seized the rest of Czechoslovakia
Hitler and Stalin signed the Nazi-Soviet Non-Aggression Pact
Germany seized Poland
Great Britain and France declared war on Germany

Time Box Extension

Divide the class into five small groups. Assign each group one of the years in the Time Box on page 355. Tell them that they must find reasons to support the idea that the events in their year were crucial to the coming war. Have students present their arguments in a round table discussion.

Putting It All Together

Students' timelines should include the events in the Time Box that apply to Germany during the period 1936–1939. Their paragraphs will differ.

Lesson Summary

Germany invaded a number of smaller European countries, then moved against France and Great Britain. After the Japanese bombed Pearl Harbor, the United States entered the war. A major Allied invasion of Europe began on D-Day, June 6, 1944. Italy and Germany surrendered in the spring of 1945.

Allied land and naval forces worked together to defeat the Japanese. When the Japanese refused to surrender, the United States dropped atomic bombs on Hiroshima and Nagasaki, ending the struggle.

Lesson Objective

Students will learn about the war in Europe and the Pacific.

Focus Your Reading Answers

1 To gain control of more land, Japan needed to destroy U.S. naval power in the Pacific. The Japanese bombing of the U.S. naval base at Pearl Harbor brought the U.S. into the war.

2 The "final solution" that Hitler proposed was to kill all the Jewish people. Jews, along with others, were slaughtered, starved, or worked to death in concentration camps.

3 The two-pronged Allied strategy in the Pacific was to use land forces in the Philippines, and use naval forces under to fight in the Central Pacific.

4 Although Japan was being bombed daily, the emperor and military leaders would not surrender. The U.S. dropped the first atomic bomb on Hiroshima. When Japan still refused to surrender, a second bomb was dropped on Nagasaki. Japan surrendered five days later.

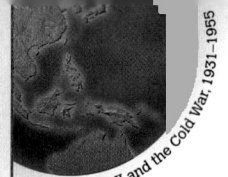

LESSON 2

Fighting the War

Thinking on Your Own

As you read this lesson, create an outline. Use Roman numerals I, II, III, IV, and V for the subheadings. Under each Roman numeral entry, include information from the most important to the least important.

Germany's invasion of Poland plunged Europe into war. The devastation of the new war would be far worse than World War I. By the time World War II ended, 17 million men and women had died in battle. More than 20 million civilians had been killed. The world had also seen the terrible damage that an atomic bomb could produce.

focus your reading

Summarize the event that caused the United States to enter the war.

What was Hitler's "final solution"?

What was the Allied strategy in the Pacific?

Describe how World War II finally ended in the Pacific.

vocabulary

Battle of Britain   war crimes
D-Day   atrocities
Holocaust

The War, 1939–1941

Hitler and Stalin did not stop after invading Poland. During the winter of 1939–1940, Soviet troops seized Estonia, Latvia, Lithuania, and part of Finland. In the spring of 1940, German forces quickly overran Norway, Denmark, the Netherlands, and Belgium.

In May 1940, the German army invaded France. By then, Britain had sent an army to help protect France. In hard fighting, the Germans advanced, pushing the British army and many French troops west. The Allied forces found themselves at Dunkirk, France, on the English Channel. The British navy launched a huge rescue effort. Fishing boats and other private boats joined Royal Navy ships in carrying some 338,000 Allied soldiers to Great Britain. The French government surrendered to Germany on June 22, 1940.

Lesson Vocabulary

Discuss each of the vocabulary terms with students.

The *Battle of Britain* was the German air war against Britain. Hitler ordered the *Battle of Britain* because he knew he had to defeat the British air force to conquer that nation.

D-Day was June 6, 1944, when the Allied forces landed in France. Dwight D. Eisenhower commanded the Allied forces on *D-Day*.

The *Holocaust* is the term used to describe the mass murder of the Jewish people under Hitler. Nations that Germany had conquered helped carry out the *Holocaust*.

War crimes were acts of violence, such as mistreating prisoners during war. The *war crimes* trials were held at Nuremberg. *Atrocities* are wicked or cruel acts, such as killing. The Third Reich was accused of many *atrocities*.

Great Britain was now alone in the fight against Germany. The English Channel had protected England from invasion since 1066. In 1940, the British had an air force to help protect the country. Hitler decided he must defeat the air force in order to conquer England. He ordered a massive air war against Britain. This came to be known as the **Battle of Britain**. German planes bombed air fields, naval bases, shipyards, and war factories. Hitler also directed his air force to bomb British cities. However, the British sent their fighter planes against the German bombers. Realizing that he could not destroy the British air force, Hitler decided against invading Britain in 1940.

By 1941, Hitler had added the nations of the Balkans to his German empire. He then turned against Stalin and invaded the Soviet Union. At first the German army made great progress in its push east. However, the severe Russian winter again stopped an invading army, as it had Napoleon's army in 1812.

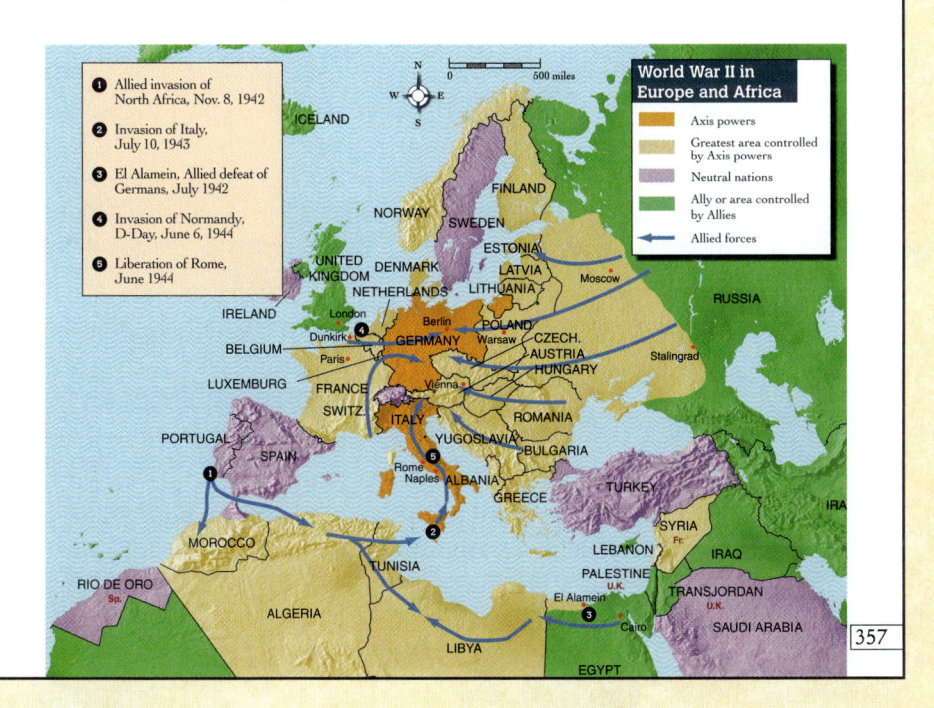

World War II in Europe and Africa

1. Allied invasion of North Africa, Nov. 8, 1942
2. Invasion of Italy, July 10, 1943
3. El Alamein, Allied defeat of Germans, July 1942
4. Invasion of Normandy, D-Day, June 6, 1944
5. Liberation of Rome, June 1944

Picturing History

The photograph at the top of page 357 shows firefighters trying to put out the flames caused by German bombs. Hermann Göring, Hitler's Chief of the Luftwaffe, the German air force, believed that it would take only four days to destroy southern England's air defenses and four weeks to destroy the entire Royal Air Force. Instead, after three months, Germany stopped the bombing operations.

Map Extension

Ask students to use the map on page 357 to answer the following questions:

- From what country did the Allies invade North Africa? (Portugal)
- Which happened first, the liberation of Rome or El Alamein? (El Alamein)
- In what direction did the invading forces of Normandy move? (east)
- When did the Allies invade Italy? (July 10, 1943)

Extension

Most of the leaders of the nations that Germany conquered fled to London and set up governments in exile there. The French and Norwegian leaders, however, assisted Germany. The French government, relocated to Vichy in the south of France, was a puppet government headed by Marshal Pétain. The Vichy government collaborated with the Germans, providing supplies and deporting Jewish people. The Norwegian leader was named Vidkun Quisling. Today, the word *quisling* means "traitor."

Extension

Part of the success of Britain's forces was radar, an acronym coined in 1942 that stands for "radio detecting and ranging." Radar allowed the British Air Force to know when German bombers were coming, so they could prepare for battle. Have students interested in electronics or military strategy learn more about the weapons used in this war. Allow time for students to share their findings with the class.

World War II and the Cold War

Picturing History

The photograph at the top of page 358 shows Stalingrad during the battle for that city. Both sides considered the city of symbolic importance, so fighting was fierce. Every building was a battleground, with the Soviet and German armies sometimes occupying different floors, and hand-to-hand combat was common. The surrender of the German army in early 1943 was the first indication that Germany was not unstoppable. The losses of Stalingrad were horrific: 91,000 German soldiers were imprisoned at the end of the battle. Each side lost about 500,000 soldiers. Civilian casualties numbered about two million.

Stop and Think

Students' timelines will vary. Possible response:

Winter 1939–1940: Germany conquered Estonia, Latvia, Lithuania, part of Finland

Spring 1940: Germany conquered Norway, Denmark, the Netherlands, Belgium; Germany lost the Battle of Britain

1941: Germans gained Balkan nations; Japan bombed Pearl Harbor

1942: Allies invaded North Africa

1943: Allies invaded Italy

1944: D-Day, Normandy, and liberation of Rome

1945: surrender of Germany, Italy, and Japan; atomic bombs dropped on Japan

The War, 1942–1945

Japan was expanding its control in Asia in 1940. It wanted the European colonies and the Philippines, which the United States governed. To gain this new territory, Japan sought to destroy U.S. naval power in the Pacific and seize the colonies. On December 7, 1941, Japanese planes bombed the U.S. naval base at Pearl Harbor, Hawaii. The day after Pearl Harbor, the United States declared war on Japan. Germany then declared war on the United States. Italy, the third Axis power, also declared war.

The nations fighting the Axis powers called themselves the Grand Alliance, or the Allies. The main Allies included the United States, Great Britain, Free France (officials and officers who had escaped France),

The siege of Stalingrad, 1942

stop and think

Make a timeline of the war in Europe from 1939 to 1945. Include where each major event took place and find that place on the map on page 357.

Biography

Sir Winston Churchill (1874–1965)

Winston Churchill became Great Britain's prime minister May 10, 1940. This was the same day that Hitler launched his attack on the Netherlands, Belgium, and France.

Churchill spent most of his life in public service. He was a British soldier in the 1890s in Africa. In 1900, he was elected to Parliament for the first time. He held a number of important government positions between 1 and 1929. Throughout the 1930s, Churchill opposed appeasement. His view was unpopular, and he was not appointed to any government jobs.

However, by mid-1939, the government realized that war was coming. A stronger leader than Neville Chamberlain was needed to direct the nation against the Nazi menace. Churchill was noted for his determination and inspiring speeches. He promised, "We shall never surrender." Churchill kept British morale up until the United States joined the war at the end of 1941. Churchill then made sure that Great Britain remained an equal partner in the war and in post-war negotiations. He is considered one of history's greatest wartime leaders.

Bio Facts

- Born 1874, died 1965.
- His mother was Jennie Jerome, a New Yorker.
- Married to Clementine for 57 years.
- As a young man, served in Cuba, Africa, and India.
- Served the government under six different monarchs spanning Queen Victoria to Queen Elizabeth II.
- Authored 40 books.
- Awarded 1953 Nobel Prize in Literature for his six-volume history of World War II.
- Was an amateur painter.

Biography Extensions

1 Winston Churchill was a gifted writer and public speaker. Have students create a list of famous quotations by Churchill, using library resources or the Internet. Ask them to imagine the effect of his words on the British during the war.

2 Students may be interested in the new Churchill Museum, which opened in London in 2005. Encourage them to investigate Churchill's life using library resources or the Internet.

Chapter 22

China, and the Soviet Union. They agreed to defeat Hitler first and then Japan. The Allies invaded North Africa in November of 1942. By May 1943, they had defeated German forces there. Then they invaded Sicily and mainland Italy. Hitler sent German troops to save Mussolini and keep the Allies from taking Italy. Fierce fighting continued until May 1945 when Italy surrendered. By then, Italian resistance fighters had killed Mussolini.

On June 6, 1944, Allied armies crossed the English Channel from Britain to land on the beaches of France. This is known as the **D-Day** invasion. General Dwight D. Eisenhower commanded the Allied troops that came ashore. They broke the German lines and pushed the Germans steadily eastward.

By April 1945, the remaining German armies were being squeezed between the Allied armies in the west and the Soviets in the east. The Soviets had started moving across Eastern Europe in 1943. They pushed the Germans out and occupied the areas themselves. Hitler committed suicide on April 30, 1945. Germany surrendered on May 7, 1945. The war in Europe was over.

Allied marines march ashore during the D-Day invasion of Normandy.

The Holocaust and War Crimes

Adolf Hitler's hatred toward Jews began many years before World War II. By 1942, Hitler had decided on a "final solution" for ridding Germany and Europe of Jewish people. He would kill them all. The result was the **Holocaust**, the killing of millions of Jews. The Holocaust also included Slavs, Gypsies, and those with mental illness or mental disabilities—anyone Hitler considered undesirable.

Governments in nations conquered by Germany helped carry out the Holocaust. Like the Germans, they arrested Jews

Picturing History

The attack on Pearl Harbor is shown at the top left on page 359. Roosevelt called December 7, 1941, "a day that will live in infamy." It also has been referred to as the worst day in U.S. naval history. By the end of the attack, 18 warships had been sunk, 188 planes destroyed, 1,178 people wounded, and 2,433 dead. Only two aircraft carriers, which were not in the harbor at the time, remained undamaged.

Picturing History

Marines are shown arriving in Normandy in the photograph at the right on page 359. Dwight D. Eisenhower, commander of Allied forces in Europe, was in charge of Operation Overlord. In addition to the troops, 50,000 bulldozers, tanks, and motorcycles had to be moved across the English Channel. It required 11,000 airplanes and 5,000 ships. Experts predicted that as many as 75 percent of the 23,000 Allied paratroopers going in could be killed. Eisenhower carried a note in his pocket on D-Day accepting all blame should the invasion fail. Two Allied armies landed on five different beaches, sustaining some 3,000 casualties on Omaha Beach alone, the scene of some of the fiercest fighting.

Extensions

1 Invite students interested in weather science to learn about the role that rain played in the D-Day invasion. Have them report their findings to the class.

2 Have students use library resources or the Internet to investigate the internment of Japanese Americans during World War II and subsequent reparations.

3 Students also may wish to learn about the camp in Oswego, New York, where European Jews were held as "guests of the president."

4 Other areas for research include the service of Japanese Americans during the war and the role of the Navajo Code-Talkers, whose language could not be understood by enemy code breakers.

Picturing History

The discovery of Holocaust victims is pictured at the top right on page 360. In 1942, the Germans built eight extermination camps. Six of the most active camps were located in Poland. The staff at Auschwitz, one of the most terrible camps, claimed proudly that they could kill 12,000 inmates daily. A few of those sent to the camps were kept to provide labor; most were sent to the "showers," which dispensed rat poison instead of water. The dead bodies were later burned in ovens.

Picturing History

The Nuremberg war crimes trial, which continued over many years, is shown in session at the left on page 360. An International Military Tribunal sentenced 12 of 22 leading Nazis to death. Japan's General Tojo was also executed in 1948. Rudolf Hess, the Nazi Party's deputy leader, surrendered in 1941, and at Nuremberg was sentenced to life in prison. He remained imprisoned in Berlin until he died in 1987.

---

and jammed them into railroad freight cars. The cars took these people to concentration camps in Eastern Europe, such as Auschwitz in Poland. Many died during the trip from lack of air and food.

Allied troops found railroad cars filled with corpses as they liberated concentration camps across Eastern Europe.

When the prisoners arrived at the camps, the ill and weak were marched directly to the gas chambers to be put to death. The healthy were marched to barracks. German guards required them to work in war factories or on farms. Most died from starvation and exhaustion. Between 9 million and 12 million people died in the Holocaust. About 6 million were Jews. More than half came from just four countries: Germany, Austria, Czechoslovakia, and Poland.

As the Allies pushed into Germany and Poland, they found the concentration camps. Half-dead, human skeletons greeted them through barbed wire fences. Their German guards had fled.

German defendants at the Nuremberg Nazi Trial in 1946

After the war, the Allies held **war crimes** trials in Nuremberg, Germany. They tried German and Austrian leaders for the **atrocities** of the Third Reich, as Germany was known. Japanese and Italian wartime leaders also were tried for war crimes. The message was clear. Government officials and military officers were responsible for their actions. They were not above international law.

War in the Pacific

By early 1942, the Japanese had captured European colonies in Southeast Asia and the islands in the western Pacific. Although the Allies decided to defeat Hitler first, they did not give up fighting in the Pacific. They planned a two-pronged strategy to fight the Japanese. One prong, or branch, was made up of land forces under the command of General Douglas MacArthur. His orders were to attack the Solomon Islands, New Guinea, and then the Philippines.

Extension

Anne Frank and Elie Wiesel are two of the most noted writers about the Holocaust. Frank's famous diary was written before she entered a concentration camp. Wiesel began writing after his liberation from a camp. Have students read about either or both writers' experiences. Alternatively, divide the class into two groups and have them research both, then do a comparison/contrast study.

By October 1944, the land forces had seized control of the Solomon Islands and New Guinea. On October 20, they invaded the Philippines. By March 1945, they had captured Manila, the capital of the Philippines. However, fighting in the Philippines continued until the end of the war.

The second prong consisted of naval forces led by Admiral Chester A. Nimitz. They were to fight their way through the Central Pacific to the Japanese home islands. In May 1942, Allied naval forces won a major victory at the Battle of the Coral Sea. The next month they defeated a Japanese fleet near Midway Island. This was a turning point in the war in the Pacific. The Allies had stopped the Japanese advance.

The Allies then began pushing the Japanese back. For the next two years, they fought their way north through the Central Pacific. By April 1945, they were only 800 miles from Tokyo, Japan's capital. Allied planes were bombing Japanese cities daily. The war in Europe was over. Japan's civilian leaders and Emperor Hirohito were willing to end the war. However, Japan's military leaders refused to surrender.

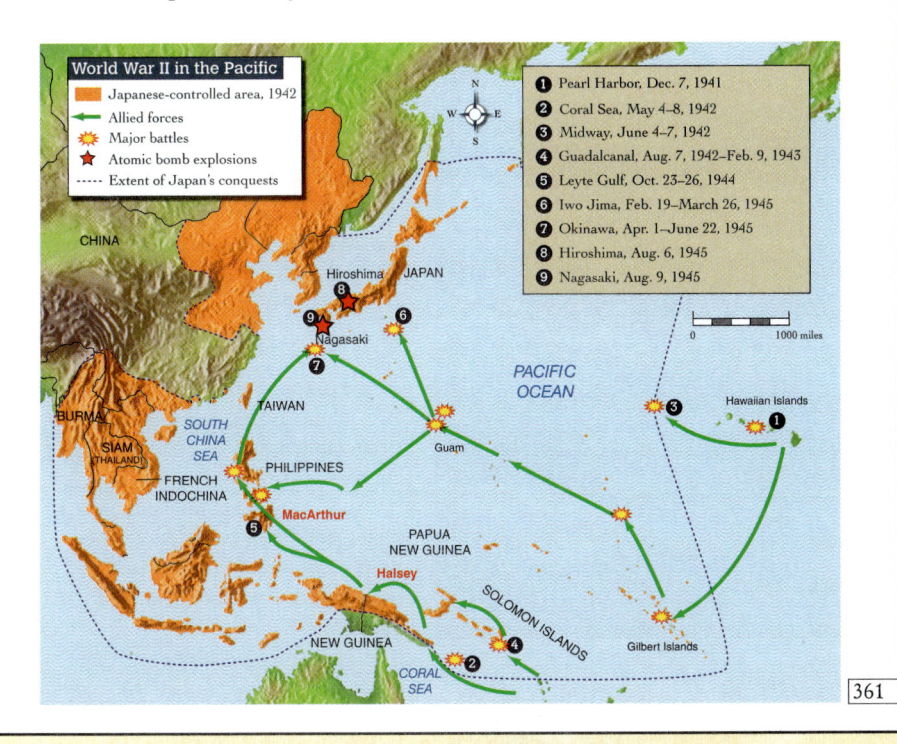

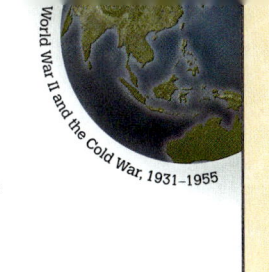

Map Extension

Ask students to use the map on page 361 to answer the following questions:

- Were the Hawaiian Islands part of the region Japan conquered? (no)
- Which happened first, Midway or Iwo Jima? (Midway)
- In what direction did the Allied forces move against Japan? (west)
- How many major battles took place on Guam? (two)

World War II in the Pacific

- Pearl Harbor, Dec. 7, 1941
- Coral Sea, May 4–8, 1942
- Midway, June 4–7, 1942
- Guadalcanal, Aug. 7, 1942–Feb. 9, 1943
- Leyte Gulf, Oct. 23–26, 1944
- Iwo Jima, Feb. 19–March 26, 1945
- Okinawa, Apr. 1–June 22, 1945
- Hiroshima, Aug. 6, 1945
- Nagasaki, Aug. 9, 1945

Extension

Students may wish to know more about the efforts of women during the war. Around the world, they participated in the war effort as nurses, factory workers, aircraft pilots, and farmers. You may wish to divide students into groups to research women's efforts, either by nationality or by the kinds of work they did.

World War II and the Cold War

Picturing History

The photograph on page 362 shows the huge mushroom cloud created by the first atomic bomb dropped on a city. The bomb weighed four metric tons and carried the power of 20,000 tons of dynamite. The bomb, which was 10 feet (3 m) long and 28 inches (71 cm) in diameter, had been nicknamed Little Boy. Colonel Paul Tibbets, who piloted the *Enola Gay*, the B-29 plane that delivered the bomb, named the plane for his mother. After dropping the bomb, the men in the airplane could still see the mushroom cloud from 270 miles (435 km) away. The estimated death toll at Hiroshima was 78,000. A few days later, 70,000 people in Nagasaki died when the second bomb was dropped. Thousands more died in subsequent weeks from radiation poisoning.

Extension

Hiroshima was chosen as a target because it was the headquarters of the 2nd Japanese Army and the site of warmaking industries. More than 700,000 leaflets were dropped on Hiroshima on August 4, warning that the city was going to be demolished, but the warnings were disregarded.

World War II and the Cold War, 1931–1955

Dropping the Atomic Bomb

President Franklin Roosevelt died suddenly on April 12, 1945. Vice President Harry Truman was immediately sworn in as president. It was then that Truman learned about the atomic bomb. President Roosevelt had established a top-secret project in 1941 to develop an atomic bomb. It was called the Manhattan Project. Top scientists and more than 600,000 people worked to develop the atomic bomb. Physicist J. Robert Oppenheimer directed construction of the bomb in Los Alamos, New Mexico. The damage from such a bomb would be horrendous.

Truman asked for advice from his military advisors. They estimated that an invasion of the Japanese home islands would be costly. It would take months, and hundreds of thousands of U.S. soldiers and Japanese civilians would be killed.

During the summer of 1945, the Allies again offered Japan a chance to surrender. Its military leaders again refused. On August 6, a U.S. plane, the *Enola Gay*, dropped an atomic bomb on the city of Hiroshima. Between 80,000 and 120,000 people were killed. Thousands more died from burns and radiation poisoning. The Japanese government still did not surrender. A second bomb was dropped on the city of Nagasaki on August 9. Another 35,000 to 75,000 Japanese died. Japan finally surrendered on August 14, 1945.

The mushroom cloud over Hiroshima

Putting It All Together

Create a flowchart of the events in the Pacific that led to President Truman's decision to use the atomic bomb. Compare your flowchart with a partner's to make sure you included all the important information. Then write a short paragraph that summarizes the major events of World War II in the Pacific.

362 Chapter 22

Putting It All Together

Students' flowcharts and paragraphs will vary but should describe events leading to the dropping of the atomic bomb on Japan.

Extension

Students who are interested in science should be encouraged to use library resources or the Internet to investigate the work of scientists such as Oppenheimer and Albert Einstein in developing the bomb.

LESSON 3

The Cold War

Thinking on Your Own

Turn each subheading into a question. Write your questions in your notebook. As you read each subheading, write an answer to your question.

During World War II, Roosevelt, Churchill, and Stalin met several times. The purpose was to plan wartime **strategy** and the postwar peace. However, Stalin did not share the same goals for peace as Roosevelt and Churchill. He wanted to create a zone of Communist nations between the Soviet Union and the rest of Europe. This became clear soon after the war ended.

focus your reading

Explain how Communist governments came to power in Eastern Europe.

Describe how the United States dealt with communism during the Cold War.

vocabulary

strategy
iron curtain
containment
Cold War
proliferation

Losing Eastern Europe to Communism

During their wartime conferences, Roosevelt, Churchill, and Stalin made a number of agreements about what would happen after the war. Some of the most important were made at the Yalta Conference in 1945.

The three leaders agreed that Germany would be divided into four military zones. The United States, Britain, the Soviet Union, and France would each govern a zone. Roosevelt and Churchill insisted that Stalin hold free elections in the Soviet-occupied nations of Eastern Europe. Stalin agreed, but broke his promise. Instead, he imposed Communist governments on East Germany, Poland, Czechoslovakia, Hungary, and the Balkan nations. He also helped the Communist side in a civil war in Greece and tried to take territory from Turkey.

World War II 363

Lesson Vocabulary

Discuss each of the vocabulary terms with students.

A *strategy* is a plan to reach a goal or win a war. Leaders of the Allies met to plan their *strategy* during World War II. Blocking Communist expansion into other nations was called *containment*. The Marshall Plan was one example of *containment* at work.

The *Cold War* was a time of war with words and threats, not actual combat. Democracy and communism "fought" during the *Cold War*.

The spread of something is its *proliferation*. The *proliferation* of nuclear weapons is a major world problem.

The *iron curtain* is an image that Churchill used to describe the takeover of Eastern Europe by the Soviet Union.

Lesson Summary

The leaders of the Allied nations met at Yalta in 1945 to determine their postwar agendas. Stalin later broke the agreements to allow free elections, fearing that the nations of Eastern Europe would choose democracy. He imposed Communist regimes in Eastern Europe to create a buffer zone between the Soviet Union and the European democracies. The United States followed a policy of containment, both through the application of the Truman Doctrine and the Marshall Plan. The Cold War prevented actual war between the U.S. and the Soviet Union or China but also led to an arms race and the proliferation of nuclear arms.

Lesson Objective

Students will learn about the spread of communism and the Cold War.

Focus Your Reading Answers

1 The Communists came to power in Eastern Europe because, after the war, Stalin broke agreements that he had made. Instead of allowing free elections, he imposed Communist governments in several Eastern European nations.

2 During the Cold War, the United States followed a policy of containment, which tried to block further expansion of communism. One strategy was the Truman Doctrine, which aided nations trying to remain free. The Marshall Plan was another strategy; it offered aid to help Europe rebuild after the war.

World War II and the Cold War 363

Map Extension

Ask students to use the map on page 364 to answer the following questions:

- Was Berlin in an area of Soviet influence? (yes)
- Under which influence was Turkey? (Western)
- Which influence affected Romania? (Soviet)

Stop and Think

Students' letters will vary but should provide ideas about dealing with the Soviet Union in 1947.

Extension

The leaders at Yalta also discussed the creation of the United Nations, an issue that Roosevelt promoted in light of the failure of the League of Nations. An initial meeting was set for April 1945 in San Francisco, even though at the time of the February conference in southern Russia, an Allied victory was several months away.

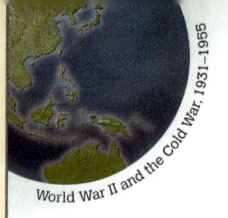

The alliance that won World War II quickly split apart. The nations of the West were on one side. On the other side were the Soviet Union and the nations of Eastern Europe that it controlled. The Soviet army cut off these nations from any contact with the West. This separated Europe into two blocks of nations divided by what Winston Churchill called an **"iron curtain."** He also warned that Stalin would not be satisfied with controlling Eastern Europe. He feared that Stalin wanted a Communist world.

America's Response to Stalin's Policies

The Free World looked to the United States for leadership. The British people were exhausted after the war. Many of their cities, factories, and shipyards had been badly damaged by German bombing raids. Much of France also lay in ruins. China was already fighting Communists in a civil war. The only nation that had the energy and resources to fight the Soviets was the United States.

In 1947, President Truman promised to aid nations struggling to remain free. In his message to Congress, he asked for $400 million for Turkey and Greece. The aid helped Turkey refuse Soviet demands. It also kept Greek Communists from winning the civil war. This new policy was called the Truman Doctrine.

President Truman also supported the European Recovery Act, known as the Marshall Plan. U.S. Secretary of State George Marshall proposed the plan to help Europe rebuild. Aid was offered to Stalin for the Soviet Union, but he rejected it. Between 1948 and

> **stop and think**
>
> If you were an American citizen in 1947, what advice would you have given to President Truman about dealing with the Soviets? Discuss this with a partner. Then write a letter to the president in your notebook.

Extension

In support of the Marshall Plan, President Truman cited the outbreaks of tuberculosis and the starvation many people faced after the war. In Italy and France, food riots had broken out. Truman believed that it was important to be generous after victory, knowing that the war just ended had been caused, in part, because of Germany's anger and humiliation over the Treaty of Paris at the end of World War I.

1951, the plan provided $13 billion to western European nations. They used the money to build new housing, rebuild factories and cities, and get their economies growing again.

The goal of the Truman Doctrine and the Marshall Plan was **containment**. President Truman adopted this policy as a way to block further Communist expansion. The United States would provide money, equipment, weapons, and military support to nations threatened by communism. In addition to European nations, the United States provided aid to Chinese nationalists in the late 1940s. They were fighting Communists in a civil war.

The United States's policy of containment stopped the expansion of Soviet power in Europe. It also kept the United States and the Soviet Union—and later the United States and Communist China—from fighting each other during the **Cold War**. However, these great powers continued to support their democratic or Communist allies. Containment led to an uneasy peace.

However, containment could not stop a new arms race. By 1949, Soviet scientists had built an atomic bomb. Both the United States and the Soviet Union began a race to see who could build more nuclear bombs and the missiles to carry them. By the 1950s, other nations were developing their own nuclear weapons. One of the major problems in the world today continues to be the **proliferation**, or spread, of nuclear weapons and the nations that have them.

U.S. aid being delivered to Europe under the Marshall Plan

The Berlin Airlift provided food and supplies for more than 10 months, ending in May, 1949, after Soviet forces surrounded and cut off the city.

Putting It All Together

Think about appeasement and containment. Were they different or the same? Discuss this question with a partner. Write your ideas in your notebook. Then write a paragraph comparing appeasement and containment.

Picturing History

The photograph at the top of page 365 shows a ship being unloaded in Europe. The Marshall Plan affected 16 nations. It was designed primarily to help rebuild industry, although it included direct aid such as medicine, fuel, food, and emergency housing. At the height of the program, each day 150 ships brought oil, cotton, drilling equipment, tractors, tires, and chemicals to European ports. Of the plan, Marshall said that United States policy was directed "not against any country or doctrine, but against hunger, poverty, desperation, and chaos."

Picturing History

The Berlin Airlift, shown in the photograph at the bottom of page 365, supplied food and other items to more than two million residents of West Berlin. During the 321 days of the operation, British and American pilots delivered 2.3 million tons of food and supplies in 272,264 flights.

Putting It All Together

Students' opinions on the relationship of containment and appeasement will vary but should be supported.

Extension

Estimates of supplies needed for Berlin included 4,000 tons of supplies daily, or a planeload every 3.5 minutes. To speed up delivery, airplane crews were asked not to leave the planes between landing and takeoff. The planes were refueled as they were unloaded, and food was brought to the pilots and crew. In the beginning, a mere 1,000 tons arrived daily. Twenty thousand volunteer Berliners built a third airport to handle the traffic. Supply levels increased to 4,500 tons, then 8,000 tons, then 13,000 tons daily. Although their planes were overloaded and the pilots exhausted, they still dropped bags of candy to children who ran to meet the planes.

World War II and the Cold War

Chapter Review

1 Students' concept maps will vary. Possible responses may include: Italian, Japanese, and German expansion; violation of Treaty of Paris; inability of League of Nations to stop aggression

2 Students' topics and essays will vary but should focus on ideas related to the chapter.

Chapter Summary

- In 1936, Italy invaded and conquered Ethiopia.
- In the mid-1930s, Hitler rebuilt the German military and sent troops into the Rhineland.
- Great Britain adopted a policy of **appeasement** toward Hitler, who took control of Austria to achieve **Anschluss**.
- On September 1, 1939, Hitler launched his **blitzkrieg** against Poland. Within two days, Great Britain and France declared war on Germany.
- **Isolationists** initially kept the United States out of the war.
- Hitler's forces conquered most of Northern Europe and launched an air war over Great Britain known as the **Battle of Britain**.
- The United States entered the war after the Japanese bombed Pearl Harbor on December 7, 1941.
- On June 6, 1944, known as **D-Day**, the Allies landed in Normandy, France.
- In May 1945, the German government surrendered.
- As the Allies pushed into German-held territory, they found concentration camps. Survivors told of the **atrocities** of the **Holocaust**. German, Austrian, Japanese, and Italian leaders were tried for **war crimes**.
- During the war, Roosevelt, Churchill, and Stalin met to plan wartime **strategy** and postwar peace.
- President Truman adopted a policy of **containment** toward the Soviet Union and communism. This policy continued throughout the **Cold War**.
- The arms race led to the **proliferation** of nuclear weapons on each side of the **iron curtain**.

Chapter Review

1 Draw a concept map to show the causes of World War II. Label the large circle in the center "Causes of World War II." Then draw a smaller circle for each cause. Add more circles to the small ones, including details about the causes.

2 Complete the K-W-L chart you began at the start of this chapter. Research three topics you want to know more about. Present your findings in a short essay.

Novel Connections

Below is a list of books that relate to the time period covered in this chapter. The numbers in parentheses indicate the related Thematic Strands of the National Council for the Social Studies (NCSS).

Martin Booth. *War Dog*. Simon & Schuster Children's, 1997. (II, IV, VI)

Joseph Bruchac. *Code Talker: A Novel About the Navajo Marines of World War Two*. Dial, 2005. (V, VIII, X)

Peter Carter. *Hunted*. Farrar, Straus and Giroux, 1994. (IV, VI)

Jacqueline Harris. *The Tuskegee Airmen: Black Heroes of World War II*. Dillon Press, 1996. (V, VI, X)

Hanneke Ippisch. *Sky: A True Story of Courage During World War II*. Troll Communications, 1998. (IV, VI, X)

R. Conrad Stein. *The Home Front During World War II* (*In American History* series). Enslow Publishers, 2003. (II, III, VI)

Skill Builder

Comparing Points of View

It is often useful when studying history to compare different points of view. Understanding how different people think and feel about historic events makes what happened more understandable. Comparing points of view is also useful during elections. It can help voters decide which candidate to vote for in an election.

Winston Churchill and Neville Chamberlain, an earlier British prime minister, had different points of view about British appeasement of Hitler. Churchill's biography in Lesson 2 states that he opposed appeasement.

Read the following excerpts and then answer the questions.

Source A

"I make an earnest appeal to those who hold responsible positions . . . in this country . . . to weigh their words very carefully before they utter them . . . bearing in mind the consequences that may flow from some rash or thoughtless phrase. By exercising caution and patience and self-restraint we may yet be able to save the peace of Europe."

Source B

"Is it the new policy to come to terms with the totalitarian Powers in the hope that by great and far-reaching acts of submission . . . peace may be preserved.

"A firm stand by France and Britain, under the authority of the League of Nations, would have been followed by an immediate evacuation of the Rhineland without the shedding of a drop of blood; and the effects . . . might have enabled the . . . German army to gain their proper positions, and would not have given the political head of Germany the enormous ascendancy which has enabled him to move forward."

1. Between Chamberlain and Churchill, who do you think was Source A? Source B?
2. What words and phrases helped you determine the speaker?
3. In one sentence each, summarize the points of view of Source A and Source B.

Skill Builder

1. Source A was Chamberlain; Source B was Churchill.
2. Possible answer: Source A: "we may yet be able to save the peace of Europe," which sounds like Chamberlain; Source B questions the status quo: "Is it the new policy to come to terms with the totalitarian Powers . . ."
3. Possible answer: Source A: This person is hoping to preserve peace. Source B: The speaker is irritated that stronger measures were not taken when the Rhineland was invaded.

Classroom Discussion

Discuss with students some of the broader topics covered in this chapter.

- How should free nations treat and deal with aggressor nations?
- How can democracy be spread to other lands?
- Are there any situations in which nuclear war can be justified?
- In what situations could an isolationist stance be a positive good?

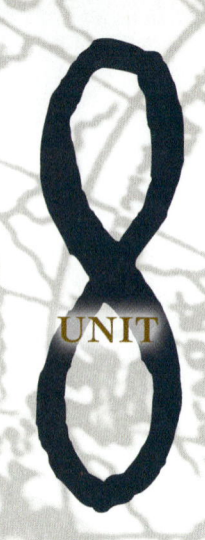

UNIT 8: THE WORLD TODAY

Unit Objectives

After studying this unit, students will be able to

- describe the events of the post-World War II era
- analyze and discuss the global challenges at the beginning of the twenty-first century

Unit 8 focuses on events following World War II.

Chapter 23, The World Enters the 21st Century, examines events of the post-World War II era.

Chapter 24, The World: Opportunities and Challenges, explores the impact of five different issues around the world.

Getting Started

Write the word *today* on the board. Ask students for current world news events and discuss them briefly. Then ask a volunteer to read aloud the three paragraphs on page 368. Tell them that in Unit 8 they will find the roots of some of the current world issues just discussed.

Measuring Time

Explain to students that Chapter 23 focuses on the move toward greater freedom and on issues of economic importance. The events of that era appear on the timeline on pages 368–369. Chapter 24 examines five contemporary issues that nations must resolve. The events that most deeply affect this era are on page 369 of the timeline.

The last 50 years of the 20th century and the beginning of the 21st century have seen huge changes in the world. After World War II, Asians and Africans gained their independence from colonial powers. In many cases they had to fight for years to win nationhood. Latin American nations were making progress in becoming more industrialized.

By the 1990s, the Cold War was over. The Soviet Union and Communist governments in Eastern Europe had collapsed. Chinese leaders had relaxed some Communist practices and were welcoming foreign business.

But new problems replaced the old ones. Supporters of a radical branch of Islam began a worldwide war of terror. Many nations were still poor. Women and children remained the primary victims of poverty. Industrialization eased poverty but created problems for the environment.

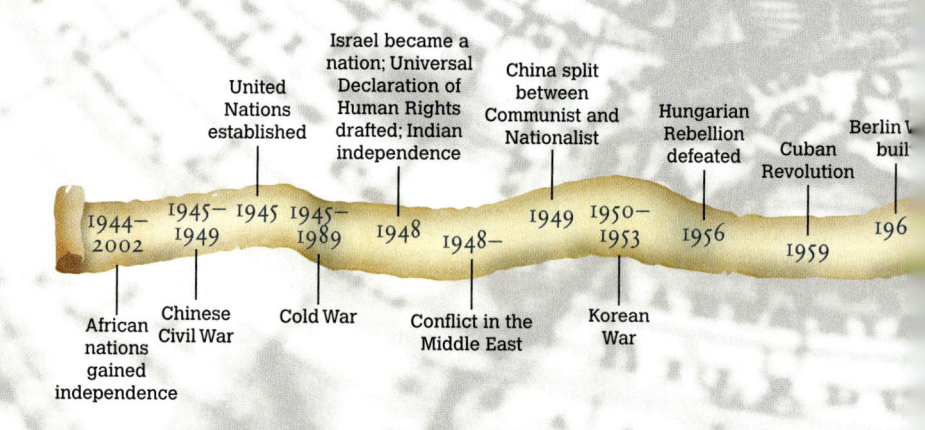

Timeline:

- 1944–2002 African nations gained independence
- 1945–1949 Chinese Civil War
- 1945 United Nations established
- 1945–1989 Cold War
- 1948 Israel became a nation; Universal Declaration of Human Rights drafted; Indian independence
- 1948– Conflict in the Middle East
- 1949 China split between Communist and Nationalist
- 1950–1953 Korean War
- 1956 Hungarian Rebellion defeated
- 1959 Cuban Revolution
- 196– Berlin Wall built

Timeline Extension

Ask students to use the timeline to preview each chapter in the unit. Then have them answer the following questions:

- What word would you choose to represent the events of the timeline?
- For how many years did the Berlin Wall stand?
- Look at the events that span several years. Which series of events covered the greatest amount of time?
- When did the Soviet Union collapse?
- What do the timeline events suggest about war?

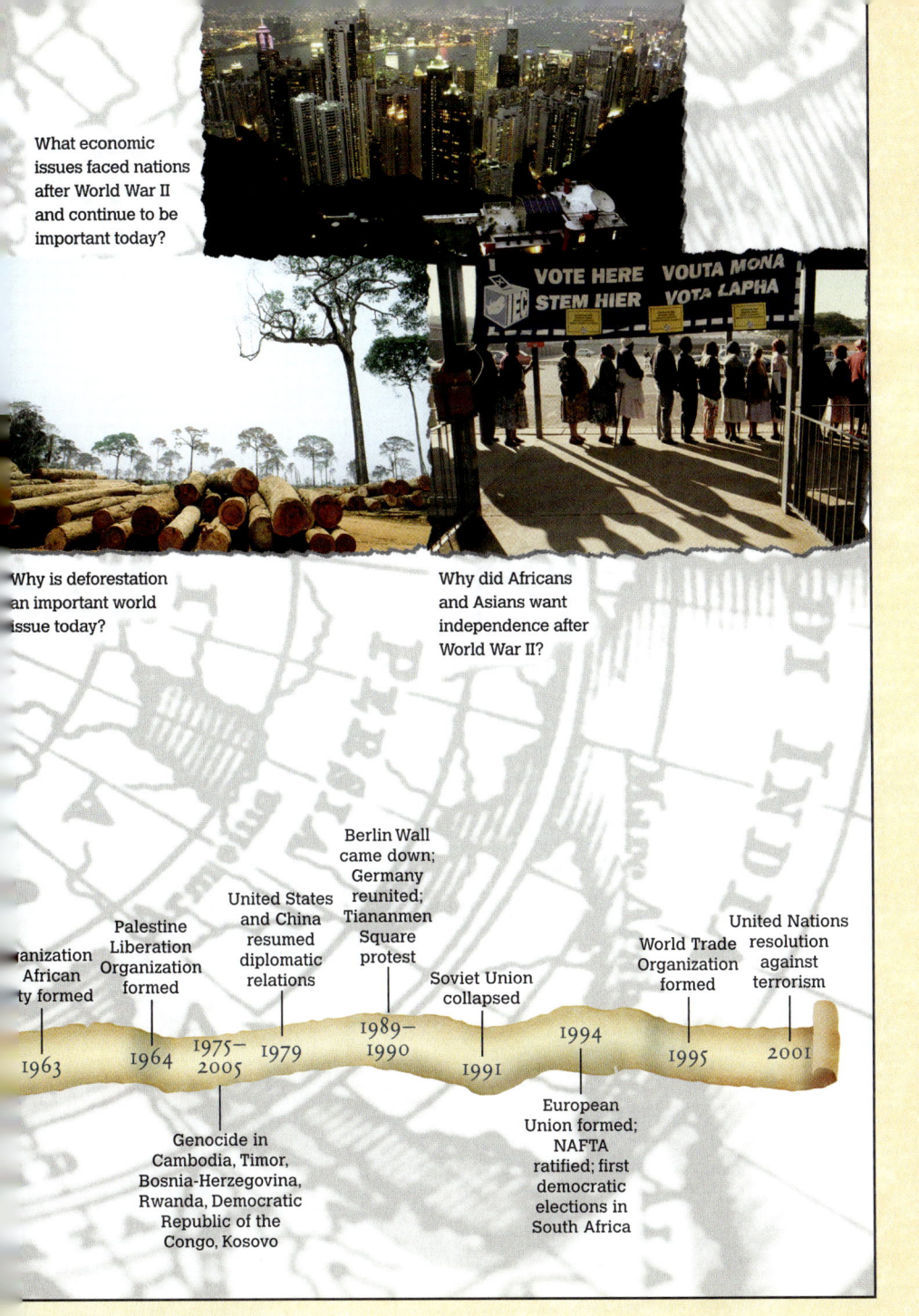

What economic issues faced nations after World War II and continue to be important today?

Why is deforestation an important world issue today?

Why did Africans and Asians want independence after World War II?

Timeline:
- 1963 — Organization of African Unity formed
- 1964 — Palestine Liberation Organization formed
- 1975–2005 — Genocide in Cambodia, Timor, Bosnia-Herzegovina, Rwanda, Democratic Republic of the Congo, Kosovo
- 1979 — United States and China resumed diplomatic relations
- 1989–1990 — Berlin Wall came down; Germany reunited; Tiananmen Square protest
- 1991 — Soviet Union collapsed
- 1994 — European Union formed; NAFTA ratified; first democratic elections in South Africa
- 1995 — World Trade Organization formed
- 2001 — United Nations resolution against terrorism

Collage Answers

1 Certain economic issues facing the world following World War II continue to be important today. These include the division of developing and industrialized nations, the cost of rebuilding after war, free trade agreements, and the status of workers around the world.

2 Deforestation is an important world issue because healthy forests are essential for the climate and the well-being of people. Cutting down forests and not replacing them also leads to desertification.

3 After World War II, Africans and Asians wanted independence because the European colonial powers were interested primarily in exploiting resources and labor, not in building the country they controlled. Racism led the colonial powers to regard the nationals as children who needed to be governed. Africans and Asians wanted control of their own destiny and resources.

Collage Extension

Use the images and questions on page 369 to preview the unit. Discuss what the questions and pictures suggest about the state of the world.

Picturing History

The images on page 369 represent people and places that will be discussed in Unit 8.

1 The skyline of a large city with smog shows the effect of air pollution.

2 The picture is of logs waiting to be taken from the rain forest.

3 Voters waiting in line to vote in South Africa shows the emergence of new democratic nations.

The World Today

Chapter Summary

Refer to page 394 for a summary of Chapter 23.

Related Transparencies

T-1 World Map

T-12 African Independence

T-18 Three-Column Chart

T-19 Venn Diagram

T-20 Concept Web

Key Blacklines

Primary Source—Jobless in Detroit And Germany

CD Extension

Encourage students to use the reading comprehension, vocabulary reinforcement, and interactive timeline activities on the student CD.

Getting Focused

Students' questions will vary. Before discussing each photograph, check to see what questions students have concerning it. If the material in the text does not sufficiently explain the questions, have students do independent research using library resources or the Internet.

Chapter 23
THE WORLD ENTER
THE 21ST CENTURY
(1945–)

Getting Focused

Skim this chapter to predict what you will be learning.
- Read the lesson titles and subheadings.
- Look at the illustrations and read the captions.
- Examine the maps.
- Review the vocabulary words and terms.

Look through the chapter at the photographs until you find one that captures your imagination. What question does it raise in your mind? Write down three of the questions in your notebook. Share your questions with partner. Remember to add the newest countries of the world to your world map.

Pre-Reading Discussion

1 Ask students to recall the struggles of the United States to gain independence from Britain. See if they can identify some commonalities in that struggle with subsequent ones in France and elsewhere in Europe. Tell them that in this chapter, they will read about more nations gaining their independence.

2 Discuss with students some of the recent news articles about violence taking place between nations or ethnic groups. Locate the relevant areas on a world map in the classroom. Ask students to watch for mention of these locations as they read the chapter to find possible roots of the conflicts.

Picturing History

The United Nations, which was a term coined by Franklin Roosevelt, began meetings in London in 1946. Its headquarters in New York City is shown on page 370. To distinguish the United Nations from the League of Nations, the General Assembly determined not to have headquarters in Geneva, Switzerland.

LESSON 1

European Economic Recovery

Thinking on Your Own

Look at the Focus your Reading questions. Note the countries or regions that are mentioned. Make a three-column chart with the headings "Germany," "Soviet Union," and "Eastern Europe." As you read the lesson, take bulleted notes on the changes that took place in each nation or region.

During World War II, President Franklin Roosevelt proposed a new global organization. It would replace the League of Nations. The new United Nations (UN) would negotiate disagreements among member nations. It would also be able to use force against aggressor nations.

The United Nations began in 1945 with high hopes for preventing another global war. Although wars have continued, none has been on the scale of the two world wars of the twentieth century. Many new nations have emerged and joined the United Nations. Today, the UN has many roles. Among its duties are peacekeeping and aiding the world's poor and sick.

focus your reading

Summarize what happened to Germany following World War II.

Describe the conflicts that occurred in Eastern Europe during the 1990s.

Why did Mikhail Gorbachev begin reforms in the Soviet Union?

Explain the European Union.

vocabulary

totalitarian
satellite nations
ethnic cleansing
perestroika

Redrawing the Map of Eastern Europe

When World War II ended, Europe was divided into free and Communist-controlled states. The Soviet Union had freed most of Eastern Europe from Germany's power. As a result, the

The World Enters the 21st Century | 371

Lesson Summary
The United Nations was created in 1945 to prevent another world war.

After World War II ended, the Soviet Union controlled countries in Eastern Europe. A huge wall divided East and West Berlin from 1961 until 1989. Yugoslavian republics of Croatia, Slovenia, and Bosnia-Herzegovina fought for independence in the 1990s. NATO nations intervened to stop the war.

The Soviet Union faced political and economic challenges in the 1980s and 1990s under Mikhail Gorbachev.

European economic cooperation led to the formation of the European Union.

Lesson Objective
Students will learn about the events in Europe following World War II.

Focus Your Reading Answers

1 After World War II, Germany was divided into two parts. The Soviets put up a concrete wall in Berlin in 1961 to stop East Germans from leaving. It stood until 1989, when Germany was reunited.

2 People in Hungary and Czechoslovakia rebelled against the Soviet Union. Various republics of Yugoslavia fought for freedom, with Serbians practicing ethnic cleansing against Bosnians and Albanians.

3 Gorbachev began reforms because of economic difficulties within the Soviet Union.

4 The European Union is a loose confederation of 25 nations. They have a common currency and practice free trade.

Lesson Vocabulary
Introduce each of the following vocabulary terms to students.

Explain that *totalitarian* governments are those that have a strong central government. In *totalitarian* states, people are less important than the state, which controls their lives.

Satellite nations are controlled by larger, more powerful nations. Hungary, Poland, and Romania were once *satellite nations* of the Soviet Union.

Killing all members of a particular ethnic group is called *ethnic cleansing*. The Serbians practiced *ethnic cleansing* against the Muslim Bosnians.

The Russian word *perestroika* means "restructuring." *Perestroika* was key to Mikhail Gorbachev's program for the Soviet Union.

The World Enters the 21st Century | 371

> **Extension**
>
> Divide the class into five small groups. Assign each group one of the major areas of the United Nations: Peace and Security, Economic and Social Development, Human Rights, Humanitarian Affairs, or International Law. Ask them to use library resources or the Internet to find out what their division does and a recent example of its work. Have each group present its findings to the class by using the Student Presentation Builder on the student CD.

> **Picturing History**
>
> The photograph on page 372 shows the end of "Prague Spring," Czechoslovakia's 1968 move toward greater freedoms. Then Communist Party leader Alexander Dubcek wanted to bring freedom of assembly and free speech to his land. He referred to it as "socialism with a human face." The period ended in August. Dubcek was taken to Moscow; over 100 people were killed.

Soviets imposed **totalitarian** governments in those nations. In 1949, the United States and 11 European nations formed a new military alliance. Known as the North Atlantic Treaty Organization (NATO), it was designed to stop Soviet expansion in Europe. Officials in the United States called it an "antidote to fear."

Despite earlier agreements, free elections were not allowed in Poland, Romania, Czechoslovakia, Bulgaria, or Hungary. East Germany and East Berlin were also under Communist control. These countries were known as **satellite nations**. That is, they were controlled by the Soviet Union, just as space satellites are held in place by the planet they circle.

Freedom fighters in Hungary and Czechoslovakia tried to free their nations from Soviet control. Soviet troops put down both rebellions. They quashed rebellions in Hungary in 1956 and in Czechoslovakia in 1968.

"Prague Spring," a move for democracy, ended with Soviet tanks entering the Czech capital.

Communists wanted to stop people who were leaving East Germany. East Germans were using West Berlin as an escape route to freedom. In 1961, the Soviets built a 12-foot wall made of barbed wire and several layers of concrete between East and West Berlin. The wall split the city into two sections, separating families and friends. It had searchlights, mines, and guards who shot anyone attempting to cross its border.

Mikhail Gorbachev, the Soviet leader who came to power in 1985, began to allow greater freedom. He changed the Soviet policy by refusing to intervene militarily in the affairs of satellite nations. This led to a greater freedom of movement for people living in Communist-controlled nations. People began moving out of Hungary and into Austria. Soon, a new government had been established in East Germany.

The Berlin Wall came down in 1989 after U.S. President Ronald Reagan challenged the Soviet leader, "Mr. Gorbachev, tear down this wall!" East and West Germans joined in

> **Extension**
>
> In 1968, Václav Havel was known as a poet and a playwright. He participated in anti-Communist uprisings in Czechoslovakia in 1968 and in 1989. Because of this, his passport was taken away and his plays, which satirized the bureaucratic government, were banned. He was imprisoned for his work on behalf of human rights. He later became the president of Czechoslovakia and was also elected president of the new Czech Republic. Havel was reelected in 1998; he stepped down in 2003 because the constitution did not allow him to serve a third term.

tearing down the hated wall and formed one Germany in 1990. Gorbachev also announced that Eastern European nations would be responsible for their own lands without help from the Soviet Union.

Poland became the first satellite nation to hold democratic elections. Its citizens elected Lech Walesa president. Walesa had led the protest movement in Poland known as Solidarity. He was the leader of the shipyard workers' union. Bulgaria and Hungary followed. In free elections during 1989 and 1990, Communists lost power and democracy spread. In Czechoslovakia, this change was known as the "Velvet Revolution," because it was not accomplished through war.

Yugoslavia was a Communist country but not a Soviet satellite. Joseph Tito, the powerful leader after World War II, held its two provinces and six republics together. When he died in 1980, Yugoslavia joined other Eastern European nations in the quest for freedom.

Fighting for independence began in the republics of Slovenia, Croatia, and Bosnia-Herzegovina in 1990. These republics included Serbian minorities from the Republic of Serbia. The Serbian army went against Croatia after that nation and Slovenia declared independence from Yugoslavia. The fighting was fierce and moved into Bosnia-Herzegovina.

Many of the Bosnians were Muslim. Following the example of Nazi Germany, the Serbian army practiced **ethnic cleansing**. About a quarter of a million Bosnians had been killed by 1995. Two million people were homeless and living in refugee camps. Finally, after NATO intervened with bombing strikes, Serbs

People tore down the Berlin Wall in 1989 without waiting for the government to do it.

Polish Solidarity leader Lech Walesa had been imprisoned for his fight for democracy.

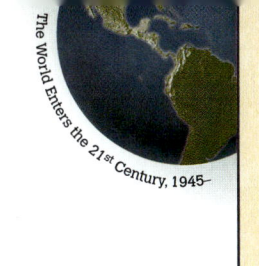

Picturing History

The photograph at the top of page 373 shows people taking down the Berlin Wall. The barrier had been built in 1961 to stop the East Germans—about 2.5 million between 1949 and 1961—from fleeing to the West German side of Berlin. The wall, at first made of barbed wire and cinder blocks that were put up overnight, eventually included walls, electric fences, and forts that extended 75 miles (121 km) around West Berlin. Although about 5,000 East Germans crossed the Berlin Wall, East German officials captured an equal number who were trying to escape, with 191 persons killed in the attempt.

Picturing History

Lech Walesa, shown in the photograph on page 373, was awarded the Nobel Peace Prize in 1983 for his efforts in leading Polish workers. Walesa served as president of Poland from 1990 until 1995.

Extension

The reunification of Germany did not always benefit citizens in the East. By 1996, nearly 25 percent of East Germans were unemployed. With the Communists' workplace day-care centers discontinued, many women were no longer able to work. Factories that couldn't meet Western anti-pollution or safety codes were closed. Taxes rose to pay for investing and development in East Germany.

Map Extension

Ask students to use the map on page 374 to answer the following questions:

- What ended the war in 1995? (the Dayton Peace Agreement)
- In what directions did Yugoslavia lose land? (to the south and west)
- How many new nations did the agreement form? (five)

Time Box Extension

Have students create flash cards for each event in the Time Box on page 374. They can then work in pairs or teams to review the lesson using these cards prior to a test or quiz.

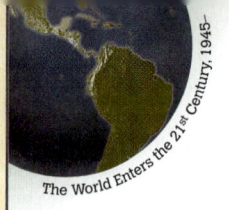

---

and Bosnians signed a peace treaty. It split Bosnia into a Muslim-Croat federation and a Serb republic.

War broke out again in 1998 over Kosovo, a self-governing province in Yugoslavia. The people of Kosovo were mostly Albanians. They had kept their own customs and language. They wanted to remove the Serbs from power. The Serbs began killing ethnic Albanians. Once again, NATO tried to find a solution. Albanians were freed within Serbia in 1999. Three years later, Serbia and Montenegro created a loose union and dropped the name Yugoslavia.

Former Yugoslavia, 1991–1999
- Boundary of former Yugoslavia, 1991
- Yugoslavia, 1991
- Dayton Peace Agreement boundary that ended the war in Bosnia, 1995
- Boundary of Bosnia and Herzegovina

Time Box

1961 Berlin Wall divided capital of Germany into East and West sections
1989 Berlin Wall came down; Poland gained freedom
1991 Soviet Union collapsed
1994 European Union began

The End of the Soviet Union

The Soviet Union had been facing economic troubles for several decades. Mikhail Gorbachev called for **perestroika**, or restructuring. At first, he intended only economic reform, wanting limited capitalism. However, he also saw the need for political reform.

The Soviet Union was a huge nation with 92 different nationalities, 112 languages, and 12 time zones. The reforms encouraged the republics to break away. Ukraine voted to become independent in 1991. Leaders of Ukraine, Russia, and Belarus soon announced that the Soviet Union no longer existed.

Out of the old Soviet empire emerged the Commonwealth of Independent States—a loose alliance of former Soviet republics. Each country was independent but would work with the others in trade. Not all has been peaceful since then. In 1991, the Republic of Chechnya declared that it wanted to separate from Russia. Continued outbreaks of violence have hurt both countries.

374 Chapter 23

Extension

In 1991, Boris Yeltsin became Russia's first freely elected president. Elected on the promise of reform, he headed the move to write a new constitution, which was adopted in 1993. In a historic first, it guarantees Russians the right to own private property. Other provisions include equality, freedom of conscience, and freedom of religion.

A New Economic Power

Since World War II, the nations of Western Europe have learned to work together. In 1950, six nations created the European Economic Community (EEC), better known as the Common Market. It was a free-trade area that included France, West Germany, Belgium, the Netherlands, Luxemburg, and Italy. These nations agreed to not charge tariffs, or fees, on goods imported from each other. Free trade reduced prices and led to economic growth.

Economic cooperation led to closer political ties. In 1994, the Common Market nations formed the European Union (EU). While the nations remained independent, they agreed to enforce certain rules and regulations. For example, the EU nations have set standards for protecting the environment. In 1999, the EU also issued a common currency, called the euro. By 2004, twenty-five nations had joined the EU.

stop and think

How would forming a commonwealth help the new nations that emerged from the Soviet Union? Make a list of three ideas and share them with a partner.

Putting It All Together

Make a concept web about the move to freedom in Eastern Europe. Write "Freedom" in the center of the web. Add each country that became free. Then add details.

Map Extension

Ask students to use the map on page 375 to answer the following questions:

- Where were the new republics? (west and south of Russia)
- Which republic was the second largest, after Russia? (Kazakhstan)
- What is the capital of Ukraine? (Kiev)
- In which republic is Minsk? (Belarus)

Stop and Think

Students' ideas will vary but may include having a common approach to construction of new industries, to security issues, and to financing transportation and communication.

Putting It All Together

Students' concept webs will vary but should include details from the lesson. Possible responses may include the nations of East Germany, Poland, Bulgaria, Hungary, Czechoslovakia, and Yugoslavia.

Lesson Summary

During the last half of the twentieth century, countries in Latin America struggled with economic and political issues.

A 1959 revolution in Cuba brought Fidel Castro to power and ended U.S. control of many plantations and private businesses. The U.S. placed an embargo on Cuba.

Mexico has prospered because of the foreign factories set up near the border and because of the North American Free Trade Agreement. There continue to be concerns of undocumented Mexican workers in the United States.

Conflicts within Central America include those in El Salvador and Nicaragua. The U.S. was involved in struggles against Communist rebels in both nations. The U.S. also arrested the leader of Panama for drug trafficking.

Argentina is one of the South American nations struggling with the results of military rule and economic difficulties.

Lesson Objective

Students will learn about the economic conditions in several areas of Latin America.

LESSON 2

Economic Issues in Latin America

Thinking on Your Own

Look at the vocabulary terms for this lesson. As you read, write a sentence for each of the terms. Check with a partner to be sure you have used the words correctly. Then use a synonym for each word in a new sentence.

Latin America faced great challenges during the last half of the twentieth century. Most nations in Central and South America lacked modern economies. For income, they depended on exports to the United States of fruit, coffee, and farm products. Political turmoil also created problems in the region.

focus your reading

Explain why Fidel Castro took over the Cuban government.

Why did the world fear a nuclear war?

Summarize what NAFTA has done for the Mexican economy.

In what Central American conflicts did the United States intervene?

vocabulary

embargo   inflation
maquiladora austerity
amnesty

The Cuban Revolution

In the 1950s, the island nation of Cuba faced huge problems. Its economy was based on sugar plantations, owned mostly by companies in the United States. American support helped keep Fulgencio Batista, a harsh dictator, in power. The Cuban people were generally poor, many lived in shacks, and most lacked health care.

In 1959, a young lawyer named Fidel Castro led a revolt that overthrew Batista. The Peoples' Revolution was successful. Castro set up a Communist government

Fidel Castro and Che Guevara wanted to bring communism to Cuba and other Latin American nations.

Focus Your Reading Answers

1 Castro took over the Cuban government because of the harsh policies of the dictator Batista and the unjust economy.

2 During 1961, the U.S. discovered that the Soviet Union had sent nuclear missiles to Cuba. The U.S. demanded their removal. Nuclear war seemed likely, but after six days, the Soviets agreed to remove the missiles.

3 The North American Free Trade Agreement has improved Mexico's economy. Mexico has become the second-largest trading partner of the U.S., and in 2000, its gross domestic product grew by 7 percent.

4 The United States has intervened in El Salvador, Nicaragua, and Panama. In the first two cases, trying to prevent the spread of communism was the issue. In Panama, drug trafficking was the concern.

376 | Chapter 23

and made radical changes in the economy. The government took over the sugar plantations and thousands of private businesses. Their Cuban and American owners fled the country.

The United States saw Communist Cuba as a major threat. It placed a trade and travel **embargo** on Cuba. This nearly wrecked the island's economy, as the United States controlled 70 percent of its trade.

The United States government also helped train an invasion force that landed at the Bay of Pigs in 1961. These Cuban exiles, who were trained by the CIA, hoped to lead a revolt against Castro. Instead, the people remained loyal to Castro and the invasion failed.

By then, Castro had turned to the Soviet Union for economic and military help. In 1961, the Soviets built missile sites in Cuba to help "protect" Castro from any future American attack. President John Kennedy blockaded the ships that were delivering missiles and supplies to Cuba. He also demanded that the Soviets turn back the ships bringing the missiles. The Cuban Missile Crisis could have led to a nuclear war. After six tense days, the Soviets backed down.

Castro's revolution was not a democratic revolution. His government controlled the newspapers and jailed its critics. Still, it did provide better medical care for the poor. It also nearly wiped out illiteracy.

The collapse of the Soviet Union in 1991 caused another crisis for Cuba. The Soviet Union was Cuba's major trading partner, buying most of its sugar crop. The result was a sharp economic downturn. In response, Castro allowed some private businesses to open. He also encouraged tourists to visit Cuba. Tourism now brings in more than $2 billion each year. About half of Cuba's workers have service jobs.

Mexico's Economic Boom

In an attempt to grow the economy during the mid-1960s, Mexico set aside a strip of land 12.5 miles (20 km) wide along the United States border. Within this area, any foreign nation can set up a factory, called a

In July 2003, the U.S. Coast Guard stopped this "boat" made of a 1951 Chevy truck. The people trying to come to the U.S. were forced to return to Cuba.

Picturing History

The desperation of Cubans trying to reach freedom is shown in the photograph on page 377. Many who felt their lives were at risk under Castro fled, including artists and writers, scientists, physicians, and teachers. During Operation Peter Pan, as the CIA called it, some 14,000–15,000 children went alone to the U.S. for fear that the Cuban government would separate them from their parents. The operation was funded by the Roman Catholic Church, which promised scholarships and care for the children, and by companies that had lost their Cuban holdings in the revolution. While many parents later rejoined their children, many of those children left refugee camps in Miami, ending up in foster homes and orphanages.

Extension

Some people feel that the U.S. embargo of Cuba, which began in 1961, should be lifted. Have interested students use library resources or the Internet to find out more information, then have a structured debate in class.

Picturing History

Che Guevara, shown second from the right in the photograph on page 376, became a folk hero as a result of his devotion to guerrilla warfare as a means to world revolution. After earning a medical degree in his native Argentina, he left to avoid serving under Juan Perón. While traveling in Latin America, he met the Castro brothers in Mexico during the 1950s and later participated in the 1959 Cuban revolution.

Vocabulary

each of the vocabulary terms with students.

argo is refusing to allow trade. The United placed an *embargo* on Communist Cuba.

ry in Mexico near the U.S. border is a *dora*. Work done in a *maquiladora* can be ore cheaply than in the United States.

al pardon for political offenses is *amnesty*. mented immigrants in the U.S. would like ve *amnesty*.

is rapid increase in prices. Argentina from a 200 percent rate of *inflation*.

without comforts is *austerity*. The Argentine ment imposed *austerity* measures to improve omy.

Picturing History

Vicente Fox, shown in the photograph on page 378, won the presidency of Mexico in 2000 with 43 percent of the popular vote, after serving as governor of Guanajuato for three years. Fox was a former executive with the Coca-Cola Company in Mexico, who resigned rather than become head of Latin American operations, which would have required a move to Miami, Florida. Educated at the Ibero-American University of Mexico City, with post-graduate work at Harvard, Fox intended to run a businesslike administration and to focus on growing the economy.

Extension

In 1948, the nations of the Western Hemisphere formed the Organization of American States (OAS). One goal was to end foreign military action in the independent nations. However, the United States did not end its involvement in Latin American affairs, despite the OAS.

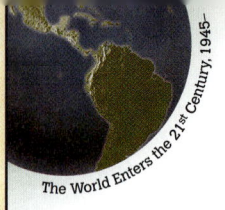

Extension

Vicente Fox made a state visit to the United States in early September 2001 to urge President George W. Bush, whom he had known from Bush's days as governor of Texas, to resolve migration issues for Mexican workers living illegally in the U.S. Bush promised to do so; however, within a week, the entire agenda of his presidency changed when the World Trade Center was attacked by terrorists.

Vicente Fox changed "politics as usual" in Mexico.

maquiladora. Because these workers are paid less than factory workers in other countries, goods can be produced more cheaply. Still, the workers in the maquiladoras generally earn more than twice the wage of the average Mexican worker.

Mexico and the United States joined with Canada in 1994 to ratify the North American Free Trade Agreement (NAFTA). The United States could see from the success of the European Union that regional trade groups offered an advantage. The second largest free-trade zone in the world, NAFTA nations hope to expand to other nations in the Western Hemisphere, except Cuba. NAFTA has helped Mexico's economy; in 2000, its gross domestic product grew a healthy seven percent. It is the United States's second largest trading partner, replacing Japan. In addition, Mexico has signed trade agreements with other countries in Central and South America, as well as European nations and Israel.

On January 1, 1994, the same day that NAFTA took effect, a revolt in the southern part of Mexico occurred. In the state of Chiapas, Indians and peasants protested the loss of land rights and the way that the economy was being developed. The revolutionaries wanted land, teachers and schools, health care, and roads. The first phase of the rebellion lasted 10 days. Uprisings broke out again in 1997 and continue to be a concern for Mexico's government.

By 2000, the government of Mexico had been controlled by the same political party for 70 years. Leaders were corrupt and debt was rising. In 2000, Mexicans elected Vicente Fox, a businessman from an opposing party—the National Action Party (PAN).

One of the largest issues facing Mexico has been the status of its workers in the United States. As many as 3 million Mexicans work in the United States as undocumented immigrants. They do jobs that people born in the U.S. don't want. These jobs offer low pay and, in some cases, are dangerous. Still, Mexican workers send about $9 billion each year back to family members in Mexico. The issue between the two countries is still not resolved. Many undocumented immigrants support **amnesty**—or a general pardon for political offenses, including illegally entering a country.

stop and think

What do you think should be done about undocumented immigrant workers in the United States? Make a list of three ideas and then write a paragraph explaining your position.

Conflicts in Central America

The nations of Central America had their own challenges. Rich landowners and factory owners controlled most of the wealth. The majority of the people were very poor. In El Salvador, Nicaragua, and elsewhere, inequality of wealth led to political upheavals.

The economy of El Salvador grew rapidly after World War II. Wealthy land owners got richer by investing in factories. The factories paid low wages. Poor farmers and factory workers sank deeper into poverty.

In the 1970s, workers, farmers, and some leaders of the Catholic Church protested. Poor farmers organized armed guerrilla bands. The army, which ran the government in El Salvador, cracked down. It sent out death squads that killed protest leaders, including Catholic Archbishop Oscar Romero.

The result was a civil war. The United States supported the government, afraid the rebels would make El Salvador a Communist nation. It sent more than $4 million in aid, which only prolonged the war. The two sides finally made peace in 1992 after 75,000 people had been killed.

The economy of Nicaragua also boomed after the war, but workers and farmers felt left out. They organized protest movements. The dictator of Nicaragua, President Anastasio Somoza, sent out his army and police force to kill protestors. Joined by university students, the rebels formed the Sandinista National Liberation Front. In 1979, the Sandinistas overthrew Somoza and took control.

As in El Salvador, the United States opposed the rebels. After they seized power, President Ronald Reagan ordered a trade embargo against Nicaragua. His administration also provided

Time Box

1959
Castro came to power in Cuba

1980s
U.S. supported Nicaraguan rebels against Sandinistas

1994
North American Free Trade Agreement

1999
Panama Canal returned to Panamanian control

2000
Vicente Fox elected president of Mexico

Stop and Think

Students' ideas and paragraphs will vary but should offer suggestions for dealing with the problem of undocumented workers.

Time Box Extension

Ask students how long Fidel Castro has been in power.

Extension

Archbishop Romero was shot through the heart while celebrating Mass on March 24, 1980. He had a premonition of his death; six other priests had already been killed. Part of the reason for Romero's death was his radio station in San Salvador, the capital city. In response to requests from families to help locate a person who was missing, the station broadcasted the names of those people. For his work in El Salvador, Romero had been nominated for the 1979 Nobel Peace Prize. The violence did not end with Romero. Only months later, El Salvador's National Guard killed four American women. Six Jesuit priests, along with their housekeeper and her daughter, were murdered in 1989.

Map Extension

Ask students to use the map on page 380 to answer the following questions:

- In what two nations was there rioting against the United States? (Peru, Venezuela)

- In which nation did the U.S. intervene in 1965? (Dominican Republic)

- What happened in Honduras during the 1980s? (The U.S. used bases in Honduras to support rebels in Nicaragua.)

- What did the United States try to do in Chile? (prevent the election of Allende)

Extension

In 1985, the United States decided to cease funding the contras and placed a trade embargo on Nicaragua. Because the U.S. had been Nicaragua's major trading partner, the economy of that nation was in chaos. Despite the decision to stop helping the contras, some members of the Reagan administration and the Central Intelligence Agency were still helping them. This created a scandal for the Reagan administration, known as the Iran-Contra scandal, because money from the sale of arms to Iran provided the funds sent to the contras.

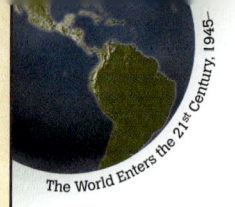

---

over $1 billion and trained a group called the contras, who tried to overthrow the government. Economic hard times in the mid-1980s finally defeated the Sandinistas. They lost the 1990 election to a more conservative candidate, Violeta Chamorro.

The challenges faced by El Salvador and Nicaragua were typical of the problems faced by Central American nations. So, too, was the United States' willingness to get involved in the region. In 1989, the United States sent troops to Panama to arrest its military dictator. They captured and arrested

U.S. Involvement in Latin America since 194–

① Argentina
1946: U.S. tries and fails to prevent election of President Perón.

② Guatemala
1954: U.S. supports overthrow of the Socialist government.

③ Peru
1958: Riots against U.S.

④ Venezuela
1958: Riots against U.S.

⑤ Dominican Republic
1965: U.S. military forces intervene to suppress possible Communist influence.

⑥ Chile
1970: U.S. tries and fails to prevent election of Socialist President Allende.

⑦ Nicaragua
1979: U.S. withdraws support for corrupt Somoza family; Somozas are overthrown by Sandinistas (Marxist guerilla forces).
1981–1990: U.S. secretly aids contra rebel efforts to overthrow Sandinista government.

⑧ Grenada
1979: U.S. ends aid as Marxist government assumes power. 1983: Extremists overthrow government; U.S. invades to restore stable government.

⑨ El Salvador
Late 1970s and 1980s: U.S. supports Salvadoran army against Marxist-led guerrillas in civil war. 1992: Peace settlement ends civil war.

⑩ Honduras
1981–1990: U.S. supports contra rebels in Nicaragua from bases in Honduras.

⑪ Panama
1989: U.S. invades Panama and arrests and imprisons General Noriega on charges of drug trafficking. 1999: U.S. relinquishes rights to Panama Canal Zone.

Extension

In the 1970s, during rule by a military junta, perhaps as many as 15,000 Argentine citizens were imprisoned, kidnapped, or murdered. They were called *los desaparecidos*, "the disappeared." In 1977, in Buenos Aires, a group of women began meeting each Thursday at the Plaza de Mayo, protesting the loss of husbands and children in this campaign. Known as the Madres de la Plaza de Mayo, they symbolized opposition to the dictatorship by demonstrating across from the president's palace. They continued meeting regularly, even after the fall of the junta, demanding to know the truth.

General Manuel Noriega on charges of trafficking in drugs. They brought him to the United States to stand trial, where he was convicted and sentenced to prison.

Many countries in Latin America are trying to grow their economies. Traditionally, these countries have focused on agriculture. Many countries grow one major crop such as bananas or coffee. These countries are attempting to industrialize and to repay national debt. Military rulers often do not know how to deal with their economic problems. As a result, many Latin American nations have turned to democracy.

Violeta Barrios de Chamorro, leader of the anti-Sandinista coalition, was elected president of Nicaragua in 1990.

Argentina

Argentina is one example of a South American economy in danger. Although it once had one of the strongest economies in Latin America, Argentina came to the edge of financial collapse as the 21st century began.

During the 1930s, Argentina had a strong economy based on its exports of beef. After World War II, the nation set out to modernize. Dictatorships and military rule hurt the country. By the end of the 1980s, the rate of **inflation** was 200 percent a month. When neighboring Brazil's economy suffered in 1999, Argentina was harmed as well, because Brazil was a major trading partner.

Like Brazil, Argentina was being supported through loans from the International Monetary Fund (IMF) and other international lenders. By 2001, the nation's debt was $141 billion. Repayment of these loans drained Argentina's economy. The **austerity** measures that the government imposed led to riots and strikes. Austerity measures are designed to control a nation's economy. Many people were unemployed. Foreign companies were unwilling to invest in a nation with an uncertain economy. Argentina is working to recover from this financial disaster.

Putting It All Together

Make a T-chart labeled "Event" and "Importance." List at least five events from the lesson and explain why they were important.

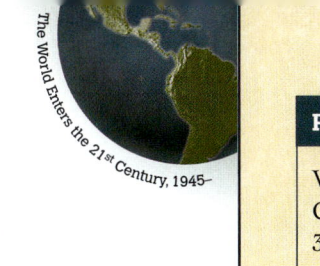

Picturing History

Violeta Barrios de Chamorro, shown on page 381, served as Nicaragua's president for seven years after her career in publishing. Her husband, Pedro, had been the editor of the newspaper *La Prensa*, which criticized the government. Pedro Chamorro was imprisoned several times and assassinated in 1978. His death helped to ignite the Sandinista revolution. Violeta was the first woman to hold the presidency in any Central American nation. During her administration, the size of the army was reduced, censorship was lifted, and some state-owned industries were privatized.

Extension

Juan and Eva Perón were among the more colorful and noted rulers of Argentina. First elected president in 1946, Juan Perón tried to decrease reliance on foreign investors while also increasing industrialization. After the military overthrew his totalitarian regime in 1955, Perón went to Spain. (He was later allowed to return and was reelected president in the last year of his life, 1973.) Evita, as she was popularly known, had become famous as a radio performer before her marriage to Juan Perón in 1945. Having grown up in poverty, she formed a charitable organization that built schools, orphanages, and hospitals. She died in 1952, of cancer, at age thirty-three. The musical and movie *Evita* are based on her life.

Putting It All Together

Students' T-charts will vary but should include at least five events from the lesson, with an explanation of their importance.

LESSON 3

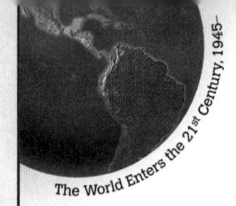

Asia: Conflict and Economic Growth

Lesson Summary
Revolution in China split that country into two states: Communist China occupied the mainland, while the Nationalist government moved to the island of Taiwan. Mao Zedong led the Great Leap Forward and the Cultural Revolution, which reformers ended at his death.

After World War II, Korea was split into two nations, one Communist and one free. The Communist nation, North Korea, invaded South Korea in 1950. The United Nations agreed to help South Korea remain free.

In 1954, French forces withdrew from what is now Vietnam. Most of that nation, particularly in the north, was under Communist control. Despite nearly a decade of support from the U.S., South Vietnam fell to the Communists and the country was reunited.

Nations in the Pacific began to regain economic prosperity with help from the United States. Lacking natural resources, nations such as Japan, Korea, and Singapore focused on exporting goods. A large population and low wages helped India's economy after independence from Britain. Pacific Rim nations suffered the effects of a tsunami in 2004 that disrupted and financial activity took many lives.

Lesson Objective
Students will learn about political and economic growth in Asia since World War II.

Thinking on Your Own
Since 1945, the United States has been deeply involved in Asia. It has fought two wars there. With a partner, list the possible reasons why the United States cares about Asia. Write this list in your notebook.

The late twentieth century brought changes to many countries in Southeast Asia. Both political and economic, these changes affected relationships with Western nations as well as with the people in Asia.

focus your reading

Why did China split into two nations?

Summarize Mao's goals for China.

How did the United States become involved in Korea and Vietnam?

How did Japan improve its economy after World War II?

Explain the four "Little Tigers" and why they were called that.

vocabulary

socialist market economy
decolonization
tsunami

Revolution in China
China began a civil war in 1945. The People's Liberation Army, under the command of Mao Zedong, was strongest in northern China. The Nationalists were strong in central and southern China. They were led by Chiang Kai-shek and supported by the United States. By 1949, Mao's Communist group had defeated the Nationalists, who fled to Taiwan, an island off the southern tip of China. China and Taiwan still disagree over the political status of Taiwan.

Mainland China would like to have a unified country under Communist control, but Taiwan's leaders favor continuing independence. Still, they are tied economically. Hundreds of thousands of Taiwanese people work on the mainland. Trade between China and Taiwan rose more than 34 percent between 2003 and 2004, to $70 billion.

Focus Your Reading Answers

1 China split into two nations after Mao Zedong's Communist forces were victorious over the Nationalists led by Chiang Kai-shek.

2 Mao's goals for China included land reform and cultural revolution.

3 The United States became involved in Korea after North Korean troops marched into South Korea, and the United Nations sent in troops to keep South Korea from becoming Communist. U.S. involvement in Vietnam began in support of the anti-Communist government in South Vietnam.

4 After World War II, Japan improved its economy by focusing on manufacturing goods for export.

5 The four "Little Tigers" are South Korea, Hong Kong, Singapore, and Taiwan. They are called that because their economic strategy has been modeled on that of Japan.

stop and think

What do you think would happen to a country if all its ideas, cultures, habits, and customs were taken away? How would the citizens react? Write a bulleted list of five ideas and share them with a partner.

Under Mao, China began various attempts to strengthen the economy and practice communism. Land reform began in 1955, with poor peasants receiving land from rich landowners. Three years later, Mao began the Great Leap Forward, creating farm communes. The peasants did not agree with the system and the weather did not favor the crops. Nearly 15 million people starved before the communes were broken up.

Mao's next move was the Great Proletariat Cultural Revolution. The Red Guards, a group of revolutionary young people, were sent to destroy the "Four Olds." Old ideas, old cultures, old habits, and old customs all had to go.

After Mao died in 1976, a group of reformers ended the Cultural Revolution. These reformers were more moderate, seeking to modernize China. They concentrated on four areas—agriculture, technology, industry, and national defense. By the late 1970s, China had opened trade with other nations. In 1992, the nation began a **socialist market economy**. The government would no longer plan the economic system. Instead it would allow the demand for goods and services to determine pricing and production. China became a major exporter, benefiting from its huge domestic markets and its pool of cheap labor. It joined the World Trade Organization in 2001.

Despite movement into the larger world economically, China's leaders remained closed to democracy. In 1989, the government sent tanks to disperse demonstrators who were calling for

A single demonstrator faces tanks during the Tiananmen Square protest.

Lesson Vocabulary

Discuss each of the vocabulary terms on page 382 with students.

A *socialist market economy* allows demand for goods and services to set the prices and production. China began a *socialist market economy* in 1992.

Decolonization is the process of former European colonies struggling for independence. *Decolonization* began after World War II.

A *tsunami* is a huge sea wave caused by an underground ocean earthquake. A *tsunami* struck the Pacific Rim nations in 2004.

Extension

When he was a school principal in Hunan, Mao Zedong helped found China's Communist Party in 1921. Two years later, the Communists became allied with Sun Yat-sen's Nationalist Party. Mao's strategy was to gain control of the country and then encircle the cities. The Nationalist-Communist alliance broke down in a battle for control. Nationalists sometimes persecuted the Communists; in 1930, for example, they executed Mao's first wife.

Stop and Think

Students' lists will vary but may include confusion about the rules of society, practices continued in secret, and hiding evidence of the former culture.

Picturing History

The 1989 Tiananmen Square confrontation is shown on page 383. Ironically, the square is named for a huge stone that was once the Imperial Palace's main gate; it was called the Gate of Heavenly Peace. Originally built in 1651, the square was enlarged in 1958 to four times its former size. Mao Zedong's body lies in state there at the Memorial Hall bearing his name. Since 1919, Tiananmen Square, which covers 100 acres, has been a site of student demonstrations.

Extension

U.S. President Richard Nixon and his wife, Pat, visited China in 1972 to end two decades of uneasiness between the two nations. Nixon was the first president to visit China while in office. Some historians believe that re-establishing relations with China was his most important foreign relations accomplishment.

The World Enters the 21st Century | 383

Picturing History

Korea's Demilitarized Zone (DMZ), shown on page 384, is a 2.4 mile-wide (3.9 km) strip of land between the two Koreas.

The largest crossing at the DMZ occurred in late 2003, when more than 1,000 South Koreans traveled to Pyongyang, North Korea's capital, for the dedication of an indoor gymnasium.

Oddly enough, despite being heavily guarded and planted with land mines, the DMZ also provides sanctuary for a number of endangered species. Since there are strict rules about access to the DMZ, Amur leopards, white-naped cranes, Asiatic black bears, Chinese egrets, and other rare animals can remain undisturbed and roam freely.

---

reform. Between 500 and 2,000 protesters were killed in Beijing's Tiananmen Square, the site of the protests.

Korean War

Leaders of the Soviet Union and the United States divided Korea into two parts after World War II. The split became permanent in 1948. North Korea was communist, while South Korea was democratic. North Korean troops surged into the south and captured the capital in 1950. The United Nations agreed that South Korea should receive help. The goal was to prevent it from becoming a Communist state.

The Demilitarized Zone in Korea

When troops from the United States and the United Nations pushed into North Korea, the Chinese sent troops. They pushed the U.N. troops back across the thirty-eighth parallel, the boundary between the two nations. This region became known as the Demilitarized Zone (DMZ). The war continued until a 1953 cease-fire, with neither side a clear winner. Tension between the two Koreas continues. A treaty ending the war has never been signed.

War in Vietnam

The period after World War II was marked by **decolonization**. Country after country became determined to be free of European control. One of the longest struggles took place in Vietnam, which had been under French control and was known as French Indochina.

Extension

After a South Korean working in Iraq was killed by terrorists there, both North and South Korea agreed to reduce the propaganda distributed along the DMZ. The U.S. also agreed to remove about one-third of its armed forces stationed in South Korea—more than 12,000 troops. Students interested in military strategy may wish to investigate the history of and recent developments in the continuing U.S. presence in Korea.

Ho Chi Minh led Communist forces against France in 1946, taking control of most of Vietnam. France, refusing to recognize the new government based in Hanoi, took control of the southern part of the nation.

The French finally withdrew from Vietnam. In 1954, the Vietminh forced the French to surrender at Dien Bien Phu. The two sides agreed to divide Vietnam temporarily until an election could be held to decide on a new government. The election never took place.

Instead, President Dwight D. Eisenhower and President John F. Kennedy supported the anti-Communists who controlled South Vietnam. In 1965, President Lyndon B. Johnson sent American troops to Vietnam, the first of about 2.7 million who would serve there. The United States finally withdrew from Vietnam in 1973, after more than 58,000 soldiers were killed and 300,000 were wounded. In 1975, North Vietnam took over South Vietnam, creating one Communist nation.

Economic Growth in the Pacific

After World War II ended, the United States tried to help Japan restore economic productivity. By 1949, only four years after its surrender, Japan was working at its prewar levels. Japan had few natural resources and a large population. It had also lost its overseas empire. Nevertheless, the nation focused on exporting goods. The low wages which Japanese workers received offset the cost of importing raw materials. Japanese products were competitively priced in the world market.

The World Enters the 21st Century 385

Map Extension

Ask students to use the map on page 385 to answer the following questions:

- What was the capital of North Vietnam? (Hanoi)

- Along which coast did many of the battles of the Tet Offensive occur? (eastern shore of South Vietnam, along the South China Sea)

- What two cities of the Tet Offensive were nearest the Demilitarized Zone? (Hue and Khe Sanh)

- What was the southernmost destination of the Ho Chi Minh Trail? (Bien Hoa)

Extension

Since the reunification of the nation, Vietnam has made an astounding economic recovery. Its annual growth rate, at 7.7 percent, is second only to China's among Asian nations. From China, Vietnam has borrowed the language of a socialist market economy. The United States accounts for $5 billion in annual exports. Vietnam's single largest employer is Nike, which produces $700 million in footwear annually and employs 130,000 workers. China, Indonesia, and Vietnam are the largest manufacturers for Nike.

Extension

Students may be familiar with the Vietnam Veterans Memorial. Suggest they use library resources or the Internet to find out more about the Vietnam Women's Memorial, dedicated in 1993 and also located in Washington, D.C. About 13,000 women served in Vietnam during the war, most of them as nurses, although women worked as clerks, mapmakers, air traffic controllers, and intelligence officers. Of the 58,000 names carved on the Vietnam Veterans Memorial, only eight are those of women.

Map Extension

Have students use maps of Asia or the world to more completely locate the "Little Tigers" and to identify the nations around them.

Time Box Extension

Assign students to "become" one of the dates in the Time Boxes on pages 374, 379, or 386. Have them line themselves up in the correct chronological order. Ask them to tell what happened in the year that they represent and where it happened.

Putting It All Together

Students' timelines may vary but should include events listed in the Time Box on page 386.

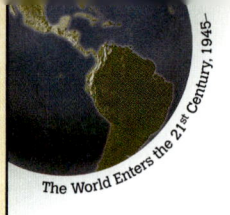

The World Enters the 21st Century, 1945–

During the 1970s, Japanese industry began to focus on producing technology-related equipment. Although a recession slowed growth during the 1990s, the example Japan set was an encouragement to other Asian nations.

Singapore, South Korea, Hong Kong, and Taiwan followed Japan's example. These Pacific Rim countries became known as the "Little Tigers." Like Japan, each of them had many people and little capital or natural resources. They also became export-driven and became Japan's competitors during the 1990s. Indonesia, Thailand, and Malaysia soon joined the original group of four.

India has also experienced unparalleled economic growth. After achieving independence from Britain in 1948, the country began to modernize. Many corporations in the United States moved part of their operations to India. These companies took advantage of the large labor force and low wages.

Asian nations experienced huge climate upheavals, as well as economic changes. In December 2004, a **tsunami** struck. This underground, oceanic earthquake began on the west coast of Sumatra, an island in the Pacific. Trillions of tons of water moved as the earth shifted. The tsunami's effects reached more than 3,000 miles away to East Africa. Hundreds of thousands died, and the economies of several nations were severely affected.

Little Tigers
SOUTH KOREA
HONG KONG
TAI*
SINGAPORE

Time Box

1949 Nationalist Army defeated, moved to Taiwan
1950 North Korea invaded South Korea
1952 Japan's independence restored
1958 The Great Leap Forward began in China
1965 U.S. troops sent to Vietnam
1979 The United States and China resumed diplomatic relations
1989 Protests in Tiananmen Square
1997 Hong Kong returned to China's control

Putting It All Together

Make a timeline showing the progress and challenges of Asian nations after World War II. Compare your timeline with that of a partner. Add details as you review the lesson.

386 | Chapter 23

Lesson Vocabulary

Discuss each of the vocabulary terms on page 387 with students.

Tell them that *apartheid*, like segregation in the United States, was a system for keeping whites and blacks separated. The British who controlled South Africa passed laws in 1948 to establish *apartheid*.

Restrictions intended to enforce international law are *sanctions*. Refusing to trade with South Africa was one of the *sanctions* that helped end *apartheid*.

The idea that all Africans would work together to meet common goals is called *Pan-Africanism*. *Pan-Africanism* promotes using the strong African tradition of community to benefit all.

Extension

In all, 17 African nations gaine[d] independence in 1960, followin[g] Ghana, which was the first Bri[tish] colony to gain independence i[n]... Between 1961 and 1965, anoth[er]... nations became free.

386 | Chapter 23

LESSON 4

Independence Movements in Africa

Thinking on Your Own

What are some of the first things a new government must deal with? Develop a concept web to answer this question. Then write a paragraph about the important issues. Share your paragraph with a partner to compare your ideas.

Some people refer to 1960 as "the year of Africa." It was a turning point for African nations wanting freedom from European colonial rule. Thirteen countries gained their independence from France that year, setting an example for the rest of Africa.

focus your reading

Discuss why 1960 was called "the year of Africa"?

Explain apartheid.

Why is Nelson Mandela important to South Africa?

What was Pan-Africanism?

vocabulary

apartheid   Pan-Africanism
sanctions

New Nations Form

By the beginning of the twentieth century, European rulers enacted laws that took away the land of the native people and forced them to work in mines or on farms. Many native people were little more than slaves. They had no rights and no support.

After decades of this treatment, Africans wanted to regain their independence. This process was called decolonization. It was complicated by the many divisions within the African societies. Many language groups, religions, and ethnic differences existed, and many different solutions were set forth.

This was also the era of the Cold War. Free European governments delayed granting independence. They assumed that Africans were not ready for self-government and feared that Communist ideas would grow. Harsh laws were passed, supposedly to prevent communism.

Lesson Summary

The turning point for Africa is often thought to be 1960, when 13 nations gained independence from France. European powers were often reluctant to grant their African colonies independence, fearing that they were not ready for self-government and would become Communist states. South Africa was a remarkable example of change in a nation. After decades of being under apartheid rules separating the races, the former Dutch/British colony dismantled the system. Nelson Mandela, imprisoned on political charges for 27 years, was freed. In 1994, he became the first non-white president of South Africa. The Organization of African Unity, and later the African Union, were attempts at Pan-Africanism, the idea that all nations in Africa can work together to solve their problems. Among the largest of those problems is debt. To modernize, educate, and care for their people, many African nations have gone deeply into debt to industrialized Western nations.

Lesson Objective

Students will learn about the challenges facing newly independent nations in Africa.

Focus Your Reading Answers

1 The turning point in Africa's quest to be free of European colonial powers was 1960, which became known as "the year of Africa."

2 Apartheid was a complex system started by the white minority of South Africa to prevent black Africans from gaining land, education, or wealth. Blacks, "colored" people, and whites lived in strict segregation.

Focus Your Reading Answers, continued

3 Jailed for his efforts to end apartheid, Nelson Mandela emerged from prison to become South Africa's first black president and an architect of the new government.

4 Pan-Africanism is the idea that if all the African nations cooperated, they could more effectively solve problems throughout the continent.

Map Extension

Ask students to use the map on page 388 to answer the following questions:

- From what country did the Democratic Republic of the Congo win its independence? (Belgium)

- Which European nation had at one time controlled much of the northwest part of the African continent? (France)

- What island gained independence in 1960? (Madagascar)

- Which European nation had colonies in nearly every part of Africa? (Great Britain)

France was determined to keep control of Algeria, its North African colony. While fighting there, the French allowed other colonies to be free. The conflict in Algeria lasted from 1954 until 1962, when France at last agreed to independence.

The Sub-Saharan nations of Central and Southern Africa slowly gained independence as well. Many changed their names, which had reflected the white colonization. For example, Rhodesia had been named for Cecil Rhodes, a British administrator. At independence, the nation became Zimbabwe, honoring one of the great African kingdoms of the past.

South African Independence

One of the most amazing examples of decolonization occurred in South Africa. Originally the Dutch settled the region, which later passed to British control. In 1948, the British enacted strict laws separating blacks and whites, a policy known as **apartheid**.

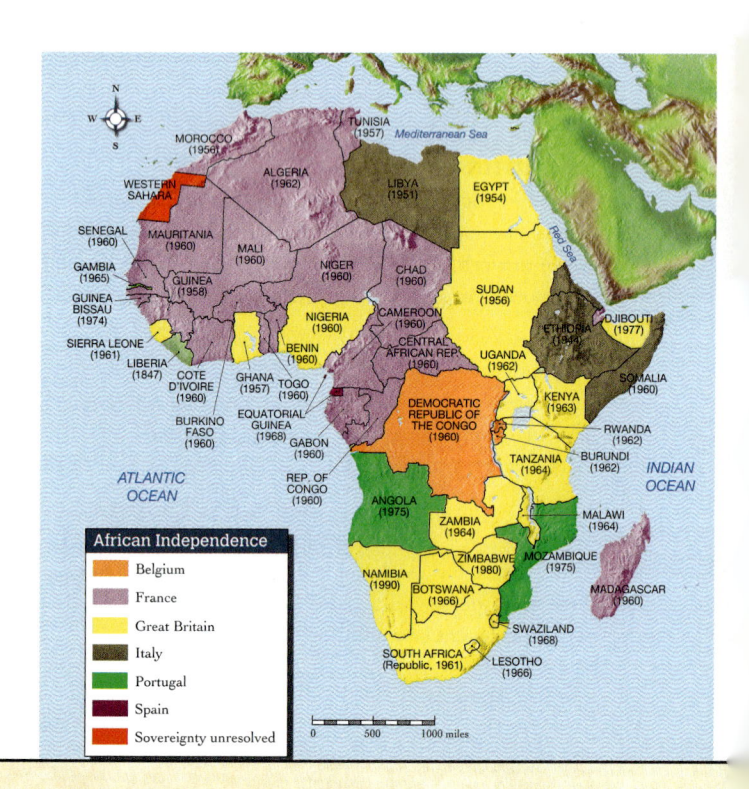

Extension

Have students use library resources or the Internet to investigate some of the markers on the road to South Africa's independence. The Sharpeville Massacre of 1960 and the Soweto uprising in 1976 are two places to begin. Other students may wish to investigate the role of sympathetic white South Africans, such as writer Alan Paton. Allow time for students to share their findings with the class.

Blacks, who made up the majority of the population, struggled against the unjust rules. Apartheid governed every part of life: where a person could live, what entrance to the train he or she could use, how or if he or she would be educated. Many blacks were killed or jailed as a result of uprisings. Nelson Mandela, a black leader, was arrested in 1962 for resisting apartheid and sentenced to life in prison. For 27 years he remained a prisoner who believed in the cause of freedom.

Sanctions were passed against South Africa. Many nations, including the United States, refused to trade with the country because of its human rights violations. In addition, violent protests within the nation were heightened in 1984. Indians and "colored" people, who were of mixed race, gained some civil rights while blacks were still excluded. Finally, the white rulers determined that all non-whites should be allowed to vote. Nelson Mandela was freed from Robbin Island Prison in 1990. Four years later, when the first democratic elections were held, Mandela became the first democratically elected president.

Long lines of people waited to vote in the historic 1994 South African election.

Nelson Mandela

The Quest for African Unity

Some of the new leaders throughout Africa believed in **Pan-Africanism**. This idea meant that all Africans would join together to meet common goals. Community is a strong African tradition. Pan-Africanism wanted to use that tradition to benefit all Africans.

stop and think

What are some of the problems that African nations could work together to solve? Make a list of concerns for that continent. Then choose one and, in a short paragraph, explain why it is a problem for all of Africa.

Picturing History

The voters shown in the photograph at the right of page 389 were part of the 19.5 million who turned out during the 1994 election. Originally scheduled to take three days, it was extended one additional day to make sure everyone who wanted to vote had the opportunity.

Picturing History

Nelson Mandela, shown in the photograph at the left of page 389, was the son of a chief and was expected to fill that position. However, he chose a university education and training in law and was a partner in the first black law firm in South Africa. When the African National Congress, for whom he had been organizing youth activities, was banned in 1961, Mandela went "underground" to continue his activities. Two years later he was arrested. During his imprisonment, his picture could not be displayed or his words quoted. Wearing a "Free Mandela" T-shirt was grounds for arrest. During the 27 years he spent in prison, Mandela worked to educate others, including prison guards, to ANC beliefs.

Extension

Head of the Anglican Church in South Africa since 1986, Archbishop Desmond Tutu strongly supported nonviolence and sanctions. He received the Nobel Peace Prize in 1984. He also chaired the Truth and Reconciliation Commission, set up to investigate charges of human rights violations from 1960 to 1994. The Commission heard testimony from some 21,000 persons, including informers, police, activists, and victims.

Stop and Think

Students' lists and paragraphs will vary. Possible responses include famine, debt, desertification, the AIDS pandemic, and industrialization.

Time Box Extension

Ask students to research one of the events in the Time Box on page 390 and make a poster to explain the event to the class.

Chart Extension

Have students choose another African nation that achieved independence after 1950. Ask them to find similar data for the country they chose at the time of its independence using library resources or the Internet. Then have them make circle graphs to represent the data visually.

Putting It All Together

Students' Venn diagrams will vary. Possible response:

Algeria: fought a war to gain independence from France; no apartheid rules to overcome

South Africa: peaceful change of government; apartheid had ruled daily life

Both: former European colonies; 1962 a pivotal year: Algeria gained independence, and Nelson Mandela was jailed.

In 1963, leaders of 32 African nations created the Organization of African Unity (OAU). It became the African Union in 2002 with 53 members. The goals of the group include economic growth and democracy.

Many African nations are among the very poorest countries in the world. To modernize, educate, and care for the sick, they have borrowed from Western industrialized nations. At a meeting in 2005, the largest of these nations, known as the G7—or Group of Seven—worked to solve the problems caused by huge indebtedness. The Sub-Saharan African nations, for example, owe about $70 billion to large lenders such as the International Monetary Fund and the World Bank. The G7 have set a goal of ridding Africa of poverty by 2015.

Time Box

1951
Libya gained independence from Italy

1960
Thirteen French colonies gained independence

1963
Organization of African Unity (OAU) formed

1994
First democratic elections in South Africa

2002
African Union replaced OAU

South Africa's Resources at the End of Apartheid, 1994

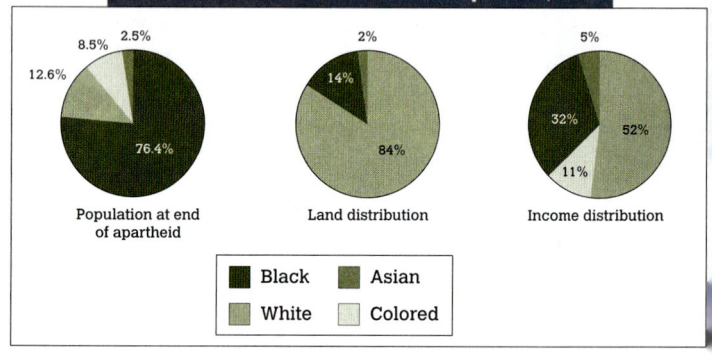

Population at end of apartheid: Black 76.4%, White 12.6%, Asian 2.5%, Colored 8.5%

Land distribution: Black 84%, White 14%, Asian 2%

Income distribution: Black 52%, White 32%, Asian 11%, Colored 5%

Putting It All Together

Make a Venn diagram comparing and contrasting the experiences of freedom in Algeria and South Africa. Conduct additional research if needed.

Chapter 23

Extension

One of the criticisms of the Organization of African Unity was its failure to intervene in internal affairs of member nations, permitting dictators to use oppressive forms of power. The OAU did support liberation movements in Zimbabwe and Mozambique, as well as calling for sanctions against apartheid in South Africa. The African Union began in Libya at a summit held there in 1999 and came into being three years later in South Africa. All African nations with the exception of Morocco have joined. Headquartered in Addis Ababa, Ethiopia, the AU hopes to provide a common currency, a security council, peacekeeping troops, a legislature, and a regional court. The AU has the power to intervene in cases of genocide or other crimes against humanity.

LESSON 5

Conflict in the Middle East

Thinking on Your Own

What do you already know about the nations in the Middle East? What would you like to know more about? Make a K-W-L chart and write the answers as you read the lesson. Then write a brief paragraph explaining one of the things you learned.

The Middle East has been a scene of political turmoil through the centuries. During the post-World War II era, conflict erupted many times.

focus your reading

Why was there greater sympathy toward the idea of a Jewish state after World War II?

What is OPEC?

Describe Pan-Arabism.

What happened in Iran after the monarchy was overthrown?

vocabulary

intifada
Pan-Arabism
pre-emptive strike

The Nation of Israel

The region of Palestine was under British control between the two world wars. In the early twentieth century, groups of Jewish people had argued for the creation of an Israeli state. They wanted it located in the land known as Palestine, which they regarded as theirs since biblical times. Since being driven from the land by the Romans in A.D. 70, the Jewish people had been longing for a homeland.

Sympathy for the Jews increased as people learned of the deaths of millions in Hitler's Holocaust. However, Palestine was primarily an Arab Muslim region, and old hatreds between the groups were strong.

Jewish children who survived the Holocaust arrived in Palestine looking for a home.

Lesson Summary
Since the end of World War II, the Middle East has been the scene of several conflicts. The founding of the modern nation of Israel, formerly under Britain's control, led to several wars with Israel's neighbors. The Palestine Liberation Organization (PLO) has twice declared an intifada against Israel. Although Pan-Arabism has not been successful, the Middle East affects the world's economy through the Organization of Petroleum Exporting Countries (OPEC). The Persian Gulf has been the site of several wars, particularly in Iran and Iraq. The United States has twice gone to war against Iraq. However, with free elections in that nation in 2005, the Shiite majority is again in power. The U.S. also fought against the Taliban, an Islamic fundamentalist group, in Afghanistan in 2001.

Lesson Objective
Students will learn about the various conflicts that have occurred in the Middle East since the end of World War II.

Focus Your Reading Answers

1 After the end of World War II, there was greater sympathy for the idea of a Jewish state because of the millions of Jews who had died in the Holocaust.

2 OPEC is the Organization of Petroleum Exporting Countries, which controls oil prices.

3 Pan-Arabism was the attempt to form a union among all Arabs.

4 After Iran's monarchy was overthrown, Islamic fundamentalist clergy began to rule.

Lesson Vocabulary
Discuss each of the vocabulary terms with students.

An *intifada* is an uprising. To achieve the goal of a Palestinian homeland, the Palestine Liberation Organization called for an *intifada* in 2000.

Pan-Arabism is the desire for unity among all Arab states. Egypt and Syria's attempt toward *Pan-Arabism* failed.

A *pre-emptive strike* is attacking to prevent another nation from striking first. The United States carried out a *pre-emptive strike* against Iraq in 2003.

The World Enters the 21st Century | 391

Map Extension

Ask students to use the map on page 392 to answer the following questions:

- What region did Israel occupy after the 1967 war? (West Bank)
- Does Israel control Damascus? (no)
- What geographic area of land was returned to Egypt? (south of Israel, the Arabian Peninsula)

Picturing History

The 1993 Camp David Accords were sealed with a historic handshake, pictured in the photograph on page 392. Talks continued, as did attacks by extremists. President Clinton was also present when representatives from Jordan, Israel, and the Palestinians met in 1998. The accords have not progressed as hoped, and violence continues in the region.

Stop and Think

Students' ideas and paragraphs will vary. Possible response: The Middle East could have become a group similar to the European Union.

Extension

Since the founding of modern Israel, there have been several conflicts with Arab states. Students may wish to use library resources or the Internet to investigate the conflicts that took place in 1948–1949, 1956, 1967 (the Six-Day War), 1973, or 1982.

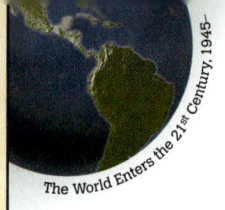

In 1948, the United Nations divided Palestine into Arab and Jewish portions despite the objections of Arab nations. As soon as Israel was declared a nation, these old enemies attacked. Israel defeated them in 1948 and again in land disputes during 1967.

The Palestine Liberation Organization was an Egyptian initiative. Founded in 1964, it has used terrorism to bring about a Palestinian state. In the early 1980s and in 2000, the PLO declared an **intifada**—or uprising—to achieve the goal of a Palestinian homeland.

Tensions with Israel began to ease with the death of longtime PLO leader Yasser Arafat in 2004. Discussion over peace and land issues continued with Jerusalem's West Bank being a major focus.

Egypt's leaders also favored **Pan-Arabism**, the unity of all Arabs. A union between Egypt and Syria did not last; however, several Arab states did join to form the Organization of Petroleum Exporting Countries (OPEC). This group controls oil prices and thus affects the world's economy.

In 1993, U.S. President Bill Clinton watches as Yitzhak Rabin, Israel's prime minister, and PLO leader Yasser Arafat shake hands after agreeing to a Declaration of Principles for peace.

Wars in the Persian Gulf Region

In addition to the conflicts between Israel and its Arab neighbors, the Persian Gulf region has been unstable. The nation of Iran ended the monarchy with a coup in 1979. Under fundamentalist Muslim clergy, the nation moved to a conservative interpretation of Islamic law.

stop and think

What do you think might have happened if Pan-Arabism had worked? Share your ideas with a partner. Then write a short paragraph explaining what the Middle East could have become.

Picturing History

The photograph on page 391 shows children on a ship awaiting residency in Palestine after World War II. The League of Nations had given Britain authority to govern present-day Israel and Jordan. Many Jews came to the area, despite restrictions on immigration that continued even during World War II. In 1939, the British limited Jewish immigration to Palestine to 25,000 Jewish people annually, to decrease to 10,000 each year. The final stage would prohibit immigration to Jews unless the Arabs agreed. After World War II, the British refused to allow 100,000 Holocaust survivors to come to Palestine. They sent the refugee ships to Cyprus, and from there many were smuggled into Palestine. The protests from Zionist terrorist groups led to Britain asking the United Nations for help. The United Nations General Assembly proposed the division of Palestine into two states, one Arab and the other Jewish. Israel became a state on May 14, 1948.

Time Box

1948
Israel became a nation

1960
OPEC formed

1979
Shah of Iran overthrown

2001
Taliban driven from power in Afghanistan

2005
Democratic elections in Iraq

Also in 1979, Saddam Hussein came to power in neighboring Iraq. From 1980 until 1988, Iraq and Iran were at war. Victory bounced back and forth between the nations until the cease-fire. In 1990, Iraq invaded Kuwait, prompting the United Nations and U.S. forces to attack Iraq. Kuwait was restored as its own nation.

In 2003, the United States launched a **pre-emptive strike** against Iraq, declaring war in the mistaken belief that the Iraqis were developing weapons of mass destruction. Saddam Hussein and many of Iraq's key government officials were captured although insurgent fighting continued.

In early 2005, free elections were held in Iraq for the first time in 50 years. The Shiite Muslim majority regained control of the Iraqi government. Many Sunni Muslims, who had held power under Hussein, boycotted the election. Nevertheless, about 58 percent of eligible voters cast ballots. A 275-member National Assembly wrote the constitution for the new democracy.

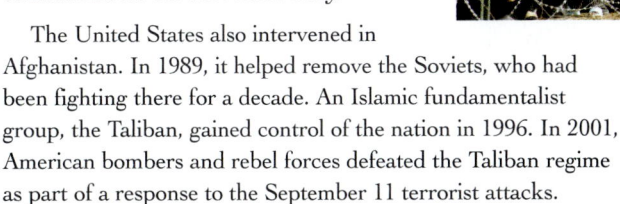

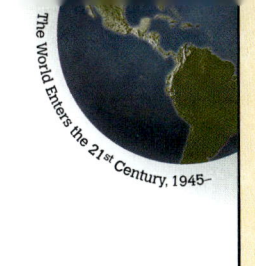

The United States also intervened in Afghanistan. In 1989, it helped remove the Soviets, who had been fighting there for a decade. An Islamic fundamentalist group, the Taliban, gained control of the nation in 1996. In 2001, American bombers and rebel forces defeated the Taliban regime as part of a response to the September 11 terrorist attacks.

The 2005 Iraqi elections

Putting It All Together

Choose an important event in the Middle East and write a news story about it.

Time Box Extension

Divide the class into five small groups. Assign each group one of the events in the Time Box on page 393. Ask them to use library resources or the Internet to find out more about the event, then present their findings to the class. Encourage them to use a creative format such as a radio drama or role-playing to share what they have learned.

Picturing History

The elections held in Iraq in 2005, shown in the photograph on page 393, brought the Shiite majority to power. Prime Minister Ibrahim al-Jaafari proposed a cabinet that, while heavily Shiite, also included representatives from Kurds and Sunni Arabs, as well as seven women. Ironically, the resolution of several months of deadlock occurred on Saddam Hussein's 68th birthday. The former dictator was in prison outside Baghdad awaiting trial.

Putting It All Together
Students' choices of events and news stories will vary but should focus on the Middle East.

Chapter Review

1. Students' choices and essays will vary but should focus on one of the world regions covered in the chapter and explain its movement toward or away from freedom since World War II.

2. Students' Venn diagrams and paragraphs will vary but should focus on comparing and contrasting two regions discussed in the chapter.

Chapter Summary

- **Totalitarian** governments existed in Eastern Europe.
- The Soviet Union controlled many Eastern European countries, known as **satellite nations**.
- When Mikhail Gorbachev came to power, he favored **perestroika**, or restructuring of the government.
- Several attempts at **ethnic cleansing** in the nations of Bosnia and Albania left thousands dead.
- The Mexican government would like **amnesty** for illegal Mexican workers in the United States.
- After World War II, the Mexican government allowed the U.S. to build factories, known as **maquiladoras**, near the border the two countries share.
- The United States placed an **embargo** on Cuba after Castro nationalized its industries.
- **Inflation** brought Argentina to the edge of collapse.
- Argentina enacted economic **austerity** measures.
- After the death of Mao Zedong, China favored a limited **socialist market economy**.
- A **tsunami** struck Southeast Asia at the end of 2004.
- The **decolonization** of Africa started in the 1960s.
- The **apartheid** policies in South Africa brought **sanctions** from the rest of the world.
- Some leaders favored **Pan-Africanism** as a way to address problems across the continent.
- Arabs declared an **intifada** to protest Israeli actions.
- **Pan-Arabism** attempted to join Arab nations of the Middle East.
- The U.S. moved to a **pre-emptive strike** against Iraq.

Chapter Review

1. Select one region of the world covered in this chapter. Write a five-paragraph essay explaining how it has or has not moved toward greater freedom since World War II ended.

2. Create a Venn diagram to compare and contrast two regions discussed in this chapter. Then write a comparison and contrast paragraph about the two regions.

Novel Connections

Below is a list of books that relate to the time period covered in this chapter. The numbers in parentheses indicate the related Thematic Strands of the National Council for the Social Studies (NCSS).

Bernard Ashley. *Little Soldier*. Scholastic Inc., 2003. (IV, V, IX)

Simon Beecroft. *The Release of Nelson Mandela*. Gareth Stevens, 2004. (IV, VI, IX)

Margot Fortunato Galt. *Stop This War!: American Protest of the Conflict in Vietnam*. Lerner Publications Company, 2000. (II, V, VI, IX)

Elizabeth Laird. *Kiss the Dust*. Sagebrush Educational Resources, 1994. (IV, VI)

Carol Matas. *After the War*. Simon & Schuster, 1997. (III, IV, VI, X)

Nhuong Huynh Quyang. *The Land I Lost: Adventures of a Boy in Vietnam*. HarperTrophy, 1986. (III, IV, VI)

Skill Builder

Problem Solving and Decision Making

Identifying a problem and deciding what to do about it are two skills that everyone can use—from students to business executives to government officials. For example, you would like to go to the movies once a week. However, you never seem to have any money. What do you do? Say "Well, that's life" and never go to the movies? Or, do you figure out how you spend your money and make a decision how to save some for movies?

Identifying the Problem

You have identified the problem: You never have enough money.

To determine how you spend your money, you should gather information about your spending habits for a week. Make a list of what you buy and how much you spend for each thing. After a week, you should know how you spend your money.

Some things you have to buy. You cannot stop paying for subway passes to school and for lunch. But do you need a new CD every week? How about that snack of a soda and slice of pizza a couple of days a week?

Making the Decision

You have figured out how you spend your money. Some things are necessities like lunch. Other things are "luxuries" like new CDs.

Which do you want more:
- to go to the movies or to eat pizza?
- to go to the movies or to have the latest CD?

To help you decide, look at the advantages of each thing and the disadvantages of giving it up. For example, what do you gain by buying the latest CD? If you did not buy the latest CD, what would you lose?

Classroom Discussion

Discuss with students some of the broader topics covered in this chapter.

- What strategies could be used to help different ethnic and racial groups learn to respect one another?
- How can undocumented workers be brought into the United States?
- What are the advantages and disadvantages of pre-emptive war?
- In what ways can fair trade practices be encouraged?

Skill Builder

1. Students' choices of problems will vary; however, they should be able to use the five steps outlined in the Skill Builder to reach a solution.

2. Students' choices of problems will vary. Discussion should focus on two problems faced by the U.S. government and how to use the problem-solving steps.

Skill Builder, continued

Now ask yourself the same questions about going to the movies and eating pizza.

Look at your answers. Which choice offers you the most advantages and the least disadvantages? Choose the one that makes the most sense to you and follow it.

Evaluating the Solution/Decision

After a few weeks, review your decision. Evaluate how well it is working. Does it still make the most sense? Maybe going to the movies every week is not as much fun as you thought it would be. Maybe having pizza is more fun. You could change your decision.

To help you identify problems and make decisions, follow these steps:

1. Identify the problem.
2. Gather information about the problem.
3. List as many solutions as you can think of.
4. Review the advantages and disadvantages of each solution.
5. Decide on your solution.
6. Put your solution/decision into practice.
7. Review and evaluate your decision after a period of time.

Complete the following activities.

1. Think of a problem that you have. It could be a real problem or a made-up one. Go through Steps 1 to 5 to reach a possible solution. Then think of how you would evaluate whether your solution is working.

2. Discuss with a partner two problems that the national government is facing. Talk about how the government might work through Steps 2 to 7 for each problem.

Chapter 24

THE WORLD: OPPORTUNITIES AND CHALLENGES

developing nations

the environment

human rights

genocide

terrorism

Getting Focused

The study of history is the study of connections. Historians look to the past for the causes of later events and the effects of those events on later happenings. There is an old saying that "history repeats itself." It does not have to. People can change tomorrow by learning from yesterday and today. The goal of this special chapter is to show you that change can happen. Each case study provides an overview of an important issue that people face today. Each case study also presents some ways that people are tackling these issues.

Businesses and governments go through problem-solving and decision-making processes. Suppose a business is considering building a factory in China. It must identify possible problems and look for solutions. Only after the company has done that, can it decide whether it makes business sense to build the factory.

Suppose a nation is trying to reduce pollution from factories. The government gathers information about how factories are polluting the air. Then it investigates ways to stop the pollution. All this work has to be done before the government can write laws to stop or reduce pollution.

How would you solve the problems presented in this chapter?

Getting Focused

Read aloud together the material on page 397. Consider dividing the class into five groups, assigning one photograph to each group. Ask students to predict what they will be learning, based on the photographs.

Case Studies

This chapter presents five Case Studies of problems facing the world in the twenty-first century. Students will consider the issues of developing nations, the environment, human rights, genocide, and terrorism. The chapter presents an overview of each issue through data in charts and graphs, as well as offering evocative photographs.

Related Transparencies

T-1 World Map

T-13 The Developing World

CD Extension

Encourage students to use the reading comprehension, vocabulary reinforcement, and interactive timeline activities on the student CD.

Pre-Reading Discussion

1 Discuss with students issues covered in the chapter that are also in the current day's newspaper. You may wish to make available photocopies of recent news articles so that students can skim them and discuss the current events that most closely relate to the chapter content.

2 Before opening to the chapter, ask students to identify several problems they feel the world faces and should solve within their lifetimes. Keep a master list of ideas; see how well they match the chapter content. You may wish to assign topics not covered in the Case Studies as outside research.

The World: Opportunities and Challenges 397

Case Study 1: Developing Nations

Case Study Summary
Developing nations are those whose economies are based on agriculture and the export of natural resources. The standard of living is low in these nations, in contrast to that in an industrialized economy. Problems of developing nations include limited health care, high infant mortality rates, and malnutrition. Families tend to have many children. Another problem is debt incurred by accepting loans from industrialized nations. One option is to receive foreign aid in the form of grants. Another alternative to borrowing millions of dollars in loans is getting a microloan. Many people in the world could start their own businesses with less than $50.

Case Study Objective
Students will learn about the problems of developing nations in the twenty-first century.

Case Study Answers
1 Problems in developing nations include access to affordable health care, infant mortality, malnutrition, and repaying debts from foreign aid.

2 Some possible solutions include grants instead of loans, and microloans for small businesses. Several groups, including the Bill and Melinda Gates Foundation, are working to address health care issues.

Case Study 1: Developing Nations

- What are the problems in developing nations?
- What are some possible solutions?

In economic terms, the world is divided into rich nations and poor nations. The poor nations are called developing nations. Their economies are based on agriculture and the export of natural resources, and the standard of living is low. Developed nations have industrialized economies and a high standard of living. An industrialized economy is one in which the majority of people do not earn their living by farming. Instead, most people work in offices, stores, and factories.

Another way to look at developing and developed nations is by geographic location. Examine the map on this page. The rich, or developed, nations tend to be in the Northern Hemisphere, with the exception of Australia and New Zealand. The poor, or developing, nations are generally in the Southern Hemisphere. Think back to your study of the European colonization of Central and South America, Southeast Asia, and Africa. European efforts to keep their colonies economically dependent help to explain the lag in development of these nations.

Economists and sociologists talk about the standard of living of a nation. Standard of living measures the quality of life of a nation's people. It evaluates how much people are able to buy certain goods and services. Among these are food, housing, clothing, education, medical care, and recreation. Examine the table on the next page to learn more about the differences between developing and developed nations.

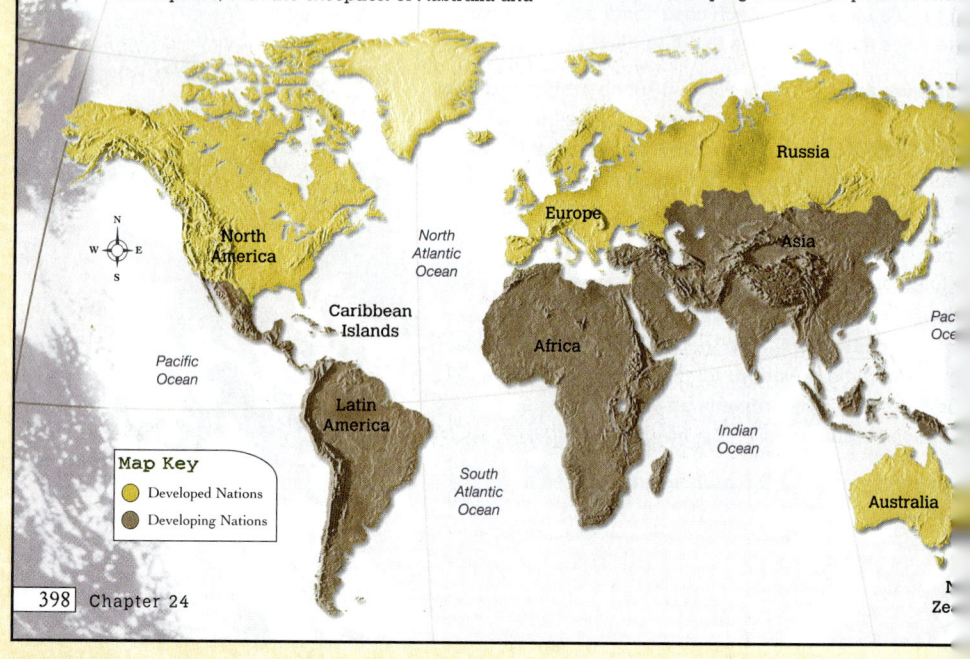

Map Key
- Developed Nations
- Developing Nations

Case Study Vocabulary
Introduce each of the following vocabulary terms to students.

Explain that *developing nations* are those with economies based on agriculture and exporting of natural resources. *Developing nations* are primarily found in the southern hemisphere.

An *industrialized economy* is one in which most people do not make their living by farming. In an *industrialized economy* most people work in factories or offices.

The *standard of living* measures the quality of life of the people within a nation. The *standard of living* includes the ability to afford education, health care, housing, food, and clothing. The rate of *infant mortality* is the death rate for children less than one year old. *Developing nations* generally have a high *infant mortality* rate.

Not getting enough to eat each day results in *malnutrition*. More than 200 million children suffer from *malnutrition*.

Selected Statistics of Developing and Developed Nations

Nation	Per Capita Income*	Infant Mortality Rate (deaths per 1,000 births)	Total Fertility Rate (births per woman)	Motor Vehicles (per 1,000 people)	Telephones*** (per 100 people)	Televisions (per 1,000 people)
Angola	$1,900	118	7	5	1	13
Bangladesh	$1,700	67	4	2	n/a ♦	6
Cambodia	$2,000	73	5	1	n/a	9
China	$5,000	37	2**	10	9	321
Peru	$5,200	37	3	44	6	126
Germany	$27,000	5	1	554 (1991 est.)	59	567
Italy	$26,800	5	1	617	46	528
USA	$32,778	7	2	798	67	806

*Per capita income is the average income. All numbers are given in U.S. dollars.
**China has an official policy to discourage population growth.
*** The statistics for telephones do not include cell phones.
♦ n/a means not available.

Problems of Developing Nations

Many people in developing nations live in rural areas and make their living from agriculture.

Because they have limited money, developing nations have limited health care systems. As a result, the infant mortality, or death rate for children under one year of age, is high in these countries. Examine the table to see the contrast in infant mortality rates between developing and developed nations.

Even if children survive infancy in developing nations, many will die before they reach adulthood. Two million children die each year from diseases, such as measles, which can be prevented with vaccinations. Their parents are too poor to pay for the shots. In some cases, their nations are too poor to import the vaccines and distribute them through free clinics.

The world's population is now more than 6 billion people. Almost 800 million people suffer from malnutrition. They do not get enough to eat each day to meet their minimum energy needs. In certain areas of the world, such as sub-Saharan Africa, people live on less than $US2 per day. Over 200 million children under the age of five are malnourished.

As nations become more developed, infant mortality rates decline. Birth rates have also declined. There are several reasons for this. First, couples no longer need to have so many children to be sure that some will live. Second, raising children has become more expensive. Third, as a nation becomes wealthier, education becomes more available to women. Having an education and fewer children frees women to work outside the home.

> **World Food Day**
> **October 16**
>
> World Food Day is organized by the Food and Agriculture Organization of the United Nations. Its goal is to educate people about world hunger and the need to end the problem. More than 150 nations, including the United States, participate in the event each year.

Case Study 1

Chart Extension

Lead students to identify which nations are developing and which are industrialized (developed). Based on those categories, have them skim the chart looking for anything that surprises them. (the U.S. infant mortality rate, for example, or that there are more televisions in Angola than in Bangladesh or Cambodia)

You may wish to have students create bar graphs of the figures to present the information another way. Another useful exercise might be to have students calculate what change would be necessary to make the lowest and highest numbers equal in any category. For instance, a person in Peru would have to make about six times the current per capita income to equal the U.S. rate.

Information about other countries can be found online by searching for the CIA World Factbook.

Map Extension

Ask students to use the map on page 398 to answer the following questions:

- Which nations in the southern hemisphere are developed? (Australia and New Zealand)
- Which Asian nation has an industrialized economy? (Japan)
- In what geographic direction will industrialization move? (south)

Extension

Seventy percent of the people in the developing world live in Asia and the Pacific. Nearly two-thirds of the world's undernourished live in this region. More than 200 million undernourished people live in India alone. The highest percentage of undernourished people, however, is in sub-Saharan Africa. Malnutrition may play a role in the deaths of the almost 13 million children who die annually of preventable infections and diseases.

Case Study 1

Foreign Aid

A major problem for developing nations is debt repayment. While they were colonies, developing nations exported raw materials and imported manufactured goods. After independence, the new nations had to borrow large sums of money to modernize and industrialize. These nations continue to borrow millions of dollars a year. In some countries, a large part of the borrowed money does not go to infrastructure—to buy machines and build roads. It goes to buy such basics as food and medical care and to pay the interest on the loans. Interest payments are a heavy burden on the borrowing nations.

In 2005, a group of 28 developed nations agreed to give grants of money to the very poorest nations rather than loans. In addition, the loans that these poor nations already had were forgiven. They do not have to repay them.

The money grants are part of what is called foreign aid. Foreign aid is economic and military assistance given by one nation to another. The Marshall Plan, after World War II, was one of the first U.S. foreign aid programs. Since then, the United States has contributed more than $460 billion in foreign aid. About $160 billion was for military help. Today, the United States is the second largest contributor of foreign aid in the world. Japan ranks first.

Zimbabweans wait in line for USA food aid.

VIEWPOINT

Don't Just Throw Money at the World's Poor

"Poor countries face high tariffs, quotas, subsidized competition from rich nations industries such as food processing, textile and agriculture. The World Bank estimate that... dismantling of these barriers coul be worth $350 billion to the developing world in the next decade and could lift 144 million people out of poverty. Reducing trade barriers would also help consumers in the industrialized nations."

—Jeffrey E. Garten, BusinessWee
March 7, 20

NAMES IN THE NEW

The following international organizations work with developing nations on economic growth:

World Bank — The UN founded World Bank in 1944 to lend money member nations for investment, forei trade, and repayment of foreign deb Today, it serves almost all of the worl nations. The full name of the bank is International Bank for Development a Reconstruction. Through contributions fr member nations, the World Bank provides ab 10 percent of the world's foreign aid.

International Monetary Fund (IMF) — T IMF, founded in 1945, is an agency of the UN. purpose is to promote economic cooperati among its 184 member nations. It works w nations to set exchange rates for their money a to expand foreign trade.

World Trade Organization (WTO) — The W was created in 1995. It oversees compliance w international trade agreements and rules violations by member nations. It has more th 148 members, including all the major nations the world.

Viewpoint Extension

1 Ask students to use library resources or the Internet to research a developing country that manufactures textiles or clothing. Have students explain their findings to the class.

2 Challenge students to find out why high tariffs were a cause of the American Revolution. Have them compare this information to today's problems.

Picturing History

In 2003, after HIV/AIDS, poor economic policies, and drought, many communities in Zimbabwe faced disaster. Several private organizations joined to form MAPP, the Market Assistance Pilot Program. The United States Agency for International Development (USAID) funded the program and offered Title II sorghum as a low-cost and drought-resistant alternative to corn. The demand soon accelerated from 30 tons to 300 tons a day. Shown in the photograph on page 400 is a delivery of cornmeal to Zimbabwe.

Names in the News Extension

Have students regularly skim the major newspaper in your area during the time you are studying this chapter. Ask them to look for news articles on the three organizations listed on page 400 or any other groups that deal with the issues addressed in the Case Studies.

Extension

Total amounts of aid are not always indicative of large donors. Using percentage of the gross national product as an indicator, the biggest givers in 2001 were Denmark, Norway, the Netherlands, Luxembourg, and Sweden. With a population of only 16.3 million, the Netherlands gave nearly one-third of the U.S. contribution. The United States ranks last among the wealthiest nations in percentage of gross national product marked for foreign aid, about 0.1 percent. Public perception, however, is inaccurate, supposing about 24 percent of the budget goes toward foreign aid.

Making a Difference: Microloans

A microloan is a loan of money in a small amount, such as $40. That may not seem like much, but in Bangladesh it could establish a woman in business making and selling bamboo stools. That is how microlending began.

In 1974, Muhammad Yunus was visiting a village in Bangladesh and met a woman making stools from bamboo. She earned very little because of an arrangement she had with a supplier. He gave her the bamboo and she had to sell him her finished stools. The supplier paid her what he wanted and then sold the stools for much more.

Dr. Yunus was a professor of economics and he began to think about the woman's problem. She had no capital, or money, to buy the bamboo. If she could actually buy bamboo, she could sell her stools herself and make a profit. Instead, the bamboo supplier was making a profit. Dr. Yunus studied the village. In all, he found 42 villagers who could start their own businesses if they had some money to invest. How much money did they need? Twenty-seven dollars—just $27 for all 42 villagers.

Dr. Yunus started the Grameen Bank to lend people like these villagers small amounts of money so they could start their own businesses. *Grameen* means "village." The Grameen Bank is not a charity. It charges interest on its loans just like any other bank and has branches throughout Bangladesh. About 90 percent of its loans are made to women starting their own businesses.

Today, the Grameen Bank is international. By the early 2000s, the bank had made 3.7 million loans around the world. Women make up 96 percent of the borrowers.

Other people have learned from Dr. Yunus' idea. For example, in Kazakhstan, the Asian Credit Fund makes similar microloans. The XacBank helps small borrowers get businesses started in Mongolia.

Microloans are used throughout Indonesia.

The Green Revolution

The Green Revolution was a program to increase crop yields—or the amount of food grown per acre. In the 1940s, scientists created new kinds of wheat that produced more grain. The new plants were also more resistant to disease. India, Pakistan, and nations in Latin America began growing the new wheat. New types of corn and rice were also developed.

The new plants more than doubled grain harvests worldwide between 1950 and 1990. However, the new plants required irrigation systems and chemical fertilizers and pesticides. Peasant farmers could not afford these and lost their land to larger farm owners with more money. The use of chemicals and large amounts of water for irrigation created environmental problems. Despite these problems, the Green Revolution improved living standards for millions of people.

investigative reporting

With a partner, research and prepare a presentation about one of the following programs that works with developing nations:

- Bill and Melinda Gates Foundation
- Grameen Bank
- Green Revolution
- Food and Agriculture Organization (FAO)
- World Food Day

Case Study 1 | 401

Picturing History

Indonesian women working in a home-based business are pictured on page 401. The United Nations designated November 18, 2004, as the beginning of the International Year of Microcredit. Eight nations were targeted for special assistance: Rwanda, Pakistan, Mozambique, Mexico, Indonesia, the Dominican Republic, Cambodia, and Afghanistan. Students from the Harvard Business School and a global team led the project. Have students use library resources or the Internet to investigate the outcome of the International Year of Microcredit.

Investigative Reporting

Students' presentations will vary but should be based on one of the five programs mentioned on page 401. Have students present their findings to the class by using the Student Presentation Builder on the student CD.

Case Study 1 | 401

Case Study 2: The Environment

Case Study Summary
The environment is composed of both renewable and nonrenewable resources. Industrialization changed the relationship of humans and the environment, requiring the use of more resources. Although developed nations account for about 20 percent of the world's population, their populations use 86 percent of the non-energy and 70 percent of the energy resources.

Developing nations are trying to industrialize; however, they often lack the money needed to create environmentally friendly industries. They may sell nonrenewable resources just to be able to feed their large populations.

One solution is sustainable development, which uses natural resources without endangering future supplies. Nongovernmental organizations (NGOs) are working to help preserve the environment. Individuals can also help by becoming active and by reducing, reusing, recycling, and composting.

Case Study Objective
Students will learn about the current challenges facing the world's environment.

Picturing History
The cartoon in the center of page 402 depicts a humorous look at global warming. Have students identify the scene and explain why it is amusing.

Case Study 2: The Environment

▶ What are some of the issues affecting the environment?
▶ What specific environmental issues face developing nations?
▶ Explain five things you can do to help the environment.

When people talk about the environment, they mean all the things around us in nature—our natural resources. The environment includes both renewable and nonrenewable natural resources.

Renewable resources are water, air, soil, and plant and animal life. They renew or replace themselves over time. For example, when trees die in a forest fire, new trees will grow in the same forest over time. When topsoil wears out and blows away, new topsoil will form—one inch every 200 years.

Nonrenewable resources are those that cannot be replaced. Once they are used up, they are gone. Fossil fuels and minerals such as iron and copper are nonrenewable resources. Fossil fuels are coal, natural gas, and petroleum, or oil.

The Industrial Revolution greatly changed how people affected the environment. In early farming economies, there was little need to use nonrenewable resources. Horses or oxen pulled plows, and water power moved the wheels that ground wheat. Women cooked over an open fire and sewed clothes by candlelight.

However, as nations began to industrialize, they needed more and more renewable and nonrenewable resources. Coal and petroleum became important sources of energy. The smoke from factories burning coal began to pollute the air in industrial cities. Wastes from factories and cities flowed into rivers and polluted them.

Earlier farmers used to let some fields lie fallow—or unused—each year to allow the soil replace nutrients. As populations increased, farmers had to plant more and more fields eve year to grow enough to feed the increasing population. As a result, soil began to wear out from overfarming. Forests w cut down faster than new tr could grow. The lumber was needed to build houses and factories as well as ships to carry all the new manufactu goods.

One way to understand rapid use of resources is to look at the production of iro in Great Britain. In 1757, Gr Britain produced 18,000 tor of iron. In 1850, it produced 2.25 million tons iron. This jump in production increased not o the iron sold, but also the amount of iron ore coal used. Coal was needed to power the hug furnaces that made iron from iron ore.

Today, even the use of resources is sharpl divided between developed and developing nations. About 20 percent of the world's population lives in developed nations. Howeve they use 86 percent of the world's natural no energy resources and 70 percent of its energ resources.

Case Study Answers

1 Some of the issues affecting the environment include conserving nonrenewable resources, the problems of developing nations selling their natural resources, air and water pollution, deforestation, soil erosion and desertification, and sustainable development.

2 Specific issues that developing nations face include the loss of resources because of the current need to sell lumber or minerals for a profit. Developing nations also lack the money needed to industrialize in an environmentally friendly way.

3 Five things that can help the environment are writing to legislators, joining an NGO, following the 3Rs, composting, and educating others.

The Dilemma of Developing Nations

Environmentalism is the movement to conserve, or save, and improve the environment. Environmentalists want to save the world's natural resources and improve our quality of life. For example, if air pollution is reduced, the health of an area's residents will improve. There will be fewer cases of asthma and other respiratory diseases.

When it comes to the environment, developing nations face a dilemma, or difficult problem. Many developing nations still rely on selling raw materials or cash crops for export. Nations like the Philippines are cutting down their forests with little effort to replace them. Other nations like South Africa and Nigeria are selling their mineral resources and petroleum reserves. They need the money that their resources will bring, but selling those resources means losing them forever.

In addition, developing nations use much of their export earnings to buy basics for their citizens. These nations are trying to industrialize, but they often lack the money to buy the technology needed to create environmentally friendly industries.

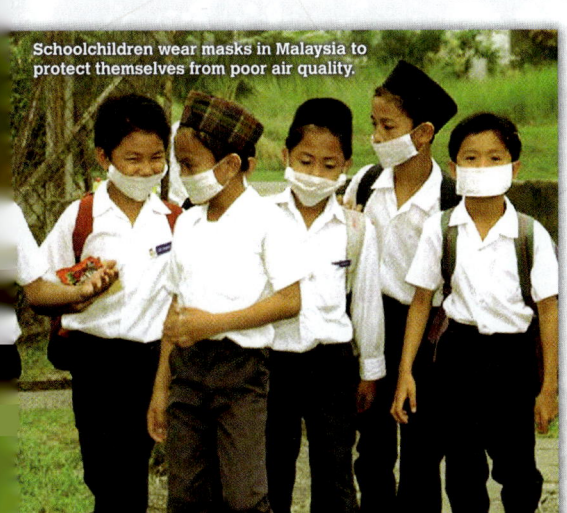

Schoolchildren wear masks in Malaysia to protect themselves from poor air quality.

Air Pollution

A variety of chemicals is released into the air every day. Among them are carbon monoxide and nitrogen oxide from car engines, factories, cigarette smoke, and jet planes. These and other chemicals create air pollution. Acid rain and global warming are two results of air pollution.

Acid rain contains high levels of acid from certain chemicals released into the air. Acid rain falling into rivers and lakes kills fish. It also kills trees and eats away marble on buildings.

Global warming is an increase in the temperature of the earth's surface. By the 1990s, the upward trend in temperature had become noticeable. Many scientists believe that human activity is responsible for global warming. The increase in world population and the industrialization of more nations result in the burning of more fossil fuels. These produce large quantities of greenhouse gases, which heat up the atmosphere.

To reduce air pollution, some nations are supporting efforts to develop other forms of energy. Among these alternative sources of power are solar, water, wind, and nuclear. In 1997, more than 150 nations negotiated the Kyoto Protocol, or agreement, to reduce the production of carbon dioxide and other greenhouse gases. The United States, Australia, and India, among other nations, have not ratified the treaty. The Bush administration agreed with business leaders that adding pollution controls would be expensive and put an unfair burden on U.S. industry. Developing nations gave similar reasons for not joining the agreement.

Case Study 2

Picturing History

Asian schoolchildren wearing protective masks are shown in the photograph on page 403. Ages ten through eighteen are crucial years for lung development. If lungs are underdeveloped because of pollution, they will probably remain that way into adulthood. A short-term effect of low lung function includes more severe, long-lasting colds. Cardiovascular and respiratory illnesses are long-term effects that can lead to an increased risk of death.

Extension

Studies show that by 2025, one-fourth of America's energy supplies could come from agricultural energy, such as biofuel, and renewable energy, such as solar and wind power. Because of national security concerns, politicians are seriously considering a major change in energy policies. The idea also appeals to labor groups, because developing these new energies can provide new industrial jobs.

Case Study Vocabulary

Discuss each of the vocabulary terms with students.

The *environment* is a term for the things that are around us in nature. The *environment* includes earth, air, and water.

Renewable resources are those that renew or replace themselves over time. Trees growing back after a fire are an example of *renewable resources*. The resources that cannot be replaced are *nonrenewable resources*. *Nonrenewable resources* include minerals and fossil fuels.

The wearing away of the thin layer of topsoil is called *soil erosion*. Overfarming is one of the major causes of *soil erosion*.

Case Study 2

Picturing History

The photograph on page 404 shows trees logged in the rain forest being measured. One source estimates that 80 percent of the natural forests of Earth have been destroyed. Since 1900, as much as 90 percent of the coastal rain forests of West Africa have been cut down. This destruction may have contributed to the 20 terrible years of drought in Central Africa. The lost rain forests of Ghana, Nigeria, and Côte d'Ivoire may have helped to create rain in drought-prone regions. The largest surviving areas of rain forest, in Indonesia and Brazil, are rapidly being destroyed by fires, logging, cattle-grazing, and land-clearing for farming.

Extension

A five-year drought that began in 1968 in the Sahel, a savanna bordering areas of West Africa, hastened the approach of the Sahara Desert from the north. In the United States and Mexico, the Sonoran and Chihuahuan Deserts have grown more stark as wildlife and native plants diminish. Human activity depleting the groundwater contributes to the losses. Scientists call desertification a runaway phenomenon. It is nearly impossible to stop once it begins, and it cannot be reversed within a human lifetime.

Rain Forests and Deforestation

The Amazon River Basin in South America is the largest rain forest in the world. Other areas with large rain forests are in Central America, Central Africa, and Southeast Asia. Rain forests are home to thousands of species, or types, of birds, insects, animals, and plants. Fifty percent of all trees in the world grow in the rain forests. It is estimated that the trees in the Amazon provide 40 percent of the world's oxygen exchange and are vitally important to the purification of the world's air and water vapor quality.

Brazilian environmental agents inspect logged mahogany in the Amazon forest.

The major danger to the rain forests is deforestation. This is the cutting down of forests without planting new trees. For example, the Amazon rain forest is 1.6 million square miles. However, every year ranchers, developers, and loggers illegally clear more and more of the land. Experts estimate that the area loses 6,600 square miles of rain forest each year. In all, 20 percent of the Amazon rain forest has disappeared.

The Brazilian government is often powerless against the armed gunmen who protect the wealthy cattle ranchers and loggers. However,

Water: Fast Facts

- Only 45 percent of the people in developing nations have safe water, whereas 96 percent of the people in developed nations have safe water.
- 95 percent of cities around the world dump raw sewage into surface water (rivers, lakes, and ocea
- Other forms of water pollution are solid wastes such as soda cans and plastic bottles, chemicals from factories, pesticides, fertilizers, and oil spills from oil tankers.
- 80 percent of water worldwide is used in farming, but 60 percent of that is wasted. Developing nations cannot afford the irrigation systems that use water efficiently.

Soil Erosion and Desertification

Soil erosion is the wearing away of the thin layer of topsoil. This is the fertile soil that needed to grow plants. Overfarming is the major reason for soil erosion. However, overgrazing by animals and cutting down trees also cause soil erosion and desertification. This occurs when land dries out so much that it becomes desert. The UN reports that about 15 million acres of land become desert every year.

The hardest hit area in the world is North Africa. Desertification, along with years of little or no rain, caused a famine the region in the 1970s and 1980s. With n way to feed themselves, hundreds of thousands died. Survivors left their homes and became refugees.

in 2005, the murder of a Roman Catholic nun Sister Dorothy Stang, forced the Brazilian government to act.

Sister Stang opposed the destruction of th rain forest and worked to protect the rights of native population living there. Ranchers and loggers forced them into near slave-like work arrangements. After Sister Stang's murder, the Brazilian government sent in federal police to investigate and set up two new preserves in t Amazon rain forest. Some 9.2 million acres w now be protected.

Extension

To grow grass for cattle, people slash and burn thousands of acres of rain forest. For each quarter-pound fast-food burger that comes from a cow originally from rain forest land, 55 square feet of rain forest is destroyed. Have students find out how many quarter-pound burgers local fast-food establishments sell daily. Then ask them to figure out how many square feet of rain forest those burgers required.

What You Can Do for the Environment

You can write to local officials, state legislators, or members of Congress stating your position.

You can join a nongovernmental organization (NGO) that shares your viewpoint on environmental issues.

You can follow the 3Rs:

Reduce: Cut down on what you use.
- Use reusable containers for food instead of plastic bags.
- Don't keep the water running while you brush your teeth.
- Turn off the lights when you leave a room.

Reuse: Figure out ways to reuse things.
- Don't throw away the plastic bags from the grocery store. Use them as trash bags.
- Use the blank side of school assignment sheets for scratch paper.

Recycle: Recycle everything that you can.
- Many communities have curbside pickup to recycle paper, cans and bottles, cardboard, and clothes.
- Cartridges from printers and fax machines can be sent back free to the manufacturer to be recycled.
- Cell phones, computers, and printers can be recycled. Contact your community to find out where and how to recycle them.

4. If you live in a place where you can have a garden, you can add a fourth R: *Rot*. Rot? Those banana peels and wilted lettuce leaves along with grass clippings and tree leaves make good compost. Compost is a natural fertilizer. You can spread it around trees and bushes and on your garden to help trees and plants grow.

Sustainable Development

Sustainable development is economic development that uses natural resources to meet present needs without endangering supplies for the future. In other words, those who favor sustainable development believe people must make better use of resources. They believe that each generation must ensure that there are natural resources left for future generations.

Those who support sustainable development urge people to use less natural resources. For example, an advocate for sustainable development would not call for more oil drilling. Instead, he or she would try to influence automakers to produce—and consumers to buy—smaller, more fuel-efficient cars.

NGOs and the Environment

There are a number of nongovernmental organizations (NGOs) that work to save the environment. These organizations are often described as "green." Among the well-known U.S. conservation and environmental NGOs are the World Wildlife Fund, Audubon Society, Nature Conservancy, and Sierra Club.

Investigative Reporting

With a partner, choose one of the following topics to learn more about. Create a poster to explain the issue and what is being done about it on the national or international level.

- air pollution
- water pollution (rivers or oceans)
- desertification
- deforestation
- energy use
- building dams

Extension

In 2004, Wangari Maathai became the first African woman and the first environmentalist to receive the Nobel Peace Prize. Her work among rural women in Kenya spread to the Green Belt Movement, which has planted more than 30 million trees. She also protested the human rights abuses under the former president of Kenya. For that she was jailed, but she later became a member of Kenya's parliament and deputy minister for the environment. Have students use library resources or the Internet to find out more about the Wangari Maathai Foundation, which was founded with the Nobel Prize money, or about the Green Belt Movement.

Investigative Reporting

Students' posters will vary but should explain one of the six issues listed and strategies at the national or international level.

Extension

Students interested in literature or ecology may wish to read some of John Steinbeck's nature writing. Especially notable is *Sea of Cortez*, written about a six-week voyage he took in 1939 with his friend, the biologist Ed Ricketts. Their purpose was to collect small marine animals in the Gulf of California. Some people feel that *Sea of Cortez* is one of the most important books written about nature during the twentieth century.

Case Study 3: Human Rights

Case Study Summary
Human rights are the basic rights that all people need. The United Nations adopted a Universal Declaration of Human Rights in 1976. However, only 65 countries have ratified the document. Abuses include slavery, child labor, selling women and children, censorship, torturing political prisoners, and using land mines.

The UN's International Labour Organization investigates the use of child labor. Although child labor is a human rights abuse, more than 200 million children around the world work in domestic labor. Children also serve as soldiers in many nations. About half of the 50 million refugees in the world are children. The UN's refugee agency, the United Nations High Commissioner for Refugees, assists more than 17 million people in 115 countries.

Case Study Objective
Students will learn about the issues surrounding human rights and their violations, particularly as they relate to children.

Case Study Answers
1 Human rights are basic rights that all people need. They include life, liberty, and security of person.

2 Globally, human rights have been addressed by documents of the United Nations, by the UN's International Labour Organization, and by NGOs such as Human Rights Watch and Amnesty International.

Case Study Vocabulary
Discuss the following vocabulary term with students.

A *refugee* is someone who flees his or her country because of a well-founded fear of persecution based on religion, race, nationality, political opinion, or membership in a particular social group. A *refugee* either cannot go back home or is afraid to do so.

Case Study 3: Human Rights

▶ What are human rights?
▶ Describe how human rights have been addressed globally.

You may be surprised to learn that not all nations agree on a definition of basic human rights. A nation's cultural values influence its ideas about human rights. For example, the United States values freedom of the individual. It grants rights to women, such as the right to vote and to own property. In a nation influenced by Islamic teachings, women have fewer rights. For example, women in Saudi Arabia are not allowed to drive. In many developing nations, marriages are arranged by parents when the future bride and groom are still children.

In 1948, the UN drafted the Universal Declaration of Human Rights. The document was an attempt to define basic human rights. (See pages 437–440 for the complete

Universal Declaration of Human Rights

In 1976, the Declaration became international law after being ratified by 35 countries. To date, 65 countries have ratified the document.

"**Article 1** All human beings are born free and equal in dignity and rights. . . .

Article 2 Everyone is entitled to all the rights and freedoms set forth in this Declaration, without distinction of any kind, such as race, color, sex, language, religion, political or other opinion, national or social origin, property, birth or other status. . . ."

UN trained specialists clear land mines in Iraq.

document.) However, it is not legally binding. Nations do not have to guarantee the rights outlined in the document.

In order to make nations responsible for guaranteeing these basic human rights, the UN over the years has written additional documents on areas of human rights. These conventions, agreements, and treaties are legally binding the nations that ratify them. However, not all nations ratify them. Some of the UN's human rights documents

- make genocide a crime
- describe how prisoners of war should be treated, banning torture
- guarantee political and civil rights
- eliminate discrimination against women
- guarantee freedoms and protections to children

VIEWPOINT

Capital Punishment
One issue that many people do not agree about is capital punishment—or the use of death as a penalty. Many people consider it an abuse of human rights. More than nations have banned the death penalty. However, a majority of states in the United States continue to impose the death sentence for certain crimes.

Picturing History
The photograph on page 406 shows a United Nations specialist clearing a land mine in Iraq. The Mines Advisory Group (MAG), which shared the Nobel Peace Prize in 1997, has worked in Iraq continuously since 1992, the only demining NGO to do so. They have cleared more than one million land mines in 25 million square meters. MAG works in 22 countries.

Human Rights Abuses

What specifically are human rights abuses? The following is a partial list of abuses that human rights organizations are working to end:

- murder of political opponents
- jailing of political opponents without fair trials
- torture of political prisoners
- censorship of the media
- slavery
- trafficking in (selling) women and children
- discrimination against women in education, employment, and the legal system
- the use of landmines
- discrimination against people with HIV/AIDS
- bombing of civilians in wartime
- discrimination against minorities in education, employment, and the legal system
- the use of threats and/or violence against workers attempting to unionize their workplaces

How successful are efforts to protect human rights around the world? The answer to that question varies greatly. A great deal has been done by governments, the United Nations, and nongovernmental organizations to highlight human rights violations and end them, but much remains to be done.

The True Story of a Child Slave

Francis Bok writes and lectures against slavery. He captivates his audience because he tells a true story. It is the story of his 10 years as a slave—not 100 years ago, but from 1986 to 1996.

Bok was born in Sudan in North Africa. One day when he was seven, he was seized by Arab militiamen near his home village. He and other young children who were in the market that day were tied up and taken away. They were sold for forced labor. Bok's family and everyone in his village were killed the day he was taken captive. The militiamen forced them into an auditorium and set fire to it.

A rich farmer and his family took Bok as a slave. Bok's job was to take care of the family's goats and cattle. He lived in a shed with the animals and ate scraps of food the family gave him. The farmer's children beat him for fun.

"I never complained, because I knew that if I complained I would get hurt," Bok says.

When he was fourteen, Bok tried to escape. He was caught and beaten. The farmer threatened to kill him if he tried to escape again. Bok tried again and was caught. The farmer aimed his gun at Bok while the farmer's family laughed. Bok thought he was going to die. However, the farmer did not shoot him. He untied him, and Bok spent another three years as a slave.

When he was seventeen, Bok made a successful escape. With help from a Muslim truck driver, Bok was able to reach Khartoum, the capital of Sudan. He was sent to refugee camps and finally, with UN help, made his way to the United States. Bok now works to end slavery.

Bio Facts

- Born in 1979 in Sudan.
- Captured and enslaved in 1986.
- Escaped in 1996; went to Cairo and ultimately to Fargo, North Dakota, in 1999.
- Began working with the American Anti-Slavery Group in Boston in 2000.
- Testified before the U.S. Senate Committee on Foreign Relations in 2000.
- Met U.S. President George W. Bush at the signing of the Sudan Peace Act in 2002.
- In 2002, torchbearer for Salt Lake City Winter Olympic Games.
- Published autobiography *Escape from Slavery* in 2004.

Biography Extension

Bok came to the United States knowing little English. Assisted by a group of Lutherans, he lived in Fargo, North Dakota, for five months. Determined to leave the area because of the extreme cold, he was working two jobs to save for his education when the president of the American Anti-Slavery Group, Dr. Charles Jacobs, persuaded him to come to Boston. Despite Bok's assurance that he was fine now that he was out of slavery, Jacobs persisted in his offers of help. Bok says his favorite movie is *The Ten Commandments*, because of its emphasis on deliverance from slavery.

Viewpoint Extension

1 Challenge students to find statements in their local newspaper that either support capital punishment or oppose it.

2 Ask students to form groups that either support or oppose the death penalty. Have each group do research on the topic. Conduct a classroom debate on the issue. Be sure students support their opinions with facts they find in their research.

Extension

Students may be interested in the work of bomb-sniffing dogs working in Afghanistan to help clear land mines. Land mines wound, maim, or kill some 30 Afghani civilians daily. Suggest that students use library resources or the Internet to find out more about the work of German shepherds and Belgian malinois.

Students may also be interested in the HALO Trust, an organization that specializes in the removal of the debris of war.

Case Study 3

Picturing History

The photograph at the top of page 408 shows child labor in a marketplace. The problem of child labor is particularly acute in South Asia, where children make up one-fourth of the unskilled labor force. South Asia has more than 80 million children working, many of them sold into servitude to repay small family loans. India has one of the highest rates of child labor in the world, with one estimate at 140 million children working, at least 10 million of them as slaves. Many of the children work in carpet, leather, garment, or footwear industries.

Extension

Early in the twenty-first century, the United States assisted some 4,000 Sudanese boys in immigrating to the U.S. Have students use library resources or the Internet to find out more about the so-called "Lost Boys of Sudan."

Child Labor

Slavery, or forced labor, is just one way that children are the victims of human rights abuse. The International Labour Organization (ILO), an agency of the UN, investigates child labor around the world. The agency has found that domestic labor is "one of the worst forms of child labour." Domestic laborers work in someone's home, often doing the cooking and cleaning. There is little regulation for this form of work, and more than 200 million children around the world work in domestic labor. Some are as young as five years old.

World Day Against Child Labor – June 12
The goal of this day is to raise people's awareness about the worldwide abuses of children through labor.

Burma has yet to institute child labor laws.

ILO studies find that domestic labor exploits, or takes advantage of, children. It may include selling of children as slaves, or employing them in work that is hazardous or harmful to their health, such as in factories. Some employers pay the children nothing for their work, but give them a place to sleep and a little food to eat.

Child Soldiers

The ILO also investigates the use of children as soldiers. In the early 2000s, the ILO conservatively estimated that 300,000 children were serving in armed conflicts worldwide. The ILO bans the use of child soldiers, as do many international documents. However, guerrilla groups often recruit children for their forces. Governments who fight the guerrillas also use child soldiers.

Child soldiers fought in the Liberian Civil War.

Some children are kidnapped and forced into fighting. Other groups recruit children by promising them food and protection in the midst of civil war.

Children are considered good soldiers because they obey orders. Also, they are more willing to take risks than adult soldiers. Both paramilitary units and guerrillas use children as decoys. Children can be sent into an area to distract victims. Then adult soldiers move in and open fire.

When the fighting is over, or when children are removed from the armed groups, they have a difficult time adjusting to normal life. They have never had a childhood. They have been denied an education. As a result, they lack the skills to earn a living.

Extensions

1 Kailash Satyarthi has made rescuing children from slavery in his native India a priority. Using a three-pronged approach, the former engineering teacher has rescued some 40,000 former slaves, almost 30,000 of them children. The strategy of his South Asian Coalition Against Child Servitude includes raids on businesses that exploit child labor, rehabilitating the children and giving them job training, and mobilizing the media. Satyarthi was attacked in 2004 for his attempts to free children from a circus.

2 At home, have students select five pieces of clothing or footwear they own. Ask them to inspect the labels and to list where each garment was made. Then ask them to use library resources or the Internet to check for child labor practices in those countries.

3 Students may be interested in learning more about Craig Kielburger who, at age twelve, founded Free the Children, an NGO that works to end child slavery.

Convention on the Rights of the Child

Article 2—[Nations] shall respect and [en]sure the rights set forth in the present [Co]nvention to each child within their [jur]isdiction without discrimination of any kind [irr]espective of the child's or his or her parent's [l]egal guardian's race, colour, sex, language, [re]ligion, political or other opinion, national, [eth]nic or social origin, property, disability, [birt]h or other status."

Refugees in Search of a Home

[W]hat happens to the victims of human [?] rights abuses, genocide, and war crimes? [The] United Nations High Commissioner for [Ref]ugees (UNHCR), the UN's refugee agency, [esti]mates that there are 50 million refugees in [the] world today. About half of them are children.

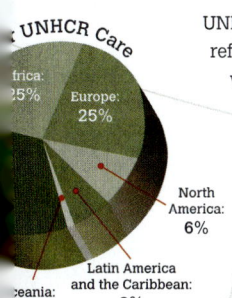

UNHCR Care
- [A]frica: [?]5%
- Europe: 25%
- North America: 6%
- Latin America and the Caribbean: 8%
- [O]ceania: <1%

UNHCR defines a refugee as "someone who flees his or her country because of a well-founded fear of persecution for reasons of race, religion, nationality, political opinion or membership in a [par]ticular social group; a refugee either cannot [retu]rn home or is afraid to do so."

[T]he Universal Declaration of Human [Righ]ts guarantees refugees the right to seek [asyl]um. This is a safe place with food, water, [shel]ter, and medical care. UNHCR protects [and] assists more than 17 million refugees in [120] countries. Many of these people live in [refu]gee camps while they wait for a safe [retu]rn to their home countries. Most, however, [can] never return home and are waiting for [rese]ttlement in another country.

NAMES IN THE NEWS

Nongovernmental Organization (NGO): An NGO is a private organization that usually does not receive any government funding. NGOs work to achieve specific goals. Labor unions, conservation groups, and women's rights organizations are NGOs.

Amnesty International (AI): AI is a global NGO with over 1.8 million members in 150 countries and territories. It campaigns to have a single set of human rights recognized by all nations. Its members want all people everywhere to be protected by the UN's Universal Declaration of Human Rights.

Human Rights Watch (HRW): HRW is also a global NGO dedicated to protecting human rights. It publicizes human rights abuses "to shame abusers and . . . put pressure on them to reform their conduct." It also pressures groups such as the UN and the European Union to remove military and economic aid from governments violating their citizens' human rights.

investigative reporting

With a partner, conduct research and prepare a report on one of the following organizations:
- Amnesty International
- Human Rights Watch
- International Labour Organization (ILO)
- International Programme on the Elimination of Child Labour (IPEC)
- United Nations Refugee Agency (UNHCR)
- UNICEF

Case Study 3 | 409

Picturing History

The photograph at the bottom of page 408 shows a child soldier. The problem of kidnapping children to become soldiers has caused the nation of Uganda to take extraordinary measures. Already some 20,000 children, most under the age of thirteen, have been lost to a cult, the Lord's Resistance Army, in northern Uganda. To protect their children, families walk them several miles every night to sanctuaries set up in schools, hospitals, and public buildings. There, they sleep in a group on woven mats, hoping to avoid being abducted. The problem has been largely overlooked because of the genocide in neighboring Sudan.

Names in the News Extension

Divide the class into two groups, assigning each group one of the NGOs listed on page 409. Have them imagine that they are working for that group. Ask them to address one of the problems in this Case Study as they think the members of the NGO might. Have them share their recommendations with the class.

Chart Extension

Challenge students to use library resources or the Internet to create additional circle graphs representing breakdowns of the top five areas listed on page 409. What percentage of refugees in Asia are from Cambodia, for example? You may wish to divide the class into five groups, assigning each group one of the regions listed.

Investigative Reporting

Students' reports will vary but should focus on one of the six agencies listed on page 409.

Case Study 3 | 409

Case Study 4:
Genocide and Other Crimes Against Humanity

Case Study Summary
Although Hitler's genocide during World War II is perhaps the most famous example, it is unfortunately not the most recent. The devastation of the Darfur region of Sudan early in the twenty-first century is a continuation of genocide, a practice as old as Egyptian and Roman civilizations.

During the Holocaust, Hitler tried to destroy all European Jews, using death camps as a "final solution." He also killed the disabled, the mentally handicapped, and Gypsies.

Since 1975, there have been at least six documented cases of genocide in Asia, Africa, and Europe. To try to deal with crimes against humanity, the UN Security Council helped establish an International Criminal Court.

Case Study Objective
Students will learn about the issues surrounding genocide and crimes against humanity.

Case Study Vocabulary
Discuss the following vocabulary term with students.

The systematic, deliberate killing, in whole or part, of a racial, ethnic, religious, or national group is called *genocide*. The Darfur region of Sudan is the site of recent acts of *genocide*.

Case Study 4:
Genocide and Other Crimes Against Humanity

▶ What is genocide?
▶ What are crimes against humanity?
▶ What is being done to stop genocide and crimes against humanity?

It is estimated that 174 million people died in the 20th century as a result of genocide and other crimes against humanity. Genocide is the deliberate, systematic killing "in whole or in part, [of] a national, ethnic, racial or religious group." Hitler's campaign to rid Europe of Jews in the 1930s and 1940s is the best known example, but genocide has happened before and continues to happen.

Genocide is a crime against humanity. These crimes involve "the multiple commission of one or more acts such as . . . murder, extermination, enslavement, the forcible transfer of a population, torture, or rape."

The UN found evidence of crimes against humanity by both government and rebel forces in the Darfur region of Sudan in the early 2000s. The UN listed "killing of civilians, enforced disappearances, destruction of villages, rape and other forms of sexual violence, pillaging, and forced displacement." In the space of two years, more than 70,000 people were killed. Another 2 million escaped the region rather than stay and die.

Genocide and crimes against humanity are not inventions of the 20th century. As early as the 1300s B.C., Egyptians enslaved the Israelites. In 148 B.C., the Roman Empire defeated Carthage and burned the city to the ground. Any Carthaginian who survived was sold into slavery.

In the 1840s, the British did little to help as over 1 million Irish starved to death. Another 1.5 million emigrated when disease struck Ireland's crops.

The memorial to the Khmer Rouge victims at Choeung Ek, often known as the Killing Fields.

410   Chapter 24

Case Study Answers
1 Genocide is the systematic, deliberate killing, in whole or part, of a racial, ethnic, religious, or national group.

2 Crimes against humanity include murder, torture, rape, or forcible transfer of a population.

3 To stop genocide and crimes against humanity, the United Nations began the International Criminal Tribunals, which try people accused of war crimes. In 2002, the International Criminal Court began functioning, not as part of the UN, but in cooperation with the UN Security Council.

The Holocaust

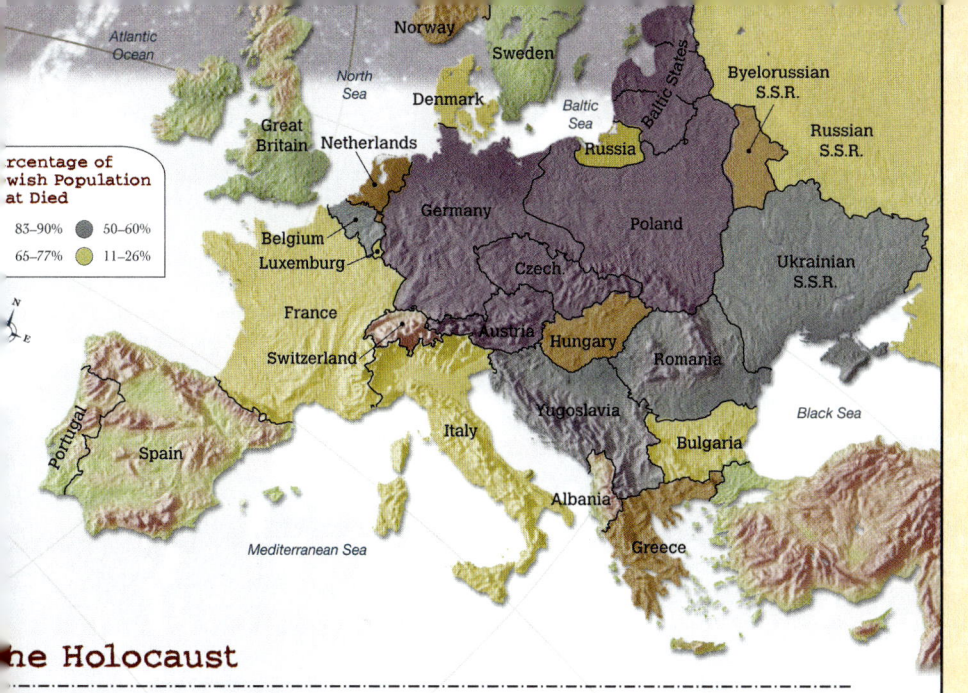

Beginning with the Nuremberg Laws in 1935, Adolf Hitler tried to force Jews to leave Germany. He took away their German citizenship and forbade them to marry non-Jewish Germans. They had to wear a yellow star of David to show they were Jews. After November 9, 1938, and the violence of Kristallnacht, the persecution against Jews increased.

In 1942, Hitler decided on a "final solution." He decreed that all Jews were to be exterminated, or killed. The Holocaust was not limited to Germany. In every nation that Germany occupied, Jews were rounded up and shipped to concentration camps and forced labor camps.

Experts estimate that 6 million Jews were murdered in the Holocaust. Another 3 million to 4 million Gypsies, the mentally ill, and the disabled died in Hitler's campaign to purify Europe. Examine the map and table to learn how the Holocaust affected the Jewish population of Europe.

Jewish Deaths, 1939–1945

Belgium	40,000
Bulgaria	14,000
Czechoslovakia	155,000
Denmark	500
Baltic States (Estonia, Latvia, Lithuania)	228,000
France	90,000
Germany and Austria	210,000
Greece	54,000
Hungary	450,000
Italy	8,000
Poland	3,000,000
Romania	300,000
Soviet Union	
Russia	107,000
Byelorussia	245,000
Ukraine	900,000

Checking the Facts:
Which nation lost the largest number of Jews? How many Jews were murdered in the German-occupied part of the Soviet Union?

Case Study 4 | 411

Map Extension

Ask students to use the map on page 411 to answer the following questions:

- What percentage of the Jewish population of France died? (11–26%)
- Which five nations suffered the greatest losses? (Germany, Austria, Poland, Czechoslovakia, and the Baltic States)
- What general statement can you make about Sweden? (It was not directly affected.)

Chart Extension

Have students rearrange the data on page 411 and create a bar graph showing the deaths in the Jewish population during the Holocaust.

Checking the Facts Answers

1. Poland lost the largest number of Jews in World War II.

2. A total of 1,252,000 Jews were murdered in the Soviet Union.

Picturing History

The photograph on page 410 shows skulls of those killed in Cambodia during the rule of Pol Pot. When the Vietnamese invaded Cambodia and freed the people from the Khmer Rouge, more than 500,000 people went to border camps in Thailand. The Communists had planted ten million land mines in Cambodia, enough to kill every person in the country. After the Vietnamese withdrew in 1991, the United Nations placed a large peacekeeping mission in Cambodia to ensure fair and free elections.

Extension

Suggest that students investigate attempts that were made to stop Hitler. For example, Lutheran minister Dietrich Bonhoeffer, the subject of a PBS special and a documentary, was sentenced to death for his collaboration in a scheme to assassinate Hitler. You may wish to show clips from the documentary film, which includes commentary from Archbishop Desmond Tutu.

Major Genocides Since 1975

1975 to 1979 — Cambodia
The Khmer Rouge, under Pol Pot's leadership, murdered about 1.8 million people—or about 20 percent of the nation's population. The goal was to turn Cambodia into a Communist agrarian stat

1975 to 1999 — East Timor
Until 1975, East Timor was a Portuguese colony. In 1974, the dictator of Portugal was overthrown, and following year East Timor declared independence. Indonesia quickly invaded the new nation in a bru campaign of torture and murder. About 16 percent of the population of 600,000 was killed. By 1999, about 25 percent had been murdered. Most were Roman Catholics. The UN stepped in and took contr

1992 to 1995 — Bosnia-Herzegovina
This genocide was about religion. Bosnian Serbs who belonged to the Bosnian Orthodox Church began a program of ethnic cleansing. Their goal was to remove Catholics and Muslims from much of Bosnia. However, the forcible removals soon turned into genocide. About 200,000 non-Serbs were killed before troops from the North Atlantic Treaty Organization (NATO) were sent in as peacekeepers.

1994 — Rwanda
In this ethnic conflict, the majority Hutus (85 percent of the population) massacred the minority Tutsis (about 12 percent). Some moderate Hutu politicians were also killed. This program of genocide was initiated by the Rwand government. In the 100-day massacre, the Rwandan army and militia murdered about 800,000 Tutsis. This was approximately 75 percent of the entire Tutsi population of Rwanda.

1997 to present — Democratic Republic of the Congo
To gain power, Laurent-Desire Kabila and his allies killed thousands of Congolese. Kabila then us various illegal means, such as torture and imprisonment, to keep control over the nation. Then Kabila's former allies joined Congolese rebels to attack him. The Congolese people were again t innocent victims of brutal murders, rapes, and executions. More than 1.7 million people are estimated to have been killed.

1998 to 1999 — Kosovo
Kosovo is a province within Serbia and Montenegro. Ethnic Muslim Albanians made up the large population in Kosovo. In 1998, they began attacks against the government. They wanted to join Kosovo with Albania. The Serbian government fought back with "excessive force" and launched a campaign of ethnic cleansing. Some 400,000 ethnic Albanians were displaced. That was almost percent of the population. NATO planes bombed government forces for 72 days before the government surrendered.

Extension

Divide the class into six small groups, assigning each group a region of major genocide. Ask students to use library resources or the Internet to find out more about the situation in that region. Challenge the groups to find at least one personal narrative of a survivor and to present this person's story to the class in a creative manner, such as a mock interview, role-play, or radio drama.

Armenian Genocide

Between 1915 and 1918, the government of the Ottoman Empire systematically murdered 1.5 million Armenian Christians. Another 500,000 were forced to leave their homeland. Why? Armenians were non-Turks and Christians. The new government of the Ottoman Empire, known as Young Turks, consisted of strong nationalists. They wanted to create a pure "Turkish" state. There was no place for non-Turks and non-Muslims.

The U.S. ambassador to the Ottoman Empire, Henry Morgenthau, Sr., reported: "When the Turkish authorities gave the orders for deportations, they were merely giving the death warrant to the whole race; they understood this well, and, in their conversations with me, they made no particular attempt to conceal the fact."

UN Convention on Genocide, 1948

"**Article I:** The Contracting Parties [the nations that agree to the document] confirm that genocide, whether committed in time of peace or in time of war, is a crime under international law which they undertake to prevent and to punish.

Article IV: Persons committing genocide or any other of the acts . . . shall be punished, whether they are . . . rulers, public officials or private individuals."

Former Yugoslav president Slobodan Milosevic on trial for war crimes.

International Criminal Court

The world did nothing to stop the Armenian genocide and little to help Jews against Hitler. After World War II, the Allies tried officials of Germany, Japan, and Italy as war criminals. Yet, genocide and crimes against humanity continued. As new horrors came to the attention of the world community, nations began calling for some way to punish such crimes.

The UN Security Council created International Criminal Tribunals to try people accused of war crimes in Rwanda and Kosovo. However, nations began to look for a permanent way to deal with crimes against humanity. In 1989, the UN Security Council first debated the idea of setting up an International Criminal Court (ICC).

The ICC began work on July 1, 2002. It took many years of negotiation to ensure that nations did not give up any of their rights. Another concern was that the ICC would not have enough authority to operate. By 2004, 96 nations had ratified the treaty officially forming the ICC. The United States has not ratified the treaty.

The ICC is not an agency of the UN. Its financial support comes from the nations that ratify the treaty that created the ICC. However, the ICC works closely with the UN, and the UN Security Council refers cases to the ICC.

investigative reporting

With a partner, conduct research to find out the latest developments
- about current events that may include crimes against humanity
- in the work of the International Criminal Court

Case Study 4 | 413

Picturing History

Slobodan Milosevic, the former Yugoslav president, is pictured on page 413 during his trial before the International Criminal Court. The trial, which began in February 2002, had been delayed several times because of Milosevic's ill health and his determination to act as his own lawyer. The prosecution completed their case in February 2004. The crimes spanned eight years and three nations, and the 66 charges against Milosevic included war crimes, crimes against humanity, and genocide.

Extension

Several nations, including the United States, claim that concerns about national sovereignty issues have prevented them from ratifying the ICC. Have students use library resources or the Internet to investigate the debate. Allow time for them to present their findings to the class.

Investigative Reporting

Students' research will vary but should focus on one of the nations listed on page 412 or on the work of the International Criminal Court.

Extension

Early in 2005, Unocal Corporation, an oil company based in California, quietly settled cases charging complicity in human rights abuses in Burma. In that nation, the military allegedly forced villagers to assist in clearing the jungles for a natural gas pipeline. The case demonstrates that multinational corporations have both direct and indirect responsibility for human rights. Other multinational companies facing charges include Del Monte Foods, Occidental Petroleum, ExxonMobil, and Coca-Cola. Have interested students investigate these charges by using library resources or the Internet.

Case Study 5: Terrorism

Case Study Summary
Terrorism has affected nations on every continent. The first attack on U.S. soil was on September 11, 2001, when Islamic extremists crashed two airplanes into New York City's World Trade Center and one into the Pentagon in Washington, D.C. While Al-Qaeda, the terrorist group responsible, has carried out several attacks, it is not the only terrorist organization. The 37 major terrorist organizations fall broadly into four groups: nationalist groups, urban guerrillas, Islamic militants desiring a Palestinian state, and anti-Western Islamic militants. Six nations have been identified as sponsoring terrorism: Cuba, Iran, Libya, Korea, Sudan, and Syria. The United States has responded to terrorism by passing the USA Patriot Act and by creating a counterterrorism policy. The United Nations also has acted against terrorism.

Case Study Objective
Students will learn about the issues surrounding terrorism.

Case Study Vocabulary
Discuss each of the vocabulary terms with students.

A *terrorist* uses force or threatens force to frighten and demoralize their enemies. Osama bin Laden is an example of a *terrorist*. *Terrorism* is a political strategy of using violence to achieve goals. Many Americans first became aware of the reality of *terrorism* on September 11, 2001.

Case Study 5: Terrorism

▶ What is terrorism?
▶ Who are terrorists?
▶ Explain the different types of terrorism that exist today.

A terrorist is a person who uses force or the threat of force to frighten and demoralize an enemy. Terrorism is a political strategy that uses violence against people or property to achieve a goal. Often the goal of terrorism is to force a change in government or society.

The first awareness of terrorism for many Americans came on September 11, 2001. Two airplanes piloted by terrorists flew into the World Trade Center in New York City on that morning. A third plane flew into the Pentagon in Washington, D.C. Passengers in a fourth airliner caused the terrorists to crash the plane in a cornfield in Pennsylvania. Close to 3,000 people died that morning in the planes and on the ground in New York City and Washington, D.C.

Investigations showed that Al-Qaeda was responsible for what Americans call 9/11. Al-Qaeda is a terrorist organization founded by Osama bin Laden. Bin Laden is a militant, radical Muslim. He created Al-Qaeda after the first Gulf War ended in 1991. His original aim was to force the United States to remove its troops from Saudi Arabia, the home of the prophet Muhammad, founder of Islam. Bin Laden continues to target the U.S. and other free countries.

However, these were not the first strikes against U.S. property and citizens. In 1993, terrorists planted a car bomb in the parking garage under the World Trade Center towers. The U.S. embassies in Kenya and Tanzania were bombed by terrorists in 1998. In 2000, terrorists bombed the USS *Cole* while it lay at anchor in Adan Harbor, Yemen.

The U.S. State Department lists 37 major terrorist organizations around the world. There are other smaller groups as well. Read the section "Terrorist Organizations" to identify some current terrorist groups.

The remains of a bus after a Palestinian suicide bombing in Jerusalem.

Case Study Answers

1 Terrorism is a political strategy of using violence to achieve goals.

2 Terrorists are people who use force or threaten to use force to scare and demoralize their enemies.

3 Current terrorist groups include anti-Western terrorists such as Al-Qaeda, Palestinian militants such as Hizballah, urban guerrillas such as the Shining Path of Peru, and nationalist groups such as the Liberation Tigers of Tamil Eelam.

Who Are Terrorists?

Terrorists operate in all regions of the world. They use many of the same tactics to create fear. However, their goals vary. The following are the four main categories of terrorist organizations:

- nationalist groups who want to create their own nations
- urban guerrillas who want to overthrow the government in power
- Islamic militants who want to create a nation of Palestine
- Islamic militants who are fighting Western, especially U.S., influences in the Middle East

Al-Qaeda fits the last group. Islamic fundamentalists want all Western influences to be removed from nations with large Islamic populations. They believe that Islamic nations should be theocracies. A theocracy is a government based on religious principles and run by religious teachers. Muslim terrorist groups in the Philippines and Southeast Asia have a similar goal of setting up Islamic nations.

The Basque Fatherland is a nationalist group. Members of this organization want to set up a separate nation by combining areas in Spain and France that have large populations of Basque people.

In Peru and Colombia, urban guerrillas want to overturn the governments in power. They believe government officials favor the wealthy and ignore the problems of the poor. Many of the poor have moved from rural areas to cities hoping to make a better life for themselves. Instead, they find few jobs, little or no public services, such as schools, medical care, and sanitation, and corrupt public officials.

The Middle East has been an area of conflict since Israel was founded in 1948. Militant groups such as HAMAS and Hizballah have been attacking Israel since the 1980s. Their aim and that of similar Islamic militants is to establish an independent nation of Palestine. They want to force the Israeli government to recognize Palestinian claims to a homeland and to negotiate with the Palestinians on setting up that homeland.

Terrorist Organizations

The following are some of the more notorious terrorist organizations operating today.

Nationalist Groups
- Harakat ul Mujahidin (HUM)
  Goal: to unite the Indian state of Kashmir with Pakistan
- Liberation Tigers of Tamil Eelam
  Goal: to set up a separate state for Tamil people by taking land from Sri Lanka

Urban Guerrillas
- Sendero Luminoso (Shining Path) [Peru]
- National Liberation Army of Colombia

Palestinian Militants
- HAMAS (Islamic Resistance Movement)
- Hizballah (Party of God)
- Palestine Islamic Jihad
- Palestine Liberation Front
- Popular Front for the Liberation of Palestine

Anti-Western Terrorists
- Al-Qaeda
- Al-Jihad (Egyptian Islamic Jihad) [Egypt]
- Jemaah Islamiya [Philippines and Southeast Asia]

These terrorist groups use suicide bombing (sometimes called homicide bombings), airplane hijacking, kidnapping, car bombing, and assassination as weapons of terror.

Case Study 5 415

Chart Extension

Pair students and assign them one of the terrorist organizations listed in the chart on page 415. Ask them to use library resources or the Internet to find out more about the group and its activities. Allow time for pairs to share their findings with the class.

Picturing History

The bus pictured on page 414 depicts the effects of terrorism. After elections in Iraq, terrorist acts such as suicide bombings increased. Some commentators saw the spurt of violence as a sign that the jihadists, who can accept no accommodation of Western notions, are fearful that they are losing hold and so have become more violent.

Extension

Have interested students use library resources or the Internet to find out more about the group Women in Black. Nominated in mid-2001 for the Nobel Peace Prize, the worldwide group incorporates the strategies of the women of Jerusalem, wearing black and standing in silent vigil to protest against the Israeli occupation of Palestinian land.

Case Study 5 415

Picturing History

The photograph at the top of page 416 shows one of two planes that hit the World Trade Center in New York City on September 11, 2001. On the same day, a plane struck the Pentagon in Arlington, VA. A fourth plane crashed in a field in western Pennsylvania after passengers overpowered the hijackers. Over 3,000 people were killed in the attacks that morning, either on the planes or on the ground.

Picturing History

Violence in Chechnya is depicted in the photograph at the bottom of page 416. Some believe that one of the major sources of conflict in Chechnya is oil. That nation not only produces crude oil but also is key to transporting and exporting it from the Caspian Sea to the Black Sea. By remaining in Chechnya, Russia continues to profit from the oil trade, which increased after the terrorist attacks of 9/11.

The World Trade Center, September 11, 2001

U.S. Response to Terrorism

According to the U.S. Department of State, "The global war on terrorism is being fought by many means—through diplomatic, military, financial, intelligence, investigative, and law enforcement actions—at home and abroad."

On October 24, 2001, the USA Patriot Act was signed into law. The law allows the United States government to:

- detain foreigners who are suspected of terrorism for seven days without charging them with a crime
- monitor e-mail and Internet use and tap telephones of suspects
- make search warrants valid across states
- order United States banks to investigate sources of large foreign bank accounts
- prosecute terrorist crimes without any limitations or time restrictions

State Sponsors of Terrorism

Terrorist organizations need financial support and safe havens in order to operate. The United States has identified six nations that it calls state sponsors of terrorism. The six are Cuba, Iran, Libya, North Korea, Sudan, and Syria. These nations provide mon to terrorist organizations. They also allow the groups to live in and operate from their territ

The U.S. government has placed economic sanctions on these six nations. Sanctions are restrictions placed on a nation because it has not obeyed international law. Among the sanctions are a ban on selling military equipment and giving foreign aid. In addition the sanctions limit the type of nonmilitary goods that can be sold.

Chechen Terrorists

The region of Chechnya broke away from Russia in 1991 and declared itself an independent nation. Russia refused to recog Chechen independence and sent troops to t control. Fighting lasted from 1994 to 1996.

In the late 1990s, Chechen rebels began to use terrorism to achieve their goal of independence. A series of bombings in Mosc and other Russian cities was blamed on Chechens. Militants took over a theater in Moscow in demanding freedom for Chechny Hundreds of innocent people died as the government tried to free them.

In 2004, at least 32 Chechen terrorists sei a school in Beslan, Russia. They demanded t Russia remove its troops from Chechnya. Afte hours, troops moved in to free the hostages. than half of the 339 people killed were childr

Survivors of the Beslan school siege

416

Major Terrorist Attacks

Location	Date	Event
Munich, Germany	1972	Palestinians take Israeli hostages at Summer Olympics; hostages and terrorists die in battle with police
Beirut, Lebanon	1983	U.S. marine barracks attacked by truck bomb, 241 killed
Mediterranean Sea	1985	Palestinian terrorists hijack the cruise liner *Achille Lauro*; 1 killed
Lockerbie, Scotland	1988	Terrorists detonate bomb on Pan Am flight 103; 270 killed
Tokyo, Japan	1995	Lethal gas released by extremists into subway; 12 killed, thousands injured
Omagh, Northern Ireland	1998	Irish Republican Army faction detonates car bomb; 29 killed
Kenya & Tanzania, Africa	1998	U.S. embassies bombed; 301 killed, 5,077 injured
New York, Washington, Pennsylvania, United States	2001	Al-Qaeda operatives hijack four airliners; 3,000+ killed
Moscow, Russia	2002	Chechen rebels seize theater; 100 hostages and all terrorists killed

Chapter 24

UN Actions Against Terrorism

The UN has 19 global or regional treaties relating to international terrorism. Many of [these] date to the 1970s and the beginning of [pl]ane hijackings. After 9/11, the UN adopted [Reso]lution 1373 that binds UN member nations [?] to end terrorism.

[T]he UN also set up a Counter-Terrorism [Com]mittee (CTC) made up of the 15 member [nati]ons of the Security Council. The CTC's role [is to] make sure that member nations "deny [opp]ortunities for the commission of acts of [terro]rism." The CTC also seeks to build [coop]eration among member nations in the fight [agai]nst terrorism.

UN Resolution 1373

UN member nations must

- deny all forms of financial support to terrorist groups . . . ;
- suppress . . . safe haven . . . or support for terrorists . . . ;
- share information with other governments . . . ;
- cooperate with other governments in the investigation, detection, arrest, and prosecution of those involved . . . ; and
- criminalize active and passive assistance for terrorism in domestic laws and bring violators of these laws to justice . . .

U.S. Counterterrorism Policy

First, make no concessions to terrorists and strike no deals;

Second, bring terrorists to justice for their crimes;

Third, isolate and apply pressure on states that sponsor terrorism to force them [to] change their behavior; and

Fourth, bolster the counterterrorism [ca]pabilities of those countries that work [wi]th the U.S. and require assistance.

VIEWPOINT

"... The enemy of America is not our many Muslim friends. It is not our many Arab friends. Our enemy is a radical network of terrorists and every government that supports them. ...

"This is not just America's fight. And what is at stake is not just America's freedom. This is the world's fight, this is civilization's fight, this is the fight of all who believe in progress and pluralism, tolerance and freedom.

"We ask every nation to join us. We will ask and we will need the help of police forces, intelligence service, and banking systems around the world."

—George W. Bush, September 20, 2001
Address to the nation and to the world

Investigative reporting

With a partner find the latest information on the war on terror. Choose one topic and prepare a presentation about it.

- Check newspapers and newsmagazines for information about the activities of terrorist groups listed in this Case Study.
- Check the Web sites of the U.S. Departments of Homeland Security, State, Justice, and Defense and the UN for updates on counterterrorism activities and policies.

Case Study 5 | 417

Extensions

1 The Patriot Act has faced a series of legal challenges. Have interested students use library resources or the Internet to investigate controversial provisions of the act and the resulting legal battles.

2 Have students use library resources or the Internet to update the chart titled "Major Terrorist Attacks."

Investigative Reporting

Students' presentations will vary but should be based on updates on the war on terror.

Viewpoint Extensions

1 Challenge students to find other statements made by world leaders after the September 11 attack. How did leaders in Russia and Britain respond, for instance? Allow time for students to read aloud to the class the statements they find.

2 Ask students to use library resources or the Internet to find out how the international police forces, intelligence service, and banking systems have cooperated with the U.S. in fighting global terrorism.

Extension

In the wake of September 11, 2001, America's ports continue to be one area of security concern. Some 19,000 cargo containers come into the U.S. daily. The Port of New York and New Jersey alone handles about 4,000 shipping containers on an average day. Inspectors at America's 361 seaports normally screen only three percent of the seven million containers, each a 20- to 40-foot box, that arrive annually. The global economy depends on the containers, which move about 90 percent of international commerce. Some security experts believe America needs to put more screens in place to make shipping of terrorist weapons less likely.

Case Study 5 | 417

Appendix

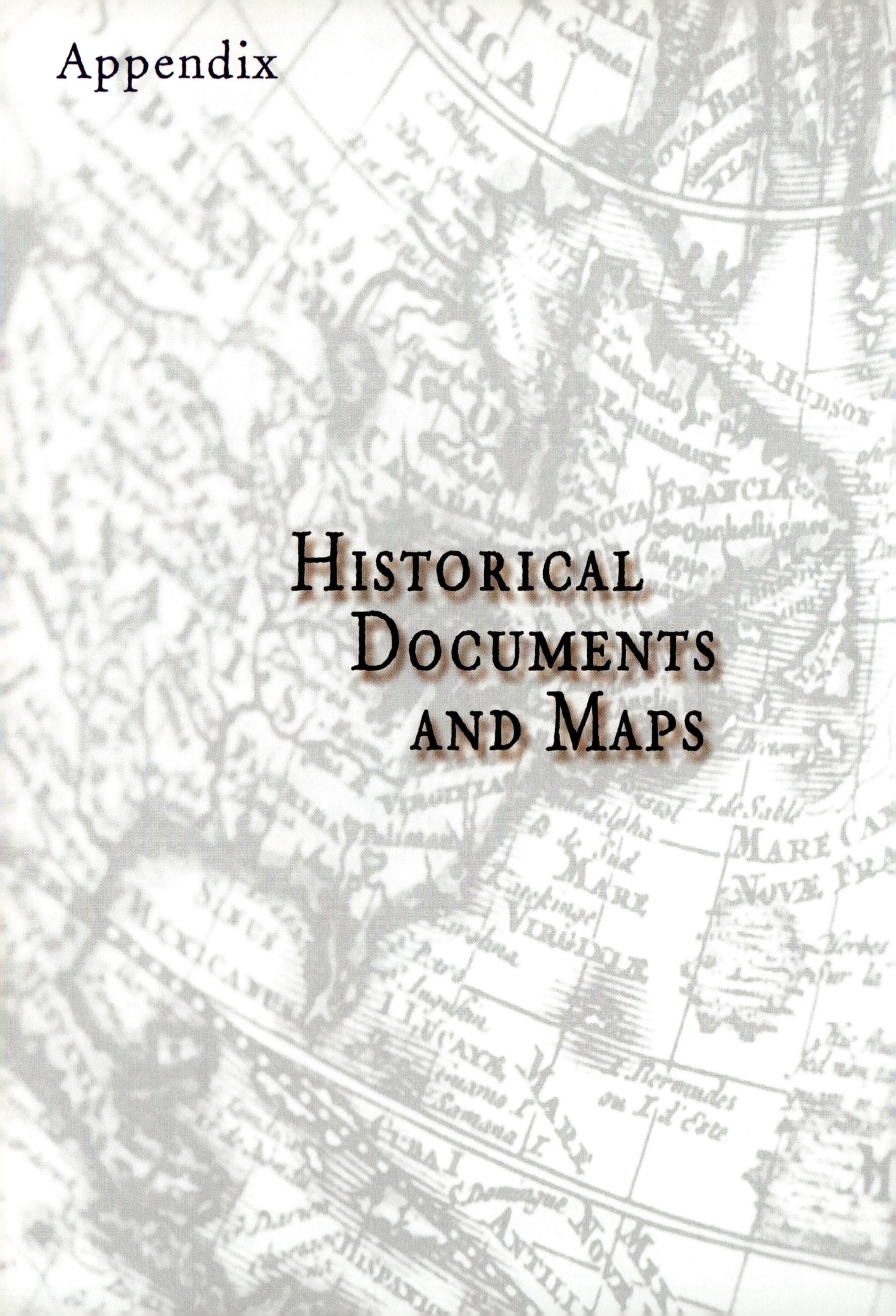

Historical Documents and Maps

The Declaration of Independence

Action of Second Continental Congress, July 4, 1776

The unanimous Declaration of the thirteen United States of America

WHEN in the Course of human Events, it becomes necessary for one People to dissolve the Political Bands which have connected them with another, and to assume among the Powers of the Earth, the separate and equal Station to which the Laws of Nature and of Nature's God entitle them, a decent Respect to the Opinions of Mankind requires that they should declare the causes which impel them to the Separation.

WE hold these Truths to be self-evident, that all Men are created equal, that they are endowed by their Creator with certain unalienable Rights, that among these are Life, Liberty and the Pursuit of Happiness — That to secure these Rights, Governments are instituted among Men, deriving their just Powers from the Consent of the Governed, that whenever any Form of Government becomes destructive of these Ends, it is the Right of the People to alter or to abolish it, and to institute new Government, laying its Foundation on such Principles, and organizing its Powers in such Form, as to them shall seem most likely to effect their Safety and Happiness. Prudence, indeed, will dictate that Governments long established should not be changed for light and transient Causes; and accordingly all Experience hath shewn, that Mankind are more disposed to suffer, while Evils are sufferable, than to right themselves by abolishing the Forms to which they are accustomed. But when a long Train of Abuses and Usurpations, pursuing invariably the same Object, evinces a Design to reduce them under absolute Despotism, it is their Right, it is their Duty, to throw off such Government, and to provide new Guards for their future Security. Such has been the patient Sufferance of these Colonies; and such is now the Necessity which constrains them to alter their former Systems of Government. The History of the present King of Great-Britain is a History of repeated Injuries and Usurpations, all having in direct Object the Establishment of an absolute Tyranny over these States. To prove this, let Facts be submitted to a candid World.

HE has refused his Assent to Laws, the most wholesome and necessary for the public Good.

HE has forbidden his Governors to pass Laws of immediate and pressing Importance, unless suspended in their Operation till his Assent should be obtained; and when so suspended, he has utterly neglected to attend to them.

HE has refused to pass other Laws for the Accommodation of large Districts of People, unless those People would relinquish the Right of Representation in the Legislature, a Right inestimable to them, and formidable to Tyrants only.

HE has called together Legislative Bodies at Places unusual, uncomfortable, and distant from the Depository of their public Records, for the sole Purpose of fatiguing them into Compliance with his Measures.

HE has dissolved Representative Houses repeatedly, for opposing with manly Firmness his Invasions on the Rights of the People.

HE has refused for a long Time, after such Dissolutions, to cause others to be elected; whereby the Legislative Powers, incapable of the Annihilation, have returned to the People at large for their exercise; the State remaining in the mean time exposed to all the Dangers of Invasion from without, and the Convulsions within.

HE has endeavoured to prevent the Population of these States; for that Purpose obstructing the Laws for Naturalization of Foreigners; refusing to pass others to encourage their Migrations hither, and raising the Conditions of new Appropriations of Lands.

HE has obstructed the Administration of Justice, by refusing his Assent to Laws for establishing Judiciary Powers.

HE has made Judges dependent on his Will alone, for the Tenure of their Offices, and the Amount and Payment of their Salaries.

HE has erected a Multitude of new Offices, and sent hither Swarms of Officers to harrass our People, and eat out their Substance.

HE has kept among us, in Times of Peace, Standing Armies, without the consent of our Legislatures.

HE has affected to render the Military independent of and superior to the Civil Power.

HE has combined with others to subject us to a Jurisdiction foreign to our Constitution, and unacknowledged by our Laws; giving his Assent to their Acts of pretended Legislation:

FOR quartering large Bodies of Armed Troops among us;

FOR protecting them, by a mock Trial, from Punishment for any Murders which they should commit on the Inhabitants of these States:

FOR cutting off our Trade with all Parts of the World:

FOR imposing Taxes on us without our Consent:

FOR depriving us, in many Cases, of the Benefits of Trial by Jury:

FOR transporting us beyond Seas to be tried for pretended Offences:

FOR abolishing the free System of English Laws in a neighbouring Province, establishing therein an arbitrary Government, and enlarging its Boundaries, so as to render it at once an Example and fit Instrument for introducing the same absolute Rules into these Colonies:

FOR taking away our Charters, abolishing our most valuable Laws, and altering fundamentally the Forms of our Governments:

FOR suspending our own Legislatures, and declaring themselves invested with Power to legislate for us in all Cases whatsoever.

HE has abdicated Government here, by declaring us out of his Protection and waging War against us.

HE has plundered our Seas, ravaged our Coasts, burnt our Towns, and destroyed the Lives of our People.

HE is, at this Time, transporting large Armies of foreign Mercenaries to compleat the Works of Death, Desolation, and Tyranny, already begun with circumstances of Cruelty and Perfidy, scarcely paralleled in the most barbarous Ages, and totally unworthy the Head of a civilized Nation.

HE has constrained our fellow Citizens taken Captive on the high Seas to bear Arms against their Country, to become the Executioners of their Friends and Brethren, or to fall themselves by their Hands.

HE has excited domestic Insurrections amongst us, and has endeavoured to bring on the Inhabitants of our Frontiers, the merciless Indian Savages, whose known Rule of Warfare, is an undistinguished Destruction, of all Ages, Sexes and Conditions.

IN every stage of these Oppressions we have Petitioned for Redress in the most humble Terms: Our repeated Petitions have been answered only by repeated Injury. A Prince, whose Character is thus marked by every act which may define a Tyrant, is unfit to be the Ruler of a free People.

NOR have we been wanting in Attentions to our British Brethren. We have warned them from Time to Time of Attempts by their Legislature to extend an unwarrantable Jurisdiction over us. We have reminded them of the Circumstances of our Emigration and Settlement here. We have appealed to their native Justice and Magnanimity, and we have conjured them by the Ties of our common Kindred to disavow these Usurpations, which, would inevitably interrupt our Connections and Correspondence. They too have been deaf to the Voice of Justice and of Consanguinity. We must, therefore, acquiesce in the Necessity, which denounces our Separation, and hold them, as we hold the rest of Mankind, Enemies in War, in Peace, Friends.

WE, therefore, the Representatives of the UNITED STATES OF AMERICA, in GENERAL CONGRESS, Assembled, appealing to the Supreme Judge of the World for the Rectitude of our Intentions, do, in the Name, and by Authority of the good People of these Colonies, solemnly Publish and Declare, That these United Colonies are, and of Right ought to be, FREE AND INDEPENDENT STATES; that they are absolved from all Allegiance to the British Crown, and that all political Connection between them and the State of Great-Britain, is and ought to be totally dissolved; and that as FREE AND INDEPENDENT STATES, they have full Power to levy War, conclude Peace, contract Alliances, establish Commerce, and to do all other Acts and Things which INDEPENDENT STATES may of right do. And for the support of this Declaration, with a firm Reliance on the Protection of divine Providence, we mutually pledge to each other our Lives, our Fortunes, and our sacred Honor.

John Hancock	Charles Carroll	Geo. Taylor	Josiah Bartlett
Button Gwinnett	Of Carrollton	James Wilson	Wm. Whipple
Lyman Hall	George Wythe	Geo. Ross	Saml Adams
Geo Walton	Richard Henry Lee	Caesar Rodney	John Adams
Wm Hooper	Th Jefferson	Geo Read	Robt Treat Paine
Joseph Hewes	Benja Harrison	Tho M. Kean	Elbridge Gerry
John Penn	Thos Nelson Jr.	Wm Floyd	Step Hopkins
Edward Rutledge	Francis Lightfoot Lee	Phil. Livingston	William Ellery
Thos Heyward Junr.	Carter Braxton	Frans. Lewis	Roger Sherman
Thomas Lynch Junr.	Robt Morris	Lewis Morris	Samel Huntington
Arthur Middleton	Benjamin Rush	Richd. Stockton	Wm. Williams
Samuel Chase	Benja. Franklin	Jno Witherspoon	Oliver Wolcott
Wm. Paca	John Morton	Fras. Hopkinson	Matthew Thornton
Thos. Stone	Geo Clymer	John Hart	
	Jas. Smith	Abra Clark	

The United States Constitution

The pages that follow contain the original text of the United States Constitution. Sections that are no longer enforced have been crossed out. The spelling and punctuation of the document remain in their original format. The headings are not part of the original Constitution.

We the People of the United States, in Order to form a more perfect Union, establish Justice, insure domestic Tranquility, provide for the common defence, promote the general Welfare, and secure the Blessings of Liberty to ourselves and our Posterity, do ordain and establish this Constitution for the United States of America.

Article I
Legislative Branch

Section 1
Congress

All legislative Powers herein granted shall be vested in a Congress of the United States, which shall consist of a Senate and House of Representatives.

Section 2
House of Representatives

Clause 1: The House of Representatives shall be composed of Members chosen every second Year by the People of the several States, and the Electors in each State shall have the Qualifications requisite for Electors of the most numerous Branch of the State Legislature.

Clause 2: No Person shall be a Representative who shall not have attained to the Age of twenty five Years, and been seven Years a Citizen of the United States, and who shall not, when elected, be an Inhabitant of that State in which he shall be chosen.

Clause 3: Representatives and direct Taxes shall be apportioned among the several States which may be included within this Union, according to their respective Numbers, ~~which shall be determined by adding to the whole Number of free Persons, including those bound to Service for a Term of Years, and excluding Indians not taxed, three fifths of all other Persons.~~

The actual Enumeration shall be made within three Years after the first Meeting of the Congress of the United States, and within every subsequent Term of ten Years, in such Manner as they shall by Law direct.

The Number of Representatives shall not exceed one for every thirty Thousand, but each State shall have at Least one Representative; ~~and until such enumeration shall be made, the State of New Hampshire shall be entitled to chuse three, Massachusetts eight, Rhode-Island and Providence Plantations one, Connecticut five, New-York six, New Jersey four, Pennsylvania eight, Delaware one, Maryland six, Virginia ten, North Carolina five, South Carolina five, and Georgia three.~~

Clause 4: When vacancies happen in the Representation from any State, the Executive Authority thereof shall issue Writs of Election to fill such Vacancies.

Clause 5: The House of Representatives shall chuse their Speaker and other Officers; and shall have the sole Power of Impeachment.

Section 3
Senate

Clause 1: The Senate of the United States shall be composed of two Senators from each State, chosen ~~by the Legislature thereof,~~ for six Years; and each Senator shall have one Vote.

Clause 2: Immediately after they shall be assembled in Consequence of the first Election, they shall be divided as equally as may be into three Classes. The Seats of the Senators of the first Class shall be vacated at the Expiration of the second Year, of the second Class at the Expiration of the fourth Year, and of the third Class at the Expiration of the sixth Year, so that one third may be chosen every second Year; ~~and if Vacancies happen by Resignation, or otherwise, during the Recess of the Legislature of any State, the Executive thereof may make temporary Appointments until the next Meeting of the Legislature, which shall then fill such Vacancies.~~

Clause 3: No Person shall be a Senator who shall not have attained to the Age of thirty Years, and been nine Years a Citizen of the United States, and who shall not, when elected, be an Inhabitant of that State for which he shall be chosen.

Clause 4: The Vice President of the United States shall be President of the Senate, but shall have no Vote, unless they be equally divided.

Clause 5: The Senate shall chuse their other Officers, and also a President pro tempore, in the Absence of the Vice President, or when he shall exercise the Office of President of the United States.

Clause 6: The Senate shall have the sole Power to try all Impeachments. When sitting for that Purpose, they shall be on Oath or Affirmation. When the President of the United States is tried, the Chief Justice shall preside: And no Person shall be convicted without the Concurrence of two thirds of the Members present.

Clause 7: Judgment in Cases of Impeachment shall not extend further than to removal from Office, and disqualification to hold and enjoy any Office of honor, Trust or Profit under the United States: but the Party convicted shall nevertheless be liable and subject to Indictment, Trial, Judgment and Punishment, according to Law.

Section 4
Elections and Meetings

Clause 1: The Times, Places and Manner of holding Elections for Senators and Representatives, shall be prescribed in each State by the Legislature thereof; but the Congress may at any time by Law make or alter such Regulations, ~~except as to the Places of chusing Senators.~~

Clause 2: The Congress shall assemble at least once in every Year, ~~and such Meeting shall be on the first Monday in December,~~ unless they shall by Law appoint a different Day.

Section 5
Rules of Procedure

Clause 1: Each House shall be the Judge of the Elections, Returns and Qualifications of its own Members, and a Majority of each shall constitute a Quorum to do Business; but a smaller Number may adjourn from day to day, and may be authorized to compel the Attendance of absent Members, in such Manner, and under such Penalties as each House may provide.

Clause 2: Each House may determine the Rules of its Proceedings, punish its Members for disorderly Behaviour, and, with the Concurrence of two thirds, expel a Member.

Clause 3: Each House shall keep a Journal of its Proceedings, and from time to time publish the same, excepting such Parts as may in their Judgment require Secrecy; and the Yeas and

Nays of the Members of either House on any question shall, at the Desire of one fifth of those Present, be entered on the Journal.

Clause 4: Neither House, during the Session of Congress, shall, without the Consent of the other, adjourn for more than three days, nor to any other Place than that in which the two Houses shall be sitting.

Section 6
Privileges and Restrictions

Clause 1: The Senators and Representatives shall receive a Compensation for their Services, to be ascertained by Law, and paid out of the Treasury of the United States. They shall in all Cases, except Treason, Felony and Breach of the Peace, be privileged from Arrest during their Attendance at the Session of their respective Houses, and in going to and returning from the same; and for any Speech or Debate in either House, they shall not be questioned in any other Place.

Clause 2: No Senator or Representative shall, during the Time for which he was elected, be appointed to any civil Office under the Authority of the United States, which shall have been created, or the Emoluments whereof shall have been encreased during such time; and no Person holding any Office under the United States, shall be a Member of either House during his Continuance in Office.

Section 7
How Bills Become Laws

Clause 1: All Bills for raising Revenue shall originate in the House of Representatives; but the Senate may propose or concur with Amendments as on other Bills.

Clause 2: Every Bill which shall have passed the House of Representatives and the Senate, shall, before it become a Law, be presented to the President of the United States; If he approve he shall sign it, but if not he shall return it, with his Objections to that House in which it shall have originated, who shall enter the Objections at large on their Journal, and proceed to reconsider it. If after such Reconsideration two thirds of that House shall agree to pass the Bill, it shall be sent, together with the Objections, to the other House, by which it shall likewise be reconsidered, and if approved by two thirds of that House, it shall become a Law. But in all such Cases the Votes of both Houses shall be determined by yeas and Nays, and the Names of the Persons voting for and against the Bill shall be entered on the Journal of each House respectively.

If any Bill shall not be returned by the President within ten Days (Sundays excepted) after it shall have been presented to him, the Same shall be a Law, in like Manner as if he had signed it, unless the Congress by their Adjournment prevent its Return, in which Case it shall not be a Law.

Clause 3: Every Order, Resolution, or Vote to which the Concurrence of the Senate and House of Representatives may be necessary (except on a question of Adjournment) shall be presented to the President of the United States; and before the Same shall take Effect, shall be approved by him, or being disapproved by him, shall be repassed by two thirds of the Senate and House of Representatives, according to the Rules and Limitations prescribed in the Case of a Bill.

Section 8
Powers of Congress

Clause 1: The Congress shall have Power To lay and collect Taxes, Duties, Imposts and Excises, to pay the Debts and provide for the common Defence and general Welfare of the United States; but all Duties, Imposts and Excises shall be uniform throughout the United States;

Clause 2: To borrow Money on the credit of the United States;

Clause 3: To regulate Commerce with foreign Nations, and among the several States, and with the Indian Tribes;

Clause 4: To establish an uniform Rule of Naturalization, and uniform Laws on the subject of Bankruptcies throughout the United States;

Clause 5: To coin Money, regulate the Value thereof, and of foreign Coin, and fix the Standard of Weights and Measures;

Clause 6: To provide for the Punishment of counterfeiting the Securities and current Coin of the United States;

Clause 7: To establish Post Offices and post Roads;

Clause 8: To promote the Progress of Science and useful Arts, by securing for limited Times to Authors and Inventors the exclusive Right to their respective Writings and Discoveries;

Clause 9: To constitute Tribunals inferior to the supreme Court;

Clause 10: To define and punish Piracies and Felonies committed on the high Seas, and Offences against the Law of Nations;

Clause 11: To declare War, grant Letters of Marque and Reprisal, and make Rules concerning Captures on Land and Water;

Clause 12: To raise and support Armies, but no Appropriation of Money to that Use shall be for a longer Term than two Years;

Clause 13: To provide and maintain a Navy;

Clause 14: To make Rules for the Government and Regulation of the land and naval Forces;

Clause 15: To provide for calling forth the Militia to execute the Laws of the Union, suppress Insurrections and repel Invasions;

Clause 16: To provide for organizing, arming, and disciplining, the Militia, and for governing such Part of them as may be employed in the Service of the United States, reserving to the States respectively, the Appointment of the Officers, and the Authority of training the Militia according to the discipline prescribed by Congress;

Clause 17: To exercise exclusive Legislation in all Cases whatsoever, over such District (not exceeding ten Miles square) as may, by Cession of particular States, and the Acceptance of Congress, become the Seat of the Government of the United States, and to exercise like Authority over all Places purchased by the Consent of the Legislature of the State in which the Same shall be, for the Erection of Forts, Magazines, Arsenals, dock-Yards, and other needful Buildings;—And

Clause 18: To make all Laws which shall be necessary and proper for carrying into Execution the foregoing Powers, and all other Powers vested by this Constitution in the Government of the United States, or in any Department or Officer thereof.

Section 9
Powers Denied to the Federal Government

Clause 1: ~~The Migration or Importation of such Persons as any of the States now existing shall think proper to admit, shall not be prohibited by the Congress prior to the Year one thousand eight hundred and eight, but a Tax or duty may be imposed on such Importation, not exceeding ten dollars for each Person.~~

Clause 2: The Privilege of the Writ of Habeas Corpus shall not be suspended, unless when in Cases of Rebellion or Invasion the public Safety may require it.

Clause 3: No Bill of Attainder or ex post facto Law shall be passed.

Clause 4: No Capitation, or other direct, Tax shall be laid, unless in Proportion to the Census or Enumeration herein before directed to be taken.

Clause 5: No Tax or Duty shall be laid on Articles exported from any State.

Clause 6: No Preference shall be given by any Regulation of Commerce or Revenue to the Ports of one State over those of another: nor shall Vessels bound to, or from, one State, be obliged to enter, clear, or pay Duties in another.

Clause 7: No Money shall be drawn from the Treasury, but in Consequence of Appropriations made by Law; and a regular Statement and Account of the Receipts and Expenditures of all public Money shall be published from time to time.

Clause 8: No Title of Nobility shall be granted by the United States: And no Person holding any Office of Profit or Trust under them, shall, without the Consent of the Congress, accept of any present, Emolument, Office, or Title, of any kind whatever, from any King, Prince, or foreign State.

Section 10
Powers Denied to the States

Clause 1: No State shall enter into any Treaty, Alliance, or Confederation; grant Letters of Marque and Reprisal; coin Money; emit Bills of Credit; make any Thing but gold and silver Coin a Tender in Payment of Debts; pass any Bill of Attainder, ex post facto Law, or Law impairing the Obligation of Contracts, or grant any Title of Nobility.

Clause 2: No State shall, without the Consent of the Congress, lay any Imposts or Duties on Imports or Exports, except what may be absolutely necessary for executing it's inspection Laws: and the net Produce of all Duties and Imposts, laid by any State on Imports or Exports, shall be for the Use of the Treasury of the United States; and all such Laws shall be subject to the Revision and Controul of the Congress.

Clause 3: No State shall, without the Consent of Congress, lay any Duty of Tonnage, keep Troops, or Ships of War in time of Peace, enter into any Agreement or Compact with another State, or with a foreign Power, or engage in War, unless actually invaded, or in such imminent Danger as will not admit of delay.

Article II Executive Branch

Section 1
President and Vice-President

Clause 1: The executive Power shall be vested in a President of the United States of America. He shall hold his Office during the Term of four Years, and, together with the Vice President, chosen for the same Term, be elected, as follows

Clause 2: Each State shall appoint, in such Manner as the Legislature thereof may direct, a Number of Electors, equal to the whole Number of Senators and Representatives to which the State may be entitled in the Congress: but no Senator or Representative, or Person holding an Office of Trust or Profit under the United States, shall be appointed an Elector.

Clause 3: ~~The Electors shall meet in their respective States, and vote by Ballot for two Persons, of whom one at least shall not be an Inhabitant of the same State with themselves. And they shall make a List of all the Persons voted for, and of the Number of Votes for each; which List they shall sign and certify, and transmit sealed to the Seat of the Government of the United States, directed to the President of the Senate. The President of the Senate shall, in the Presence of the Senate and House of Representatives, open all the Certificates, and the Votes shall then be counted. The Person having the greatest Number of Votes shall be the President, if such Number be a Majority of the whole Number of Electors appointed; and if there be more than one who have such Majority, and have an equal Number of Votes, then the House of Representatives shall immediately chuse by Ballot one of them for President; and if no Person have a Majority, then from the five highest on the~~

~~List the said House shall in like Manner chuse the President. But in chusing the President, the Votes shall be taken by States, the Representation from each State having one Vote; A quorum for this Purpose shall consist of a Member or Members from two thirds of the States, and a Majority of all the States shall be necessary to a Choice. In every Case, after the Choice of the President, the Person having the greatest Number of Votes of the Electors shall be the Vice President. But if there should remain two or more who have equal Votes, the Senate shall chuse from them by Ballot the Vice President.~~

Clause 4: The Congress may determine the Time of chusing the Electors, and the Day on which they shall give their Votes; which Day shall be the same throughout the United States.

Clause 5: No Person except a natural born Citizen, or a Citizen of the United States, at the time of the Adoption of this Constitution, shall be eligible to the Office of President; neither shall any Person be eligible to that Office who shall not have attained to the Age of thirty five Years, and been fourteen Years a Resident within the United States.

Clause 6: ~~In Case of the Removal of the President from Office, or of his Death, Resignation, or Inability to discharge the Powers and Duties of the said Office, the Same shall devolve on the Vice President, and~~ the Congress may by Law provide for the Case of Removal, Death, Resignation or Inability, both of the President and Vice President, declaring what Officer shall then act as President, and such Officer shall act accordingly, until the Disability be removed, or a President shall be elected.

Clause 7: The President shall, at stated Times, receive for his Services, a Compensation, which shall neither be encreased nor diminished during the Period for which he shall have been elected, and he shall not receive within that Period any other Emolument from the United States, or any of them.

Clause 8: Before he enter on the Execution of his Office, he shall take the following Oath or Affirmation:—"I do solemnly swear (or affirm) that I will faithfully execute the Office of President of the United States, and will to the best of my Ability, preserve, protect and defend the Constitution of the United States."

Section 2
Powers of the President

Clause 1: The President shall be Commander in Chief of the Army and Navy of the United States, and of the Militia of the several States, when called into the actual Service of the United States; he may require the Opinion, in writing, of the principal Officer in each of the executive Departments, upon any Subject relating to the Duties of their respective Offices, and he shall have Power to grant Reprieves and Pardons for Offences against the United States, except in Cases of Impeachment.

Clause 2: He shall have Power, by and with the Advice and Consent of the Senate, to make Treaties, provided two thirds of the Senators present concur; and he shall nominate, and by and with the Advice and Consent of the Senate, shall appoint Ambassadors, other public Ministers and Consuls, Judges of the supreme Court, and all other Officers of the United States, whose Appointments are not herein otherwise provided for, and which shall be established by Law: but the Congress may by Law vest the Appointment of such inferior Officers, as they think proper, in the President alone, in the Courts of Law, or in the Heads of Departments.

Clause 3: The President shall have Power to fill up all Vacancies that may happen during the Recess of the Senate, by granting Commissions which shall expire at the End of their next Session.

Section 3
Duties of the President

He shall from time to time give to the Congress Information of the State of the Union, and recommend to their Consideration such Measures as he shall judge necessary and expedient; he may, on extraordinary Occasions, convene both Houses, or either of them, and in Case of Disagreement between them, with Respect to the Time of Adjournment, he may adjourn them to such Time as he shall think proper; he shall receive Ambassadors and other public Ministers; he shall take Care that the Laws be faithfully executed, and shall Commission all the Officers of the United States.

Section 4
Impeachment

The President, Vice President and all civil Officers of the United States, shall be removed from Office on Impeachment for, and Conviction of, Treason, Bribery, or other high Crimes and Misdemeanors.

Article III
Judicial Branch

Section 1
Federal Courts

The judicial Power of the United States, shall be vested in one supreme Court, and in such inferior Courts as the Congress may from time to time ordain and establish. The Judges, both of the supreme and inferior Courts, shall hold their Offices during good Behaviour, and shall, at stated Times, receive for their Services, a Compensation, which shall not be diminished during their Continuance in Office.

Section 2
Extent of Judicial Powers

Clause 1: The judicial Power shall extend to all Cases, in Law and Equity, arising under this Constitution, the Laws of the United States, and Treaties made, or which shall be made, under their Authority;—to all Cases affecting Ambassadors, other public Ministers and Consuls;—to all Cases of admiralty and maritime Jurisdiction;—to Controversies to which the United States shall be a Party;—to Controversies between two or more States;—between a State and Citizens of another State;—between Citizens of different States,—between Citizens of the same State claiming Lands under Grants of different States, and between a State, or the Citizens thereof, and foreign States, Citizens or Subjects.

Clause 2: In all Cases affecting Ambassadors, other public Ministers and Consuls, and those in which a State shall be Party, the supreme Court shall have original Jurisdiction. In all the other Cases before mentioned, the supreme Court shall have appellate Jurisdiction, both as to Law and Fact, with such Exceptions, and under such Regulations as the Congress shall make.

Clause 3: The Trial of all Crimes, except in Cases of Impeachment, shall be by Jury; and such Trial shall be held in the State where the said Crimes shall have been committed; but when not committed within any State, the Trial shall be at such Place or Places as the Congress may by Law have directed.

Section 3
Treason

Clause 1: Treason against the United States, shall consist only in levying War against them, or in adhering to their Enemies, giving them Aid and Comfort. No Person shall be convicted of Treason unless on the Testimony of two Witnesses to the same overt Act, or on Confession in open Court.

Clause 2: The Congress shall have Power to declare the Punishment of Treason, but no Attainder of Treason shall work Corruption of Blood, or Forfeiture except during the Life of the Person attainted.

Article IV
The States

Section 1
Recognition of Each Other's Acts

Full Faith and Credit shall be given in each State to the public Acts, Records, and judicial Proceedings of every other State. And the Congress may by general Laws prescribe the Manner in which such Acts, Records and Proceedings shall be proved, and the Effect thereof.

Section 2
Citizens' Rights in Other States

Clause 1: The Citizens of each State shall be entitled to all Privileges and Immunities of Citizens in the several States.

Clause 2: A Person charged in any State with Treason, Felony, or other Crime, who shall flee from Justice, and be found in another State, shall on Demand of the executive Authority of the State from which he fled, be delivered up, to be removed to the State having Jurisdiction of the Crime.

Clause 3: ~~No Person held to Service or Labour in one State, under the Laws thereof, escaping into another, shall, in Consequence of any Law or Regulation therein, be discharged from such Service or Labour, but shall be delivered up on Claim of the Party to whom such Service or Labour may be due.~~

Section 3
New States and Territories

Clause 1: New States may be admitted by the Congress into this Union; but no new State shall be formed or erected within the Jurisdiction of any other State; nor any State be formed by the Junction of two or more States, or Parts of States, without the Consent of the Legislatures of the States concerned as well as of the Congress.

Clause 2: The Congress shall have Power to dispose of and make all needful Rules and Regulations respecting the Territory or other Property belonging to the United States; and nothing in this Constitution shall be so construed as to Prejudice any Claims of the United States, or of any particular State.

Section 4
Guarantees to the States

The United States shall guarantee to every State in this Union a Republican Form of Government, and shall protect each of them against Invasion; and on Application of the Legislature, or of the Executive (when the Legislature cannot be convened) against domestic Violence.

Article V
Amending the Constitution

The Congress, whenever two thirds of both Houses shall deem it necessary, shall propose Amendments to this Constitution, or, on the Application of the Legislatures of two thirds of the several States, shall call a Convention for proposing Amendments, which, in either Case, shall be valid to all Intents and Purposes, as Part of this Constitution, when ratified by the Legislatures of three fourths of the several States, or by Conventions in three fourths thereof, as the one or the other Mode of Ratification may be proposed by the Congress; Provided ~~that no Amendment which may be made prior to the Year One thousand eight hundred and eight shall in any Manner affect the first and fourth Clauses in the Ninth Section of the first Article; and~~ that no State, without its Consent, shall be deprived of its equal Suffrage in the Senate.

Article VI
National Supremacy

Clause 1: All Debts contracted and Engagements entered into, before the Adoption of this Constitution, shall be as valid against the United States under this Constitution, as under the Confederation.

Clause 2: This Constitution, and the Laws of the United States which shall be made in Pursuance thereof; and all Treaties made, or which shall be made, under the Authority of the United States, shall be the supreme Law of the Land; and the Judges in every State shall be bound thereby, any Thing in the Constitution or Laws of any State to the Contrary notwithstanding.

Clause 3: The Senators and Representatives before mentioned, and the Members of the several State Legislatures, and all executive and judicial Officers, both of the United States and of the several States, shall be bound by Oath or Affirmation, to support this Constitution; but no religious Test shall ever be required as a Qualification to any Office or public Trust under the United States.

Article VII Ratification

The Ratification of the Conventions of nine States, shall be sufficient for the Establishment of this Constitution between the States so ratifying the Same. Done in Convention by the Unanimous Consent of the States present the Seventeenth Day of September in the Year of our Lord one thousand seven hundred and Eighty seven and of the Independence of the United States of America the Twelfth In witness whereof We have hereunto subscribed our Names,

---

George Washington, President and Deputy from Virginia
Delaware
George Read
Gunning Bedford, Junior
John Dickinson
Richard Bassett
Jacob Broom

Maryland
James McHenry
Daniel of St. Thomas Jenifer
Daniel Carroll
Virginia
John Blair
James Madison, Junior
North Carolina
William Blount
Richard Dobbs Spaight
Hugh Williamson
South Carolina
John Rutledge
Charles Cotesworth Pinckney
Charles Pinckney
Pierce Butler.
Georgia
William Few
Abraham Baldwin
New Hampshire
John Langdon
Nicholas Gilman
Massachusetts
Nathaniel Gorham
Rufus King
Connecticut
William Samuel Johnson
Roger Sherman
New York
Alexander Hamilton
New Jersey
William Livingston
David Brearley
William Paterson.
Jonathan Dayton
Pennsylvania
Benjamin Franklin
Thomas Mifflin
Robert Morris
George Clymer
Thomas FitzSimons
Jared Ingersoll
James Wilson
Gouverneur Morris
Attest: William Jackson, Secretary

Ammendments to the Constitution

The pages that follow contain the original text of the Amendments to the United States Constitution. Sections that are no longer enforced have been crossed out. The spelling and punctuation of the document remain in their original format. The headings are not part of the original Amendments.

Amendment 1 (1791)
Religious and Political Freedom

Congress shall make no law respecting an establishment of religion, or prohibiting the free exercise thereof; or abridging the freedom of speech, or of the press; or the right of the people peaceably to assemble, and to petition the Government for a redress of grievances.

Amendment 2 (1791)
Right to Bear Arms

A well regulated Militia, being necessary to the security of a free State, the right of the people to keep and bear Arms, shall not be infringed.

Amendment 3 (1791)
Quartering of Soldiers

No Soldier shall, in time of peace be quartered in any house, without the consent of the Owner, nor in time of war, but in a manner to be prescribed by law.

Amendment 4 (1791)
Search and Seizure

The right of the people to be secure in their persons, houses, papers, and effects, against unreasonable searches and seizures, shall not be violated, and no Warrants shall issue, but upon probable cause, supported by Oath or affirmation, and particularly describing the place to be searched, and the persons or things to be seized.

Amendment 5 (1791)
Life, Liberty, and Property

No person shall be held to answer for a capital, or otherwise infamous crime, unless on a presentment or indictment of a Grand Jury, except in cases arising in the land or naval forces, or in the Militia, when in actual service in time of War or public danger; nor shall any person be subject for the same offence to be twice put in jeopardy of life or limb; nor shall be compelled in any criminal case to be a witness against himself, nor be deprived of life, liberty, or property, without due process of law; nor shall private property be taken for public use, without just compensation.

Amendment 6 (1791)
Rights of the Accused

In all criminal prosecutions, the accused shall enjoy the right to a speedy and public trial, by an impartial jury of the State and district wherein the crime shall have been committed, which district shall have been previously ascertained by law, and to be informed of the nature and cause of the accusation; to be confronted with the witnesses against him; to have compulsory process for obtaining witnesses in his favor, and to have the Assistance of Counsel for his defence.

Amendment 7 (1791)
Right to Trial by Jury

In Suits at common law, where the value in controversy shall exceed twenty dollars, the right of trial by jury shall be preserved, and no fact tried by a jury, shall be otherwise re-examined in any Court of the United States, than according to the rules of the common law.

Amendment 8 (1791)
Bail and Punishment

Excessive bail shall not be required, nor excessive fines imposed, nor cruel and unusual punishments inflicted.

Amendment 9 (1791)
All Other Rights

The enumeration in the Constitution, of certain rights, shall not be construed to deny or disparage others retained by the people.

Amendment 10 (1791)
Rights of States and the People

The powers not delegated to the United States by the Constitution, nor prohibited by it to the States, are reserved to the States respectively, or to the people.

Amendment 11 (1795)
Suits Against a State

The Judicial power of the United States shall not be construed to extend to any suit in law or equity, commenced or prosecuted against one of the United States by Citizens of another State, or by Citizens or Subjects of any Foreign State.

Amendment 12 (1804)
Election of President

The Electors shall meet in their respective states, and vote by ballot for President and Vice-President, one of whom, at least, shall not be an inhabitant of the same state with themselves; they shall name in their ballots the person voted for as President, and in distinct ballots the person voted for as Vice-President, and they shall make distinct lists of all persons voted for as President, and of all persons voted for as Vice-President, and of the number of votes for each, which lists they shall sign and certify, and transmit sealed to the seat of the government of the United States, directed to the President of the Senate;

The President of the Senate shall, in the presence of the Senate and House of Representatives, open all the certificates and the votes shall then be counted;

The person having the greatest number of votes for President, shall be the President, if such number be a majority of the whole number of Electors appointed; and if no person have such majority, then from the persons having the highest numbers not exceeding three on the list of those voted for as President, the House of Representatives shall choose immediately, by ballot, the President. But in choosing the President, the votes shall be taken by states, the representation from each state having one vote; a quorum for this purpose shall consist of a member or members from two-thirds of the states, and a majority of all the states shall be necessary to a choice.

~~And if the House of Representatives shall not choose a President whenever the right of choice shall devolve upon them, before the fourth day of March next following, then the Vice-President shall act as President, as in the case of the death or other constitutional disability of the President.~~

The person having the greatest number of votes as Vice-President, shall be the Vice-President, if such number be a majority of the whole number of Electors appointed, and if no person have a majority, then from the two highest numbers on the list, the Senate shall choose the Vice-President; a quorum for the purpose shall consist of two-thirds of the whole number of Senators, and a majority of the whole number shall be necessary to a choice. But no person constitutionally ineligible to the office of

President shall be eligible to that of Vice-President of the United States.

Amendment 13 (1865)
Abolition of Slavery

Section 1 Neither slavery nor involuntary servitude, except as a punishment for crime whereof the party shall have been duly convicted, shall exist within the United States, or any place subject to their jurisdiction.

Section 2 Congress shall have power to enforce this article by appropriate legislation.

Amendment 14 (1868)
Civil Rights in the States

Section 1 All persons born or naturalized in the United States, and subject to the jurisdiction thereof, are citizens of the United States and of the State wherein they reside. No State shall make or enforce any law which shall abridge the privileges or immunities of citizens of the United States; nor shall any State deprive any person of life, liberty, or property, without due process of law; nor deny to any person within its jurisdiction the equal protection of the laws.

Section 2 Representatives shall be apportioned among the several States according to their respective numbers, counting the whole number of persons in each State, excluding Indians not taxed. But when the right to vote at any election for the choice of electors for President and Vice President of the United States, Representatives in Congress, the Executive and Judicial officers of a State, or the members of the Legislature thereof, is denied to any of the male inhabitants of such State, being twenty-one years of age,(See Note 15) and citizens of the United States, or in any way abridged, except for participation in rebellion, or other crime, the basis of representation therein shall be reduced in the proportion which the number of such male citizens shall bear to the whole number of male citizens twenty-one years of age in such State.

Section 3 No person shall be a Senator or Representative in Congress, or elector of President and Vice President, or hold any office, civil or military, under the United States, or under any State, who, having previously taken an oath, as a member of Congress, or as an officer of the United States, or as a member of any State legislature, or as an executive or judicial officer of any State, to support the Constitution of the United States, shall have engaged in insurrection or rebellion against the same, or given aid or comfort to the enemies thereof. But Congress may by a vote of two-thirds of each House, remove such disability.

Section 4 The validity of the public debt of the United States, authorized by law, including debts incurred for payment of pensions and bounties for services in suppressing insurrection or rebellion, shall not be questioned. But neither the United States nor any State shall assume or pay any debt or obligation incurred in aid of insurrection or rebellion against the United States, or any claim for the loss or emancipation of any slave; but all such debts, obligations and claims shall be held illegal and void.

Section 5 The Congress shall have power to enforce, by appropriate legislation, the provisions of this article.

Amendment 15 (1870)
Black Suffrage

Section 1 The right of citizens of the United States to vote shall not be denied or abridged by the United States or by any State on account of race, color, or previous condition of servitude.

Section 2 The Congress shall have power to enforce this article by appropriate legislation.

Amendment 16 (1913)
Income Tax

The Congress shall have power to lay and collect taxes on incomes, from whatever source derived, without apportionment among the several States, and without regard to any census or enumeration.

Amendment 17 (1919)
Direct Election of Senators

Section 1 The Senate of the United States shall be composed of two Senators from each State, elected by the people thereof, for six years; and each Senator shall have one vote. The electors in each State shall have the qualifications requisite for electors of the most numerous branch of the State legislatures.

Section 2 When vacancies happen in the representation of any State in the Senate, the executive authority of such State shall issue writs of election to fill such vacancies: Provided, That the legislature of any State may empower the executive thereof to make temporary appointments until the people fill the vacancies by election as the legislature may direct.

Section 3 This amendment shall not be so construed as to affect the election or term of any Senator chosen before it becomes valid as part of the Constitution.

Amendment 18 (1919)
National Prohibition

Section 1 ~~After one year from the ratification of this article the manufacture, sale, or transportation of intoxicating liquors within, the importation thereof into, or the exportation thereof from the United States and all territory subject to the jurisdiction thereof for beverage purposes is hereby prohibited.~~

Section 2 ~~The Congress and the several States shall have concurrent power to enforce this article by appropriate legislation.~~

Section 3 ~~This article shall be inoperative unless it shall have been ratified as an amendment to the Constitution by the legislatures of the several States, as provided in the Constitution, within seven years from the date of the submission hereof to the States by the Congress.~~

Amendment 19 (1920)
Women's Suffrage

The right of citizens of the United States to vote shall not be denied or abridged by the United States or by any State on account of sex.

Congress shall have power to enforce this article by appropriate legislation.

Amendment 20 (1933)
"Lame-Duck" Amendment

Section 1 The terms of the President and Vice President shall end at noon on the 20th day of January, and the terms of Senators and Representatives at noon on the 3d day of January, of the years in which such terms would have ended if this article had not been ratified; and the terms of their successors shall then begin.

Section 2 The Congress shall assemble at least once in every year, and such meeting shall begin at noon on the 3d day of January, unless they shall by law appoint a different day.

Section 3 If, at the time fixed for the beginning of the term of the President, the President elect shall have died, the Vice President elect shall become President. If a President shall not have been chosen before the time fixed for the beginning of his term, or if the President elect shall have failed to qualify, then the Vice President elect shall act as President until a President shall have qualified; and the Congress may by law provide for the case wherein neither a President elect nor a Vice President elect shall have qualified, declaring who shall then act as President, or the manner in which one who is to act shall be selected, and such person shall act accordingly until a President or Vice President shall have qualified.

Section 4 The Congress may by law provide for the case of the death of any of the persons from whom the House of Representatives may choose a President whenever the right of choice shall have devolved upon them, and for the case of the death of any of the persons from whom the Senate may choose a Vice President whenever the right of choice shall have devolved upon them.

Section 5 Sections 1 and 2 shall take effect on the 15th day of October following the ratification of this article.

Section 6 This article shall be inoperative unless it shall have been ratified as an amendment to the Constitution by the legislatures of three-fourths of the several States within seven years from the date of its submission.

Amendment 21 (1933)
Repeal of Prohibition

Section 1 The eighteenth article of amendment to the Constitution of the United States is hereby repealed.

Section 2 The transportation or importation into any State, Territory, or possession of the United States for delivery or use therein of intoxicating liquors, in violation of the laws thereof, is hereby prohibited.

Section 3 This article shall be inoperative unless it shall have been ratified as an amendment to the Constitution by conventions in the several States, as provided in the Constitution, within seven years from the date of the submission hereof to the States by the Congress.

Amendment 22 (1951)
Presidential Term of Office

Section 1 No person shall be elected to the office of the President more than twice, and no person who has held the office of President, or acted as President, for more than two years of a term to which some other person was elected President shall be elected to the office of the President more than once. But this article shall not apply to any person holding the office of President when this article was proposed by the Congress, and shall not prevent any person who may be holding the office of President, or acting as President, during the term within which this article becomes operative from holding the office of President or acting as President during the remainder of such term.

Section 2 This article shall be inoperative unless it shall have been ratified as an amendment to the Constitution by the legislatures of three-fourths of the several states within seven years from the date of its submission to the states by the Congress.

Amendment 23 (1961)
Voting in the District of Columbia

Section 1 The District constituting the seat of government of the United States shall appoint in such manner as the Congress may direct:

A number of electors of President and Vice President equal to the whole number of Senators and Representatives in Congress to which the District would be entitled if it were a state, but in no event more than the least populous state; they shall be in addition to those appointed by the states, but they shall be considered, for the purposes of the election of President and Vice President, to be electors appointed by a state; and they shall meet in the District and perform such duties as provided by the twelfth article of amendment.

Section 2 The Congress shall have power to enforce this article by appropriate legislation.

Amendment 24 (1964)
Abolition of Poll Taxes

Section 1 The right of citizens of the United States to vote in any primary or other election for President or Vice President, for electors for President or Vice President, or for Senator or Representative in Congress, shall not be denied or abridged by the United States or any state by reason of failure to pay any poll tax or other tax.

Section 2 The Congress shall have power to enforce this article by appropriate legislation.

Amendment 25 (1967)
Presidential Disability and Succession

Section 1 In case of the removal of the President from office or of his death or resignation, the Vice President shall become President.

Section 2 Whenever there is a vacancy in the office of the Vice President, the President shall nominate a Vice President who shall take office upon confirmation by a majority vote of both Houses of Congress.

Section 3 Whenever the President transmits to the President pro tempore of the Senate and the Speaker of the House of Representatives his written declaration that he is unable to discharge the powers and duties of his office, and until he transmits to them a written declaration to the contrary, such powers and duties shall be discharged by the Vice President as Acting President.

Section 4 Whenever the Vice President and a majority of either the principal officers of the executive departments or of such other body as Congress may by law provide, transmit to the President pro tempore of the Senate and the Speaker of the House of Representatives their written declaration that the President is unable to discharge the powers and duties of his office, the Vice President shall immediately assume the powers and duties of the office as Acting President.

Thereafter, when the President transmits to the President pro tempore of the Senate and the Speaker of the House of Representatives his written declaration that no inability exists, he shall resume the powers and duties of his office unless the Vice President and a majority of either the principal officers of the executive department or of such other body as Congress may by law provide, transmit within four days to the President pro tempore of the Senate and the Speaker of the House of Representatives their written declaration that the President is unable to discharge the powers and duties of his office. Thereupon Congress shall decide the issue, assembling within forty-eight hours for that purpose if not in session. If the Congress, within twenty-one days after receipt of the latter written declaration, or, if Congress is not in session, within twenty-one days after Congress is required to assemble, determines by two-thirds vote of both Houses that the President is unable to discharge the powers and duties of his office, the Vice President shall continue to discharge the same as Acting President; otherwise, the President shall resume the powers and duties of his office.

Amendment 26 (1971)
Eighteen-Year-Old Vote

Section 1 The right of citizens of the United States, who are 18 years of age or older, to vote, shall not be denied or abridged by the United States or any state on account of age.

Section 2 The Congress shall have the power to enforce this article by appropriate legislation.

Amendment 27 (1992)
Congressional Salaries

No law varying the compensation for the services of the Senators and Representatives shall take effect until an election of Representatives shall have intervened.

Universal Declaration of Human Rights

On December 10, 1948, the General Assembly of the United Nations adopted and proclaimed the Universal Declaration of Human Rights, the full text of which appears in the following pages. The Assembly then called upon all member nations to publicize the text of the Declaration and "to cause it to be disseminated, displayed, read and expounded principally in schools and other educational institutions, without distinction based on the political status of countries or territories."

PREAMBLE

Whereas recognition of the inherent dignity and of the equal and inalienable rights of all members of the human family is the foundation of freedom, justice and peace in the world,

Whereas disregard and contempt for human rights have resulted in barbarous acts which have outraged the conscience of mankind, and the advent of a world in which human beings shall enjoy freedom of speech and belief and freedom from fear and want has been proclaimed as the highest aspiration of the common people,

Whereas it is essential, if man is not to be compelled to have recourse, as a last resort, to rebellion against tyranny and oppression, that human rights should be protected by the rule of law,

Whereas it is essential to promote the development of friendly relations between nations,

Whereas the peoples of the United Nations have in the Charter reaffirmed their faith in fundamental human rights, in the dignity and worth of the human person and in the equal rights of men and women and have determined to promote social progress and better standards of life in larger freedom,

Whereas Member States have pledged themselves to achieve, in co-operation with the United Nations, the promotion of universal respect for and observance of human rights and fundamental freedoms,

Whereas a common understanding of these rights and freedoms is of the greatest importance for the full realization of this pledge,

Now, Therefore THE GENERAL ASSEMBLY proclaims THIS UNIVERSAL DECLARATION OF HUMAN RIGHTS as a common standard of achievement for all peoples and all nations, to the end that every individual and every organ of society, keeping this Declaration constantly in mind, shall strive by teaching and education to promote respect for these rights and freedoms and by progressive measures, national and international, to secure their universal and effective recognition and observance, both among the peoples of Member States themselves and among the peoples of territories under their jurisdiction.

Article 1.

All human beings are born free and equal in dignity and rights. They are endowed with reason and conscience and should act towards one another in a spirit of brotherhood.

Article 2.

Everyone is entitled to all the rights and freedoms set forth in this Declaration, without distinction of any kind, such as race, colour, sex, language, religion, political or other opinion, national or social origin, property, birth or other status. Furthermore, no distinction shall be made on the basis of the political, jurisdictional or international status of the country or territory to which a person belongs, whether it be independent, trust, non-self-governing or under any other limitation of sovereignty.

Article 3.

Everyone has the right to life, liberty and security of person.

Article 4.

No one shall be held in slavery or servitude; slavery and the slave trade shall be prohibited in all their forms.

Article 5.

No one shall be subjected to torture or to cruel, inhuman or degrading treatment or punishment.

Article 6.

Everyone has the right to recognition everywhere as a person before the law.

Article 7.

All are equal before the law and are entitled without any discrimination to equal protection of the law. All are entitled to equal protection against any discrimination in violation of this Declaration and against any incitement to such discrimination.

Article 8.

Everyone has the right to an effective remedy by the competent national tribunals for acts violating the fundamental rights granted him by the constitution or by law.

Article 9.

No one shall be subjected to arbitrary arrest, detention or exile.

Article 10.

Everyone is entitled in full equality to a fair and public hearing by an independent and impartial tribunal, in the determination of his rights and obligations and of any criminal charge against him.

Article 11.

(1) Everyone charged with a penal offence has the right to be presumed innocent until proved guilty according to law in a public trial at which he has had all the guarantees necessary for his defence.
(2) No one shall be held guilty of any penal offence on account of any act or omission which did not constitute a penal offence, under national or international law, at the time when it was committed. Nor shall a heavier penalty be imposed than the one that was applicable at the time the penal offence was committed.

Article 12.

No one shall be subjected to arbitrary interference with his privacy, family, home or correspondence, nor to attacks upon his honour and reputation. Everyone has the right to the protection of the law against such interference or attacks.

Article 13.

(1) Everyone has the right to freedom of movement and residence within the borders of each state.
(2) Everyone has the right to leave any country, including his own, and to return to his country.

Article 14.

(1) Everyone has the right to seek and to enjoy in other countries asylum from persecution.
(2) This right may not be invoked in the case of prosecutions genuinely arising from non-political crimes or from acts contrary to the purposes and principles of the United Nations.

Article 15.

(1) Everyone has the right to a nationality.
(2) No one shall be arbitrarily deprived of his nationality nor denied the right to change his nationality.

Article 16.

(1) Men and women of full age, without any limitation due to race, nationality or religion, have the right to marry and to found a family. They are entitled to equal rights as to marriage, during marriage and at its dissolution.
(2) Marriage shall be entered into only with the free and full consent of the intending spouses.
(3) The family is the natural and fundamental group unit of society and is entitled to protection by society and the State.

Article 17.

(1) Everyone has the right to own property alone as well as in association with others.
(2) No one shall be arbitrarily deprived of his property.

Article 18.

Everyone has the right to freedom of thought, conscience and religion; this right includes freedom to change his religion or belief, and freedom, either alone or in community with others and in public or private, to manifest his religion or belief in teaching, practice, worship and observance.

Article 19.

Everyone has the right to freedom of opinion and expression; this right includes freedom to hold opinions without interference and to seek, receive and impart information and ideas through any media and regardless of frontiers.

Article 20.

(1) Everyone has the right to freedom of peaceful assembly and association.
(2) No one may be compelled to belong to an association.

Article 21.

(1) Everyone has the right to take part in the government of his country, directly or through freely chosen representatives.
(2) Everyone has the right of equal access to public service in his country.
(3) The will of the people shall be the basis of the authority of government; this will shall be expressed in periodic and genuine elections which shall be by universal and equal suffrage and shall be held by secret vote or by equivalent free voting procedures.

Article 22.

Everyone, as a member of society, has the right to social security and is entitled to realization, through national effort and international co-operation and in accordance with the organization and resources of each State, of the economic, social and cultural rights indispensable for his dignity and the free development of his personality.

Article 23.

(1) Everyone has the right to work, to free choice of employment, to just and favourable conditions of work and to protection against unemployment
(2) Everyone, without any discrimination, has the right to equal pay for equal work.

(3) Everyone who works has the right to just and favourable remuneration ensuring for himself and his family an existence worthy of human dignity, and supplemented, if necessary, by other means of social protection.
(4) Everyone has the right to form and to join trade unions for the protection of his interests.

Article 24.

Everyone has the right to rest and leisure, including reasonable limitation of working hours and periodic holidays with pay.

Article 25.

(1) Everyone has the right to a standard of living adequate for the health and well-being of himself and of his family, including food, clothing, housing and medical care and necessary social services, and the right to security in the event of unemployment, sickness, disability, widowhood, old age or other lack of livelihood in circumstances beyond his control.
(2) Motherhood and childhood are entitled to special care and assistance. All children, whether born in or out of wedlock, shall enjoy the same social protection.

Article 26.

(1) Everyone has the right to education. Education shall be free, at least in the elementary and fundamental stages. Elementary education shall be compulsory. Technical and professional education shall be made generally available and higher education shall be equally accessible to all on the basis of merit.

(2) Education shall be directed to the full development of the human personality and to the strengthening of respect for human rights and fundamental freedoms. It shall promote understanding, tolerance and friendship among all nations, racial or religious groups, and shall further the activities of the United Nations for the maintenance of peace.

(3) Parents have a prior right to choose the kind of education that shall be given to their children.

Article 27.

(1) Everyone has the right freely to participate in the cultural life of the community, to enjoy the arts and to share in scientific advancement and its benefits.
(2) Everyone has the right to the protection of the moral and material interests resulting from any scientific, literary or artistic production of which he is the author.

Article 28.

Everyone is entitled to a social and international order in which the rights and freedoms set forth in this Declaration can be fully realized.

Article 29.

(1) Everyone has duties to the community in which alone the free and full development of his personality is possible.
(2) In the exercise of his rights and freedoms, everyone shall be subject only to such limitations as are determined by law solely for the purpose of securing due recognition and respect for the rights and freedoms of others and of meeting the just requirements of morality, public order and the general welfare in a democratic society.
(3) These rights and freedoms may in no case be exercised contrary to the purposes and principles of the United Nations.

Article 30.

Nothing in this Declaration may be interpreted as implying for any State, group or person any right to engage in any activity or to perform any act aimed at the destruction of any of the rights and freedoms set forth herein.

The United States of America

The World

443

South America

Africa

Europe

Asia

447

Antarctica

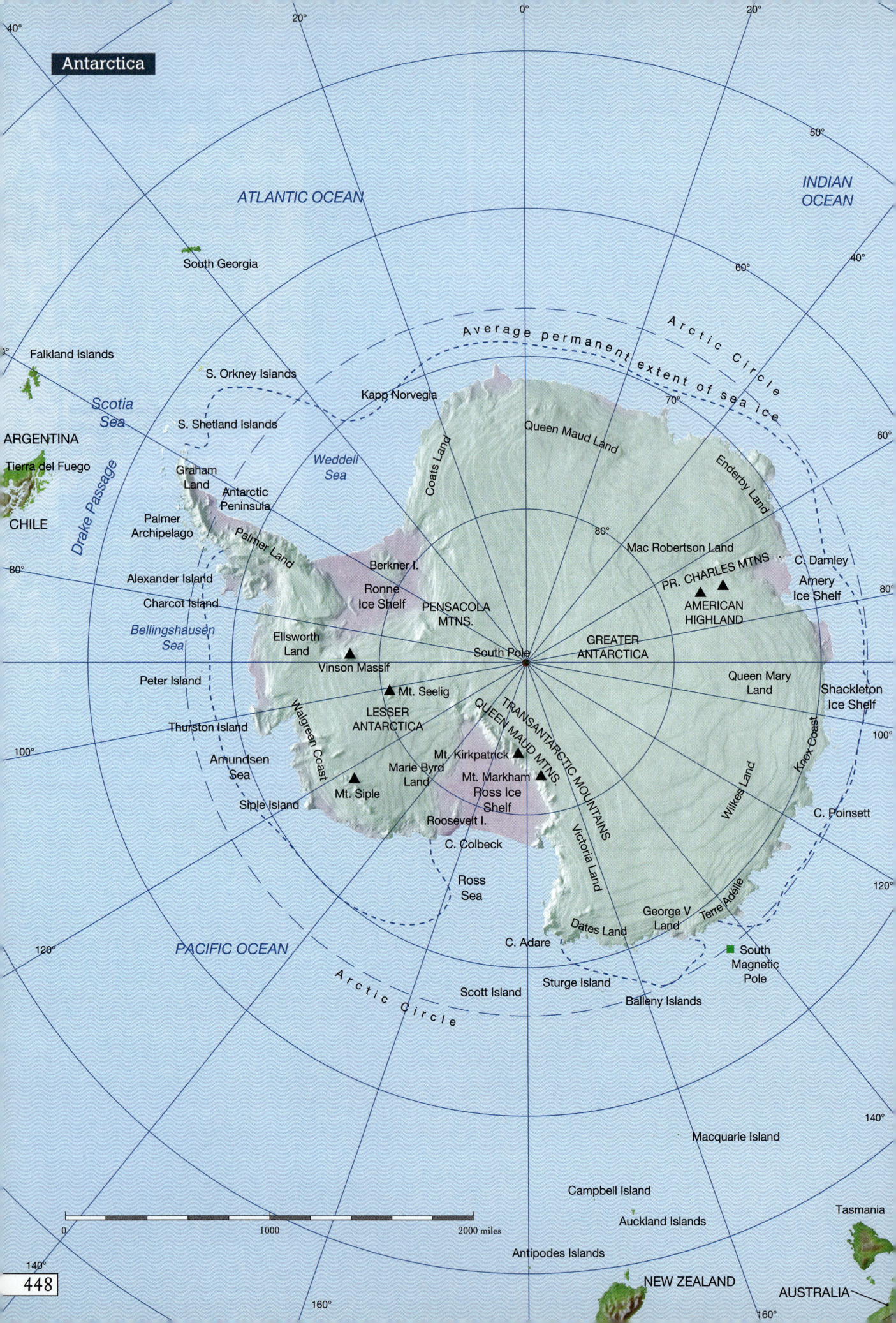

Glossary/Index

Vocabulary definitions are shown in bold type.

A

Abbasid Dynasty, 126
Abraham (Bible), 23, 119, 120
Absolutism, in France, 197
Abu Bakr (caliph), 123
Acid rain, 403
Acropolis, 72
Adams, John, 251
Adapted style—to change, to make one's own, 95
Adopted style—to take on and follow, 95
Adowa, Battle of, 300
Aeneid (Virgil), 95
Afghanistan, 82, 393
Africa, 134 (map). *See also* Slavery
　Bantu-speakers in, 135–136
　early humans in, 6, 7
　East Africa, 137–140
　European imperialism in, 293, 294, 298–301, 299 (map)
　geography of, 133-135
　independence for, 299 (map), 300, 369, 387–390, 388 (map)
　industrialization and, 269
　naming of, 91
　Nile River civilization in, 28
　poverty in, 390
　slavery and, 226–227, 235
　unity in, 389-390
　after World War I, 324
　in World War II, 357 (map)
Africans
　slave trade in, 234–235
　in Spanish American society, 227
African Union, 390
Afterlife, 8
　in China, 58
　in Egypt, 33
　humanists on, 202
Age of Exploration (European), 206–236
Age of Pericles (Athens), 77–78, 79–80
Age of Reason, 245
Agora—an open space in a Greek city that was used as a market area and a place for meetings, 72
Agricultural Revolution, 238, 239
Agriculture, 2. *See also* Farming; Food
　Green Revolution and, 401
　slash-and-burn, 134
Airplanes, in World War I, 322
Air pollution, 403
Ajanta, Caves of, 52

Akbar (Mogul Empire), 176–177
Albanians, in Kosovo, 374, 412
Albuquerque, Afonso da, 220
Alexander VI (Pope), 222
Alexander the Great, 81–83, 82 (map)
Alexius I (Byzantine Emperor), 188–189
Algebra, 129
Algeria, as French colony, 388
Ali (Caliph), 123, 124
Allah, 120, 124
Alliances. *See also* Allies; specific alliances
　Delian League as, 77
　Roman, 91
Allies—countries that join together in a war to fight a common enemy, 77
　Athenian, 77
　in Russian civil war, 332
　in World War I, 320, 322, 323, 324, 344
　in World War II, 356, 358, 359, 360–361, 364
All-India Muslim League, 297
All-Russian Congress of Soviets, 331
Alphabet, Cyrillic, 113–114
Al-Qaida, 414
Alsace Lorraine, after World War I, 326
Amaterasu (Japanese god), 169
Amazon River Basin, 404
Amendments, to U.S. Constitution, 252
American Revolution, 249–251, 332
Americas, 148–159. *See also* Latin America; specific countries and empires
　Monroe Doctrine and, 293
　Native Americans in, 234
Amnesty—a general pardon for political offenses, including illegally entering a country, 378
Amnesty International (AI), 409
Anasazi people, 156–157
Ancestor worship—worship of family members, which included offering sacrifices to those who had lived in the past, 58
Ancient world. *See* specific countries
Andes Mountains, 224
Anglican Church. *See* Church of England
Anglo-Saxons, 183, 194
Animals
　in Columbian Exchange, 232–233
　domestication of, 2, 11
　hunting of, 8
Annexation—to incorporate into an existing political unit, 312

Annulled—to declare a marriage void or invalid, 209–210
Anschluss—Hitler's plan to unite Austria with Germany, 353
Anthropologist—a scientist who studies the origin and development of humans and their cultures, 5, 6
Anti-Semitism—discrimination against Jews, in Nazi Germany, 347
Antony, Mark, 93, 94
Apache Indians, 157
Apartheid—law that legally separated blacks from whites in South, 389, 390
Apostles—Jesus' followers, four of whom wrote the Gospels, 99–100
Appeasement—giving in to the demands of a hostile person or group in order to keep peace, 282, 353
Appian Way, 91
Apprentices, guilds and, 193
Aqueduct—a channel designed to transport water, usually by gravity, 109
Arabia, 120, 122
Arabian Nights, The, 129
Arabian Peninsula, trade and, 37
Arabian Sea, 41
Arabic numerals, 52–53, 129
Arabs and Arab world. *See also* Islam; Muslims; specific countries
　Ethiopian colony of, 137
　Israel and, 391–392
　Pan-Arabism in, 392
　Portuguese conflict with, 140
　trade and, 139, 218
　World War I and, 321, 328
Arafat, Yasser, 392
Archaeologist—a scientist who studies human life by examining the things people made and left behind, 5–6
Archbishop—the highest ranking bishop; the head of a diocese, 187
Archimedes, 83
Archipelago—a chain of many islands, 169
Architecture, 13
　Greek, 83
　Islamic, 126
　Muslim, 129
　in Zimbabwe, 138
Argentina, 261, 381
Aristarchus, 83

449

Aristocrat—a wealthy man of power, usually a land owner, 72, 169
Aristotle, 80
Arizona, 229
Arkwright, Richard, 267
Armed forces. *See* Military; Navy; Soldiers
Armenia, genocide in, 410, 413
Armistice—a cease fire, an end to World War I, 323
Arms race, after World War II, 364
Art(s), 13. *See also* Literature; Painting(s)
  in Athens, 77
  Bantu, 136
  in Byzantine Empire, 111–112
  Caves of Ajanta murals, 52
  in China, 164
  Islamic, 126, 129
  Protestantism and, 206
Arthashastra (political writing), 53
Articles of Confederation, 251
Artifact—a man-made object, especially one of archaeological interest, 5, 6
Artisan—a skilled worker who specializes in a particular craft, 13, 111
Aryans, 44–45, 44 (map)
Asante people, British and, 301
Ashikaga shogunate, 170
Asia. *See also* Southeast Asia; specific countries
  British East India Company in, 294
  Buddhism in, 51
  Chinese Revolution and, 382–384
  cultures in, 162–178
  European trade and, 217–218
  humans in, 7
  imperialism in, 293, 294
  Indian subcontinent in, 41
  industrialization and, 269
  land bridge from North America to, 149
  Muslims in, 126, 127, 127 (map)
  Portugal and, 220
  sea route to, 189
  Southwest, 16–26
  West, 117 (map)
  in World War I, 322
  before World War II, 351
Asian Tigers (Little Tigers), 386, 386 (map)
Askia Muhammad, 144–145
Asoka (Maurya Empire), 51–52
Assemblies. *See also* Parliament (England)
  in Athens, 74, 78, 88
  in Rome, 88, 89
  in Sparta, 74
Assimilation—to make similar, of Africans, **301**
Assyria, 24, 37

Astrolabe—an instrument used to determine the altitude of the sun or other celestial bodies, 129, 218
Astronomy
  Aristarchus and, 83
  Muslims and, 12
  in Scientific Revolution, 246
Asylum, rights of, 409
Atahualpa (Inca), 224
Athens, 74–75
  direct democracy in, 88
  Parthenon in, 77, 78
  in Peloponnesian War, 78–79
  Persian Wars and, 76–77
  Philip II (Macedonia) and, 81
Atlantic ocean region, 229–230
Atman—Hindu word for soul, **47**
Atomic bomb, 362, 364
Atrocity—an utterly cruel or revolting act, **360**
  of Third Reich, 360
Attila (Huns), 98
Augustus (Octavian, Rome), 93, 94
Aurangzeb (India), 177
Auschwitz, 360
Austerity—a policy designed to control a nation's economy, **381**
Australia, humans in, 7
Australopithecus, 7
Austria, 372
  Anschluss with Germany, 353–354
  Austro-Prussian War and, 284
  France and, 254
  Italy and, 283
  nationalism in, 282
  Prussia and, 287
  after World War I, 324
Austria-Hungary, 321
  ethnic nationalism in, 320
  World War I and, 319, 324, 326, 327
Austrian Empire, 281
  ethnic groups in, 282
  Germans in, 285
Austro-Prussian War, 284
Authoritarian government—a government that has absolute power over a nation, **289**
Axes, as prehistoric tools, 7
Axis Powers, 354, 358
Axum, Kingdom of, 37, 137, 138
Aztecs, 12, 151–153
  on battle for Tenochtitlán (document), 223
  Spanish conquest of, 222–224

B
Babur (Mogul Empire), 176
Babylonia, Persian capture of, 24
Babylonian Empire, 20–21
Bacon, Francis, 245–246
Baghdad, as Abbasid capital, 126

Balance of power—a sharing of powers between nations to discourage one nation from imposing its will on the other nations, **281**
Balance of trade, favorable, 233
Balkan region
  communism in, 363
  Serbia in, 320
  in World War I, 319 (map), 320
  in World War II, 357
Ball games, in Americas, 151
Bangladesh, 41
Banking
  German, 289
  in Japan, 304
  for trade financing, 191
Bantu-speakers, 133–136, 135 (map), 138
Bar graph, 277
Barter system—to trade or exchange, 137, **191**
Basque Fatherland, 415
Bastille, destruction of, 254
Batista, Fulgencio, 376
Battle of Britain—when German planes, under Hitler's command, bombed air fields, naval bases, shipyards, and war factories of Great Britain, **357**
Battles
  of Adowa, 300
  at Cannae, 90
  of the Coral Sea, 361
  at Khartoum, 301
  at Marathon, 76
  at Midway Island, 361
  of Plassey, 295
  at Plataea, 77
  of Saratoga, 251
  for Tenochtitlán, 223
  of Tours, 183
  of Waterloo, 256, 281
  at Yorktown, 251
Batu Khan (Mongols), 115
Bay of Bengal, 41
Bay of Pigs fiasco, 376
Beijing, Imperial City in, 167
Belarus, 374
Belgian Congo, 300
Belgium, 356
  imperialism by, 299, 299 (map)
  industrialization of, 269
Bell, Alexander Graham, 275
Bentley, Elizabeth, 272
Berbers—desert nomads who ran camel caravans across the Sahara, **141**, 144
Bering Strait, 149
Berlin, conference in, 299
Berlin Airlift, 365

Berlin Wall, 372–373
Bethlen, István (Hungary), 324
Bezant (gold coin), 110
Bible
   Christian, 100
   of Gutenberg, 203
   Hebrew, 23
   Luther on, 206
Big Three (World War I), 325, 338
Bill of Rights
   in England, 244
   in United States, 252
Bin Laden, Osama, 414
Birth rates, 399
Bishop—the head of a diocese, 187
Bismarck, Otto von, 286, 288, 299
Bison, 150
   hunting of, 157, 158
Black Death. *See* Bubonic plague
Black Hand organization, 320
Blacks. *See also* Africa
   in Latin America, 310
   in South Africa, 389
Black Sea, 114
Blackshirt—a member of Mussolini's Fascist Party, 338
Blitzkrieg—a lightning war, 355
Blockade—shutting of ports or cities to outside deliveries so that no food, fuel, or other resources can get through, 79
Blood circulation, 247
Bok, Francis, as slave, 407
Boleyn, Anne, 209–210
Bolívar, Simón, 260, 261
Bolshevik Party, 330, 331–332
Bombs and bombings. *See* Atomic bomb
Books. *See also* Literature; specific works
   printing press and, 203–204
Borders, Roman, 98
Bosnia
   Muslim-Croat federation and Serb republic in, 374
   World War I and, 320
   in Yugoslavia, 327
Bosnia-Herzegovina, 373
   genocide in, 412
Bosnians, ethnic cleansing against, 373
Bosnian Serbs, 412
Boxer Rebellion (China), 308
Boycott—to refuse to buy something as a form of protest, 120–121
Brahma (Hindu deity), 47, 48
Brahman—a single force or power in the world that the Aryans worshipped, 44, 47
Brahmans (Aryan priests), 44, 45
Branches of government, 248
Brazil, 222, 381, 404
"Bread and circuses," in Rome, 97

Britain, Battle of, 357
British East India Company, 294–295, 306
British Empire, India and, 177, 295–297
Bronze, 12
   in China, 58
   weapons of, 37
Brunelleschi, Filippo, 202
Bubonic plague—an infectious fever carried by infected fleas that lived on rats, 191, 192 (map)
Buddha, 49–50
Buddhism—a religion that was founded by Siddhartha Gautama in the 500s B.C., 46, 49–51
   in Japan, 170
   Korean conversions to, 173
   Maurya Empire and, 51–52
Bulgaria, freedom of, 373
Bureaucrat—a government official who enforces the rules of the government, 65
   in China, 65, 66, 167
   in England, 195
   in France, 197, 255
   German, 288-289
Burial
   Chinese, 58
   Egyptian, 33–34
   sites, 8
Bush, George W.
   environment and, 403
   on terrorism, 417
Bushido code, 171
Business
   in Cuba, 377–378
   microloans to, 401
   trade and, 191
Byzantine Church, 189
Byzantine Empire, 104, 106–112, 108 (map), 126
   feudalism in, 184
   Holy Land and, 188
Byzantium. *See* Constantinople

C

Cabinet, in Japan, 303, 304
Caesar, Julius, 92
Cahokia, 157
Cairo, as Islamic center, 126
Calendar, 12
   Aztec, 152
   Egyptian, 35
   Incan, 155
   Islamic, 121
   Mayan, 151
California, 229
Caliph—a deputy who guided a community in Muslim beliefs, 123

Calligraphy—meaning beautiful writing, used by Muslims to decorate mosques with verses from the Quran, 129
Calvin, John, and Calvinism, 202, 207–208, 211
Cambodia, genocide in, 412
Camel caravans, 141
Canaan, 23
Canada
   English in, 249
   French in, 229
   NAFTA and, 378
Canals
   Panama, 312–313
   Suez, 297
Canal Zone, 312–313
Cannae, battle at, 90
Cannons, warfare and, 128
Canterbury Tales (Chaucer), 203–204
Cape of Good Hope, 219
Capet, Hugh, 197
Capetian Dynasty (France), 197
Capital (city), of Roman Empire, 107–108
Capital, for industrial investment—money or property used to invest in a business, 266
Capitalism—an economic system based on the private ownership of production for the purpose of making a profit, 191, 273
   in Russia, 331
Capital punishment, 406
Caravan—a group of people that traveled together, 122, 141
Carbon monoxide, 403
Cardinal—a position in the Catholic Church immediately below the pope, 187
Cargo—the freight or items carried on a ship, 219
Caribbean region
   Africans in, 226
   rebellion in Saint Domingue, 257–258
Caroline Islands, 322
Carthage, 89
   Punic Wars and, 89–91
Cash crop—crop grown to be sold to others rather than used by the farmer, 311
Caste system—a social system that determined a person's occupation and social class
   Hinduism and, 48
   in India, **45**
   in Islam, 176
Castro, Fidel, 376–377
Casualties
   from atomic bombs, 362
   of Holocaust, 360

451

in Vietnam, 385
in World War I, 324, 329
Cathedrals, medieval, 186
Catherine of Aragon, 209
Catholicism. *See* Roman Catholic Church
Catholic Reformation, 211–213
Cause and effect, 103
Cavaliers, in England, 242, 243
Cavour, Camillo di, 283, 284
Cayuga Indians, 159
Censors—people who checked up on the bureaucrats, 65
in China, 65
Censorship—to forbid the communication of views that oppose the government, 339
Central America. *See also* Americas; Latin America
civilizations of, 150 (map)
conflicts in, 379-381
economies in, 376
European colonization of, 225–228
nations of, 260 (map)
Panama Canal and, 312
rain forests in, 404
Centralized government—one single government ruled by one person or power group, 13, 65
Central Powers, 320, 322
Centuriate Assembly (Rome), 88, 89
Ceremonial center, Mayan—a religious center with temples dedicated to the deities and palaces for the ruler and other nobles, 150
Chamberlain, Neville, 354, 367
Chamorro, Violetta, 380
Champlain, Samuel de, 229
Chandragupta Maurya (Maurya Empire), 51, 53
Chang Jiang River, 28
Charity—kindness to one another, especially to those in need, 101
Charlemagne, 183, 196
Charles I (England), 240, 242–243
Charles II (England), 243
Charles V (Holy Roman Empire), 207
Charles Martel, 183
Charter—a written guarantee of rights, 192
Chaucer, Geoffrey, 203–204
Chechnya, 374, 416
Checks and balances, 248, 251
Chemistry, 129, 247
Chiang Kai-shek, 352, 382
Chiapas, Mexico, revolt in, 378
Chieftain—a tribal leader, 128
Childcare, by women, 9
Child labor, 271, 408

Children
Convention on the Rights of the Child, 409
family size and, 12
in fascist Italy, 340
malnourished, 399
poverty among, 368
as soldiers, 408
in Sparta, 73
Chile, 261
China, 61–63
Boxer Rebellion in, 308
centralized government in, 65
civil wars in, 165–166
Confucianism in, 61–63
early civilizations of, 56, 57–60
European trade with, 220
family life in, 60
internal problems of, 307–308
inventions in, 165
Japan and, 352
Korea and, 172–173
modernization of, 308
in 1990s, 368
paper in, 62, 164–165
People's Republic of, 307
population of, 66
Portugal and, 220
republic in, 308–309
revolution in, 306-309, 382–384
rise and fall of dynasties in, 64–67
river valley civilizations in, 28
Sino-Japanese War and, 305
Sui Dynasty in, 163
Tang Dynasty in, 163–165
trade by, 67, 67 (map)
unification of, 309
Vietnam and, 307
Warring States Period in, 64
in World War I, 322
after World War II, 364
in World War II, 359
writing in, 27
Chinese language, 58, 59
Chivalry—a code of behavior that knights followed, 185
Christ. *See* Jesus Christ
Christian Bible, 100
Christian Church, 100
Eastern Orthodox, 111–112
Christianity, 99–101
in Africa, 298
in Axum, 138
Constantine's conversion to, 107
Native American conversions to, 226, 233
persecution of, 107
as religion of Roman Empire, 100
Saladin and, 126
spread of, 101, 101 (map), 218
Chronological order, of timelines, 27
Churches
Christian, 100
Protestant, 206

Churchill, Winston, 358, 367
on iron curtain, 364
World War II strategy and, 363
Church of England, 202, 209–211, 242
Circle graphs, 131
Circuit court—a state court that holds sessions at many different places in a judicial district
in England, 195
Cities and towns, 13, 18
in early civilizations, 12
Harappa and Mohenjo-Daro, 42–43
industrial, 270–272
Islamic, 144
medieval, 188
rights of, 192
rise of, 192
of Spanish America, 227
tenant farmers and, 193
trade and, 190–191
in West Africa, 142–143
Citizens and citizenship
in Byzantine Empire, 109
in Puerto Rico, 312
in Rome, 88, 91, 94
City-state—an independent state consisting of a city and its surrounding territory, 18
African trading, 139–140
Athens as, 74–75
in Aztec Empire, 152
in Greece, 29, 70–85
in Italy, 91, 190
Sparta as, 73–74
in Sumer, 18–19
Civilization—a society in an advanced state of cultural development, 13
in Americas, 148–159
of Central America, 150 (map)
characteristics of, 13
Chinese, 56, 57–60
cities in, 18
development of earliest, 28–29
Egyptian, 31–35, 39
farming and beginning of, 10–13
Greek, 70–85
of Indian subcontinent, 41–45
in Indus River region, 42–44
Islamic, 118–130
Mayan, 150–151
in Mesopotamia, 39
of Mexico, 150 (map)
Minoan, 72
Mycenaean, 72
of North Africa, 30–38, 132, 133–146
Olmec, 150
origins of, 2–3
after Roman Empire, 104–105
in Southwest Asia, 16-26
timeline of earliest, 28–29
timeline of later, 104–105
Civil law—the law of a nation that deals with the rights of private citizens, 109

452

Civil service—people who work for the government, 164, 308
  in China, 63
Civil wars
  in China, 67, 165–166
  in El Salvador, 379
  in England, 242–243
  in Inca Empire, 224
  in Japan, 170
  in Rome, 92, 93, 94, 96, 98
  in Russia, 332
Ci Xi (Empress of China), 306
Clans—small groups of related people
  in Japan, **169**
  women in, 159
Classes, 13. *See also* Caste system; Middle class; Workers
  Egyptian, 34–35
  in Spanish America, 227
  in Sumer, 19
Classical Greece—an age of Greek civilization's greatest cultural achievements, around 500 B.C.–338 B.C., 76–80
Claudius (Rome), 94
Cleisthenes (Athens), 74–75, 78
Clemenceau, Georges, 325
Clergy—officials in a religious order, 253
Climate
  of Africa, 133–135
  of Indian subcontinent, 41–42
Clive, Robert, 294
Clothing, animals for, 9, 11
Coal, 269 (map), 402
  in England, 265, 266
  in Germany, 289
Codes of laws. *See* Law(s); specific codes
Codify—to organize or arrange into a system or a code, 20
Coins, in Byzantine Empire, 110
Cold War—a condition of open hostility between nations, 316, 317, 363–365, **364**
  African independence movements and, 387–388
  end of, 368
Cole (ship), 414
Collectivization—to make huge farms by combining the small farms of many peasant families, in Soviet Union, 342
Colombia, 260
  Panama and, 312
  U.S. military in, 313
Colonies and colonization. *See also* Imperialism; Provinces
  in Africa, 298–300, 299 (map)
  American Revolution and, 249–251
  Arab, 137
  British goods for, 266
  Chinese in Korea, 173
  colonial troops in World War I, 321

decolonization and, 387
English, 230–231, 231 (map)
European education for elites, 301
German, 326
Greek, 71, 76, 78, 83, 137
industrialization and, 269
Japanese, 304–305
mercantilism and, 233
in North America, 228–235
proprietary, 231
royal, 231
Spanish, 225–227
after World War I, 328
Columbian Exchange—the sharing of goods and ideas that began with Columbus's first voyage, **232**–233 (map)
Columbus, Christopher, 156, 221–222, 221 (map), 232
Comedy—a play that uses humor to criticize society, especially politicians, 80
Commoner—a social and economic class that included everyone who was not a noble or a slave, and who owned property, 152
Common Market, 375
Commonwealth—a nation governed by the people
  in England, 243
Commonwealth of Independent States, 374
Communication, 275
  in Japan, 304
  with speech, 9
Communism. *See also* Cold War
  in China, 364, 382–384
  containment policy and, 364
  in Cuba, 376
  in Eastern Europe, 316, 363–364, 372
  in North Korea, 384
  in Russia, 332–333
  as Socialists, 338
  in Vietnam, 385
Communist Manifesto, The (Marx), 274
Compare and contrast, using a table, 39
Compass—a device used to determine geographic location that consists of a magnetic needle that pivots until it is aligned with the Earth's magnetic field, 62, **218**
Competition, imperialism and, 294
Concentration camp—a type of prison camp, **346**, 347, 360
Concession—a grant of land made by a government in return for specified services, 307
Conflicts, in Central America, 379–381
Confucianism—a Chinese philosophy based on the teachings of Confucius, 61–63
  Chinese exploration and, 168

  in Han China, 66
  in Korea, 173
Confucius, 61–62, 64
Congo
  Belgian, 300
  Democratic Republic of, 136, 412
Congolese people, 412
Congo River basin, 135
Congress of Vienna, 281
Congress Party (India), 297
Conquer—to defeat or gain control of by force, 81
Conquistador—a 16th century Spanish soldier who conquered the civilizations of Mexico or Central America, 222–224
Conservative—favoring traditional views and values; usually not supporting change, **281**–282
  in Germany, 289
  in Italy, 283
Consistory, Calvinist, 208
Constantine (Rome), 97, 100, 107–108
Constantinople, 97, 109–110
  Church at, 111–112
  as Istanbul, 111, 128
  Ottoman capture of, 128
Constantinople University, 111
Constitution
  in France, 254, 255
  in Japan, 303
  in United States, 251–252, 422–436
Constitutional monarchy—a system of government where the power of the monarch is limited by law
  in England, **243**
  in Italy, 284
Consuls—officials who headed the Roman government and issued laws and orders and could veto each other's decisions, **88**, 89, 92, 94
Containment—a policy put in place to prevent expansion of hostile powers, 364
Continental Congress, Second, 250
Continental Europe, industrialization of, 268–269
Contras, in Nicaragua, 380
Convention on Genocide (1948), 413
Convention on the Rights of the Child, 409
Conversion. *See also* Christianity; Missionaries
  to Buddhism, 173
  to Islam, 122, 175
Cooper, Peter, 267
Copernicus, Nicholas, 246
Copper, 12
Coral Sea, Battle of the, 361
Corn, 233

453

Cornwallis, Charles (Lord), 251
Corporate state—where workers are grouped by occupations, **340**
Corrupt—allowing others to take bribes and misuse their power; a dishonest or immoral person, 164, **167**
Cortés, Hernán, 222–224
Cottage industry—product that is made in steps by different workers in their homes, **267**
Cotton, 43, 268, 297
Cotton gin, 268
Council of People's Commissars (Russia), 331–332
Council of Plebs (Rome), 88, 89, 93
Council of State (England), 243
Council of Trent, 202, 212
Counter-Terrorism Committee (UN), 417
Counterterrorism policy (U.S.), 417
Courts, in England, 195
Covenant—a binding agreement, **25**
Crafts, bronze and, 12
Craftworkers, 112, 192–193, 204
Cranmer, Thomas, 210
Crassus (Rome), 92
Creoles—a social class whose ancestors were the original Spanish colonists, **227**, 257
Crete, Minoan civilization on, 72
Crimes against humanity, 410–413
Croatia, 373
Croatians, in Yugoslavia, 327
Cromwell, Oliver, 240, 242–243
Crops. *See also* Farming; specific crops
  in Latin America, 311, 381
  in Mesopotamia, 18
Crucifixion, 100
Crusade—a military expedition undertaken by Christian nations in Europe to regain control of the holy sites under Muslim control; a great campaign, 126, **188**–189, 189 (map), 217
Cuba, 261
  Columbus in, 222
  revolution in, 376–377
  state-sponsored terrorism by, 416
  United States and, 312, 313
Cuban Missile Crisis, 376
Cultural Revolution (China), 383
Culture—the way of life of a group of people, including their beliefs, traditions, government, religion, and social class, **5**
  in Asia, 162–178
  Bantu, 136
  of China, 164–165
  civilization as, 13
  of classical Greece, 79–80
  of East Africa, 137–140
  Egyptian, 35
  French, in Africa, 301
  in Gupta India, 52–53
  Hellenistic, 82–83
  North American, 156–159, 158 (map)
  prehistoric, 5–6
  of Renaissance, 201–202
  Roman, 95
Cuneiform—a system of writing developed by the Sumerians consisting of wedge-shaped characters, **20**, 39
Curie, Marie and Pierre, 275
Currency, euro as, 375
Customs duties—a tax placed on all of the goods that came through a city, **111**
Cuzco, 153
Cyril (missionary), 113
Cyrillic alphabet, 113–114
Cyrus the Great (Persia), 21, 24
Czar of Russia, Nicholas II as, 330
Czechoslovakia
  communism in, 363
  Nazi invasion of, 354
  Prague Spring in, 372
  Velvet Revolution in, 373
  after World War I, 324, 327

D

Daimyo—the head of a wealthy Japanese family, **171**
Damascus, Umayyads in, 125
Dams. *See* Flooding
Dante, 203
Daoism—a philosophy based on the teachings of Laozi, **63**
Darius (Persia), 21–22, 76
Dark Ages, in Greece, 72
Darwin, Charles, 274
Dating, historic, 12
David (Bible), 24
D-Day invasion—**June 6, 1944, the day the Allies crossed the English Channel from Britain to land on the beaches of Normandy, France, 359**
Death. *See* Afterlife; Infant mortality
Debt
  in Argentina, 381
  in developing nations, 400
Deccan Plateau, 41, 44, 174
Decision making, 395, 397
Declaration of Human Rights, 437–440
Declaration of Independence, 250, 419–421
"Declaration of the Rights of Man," 254, 258
Decolonization—to break free from colonial status, **387**, 388–389
Decree—an order
  by Council of Trent, **212**
Defense Department, 416
Deforestation, 369, 402, 404
Degnawida (Iroquois), 159
Deities—gods or goddesses, **13**, 19
  See also Religion; specific religions
  in Egypt, 32, 33
  Hebrew, 23
  Hindu, 47
  Inca, 154
  in Indus Valley civilizations, 44
  Roman, 99
  in Sumer, 19
Delaware, 230
Delhi, 174, 175
Delhi Sultanate, 175, 175 (map)
Delian League, 77, 78
Demilitarized zone (DMZ)—no weapons or fortifications are allowed in the area, **326**, 384
Democracy—a government run by the people, **73**
  in Athens, 74–75, 77
  China and, 383–384
  in Czechoslovakia, 372
  direct, 78
  in Greece, 73
  in Latin America, 381
  republic compared with, 88
Democratic Republic of the Congo, 136, 412
Denmark, 356
Depose—to overthrow those in power, **283**
Depression—a period of rising unemployment and low economic activity, **337**, 344
Desert zones, in Africa, 133
Dessalines, Jean-Jacques, 259
Developed nations, 398
  developing nations compared with, 399
  grants to poor nations, 400
  resources of, 402
Developing nations, 398–401
Dharma—refers both to divine law and to a person's obedience toward divine law, it sets up certain moral and religious duties for every person, **48**, 51
Dhows (boats), 140
Dias, Bartholomeu, 219
Dickens, Charles, 274
Dictator—a single person that has complete control of the government, **338**
  Caesar as, 93
  in Cuba, 376
  Hitler as, 346
  Mussolini as, 338
  in Rome, 89
  Stalin as, 341–343

Dictatorship, in England, 243
Diderot, Denis, 248
Dien Bien Phu, 385
Diet, in Americas, 150
Diocletian (Rome), 97
Diplomacy—the practice of conducting negotiations between nations, 91
  Byzantine, 110
  Japanese-American, 302–303
  Roman, 91
Direct democracy, in Athens, 78
Directory, in France, 255
Direct rule, of colonies—**a governmental system where a central government controls a country, 300**
Disabled, in Holocaust, 411
Disease, 226, 266
  in Rome, 96
  in urban areas, 271
Divine Comedy (Dante), 203
Divine right—monarch's belief that their right to rule came directly from God, 241
Dnieper River, 114
Doctrine—a religious teaching, 212
Domestication, of plants and animals—**to adapt, tame, or control a plant or an animal, 2, 10–11**
Domestic labor, children as, 408
Domination—to control or wield power over others, 287
Dominican Republic, United States and, 313
Drake, Francis, 228
Drama, Greek, 80
Drawing conclusions, 161
Drug traffic, in Panama, 380–381
Duce, Il, Mussolini as, 339
Dukes, 185
Duma (Russia), 330
Dunkirk, 356
Duomo, Il (Florence), 202
Dutch. *See also* Netherlands
  colonization by, 228
  in South Africa, 388
  trade by, 220, 233
Duties, Byzantine, 111
Dynastic cycle—the rise, rule, and fall of a dynasty over a number of years, 59, 60
Dynasty—a group or family that maintains power for many generations, 31, 51. *See also* Empires; specific dynasties and rulers
  breakaways from Islamic Empire, 126
  in China, 29, 58–59, 63, 64–67, 163–168, 306
  in Egypt, 31–32
  in Korea, 172
  in Kush, 36
  in Maurya Empire, 51–52

E

Earth
  Muslims and, 129
  planetary movement and, 246
  size of, 221
East Africa
  Homo sapiens in, 7
  trading states in, 137-140, 140 (map)
East Berlin, 372
Eastern Europe
  communism in, 316, 363–364
  ethnic groups in, 327–328
  in 1990s, 368
  after World War I, 324, 327
  after World War II, 371–374
  in World War II, 359
Eastern Front, in World War I, 321
Eastern Orthodox Church—adhering to the accepted and established faith 112, 114
Eastern Roman Empire, 97. *See also* Byzantine Empire
Eastern Woodlands Indians, Iroquois as, 159
East Germany, 363, 372
East India Company, British, 294–295
East Indies, 220, 221, 222
East Timor, genocide in, 412
Economic imperialism—where buyers set the prices because producers have nowhere else to sell their crops and raw materials, 310–311
Economics, laissez-faire, 247
Economic system. *See also* Communism; Socialism
  capitalism as, 191
  manorialism as, 185–186, 193
Economy. *See also* Imperialism; Industrial Revolution; Wealth
  in Africa, 390
  in Argentina, 381
  in Central American countries, 379–381
  of China, 164, 383
  in Cuba, 376
  depression of 1920s and 1930s, 337
  developing nations and, 398–401
  in English colonies, 231
  EU and, 375
  European, 371–374
  fall of Roman Empire and, 96–97
  German, 289
  guilds in, 192–193
  of Harappa and Mohenjo-Daro, 43
  in Japan, 171, 351, 385–386
  of Latin America, 310–311
  Mayan, 151
  mercantilism and, 233
  of Mexico, 377–378
  money in, 191
  in Nazi Germany, 346
  oil and, 392
  in Pacific Ocean region, 385–386
  in Russia, 329, 333, 341–342
  socialism and, 273
  sustainable development and, 405
  after World War II, 369
Edict of Milan, 100
Edison, Thomas, 275
Edo. *See* Tokyo
Education. *See also* Schools
  in Byzantine Empire, 110–111
  in China, 308–309
  in developing nations, 399
  Islamic, 129
  in Japan, 304
  religion and, 186
  in Roman Empire, 95
  in Sparta, 73, 74
  of workers, 271
Edward VI (England), 210
Egypt (ancient), 31–35, 31 (map), 36
  archaeology in, 5
  civilizations in, 29, 39
  Hebrews in, 23–24
  independent dynasty in, 126
  pyramids of, 34
Egypt (modern), Israel and, 392
Eightfold Path, 50–51
Eisenhower, Dwight D., 359, 385
Elba, Napoleon on, 256
Elections
  in Eastern Europe, 372, 373
  in South Africa, 389
"El Grito de Dolores" (the Cry of Dolores), 259
Elite—the upper class, 301
Elizabeth I (England), 210, 228, 241
El Salvador, 379
Emancipation—to make free, 330
Embargo—a legal stoppage of all commerce
  on Cuba, **376**
Emperor—the ruler of an empire, 64
  in China, 64–65, 66
  Japanese, 169
  Roman Empire and, 94
Empires. *See also* Dynasty; Imperialism; specific empires
  in India, 174–177
  Portuguese trading, 220
  of West Africa, 235
  of West Asia, 117 (map)
  before World War II, 351
Encomienda—the right to demand labor from Native Americans living on the land, 226
Encyclopedia.... (Diderot), 248
England (Britain). *See* British Empire; Great Britain
English language, 204, 211

455

Enlightenment—the Scientific Revolution and the Age of Reason, 245, 247–248, 252, 257
Enola Gay (airplane), 362
Entertainment, in Rome, 97
Entrepreneur—a person who plans, organizes, and assumes the risk of and operates a business venture, in United States, 269
Environment—the physical geography and the climate that influences the development of a people, 133, 368, 402–405
Ephor—a council of five men who held power and managed the government, on a daily basis, in Sparta, 74
Epic literature. *See also* specific works
  Homeric, 80
  of Virgil, 95
Epic of Gilgamesh, 20
Epic of Sundiata, 143
Eratosthenes, 83
Essays, persuasive, 85
Estates (Estates-General)—the legislative assembly in France prior to the Revolution; a social position or rank, 253
Estonia, 327, 356
Ethiopia, 137, 138, 298
  Australopithecus in, 7
  independence of, 300
  Italian invasion of, 352–353
Ethnic cleansing—the killing of ethnic groups, 373–374, 412
Ethnic group—a group of people that share the same culture, 282
  in Austrian Empire, 282
  Russian Revolution and, 332
  after World War I, 324
  in Yugoslavia, 327–328
Ethnic nationalism, World War I and, 320
Ethnocentrism—an ethnic group's belief that its ethnic group is superior, 234
Etruscans, 87
EU. *See* European Union (EU)
Euclid, 83
Euphrates River, 17, 28
Euro, 375
Europe
  Africa partitioned by, 298–301
  balance of power in, 281
  Chinese revolution and, 306–309
  economic recovery in, 371–374
  in global age (1400s), 217–236
  Homo erectus in, 7
  humans in, 7
  industrial centers in, 269 (map)
  invasions of, 188
  Japan and, 171, 303
  medieval period in, 182–199
  Middle East and, 189
  nationalism in, 280–290
  North American colonization by, 228–235
  power in other countries, 278
  religions in (1600), 211 (map)
  Renaissance in, 201–204
  Roosevelt Corollary and, 313
  rule in Africa by, 387–388
  scientific contributions from, 247
  Suez Canal and, 297
  totalitarian governments in, 336
  trade routes of (1700), 219 (map)
  World War I and, 322–323, 322 (map), 327 (map)
  World War II and, 356–360, 364 (map)
European Economic Community (EEC), 375
European Recovery Act. *See* Marshall Plan
European Union (EU), 375
Exchange. *See* Trade
Excommunication, of Luther—to take away the right of church membership, 202, 206
Executive branch, 248, 251, 303
Exodus, 24
Expansion. *See also* Imperialism; Invasions; specific countries
  of Byzantine Empire, 108–109, 108 (map)
  global, 180
  by Japan, 304–305, 305 (map), 351–352, 352 (map)
  by Nazi Germany, 353–354, 353 (map), 355
  by Rome, 93, 94–95
  by Soviet Union, 363, 364
Exploration
  Age of, 216–236
  by China, 167–168
  by Columbus, 221–222
  Crusades and, 189
  by England, 228
  in global age, 217–224
  by Portugal, 218–219
  by sea, 218–222
  by Spain, 221–222, 221 (map), 229
Export—to trade or sell goods to other nations, 37, 233
Extended family—all the related members of a family, 60
Extraterritoriality—exemption from local legal jurisdiction, 307
Ezana (king of Axum), 138

F

Fact and opinion, 215
Factories, 266. *See also* Industrialization
  conditions in, 271
  in Latin America, 310–311
  maquiladora as, 378
Factors of production, 267
Factory system, 267–268
Faith, 206, 212
Families
  in Athens, 75
  in Babylonia, 21
  in China, 58, 60
  in Confucianism, 62
  middle-class, 272
  nuclear, 204
  in rural Africa, 136
  sizes of, 12
Famine—a drastic food shortage, 23, 333, 342
Farming, 2
  in Americas, 150
  in Byzantine Empire, 109, 110
  and civilization, 10–13
  Columbian Exchange and, 233
  in developing nations, 399
  Egyptian, 35
  in England, 266
  in English colonies, 231
  Green Revolution and, 401
  in Harappa and Mohenjo-Daro, 43
  in Kush, 36
  in Latin America, 310–311
  in Mali, 143
  Mayan, 151
  in Mesopotamia, 17
  migration from, 265
  in Roman Empire, 96
  slash-and-burn method of, 134
  in Soviet Union, 342
  in Sparta, 74
  spread of, 11 (map)
  tenant farmers and, 193
Fascism—a totalitarian government that is not Communist, 338, 339–340
Favorable balance of trade—when the value of goods that a nation exports to other nations is greater than the value of the goods that it imports, 233
Federal system—power shared between a national government and the state governments, 251
Ferdinand (Spain), 213, 222
Fertile Crescent, 18 (map)
Fertile—land that is rich enough to sustain plant growth, 17
Feudal system—a form of government where there is a powerful ruler to whom everyone owes honor and loyalty, 115, 184–185
  in Japan, 171, 303
  in Monomotapa Empire, 139
  in Russia, 329–330
Fief—a land grant or gift of land, 184

Filial piety—a family member's duty and responsibility to other members of the family, 60
Final solution. *See also* Holocaust of Hitler, 411
Finland, 327, 356
Fire, 7
First Estate, 253, 254
First Punic War, 89
First Triumvirate (Rome), 92–93
First War of Independence (India), Sepoy Rebellion as, 295–296
First World War. *See* World War I
Fishing, 8
Five Constant Relationships, 62, 66
Five nations, Iroquois League as, 159
Five Pillars of Islam, 120
Five-Year Plans—policy introduced by Joseph Stalin to increase industrial and agricultural production, 341–342
Flanders, 191
Fleet—many ships operating together under one commander, 167–168, **302–303**
Flood ing
by Huang He River, 57
on Indian subcontinent, 42
of Indus River, 43
of Nile, 31
of Tigris and Euphrates, 17–18
Floodplain—the area in a river valley that is subject to flooding, **17**
Florida, Spanish exploration by, 229
Flowchart, for analyzing sequence, 179
Flying shuttle, 267
Food, 2. *See also* Farming
in Americas, 150
British surplus of, 266
in Columbian Exchange, 232–233
in early civilizations, 12
hunting and gathering of, 8–9
Indian, 157–158
irrigation and, 3
malnutrition and, 399
in Roman Empire, 97
in Soviet Union, 343
surplus, 12
Food and Agriculture Organization (FAO), 399
Forced labor. *See* Slavery
Foreign aid
microloans and, 401
after World War II, 363–364, 400
Foreign investment, in Latin America, 310–311
Foreign policy. *See* specific countries
Forests, 159, 402, 404
Fossil fuels, 402
Fossils—the remains of humans, plants, and animals that have become hard like stone over time, **6**
Four Noble Truths, 50
Fourteen Points, 325, 327
Fox, Vicente, 378
France, 281. *See also* French Revolution
Africa and, 301, 388
American Revolution and, 251
Caesar and, 93
Capetian Dynasty in, 197
colonial rule by, 228, 300
creation of, 197
England and, 249
Estates in, 253
First Empire in, 256
Germany and, 353
Hannibal in, 90
imperialism by, 299, 299 (map)
India and, 294
industrialization of, 269
monarchy in, 196–197
Muslim invasion of, 183
Napoleon and, 259
as nation-state, 194
Normandy in, 194
Second Empire in, 282
Second Republic in, 282
Vietnam and, 307, 384–385
Vikings and, 183
World War I and, 319, 320, 325, 326
World War II and, 355, 356, 359, 364
Francis Ferdinand (Austria-Hungary), 320
Franco-Prussian War, 284, 287
Frankish Empire, 196–197
Franklin, Benjamin, 251
Freedom fighters, in Eastern Europe, 372
Freedoms. *See also* Religious freedom
in England, 243
in France, 255–256
in U.S. Bill of Rights, 252, 431–436
Free France, in World War II, 359
Free trade, 310–311, 375
French and Indian War, 249
French Indochina, 384–385
French Revolution, 238, 239, 253–256, 332
Saint Domingue rebellion and, 257–258
Fuhrer, Der, Hitler as, 346
Fujiwara family (Japan), 169–170
Fulton, Robert, 267
Fundamentalist Muslims, 392, 393
Fur trade, 229–230, 233

G

Gaius Gracchus. *See* Gracchus family
Galilei, Galileo, 246
Gama, Vasco da, 219
Game animals, 8, 150
Ganges River, 41, 44, 45, 46, 51
Gao, 144
Garibaldi, Giuseppe, 279, 284
Garten, Jeffrey E., 400
Gas chambers, in World War II, 360
Gathering, 157
hunters and, 8–9, 150
Gaul, 93
Geneva, Switzerland, Calvin in, 207, 208
Genghis Khan (Mongols), 115, 166
Genoa, 190
Genocide—the murder of all members of an ethnic group, **346**, 410–413
Geography
of Africa, 133
civilization and, 28
of developing and developed nations, 398, 398 (map)
of Greece, 71, 71 (map)
of Indian subcontinent, 41–42, 42 (map)
in Mesopotamia and Egypt, 39
Geometry, 35, 83
German Empire, 287–288
Germanic peoples, 98, 183
Germany, 194. *See also* Reparations; World War II
African rebellion against, 301
Austrian Anschluss with, 353–354
expansion by, 353–354, 353 (map), 355
government of, 288–289
Holocaust in, 359–360
imperialism by, 299 (map)
industrialization in, 269, 285, 285 (map), 289
inflation in, 344, 345
invasions by, 353, 354–355, 356
Japan and, 303, 322
Luther in, 202, 205–207
Nazis in, 344–347
postwar division of, 363
propaganda in, 335
Prussia in, 285–286
republic in, 323
unification of, 285–289, 285 (map)
World War I and, 319, 320–322, 325, 326, 327
before World War II, 351, 353–354
Ghana, Kingdom of, 142–143
Gilgamesh (Sumer), 20
Gladiators—captured slaves that fought each other to the death for Roman entertainment, **95**
Global age—a period in the 1400s when, for the first time, Europeans had direct contact with Africans, Asians, and by the end of the century, Americans, **217–236**
timeline of, 180–181
Global war, World War I as, 320–322

Global warming, 403
Glorious Revolution (England)—established that a monarch ruled by the power of Parliament, not God, 244
Gods and goddesses. *See* Deities
Gold
   from Ghana, 142
   Incan, 154, 224
   Mali trade in, 143, 144
   Portugal and, 139, 219
   in Spanish-American churches, 227
   from Zimbabwe, 138
"Golden Age of the Gupta," 52–53
Golden Ages, in China, 163
Golden Hind (ship), 228
Golden Horde, 115
Golden Horn, 108
Gorbachev, Mikhail, 372–373, 374
Gordon, Charles, 301
Gospels—written records of Jesus' life and teachings, 99
Government, 13. *See also* Civil service; specific leaders and countries
   under Articles of Confederation, 251
   Confucianism and, 62–63
   under dictator, 338–339
   under feudalism, 184–185
   laissez-faire economics and, 247
   Locke on, 247
   of nation-state, 194–197
   representative, 196
Gracchus family, Tiberius and Gaius, 93
Grameen Bank, 401
Gran Colombia, 260
Grand Alliance. *See* Allies, in World War II
Grand Council (Iroquois), 159
Graphs
   bar, 277
   circle, 131
   line, 237
Gravitation, 247
Great Britain, 95, 281. *See also* British Empire
   American Revolution and, 249–251
   Anglo-Saxons in, 183
   Bill of Rights in, 244
   civil war in, 242–243
   colonies of, 228, 230–231, 300
   constitutional monarchy in, 243
   East India Company of, 294–295
   Germanic invasions of, 98
   Glorious Revolution in, 244
   imperialism by, 299 (map)
   India and, 177, 279
   industrialization in, 265–268
   monarchy in, 194–196
   New Netherlands, New Sweden, and, 230
   Normans in, 183
   opium trade and, 306
   Parliament in, 196, 240–244

   Protestant Reformation in, 209–211
   rights in, 239
   separation of powers in, 248
   slave trade and, 227
   South Africa and, 388–389
   thirteen original colonies of, 231 (map)
   unions in, 274
   Vikings and, 183
   World War I and, 319, 321, 325
   World War II and, 355, 356, 357, 358
Great Council (England), 196
Great Leap Forward (China), 383
Great Mosque (Cordoba), 126
Great Purge (Soviet Union), 342
Great Pyramid (Giza), 34
Great Schism—a separation or division, 111
Great Serpent Mound, 157
Great Wall of China, 65, 65 (map), 69 (map), 167
Great Zimbabwe, 138
Greece (ancient), 70–85
   classical period in, 76–80
   Dark Ages in, 72
   geography of, 28, 71, 71 (map)
   Hellenism and, 82–83
   Renaissance interest in, 201
   Rome and, 89, 95
Greece (modern), 363, 364
Greek fire, 109
Greek language, 83
Greek language, Muslims and, 129
Green organizations, 405
Green Revolution, 401
Gregorian calendar, 12
Gregory VII (Pope), 187
G7 nations, 390
Guatemala, 151, 313
Guevara, Che, 376
Guild—an organization of merchants or craftworkers who banded together to protect their economic interests, 192–193
Gupta Empire (India), 52–53, 174
Gutenberg, Johann, 203
Gypsies, 346, 411

H
Hadrian's Wall, 95
Hagia Sophia, 108, 111, 114
Haiti, 255, 257–259, 313
Hajj-pilgrimage to Makkah, 122
Hall of Mirrors, Versailles Treaty and, 325
HAMAS, 415
Hammurabi and Hammurabi's Code, 3, 20–21, 22

Han Empire (China), 63, 65–66, 65 (map)
   Korea and, 171, 173
Hanfeizi (China), 63
Han Gaozu (China), 65–66
Hannibal (Carthage), 90
Hanoi, 385
Harappa, Pakistan, 13, 42–43
Hargreaves, James, 267
Harvey, William, 247
Hatshepsut (Egyptian pharaoh), 32
Hawaii, 312, 358, 359
Hay, John, 307
Health, pollution and, 403
Health care, in developing nations, 399
Hebrew Bible, 23
Hebrews, exodus and, 23–24, 32
Hellenism—the adoption of Greek culture and language by the people that Alexander conquered, 82–83
Helots—people who were captured in battle and enslaved, 74
Hemingway, Ernest, on inflation, 345
Henry IV (German Emperor), 187
Henry VIII (England), 202, 209–211
Henry the Navigator (Portugal), 218
Hereditary—passed on from one family member to another family member, 94
Heretic—a person who believes in religious ideas that are not approved by the Church, 212–213
Hiawatha (Mohawk), 159
Hidalgo, Miguel, 259
Hide—a dried animal skin, 158
Hierarchy
   feudal, 184–185
   of Roman Catholic Church, 186–187
   social, 13
Hieroglyphics—a writing system that the ancient Egyptians developed, 34, 35, 151, 152
Higher education, Byzantine, 110–111
Himalaya Mountains, 41
Hindus and Hinduism—one of two major world religions that began on the Indian subcontinent and contains many deities and different rituals and practices, 46–48
   Buddhism and, 51
   of Gupta Empire, 52
   Muslims and, 175–177
Hirohito (Japan), 361
Hiroshima, Japan, 362
Hispaniola, 222, 226
History and historians, 79, 95, 397. *See also* specific historians

Hitler, Adolf, 317. *See also* Germany
    Battle of Britain and, 357
    Holocaust and, 359–360, 411
    Jews and, 346, 347
    military and, 351
    Nazi Germany and, 344–347
    Russian invasion by, 357
Hizballah, 415
Ho Chi Minh (Vietnam), 385
Holocaust—the killing of millions of Jews, by the Nazis, during WWII, 359–360, 391
    Jews murdered in, 411, 411 (map)
Holstein, 287
Holy Land—the name that Christians gave Jerusalem and parts of Palestine where Jesus had lived, 188, 217. *See also* Israel entries; Jerusalem; Palestine
Holy Roman Empire, Protestantism and, 207
Home front—people that are not in the military, in World War I, **329**
Homeland Security, Department of, 416
Homer, 72, 80
Hominid—an early humanlike creature; the ancestor of modern humans, 6–7
Homo (genus), 7
Homosexuals, Nazis and, 346
Honduras, U.S. military in, 313
Hong Kong, 307, 386
Hong Xiuquan, 308
Horde—the name for a political division, similar to a principality; it has come to mean a large crowd, 115
Horses, 158
Horus (Egyptian god), 33
Hostage system—a family being held, against their will, so that specific terms will be met, 171
House of Commons (England), 242, 243
"House of Wisdom," 129
Housing
    of ancestral Puebloans (Anasazi), 156, 157
    in early civilizations, 12
    in Eastern Woodlands, 159
    in Harappa and Mohenjo-Daro, 43
    in Sumer, 19
Huang He River, 28, 57, 58
Huascar (Inca), 224
Huitzilopochtli (Aztec god), 152
Human body, 247
Humanism—an intellectual movement that emphasized working for the good of the city and state, 202
Humanitarianism—people who want to improve conditions for native people, imperialism and, **294**

Human rights, 406–409, 437–440. *See also* Genocide
Human Rights Watch (HRW), 409
Humans
    in Americas, 149
    prehistory of, 2–3, 4-26
Human sacrifice, 151, 152, 153
Hungary, 372, 373. *See also* Austria-Hungary
    communism in, 363
    nationalism in, 282
    after World War I, 324, 326, 327
Huns, 98, 335
Hunting, 2, 3
    gathering and, 8–9, 10, 150, 157
    with horses, 158
Hyksos people, 32

I

Ice Age, 149
Icon—image of religious figure, 112
Iliad (Homer), 72, 80
IMF. *See* International Monetary Fund (IMF)
Immigrants, Mexican in United States, 378
Immunity—acquired resistance to infection, 226
Imperial City (China), 167
Imperial—having supreme authority over an empire, 170
Imperialism—a nation's economic and political influence over other nations, 292, 293–301
    Japanese, 302, 304–305, 305 (map)
    in Latin America, 310–313
Import—to bring in goods from a foreign country to sell, 233
Inca Empire, 153–155, 153 (map), 224
Income, in Latin America, 376
Independence, 238
    for Africa, 299 (map), 300, 369, 387–390
    for Asia, 369
    for Haiti, 257–259
    for Latin America, 310
    for Texas, 312
    U.S. Declaration of Independence, 250, 419–421
    after World War II, 368
India. *See also* Aryans; Gupta Empire (India); Maurya Empire (India)
    Alexander the Great in, 82
    British and, 279, 294–297
    development of, 386
    empires in, 174–177
    English control of, 249
    European trade with, 220
    Gama in, 219
    Gupta Empire in, 52–53
    Indus River civilization in, 28
    Maurya Empire in, 51–52

    Mogul Empire in, 176–177
    Muslim influences on, 175–176
    nationalism in, 297
    subcontinent of, 40, 41–45
    trade and, 37
Indian National Congress, 297
Indian Ocean, 41, 42, 137
Indians. *See also* Native Americans
    naming by Columbus, 222
Indian subcontinent
    geography of, 41–42, 42 (map)
    Hinduism on, 46–48
Indigo, 231
Indirect rule—a governmental system that allows a country to maintain its traditions and customs while another country makes all decisions, 300
Individual achievement, in Renaissance, 202
Indochina. *See also* Vietnam; Vietnam War
    Japan and, 352
Indo-European languages, Sanskrit as, 44
Indonesia, 386
Indra (Aryan god), 44
Indulgence—a fee paid to the Catholic Church that freed a person from all or part of the punishment for sins, 205, 212
Indus River, 28, 41
Indus River region
    Aryan invasions of, 44–45
    civilizations of, 42–44
Industrialization—to develop a strong manufacturing sector, 268–269, 285, 368
    in developed nations, 398
    European centers of, 269 (map)
    factors of production for, 267
    in Germany, 269, 285, 285 (map), 289
    in Japan, 304
    in Latin America, 381
    in Prussia, 285
    in Russia, 329
Industrial Revolution—a period of time when the economies of many nations shifted from farming to manufacturing, 238, 239, 265–269
    environment and, 402
    imperialism and, 293–294
    middle class and, 272
    societal changes during, 273–275
    working class and, 271
Industry
    in Nazi Germany, 346
    in Russia, 333
Infant mortality, in developing nations, 399

Inflation—a rapid increase in the prices of goods
  in Argentina, **381**
  in Germany, 344, 345
  after World War I, 338
Information
  comparing and contrasting, 39
  synthesizing, 199
Inquisition—an investigation that violates personal rights of the individual, **212**–213, 246
Institutes of the Christian Religion (Calvin), 207
Insurance, for workers, 271
Intellectual thought. *See also* Philosophy
  in Columbian Exchange, 232–233
  in Enlightenment, 247
  in Greece, 80
  humanism in, 202
  Islamic, 128, 129
  monasteries and, 201–202
  preservation of ancient, 129
  Scientific Revolution and, 245–246, 247
  in Timbuktu, 144
Intermediary—a person who acts as a mediator or middleman, **140**
International Criminal Court (ICC), 413
International Criminal Tribunals, 413
International Labour Organization (ILO), 408
International Monetary Fund (IMF), 381, 390, 400
Inti (Inca sun god), 154
Intifada—an uprising, **392**
Invasions. *See also* specific countries and rulers
  Aryan, 44–45, 44 (map)
  Germanic, 98
  of Indian subcontinent, 52
  Viking, 183
Invention—a new device, method, or idea created from experimentation, **275**. *See also* specific inventions
  Chinese, 165
  in textile industry, 267–268
  World War I and, 322
Iona, 76
Iran, 82, 393, 416. *See also* Persia
Iraq, 17, 82, 328, 393. *See also* Persian Gulf region
Iron—a heavy flexible metal used to make weapons, **37**, 269, 269 (map)
  in China, 62
  in England, 265, 266
  environment and, 402
  in Germany, 289
Iron Chancellor, Bismarck as, 288
Iron curtain—the political separation between Communist countries and Western nations after World War II, **364**
Iroquois Indians, 159
Iroquois language family, 159
Irrigation, 3, 18, 31, 157, 404
Isabella (Spain), 213, 222, 226
Ishmael (Bible), 120
Isis (Egyptian goddess), 33
Islam, 104, 118, 119–130, 125 (map). *See also* Abbasid Dynasty; Islamic Empire; Muslims; Umayyad Dynasty
  African conversions to, 140
  Five Pillars of, 120
  Hinduism compared with, 176
  images and, 112
  radical, 368
  scholarship preserved by, 202
  in West Africa, 142
Islamic Empire, 125–130, 125 (map)
Islamic fundamentalism, 392, 393, 414
Isolation—being alone or remote from others, of Japan, **302**
Isolationist—a policy of not getting involved in alliances or other national political and economic relations, **355**
Israel (ancient), 16, 23–25, 24 (map), 82
Israel (modern), 391–392
Istanbul, 111, 112, 128. *See also* Constantinople
Italian language, 203
Italy, 279. *See also* Rome (ancient)
  Ethiopia and, 300, 352–353
  humanism in, 202
  imperialism by, 299 (map)
  Mussolini in, 338–340
  nationalism in, 282
  Papal States in, 284
  Renaissance in, 201
  Roman Republic in, 87–91
  trade in, 189, 190
  unification of, 283
  war crimes trials and, 360
  World War I and, 319, 321
  World War II and, 358
Iturbide, Agustín de, 259–260

J
Jacobins (France), 240, 255
Jahan (Shah), 177
James I (England), 241, 242
James II (England), 243–244
Japan, 169–172
  atomic bombing of, 362
  China and, 164, 305, 352
  expansion by, 351–352, 352 (map)
  feudalism in, 171, 184
  foreign aid from, 400
  imperialism by, 302, 304–305, 305 (map)
  industrialization of, 269
  isolation of, 302
  military in, 351
  modernization of, 279, 302–305
  Portugal and, 220
  Russia and, 305
  war crimes trials and, 360
  World War I and, 322
  after World War II, 385–386
  in World War II, 358, 360–362
Jefferson, Thomas, 250
Jenne (city), 144
Jenner, Edward, 247
Jerusalem, 24, 24 (map), 126, 188, 392
Jesus Christ, 99–100, 119
Jewelry, 12
Jews and Judaism
  ancient homeland of, 23–25, 24 (map)
  Crusades and, 189
  Holocaust and, 359–360, 411, 411 (map)
  Inquisition and, 213
  Islam and, 121
  Israel and, 391–392
  monotheism of, 24–25
  in Nazi Germany, 346, 347
  persecution of, 107
  Prophet Abraham in, 119
  in Roman Empire, 99
John (king of England), 195, 196
Johnson, Lyndon B., Vietnam and, 385
Joint-stock company—stock or funds of a company held jointly by its owners, **230**
Josephine (France), 255
Journeyman—a person who has learned a trade and works for another person for wages, **193**
Juarez, Benito, 312
Judaea, Judaism in, 99
Judah, Kingdom of, 24 (map)
Judaism. *See* Jews and Judaism
Judas, 100
Judicial branch, 248, 251
Jupiter (god), 99
Juries, in England, 195
Justice Department, 416
Justification by faith alone, 206
Justinian (Byzantine Empire), 108–109, 108 (map), 110

K
Kaaba, 120, 122
Kabila, Laurent-Desire, 412
Kaiser—an emperor, **287**–289, 323
Kalahari desert, 133
Kamakura shogunate, 170
Kaniaga, Kingdom of, 143
Karma—the sum of a person's actions in life that determines a soul's next life, **47**, 51

460

Kay, John, 267
Kazakhstan, Alexander the Great and, 82
Kennedy, John F., 376, 385
Kenya
  embassy bombing in, 414
  Swahili in, 140
Kepler, Johannes, 246
Khadija (wife of Muhammad), 120
Khanates, 166
Khartoum, battle at, 301
Khmer Rouge, 412
Khufu (Egyptian king), 34
Kiaochow, Shantung Peninsula, 322
Kievan Rus, 114-115
Kilwa (city-state), 139
Kingdom—a community with a monarchy form of government headed by a king or queen, 141
  See also Dynasties; specific kingdoms and kings
  African trading kingdoms, 137–139
  Egyptian pharaohs and, 31–32
Kingdom of the Two Sicilies, 284
King Philip's War, 234
Knights, 184, 185, 196
Korea, 164, 172–173, 302, 305
Korean War, 384–385
Koryo Dynasty (Korea), 172
Kosovo, 374, 412
Kristallnacht, 346, 411
Kshatriya caste, 45
Kublai Khan, 166, 167
Kulak—a farm owner who resisted collectivization, 342
Kush, Kingdom of, 31 (map), 36–37, 138
Kuwait, 392
Kyoto Protocol, 403

L

Labor. *See also* Slavery; Strikes; Workers
  in Athens, 75
  child, 408
  for factories, 268
Labor tribute, for Inca, 154
Labor unions—organizations formed by groups of workers to protest working conditions, 271, 274, 346
Laissez-faire economics—the idea that the government should do nothing for the economy, 247
Lake Texcoco, 151
Land
  manorial, 185
  Native American, 234
  in North American colonies, 231
  won from Mexico, 311–312
Land bridge—a stretch of land that connects two land masses, 149

"Land of gold," Ghana as, 143
Land ownership, in Byzantine Empire, 109
Languages. *See also* specific languages
  Indo-European, 44
  Iroquois language family and, 159
  vernacular, 203–204
Laozi, 63
Las Casas, Bartolomé de, 226
Lateen sail, 218
Latin America. *See also* Spanish America; specific countries
  imperialism in, 293, 294, 310–313
  industrialization and, 269
  nations of, 260 (map)
  revolutions in, 257–261
  U.S. involvement in, 378–381, 380 (map)
Latin language, vernacular and, 203
Latin people, 87
Latium, plain of, 87
Latvia, 327, 356
Lavoisier, Antoine, 247
Law(s)
  Arthashastra and, 53
  in England, 195–196, 241–242
  German, 289
  Hammurabi's Code of, 3, 20–21, 22
  in Japan, 304
  Justinian's law codes, 109
  Napoleonic Code and, 255
  Parliament and, 196
  in Rome, 88, 95
  in Russia, 115
  scientific, 246
  in Sparta, 73
Law of Nations, 95
League of Nations—an organization established to promote international cooperation and peace among nations, 325–326, 337
  mandate system and, 328
  before World War II, 352, 353
Leakey family, 9
Lebanon, 82, 328
Leeuwenhoek, Anton van, 247
Legalism—a philosophy based on the teachings of Hanfeizi, in China, 63, 66
Legislative Assembly, in France, 254, 255
Legislative branch, 248, 251
Legislature. *See also* Assemblies; Parliament (England)
  in Germany, 288
  in Japan, 304
Lenin, Vladimir I., 330, 331–332, 341
Leo Africanus, visit to Timbuktu, 145
Leopold (king of Belgium), 299
Lepidus (Rome), 93
Lexington, Massachusetts, 250

Liberal—a belief that laws should be made by legislators elected by the people and that the government should be based on a constitution, 281–282
Liberator, Bolívar as, 260
Liberia, 298
Liberties. *See also* Rights; specific liberties
  in Magna Carta, 196
Libya, state-sponsored terrorism by, 416
Lifespan, in England, 266
Lifestyle. *See also* Society; specific cultures
  of ancestral Puebloans (Anasazi), 156–157
  in cities, 270
  of colonial British, 296
  in early civilizations, 12
  in English colonies, 231
  on manors, 185
  quality of life and, 398
  in rural Africa, 136
  in Spanish-American cities, 227
Light bulb, 275
Lima, Peru, 227, 261
Line graph, 237
Line of Demarcation—a line at 38° west longitude that separated the Spanish lands from the Portuguese lands, 222
Literacy
  in Byzantine Empire, 110
  in Cuba, 376
  in Roman Empire, 95
  for women, 204
Literature. *See also* specific works
  Greek, 80
  Homer and, 72
  Mahabharata (Indian epic), 45
  Muslim, 129
  Roman, 95
  in Sumer, 20
Lithuania, 327, 356
"Little Tigers" (Asia), 386, 386 (map)
Liu Bang (Han Gaozu, China), 65–66
Livy (Rome), 95
Lloyd George, David, 325
Loans. *See also* Foreign aid
  microloans, 401
Locke, John, 247, 250
Locomotive, steam, 267
London, England, 190
Longhouse, 159
Loot—goods stolen during a time of war, 175
Lords
  feudal, 184
  in France, 197
  on manors, 186
  town rights of, 192
Los Alamos, New Mexico, 362

461

Louis XVI (France), 253, 254, 255
Louisiana Territory, 255
Louis-Napoleon. *See* Napoleon III (Louis-Napoleon, France)
L'Ouverture (François-Dominique Toussaint)—French word meaning "opening," it is the name given to Toussaint for his bravery in battle 258
Lucy (Australopithecus), 7
Lumber. *See* Forests
Luther, Martin, 202, 203, 205–207
Lutheranism—religious teachings and ideas of Martin Luther, 206–207
Luxuries, trade in, 36, 217

M

MacArthur, Douglas, in World War II, 360
Macedonia, 81–82
Machine guns, in World War I, 322
Machines, 266–267, 268
Machu Picchu, 148, 155
Madinah (Medina), 121, 122
Magna Carta—a charter of basic rights of English people, 195–196
Mahabharata (Indian epic), 45
Main idea, and supporting details, 15
Maji-Maji rebellion, against Germany, 301
Makkah (Mecca), 119, 122, 143
Malay Peninsula, Portugal and, 220
Malaysia, 136, 386
Mali, Kingdom of, 143–144
Malinche (Aztec), 222–223
Malnutrition, 399
Mammoths, 150
Manchuria, Japanese invasion of, 352
Manchus, 168
Mandan Indians, 157
Mandate—an authoritative command, 59, 60
Mandate system—under this system members of the League of Nations were responsible for setting up governments in former German territories, after World War I, 328
Mandela, Nelson, 389
Manhattan Project, 362
Manila, 361
Manor—the estate, or large landholding, of a noble, 185, 204
Manorialism, 185–186, 193
Mansa Musa (Mali), 143–144
Manufacturing. *See also* Guilds
 in Japan, 304
 natural resources for, 266
 in Prussia, 285
Mao Zedong (China), 309, 382
Maps. *See also* specific maps
 special-purpose, 69, 117
 for studying world history, 40
Maquiladora—a foreign-owned factory in Mexico in which the workers are paid less and the products are made for export, 378
Marathon, battle at, 76
Marcus Aurelius (Rome), 94
Mariana Islands, 322
Marie Antoinette (France), 255
Market—the place where people sell finished goods, 266, 293, **294**, 298
Market economy, in China, 383
Marriage
 age at, 204
 in Babylonia, 21
 in Rome, 95
 in Sparta, 73
Marshall, George, 364
Marshall Islands, 322
Marshall Plan, 364–365, 400
Martyrs—Christians who were put to death for their religious beliefs, 100
Marx, Karl, 273, 274
Mary I (England), 209, 210
Mary II (England), 243
Massachusetts Bay Colony, 230
Mastodons, 150
Mathematics
 Egyptian, 35
 in Gupta India, 52–53
 Hellenistic, 83
 Islamic, 129
Matope (Shona clan), 139
Maurya Empire (India), 51–52, 53
Mayan civilization, 150–151
Measles, 226
Mecca. *See* Makkah (Mecca)
Medicine
 in China, 62
 discoveries in, 247
 Egyptian, 35
 in India, 53
 in Industrial Revolution, 266
 Islamic, 129
Medina. *See* Madinah (Medina)
Meditation—intense thinking about spiritual things, 50
Mediterranean region, 36, 89, 133, 135, 141

Meiji Restoration—"enlightened rule," the period of time when Japanese officials studied Western political, economic, technological, and scientific ideas, 303–304
Melaka islands, 220
Men
 in China, 62
 Egyptian, 35
 rights in Babylonia, 21
 in Rome, 95
Menelik II (Emperor of Ethiopia), 300
Mentally ill, in Holocaust, 411
Mercantilism—the belief that the wealth of a nation depends on its supply of gold and silver, **233**, 249
Merchant—a buyer and seller of items for a profit
 cities and, 188, 192
 in middle class, 193
 Muslim, **141**
 Nubian, 36
 at trade fairs, 190–191
Meroë, 36, 37
Mesa Verde, 157
Mesopotamia, 3, 17–22, 18 (map), 28
 ancient civilizations in, 39
 Hammurabi in, 20
 Muslims in, 126
 writing in, 27
Messiah—the one sent by God to lead the Jews to freedom, **99**, 100
Mestizo—member of a low social class descended from Spanish Europeans and Native Americans, **227**, 257, 310
Metals and metalwork. *See also* specific materials
 bronze and, 12
 in Columbian Exchange, 233
 Egyptian, 35
Methodius (missionary), 113
Metternich, Klemens Von, 281, 282
Mexican War (1846-1848), 311–312
Mexico
 civilizations of, 150 (map)
 economy of, 377–378
 government of, 378
 independence from Spain, 259–260
 Mayan descendants in, 151
 NAFTA and, 378
 Native American deaths in, 226
 as republic, 260
 trade of, 378
 U.S. military in, 313
 Zimmermann telegram and, 323
Mexico City, 224, 227
Microloans, 401
Microscope, 247
Middle Ages, 182–199
 Renaissance after, 201

Middle class—a social and economic class made up of merchants, traders, and craftsworkers, **193**, **272**
   in China, 309
   Egyptian, 34
   French bureaucracy from, 197
   in Italy, 338
   medieval, 193
Middle East
   conflict in, 391–393
   Crusades and, 189
   terrorism in, 415
   after World War I, 328, 328 (map)
   in World War I, 321
Middle Kingdom (Egypt), 32
Middle Path, Eightfold Path as, 50–51
Midway Island, battle at, 361
Migration
   to Americas, 149–150
   Bantu, 135–136, 135 (map)
   to cities, 265
   from Greece, 71
   in Middle Ages, 183
Militarism—glorifying the ideals of a military class and having a strong military force, **286**
Military. *See also* Navy; Soldiers
   British, 356
   cannons and, 128
   in China, 308
   in El Salvador, 379
   fall of Roman Empire and, 98
   German, 345, 353
   of Hidalgo, 259
   in Italy, 340
   in Japan, 304
   in Persia, 22
   Prussian, 286
   in Rome, 89–91, 93, 97
   in Soviet Union, 343
   in Sumer, 18
   U.S. interventionism and, 313
   World War I and, 321, 326
   before World War II, 351
Military dictatorship—one person who rules alone with support from the military, **243**
Minamoto Yoritomo, 170
Minarets—the towers of a mosque, **129**
Ming Dynasty (China), 167–168, 172–173
Ming Hong Wu, Zhu Yuanzhang as, 167
Mining, 12, 226
Minoan civilization, 72
Missionaries—people who go out to preach to and convert people to their religion, **51**
   in Africa, 298
   Asian trade and, 220
   Buddhist, 51–52
   Chinese in Korea, 173
   Christian, 101
   in Spanish Empire, 226

Mission—church and housing for a priest and Native Americans who had been converted to Catholicism, **229**
Mobility (social)—the ability to move from social class to social class and better one's life, **48**
Modernization
   of China, 308
   of Japan, 302–305
Mogul Empire (India), 176–177
Mohawk Indians, 159
Mohenjo-Daro, 42–43
Mombassa (city-state), 139
Monarchs. *See also* Kings and kingdoms; specific rulers
   in Athens, 74
   constitutional, 243
   divine right of, 241
   in England, 194–196, 241–244
   feudal, 184
   in France, 196–197, 255
   in Greece, 72
   timeline of, 238–239
Monastery—a community of monks bound to vows of religious life, **201**–202, 210
Money, in Constantinople, 110
Money economy—use of gold or silver coins to acquire goods, **191**
Mongols, 115
   in China, 166–168
   Empire of, 165 (map)
   in India, 174–175
   Islamic Empire and, 126
   Korea invaded by, 172
Monk—a holy man, **167**
Monomotapa Empire, 139, 184
Monotheists—people who believe that there is one true God
   Jews as, 24–25
   Muslims as, **121**
Monroe, James, 293
Monroe Doctrine, 293, 311
   Roosevelt Corollary to, 313
Monsoons—seasonal winds that blow across the Indian Ocean, **42**, 42 (map), 137
Montenegro, 374, 412
Montesquieu, Baron de (Charles-Louis de Secondat), 248, 251
Montezuma (Aztec ruler), 151, 223
Morality, Hindu, 48
Morelos, José Maria, 259
Morgenthau, Henry, Sr., 413
Morocco, independent dynasty in, 126
Mortar—a building material that hardens like cement, **138**
Mosaic—a picture or decorative design made by setting small colored pieces into a surface, **112**

Moscow, 115
Moses (Bible), 23–24, 32
Mosques, 129
Mound Builders, 157
Mountains
   Andes, 224
   Himalaya, 41
Mount Hira, 119, 120
Movable type, 165, 203
Mu'awiyah (Caliph), 124
Muhammad, 104, 119
   ideals of, 121–122
   "rightly guided" caliphs after, 123, 125 (map)
Muhammad Ahmad al-Mahdi, 301
Muhammad Ture. *See* Askia Muhammad
Mulatto—person of a low social class who had ancestors who were Spanish and African, **227**, 310
Mummification—a process that preserves, or saves, a deceased body, 6, **33**, 35, 37, 155
Munich Conference, Hitler at, 354
Murals
   at Ajanta Caves, 52
   Etruscan, 87
Muslims, 118–130. *See also* Crusades; Islam
   All-India Muslim League of, 297
   Axum conflict with, 138
   in Byzantine Empire, 126
   Christian attacks on, 189
   fundamentalist, 392–393
   Holy Land and, 188
   Indian society and, 175–177
   Inquisition and, 213
   invasions of Europe by, 183
   Mali kings as, 143
   as merchants, 141
   terrorism by, 414, 415
   in West Africa, 142
Mussolini, Benito, 338–339, 359
Mutota (Shona clan), 139
Mutsuhito (Japan), 302
Mycenaean civilization, 72

N

NAFTA. *See* North American Free Trade Agreement (NAFTA)
Nagasaki, Japan, 362
Nam-Dinh, Vietnam, Chinese-French fight over, 307
Nanjing, Treaty of, 306
Napoleon I Bonaparte (France), 255–256, 259, 281
Napoleon III (Louis-Napoleon, France), 282, 283, 284, 287
Napoleonic Code—seven law codes that replaced the many systems of law in France, **255**–256

Natchez Indians, 157
National Action Party (PAN, Mexico), 378
National Assembly (France), 253–254
National Convention (France), 254–255
Nationalism—**a strong feeling of loyalty for one's own culture, including language and customs,** 256, 278, 280–290
  in African colonies, 301
  of Basque Fatherland, 415
  German, 285, 289, 345
  in India, 297
  in Italy, 283
  in Korea, 305
  in Soviet Union, 343
  terrorist groups and, 415
  World War I and, 319, 320
Nationalist party (China), 309, 382
Nationalist—**belief that people owe loyalty to the nation, not to a king or royal family,** 281–282
Nation-state—**a large area of land ruled by a single government,** 194–197
Native Americans, 148, 149–150
  ancestral Puebloans (Anasazi) as, 157–158
  Christianity and, 226, 233
  enslavement of, 226–227
  Europeans and, 226, 234
  Iroquois of Eastern Woodlands as, 159
  Plains people as, 157–159
  in Spanish American society, 227
  Spanish and, 229
  wars with colonists, 231
Native peoples, in Africa, 387–388
NATO. *See* North Atlantic Treaty Organization (NATO)
Natural law—**the law of nature,** 246
Natural resource—**a material source that occurs naturally in nature and is of great importance and value,** 73, 265, 289, 402
Natural rights—**rights that belong to people as human beings,** 247, 252
Natural selection, 274
Navajo Indians, 157
Navigation, Muslims and, 129
Navy
  Athenian, 76
  British, 356
  Carthaginian, 89, 90
  Chinese, 168
  U.S., 358, 361
Nazi Party—**a political party that was once known as the National Socialist German Workers Party,** 344–347
Nazi-Soviet Non-Aggression Pact, 354–355

Neolithic revolution—**the period characterized by the development of farming, tools, and jewelry; about 10,000 years ago,** 10
Nero (Rome), 100
Netherlands, 356
  colonization by, 228
  New Netherland and, 230
  trade by, 220, 233
Neutral nation—**to take no side,** 322 (map), 323
New Amsterdam, 230
New Economic Policy (NEP)—**a policy in Russia that allowed peasants some private ownership of land and some of what they raised and grew,** 333, 341
New England
  King Philip's War in, 234
  textiles in, 269
New Guinea, 360, 361
New Jersey, 230
New Kingdom (Egypt), 32, 36
New Mexico, 227, 229
New Netherlands, 230
New Rome, Constantinople as, 108
New Spain, 225, 229–230
New Sweden, 230
New Testament, 100
Newton, Isaac, 245, 247
New World, 222
New York (state), 230
New York City, September 11, 2001, terrorism in, 414
NGO. *See* Nongovernmental organization (NGO)
Nicaragua, 313, 379
Nice, 283
Nicholas II (Czar of Russia), 330
Nigeria, 144
Niger River region, 135
Nika Riot, 109, 110
Nile River, 28, 31, 36
Nimitz, Chester A., 361
Ninety-five theses (Luther), 202, 205
Nirvana, in Buddhism—**Buddha's name for release from the cycle of reincarnation,** 51
Nitrogen oxide, 403
Nobility
  in England, 195–196
  feudal, 184, 185
  on manors, 185
  middle class and, 193
  as Second Estate, 253

Nomads—**a group of people who have no fixed home and move from place to place in search of food,** 8
  Berbers as, 141
  Hebrews as, 23
  in Russia, 113
Nongovernmental organization (NGO), 405, 409
Nonrenewable resources, 402
Noriega, Manuel, 380–381
Normandy, 194
  D-Day invasion of, 359
Normans, in England, 183
North Africa
  civilizations of, 30–38, 132, 133–146
  French colonies in, 388
  Germanic invasions of, 98
  Nile River civilization in, 28
  Rome and, 89, 90
  in World War II, 359
North America. *See also* Americas
  cultures of, 156–159, 158 (map)
  European colonization of, 228–235
  humans in, 7
  land bridge to Asia from, 149
  Mound Builders in, 157
North American Free Trade Agreement (NAFTA), 378
North Atlantic Treaty Organization (NATO), 372, 374, 412
Northern Europe, Renaissance in, 201
North German Confederation, 287
North Korea, 384, 416
North Vietnam, 385
Norway, 356
Notre Dame (Paris), 186
November Revolution (Russia, 1917), 331–332
Nubia, 31 (map), 36
Nuclear family—**a household containing only a mother, father, and their children,** 204
Nuclear weapons, 364, 376. *See also* Atomic bomb
Nuremberg Laws (Germany, 1935), 346, 411
Nuremberg Nazi Trial (1946), 360

O

Octavian (Rome), as Augustus, 93, 94
Odoacer (Visigoths), 98
Odyssey (Homer), 80
Oil industry, OPEC and, 392
Old-age pension, in Germany, 289
Old Kingdom (Egypt), 32
Oleg (Kievan Rus), 114
Oligarchy—**a state that is ruled by a few,** 72
Olmec civilization, 150

Oneida Indians, 159
Onondaga Indians, 159
On The Origin of Species by Means of Natural Selection (Darwin), 274
OPEC. *See* Organization of Petroleum Exporting Countries (OPEC)
Open Door Policy, 307
Opinion. *See* Fact and opinion
Opium War, 306–307
Oppenheimer, J. Robert, 362
Oracle script, 59
Organization of African Unity (OAU), 390
Organization of Petroleum Exporting Countries (OPEC), 392
Orthodox—adhering to the accepted and established faith 112, 114
Osiris (Egyptian god), 33
Osman (Turks), 128
Ottoman Empire, 127, 127 (map), 128, 128 (map)
   Armenian genocide by, 413
   European trade and, 218
   mandate system and, 328
   mass murder of Armenians by, 410
   World War I and, 320, 321, 324, 328
Otzi (mummy), 6
Outlining, 55
Overfarming—an area of land that is no longer fertile due to excessive farming, 151
Overseas—a place beyond or across an ocean, 221
Owen, Robert, 268
Oxford University, 186

P

Pachacuti (Inca ruler), 153
Pacific Ocean region, 385–386
   Japan and, 322
   U.S. interests in, 312–313
   World War II in, 358, 360, 361 (map)
Pacific Rim countries, 386
Painting(s). *See also* Art(s)
   analyzing, 263
   Minoan, 72
   of religious subjects, 186
   secular subjects for, 202
Pakistan, 13, 41, 43, 82
Palestine, 23, 188, 391–392
   terrorism in, 415
   after World War I, 328
Palestine Liberation Organization (PLO), 392
Palestinian militants, 415
Pan-Africanism—an idea that meant that all Africans would join together to meet common goals, 389
Panama, U.S. military in, 313, 380

Panama Canal, 312–313
Pan-Arabism—the unity of all Arabs, 392
Panzer divisions, 354, 355
Papal States, 284
Paper, in China, 62, 164–165
Papyrus, 35
Paraphrasing, 147
Paris, France, 190, 287
Parish—a local church community composed of members and led by a priest, 187
Paris Peace Conference (1919), 325–326, 344
Parliament (England)—a council of state representatives, 196, 240–244
   American Revolution and, 250
   India ruled by, 296
   separation of powers and, 248
Parthenon (Athens), 77, 78
Partition—to divide up, 299–300, 299 (map)
Passover, 24
Pasteur, Louis, 275
Patriarch, 111
Patricians—citizens who were wealthy landowners and the most important social class in the Roman Republic, 88, 92
Patron—a wealthy person who supports artists with money, 202
Paul III (Pope), 212
Pax Romana—the name given to 100 years of peace and prosperity in the Roman Empire, 94–95
Peace
   of Augsberg, 207
   Pax Romana as, 94–95
   after World War I, 324–328
"Peace without victory," 326
Pearl Harbor, attack on, 358, 359
Peasants. *See also* Serfs and serfdom
   in Byzantine Empire, 109
   in China, 65, 66, 165, 167, 307
   Egyptian, 35
   in Japan, 172
   in Soviet Union, 342
   in Sumer, 19
Peloponnesian League, 78
Peloponnesian War, 78–79
Peninsula, 87
Peninsulares—officials from Spain sent to the Spanish colonies to see that the laws were carried out, 227, 257
Pensions, in Germany, 289
People's Liberation Army (China), 382
People's Republic of China. *See* China
Peoples' Revolution, in Cuba, 376

Perestroika—the restructuring of the Soviet economy, 374
Pericles (Athens), 77–78
Perry, Matthew, 302
Persecution—the oppression or harassment of a group of people, 100
   of Christians, 100, 101, 107
   of Jews, 107, 189, 346–347
   of Pilgrims, 230
Persia
   Athens and, 79
   Muslims in, 126
   Safavids in, 127, 128
   Sassanid Empire in, 107–108
Persian Empire, 21–22, 21 (map), 24, 81
Persian Gulf region, wars in, 392–393
Persian Wars, Athens and, 76–77
Persuasive essay, 85
Peru, 261
   Inca in, 153–155, 153 (map)
   Viceroyalty of, 225
Peter (Saint), 100
Petrarch, 202
Petroleum. *See* Oil industry
Pharaoh—a king or ruler of ancient Egypt, 31–34, 32, 36
Pheidippides (Athens), 77
Philip II (Macedonia), 81
Philippines, 312, 358, 360, 403
Philosophes—French word meaning "philosophers," a group of people who attempted to use reason for the good of society, 248
Philosophy—the search for knowledge about the world, including the natural world, human behavior, and thought, 61. *See also* Humanism; Religion
   in China, 61–63
   in Greece, 80
   in Industrial Revolution, 273–274
   realism as, 275
   Social Darwinism as, 274
Photographs, analyzing, 263
Pi, 83
Piankhi (King of Kush), 36
Picuria Pueblo, New Mexico, 227
Piedmont region (Italy), 283
Pilgrims, 230
Pizarro, Francisco, 224
Plague—a deadly disease that spreads quickly, 79, 96, 191
Plain—an extensive, level area of flat land, 41
Plains people, 157–159
Plains Wars, 158–159
Planetary movement, 246
Plantation system, in South, 231
Planting, in Mesopotamia, 18

465

Plants. *See also* Farming; Gathering
  in Columbian Exchange, 232–233
  domestication of, 2, 10–11
Plassey, Battle of, 295
Plataea, battle at, 77
Plateau—an area of high, mostly flat land, 41, 157
Plato, 80
Plebeians—citizens who were small landowners, farmers, craftsworkers, and merchants, 88, 92
PLO. *See* Palestine Liberation Organization (PLO)
Plutarch (Greek historian), 73
Plymouth Colony, 230
Poets and poetry. *See also* specific poets
  Rumi, 127
  in Sumer, 20
  Virgil and, 95
Point of view, 349, 367
Poison gas, in World War I, 322
Poland
  communism in, 363
  freedom of, 373
  German invasion of, 354
  after World War I, 326, 327
  in World War II, 355
Polis—a Greek city-state that was both a place and a governing body, 72–73
Political cartoons, 291
Political parties, in Fascist Italy, 339–340
Political revolutions, 238, 239, 240–244
Political systems
  feudalism as, 184–185
  revolutions in, 238, 239–244
Politics
  fall of Roman Empire and, 97
  Lutheranism and, 206–207
  origins of term, 72
  in Rome, 92–95
Pollution, 402
  air, 403
  water, 404
Polo, Marco, 166, 217
Polonium, 275
Pol Pot (Cambodia), 412
Polytheism
  in Egypt, 33
  in Indus Valley civilizations, 44
Pompey (Rome), 92, 93
Ponce de Leon, Juan, 229
Pope—the religious leader of the Roman Catholic Church, 111, 187, 212
Population, 12
  of African slaves, 227
  of Americans (1492), 156
  of Aztec Empire, 152
  Bantu migrations and, 136
  of China, 66, 307
  of cities, 270
  of East Africa, 140
  Indian caste system and, 45
  Japanese, 305
  of Native Americans, 226, 234
  of South Africa, 389, 390
  worldwide, 399
Portugal
  Axum and, 138
  East African trade and, 140
  exploration by, 218–219
  imperialism by, 299, 299 (map)
  Line of Demarcation and, 222
  Malay Peninsula and, 220
  Monomotapa Empire and, 139
Possession—land or property, 249
Pottery, in Korea, 173
Poverty, 368
  in Africa, 390
  in China, 307
  wealthy nations and, 398
Praetor, in Rome, 89
Prague Spring, 372
Predestination—God determines who will be saved and who will be damned to hell forever, 207, 212
Pre-emptive strike—to declare war on another nation unprovoked, 393
Prehistory—the time before writing was invented, 5
  humans in, 4–26
  timeline of, 2–3
Presbyterianism, 208
Priestly, Joseph, 247
Prime minister, in Japan, 303, 304
Princip, Gavrilo, 320
Principality—a territory ruled by a prince, 114
Printing, in China, 164–165
Printing press, 203–204
Problem solving, 395, 397
Production, factors of, 267
Profit, economic, 191
Proletariat—the poor working class, 274
Proliferation—to spread, 364
Propaganda, 335, 339, 340
Prophecy—a prediction of future events, 152
Prophet—a person who interprets and communicates the divine will of God, 25, 119. *See also* specific prophets
Proprietary colony—colony that was owned by an individual or private company, 231
Protectorate—a protected country or region, 312
Protestantism, 202–208
Protestant Reformation—a protest against and a way to reform practices of the Roman Catholic Church, 205–211
Protests, in Nicaragua, 379
Provinces
  Inca, 153–154
  in Monomotapa Empire, 139
  Roman, 89, 90, 91, 94, 97
Provisional government—temporary, only serving for the time, 330, 331
Prussia, 281, 285
  Austro-Prussian War and, 284
  France and, 254
  Franco-Prussian War and, 284, 287
  Germany dominated by, 287
  industrialization in, 285
  military in, 286
Ptolemy (astronomer), 246
Public works, in Athens, 77
Pueblo Bonito, 156, 157
Pueblo Indians
  ancestral Puebloans and, 156–157
  Spanish and, 229
Puerto Rico, 261, 312
Punic Wars, 89–91
Punishment
  in Babylonia, 20
  capital, 406
  by Inquisition, 212–213
  on medieval manors, 186
Purges, in Soviet Union, 342–343
Puritans and Puritanism, 208, 230, 242–243
Pyramid—a monument of ancient Egypt having a rectangular base and four triangular sides that contains a burial tomb, 34, 35
  Aztec, 152
  Egyptian, 34
  Mayan, 150–151
  at Meroë, 37
  Olmec, 150
Pythagorean theorem, 83

Q

Qin Empire (China), 64–65, 65 (map)
Qing Dynasty (China), 168, 306–308
Qin Shihuangdi (China), 64–65, 66
Quebec, 229
Quechua (Inca language), 154
Quetzalcoatl, 223
Quipu—knotted and colored strings the Inca used to keep records, 154, 155
Quito, Ecuador, 227
Quota—a set amount, for Soviet production, 342

Quran—the sacred scriptures of Islam, **120**, 121, 122, 124

R

Ra (Egyptian god), 32, 33
Racism—the belief that one race is superior to another, **294**
Radicals and radicalism
  in France, 255
  Islamic, 368
Radiocarbon dating, 6
Radium, 275
Railroads, 265, 267, 304
Rainfall. *See* Climate; Vegetation
Rain forest—a very hot region immediately north and south of the equator that receives a large amount of rain, **134**, 404
Rajah—a ruler or prince in India, **49**
Rajput—a Hindu warrior, **174**
Ramadan, 119
Ramses II (Egypt), 32
Rashidun caliphs, 124
Ratification—a formal approval, **251**–252
Raw materials
  from Africa, 298
  in colonies, 293, 294
  from Latin America, 311
Reading, in Renaissance, 204
Reagan, Ronald, 372, 379–380
Realism—the philosophy of seeing the world as it really is, **275**
Rearmament, of Germany, 351
Reason
  in Enlightenment, 247
  philosophes and, 248
Rebellions. *See* Revolts and rebellions
Rebel—a person who fights against a government and tries to gain power, **144**
Reconquista—the forcing of Muslims out of Spain by Spanish nobles, **213**
Recycling, 405
Red Army (Russia), 332
Red Guards (China), 383
Red Sea, 37, 137
Red Shirts (Italy), 279, 284
Reform
  in Athens, 77
  in Qing China, 308
  of Roman Catholic Church, 209
  in Rome, 92, 93
  in Soviet Union, 374
Reformation
  Catholic, 211–213
  Protestant, 205-211
Refugees, 409
Reign of Terror (France), 255

Reincarnation—the cycle death and rebirth in a new body or form of life, **47**, 51
Religion—the belief in and worship of a divine or superhuman power, **13**, **61**, **131**. *See also* Deities; specific religions and locations
  comparison of, 25
  Inca, 154–155
  in Middle Ages, 186–187
  monotheism and, 24–25
  national, 207
  Protestant Reformation and, 205–211
  in Renaissance, 202
  spread to new lands, 218
Religious freedom, 176, 230, 243
Religious icons, 112
Religious toleration, in India, 177
Renaissance—a period of time after the Middle Ages that describes the spirit of curiosity and adventure that developed during the 1300s in Italian city-states, **201**–204
Renewable resources, 402
Reparation—compensation for damages or injuries during a war, **326**, 344, 345, 346
Representative government—a government that consists of members of its society, **196**
Representative groups—groups that have many characteristics in common with other groups, **156**
Republic—a form of government in which citizens elect representatives to govern, **88**
  in China, 308–309
  in Germany, 323
  in Mexico, 260
  Roman, 87–91
Reservation—an area of land owned by the federal government for use by Native Americans, **159**
Resources. *See* Natural resources
Restoration—the time period between 1660 and 1688 when the English monarchy was brought back, **243**
Revenue tax—a tax paid for printed materials, **249**
Revolts and rebellions. *See also* Revolutions
  in African colonies, 301
  in Argentina, 381
  Boxer Rebellion (China), 308
  in Chechnya, 416
  in China, 67, 165–166, 383–384
  by Ionian colonies, 76
  in Japan, 172
  in Korea, 172
  in Mexico, 378
  against Moguls, 177
  nationalist, 282

  in Rome, 92
  in Saint Domingue, 257–258
  Sepoy, 295–296
  by Soviet peasants, 342
  Tai Ping (China), 308
Revolutions. *See also* specific countries
  Agricultural, 238, 239
  comparison of, 332
  Industrial, 238, 239, 265–269
  in Latin America, 257–261
  Neolithic, 10
  political, 238, 239, 240–244
  Scientific, 245–246, 247
  social, 264–276
  in transportation, 267
Rhineland, Hitler and, 353
Rhodes, Cecil, 388
Rhodesia, 388
Rice, 231
"Rightly guided" caliphs, 123, 125 (map)
Rights
  colonial, 231
  English, 239
  human, 406–409
  in Magna Carta, 196
  natural, 247
  of Parliament, 241
  in Rome, 92
  under U.S. Constitution, 251–252
  of women, 21, 35, 121–122
  after World War I, 325
Riots, Nika, 109, 110
River basin—a large area that includes a major river and its tributaries, **135**
Rivers and river valley civilizations, 28. *See also* specific rivers
  Chang Jiang, 28
  Congo, 135
  Dnieper, 114
  Euphrates, 17, 28
  Ganges, 41
  Huang He, 28, 57
  Indus, 28, 42–44
  Niger region, 135
  Nile, 28, 31, 36
  Tiber, 28, 87
  Tigris, 17, 28, 126
Roads and highways
  in China, 65
  Inca, 154
  in Persia, 22
  Roman, 91
Roman Catholic Church, 111–112, 180. *See also* Protestant Reformation
  Catholic Reformation and, 211–213
  on Earth-centered universe, 246
  English Puritans and, 242, 243
  hierarchy in, 186–187
  Inquisition by, 212–213
  Lutheranism and, 206–207
  in Middle Ages, 186–187
  Native American conversions to, 229

467

Nazi persecution of, 346
reform of, 209
in Renaissance, 202
Roman Confederation—a series of alliances between Rome and other areas in Italy, 91
Roman Empire, 86, 92–98, 94 (map), 98 (map). *See also* Byzantine Empire; Civil wars
 Christianity and, 99–100
 civilizations after, 104–105
 Muslims in former, 125–126, 125 (map)
 trade and, 67
Romanov dynasty (Russia), 330
Roman Republic, 87–91
Romans (Gypsies), 411
Rome (ancient), 86–102. *See also* Roman Empire
 geography and, 28
 Renaissance interest in, 201
Rome (modern), as Italian capital, 284
Rome-Berlin-Tokyo Axis, 354
Ronin—a soldier who fought for a daimyo, 171
Roosevelt, Franklin D., 355, 362, 363, 371
Roosevelt, Theodore, and Roosevelt Corollary, 313
Roundheads (England), 243
Royal colony—a colony that belonged to the English monarch, 231
Rule of law—to be governed according to laws, 196
Rulers. *See* Kings and kingdoms; specific rulers and dynasties
Rumero, Oscar, 379
Rumi (poet), 127
Rural areas
 in developing nations, 399
 urbanization and, 270
Rurik (Kievan Rus), 114
Russia, 113–116, 281. *See also* Russo-Japanese War; Soviet Union; World War II
 Chechnyan terrorism in, 416
 Civil War in, 332
 Communist government in, 332–333
 Cyrillic alphabet and, 114
 early period in, 114 (map)
 French invasion of, 256
 German invasion of, 357
 industrialization of, 269
 Kievan, 114–115
 Mongol invasion of, 115
 after Soviet Union, 374
 as Soviet Union, 333
 in World War I, 319, 320, 321
Russian Orthodox religion, 114
Russian Revolution, 321, 329–332
Russo-Japanese War, 305
Rwanda, genocide in, 412

Ryukyu Islands, 305

S

Sachem—a political leader or Indian chief, 159
Sacrifice. *See* Human sacrifice
Saddam Hussein, 393
Safavid Empire, 127, 127 (map), 128
Safety, in factories, 271
Sahara desert, 133
Sails, lateen, 218
Saint, Peter as, 100
St. Augustine, 229
Saint Domingue, 257–259
St. Helena, Napoleon on, 256
St. Petersburg, Russian Revolution and, 330
Saint Sofia (Kiev), 114, 115
Saladin, 126
Salat (prayer), 129
Salons, 248
Salt, 142, 143
Salvation—entrance into heaven, 206
Samaria, Israelites in, 24
Samurai (Japan)—a professional soldier, 171
Sanction—a loss of reward as a means of enforcing the law, 389, 416
Sandinista National Liberation Front, 379–380
Sanitation, 266, 271
San Martín, José de, 260, 261
Sanskrit, 44
Saratoga, Battle of, 251
Sassanid Empire (Persia), 107–108
Satellite nations—many different nations that are controlled by one central nation, 372
Satrap (governor), in Persia, 22
Saudi Arabia, Muslims in, 121
Savanna, in Africa—a region of grasslands with small trees and bushes, 134, 141–145
Savoy, 283
Saxons, 98
Scandinavia, Vikings from, 113
Schism, Great—a separation or division, 111
Schleswig, 287
Scholar—an educated person who has completed advanced studies, 128, 142. *See also* Intellectual thought
Scholarship—the knowledge gained from studying in a particular field, 202
Schools. *See also* Education
 attendance in, 271
 in China, 308–309

Sciences, 83, 129, 247
Scientific method—the systematic process for gathering and analyzing evidence, 6, 245
Scientific Revolution—a time of great scientific advances, 245–246, 247
Scribe—a writer, copyist, teacher, or secretary, 19, 34
Second Continental Congress, 250
Second Empire (France), 282
Second Estate, 253, 254
Second Punic War, 90
Second Republic (France), 282, 283
Second Triumvirate (Rome), 93–94
Second World War. *See* World War II
Secularism. *See* Humanism
Security Council (UN), 413, 417
Self-government, in Africa, 388
Self-strengthening reform—a period of reform when Qing officials introduced Western technology and science in China, 308
Seljuk Turks, 126, 188
Senate, in Rome, 88, 89, 92, 93
Seneca Indians, 159
Separation of powers
 in England, 248
 in United States, 251
Sepoy, rebellion by—a hired Indian soldier, 295–296
Sequence, on timeline, 27
Serbia
 Kosovo and, 412
 Montenegro and, 374
 and World War I, 320
 in Yugoslavia, 327
Serbs
 ethnic cleansing by, 373, 374
 genocide by, 412
Serf—a Russian peasant, 204. *See also* Peasant
 in feudal society, 184, 185
 noble control over, 185–186
 in Russia, 329–330
 as tenant farmers, 193
Settlements, 12. *See also* specific locations
Sewer systems, 271
Sewing, 9
Shang Dynasty (China), 58, 58 (map), 59, 69 (map)
Shantung Peninsula, 322
Sharecroppers, Byzantine, 110
Shia (Shiite) Muslims, 124, 127, 393
Shinto—a native religion of Japan, 169
Ships and shipping
 ancient trade and, 67
 Chinese, 62, 168
 Portuguese, 168, 220
 slave ships, 235

steamboat, 267
submarine warfare and, 322
trade and, 190
Shiva (Hindu deity), 47, 48
Shogun (Japan)—a military commander, 170–172, 302, 303
Shona clan, 138–139
Siberia, kulaks sent to, 342
Sicily, 89, 284
Siddhartha Gautama (Buddha), 49–50
Silk, 62, 67, 112
Silk Road, 67, 67 (map), 111, 141, 167
Silla Dynasty (Korea), 172
Silver, in Inca Empire, 224
Singapore, 386
Sino-Japanese War, 305
Skill Builder
  Bar Graph, 277
  Cause and Effect, 103
  Circle Graph, 131
  Drawing Conclusions, 161
  Evaluating Solution/Decision, 396
  Fact and Opinion, 215
  Flowchart for Analyzing Sequence, 179
  Line Graph, 237
  Main Idea and Supporting Details, 15
  Outlining Information, 55
  Paintings and Photographs, 263
  Persuasive Essay, 85
  Point of View, 349, 365
  Political Cartoon, 291
  Problem Solving and Decision Making, 395
  Propaganda, 335
  Special-Purpose Maps, 69, 117
  Summarizing and Paraphrasing, 147
  Synthesizing Information, 199
  Tables, 39, 315
  Timelines, 27
Slash-and-burn agriculture—the cutting down of trees and plants to burn them in order to open land for planting crops, 134
Slavery, 298. *See also* Crimes against humanity
  African, 226–227, 234–235
  in Athens, 75, 78
  Aztec, 152
  contemporary, 407
  in Egypt, 35
  Mayan, 151
  Native American, 226–227
  Portuguese trade and, 219
  in Rome, 92, 95, 97
  in Sparta, 74
  trans-Atlantic trade in, 231
Slavic language, 114
Slavs, 113
Slovenes, in Yugoslavia, 327
Slovenia, 373

Slum—heavily populated, poor neighborhood, 270
Smallpox, 226, 247
Smith, Adam, 247
Social classes. *See* Classes
Social contract—an agreement between people and their government, 247, 250
Social Darwinism—a philosophy based on the ideas of Charles Darwin, it says only the fittest, strongest and smartest people grow wealthy, 274, 294
Social Democrats (Germany), 323
Social hierarchy—a ranking system based on one's wealth and class, 13
Socialism—a system where all members of a society share equally in the work and the goods produced, 273–274, 289, 330, 338
Socialist market economy—when the demand for goods and services determines pricing and production, 383
Social mobility, in Hinduism, 48
Social revolutions, 264–276
Society
  in ancient Americas, 150
  Aryan, 44–45
  Aztec, 152–153
  in China, 62
  Egyptian, 34–35
  fall of Roman Empire and, 97
  feudal, 184–185
  Hinduism in, 48
  Inca, 155
  of India, 175–176
  during Industrial Revolution, 273–275
  of Japan, 304
  Mayan, 151
  in Renaissance, 204
  Roman, 95
  Soviet, 343
  in Spanish America, 227
Socrates, 80
Soil, 17, 402
Solar system, Aristarchus and, 83
Soldiers. *See also* Military; Warriors
  children as, 408
  feudal, 184
  in Rome, 91, 97
  in Second Punic War, 90
  in Sparta, 73, 74
Solidarity movement, 373
Solomon (Bible), 24
Solomon Islands, 360, 361
Somoza, Anastasio, 379
Song Dynasty (China), 163–166, 164 (map)

Songhai Kingdom, 144–145
Sophia (Austria-Hungary), 320
South Africa, independence of, 388–389
South America. *See also* Americas; Latin America; specific countries
  economies in, 376
  European colonization of, 225–228
  humans in, 7
  nations of, 260 (map)
  rain forests in, 404
  Spain and, 260–261
Southeast Asia, 164, 167, 220. *See also* specific countries
South Korea, 384, 386
South Vietnam, 385
Southwest, Anasazi of, 156–157
Southwest Asia, 16–26, 37
Soviets, in Russia—councils made up of workers, peasants, and soldiers, 330, 331
Soviet Union, 316. *See also* Russia
  Cold War and, 363–365
  collapse of, 368, 374, 375 (map)
  Cuba and, 376
  Korean War and, 384
  Nazi-Soviet Non-Aggression Pact and, 354–355
  under Stalin, 341–343
  in World War II, 356, 359
Spain
  Aztec Empire and, 152, 222–224
  in Chile and Peru, 261
  exploration by, 221–222, 221 (map), 229
  Hannibal in, 90
  horses brought by, 158
  imperialism by, 299 (map)
  Inca Empire and, 224
  Islamic architecture in, 126
  Jews in, 213
  Line of Demarcation and, 222
  Mexican independence from, 259–260
  Muslims in, 125, 183, 213
  New Spain and, 229–230
  as Roman province, 90
  San Martín's defeat of, 261
  slave trade and, 227
  South American freedom from, 260–261
  unification of, 213
Spanish America, 238, 310. *See also* Americas; Central America; Latin America; South America
Spanish-American War, 312
Spanish Empire, 221, 227, 261
Spanish Inquisition, 213
Sparta, 73–74, 78–79
Spear, 9
Special-purpose maps, 69, 117
Speech, 9

469

Sphere of influence—an area where only one foreign power had the right to trade, 307
Spice Islands, Melaka islands as, 220
Spice trade, 67, 219
Spinning jenny, 267
Stalemate, in World War I—neither side is able to budge, a deadlock, 321
Stalin, Joseph, 333, 341–343, 363. *See also* Russia; Soviet Union
Stalingrad, siege of, 358
Stamp Act, 249–250
Standard of living, 398, 399
Stang, Dorothy, 404
State Department, 416
States, in U.S. territory from Mexico, 311–312
State-sponsored terrorism, 416
Steamboat, 267
Steam engine, 267, 268
Stone hand axes, 7
Stone tools, 8
Strategraphic observation, 6
Strategy—a clever plan or method, 363
Strike—work stoppage by employees in support of demands made on their employer, 274
Subcontinent—a large landmass that extends out from a continent, 41
Submarines, in World War I, 322, 323
Sub-Saharan Africa, 133, 388, 390
Subsidy—a payment by the government to non governmental organization, 304
Successor—a person who is next in order, 94
Sudan, 36, 410, 416
Sudetenland, 354
Sudra caste, 45
Suez Canal, 297
Sufi mystics, 126, 127
Sugar plantations, slaves on, 226–227
Sui Dynasty (China), 163, 164 (map)
Süleyman the Magnificent (Ottomans), 128
Sultanate of Delhi—an area ruled by a sultan, 174
Sultan—a ruler, 174, 175
Sumanguru (King of Kaniaga), 143
Sumer, 18–20, 43
Sumeria, 16
Summarizing, 147
Sun, planetary movement and, 246
Sundiata Keita (King of Mali), 143
Sun god, Inca, 154–155
Sunna Islam, 124
Sunni Ali (Songhai), 144

Sunni Muslims, 124, 127, 393
Sun Yat-sen (China), 309
Superiority, racism and, 294, 298
Superpowers, 316
Surplus—an amount more than or in excess of what is required, 12
Susa, Persia, 22
Sustainable development, 405
Suttee—burning a widow with the body of her deceased husband, 177
Swahili—the most widely spoken language in East Africa and the official language of Kenya and Tanzania, 140
Sweden, colonization by, 228
Switzerland, Calvin in, 207, 208
Synthesizing information, 199
Syria, 82, 328, 392, 416

T
Tables, using, 39, 315
Tai Ping Rebellion (China), 308
Taiwan, 382, 386
Taj Mahal, 177
Taliban, 393
Tang Dynasty (China), 58, 163–165, 164 (map), 172
Tank warfare, in World War II, 354, 355
Tanzania, 140, 414
Tariffs, German, 289
Taxation
  Aztec, 152
  customs duties as, 111
  English Parliament and, 196, 241–242
  in France, 197
  of India, 296–297
  of Indian non-Muslims, 175, 176, 177
  in Mali, 143
  in Persia, 22
  records of, 13
  without representation, 250
  revenue tax as, 249
  in Rome, 97
  Stamp Act as, 249–250
  on trade, 142
Technology. *See also* Military; Weapons
  in China, 308
  environment and, 403
  industrial, 266–267, 269
  in Japan, 386
  for sea voyages, 168, 218
  warfare and, 128
Telegraph, in Japan, 304
Telephone, 275
Telescope, 245, 246
Temple of the Sun (Cuzco), 154–155
Temples
  Aztec, 152
  in Jerusalem, 24

  Mayan, 150–151
  in Sumer, 19
Tenant farmer—farmer who works land that is owned by another person and pays rent to the land owner, 172, 193
Ten Commandments, 25, 112
Tenement—a rundown, cheap apartment building that lacks basic necessities, 270, 271
Tennis Court Oath, 254
Tenochtitlán, 151, 152, 223
Tepee—a cone-shaped dwelling of poles covered with animal hides or bark, 158
Terraced—a raised area of earth that has a flat top, and vertical sides cut like steps, 155
Territories, of the United States, 312
Terror, the. *See* Reign of Terror (France)
Terror and terrorism, 414–417
  by Islamic radicals, 368
  in Mussolini's Italy, 340
  by PLO, 392
  on September 11, 2001, 414
  in Soviet Union, 342
Tet Offensive (1968), 385 (map)
Tetzel, Johann, 205
Texas, independence of, 312
Texcoco, Lake, 151
Textile—a cloth manufactured by weaving, 112, 267–268, 269, 296
Thailand, 386
Thebes, Philip II (Macedonia) and, 81
Theocracy—a government run by religious leaders, 208
Theodora (Byzantine Empire), 110
Theodosius the Great (Rome), 100
Thesis—an argument, 202, 205
Third Estate, 253
Third Punic War, 90–91
Third Reich (Germany), 346, 360
Third Rome, Moscow as, 115
Thirteen colonies, English, 231 (map)
Three Principles of the People (Sun Yat-sen), 309
Tiananmen Square, 384
Tiberius Gracchus. *See* Gracchus family
Tiber River, 28, 87
Tibet, Tang Chinese conquest of, 164
Tigris River, 17, 28, 126
Timbuktu, 144, 145
Time. *See* Calendar
Timelines, 27
  events from 1800 to 1911, 278–279
  of first civilizations, 28–29
  of global age, 180–181
  of later civilizations, 104–105
  of monarchies and revolutions, 238–239

of prehistoric civilizations, 2–3
20th century warfare, 316-317
Timur-i-Lang (Tamerlane), 174–175
Tito, Joseph, 373
Tobacco, 231, 233
Tokugawa Ieyasu (Japan), 171
Tokugawa Shogunate (Japan), 171–172, 302, 303
Tokyo, 171
Toleration—recognizing and respecting the beliefs of others, 100, 177
Tombs, Egyptian, 33
Tools, 9
    of Bantu-speakers, 135
    iron, 37
    stone, 7, 8
    of Xia, 58
Torah—the Hebrew Bible, also known as the Old Testament, 23
Tordesillas, Treaty of, 222
Totalitarian—a type of government where the political leader has total control over all aspects of a citizen's life, 336, 337–348, 372
Tourism, in Cuba, 376
Tours, Battle of, 183
Toussaint L'Ouverture, François-Dominique, 258, 259
Towns. *See* Cities and towns
Trade—an exchange of one item for another item, 12, 36. *See also* Slavery; specific regions
    by African city-states, 139–140
    Arab, 137
    in Athens, 75
    in Axum, 137–138
    of Bantu-speakers, 135–136
    barriers to, 400
    British East India Company and, 294–295
    by Carthage, 89
    between China and Taiwan, 382
    Chinese influence through, 164
    in Constantinople, 110
    Crusades and, 189
    in East Africa, 137–140, 140 (map)
    exports and, 37
    favorable balance of, 233
    foreign in China, 306–307
    French, 229–230
    Greek, 71
    of Gupta Empire, 52
    in India, Southeast Asia, and China, 220
    in Indus River civilizations, 43
    Japanese-American, 302–303
    Kushite, 36, 37
    in luxury goods, 217
    in Mali, 143
    by Maurya Empire, 52
    medieval, 188
    by Mexico, 378
    in Middle Ages, 190–192
    Muslim, 176
    Mycenaean, 72
    NAFTA and, 378
    in Nubia, 36
    in opium, 306
    Portugal and, 139, 218–219
    Roman, 89, 91
    spread of plague and, 191
    Suez Canal and, 297
    Swedish, 230
    trans-Saharan, 133, 141
    unintended consequences of, 191
    in Yuan Dynasty, 167
    in Zimbabwe, 138–139
Trade fairs, 190–191, 192
Trade route—a route used by traveling traders, 37, 67, 67 (map), 113, 113 (map), 219 (map)
Trade unions, 274
Trading states. *See* Trade; specific states
Tradition—customs and stories passed down from one generation to the next, 49
Tragedy—play that deals with themes such as good and evil and the rights of individuals, 80
Traitor—a person who betrays one's country or trust, 242
Trajan (Rome), 94, 94 (map)
Trans-Atlantic trade, in slaves, 227, 231
Transportation
    animals for, 11
    camel caravans as, 141
    in China, 65
    in Japan, 304
    railroads as, 265, 267, 304
    revolution in, 267
Trans-Saharan trade, 133, 141
Trappers, French, 229–230
Travel, Crusades and, 189
Travels of Marco Polo, The, 166
Treaties
    between Europe and Japan, 303
    between Japan and United States, 303
    in Korean War, 384
    of Nanjing, 306
    Peace of Augsburg as, 207
    of Tordesillas, 222
    of Versailles, 325–326
Treaty ports, in China, 307, 308
Tree-ring dating, 6
Trees. *See* Forests
Trench warfare—a type of combat in which fighting is done from a series of trenches, 321, 322
Trent, Council of, 202, 212
Tribunes, in Rome, 93

Tribute—a monetary payment by one nation to another nation in acknowledgement of submission or protection, 115, 128, 152, 167
Tribute state, Korea as, 173
Trimurti (Hindu trinity), 48
Triple Alliance—World War I allies that included Germany, Austria-Hungary, and Italy, 319, 319 (map), 321
Triple Entente—World War I allies that included Great Britain, France, and Russia, 319, 319 (map), 320
Triumvirates (Rome)
    First, 92–93
    Second, 93–94
Trojan War, 72
Truman, Harry, 362
    Truman Doctrine of, 364
Tsar. *See* Czar of Russia
Tsunami—an underground ocean earthquake that results in a massive wave of water, 386
Turkey, 82, 89, 97, 363, 364
Turkmenistan, 82
Turks. *See also* Ottoman Empire; Turkey
    Armenian genocide by, 413
    Byzantine Empire conquered by, 111
    crusade against, 126, 189
    in India, 174, 176–177
    Seljuk, 126, 188
Tutankhamen (Egyptian king), 34
Tyrant—a ruler who governs in a harsh or cruel manner, 73, 74

U

U-boats. *See* Submarines
Ukraine, 333, 374
Umar (Caliph), 123
Umayyad Dynasty, 124, 125–126, 125 (map)
UN. *See* United Nations (UN)
Undocumented immigrants, 378
Unemployment, in depressions, 337
Unification
    of China, 309
    of Germany, 285–289, 285 (map)
    of Italy, 283
    of Spain, 213
Unintended consequences— unplanned effects, 189, 191
Unions. *See* Labor unions
United Fruit Company, 311
United Nations (UN), 371. *See also* specific organizations
    actions against terrorism, 417
    Convention on Genocide (1948), 413
    Korean War and, 384
    Resolution 1373 of, 417

Universal Declaration of Human Rights, 406, 437–440
World Food Day and, 399
United Nations Refugee Agency (UNHCR), 409
United States, 251–252. *See also* American Revolution
  Cold War and, 363–365
  counterterrorism policy in, 417
  El Salvador and, 379
  foreign aid from, 400
  government of, 251–252
  ideas of philosophes and, 248
  imperialism by, 293, 299
  industrialization of, 268, 269
  Iraq and, 393
  isolationists in, 355
  Japan and, 302–303
  labor unions in, 274
  Latin America and, 311–313, 380 (map)
  Louisiana Territory and, 255
  NAFTA and, 378
  Nicaragua and, 379
  Panama and, 313, 380
  responses to terrorism by, 416
  World War I and, 323, 325
  World War II and, 358, 364–365
Universal Declaration of Human Rights, 406, 409, 437–440
Universal Law of Gravitation, 247
Universe, Earth- vs. sun-centered, 246
Universities and colleges. *See also* Education
  in Byzantine Empire, 110–111
Untouchables (India), 45
Upper class, education of colonials in, 301
Ur, Iraq, ziggurat of, 19
Urban II (Pope), 188–189
Urban guerrillas, 415
Urbanization—the process by which cities grow and societies become more city-like, 270–271
USSR. *See* Soviet Union
Uthman (Caliph), 123
Uzbekistan, Alexander the Great and, 82

V

Vaisya caste, 45
Valley of Mexico, 151
Value—a principle or standard considered desirable, 97
  Japanese, 303, 304
  in Rome, 97
Vandals, 98
Vassal—a lesser noble who owed loyalty, service, and sometimes a yearly payment of money to a higher noble, or king, 139, 184
Vedas (books), 44, 46

Vegetation—includes grasses, plants, bushes, and trees, 133
Velvet Revolution, 373
Venetia, 284
Venice, 190
Vernacular language—the language of ordinary people, 203–204, 206
Versailles, 253, 288
Versailles, Treaty of, 325–326, 353
Vesalius, Andreas, 247
Viceroyalty—an area governed by a viceroy or a governor who represented the monarch, 225
Victor Emmanuel II (Italy), 283, 284
Victor Emmanuel III (Italy), 338, 339
Vienna, uprising of 1848, 282
Vietminh, 385
Vietnam, 167, 307, 384–385. *See also* Indochina
Vietnam War, 384–385
Vikings
  in Kievan Rus, 114
  migrations of, 183
  in Normandy, 194
  in Russia, 113
  trade routes of, 113 (map)
Villages, 12. *See also* Cities and towns
Violence. *See also* Terror and terrorism
  in former Soviet Union, 374
  in South Africa, 389
Virgil (Rome), 95
Vishnu (Hindu deity), 47, 48
Visigoths, 98
Vladimir I (Kievan Rus), 114–115
Voltaire (François-Marie Arouet), 248
Voting rights
  in Athens, 75, 78
  in Japan, 304
Voyage—a long journey or trip, 168
  Chinese, 168
  English, 228
  of exploration, 218–222, 221 (map)

W

Wages
  in factories, 271
  in Soviet Union, 342, 343
Walesa, Lech, 373
Walled cities, in Sumer, 19
Wampanoag Indians, 234
War bonds, in World War I, 323
War communism (Russia)—when the government took over banks, mines, factories, railroads, and the food supply to supply the Red Army, 332
War crime—a crime committed during a war by a government official or military leader, 360
War debts, after World War I, 324

Warlord—a local chief who ruled the states within an empire, 64–65, 309
War of Independence (India), Sepoy Rebellion as, 295–296
Warring States Period (China), 64
Warriors. *See also* Soldiers
  Aryans as, 44
  in Japan, 171
Wars and warfare. *See also* Cold War; specific wars
  Caesar and, 92–93
  cannons and, 128
  in France, 197
  during French Revolution, 254–255
  on Great Plains, 158–159
  between Italy and Ethiopia, 300
  Native American-colonial, 234
  in Persian Gulf region, 392–393
  timelines in 20th century, 316–317
  trench warfare, 321, 322
Washington, George, 250
Waste disposal, 271
Wastes, pollution and, 402
Water, quality of, 404
Water frame, 267
Waterloo, battle at, 256, 281
Water power, 268
Watt, James, 267, 268
Wealth
  African slave trade and, 235
  in England, 266
  exploration and, 217–218
  for factory investment, 268
  inequality in Central America, 379
  mercantilism and, 233
  of merchants in African trade, 139–140
  poor nations and, 398
  from Spanish colonies, 225
Wealth gap
  in Latin America, 310
  in Rome, 92
Weapons
  atomic bomb as, 362, 364
  bronze, 12
  Greek fire as, 109
  iron, 37
  of mass destruction, 393
  in World War I, 322
Weaving, 43, 267
West Africa
  kingdoms of, 141–145, 142 (map)
  Portuguese trade with, 219
  slave trade and, 235
  trade routes in, 142 (map)
West Asia, 117 (map)
Western Europe, Marshall Plan and, 363–364
Western Front, in World War I, 321, 322
Western Hemisphere. *See also* Americas; specific countries and regions

Monroe Doctrine and, 293
villages in, 150
Westernize—to convert to the customs of the Western culture, 297
Western Roman Empire, 97
Western world
Chinese modernization and, 308, 309
Japan and, 302–305
after World War II, 364
Wheelbarrow, 62
White Army (Russia), 332
Whites, rule in Africa by, 387–388
Whitney, Eli, 268
William I (Prussia-Germany), 286, 287–288
William II (Germany), 288
William of Orange, 243
William the Conquerer (England), 183, 194
Wilson, Woodrow, 323, 325–326
Winds, monsoons as, 42
Wittenberg, Luther in, 202, 205–206
Women
in Athens, 75, 78
in Byzantine Empire, 110
in China, 62, 309
as craftworkers, 112, 193, 204
in developing nations, 399
Egyptian, 35
as factory workers, 271
in Iroquois nation, 159
in Islam, 121–122
march on Versailles by, 253
middle-class, 272
nomadic, 8
poverty among, 368
in prehistoric group, 9
in Renaissance, 204
rights of, 21, 406
in Rome, 95, 97
in Russian Revolution, 330
as serfs, 185
in Sparta, 74
as weavers, 112
Workday, 271
Workers. *See also* Labor
in cities, 270, 271
for factories, 268
German aid to, 289
Mexican in United States, 378
as proletariat, 274
in Russia, 330, 331, 343
after World War I, 338
World Bank, 390, 400
World Food Day, 399
World today, timeline of, 368–369
World Trade Center, 414
World Trade Organization (WTO), 400
World War I, 316, 318, 319–328
armistice in, 323
in Asia, 322
in Europe, 322–323, 322 (map)

Europe after, 327–328, 327 (map)
Middle East after, 328, 328 (map)
totalitarianism after, 336, 337–348
trench warfare in, 321
Versailles Treaty after, 325–326
World War II, 316, 354–355
in Africa, 357 (map)
in Europe, 356–360, 357 (map)
Europe after, 364 (map), 371–374
events leading to, 351–355
independence movements after, 368
Korea after, 384
in Pacific region, 358, 360, 361 (map)
Worldwide changes, 368–369
Writing, 5, 13
Aztec, 152
calligraphy and, 129
Chinese, 27, 58, 59
Cyrillic, 113–114
Egyptian hieroglyphics as, 34, 35, 39
Inca, 155
Mayan, 151
in Mesopotamia, 27
in Sumer, 19–20
Written history, 79
WTO. *See* World Trade Organization (WTO)

X

Xenophon (Greek historian), 73
Xerxes (Persia), 77
Xia Dynasty (China), 58, 58 (map), 69 (map)
Xiongnu people (China), 65

Y

Yahweh—the Hebrew word for God, 23
Yalta Conference, 363
Yamato clan (Japan), 169, 170
Yathrib, 121
Yemen, USS *Cole* bombing in, 414
Yi Dynasty (Korea), 172, 173
Yin Yang symbol (China), 63
Yi Song-gye (Korea), 172
Yong Le (China), 167
Yorktown, battle at, 251
Young Turks, 413
Yuan Dynasty (China), 166–167, 172
Yuan Shigai (China), 309
Yucatán Peninsula—a peninsula in Central America extending into the Gulf of Mexico, 150, 151, 222
Yugoslavia, 324, 327
former, 373–374, 374 (map)
Italy and, 338
Yunus, Muhammad, 401

Z

Zaire, 136
Zanzibar (city-state), 139
Zeus (god), 99
Zhao Zheng (Qin Shihuangdi, China), 66
Zheng He (China), 168, 168 (map)
Zhou Dynasty (China), 58, 58 (map), 64, 65, 69 (map)
Mandate of Heaven and, 59, 60
Zhu Yuanzhang (Buddhist monk), 167
Ziggurat—a pyramid-shaped temple built to honor deities, 19
Zimbabwe, 138–139, 388
Zimmermann telegram, 323
Zones
of African climate and vegetation, 133–135
in Germany, 363

Acknowledgements

Cover Images: (left to right) ©Gideon Mendel/CORBIS; ©Stefano Bianchetti/Corbis; ©Mary Evans Picture Library; ©Bettmann/CORBIS; ©Wilson Koh www.wilsonkoh.com; (bottom) ©Bettman/CORBIS

Margin Images: Magna Carta ©Bettmann/CORBIS; The Scroll of Rule ©West Semitic Research/Dead Sea Scrolls Foundation/CORBIS

3 (t)©Hulton Archive/Getty Images, (b)©Nik Wheeler/CORBIS, (l)©Gianni Dagli Orti/CORBIS; 4 ©Taxi/Getty Images;
5 ©Ron Watts/CORBIS; 6 ©Reuters/CORBIS; 7 (tl)©John Reader/Photo Researcher, Inc., (br)©John Reader/ Photo Researchers, Inc.;
8 (t)©Dewitt Jones/CORBIS, (b)©Richard T. Nowitz/Photo Researchers, Inc.; 9 ©Des Bartlett/Photo Researchers, Inc.; 10 ©CORBIS;
12 (t)©Chris R. Sharp/Photo Researchers, Inc., (bl)©Jonathan Blair/CORBIS; 13 ©Roger Wood/CORBIS;
16 ©Georg Gerster/Photo Researcher's, Inc.; 17 ©The Granger Collection; 19 (t)©Diego Lezama/CORBIS, (b)©Dean Conger/CORBIS;
20 (t)©Swiss Erlenmeyer Collection, (bl)©JupiterImages Corporation; 23 ©The Rhodes Jewish Museum; 24 ©Bettmann/CORBIS;
29 (t)©ML Sinibaldi/CORBIS, (br)©Keren Su/CORBIS, (bl)©Historical Picture Archive/CORBIS; 32 ©Sandro Vannini/CORBIS;
33 (t)©Roger Wood/CORBIS, (b)©Christine Osborne/CORBIS, (b)©Roger Wood/CORBIS; 34 (t)©JupiterImages Corporation, (b)©Sandro Vannini/CORBIS; 35 (t)©Bojan Brecelj/CORBIS, (r)©Gianni Dagli Orti/CORBIS; 36 ©Charles & Josette Lenars/CORBIS;
37 (t)©Jonathan Blair/CORBIS, (br)©Archivo Iconografico, S.A./CORBIS; 40 ©Michael Freeman/CORBIS; 42 ©Reuters/CORBIS;
43 (t)©Diago Lezama Orezzoli/CORBIS, (b)©CORBIS; 45 ©Michael Freeman/CORBIS; 46 ©Roman Soumar/CORBIS;
47 (t)©Bettmann/CORBIS, (b)©Bettmann/CORBIS, (r)©Luca I. Tettoni/CORBIS; 49 ©Leonard de Selva/CORBIS;
50 (t)©Macduff Everton/CORBIS, (t)©Archivo Iconografico, S.A./CORBIS, (t)©Pierre Vauthey/CORBIS, (t)©Nik Wheeler;
52 (t)©Adam Woolfitt/CORBIS, (b)©Lindsey Hebberd/CORBIS; 53 Primary Source from "Arthashastra", *Classical India*, edited by William H. McNeill and Jean W. Sedlar, New York: Oxford University Press, 1969.; 56 ©Lonely Planet Images/Getty Images;
58 ©Asian Art & Archeology, Inc./CORBIS; 60 ©Bettmann/CORBIS; 61 ©Archivo Iconografico, S.A./CORBIS; 63 ©The Granger Collection;
64 ©Bettmann/CORBIS; 65 ©University of Purdue; 66 (t)©The Trustees of the British Museum, (b)©University of Maryland;
72 (t)©Gianni Dagli Orti/CORBIS, (l)©Archivo Iconografico, S.A./CORBIS, (bl)©Bettmann/CORBIS, (br)©Peter M. Wilson/CORBIS;
74 (l)©Araldo de Luca/CORBIS, (b)©The Granger Collection; 75 ©Araldo de Luca/CORBIS; 76 ©Christie's Images/CORBIS;
77 (t)©Mary Evans Picture Library, (b)©John Hios/akg-images; 79 ©The Granger Collection; 80 ©Fotosearch; 81 ©The Granger Collection;
82 ©Araldo de Luca/CORBIS; 83 ©Wolfgang Kaehler; 86 ©Robert Harding World Imagery/Getty Images; 87 ©Charles & Josette Lenars/CORBIS;
88 ©Photodisc Green/Getty Images; 91 ©Free Agents Limited/CORBIS; 92 ©Giraudon/Art Resource, NY; 93 (t)©Bettmann/CORBIS, (b)©Musee d'Orsay, Paris, France, Giraudon;/Bridge; 95 ©Robert Harding World Imagery/Getty Images; 96 ©Taxi/Getty Images;
97 ©Scala/Art Resource, NY; 98 ©Mary Evans Picture Library; 99 ©Mary Evans Picture Library and ©Bettman/CORBIS;
100 (t)©The Bridgeman Art Library/Getty Images, (b)©Mary Evans Picture Library; 105 (bl)©Christine Osborne/CORBIS, (t)©Wolfgang Kaehler; 106 ©Francesco Venturi/CORBIS; 107 ©Courtesy of the Museum of Antiquities, University of Sasktchewan;
108 ©Adam Woolfitt/CORBIS; 110 (b)©Catholic University of America, (t)©Scala/Art Resource, NY; 112 (t)©Art Resource, NY, (b)©Paul H. Kuiper/CORBIS; 114 ©José F. Poblete/CORBIS; 115 ©Diego Lezama/CORBIS; 118 ©Reuters/CORBIS;
120 ©www.artislamic.com; 122 ©Bojan Brecelj; 123 ©Aaron Horowitz/CORBIS; 126 (t)©Michael Busselle/CORBIS, (b)©M. Burgess/Robertstock.com; 127 Primary Source from "One Who Wraps Himself" from *The Essential Rumi* translated by Coleman Barks, HarperSanFrancisco, 1995.; 128 ©Sheldan Collins/CORBIS; 129 (l)©David Lees/CORBIS, (b)©www.artislamic.com;
132 ©Wolfgang Kaehler 20_www.wkaehlerphoto.com; 133 ©Museum of Mankind, London, UK/www.bridgeman.co.uk; 134 (l)©Getty Images, Inc., (r)©Getty Images, Inc.; 136 (t)©Jason Laure, (r)©Brooklyn Museum of Art, New York, USA/www.bridgeman.co.uk, (l)©Private Collection, Heidi Schneebeli/Bridgeman Art Library; 137©Roger De La Harpe; Gallo Images/CORBIS; 138 ©Carmen Redondo/CORBIS;
139 ©Jason Laure; 140 ©Jason Laure; 141 ©Jeffrey L. Rotman/CORBIS; 143 ©Sandro Vannini/CORBIS;
144 ©Horniman Museum, London, UK, Heini Schneebli/www.bridgeman.co.uk;
145 Primary Source from *African Cities and Towns Before the European Conquest* by Richard W. Hull. Copyright ©1976 by W.W. Norton & Company, Inc. Used by permission of W.W. Norton & Company, Inc.; 148 ©Getty Images, Inc.; 150 ©Gianni Dagli Orti/CORBIS;
151 (t)©Werner Forman/CORBIS, (b)©Mary Evans/Edwin Wallace; 152 ©Nik Wheeler/CORBIS;
153 ©New York Historical Society, New York, NY, USA; 154 (l)©J. C. Kanny/Lorpresse/CORBIS SYGMA, (r)©Gianni Dagli Orti/CORBIS;
155 ©Werner Forman/CORBIS; 156 ©John McAnulty/CORBIS; 157 (b)©Richard A. Cooke/CORBIS; (t)©Richard A. Cooke/CORBIS;
158 ©CORBIS; 159 ©Nathan Benn/CORBIS; 162 ©Lin Liqun/CORBIS; 164 (b)©Giraudon/Art Resource, NY, (t)©Private Collection/Bridgeman Art Library; 166 ©Burstein Collection/CORBIS, Primary Source from *The Travels of Marco Polo* edited by Milton Rugoff, New York: New American Library, 1961.; 167 ©Brian A. Vikander/CORBIS; 170 ©Free Agents Limited/CORBIS;
171 (r)©Scala/Art Resource, NY, (l)©Burstein Collection/CORBIS; 172 ©John Van Hasselt/CORBIS; 173 ©Peter Harholdt/CORBIS;
176 ©Ancient Art & Architecture/DanitaDelimont.com; 177 (t)©Getty Images, Inc., (b)©Musee Royaux des Beaux-Arts de Beliguque, Brussels, Belgium/Bridge; 181 (t)©Gianni Dagli Orti/CORBIS, (l)©Gianni Dagli Orti/CORBIS, (r)©Hulton Archives/Getty Images, Inc.;
182 ©Paul Almasy/CORBIS; 183 ©Archivo Iconografico, S.A./CORBIS; 184 ©Archivo Iconografico, S.A./CORBIS;
185 ©NPTL/The Images Works; 186 (tl)©Tibor Bognar/CORBIS, (bl)©Historical Picture Archive/CORBIS, (r)©Elio Ciol/CORBIS;
187 ©Archivo Iconografico, S.A./CORBIS; 188 ©The Granger Collection, New York; 191 ©Bettmann/CORBIS; 192 ©Historical Picture Archive/CORBIS; 193 (b)©Castello di Issogne, Val d'Aosta, Italy, Giraudon;/www.bridgeman.co.uk, (t)©Gianni Dagli Orti/CORBIS;
195 ©Bettmann/CORBIS; 196 (r)©Bettmann/CORBIS, (l)©2005 JupiterImages Corporation; 197 ©Stefano/Bianchetti/CORBIS;
200 ©David Lees/CORBIS; 202 (l)©Robert Harding World Imagery/Getty Images, Inc., (r)©The Bridgeman Art Library/Getty Images, Inc.;

203 (tl)©SuperStock, Inc./SuperStock, (tr)©The Bridgeman Art Library, (l)©Bettmann/CORBIS, (b)©The Bridgeman Art Library;
204©The Bridgeman Art Library/Getty Images, Inc.; 205 ©Mary Evans Picture Library; 206(r)©The Bridgeman Art Library,
(l)©SuperStock, Inc./SuperStock; 207 ©Hulton Archive/Getty Images, Inc.; 208 ©Bettmann/CORBIS; 209 ©Scala/Art Resource, NY;
210 (l)©Robert Harding World Imagery/Getty Images, Inc., (b)©Bettmann/CORBIS; 212 ©Giraudon/Art Resource, NY;
213 ©Bettmann/CORBIS; 216 ©The Granger Collection, New York; 218 ©Victoria & Albert Museum, London/Art Resource, NY;
219 ©Giraudon/Art Resource, NY; 220 ©Bettmann/CORBIS; 222 ©Mary Evans Picture Library; 223 ©Werner Forman/Art Resource, NY,
Primary Source from "The Battle in the Market Place" from *The Broken Spears: The Aztec Account of the Conquest of Mexico*, edited by Miguel Leon
Portilla, Beacon Press, 1962, 1990, 1992.; 224 ©Mary Evans Picture Library; 226 ©Bildarchiv Preussischer Kulturbesitz/Art Resource, NY;
227 (r)©David Muench/CORBIS, (l)©Wolfgang Kaehler/CORBIS; 229 (t)©Bettmann/CORBIS, (b)©Mary Evans Picture Library;
230 ©Mary Evans Picture Library; 233 ©The Granger Collection, New York; 234 ©North Wind/North Wind Picture Archives;
235 ©AFP/Getty Images, Inc., (r)©North Wind/North Wind Picture Archives; 239 (t)©Massimo Listri/CORBIS,
(r)©Fine Art Photographic Library/CORBIS, (l)©Mary Evans Picture Library; 240 ©Index Stock Imagery, Inc.;
242 (t)©The Granger Collection, New York, (b)©Mary Evans Picture Library; 243 (tr)©Hulton Archive/Getty Images,
(br)©Mary Evans Picture Library, (bl)©Mary Evans Picture Library; 244 ©Bettmann/CORBIS; 245 ©Mary Evans Picture Library;
246 (r)©JupiterImages Corporation, (l)©Archivo Iconografico, S.A./CORBIS; 247 ©Bettmann/CORBIS;
248 ©Reunion des Musees Nationaux/Art Resource, NY; 250 (t)©The Granger Collection, New York, (b)©Bettmann/CORBIS;
251 ©The Granger Collection, New York; 252 ©Bettmann/CORBIS; 253 ©Erich Lessing/Art Resource, NY; 255 (t)©Mary Evans Picture Library,
(b)©Giraudon/Art Resource, NY; 258 (t)©Mary Evans Picture Library, (b)©JupiterImages Corporation; 259 ©Bettmann/CORBIS;
261 ©Private Collection, Index;/www.bridgeman.co.uk; 264 ©The Granger Collection, New York; 266 ©The Granger Collection, New York;
267 ©The Granger Collection, New York; 268 (t)©Snark,Art Resource, NY, (b)©The Granger Collection, New York;
269 ©Victoria & Albert Museum, London/Art Resource, NY; 270 ©The Granger Collection, New York; 271 ©The Granger Collection, New York;
273 ©Bettmann/CORBIS; 274 ©Bettmann/CORBIS; 275 ©CORBIS, Bettmann/CORBIS, Bettmann/CORBIS, Underwood & Underwood/CORBIS;
279 (t)©Scala/Art Resource, NY, (l)©Private Collection, Archives Charmet;/www.bridgeman.co.uk, (r)©HIP/Art Resource, NY;
280 ©Giraudon/Art Resource, NY; 282 (t)©The Granger Collection, New York, (b)©The Granger Collection, New York;
283 ©Reunion des Musees Nationaux/Art Resource, NY; 284 (l)©Archivo Iconografico, S.A./CORBIS, (r)©The Granger Collection, New York;
286 (t)©akg-images, (b)©2005 JupiterImages Corporation; 287 ©Reunion des Musees Nationaux/Art Resource, NY; 288 ©CORBIS;
289 ©Private Collection, Archives Charmet;/www.bridgeman.co.uk; 291 ©Bettmann/CORBIS; 292 ©Mary Evans Picture Library;
294 ©akg-images; 295 (t)©North Wind/North Wind Picture Archives, (b)©North Wind/North Wind Picture Archives; 296 ©akg-images;
297 (t)©Erich Lessing/Art Resource, NY, (b)©Hulton-Deutsch/CORBIS; 299 ©Culver Pictures, Inc.; 300 (t)©Art Resource, NY,
(b)©Art Resource, NY; 301 ©Leeds Museums and Galleries (City Art Gallery) U.K.;/www.bridgeman.co.uk; 302 ©2005 Jupiter Images Corporation;
303 (t)©US Navel Academy Museum, (l)©2005 JupiterImages Corporation, (b)©The Granger Collection, New York;
304 ©The Granger Collection, New York; 305 ©Hulton-Deutsch Collection/CORBIS;
306 ©Summer Palace, Beijing, China, Pro-File Photo Library, Hong Kong;/www.bridgeman.co.uk; 307 (t)©akg-images, (b)©Reuters/CORBIS;
308 ©Snark/Art Resource, NY; 309 ©Bettmann/CORBIS; 311 ©2005 JupiterImages Corporation; 312 (t)©CORBIS,
(r)©2005 JupiterImages Corporation; 313 ©Bettmann/CORBIS; 317 (r)©Bettmann/CORBIS, (l)©Hulton-Deutsch Collection/CORBIS,
(t)©Bettmann/CORBIS; 318 ©Hulton-Deutsch Collection/CORBIS; 320 ©Bettmann/CORBIS; 321 ©Hulton Archive/Getty Images;
322 (l)©Bettmann/CORBIS, (t)©Hulton-Deutsch Collection/CORBIS, (r)© Hulton-Deutsch Collection/CORBIS, 323 (t)©akg-images,
(b)©Swim Ink 2, LLC/CORBIS; 324 ©Bettmann/CORBIS; 325 ©Bettmann/CORBIS; 326 ©Underwood & Underwood/CORBIS;
330 ©akg-images; 331 ©Bettmann/CORBIS; 333 ©Hulton-Deutsch Collection/CORBIS; 335 ©Bettmann/CORBIS;
336 ©Hulton-Deutsch Collection/CORBIS; 338 (t)©Bettmann/CORBIS, (b)©Bettmann/CORBIS; 339 ©Bettmann/CORBIS;
340 ©Hulton-Deutsch Collection/CORBIS; 341 ©Brian A. Vikander/CORBIS; 342 ©Retrofile.com; 343 (t)©Hulton-Deutsch Collection/CORBIS,
(b)©Hulton-Deutsch Collection/CORBIS; 344 ©Bettmann/CORBIS; 345 ©Hulton Archive/Stringer, Primary Source from "German Inflation, 19
September 1922" from *Eyewitness to History* edited by John Carey, Cambridge, MA: Harvard University Press, 1987.;
346 (t)©CORBIS, (b)©CORBIS; 347 (b)©AP/Wide World Photos, (t)©Retrofile.com; 349 Primary Source from "A Public Lecture for Women
Only in the Club of the Umma Party", *Opening the Gates: A Century of Arab Feminists Writing* edited by Margot Badran and Miriam Cook (translated
by Ab Badran and Margot Badran), Indianapolis: Indiana University Press, 1990. Used by permission.; 350 ©Hulton-Deutsch Collection/CORBIS;
351 ©Bettmann/CORBIS; 352 ©Bettmann/CORBIS; 354 ©Bettmann/CORBIS; 357 ©CORBIS; 358 (b)©CORBIS, (t)©CORBIS;
359 (t)©CORBIS, (b)©Bettmann/CORBIS; 360 (t)©Bettmann/CORBIS, (b)©Bettmann/CORBIS; 362 ©CORBIS;
365 (t)©Hulton-Deutsch Collection/CORBIS, (b)©Bettmann/CORBIS; 369 (t)©Associated Press, AP, (r)©Peter Turnley/CORBIS,
(l)©Getty Images News; 370 ©Joseph Sohm; ChromoSohm Inc./CORBIS; 372 ©Josef Koudelka/Magnum Photos; 373 (t)©Reuters/CORBIS,
(b)©Reuters/CORBIS; 376 ©Bettmann/CORBIS; 377 ©Getty Images; 378 ©Reuters/CORBIS; 381 ©Bill Gentile/CORBIS;
383 ©Bettmann/CORBIS; 384 ©Bettmann/CORBIS; 389 (t)©Peter Turnley/CORBIS, (l)©Gideon Mendel/CORBIS;
391 ©Hulton Deutsch Collection/CORBIS; 392 ©Getty Images; 393 ©Erik De Castro/Reuters/CORBIS;
398 ©Associated Press, AP, ©Getty Images, ©M. Rosin, ©Photodisc/Getty Images; 400 ©Reuters/CORBIS; 401 ©Reuters/CORBIS;
402 ©Mike Lane; 403 ©Associated Press, BERNAMA; 404 ©Associated Press, Interfoto; 406 ©Michael S. Yamashita/CORBIS;
407 ©John Goodman/Photography; 408 (b)©Patrick Robert/Sygma/CORBIS, (t)©Time Life Pictures/Getty Images;
410 ©Andrew Holbrooke/CORBIS; 413 ©Reuters/CORBIS; 414 ©David Rubinger/CORBIS; 416 (t)©Reuters/CORBIS,
(b)©Sysoyev Grigory/ITAR-TASS/CORBIS; Cover: (c)©Gideon Mendel/CORBIS, (f)©Stefano Bianchetti/CORBIS,
(sr)©Mary Evans Picture Library, (sl)©Bettmann/CORBIS, (fr)©Wilson Koh www.wilsonkoh.com, (b)©Bettmann/CORBIS;
(sidebar)©Bettmann/CORBIS; (sidebar)©West Semitic Research/Dead Sea Scrolls Foundation/CORBIS

The editor has made every effort to trace the ownership of all copyrighted material and to secure the necessary permissions. Should there be a question regarding the use of any material, regret is hereby expressed for such error. Upon notification of any such oversight, proper acknowledgement will be made in future editions.

(t) top, (b) bottom, (l) left, (r) right